A Comprehensive Russian Grammar

Reference Grammars
General Editor: Glanville Price

A Comprehensive French Grammar
Fourth Edition
L. S. R. Byrne and E. L. Churchill
Completely revised and updated by Glanville Price

A Comprehensive Russian Grammar
Terence Wade
Edited by Michael J. de K. Holman

In preparation:

A Comprehensive German Grammar

A Comprehensive Italian Grammar

A Comprehensive Portuguese Grammar

A Comprehensive Spanish Grammar

A Comprehensive Welsh Grammar

A Comprehensive Russian Grammar

Terence Wade

Edited by Michael J. de K. Holman

BLACKWELL
Oxford UK & Cambridge USA

Copyright © T. L. B. Wade 1992

First published 1992
Reprinted 1992, 1993

Blackwell Publishers
108 Cowley Road, Oxford, OX4 1JF, UK

238 Main Street, Suite 501
Cambridge, Massachusetts 02142, USA

British Library Cataloguing in Publication Data

A CIP catalogue record for this book is available from the British Library.

Library of Congress Cataloging in Publication Data

Wade, Terence Leslie Brian.
  A comprehensive Russian grammar/Terence Wade.
    p. cm.
  Includes index.
  ISBN 0–631–15815–4 (hardback) ISBN 0–631–17502–4 (paperback)
  1. Russian language – Grammar – 1950– I. Title.
PG2106.W33   1992
491.782′421–dc20
                                     90–38492
                                        CIP

Typeset in 10 on 12 pt Times
by Joshua Associates Ltd, Oxford
Printed in Great Britain by
T.J. Press Ltd, Padstow, Cornwall

This book is printed on acid-free paper

Contents

The Noun

Declension

Case Usage

Diminutive and Augmentative Nouns

The Pronoun

The Adjective

The Short Form of the Adjective

The Comparative Degree of the Adjective

The Numeral

The Verb

Conjugation

Aspect

Reflexive Verbs

Impersonal Constructions

The Passive Voice

Participles

The Adverb

The Preposition

Spatial Prepositions

*Prepositions that Denote the Position of an Object in
Relation to Another Object (Behind, in Front of, Below,
on Top of etc.), or Movement To or From that Position*

*Prepositions that Denote Spatial Closeness to an Object, Movement
Towards or Away from an Object, or Distance from an Object*

Prepositions that Denote Along, Across, Through a Spatial Area

Prepositions that Denote Spatial Limit

Temporal Prepositions

*The Use of Prepositions to Denote Action in Relation to Various
Time Limits*

The Conjunction

The Particle

Word Order

To May

Preface

The *Comprehensive Russian Grammar* is meant for English-speaking pupils and students of Russian at the post-introductory stage. It is also a reference aid for teachers, translators and interpreters and others who use the language in a professional capacity.

The first new reference grammar of Russian to have been published in the United Kingdom since the 1950s, it is based on personal research and observation, long experience of teaching Russian at all levels from beginners up to the Honours Degree and the Civil Service Interpretership, and on a close study of reference materials by Russian, British and American linguists.

The approach is descriptive throughout, and rules of usage are constantly measured against current practice as reflected in contemporary journalistic and literary sources. It is entirely practical in conception and design and has no pretensions to theoretical disquisition. Particular emphasis is laid on problems which are of especial difficulty for the English speaker.

The grammar provides comprehensive guidance to usage, with exhaustive tabulated material and succinct explanations. It is presented in 484 sections which are further subdivided to take account of finer points of usage. It provides mainstream rules for quick reference, as well as access to the subtleties of the language for those who need more detailed information.

The intention is to provide the essential facts of the language and to tackle perennial problems such as adverbs and pronouns in -то and -нибудь, agreement, animacy, conjugation, declension, gerunds, long and short adjectives, numerals, participles, the partitive genitive, verbs of motion, and so on, as well as problems which have often received less attention: the gender of acronyms, alphabetisms, soft-sign nouns, the differences between в/на and other key prepositions, and between тóже and тáкже, the use of capital letters, particles, the principles of word order etc. Treatment of verbal aspect differentiates usage in the past, future, imperative and infinitive, thus throwing the rules into sharper relief. Special emphasis is given to stress patterns.

Ease of reference is assured by comprehensive indexing of subject headings and Russian words, and by general adherence to the alphabetic principle throughout.

Acknowledgements

I wish to thank the following for advising on aspects of the book: Natalya Bogoslavskaya (University of Leeds), Sheelagh Graham (University of Strathclyde), Larisa Ryazanova (Herzen Russian State Pedagogical University, St Petersburg), who also read the page proofs, Professor Dennis Ward (University of Edinburgh), Nijole White (University of Strathclyde); also Dr Marina Kozyreva (Moscow and Leeds Universities) for reading through a late draft and writing a helpful report. I am particularly grateful to my specialist readers, Dr R. Bivon (University of Essex, formerly of the University of East Anglia) and Dr Svetlana Miloslavskaya (Pushkin Institute, Moscow) for writing detailed reports at an early stage, thus enabling me to make substantial improvements. I also valued a lengthy consultation with Svetlana Miloslavskaya which allowed me to make amendments to the final draft. My editor, Professor Michael Holman (University of Leeds), supplied helpful and detailed critical analyses of each chapter during the writing of the grammar and I am most grateful to him for his support and encouragement and for the many insights that he provided. I should also like to thank Professor Glanville Price (University College of Wales), general editor of Blackwell's series of grammars of European languages, for his comments on some early chapters, particularly that on verbs. Any errors are, of course, entirely the responsibility of the author.

I wish to thank my late mother, who first encouraged me to learn Russian.

The book is dedicated to my wife, May, who bore with me throughout the thousands of hours and nine drafts that went into this grammar.

A special mention for Amstrad PCW 8512, which behaved impeccably throughout.

Finally, I would like to express my appreciation to the publishers of the books I was able to consult (see bibliography): Akademiya nauk, Birmingham University, Collets International, CUP, Dover Publications, Durham University, Harcourt Brace Jovanovich, Hutchinson, Kniga, MGU, Nauka, Oliver and Boyd, OUP, Pan Books, Pergamon, Progress Publishers, Prosveshchenie, Russkii yazyk, Sovetskaya entsiklopediya, University of East Anglia, University of London Press, Vysshaya shkola.

TW

Abbreviations

The following abbreviations are used:

acc.	accusative
adj.	adjective
cf.	compare
dat.	dative
f.	feminine
fig.	figurative
gen.	genitive
imper.	imperative
impf.	imperfective
infin.	infinitive
instr.	instrumental
lit.	literally
m.	masculine
n.	neuter
nom.	nominative
part.	participle
pf.	perfective
pl.	plural
prep.	prepositional
sing.	singular
theatr.	theatrical
trans.	transitive

Introduction

1 The Cyrillic alphabet

(1) The Russian Cyrillic alphabet contains 33 letters, including 20 consonants, 10 vowels, a semi-consonant/semi-vowel (**й**), a hard sign (**ъ**) and a soft sign (**ь**).

(2) There are a number of different systems for transliterating the Cyrillic alphabet. Two of these, that of the International Organization for Standardization (ISO) and that of the British Standards Institution (BSI) (whose system is used throughout this *Grammar*), are listed alongside the Cyrillic alphabet, as well as the Russian names of the individual letters:

Cyrillic letters	Letter name	ISO	BSI
Аа	[а]	a	a
Бб	[бэ]	b	b
Вв	[вэ]	v	v
Гг	[гэ]	g	g
Дд	[дэ]	d	d
Ее	[e]	e	e
Ёё	[ё]	ë	ë
Жж	[жэ]	ž	zh
Зз	[зэ]	z	z
Ии	[и]	i	i
Йй	[и кра́ткое]	j	ĭ

Cyrillic letters	Letter name	ISO	BSI
Кк	[ка]	k	k
Лл	[эль]	l	l
Мм	[эм]	m	m
Нн	[эн]	n	n
Оо	[о]	o	o
Пп	[пэ]	p	p
Рр	[эр]	r	r
Сс	[эс]	s	s
Тт	[тэ]	t	t
Уу	[у]	u	u
Фф	[эф]	f	f
Хх	[ха]	h/ch	kh
Цц	[цэ]	c	ts
Чч	[че]	č	ch
Шш	[ша]	š	sh
Щщ	[ща]	šč	shch
Ъъ	[твёрдый знак]	”	”
Ыы	[ы]	y	ȳ
Ьь	[мя́гкий знак]	’	’
Ээ	[э оборо́тное]	ė	é
Юю	[ю]	ju	yu
Яя	[я]	ja	ya

Note

(a) Certain letters with diacritics and accents which appear in the standard BSI system (ë for ё, ĭ for й, é for э, ȳ for ы) are used without diacritics and accents here.

(b) An apostrophe (’) for the soft sign (ь) is used only in the bibliography.

(c) The endings -ый/-ий are rendered as -y in names.

2 The international phonetic alphabet (IPA)

The following symbols from the IPA are used in the Introduction for the phonetic transcription of Russian words.

Vowels

i	as in ил	[il]
ɨ	as in пыл	[pɨl]

ι   as the first vowel in игла́ [ι'gla]
ɨ   as the first vowel in дыра́ [dɨ'ra]
ɛ   as in лес   [lɛs]
e   as in весь   [ɣes]
a   as in рад   [rat]
æ   as in пять   [pæt]
ʌ   as the first vowel in оди́н [ʌ'din]
ə   as the first vowel in хорошо́ [xərʌ'ʃo]
o   as in мох   [mox]
ö   as in тётя   ['töt̪ə]
u   as in бук   [buk]
ü   as in ключ   [kl̪üt͡ʃ]

Semi-consonant/semi-vowel

j   as in бой   [boj]

Consonants

p   as in пол   [pol]
p̪   as in пёс   [p̪os]
b   as in бак   [bak]
b̪   as in бел   [b̪ɛl]
t   as in том   [tom]
t̪   as in тем   [t̪ɛm]
d   as in дом   [dom]
d̪   as in день   [d̪en]
k   as in как   [kak]
k̪   as in кем   [k̪ɛm]
g   as in гол   [gol]
g̪   as in гид   [g̪it]
f   as in фло́ра   ['florə]
f̪   as in фен   [f̪ɛn]
v   as in вот   [vot]
ɣ   as in вино́   [ɣι'no]
s   as in сам   [sam]
ş   as in сев   [şɛf]
z   as in зуб   [zup]
z̪   as in зе́бра   ['z̪ɛbrə]
ʃ   as in шум   [ʃum]
ʒ   as in жук   [ʒuk]

x	as in хам	[xam]
x̦	as in хи́мик	['x̦imɪk]
ɕɕ	as in щека́	[ɕɕɪ'ka]
ts	as in цех	[tsɛx]
tʃ	as in чин	[tʃin]
m	as in мол	[mol]
m̦	as in мел	[m̦ɛl]
n	as in нос	[nos]
n̦	as in нет	[n̦ɛt]
l	as in лак	[lak]
l̦	as in ляг	[l̦ak]
r	as in рак	[rak]
r̦	as in река́	[r̦ɪ'ka]
j	as in я́ма	['jamə]

Pronunciation

3 Stressed vowels

Russian has ten vowel letters:

а	э	ы	о	у
я	е	и	ё	ю

(1) **A** is pronounced with the mouth opened a little wider than in the pronunciation of 'a' in English 'father', e.g. зал [zal] 'hall'.

(2) **Э** is pronounced like 'e' in 'end', but the mouth is opened a little wider and the tongue is further from the palate than in articulating English 'e' in 'end', e.g. э́то ['ɛtə] 'this is'.

(3) **У** is pronounced with the tongue drawn back and the lips rounded and protruding. The sound is similar to but shorter than the vowel in 'school', e.g. бук [buk] 'beech'.

(4) **O** is also pronounced with rounded and protruding lips, but to a lesser extent than in the pronunciation of **y**. The sound is similar to the vowel in English 'bought', e.g. бок [bok] 'side'.

(5) The vowel **ы** is pronounced with the tongue drawn back as in the pronunciation of **y**, but with the lips spread, not rounded or protruding, e.g. сын [sɨn] 'son'.

(6) The vowels **я** [ja], **e** [jɛ], **ë** [jo] and **ю** [ju] are 'iotated' variants of a, э, o and y (i.e. they are pronounced like those vowels preceded by the sound [j]). The vowel **и** resembles 'ea' in English 'cheap', but is a 'closer' sound, that is, the centre of the tongue is nearer to the hard palate in articulation, e.g. мир [mʲir] 'world, peace'. After a preposition or other word ending in a hard consonant, however, stressed initial **и** is pronounced [ɨ]: от Игоря [ʌˈt ɨɡəɾə], cf. also **4** (4) note.

Note
Vowels can be classified as:

(a) **back** vowels (pronounced with the back part of the tongue raised towards the back of the palate): **y/ю, o/ё**;

(b) **central** vowels (pronounced with the central part of the tongue raised towards the central part of the palate): **ы, a/я**;

(c) **front** vowels (pronounced with the central part of the tongue raised towards the front of the palate: **и, э/e**.

4 Unstressed vowels

(1) Unstressed y, ю, и and ы

The sound of unstressed **y/ю** is similar to that of English 'u' in 'put': дуга́ [duˈga] 'arc', юла́ [juˈla] 'top'. Unstressed **и** and **ы** are shorter and pronounced in a more 'relaxed' fashion than their stressed equivalents: игра́ [ɪˈgra] 'game', была́ [bɨˈla] 'was'. **Ë** does not appear in unstressed position. The other vowels are 'reduced' in unstressed position.

(2) Reduction of o and a

(i) The vowels **o** and **a** are pronounced as [o] and [a] only when they appear in stressed position: дом [dom], зал [zal]. In unstressed position they are reduced, **o** being the vowel most affected by various forms of reduction resulting from its position in relation to the stress.

(ii) In pre-tonic position or as the unstressed initial letter in a word **o** and **a** are pronounced [ʌ]: пото́м [pʌˈtom] 'afterwards', оди́н [ʌˈdʲin] 'one', паро́м [pʌˈrom] 'ferry', аку́ла [ʌˈkulə] 'shark'. This also applies to pre-tonic prepositions: под мо́рем [pʌˈd moɾʲɪm] 'under the sea',

над до́мом [пʌˈd doməm] 'above the house'. The combinations **aa**,
ao, **oa**, **oo** are pronounced [ʌʌ], e.g. сообрази́ть [sʌʌbrʌˈzit] 'to
comprehend'.

(iii) In pre-pre-tonic position (except as initial letters, see (ii)) or in
post-tonic position both vowels are pronounced [ə]: thus парохо́д
[pərʌˈxot] 'steamer', молодо́й [məlʌˈdoj] 'young', ра́но [ˈranə] 'early',
ви́лка [ˈvilkə] 'fork'. This also applies to prepositions (под водо́й
[pəd vʌˈdoj] 'under water', над голово́й [nəd gəlʌˈvoj] 'overhead')
and to the initial letters of words governed by prepositions (в
огоро́де [v əgʌˈrodɪ] 'in the market garden' (cf. огоро́д [ʌgʌˈrot]
'market garden')).

Note

(a) Unstressed **o** is pronounced [o] in a number of words of foreign
     origin (кака́о 'cocoa', ра́дио 'radio', ха́ос 'chaos'), with an
     optional [o] in ве́то 'veto', досье́ 'dossier', шоссе́ 'highway' and
     some other words. In certain cases, pronunciation is differenti-
     ated stylistically. The pronunciation [ʌ] in words such as поэ́т
     'poet' and шоссе́ 'highway', said to be the more colloquial
     variant, has gained ground in educated speech and is found even
     in the pronunciation of foreign names such as Шопе́н [ʃʌˈpɛn]/
     [ʃoˈpɛn] 'Chopin', especially where these have gained common
     currency (e.g. Тольятти 'Togliatti'). However, [o] is retained in
     words where it follows another vowel: три́о 'trio'.

(b) The vowel **a** is pronounced [ɪ] in pre-tonic position after **ч** and
     щ: thus часы́ [tʃɪˈsɨ] 'clock', щади́ть [ʃʃɪˈdit] 'to spare'. The
     pronunciation of unstressed **a** as [ɨ] after **ж**, **ш** is now limited for
     many speakers to жале́ть [ʒɨtˈlet] 'to regret', к сожале́нию
     [k səʒɨtˈlenɪju] 'unfortunately' and end-stressed plural oblique
     cases of ло́шадь 'horse', e.g. gen. pl. лошаде́й [ləʒɨtˈdej]. **Ца** is
     pronounced [tsɨ] in the oblique cases of some numerals:
     двадцати́ [dvətsɨtˈʧi] 'twenty' (gen.).

(3) Reduction of e and я

(i) In pre-tonic position both **e** and **я** are pronounced [(j)ɪ]: язы́к
[jɪˈzɨk] 'language', перево́д [pɪrɪˈvot] 'translation'. Thus, разреди́ть
'to thin out' and разряди́ть 'to unload' have the same pronunciation.

(ii) In post-tonic position **e** is pronounced [ɪ] (по́ле [ˈpolɪ] 'field'),
while **я** is usually pronounced [ə] (ды́ня [ˈdɨnə] 'melon'). However,
post-tonic **я** is pronounced [ɪ] before a soft consonant (па́мять

['pamʲɪt] 'memory') and in non-final post-tonic position (вы́глянул ['vʲiɡlɪnul] 'looked out').

(4) Reduction of э

Э is pronounced [ɪ] in unstressed position (этáп [ɪ'tap] 'stage').

Note
Unstressed initial **и** and **э** and conjunction **и** are pronounced [ɨ] after a preposition or other word ending in a hard consonant (see **3** (6)): в Итáлию [v ɨ'talʲju] 'to Italy', брат идёт к Ивáну [brat ɨ'dʲot k ɨ'vanu] 'my brother is on his way to see Ivan', над эквáтором [nəd ɨ'kvatərəm] 'above the equator'. **И** is also pronounced [ɨ] in certain stump compounds, e.g. Госиздáт [ɡosɨ'zdat] 'State Publishing House'.

5 Hard and soft consonants

With the exception of **ж**, **ц** and **ш**, which are invariably hard, and **ч** and **щ**, which are invariably soft, all Russian consonants can be pronounced hard or soft.

(1) Hard consonants

(i) A hard consonant is a consonant which appears at the end of a word (e.g. the **м** in дом [dom] 'house', the **т** in вот [vot] 'here is') or is followed by **а, ы, о** or **у** (**э** appears only as an *initial* letter, except in acronyms such as нэп 'NEP' (New Economic Policy) and rare words such as сэр 'sir'). Thus, the consonants in the words головá [ɡəlʌ'va] 'head', мы́ло ['mɨlə] 'soap' and дýма ['dumə] 'thought' are all hard.

(ii) Most hard consonants, e.g. **б, в, г, з, к, м, п, с, ф**, are pronounced in similar fashion to their English counterparts, i.e. 'b' in 'bone', 'v' in 'van', 'g' in 'gone', 'z' in 'zone', 'c' in 'come', 'm' in 'money', 'p' in 'pun', 's' in 'sun', 'f' in 'fun'. However, **к** and **п** (and **т**; see (iii)) lack the slight aspiration of 'k', 'p' and 't'.

(iii) In pronouncing the dentals **д** [d], **т** [t] and **н** [n], the tip of the tongue is pressed against the back of the upper teeth in the angle between teeth and gums.

(iv) **Р** is a moderately 'trilled' [r]. **Л** is pronounced with the tip of the tongue in the angle between the upper teeth and the gum, and the middle of the tongue curved downwards. The 'l' sound in English 'bubble' is a good starting-point for the pronunciation of this letter.

(v) **X** sounds as 'ch' in 'loch' or German 'acht', but is formed a little further forward in the mouth.

(vi) Unlike other consonants, **ж, ц** and **ш** are always pronounced hard (see, however, note (b), below). This means in practice that the vowels **e** and **и** are pronounced as э and ы after **ж, ц** and **ш** (жест [ʒɛst] 'gesture', жир [ʒɨr] 'fat', цех [tsɛx] 'workshop', цирк [tsɨrk] 'circus', шест [ʃɛst] 'pole', машина [mʌˈʃɨnə] 'car') while **ё** is pronounced as **о** after **ж** and **ш** (жёлоб [ˈʒoləp] 'groove', шёлк [ʃolk] 'silk'). A soft sign (as in рожь [roʃ] 'rye') has no softening effect on the pronunciation of **ж** or **ш**.

Note
(a)   Neither a soft sign nor the vowel **ё** can be written after **ц**.
(b)   **Ш** is sounded hard in the loan words парашют [pərʌˈʃut] 'parachute' and брошюра [brʌˈʃurə] 'brochure', while **ж** is pronounced soft in жюри [ʒüˈr̩i] 'jury'.

(2) Soft consonants

(i) A soft consonant is a consonant (other than **ж, ц** or **ш**) followed by a soft sign, e.g. **ль** in сталь 'steel', or by **я, е, и, ё** or **ю**. Thus, the initial consonants in мята [ˈm̩atə] 'mint', лес [l̩ɛs] 'forest', пил [p̩il] 'was drinking', нёбо [ˈn̩obə] 'palate' and дюна [ˈd̩unə] 'dune' are all soft.

(ii) Soft consonants are pronounced with the centre of the tongue raised towards the hard palate, as in articulating **и**, for example. Correct rendering of the vowels **я** [ja], **е** [jɛ], **и** [i], **ё** [jo] and **ю** [ju] will assist in the articulation of the preceding soft consonants. Soft [l̩] as in только 'only' is similar to 'll' in 'million', with the tip of the tongue against the teeth-ridge and the front of the tongue pressed against the hard palate.

(iii) Soft consonants may also appear at the end of words, e.g. **пь** and **ть** in топь [top̩] 'swamp' and мать [mat̩] 'mother'; the final sounds in these words are similar to those of the initial consonants in 'pure' and 'tune' (standard British English 'Received Pronunciation').

(iv) Unlike other consonants, **ч** and **щ** are always pronounced soft. In practice this means that the vowels **a**, **o** and **y** are pronounced as [ja], [jo] and [ju] following these consonants (час 'hour', чо́порный 'prim', чугу́н 'cast iron', поща́да 'mercy', щу́ка 'pike').

(v) The consonant **щ** is pronounced as a long soft **ш** [ʃʃ] (e.g. защища́ть [zəʃʃɪˈʃʃæt] 'to defend'); the pronunciation [ʃtʃ] is falling into disuse.

(vi) The double consonants **жч** (мужчи́на 'man'), **зч** (зака́зчик 'client'), **сч** (подпи́счик 'subscriber') are pronounced like **щ** [ʃʃ]. The pronunciation [ʃtʃ], however, is preferred in prefixed forms such as бесчи́сленный 'innumerable', расчлени́ть 'to dismember'.

(vii) **Жж** and **зж** may be pronounced either as a double soft **ж** (with the front of the tongue raised towards the hard palate) in words such as во́жжи [ˈvoʒʒɪ] 'reins', дро́жжи 'yeast', жжёт 'burns', жужжа́ть 'to buzz', бры́зжет 'sprays', визжа́ть 'to scream', е́зжу 'I travel', поезжа́й! 'go!', по́зже 'later', especially in the speech of the older generation, as well as in that of actors and announcers, or alternatively as a double hard **ж** [ˈvoʒʒt], a pronunciation preferred by very many younger speakers. **Зж** is invariably pronounced as hard [ʒʒ] across the boundary between prefix and stem: изжи́ть 'to eradicate'. The cluster **жд** in дождя́ 'of rain' etc. is pronounced as soft **жж** by some speakers and as [ʒd] by others.

(3) Use of hard and soft consonants to differentiate meaning

Hard and soft consonants may be used to differentiate meaning, cf. лук [luk] 'onions' and люк [lʲuk] 'hatch', мат [mat] 'checkmate' and мать [matʲ] 'mother' etc.

6 Double palatalization

Some words contain two adjacent soft consonants, a phenomenon known as 'double palatalization' or 'regressive softening'. The following combinations of letters are involved:

(1) [dʲ], [tʲ] and [nʲ] followed by other soft dentals or by [sʲ], [zʲ], [tʃ], [ʃʃ] or [lʲ]: о́ттепель [ˈotʲtʲɪpʲlʲ] 'thaw', дни [dʲnʲi] 'days', ко́нчик [ˈkonʲtʃɪk] 'tip', го́нщик [ˈgonʲʃʃɪk] 'racer', пя́тница [ˈpʲætʲnʲɪtsə] 'Friday', пе́нсия [ˈpʲenʲsʲɪjə] 'pension'.

(2) [ʂ] or [ʐ] followed by a soft dental, [ʂ], [ʐ] or [l̩]: возни́к [vʌˈzn̩ik] 'arose', разде́л [rʌˈzdɛl] 'partition', здесь [zdes] 'here', снег [ʂn̩ɛk] 'snow', стена́ [ʂt̪ʲˈna] 'wall', вме́сте [ˈvm̩est̪ʲ] 'together'.

Note

In some words, single or double palatalization is possible: две [dɣɛ] or [dɣɛ] 'two', дверь [dɣeɾ̩] or [dɣeɾ̩] 'door', зверь [zɣeɾ̩] or [zɣeɾ̩] 'wild animal', пе́тля [ˈpet̪lə] or [ˈpet̪lə] 'loop', свет [sɣɛt] or [sɣɛt] 'light', след [slɛt] or [slɛt] 'trace', че́тверть [ˈtʃetɣɪrt̪] or [ˈtʃetɣɪrt̪] 'quarter'.

7 Non-palatalization of consonants in some loan words

(1) The consonants **т** and **д** are pronounced hard before **e** in certain loan words and foreign names (те́рмос [ˈtɛrməs] 'thermos flask', апарте́йд 'apartheid', ателье́ 'workshop', бифште́кс 'beef-steak', бутербро́д 'sandwich', оте́ль 'hotel', парте́р 'stalls', стенд 'stand'), in words with the prefix интер- (интерлю́дия 'interlude'), ко́декс 'legal code', моде́ль 'model' and in many words with the prefix де- (деграда́ция 'degradation').

(2) Hard **м** has been retained in консоме́ 'consommé', резюме́ 'résumé'; hard **н** in кашне́ 'scarf', тонне́ль 'tunnel', турне́ 'tour', фоне́тика 'phonetics', эне́ргия 'power'; hard **п** in купе́ 'compartment'; hard **p** in кабаре́ 'cabaret', реле́ 'relay'; and hard **c** in шоссе́ 'highway'.

Note

A hard consonant is more likely to be retained in foreign loan words immediately preceding the stressed vowel (e.g. те́ннис 'tennis'). Dental consonants (**д, т, н**) are more likely to remain hard than labials (**б, п, м**).

8 Hard sign and soft sign

(1) The hard sign appears only between a hard consonant – usually at the end of a prefix – and a stem beginning **я, e, ё** or **ю**: отъе́зд [ʌˈtjest] 'departure', объясня́ть 'to explain'.

(2) A soft sign appearing between a consonant and **я, e, ё** or **ю** indicates that the consonant is soft and that the sound **й** [j] intervenes

between consonant and vowel: семья́ [sɪˈmja] 'family'. See also **5** (2) (i) and (iii).

9 The reflexive suffix -сь/-ся

(1) The pronunciation of **сь** as [s] is widespread: бою́сь [bʌˈjus] 'I fear', боя́сь [bʌˈjas] 'fearing' etc.

(2) The suffix -**ся** is usually pronounced [sə] in the infinitive (мы́ться 'to wash') and the present tense (мо́ется 'he washes'), though an alternative soft pronunciation [sə] is also found in the second-person singular and first-person plural.

(3) [sə] is preferred in participles (смею́щийся [sə] 'laughing'), the imperative (не сме́йся 'don't laugh') and the past tense (он смея́лся 'he was laughing') – except for forms in -сся or -зся (па́сся [ˈpassə] 'was grazing').

10 Effect of a soft consonant on a vowel in the preceding syllable

(1) **Э** and **e** are pronounced [ɛ] and [jɛ] in stressed position when followed by a hard consonant (e.g. э́то [ˈɛtə] 'this is', лес [lɛs] 'forest'), but as [e] and [je] (similar to French 'e acute' [é]) when followed by a soft consonant (e.g. э́ти [ˈetɪ] 'these', весь [ɣes] 'all').

(2) **Я** is pronounced as [æ], **ё** as [ö] and **ю** as [ü] preceding a soft consonant: мяч [mætʃ] 'ball', тётя [ˈtötə] 'aunt', ключ [klütʃ] 'key'.

(3) **A, o** and **ы** are also affected as the tongue is raised closer to the palate in anticipation of a following soft consonant (e.g. мать 'mother', ночь 'night', пыль 'dust', where **a, o** and **ы** are pronounced as if followed by a much-reduced **и** sound).

11 Voiced and unvoiced consonants

(1) Some consonants are pronounced with vibration of the vocal cords ('voiced' consonants), and others without such vibration ('unvoiced' consonants).

(2) There are six pairs of voiced and unvoiced equivalents:

Voiced	Unvoiced
б	п
г	к
з	с
д	т
в	ф
ж	ш

The eight other consonants include the unvoiced **ц, х, ч, щ** and the voiced sonants **л, р, м, н**.

(3) **Б**, **г**, **з**, **д**, **в**, **ж** are pronounced as their unvoiced counterparts when they appear in final position or before a final soft sign.

ло**б** 'forehead' is pronounced [lop]
лу**г** 'meadow' is pronounced [luk]
ра**з** 'time' is pronounced [ras]
са**д** 'garden' is pronounced [sat]
ле**в** 'lion' is pronounced [lɛf]
му**ж** 'husband' is pronounced [muʃ]

(4) When a voiced and an unvoiced consonant appear side by side, the first assimilates to the second. Thus, voiced consonant + unvoiced consonant are both pronounced unvoiced, while unvoiced consonant + voiced consonant are both pronounced voiced.

(i) Voiced + unvoiced (both pronounced unvoiced)

гу́**бк**а	'sponge'	is pronounced ['gupkə]
за**гс**	'registry office'	is pronounced [zaks]
ре́**зк**о	'sharply'	is pronounced ['rɛskə]
ло́**дк**а	'boat'	is pronounced ['lotkə]
вхо́дит	'goes in'	is pronounced ['fxodɪt]
ло́**жк**а	'spoon'	is pronounced ['loʃkə]

Note

(a) Devoicing also takes place on the boundary between preposition and noun or adjective: **в** ко́мнате ['f͡ komnətɪ] 'in the room', **под** столо́м [pət͡ stʌ'lom] 'under the table'.

(b) The devoicing of a final consonant may in turn cause the devoicing of the consonant which precedes it: ви**зг** [visk] 'scream', дро**зд** [drost] 'thrush'.

(c) **Г** is pronounced as [x] in лёгкий 'light, easy', лéгче 'easier', мя́гкий 'soft' and мя́гче 'softer', as well as in бог 'God' (only in the nominative singular case, however). The initial consonant in гóсподи! 'Lord!' is now usually pronounced as [g], though [h] is still heard. The noun бухгáлтер 'book-keeper' is the only word in which **хг** is pronounced as [h].

(ii) Unvoiced + voiced (both pronounced voiced)

футбóл	'football'	is pronounced [fu'dbol]
к дóму	'towards the house'	is pronounced ['g‿domu]
прóсьба	'request'	is pronounced ['proz̬bə]
тáкже	'also'	is pronounced ['tagʒt]
мàшбюрó	'typing pool'	is pronounced [maʒb̬u'ro]

Note

(a) The voicing of consonants also occurs at the boundary between words, especially when the second word is a particle or other unstressed form: Я спас бы егó ['spaz‿bɨ] 'I would have saved him'. **Ц** is voiced as [dz] in such circumstances (Отéц был дóма [ʌ'ţedz‿bɨl] 'Father was in') and **ч** as [dʒ] (дочь былá [dodʒ‿bɨ'la] 'the daughter was').

(b) **В** has no voicing effect on a preceding unvoiced consonant, e.g. твой [tvoj] 'your'.

12 The pronunciation of -чн-

(1) -чн- is pronounced [ʃn] in certain words (конéчно [kʌ'n̥εʃnə] 'of course', нарóчно 'on purpose', прáчечная 'laundry', скýчно 'boring', яи́чница 'fried eggs'), as well as in the patronymics Ильи́нична 'Ilinichna', Сáввична 'Savvichna' and Никити́чна 'Nikitichna'.

(2) However, the pronunciation [tʃn] is used in more 'learned' words such as áлчный ['altʃnɨj] 'greedy', анти́чный 'ancient' and конéчный 'ultimate'.

(3) -чн- is pronounced either as [ʃn] or [tʃn] in бýлочная 'bakery' and молóчный 'milk' (adjective). Кори́чневый 'brown' is normally pronounced with [tʃn], [ʃn] being regarded as archaic.

Note

Ч is also pronounced [ʃ] in что 'that' and чтóбы 'in order to'.

13 Consonants omitted in pronunciation

In some groups of three or more consonants one is omitted in pronunciation. Thus, the first **в** is not pronounced in здра́вствуйте! 'hallo!', чу́вство 'feeling' (however, it **is** pronounced in де́вственный 'virgin' and нра́вственный 'moral'), **д** is not pronounced in звёздный 'starry', по́здно 'late', пра́здник 'festival' or се́рдце 'heart' (however, it **is** pronounced in бе́здна 'abyss'), **л** is not pronounced in со́лнце 'sun' (however, it **is** pronounced in со́лнечный 'solar') and **т** is not pronounced in ме́стный 'local', счастли́вый 'happy' (however, the first **т** in постла́ть 'to spread' **is** pronounced).

14 The pronunciation of double consonants

Double consonants are pronounced as two letters across the boundary between prefix and stem, e.g. отта́щить [tt] 'to drag away'. When a double consonant appears within a stem, practice varies, cf. грамма́тика [m] 'grammar', гру́ппа [pp *or* p] 'group'. A single consonant is pronounced in final position: грамм [m] 'gram', грипп [p] 'influenza'.

15 Stress

(1) Stress in Russian is 'free', that is, in some words it falls on the initial syllable (до́лго 'for a long time'), in others on a medial syllable (доро́га 'road') and in others on the final syllable (каранда́ш 'pencil'). The vowel ё is *always* stressed.

(2) A change in stress may indicate a change in meaning: о́рган 'organ of the body', орга́н 'organ' (musical instrument). A few words have alternative stress without a change in meaning: творо́г/тво́рог 'cottage cheese'.

(3) For stress patterns in individual parts of speech see nouns (**57, 60, 62, 63** (4)), adjectives (**164, 165**), verbs (**219, 223, 228, 232, 341, 343, 345, 350, 369**) and prepositions (**405**).

(4) Secondary stress (a weaker stress marked here with a grave accent [`]) is found in some compounds, e.g. машѝностро́ение

'engineering' (in fast speech, however, the word is pronounced with one full stress only: машиностроéние). Secondary stress is particularly common in words with foreign prefixes (àнтикоммунѝзм 'anti-communism', кòнтрмéры 'counter-measures', трànсатлантѝческий 'transatlantic', у̀льтракорóткий 'ultra-short' (also in words with the prefix свèрх-: свèрхурóчные 'overtime'), in technical terms (морòзоустóйчивый 'frost-proof'), in compounds where there is a polysyllabic gap between the natural stresses in the components (врèмяпрепровождéние 'pastime') and in compounds consisting of a truncated word and a full word (пàртбилéт (= партѝйный билéт) 'Party card'). The use of secondary stresses is sometimes optional, varying with speaker and speech mode. Generally speaking, the newer a compound word is, the more likely a secondary stress (e.g. кѝносценáрий 'film script'). Tertiary stresses are found in some compounds: àвтомòтоклýб 'car and motor-cycle club'.

(5) Some primary-stressed adverbs take secondary stress when used as prepositions: внутрѝ/внутрѝ 'inside', вóзле/вòзле 'near', вокрýг/вокрỳг 'around', мѝмо/мѝмо 'past', óколо/òколо 'close (to)', пóсле/пòсле 'after'.

Note
Stresses are marked in a Russian text only:

(a) to resolve ambiguity, cf. Я знáю, что он говорѝт 'I know that he is speaking' and Я знáю, чтó он говорѝт 'I know what he is saying', большáя часть 'a large part', бóльшая часть 'a larger part';

(b) to denote archaic pronunciations (e.g. библиóтека for contemporary библиотéка 'library');

(c) in rendering certain professional words, non-Russian words, dialect and slang words;

(d) ‧in verse, where normal stress is sometimes distorted in the interests of rhythm.

Orthography

16 Spelling rules

Spelling rule 1

ы is replaced by **и, я** by **а** and **ю** by **у** after **ж, ч, ш, щ** and **г, к, х**:

> **нога́**, 'leg', gen. sing. **ноги́**
> **молча́ть**, 'to be silent', first-person sing. **молчу́**, third-person pl. **молча́т**

Note

Exceptions are found in some non-Russian words and names: брошю́ра 'brochure', Кызылку́м 'Kyzylkum Desert', Кя́хта 'Kyakhta'.

Spelling rule 2

о is replaced by **е** in unstressed position after **ж, ч, ш, щ, ц**:

> **не́мец** 'German', instr. sing. **не́мцем**, gen. pl. **не́мцев**

Spelling rule 3

Initial **и** is replaced by **ы** following a prefix ending in a consonant:

> impf. **игра́ть**/pf. **сыгра́ть** 'to play'
> **интере́сный** 'interesting', **небезынтере́сный** 'not uninteresting'

Spelling rule 4

The prefixes **без-/бес-**; **вз-, воз-/вс-, вос-**; **из-/ис-**; **раз-/рас-** are spelt with **з** before voiced consonants or vowels and with **с** before unvoiced consonants: **безз́убый** 'toothless' but **бесконе́чный** 'infinite'; **взлета́ть** 'to take off' but **всходи́ть** 'to rise'; **изби́ть** 'to beat up' but **испи́ть** 'to sup'; **разобра́ть** 'to dismantle' but **расцепи́ть** 'to uncouple'.

Spelling rule 5

Prefixes ending in a consonant (e.g. **под-**, **от-**, **раз-**, **с-**) are spelt **подо-**, **ото-**, **разо-**, **со-**:

(i) In compounds of **-йти** (**подойти́** 'to approach', **подошёл** 'I approached' etc.) (see **333** (2)).

(ii) Before consonant + **ь** (**сошью́** 'I shall sew') (see **234** (5)).

(iii) Before certain consonant clusters (**разогна́ть** 'to disperse') (see **234** (1–4)).

Note
For spelling rules relating to prepositions see **404**.

17 Use of capital and small letters in titles and names

(1) In the names or titles of most posts, institutions, organizations, books, newspapers and journals, wars, festivals etc., *only the first word* is spelt with a capital letter: Акаде́мия нау́к 'Academy of Sciences', Всеми́рная федера́ция профсою́зов 'World Federation of Trade Unions', Генера́льный секрета́рь 'General Secretary', Министе́рство тра́нспорта 'Ministry of Transport', Моско́вский госуда́рственный университе́т 'Moscow State University', О́бщий ры́нок 'The Common Market', Политехни́ческий музе́й 'Polytechnical Museum', Худо́жественный теа́тр 'Arts Theatre', «*Война́ и мир*» '*War and Peace*', «*Нью-Йорк таймс*» '*New York Times*', Семиле́тняя война́ 'Seven Years War' (but Вели́кая Оте́чественная война́ 'Great Patriotic War'), Но́вый год 'New Year', Пе́рвое ма́я 'May Day', Ле́нинская пре́мия 'Lenin Prize'.

Note
Any word spelt with a capital letter in its own right retains the capital in extended titles: Госуда́рственный академи́ческий **Большо́й** теа́тр 'The State Academic Bolshoi Theatre'.

(2) In geographical names, the names of administrative areas, local features and so on, the generic terms are spelt with a *small* letter and the descriptive words with a *capital*: о́зеро Байка́л 'Lake Baikal', Бе́лое мо́ре 'the White Sea', мыс До́брой Наде́жды 'the Cape of Good Hope', тро́пик Ра́ка 'the Tropic of Cancer', Се́верный

Ледови́тый океа́н 'the Arctic Ocean', полуо́стров Таймы́р 'Taimyr Peninsula', Ю́жный по́люс 'the South Pole', у́лица Го́рького 'Gorky Street', Зи́мний дворе́ц 'the Winter Palace', Исаа́киевский собо́р 'St Isaac's Cathedral', Кра́сная пло́щадь 'Red Square', Ми́нский автомоби́льный заво́д 'the Minsk Car Factory'.

(3) Some titles consist of words, all of which have *capital* letters. These include the names of exalted governmental institutions and organizations, as well as a number of international bodies (and certain geographical names, e.g. Бе́лый Нил 'the White Nile', Да́льний Восто́к 'the Far East', Но́вая Земля́ 'Novaya Zemlya', Сове́тский Сою́з 'the Soviet Union'): Верхо́вный Сове́т 'the Supreme Soviet', Сове́т Безопа́сности ОО́Н 'the United Nations Security Council', Сове́т Мини́стров 'the Council of Ministers', Сове́тская А́рмия 'the Soviet Army', Соединённые Шта́ты Аме́рики 'the United States of America', Центра́льный Комите́т 'the Central Committee'.

Note

Па́ртия 'party' is not usually spelt with a capital letter: Коммунисти́ческая па́ртия 'the Communist Party'.

(4) Unofficial titles, the names of foreign parliaments and some other titles consist of words, all of which are spelt with a *small* letter: втора́я мирова́я война́ 'Second World War', моско́вский аэропо́рт 'Moscow Airport' (cf. official titles, now also used colloquially, e.g. аэропо́рт Вну́ково 'Vnukovo Airport'), пала́та общин 'House of Commons'.

(5) Nouns denoting nationality, town of origin etc. are also spelt with a *small* letter (англича́нин 'Englishman', москви́ч 'Muscovite'), as are the corresponding adjectives (англи́йский 'English', моско́вский 'Moscow' (adjective)), except where they form part of a title (Англи́йский банк 'Bank of England', Моско́вский цирк 'Moscow Circus'). This principle is also applied to the names of months, thus март 'March', октя́брь 'October', октя́брьский 'October' (adjective), but 8 Ма́рта 'March 8' (International Women's Day), Октя́брь/Октя́брьская револю́ция 'the October Revolution'.

(6) Земля́, луна́, со́лнце 'land, moon, sun' are spelt with capitals when they denote heavenly bodies: Земля́ 'the Earth', Луна́ 'the Moon', Со́лнце 'the Sun'.

Division of Words

18 Division into syllables

(1) Each syllable in a Russian word contains a vowel and, in most cases, consonants peripheral to it, e.g. па́-спорт.

(2) Russian distinguishes 'open' syllables, which end in a vowel (го-ло-ва́) from 'closed' syllables, which end in a consonant (нос).

(3) The principles of syllabic division are different in English and Russian, cf. E doc-tor/R до́-ктор, E her-o/R ге-ро́й. Russian non-initial syllables are formed on the basis of an ascending level of 'sonority', vowels being the most sonorous letters, the voiced sonants (р, л, м, н) the next most sonorous and noise-consonants (the other sixteen consonants) the least sonorous.

(4) In practice, this means that the **syllable boundary** occurs either:

(i) **between a vowel and a following consonant**: со-ло́-ма, сте-пно́й, ка́-ска, ко-стю́м, ста-ле-ва́р, стра-на́, о-тбро́-сить, вра-жда́ etc.;

or:

(ii) **between a sonant and a following consonant** (including another sonant): су́м-ка, кон-ве́рт, боль-шо́й, ка́р-та, вол-на́, чёр-ный, кар-ма́н.

Note
Non-initial syllables cannot begin with the sequence sonant + noise-consonant (this sequence is possible, however, in an *initial* syllable, e.g. **мши́**-стый). Note, however, the sequences sonant + sonant (во́-льный), consonant + consonant (ме́-сто) and noise-consonant + sonant (ме-тла́). The syllabic boundary may occur *before* or *between* two sonants (ка-**рм**а́н or ка**р**-ма́н, во-лна́ or вол-на́).

Syllabic division in a text

Я встал и на-де́л паль-то́. Же-на́ ре-ши́-ла, что я по-шёл за си-га-ре́-та-ми, и ве-ле́-ла не су-ту́-ли-ться при хо-дьбе́. О-на́ ска-за́-ла, что ко-гда́ я хо-жу́, то ны-ря́-ю вниз го-ло-во́й, как при-стя-жна́-я ло́-шадь. Е-щё о-на́ ска-за́-ла, что я всё вре́-мя смо-трю́ вниз, бу́-дто хо-чу́ най-ти́ на а-сфа́ль-те мо-не́-тку (Tokareva).

19   Splitting a word at the end of a line

(1) Two basic criteria are observed in splitting a word at the end of a line:

(i) Syllabic division: **го-лова́** or **голо-ва́**.

(ii) Word structure: it is desirable, for example, not to disrupt monosyllabic prefixes etc. (**под-бежа́ть**, **со-гла́сен**) (cf. **пе-рево́д** and note that the rule does not apply when a prefix is no longer perceived as such: **ра́-зум**, **разо-ря́ть**).

(2) A word is normally split **after a vowel**: го́-род, го́-лоден or го́ло-ден, ребя́-та or ре-бя́та. Sometimes this involves splitting a two-vowel sequence: **чита́-ете**.

(3) A sequence of **two or more consonants** may also be split: ме́д-ленно, ро́д-ственники, проб-ле́ма, и́стин-ный etc.

(4) Other conventions include the following:

(i) A hard or soft sign must not be separated from the preceding consonant (**подъ-е́зд**, **боль-шо́й**) and **й** must not be separated from the preceding vowel (**вой-на́**).

(ii) A single vowel should not appear at the end of a line or be carried over onto the next: **аги-та́ция** (*not* *а-гита́ция or *агита́ци-я).

(iii) Two identical consonants appearing between vowels should be split: **жуж-жа́ть**, **ма́с-са**, **ко́н-ный**.

(iv) A monosyllabic component of a stump compound should not be split (**спѐцоде́жда**); nor should abbreviations (**СССР́**, **и т.д.**).

(5) Some words can be split in different ways, e.g. **се-стра́**, **сес-тра́** or **сест-ра́**.

Punctuation

20 Introductory comments

Rules of punctuation are, in general, more rigorously applied in Russian than in English. Differences of usage between the two languages relate in particular to the comma (especially in separating principal from subordinate clauses), the dash and the punctuation of direct speech.

21 The full stop, exclamation mark and question mark

Usage of the full stop, exclamation mark and question mark is comparable in the two languages:

Лю́ди и́щут сча́стья в любви́.	People seek happiness in love.
Кака́я прекра́сная пого́да!	What magnificent weather!
Куда́ вы идёте?	Where are you going?

Note

(a) There is a tendency to use exclamation marks more frequently in Russian than in English.

(b) An exclamation mark may appear in the middle of a sentence: Так мне бы́ло пло́хо, **так го́рько и посты́ло!** — ху́же вся́кой боле́зни (Rasputin) 'I felt so bad, so bitter and wretched! – it was worse than any illness'.

(c) Exclamation marks are also used in commands expressed other than by a grammatical imperative: **Молча́ть!** 'Shut up!', **За мной!** 'Follow me!', **Вста́ли!** 'On your feet!'.

(d) An exclamation mark enclosed in parentheses (!) may be used to indicate irony or indignation.

(e) Exclamation and question marks may appear together for special emphasis: **Да что же э́то тако́е?!** 'Now what's all this?!'.

22   The comma: introductory comments

The comma is more frequently used in Russian than in English. In extreme examples a series of commas in a Russian sentence may have no English equivalents at all:

Мака́ренко пи́шет, что де́ти, кото́рые уме́ют труди́ться, уважа́ют труд други́х люде́й, стремя́тся прийти́ на по́мощь тем, кто в э́той по́мощи нужда́ется (Belyakova)
Makarenko writes that children who know how to work respect the labour of other people and strive to come to the assistance of those who need it

23   Uses of the comma I: correspondence with English usage

Commas are used, in Russian *and* English, to perform the following functions:

(1) To separate

(i) **two or more adjectives** which define one noun:

Он шёл по **тёмной, гря́зной, шу́мной** у́лице
He was walking down the dark, dirty, noisy street

(ii) **two or more adverbs** qualifying one verb:

Ме́дленно, мучи́тельно он встал с посте́ли
Slowly, painfully he rose from the bed

(2) To separate **items in a list**:

Пла́та за **кварти́ру, электри́чество, газ** составля́ет о́коло 20 рубле́й (Belyakova)
The rent, electricity and gas bills amount to about 20 roubles

(3) To mark off words and phrases which stand **in apposition**:

Валенти́на Терешко́ва, рабо́чая девчо́нка из стари́нного тексти́льного городка́, ста́ла пе́рвой же́нщиной-космона́втом
Valentina Tereshkova, a working girl from an ancient textile town, became the first woman in space

(4) To mark off words which serve to **define and specify**:

Зда́ние де́тского са́да двухэта́жное, **с больши́ми све́т-лыми о́кнами, с вера́ндами для дневно́го сна** (Belyakova)
The building of the kindergarten is two-storey, with large light windows and verandas for a daytime nap

(5) After **да** 'yes' and **нет** 'no':

Да, я согла́сен с ва́ми/**Нет**, я не согла́сен
Yes, I agree with you/No, I don't agree

(6) In **addressing people**:

Здра́вствуйте, Ива́н Ива́нович!
Hallo, Ivan Ivanovich!

(7) After **interjections**:

— **Ой**, как неуда́чно. Вчера́ упа́л и́ли сего́дня? (Rasputin)
'Oh, what bad luck. Did you fall over yesterday or today?'

(8) Between **repeated words**:

Ничего́, ничего́, утеша́л он себя́, са́мое тру́дное позади́ (Abramov)
Never mind, never mind, he consoled himself, the worst is over

(9) To mark off **participial phrases**:

По равни́не, **освещённой по́здним со́лнцем**, скака́л табу́н ди́ких лошаде́й
Over the plain, (which was) illuminated by the late sun, galloped a herd of wild horses

(10) To mark off **gerundial phrases**:

Я молча́л, **не зна́я**, что де́лать (Rasputin)
I was silent, not knowing what to do

Note
In English, 'and' is often used as an alternative to a comma before the final element in enumerations and when two or more adjectives qualify a single noun or two adverbs a single verb (cf. (1) and (2) above).

24 Uses of the comma II: differences in usage between Russian and English

Russian *requires* the use of a comma in the following contexts, where usage in English is optional or inconsistent:

(1) Between clauses linked by **co-ordinating conjunctions** (see **454** (2) (i) and **455–457**):

> Óля знáет бýквы, **но** я покá помогáю ей читáть (Belyakova)
> Olya knows the letters, but for the time being I help her to read

Note

(a) While a comma *always* appears before **но** (except when it is the first word in a sentence), the insertion of a comma before English 'but' depends largely on the length of the pause required by the context, cf. 'He is young but experienced' and 'He is young, but everyone trusts him'.

(b) A comma is used between clauses linked by **и** if the clauses have different subjects (Но волк был мёртв, **и** егó сейчáс никтó не боя́лся (Abramov) 'But the wolf was dead, and no one was afraid of him any more'), but not if they have the same subject (Разожгли́ костёр **и** свари́ли грибнóй суп (Belyakova) 'They lit a fire and made mushroom soup'). In such contexts **и** may be replaced by a comma: Два дня он **не пил, не ел** (= не пил и не ел) (Abramov) 'For two days he did not drink or eat'.

(2) Between clauses linked by the conjunctions **и** . . . **и** 'both . . . and', **ни** . . . **ни** 'neither . . . nor', **и́ли** . . . **и́ли** 'either . . . or', **то** . . . **то** 'now . . . now':

> На вéчере выступáли **и** мáльчики, **и** дéвочки
> Both boys and girls performed at the party

> Нельзя́ **ни** спокóйно почитáть, **ни** сосредотóчиться (Belyakova)
> You can neither do a little quiet reading, nor concentrate

> Это **и́ли** собáка, **и́ли** волк
> That is either a dog or a wolf

> Онá **то** смеётся, **то** плáчет
> Now she laughs, now she weeps

(3) Between **a principal and a subordinate clause** (see **458–467**):

Я зна́ю, **что** коне́ц бу́дет не ско́ро
I know the end is still some way off

Мы не отдава́ли дете́й в я́сли, **хотя́** така́я возмо́жность
была́ (Belyakova)
We didn't put the children into a day-nursery, even though we
had the opportunity to do so

Дени́с стал с нетерпе́нием ждать ле́та, **что̀бы** пое́хать с
ба́бушкой к Чёрному мо́рю
Denis waited impatiently for the summer, in order to go with his
grandmother to the Black Sea

Он рабо́тал бы, **е́сли бы** мог
He would work if he could

Она́ ухо́дит, **потому́ что** она́ опа́здывает
She is leaving because she is late

Note

The appearance of a comma between **потому́** and **что** in Мы
победи́м потому́, что мы сильне́е throws the element of cause
into sharper relief: 'We shall win because we are stronger' (i.e. and
for no other reason). This effect can be intensified by distancing
потому́ from что (**Потому́** мы победи́м, **что** мы сильне́е ...), or
by the addition of **лишь, то́лько** or other intensifying words before
потому́.

(4) To separate **main from relative clauses** (see **123**):

Я посеща́л го́род, **в кото́ром (где)** провёл де́тство
I was visiting the town in which (where) I had spent my childhood

Note

English distinguishes *relative* clauses (which are marked off by
commas) – 'Cats (i.e. *all* cats), who have excellent night vision, are
nocturnal predators' – from *adjective* clauses (which are *not* marked
off by commas): 'Cats (i.e. only *those* cats) who have no tails are
called Manx cats'. In Russian, however, both types of clause are
marked off with commas.

(5) To mark off **parenthetical words**:

во-пе́рвых/во-вторы́х in the first place/in the second place
допу́стим   let us assume   наприме́р   for example

ка́жется	it seems	пожа́луйста	please
коне́чно	of course	по-мо́ему	in my opinion
к сожале́нию	unfortunately	ска́жем	let us say
ме́жду про́чим	incidentally	с одно́й, друго́й	on the one, the
мо́жет быть	perhaps	стороны́	other hand
наве́рное	probably		

Он, **должно́ быть**, ушёл
He must have left

Нам, **коне́чно**, удо́бнее, что де́ти сидя́т ти́хо (Belyakova)
Of course, it's more convenient for us if the children are sitting quietly

Не спорь, **пожа́луйста**, со мной, я зна́ю (Rasputin)
Please don't argue with me, I know best

Он сказа́л, что, **к сожале́нию**, нам придётся идти́ без него́
He said that unfortunately we would have to go without him

(6) In **comparisons**:

Он ла́зит по дере́вьям, **как обезья́на**
He scrambles about in the trees like a monkey

Кто́-то научи́л своего́ малыша́ пла́вать **ра́ньше**, **чем** тот стал ходи́ть (Belyakova)
Someone taught his baby to swim before he could walk

Он спал беспробу́дным сном, **бу́дто** его́ ничто́ не трево́жило
He was sound asleep, as though without a care in the world

25 The colon

The colon is used to perform the following functions:

(1) To **introduce a list**, in which case the colon is usually preceded by a generic term:

Моя́ семья́ состои́т из четырёх челове́к: **мой муж Ви́ктор, дво́е дете́й и я** (Belyakova)
My family consists of four people: my husband Victor, the two children and myself

(2) To introduce a statement which **elaborates on, supplements or indicates the cause** of the statement which precedes the colon:

И тут их ожидáла нóвая бедá: **отéц пропáл** (Abramov)
And now a new misfortune awaited them: father had disappeared

В наýке всегдá должнá быть тóчность: **кáждому научному тéрмину должнó соотвéтствовать однó понятие** (Vvedenskaya)
There should always be accuracy in science: a single concept should correspond to each scientific term

Ýтром я со стрáхом смотрéл на себя в зéркало: **нос вспух, под лéвым глáзом синяк** (Rasputin)
In the morning I gazed at myself in the mirror in horror: my nose had swollen up, there was a bruise under my left eye

(3) To **introduce direct speech, thought or other communication**:

В кинофи́льме «*Доживём до понедéльника*» подрóсток пи́шет: **«Счáстье — э́то когдá тебя понимáют!»** (Kovaleva)
In the film *We'll survive till Monday* a teenager writes, 'Happiness is when people understand you!'

(4) To introduce a **quotation**:

Пóмните, в «*Евгéнии Онéгине*»:
Привы́чка свы́ше нам данá:
Замéна счáстию онá
Do you remember, in *Evgenii Onegin*:
Habit is granted us from on high:
It is a substitute for happiness

26 The semicolon

The semicolon is used to **separate extensive clauses** which are **not linked by conjunctions**, especially if each clause is itself broken up by commas:

В Ленингрáде все хотят посмотрéть на легендáрную «Аврóру», побывáть в пýшкинских местáх, в многочи́сленных дворцáх; в Ульяновске познакóмиться с местáми, где жил и учи́лся В. И. Лéнин; в Нáбережных Челнáх прое́хать по огро́мному молодо́му го́роду, посмотре́ть КамА́З (Vvedenskaya)

In Leningrad everyone wants to see the legendary 'Aurora', visit places associated with Pushkin, the numerous palaces; in Ulyanovsk to get to know the places where V. I. Lenin lived and worked; and in Naberezhnye Chelny to drive through the enormous new town, see the Kamaz truck factory

27 The dash

The dash is extremely widespread in Russian. It not only has a number of specific uses of its own but in some contexts substitutes for other punctuation marks, in particular the comma, the colon and parentheses.

(1) Specific uses of the dash.

(i) It separates **subject** noun from **predicate noun**, replacing the verb 'to be':

Мой оте́ц — преподава́тель ву́за, а ма́ма — врач (Belyakova)
My father is a college lecturer, and my mother is a doctor

Са́мое глубо́кое о́зеро ми́ра — э́то пресново́дный краса́вец Байка́л (Vvedenskaya)
The deepest lake in the world is the beautiful fresh-water Lake Baikal

Note
(a) The subject may sometimes be an **infinitive**:

Са́мое тяжёлое при проща́нии — **не огля́дываться** (*Ogonek*)
The hardest thing on parting is not to look back

(b) The dash is not normally used to replace the verb 'to be' when the subject is a pronoun: Он водола́з 'He is a diver'.

(ii) In elliptical statements it replaces a word, usually a verb, which is 'understood':

Студе́нт смотре́л на профе́ссора, профе́ссор — на студе́нта (Shukshin)

The student was looking at the professor, and the professor (was looking) at the student

(2) The dash is also used as a substitute for:

(i) The comma (when, for example, introducing an unexpected turn of events or sharp contrast):

Она сделала ещё попытку посадить меня за стол — **напрасно** (= **, но напрасно**) (Rasputin)
She made another attempt to seat me at the table, but in vain

Note
Generally speaking, the dash indicates a *more pronounced pause* than the comma, for example, in expressing apposition: Со мной был грузинский чай — моё единственное удовольствие (= , моё единственное удовольствие) 'I had with me some Georgian tea, my only pleasure'.

(ii) The colon:

(a) in introducing an **enumeration**, following a generic term:

Иногда клуб приглашает гостей — **учёных, педагогов, врачей** (Belyakova)
Sometimes the club invites guests – scientists, teachers and doctors

(b) in **elucidating** a statement:

У Соколовых ещё не спали — **в избе мигал огонёк**
The Sokolovs were still up – a light was flickering in the hut (cf. ещё не спали: в избе мигал огонёк)

(iii) Parentheses:

На территории Советского Союза — **не забывайте о том, что она занимает одну шестую часть всей суши Земли!** — тысячи рек и речушек
On the territory of the USSR (do not forget that it occupies one-sixth of the Earth's surface!) there are thousands of rivers and streams

28 The punctuation of direct speech

(1) If the introductory verb *precedes* the direct speech, the verb is followed by a *colon*, and the direct speech *either*

(i) appears on a new line, preceded by a *dash*:

Я промя́млил:
— Пра́вда (Rasputin)
'It is true', I mumbled

(ii) *or* runs on after the colon and is enclosed in *guillemets* («»):

Сам хозя́ин ра́за два крича́л с крыльца́: **«Эй, кто там?»**
The master himself shouted a couple of times from the porch, 'Hey, who's there?'

(2) If, however, the verb *follows* the direct speech, the latter is flanked by *dashes*:

— **Усну́л,** — услу́жливо отве́тила Си́ма (Rasputin)
'He's fallen asleep', answered Sima obligingly

(3) A **conversation** may be rendered as follows:

— И сего́дня уже́ ссо́рились? — спра́шивала их сотру́дница за́гса.
— Коне́чно!
— Ну из-за чего́ сего́дня?
— Из-за чего́? . . . Я уже́ забы́ла . . . (Belyakova)
'And have you quarrelled today too?', asked the registry office official.
'Of course!'
'And what have you been quarrelling about today?'
'What have we been quarrelling about today? . . . I forget . . .'

Note
(a) A full stop, comma, semicolon or dash *follow* inverted commas.
(b) Quotes within quotes may be distinguished as follows: «Кре́йсер "Авро́ра" стоя́л на я́коре» 'The cruiser "Aurora" lay at anchor'.
(c) In cursive script, inverted commas are rendered as follows: „*Приве́т!*" 'Greetings!'

29 Suspension points (многото́чие)

Suspension points (. . .) indicate one of the following.

(1) **Hesitation**:

— Про́игрываешь, наве́рное?
— Нет, **вы . . . вы́игрываю** (Rasputin)
'I suppose you lose?'
'No, I – I win'

(2) An **unfinished statement**:

Знать бы нам, чем э́то всё ко́нчится . . . (Rasputin)
Had we but known how it would all end . . .

The Noun

Gender

30 Masculine, feminine and neuter gender

(1) Adjectives, pronouns and the past-tense forms of verbs have the same gender as the noun they qualify or stand for:

хоро́ший муж	a good husband
хоро́шая жена́	a good wife
хоро́шее де́ло	a good cause
Оте́ц **дово́лен**	Father is pleased
Мать **дово́льна**	Mother is pleased
Где **стол**? Вот **он**	Where is the table? There it is
Где **ка́рта**? Вот **она́**	Where is the map? There it is
Где **окно́**? Вот **оно́**	Where is the window? There it is

Дом стоя́л в це́нтре го́рода
The house stood in the city centre

Ёлка стоя́ла в це́нтре го́рода
The Christmas tree stood in the city centre

Зда́ние стоя́ло в це́нтре го́рода
The building stood in the city centre

Note

(a) There is no equivalent in Russian of the articles 'a' and 'the'. Thus, for example, **дом** means 'a house' and 'the house', the difference being resolved by context or word order (see **476** (1) note (b), as well as **126** (2) (i), **128** (2) note, **138** (1) (iii) (b), **143** (2) (i), **193** (4) (iii)). Note that such forms as **э́тот** 'this', **тот са́мый** 'the very', **вы́ше упомя́нутый** 'the above-mentioned' etc. are sometimes used where an article would be used in English.

(b) When the predicate precedes the subject and the subject consists of a number of nouns, agreement may be with the first noun only: **Ну́жно** терпе́ние, понима́ние, взаи́мная откры́тость и доброжела́тельность (*Komsomolskaya pravda*) 'Patience, understanding, mutual openness and benevolence are necessary' (pl. **нужны́** would also be possible, however).

(2) Grammatical gender (the assignment of gender to a noun in accordance with its ending) is distinguished from **natural** gender (the assignment of gender in accordance with the sex of the being denoted by the noun, e.g. **мать** 'mother' (feminine), **дя́дя** 'uncle' (masculine)). Some nouns which can denote persons of either sex have **common** gender, that is, their gender varies in accordance with the sex of the person concerned (e.g. **сирота́** 'orphan' (masculine or feminine) see **35**).

(3) Gender affects only the **singular** of nouns; **plural** forms do not exhibit gender characteristics. The same adjectival endings, for example, are used for the plurals of nouns of *all* genders, cf.:

Singular	Plural
хоро́ший муж a good husband	**хоро́шие** мужья́ good husbands
хоро́шая жена́ a good wife	**хоро́шие** жёны good wives
хоро́шее де́ло a good cause	**хоро́шие** дела́ good causes

Note

Gender may, however, be revealed in, for example, a subordinate clause: хоро́шие мужья́, **ка́ждый** (masculine singular relative pronoun) из кото́рых помога́л по до́му 'good husbands, each of whom helped around the house'.

31 Masculine nouns

The following categories of noun are masculine:

(1) All nouns ending in a hard consonant, e.g. **заво́д** 'factory'

(2) All nouns ending in **-й**, e.g. **музе́й** 'museum'

(3) 'Natural' masculines in **-а/-я**. These include:

(i) Nouns which by definition denote males:

де́душка	grandfather
дя́дя	uncle
мужчи́на	man
па́па	Dad
слуга́	male servant
ю́ноша	youth, young man

including a few obsolescent nouns, e.g. **воево́да** 'commander'.

(ii) Some masculine first names:

Илья́	Ilya
Ники́та	Nikita
Фома́	Foma

(iii) The familiar forms of many masculine first names:

Ва́ня	Vanya (short for Ива́н)
Воло́дя	Volodya (short for Влади́мир)
Са́ша	Sasha (short for Алекса́ндр (*or* for feminine Алекса́ндра)) etc.

(4) Diminutives and augmentatives based on masculine nouns:

доми́шко (from дом 'house')   little house
доми́на, доми́ще (also from дом)   enormous house

(5) **Подмасте́рье** 'apprentice'.

(6) Many nouns ending in a soft sign (see **33**).

32 Feminine nouns

Categories of feminine noun include the following.

(1) Most nouns in **-а/-я** (see, however, **31** (3) and **34** (4)).

(2) Many nouns which end in a soft sign (see **33**).

33 Soft-sign nouns

Some soft-sign nouns are feminine (approximately three-quarters of the total); the rest are masculine. It is possible to give guidelines for determining the gender of many soft-sign nouns.

(1) Feminine soft-sign nouns

(i) 'Natural' feminines: **дочь** 'daughter' (see also (ii)), **лань** 'doe', **мать** 'mother', **нётель** 'heifer', **свекро́вь** 'mother-in-law' (husband's mother).

(ii) All nouns in **-жь, -чь, -шь, -щь, -знь, -мь, -пь, -фь.**

(iii) All nouns in **-сть**, except for masculine **гость** 'guest', **нёхристь** 'infidel, rogue' and **тесть** 'father-in-law' (wife's father).

(iv) All nouns in

- **-бь** except for masculine **го́лубь** 'dove'
- **-вь** except for masculine **червь** 'worm'
- **-дь** except for masculine **вождь** 'leader', **гвоздь** 'nail', **госпо́дь** 'Lord', **груздь** 'milk-agaric', **дождь** 'rain', **жёлудь** 'acorn', **лёбедь** 'swan', **медвёдь** 'bear' and a few historicisms
- **-зь** except for masculine **князь** 'prince', **ферзь** 'queen' (chess), **язь** 'ide' (fish of the carp family) and a few archaisms such as **ви́тязь** 'knight'
- **-сь** except for masculine **гусь** 'goose', **кара́сь** 'Crucian carp', **ло́сось/лосо́сь** 'salmon', **лось** 'elk'
- **-ть** except for natural masculines (see (2) (i) below) and masculine **дёготь** 'tar', **ко́готь** 'claw', **ла́поть** 'bast shoe', **ло́коть** 'elbow', **ломо́ть** 'slice', **но́готь** 'finger-nail', **путь** 'way', **тать** 'thief', **ять** 'the letter *yat*'

(v) Nouns derived through deaffixation from adjectives: **высь** 'heights' (cf. высо́кий 'high'), **гладь** 'smooth surface', **глубь** 'depth', **глушь** 'backwoods', **даль** 'distance', **зе́лень** 'greenery', **лень** 'laziness', **мель** 'shallows', **новь** 'virgin soil', **тишь** 'quiet', **у́даль** 'daring', **ширь** 'expanse', **явь** 'reality'.

(vi) Nouns derived through deaffixation from verbs: **гарь** 'burning' (cf. горе́ть 'to burn'), **мазь** 'ointment', **на́сыпь** 'embankment', **по́дпись** 'signature', **связь** 'connection', **смесь** 'mixture', **тварь** 'creature'.

(vii) Deverbal nouns in **-ель**, e.g. **ги́бель** 'ruin' (cf. ги́бнуть 'to perish'), **колыбе́ль** 'cradle', **мете́ль** 'snow storm'.

(2) Masculine soft-sign nouns

(i) 'Natural' masculines: **гость** 'guest', **де́верь** 'brother-in-law' (husband's brother), **зять** 'son-in-law/brother-in-law', **князь** 'prince', **кобе́ль** 'male dog', **коро́ль** 'king', **па́рень** 'lad', **се́лезень** 'drake', **тесть** 'father-in-law' (wife's father), **царь** 'tsar'.

(ii) Deverbal agent nouns (animate and inanimate) in **-тель** (**созда́тель** 'creator', **выключа́тель** 'light-switch') or **-итель** (**учи́тель** 'teacher', **краси́тель** 'dye').

(iii) Nouns in **-арь** derived from verbs (**пе́карь** 'baker'), nouns (**врата́рь** 'goal-keeper') or adjectives (**дика́рь** 'savage').

(iv) The names of **months** ending in a soft sign.

(v) All names of birds ending in a soft sign except for feminine **выпь** 'bittern' and **нея́сыть** 'tawny owl'; all names of insects ending in a soft sign except for feminine **моль** 'moth'.

The gender of other soft-sign nouns has to be learnt individually.

34 Neuter nouns

Categories of neuter noun include the following.

(1) Nouns in **-o** (see, however, **31** (4)).

(2) Nouns in **-e**. However, **ко́фе** 'coffee' is masculine (neuter in substandard registers only; see **36** (1) note (a)). See also **31**(4).

(3) Nouns in **-ё**.

(4) Nouns in **-мя**: **вре́мя** 'time', **и́мя** 'first name etc. See **64**.

(5) Other parts of speech functioning as nouns: **гро́мкое** «ура́» 'a loud "hurrah"'.

35 Common gender

A number of nouns in **-а** and **-я** have common gender. They can denote males or females, adjectival, pronominal and verb agreement varying with the sex of the person denoted by the noun, e.g. **го́рький пья́ница** 'confirmed drunkard' (male), **го́рькая пья́ница** 'confirmed drunkard' (female). Among the commonest of the nouns are бродя́га 'tramp', глава́ 'head, chief', кале́ка 'cripple', колле́га 'colleague', левша́ 'left-handed person', малю́тка 'baby', невѐжда 'ignoramus', неря́ха 'litter-bug', обжо́ра 'glutton', одино́чка 'lone person', пья́ница 'drunkard', сирота́ 'orphan' (кру́глый/кру́глая сирота́ 'person who has lost both parents'), судья́ 'judge', уби́йца 'murderer', у́мница 'clever person':

> Говори́те со мной, как с **кру́глым** невѐждой (Grekova)
> Speak to me as to a complete ignoramus

36 Indeclinable nouns of foreign origin

(1) Most indeclinable loan-words in **-ао, -е, -и, -о, -оа, -у, -уа, -ю** are neuter: кака́о 'cocoa'; ателье́ 'workshop', желе́ 'jelly', кабаре́ 'cabaret', кафе́ 'cafe', кашне́ 'scarf', коммюнике́ 'communiqué', купе́ 'compartment', портмоне́ 'purse', резюме́ 'résumé', тире́ 'dash', фойе́ 'foyer', шоссе́ 'highway'; ви́ски 'whisky', жюри́ 'jury', пари́ 'bet', пена́льти 'penalty' (also masculine), такси́ 'taxi', шасси́ 'undercarriage'; бюро́ 'office', депо́ 'depot', кино́ 'cinema', метро́ 'underground railway', пальто́ 'overcoat', пиани́но 'piano', ра́дио 'radio'; боа́ 'boa' (but боа́ 'boa-constrictor' is masculine); рагу́ 'ragout'; амплуа́ 'role'; интервью́ 'interview', меню́ 'menu'.

Note

(a) **Ко́фе** 'coffee' is masculine: Ля́ля спроси́ла, не сде́лать ли **кре́пкий** ко́фе (Trifonov) 'Lyalya asked if she should not make some strong coffee'.

(b) Only context can show the number (singular or plural) of an indeclinable noun: thus В шкафу́ **виси́т но́вое** пальто́/**вися́т но́вые** пальто́ 'A new coat is hanging/new coats are hanging in the cupboard'; **одно́** пальто́ 'one coat', **де́сять** пальто́ 'ten coats'.

(2) Some indeclinables assume the gender of the central or 'generic' noun. Thus, **торна́до** 'tornado' is masculine (cf. ве́тер 'wind'), likewise **пушту́** 'Pushtu', **урду́** 'Urdu', **хи́нди** 'Hindi' (cf. язы́к 'language'). **Авеню́** 'avenue' is feminine (cf. у́лица 'street'), as are саля́ми 'salami' (cf. колбаса́ 'sausage'), **цеце́** 'tsetse fly' (cf. му́ха 'fly') and **цуна́ми** 'tsunami' (alternatively neuter) (cf. волна́ 'wave'):

Цуна́ми **унесла́** его́ в океа́н (Gagarin)
The giant wave carried him out to sea

(3) The gender of many indeclinable nouns which denote human beings follows the principle of natural gender. Thus, буржуа́ 'bourgeois', маэ́стро 'maestro' and ре́фери/рефери́ 'referee' are masculine, while ле́ди 'lady' and мада́м 'madam' are feminine. Some nouns have common gender (визави́ 'counterpart, '*vis-à-vis*', протеже́ 'protégé(e)'), whereas атташе́ 'attache', инко́гнито 'person who is incognito' and конферансье́ 'compère' are masculine.

(4) Indeclinable names of animals also have common gender: гну 'gnu', кенгуру́ 'kangaroo', шимпанзе́ 'chimpanzee' etc. Nouns are treated as masculine when the sex of the animal is irrelevant (**ра́неный** гну 'a wounded gnu'), but feminine gender is assigned in 'female' contexts:

Шимпанзе́ **корми́ла** детёныша
The chimpanzee was feeding her baby

(5) The names of some birds are masculine (какаду́ 'cockatoo', марабу́ 'marabou', флами́нго 'flamingo') while коли́бри 'hummingbird' is masculine or feminine.

37   Indeclinable place names

Indeclinable place names take the gender of the central ('generic') noun. Names of towns and islands are masculine (cf. го́род 'town' and о́стров 'island'): Баку́ 'Baku', Гла́зго 'Glasgow', Кале́ 'Calais',

Óсло 'Oslo', Скóпье/Скóпле 'Skopje', Сóчи 'Sochi' (also plural: стáрые Сóчи 'old Sochi'), Тбили́си 'Tbilisi', Тóкио 'Tokyo'; Кáпри 'Capri', Таи́ти 'Tahiti'. Similarly, the names of rivers are feminine (cf. рекá 'river'): спокóйная Миссиси́пи 'the calm Mississippi'. Ю́нгфрау 'the Jungfrau' is feminine (cf. горá 'mountain'). Э́ри 'Lake Erie' is neuter (cf. óзеро 'lake'). Мали́ 'Mali' has alternative feminine and neuter gender (cf. странá 'country' and госудáрство 'state'). Despite exceptions to the rule, the 'generic' principle is the norm.

38 Titles of books etc.

The generic principle is usually applied in assigning gender to titles which are indeclinable: тургéневская «*Мумý*» 'Turgenev's *Mumu*' (cf. пóвесть (f.) 'tale'), лóндонская «*Таймс*» 'the London *Times*' (cf. газéта 'newspaper'). A title based on an oblique case may observe the generic principle (гóрьковская «*На дне*» 'Gorky's *Lower Depths*' (cf. пьéса 'play')) or take a neuter adjective (гóрьковское «*На дне*»).

Otherwise, gender is determined by the gender and number of the title: пýшкинский «*Евгéний Онéгин*» 'Pushkin's *Eugene Onegin*', тургéневское «*Дворя́нское гнездó*» 'Turgenev's *Nest of Noblemen*', саврáсовские «*Грачи́ прилетéли*» 'Savrasov's (painting) *The rooks have arrived*'.

Note
In order to avoid possible incongruence, a genre word may be introduced: ромáн Толстóго «*Áнна Карéнина*» 'Tolstoy's novel *Anna Karenina*'.

39 Acronyms

The gender of acronyms is usually determined by their ending. Thus, **бриз** (from бюрó по рационализáции и изобретáтельству 'bureau for rationalization and resourcefulness'), **вуз** (from вы́сшее учéбное заведéние 'higher teaching establishment'), **загс** (from отдéл зáписи áктов граждáнского состоя́ния 'registry office') are masculine. However, the gender of the central noun may sometimes prove decisive. Thus, **ронó** (from райóнный отдéл наро́дного образова́ния 'local education authority') was originally neuter but is now usually treated as masculine.

40 Alphabetisms

Alphabetisms consist of initial *capital* letters, many being pronounced as letters rather than words, and most are indeclinable, though there are exceptions among those assigned masculine gender (see **73**). In terms of gender assignment, alphabetisms subdivide as follows:

(1)   Those which retain the gender of the central noun:

(i)   Masculine: **МГУ** [эм-гэ-у́] (Моско́вский госуда́рственный университе́т 'Moscow State University'), **МХАТ** [мхат] (Моско́вский худо́жественный академи́ческий теа́тр 'Moscow Arts Theatre'), **НИИ** [ний] (Нау́чно-иссле́довательский институ́т 'Scientific Research Institute'), **ОВИР** [ови́р] (Отде́л виз и регистра́ция иностра́нных гра́ждан 'Visa Department and Registration of Foreign Nationals'), **СКА** [эс-ка́ or ска] (спорти́вный клуб а́рмии) 'Army Sports Club', **ЦК** [це-ка́] (Центра́льный Комите́т 'Central Committee').

(ii)   Feminine: **АТС** [а-тэ-э́с] (автомати́ческая телефо́нная ста́нция 'automatic telephone exchange'), **ГАИ** [гаи́] (Госуда́рственная автомоби́льная инспе́кция 'State Vehicle Inspectorate'), **ГЭС** [гэс] (гѝдроэлектри́ческая ста́нция/гѝдроэлектроста́нция 'hydroelectric power station'), **ООН** [оо́н] (Организа́ция Объединённых На́ций 'United Nations Organization'), **ТЭЦ** [тэц] (теплова́я элѐктроцентра́ль 'thermal power station'):

> Здесь **рабо́тала** мо́щная ГЭС (*Sputnik*)
> A mighty power station was in operation here

(iii)   Neuter: **АПН** [а-пэ-э́н] (аге́нтство печа́ти Но́вости 'Novosti Press Agency').

(2)   Some much-used alphabetisms acquire the gender implied by the ending. Thus, **БАМ** [бам] (Байка́ло–Аму́рская магистра́ль 'Baikal–Amur Railway') is masculine, despite feminine магистра́ль,

ДОСААФ [досáф] (Доброво́льное о́бщество соде́йствия а́рмии, авиа́ции и флóту 'Voluntary Association for Cooperation with the Army, Air Force and Navy') is masculine, despite neuter о́бщество, **МИД** [мид] (Министе́рство иностра́нных дел 'Ministry of Foreign Affairs'), which was once neuter, is now masculine, **НЭП** [нэп] (нóвая экономи́ческая поли́тика 'New Economic Policy'), which was once feminine, is now masculine and **ТАСС** [тасс] (Телегра́фное аге́нтство Сове́тского Сою́за 'Telegraphic Agency of the Soviet Union'), which was once neuter, is now masculine:

БАМ **был объя́влен** всесою́зной стрóйкой (*Sputnik*)
The Baikal–Amur Railway was declared a national construction zone

(3) Some alphabetisms differentiate gender stylistically. Thus, **ЖЭК** [жэк] (жили́щно-эксплуатациóнная контóра 'housing office'), initially feminine in written styles (cf. контóра), is commonly assigned masculine gender in everyday speech.

(4) Those based on the initials of *foreign* words tend to acquire gender in accordance with the ending. Thus, **ФИАТ** [фиа́т] (Fabbrica Italiana Automobili Torino) is masculine, **ФИФА** [фифá] (Fédération Internationale de Football Association) is feminine and **НАТО** [нáто] (North Atlantic Treaty Organization) is neuter. **США** [сша/сэ-ше-á] (Соединённые Шта́ты Аме́рики 'United States of America') is plural.

Note
Alphabetisms may be rendered phonetically, particularly in dialogue:

Ва́шу **эн-тэ-э́р** (НТР — на́учно-техни́ческая револю́ция) я ви́дел (Grekova)
I have seen your scientific–technical revolution

Вагóнчик что нáдо. **Гэдээ́ровский** (ГДР — Герма́нская Демократи́ческая Респу́блика) (Yakhontov)
A first-rate little carriage. Made in the German Democratic Republic

41 Stump compounds

'Stump compounds' incorporate the truncated forms of one or more words: **исполко́м** (from исполни́тельный комите́т) 'executive committee', **колхо́з** (from коллекти́вное хозя́йство) 'collective farm', **ликбе́з** (from ликвида́ция безгра́мотности) 'elimination of illiteracy', **собе́с** (from социа́льное обеспе́чение) 'social security' (all masculine). Most nouns in this productive category take their gender from the ending of the stump compound. Those which denote people may have common gender, e.g. **управдо́м** (from управля́ющий/-ая до́мом) 'house manager' (управдо́м сказа́л, что **дово́лен** 'the house manager said he was pleased', управдо́м сказа́ла, что **дово́льна** 'the house manager said she was pleased') and similarly **за̀вка́федрой** (from заве́дующий/-ая ка́федрой) 'head of university department'. **Са́мбо** (from самооборо́на без ору́жия) 'unarmed combat' is neuter, **стѐнгазе́та** (from стенна́я газе́та) 'wall newspaper' is feminine .

Note
The full title заве́дующий ка́федрой 'head of department' is preferred to за̀вка́федрой in official contexts, referring to persons of either sex, and in contexts where the sex of the person is irrelevant, заве́дующая being confined to colloquial registers or references to a particular person, cf.:

Собесе́дник называ́ет Евге́нию Ива́новну Ду́рову, **заве́-дующую** гру́ппой биохими́ческих иссле́дований (*Pravda*)
The person I am speaking to mentions Evgeniya Ivanovna Durova, head of the biochemical research group

42 Compound hyphenated nouns

The gender of compound hyphenated nouns is determined by the gender of the central noun, which often precedes the qualifier: **га́лстук**-ба́бочка (m.) 'bow-tie', **дива́н**-крова́ть (m.) 'divan-bed', **кре́сло**-кача́лка (n.) 'rocking chair', **раке́та**-носи́тель (f.) 'carrier-rocket', **шко́ла**-интерна́т (f.) 'boarding school'. However, in some compounds the qualifier precedes the central noun: **автома́т**-заку́сочная (f.) 'vending machine', **шта̀б**-кварти́ра (f.) 'head-quarters':

Автома́т-заку́сочная **отремонти́рована**
The vending machine has been repaired

13 июля на ста́ртовом по́ле **появи́лась** дубли́рующая ракéта-носи́тель (*Russia Today*)
A reserve carrier-rocket appeared on the launch pad on 13 July

43 Differentiation of gender through suffixes

(1) Suffixes are used to distinguish male and female representatives of various occupations, professions, organizations, functions, nationalities etc.

Male	Female	
армяни́н	армя́нка	Armenian
бегу́н	бегу́нья	runner
большеви́к	большеви́чка	Bolshevik
комсомо́лец	комсомо́лка	member of the Komsomol
корми́лец	корми́лица	breadwinner
крановщи́к	крановщи́ца	crane operator
лётчик	лётчица	pilot
опеку́н	опеку́нша	guardian
поэ́т	поэте́сса	poet
сто́рож	сторожи́ха	guard
супру́г	супру́га	spouse
учени́к	учени́ца	pupil
учи́тель	учи́тельница	teacher

Note also стари́к 'old man', стару́ха 'old woman'.

(2) The masculine form may, however, be used for persons of either sex:

(i) Where gender differentiation is of no significance in a particular occupation. Thus, библиоте́карь 'librarian', води́тель 'driver', касси́р 'cashier', конду́ктор '(bus-) conductor' etc. can be used of men *and* women. The feminine suffix -ша (as in библиоте́карша, касси́рша, конду́кторша) has in any case been devalued by its earlier use in designating a woman in terms of her husband's occupation: генера́льша 'general's wife' (cf. купчи́ха 'merchant's wife'). In modern Russian -ша is reserved for some occupations practised predominantly by women (e.g. **маникю́рша** 'manicurist' (маникю́р means 'manicure')) or denotes a lower-prestige occupation (cf. **секрета́рша** 'shorthand typist' and **секрета́рь** 'secretary' (of, for example, a Party committee)).

Note

Учи́тель tends to sound more prestigious than **учи́тельница** and may refer to a female as well as to a male teacher, especially where the subject is specified: Она́ **учи́тель** матема́тики 'She is a mathematics teacher'. Compare Она́ наилу́чший **учи́тель** в шко́ле 'She is the best teacher in the school' (i.e. of all the teachers, male and female) and Она́ наилу́чшая **учи́тельница** в шко́ле 'She is the best woman-teacher in the school'.

(ii) In cases where a plural covers male and female practitioners: профсою́з **рабо́тников** тра́нспорта 'transport workers' union'.

(3) Gender differentiation is retained, however, when male and female practitioners fulfil different functions: thus **актёр**, **актри́са** 'actor, actress' (playing, respectively, male and female roles). This also applies in most sports (where men and women compete against others of their own sex, not against each other): thus **конькобе́жец/ конькобе́жка** 'skater', **плове́ц/пловчи́ха** 'swimmer', **чемпио́н/ чемпио́нка** 'champion' (note, however, that only the more prestigious-sounding **чемпио́н** is used in official titles).

(4) In cases where men take up a 'female' occupation, a male equivalent of the name of the profession may be created, e.g. **доя́р**, cf. **доя́рка** 'milkmaid' (however, both have been superseded in mechanized dairies by **опера́тор** or **ма́стер маши́нного дое́ния** 'milking-machine operator'), **перепи́счик на маши́нке**, cf. **машини́стка** 'typist' (машини́ст 'engine-driver'). Note also **медици́нский брат** (or **санита́р**) 'male nurse' (cf. медици́нская сестра́ 'nurse'). The male equivalent of балери́на 'ballerina' is **арти́ст бале́та**. However, there are seemingly no masculine equivalents for **моди́стка** 'milliner' and **швея́-мотори́стка** 'sewing-machine operator'.

44 Professions

(1) Where professions which were almost exclusively male dominated before the Revolution are now also practised by women, the same designation is used for either sex. This applies to all professions

in **-вед**, **-граф**, **-лог** (языковéд 'linguist', биóлог 'biologist', топóграф 'topographer' etc.) and to áвтор 'author', архитéктор 'architect', ветеринáр 'veterinary surgeon', врач 'doctor' (жéнщина-врач 'woman doctor' is no longer appropriate in a society where most doctors *are* women; cf., however, **жéнщина-космонáвт** 'space-woman' and **жéнщина-офицéр** 'woman officer'), дúктор 'announcer', дирéктор 'director', дóктор 'doctor', инженéр 'engineer', композúтор 'composer', минúстр 'minister', парикмáхер 'hairdresser', пóвар 'cook', почтальóн 'postman', председáтель 'chairman', продавéц 'sales assistant', профéссор 'professor', стройтель 'builder', судьÿ 'judge', счетовóд 'accountant', трéнер 'trainer', шеф 'boss, head', экскурсовóд 'guide' etc.

Note

(a) Though some of the above have feminine equivalents which are also in use (e.g. **продавщúца** 'sales-girl'), all *can* be used to designate either men or women. Masculine and feminine forms may, however, be distinguished stylistically, with masculine (**продавéц** 'sales assistant', **секретáрь** 'secretary' etc.) preferred in official contexts (Товáрищ **продавéц!** (to a woman) 'Miss!') and feminine in conversation (Онá рабóтает **продавщúцей** 'She works as a shop assistant').

(b) The sex of an individual may be indicated by context: В клýбе с родúтелями не раз **встречáлась** профéссор **А. А. Люблúнская**, специалúст по дéтской психолóгии (*Rabotnitsa*) 'Professor A. A. Lyublinskaya, a specialist in child psychology, met parents in the club on more than one occasion'.

(c) In colloquial Russian, **исторúчка** refers to a female history teacher (cf. истóрик 'historian, history teacher'). **Электрúчка** (cf. элéктрик 'electrician') and **технúчка** (cf. тéхник 'technician') mean respectively 'suburban commuter train' and 'cleaning lady'.

(d) Male and female also share ranks in the services: **Рядовóй** Вéра Захарéнко награжденá óрденом Отéчественной войнÿ (*Rabotnitsa*) 'Private Vera Zakharenko has been awarded the Patriotic War Medal'.

(2) The nouns are qualified by *masculine* attributive adjectives irrespective of sex:

Он хорóший врач	He is a good doctor
Онá хорóший врач	She is a good doctor

Note

The use of feminine adjectives in such cases (e.g. **молодáя** экскурсовóд 'a young guide') is characteristic of 'relaxed' speech. **Молодóй** экскурсовóд is preferred for persons of either sex. In oblique cases masculine agreement is mandatory: Он подошёл к нáшему экскурсовóду Иванóвой 'He approached Ivanova, our guide'. Since there are some professions with which feminine adjectives may not combine (**агронóм** 'agronomist', **учúтель** 'teacher', **хирýрг** 'surgeon'), feminine agreement is best avoided altogether.

(3) The gender of **predicative** adjectives and past verb forms depends on the sex of the individual:

Врач **бóлен**	The doctor (male) is sick
Врач **больнá**	The doctor (female) is sick

Кассúр óчень вéжливо и óчень прóсто всё **объяснúла** (*Izvestiya*)
The cashier explained everything politely and very simply

Библиотéкарь **добáвила**: У нас 12 000 томóв (Nosov)
The librarian added 'We have 12,000 volumes'

45 Animals

(1) Most nouns denoting animals, birds, insects etc. refer to the species in general: **ёж** 'hedgehog', **журáвль** (m.) 'crane', **кит** 'whale', **крýса** 'rat', **мышь** (f.) 'mouse' and so on. Thus, there is no indication of the sex of the animal or bird in Ёж скрýлся в лесý 'The hedgehog disappeared into the forest', Лáсточка вилá гнездó 'The swallow was building a nest'. Male and female can be differentiated where necessary by using the words **самéц** 'male' and **сáмка** 'female' followed by the genitive case of the name of the animal: самéц/ сáмка ежá 'male/female (of the) hedgehog' etc.

(2) Some animal names, however, do distinguish male and female: волк/волчúца 'wolf', зáяц/зайчúха 'hare', лев/львúца 'lion/ lioness', слон/слонúха 'elephant', тигр/тигрúца 'tiger/tigress'. The male form also denotes the species in general (except for **кот/ кóшка** 'cat', where the female form **кóшка** denotes the species in general).

(3) Male and female are differentiated in the names of farm animals: бара́н/овца́ 'ram/sheep', бо́ров/свинья́ 'boar/sow', бык/коро́ва 'bull/cow', козёл/коза́ 'billy-/nanny-goat', пету́х/ку́рица 'cockerel/hen', се́лезень/у́тка 'drake/duck'.

(4) A few species have three names denoting (a) the species in general, (b) male and (c) female: гусь (m.) 'goose', гуса́к 'gander', гусы́ня 'goose'; ло́шадь (f.) 'horse', жеребе́ц 'stallion', кобы́ла 'mare'; соба́ка 'dog', кобе́ль (m.) 'male dog', су́ка 'bitch'.

Declension

46 Introduction

(1) Nouns decline according to one of three declension patterns. Most masculine and neuter nouns belong to the first declension and most feminine nouns to the second, except for feminine soft-sign nouns, which belong to the third declension (see **63**).

(2) The first and second declensions contain both hard-ending nouns (e.g. first-declension **дом** 'house', **окно́** 'window', second-declension **ка́рта** 'map') and soft-ending nouns (e.g. first-declension **музе́й** 'museum', **гость** 'guest', **мо́ре** 'sea', second-declension **ку́хня** 'kitchen'). All nouns in the third declension are feminine and end in a soft sign.

(3) Some declension endings are affected by the rules of spelling (see **16** (1) and (2)).

(4) For *stress* changes in all three declensions, see **57, 60, 62, 63** (4).

47 Animacy

(1) The accusative case of an animate **masculine** singular noun is identical with the genitive, cf.

дом **бра́та** (genitive) 'my brother's house'
ви́жу **бра́та** (accusative) 'I see my brother'

Note

The differentiation of animate subject and animate object is important in a language where either may precede the other with virtually no change in meaning, cf. Отéц лю́бит сы́на 'The father loves the son' and Сы́на лю́бит отéц 'The father loves the son' (or 'It is the father who loves the son', see **475** (2)). The need to avoid ambiguity determines the accusative/genitive rule in animate masculine nouns.

(2) The following types of masculine singular noun are affected:

(i) Human beings: Отéц лю́бит **сы́на** 'The father loves the son'.

(ii) Animals: Я ви́жу **быкá** 'I see the bull'.

(iii) Common nouns used figuratively to denote human beings: болвáн 'blockhead', дуб 'dunce', куми́р 'idol', тип 'type' etc.:

> Я рéдко встречáл **такóго болвáна/такóго забáвного ти́па**
> I have seldom met such a blockhead/such a funny character

Note

(a) Я вёл «Москвичá» 'I was driving a "Moskvich"' (car) is more colloquial than Я вёл «Москви́ч».

(b) Usage with рóбот: cf. Инженéр конструи́рует **рóбот** 'The engineer is designing a robot' (i.e. an automaton), and figurative usage in превращáть человéка в **рóбота** 'to turn a man into a robot'. However, the animate accusative/genitive is now normal in non-figurative contexts also:

> Компáния «Мацуси́ма» ужé испытáла рóбота (*Nedelya*)
> The 'Matsushima' company has already tested a robot

(iv) Some folk dances, e.g. плясáть **трепакá**, **гопакá** 'to dance the trepak, the gopak'; animate beings in book titles, e.g. Держáл в рукáх «*Чапáева*» 'In his hands he held *Chapaev*' (a novel); playing cards, e.g. сбрóсить **валéта**, снять **тузá**, 'to discard a knave, cut an ace'; billiards and snooker balls, e.g. положи́ть **зелёного** (шарá) в лýзу 'to pocket the green'; chess pieces, e.g. взять **слонá**, **короля́**, **ферзя́** 'to take a bishop, the king, the queen'; the words змей 'kite' and **развéдчик** 'reconnaissance aircraft' (cf. animate connotations ('serpent' and 'reconnaissance agent' respectively)), e.g. пускáть **змéя** 'to fly a kite', сбить **развéдчика** 'to shoot down a reconnaissance aircraft'. Analogous usage such as сбить **истреби́теля** 'to shoot down a fighter' and постáвить **двóрника** 'to fit a windscreen wiper' characterizes professional colloquial speech but is otherwise regarded as substandard for usage with standard inanimate accusatives истреби́тель and дво́рник.

Note

(a) Collective nouns (e.g. наро́д 'people', полк 'regiment', скот 'cattle') are *not* treated as animate:

Внача́ле тигр напада́ет на **скот** (*Russia Today*)
First a tiger attacks the cattle

(b) The nouns мертве́ц 'dead person' and поко́йник 'deceased' are treated as animate, while труп 'corpse' is not, cf.

Он взял **мертвеца́** за плечо́ и поверну́л на́ спину (Nagibin)
He took the dead person by the shoulder and turned him on his back

and

Он рассказа́л, как он обнару́жил **труп** (Nagibin)
He told how he had discovered the corpse

(3)   The following types of **plural** noun are affected by the rule.

(i)   Human beings and animals of *all* genders:

Она́ ко́рмит **ма́льчиков** и **де́вочек**
She is feeding the boys and girls

Он ко́рмит **осло́в** и **ове́ц**
He is feeding the donkeys and the sheep

Он ви́дит **живо́тных**
He sees the animals

Note

Лови́ть **ома́ров** 'to catch (live, i.e. animate) lobsters', but есть, покупа́ть **ома́ры** 'to eat, buy (dead, i.e. inanimate) lobsters'. The distinction applies mainly to crustaceans, but is not consistently observed.

(ii)   Toys fashioned in human form:

Там де́лают **матрёшек**	Nesting dolls are made there
Де́вочка одева́ет **ку́кол**	The little girl is dressing the dolls

Note

Марионе́тка 'puppet' also belongs in this category.

(iii) Plural equivalents of the singular categories listed above: читáть «**Брáтьев Карамáзовых**» 'to read *The Brothers Karamazov*' (see (2) (iii) and (iv) above).

Note

(a) Бактéрия 'bacterium', бацúлла 'bacillus', вúрус 'virus', зарóдыш 'foetus', микрóб 'microbe' are treated as inanimate: Человéк убивáет **бацúллы** и **бактéрии** 'Man kills bacilli and bacteria'. Use of the accusative/genitive in such cases is regarded as somewhat old-fashioned but may be encountered in books on biology and medicine: Изучáть **бактéрий**, **вúрусов**, **микрóбов** 'To study bacteria, viruses, microbes'.

(b) **Войскá** (pl.) 'troops' is treated as inanimate and has accusative войскá.

(c) The animate accusative genitive rule also applies to adjectives, pronouns and certain numerals (see **193**(1 note (c)), **196**(2) and **200**).

48 Nouns which are used only in the singular

Some nouns have singular form only. They include nouns which denote:

(1) **Qualities, sensations**: хрáбрость 'bravery', грусть 'sadness'.

(2) **Collectives**: бельё 'linen', листвá 'foliage' etc.

(3) **Substances, foods, cereals**: дéрево 'wood', овёс 'oats' and so on. Note, however, that the plurals of some nouns in these categories are encountered in the meaning 'brands', 'large quantities': жирьí 'fats'. This also applies to certain **natural phenomena** normally found in the singular only: дождú 'persistent rain', морóзы 'persistent heavy frost', снегá 'heavy snow'. The names of some **vegetables and fruits** are also used in the singular only (виногрáд 'grapes', горóх 'peas', изюм 'raisins', капýста 'cabbage', картóфель 'potatoes', лук 'onions', моркóвь 'carrots'), a different word being used to denote 'one onion' (лýковица/голóвка лýка oг лýку): cf. виногрáдина 'a grape', горóшина 'a pea', изюмина 'a raisin', картóфелина/клýбень картóфеля 'a potato', кочáн капýсты 'a cabbage', моркóвка 'a carrot'. Compare also солóма 'straw', солóмина 'a straw'; шоколáд 'chocolate', шоколáдка 'a chocolate'.

(4) 'Singulatives' are also used to create plural forms from abstracts and collectives which have no plural of their own: долг 'duty' (**обя́занности** 'duties' (note that долг in the meaning 'debt' *has* a plural: **долги́**)), ложь 'lie' (**вы́думки** 'fabrications, lies'), ору́жие 'weapons' (pl. **ви́ды** ору́жия), поли́тика 'policy, politics' (полити́ческие **направле́ния** 'policies'), промы́шленность 'industry' (**о́трасли** промы́шленности 'industries'), спорт 'sport' (**ви́ды** спо́рта 'sports, events'). Note also that разли́чия can be used as the plural of ра́зница (which has no plural of its own).

(5) The names of animals, trees etc. may denote a whole species:

В на́шем лесу́ растёт то́лько **сосна́**
Only pine trees grow in our forest

Здесь ло́вят то́лько **леща́**
Only bream is caught here

(6) Names of professions and some other words can also be used collectively: День **шахтёра** 'Miners' Day', Дом **кни́ги** 'book shop', Дом **учи́теля** 'Teachers' Club'.

49 Nouns which have a plural form only

(1) Many plural-only nouns denote objects comprising two or more essential components: **брю́ки** 'trousers', **но́жницы** 'scissors'. Others denote complex processes (**ро́ды** 'childbirth'), games (**пря́тки** 'hide and seek') etc.

(2) Morphologically, the nouns subdivide as follows.

(i) Plurals in **-ы/-и/-а́**, genitive **-ов**:

аплодисме́нты 'applause'   gen. **аплодисме́нтов**

Similarly бега́ 'trotting races', весы́ 'scales', вы́боры 'election', деба́ты 'debate', джи́нсы 'jeans', духи́ 'perfume', за́морозки 'light frosts', консе́рвы 'preserves', мемуа́ры 'memoirs', оста́нки 'human remains', очки́ 'spectacles', переговоры 'negotiations', подо́нки 'dregs', припа́сы 'stores', ро́ды 'childbirth', счёты 'abacus', тро́пики 'tropics', тру́сики/трусы́ 'shorts', штаны́ 'trousers', щипцы́ 'pincers, tongs'.

Note

Nouns ending in two vowels or unstressed -цы have gen. **-ев**: обóи, **обóев** 'wallpaper' (likewise побóи 'beating', помóи 'slops'), плоскогýбцы, **плоскогýбцев** 'pliers'.

(ii) Plurals in **-ы**/**-и** with zero genitive ending:

вúлы 'pitchfork'　　　gen. **вил**

Similarly Афúны 'Athens', брюки 'trousers', дéньги (gen. **дéнег**), 'money', именúны 'name-day', кальсóны 'pants', канúкулы 'holidays', носúлки (gen. **носúлок**) 'stretcher', нóжницы 'scissors', нóжны (gen. **нóжен**) 'sheath', опúлки (gen. **опúлок**) 'sawdust', панталóны 'knickers', плáвки (gen. **плáвок**) 'swimming trunks', пóхороны (gen. **похорóн**) 'funeral', салáзки (gen. **салáзок**) 'toboggan', сáнки (gen. **сáнок**) 'sledge', слúвки (gen. **слúвок**) 'cream', сýмерки (gen. **сýмерек**) 'dusk', сýтки (gen. **сýток**) '24-hour period', ýзы 'bonds', хлóпоты (gen. **хлопóт**) 'trouble', шáхматы 'chess', шóры 'blinkers'.

(iii) Plurals in **-а** with zero genitive ending:

ворóта 'gate'　　　gen. **ворóт**

Similarly дровá 'firewood', кружевá 'lace' (also sing. **крýжево**), нéдра 'bowels of the earth', перúла 'railing', чернúла 'ink'.

(iv) Nouns in **-и**, genitive **-ей**:

качéли 'swing'　　　gen. **качéлей**

Similarly бýдни 'weekdays' (gen. also **бýден**), вóжжи (gen. **вожжéй**) 'reins', грáбли 'rake' (gen. also **грáбель**), джýнгли 'jungle', дрóжжи (gen. **дрожжéй**) 'yeast', клéщи (gen. **клещéй**) 'pincers', кýдри (gen. **кудрéй**) 'curls', пóмочи (gen. **помочéй**) 'braces', сáни (gen. **санéй**) 'sledge', щи 'cabbage soup'.

Note

(a) Прéния, gen. **прéний** 'debate', свéдения, gen. **свéдений** 'information'.

(b) Countable nouns in the series, e.g. **сáни** 'sledge', can denote one object ('sledge') or a number of objects ('sledges'). Meaning is determined by context: Из санéй вúскочил **солдáт** 'A soldier jumped from the **sledge**'; Из санéй вúскочил **цéлый взвод солдáт** 'A whole platoon of soldiers jumped from the **sledges**'.

50 Declension chart

The following chart shows, in simplified form, the declension pattern in all three declensions.

	Singular			Plural		
	m	n	f	m	n	f
N	cons. -й -ь	-о -е -ё	-а/-я	-ь	-ы/-и	-а/-я	-ы/-и
A INAN	= N	= N	-у/-ю	-ь	= N		
A ANIM	= G	= N	-у/-ю	-ь	= G		
G	-а/-я		-ы/-и	-и	-ов//-ев/-ей	zero/ей	
D	-у/-ю		-е	-и	-ам/-ям		
I	-ом/	unstr. ем str. ём	-ой/ -ей -ёй	-ью	-ами/-ями		
P	-е			-и	-ах/-ях		

51 First declension: masculine nouns

(1) Hard-ending nouns

Declension of **завóд** 'factory' (inanimate) and **студéнт** 'student' (animate):

	Singular		Plural	
Nom.	завóд	студéнт	завóд-ы	студéнт-ы
Acc.	завóд (=nom.)	студéнт-а (=gen.)	завóд-ы	студéнт-ов
Gen.	завóд-а	студéнт-а	завóд-ов	студéнт-ов
Dat.	завóд-у	студéнт-у	завóд-ам	студéнт-ам
Instr.	завóд-ом	студéнт-ом	завóд-ами	студéнт-ами
Prep.	о завóд-е	о студéнт-е	о завóд-ах	о студéнт-ах

Note

(a) Nouns in **г, к, х/ж, ч, ш, щ** have nominative and inanimate accusative plural **-и**: урóк 'lesson', **урóки**; нож 'knife', **ножи́** (see **16** (1)).

(b) Nouns ending in **ж, ч, ш, щ, ц** and with stem stress in declension have instrumental singular **-ем**: душ 'shower', **ду́шем**; ме́сяц 'month', **ме́сяцем** (see **16** (2)).

(c) Nouns ending in **ж, ч, ш, щ** have genitive plural **-ей**: нож 'knife', gen. pl. **ноже́й**.

(d) Nouns ending in **-ц** with stem stress in declension have genitive plural **-ев**: шприц 'syringe', gen. pl. **шпри́цев** (see **16** (2)).

(e) The genitive plural of some nouns is identical with the nominative singular (see **56**).

(f) **Год** 'year' has genitive plural **лет** (**годо́в** in denoting decades: мо́ды **50-х годо́в** 'the fashions of the fifties'); cf. dative, instrumental, prepositional plural **года́м, года́ми, о года́х**.

(2) Soft-ending nouns

(i) Nouns in **-й**

Declension of **музе́й** 'museum' and **геро́й** 'hero':

	Singular		Plural	
Nom.	музе́й	геро́й	музе́-и	геро́-и
Acc.	музе́й (=nom.)	геро́-я (=gen.)	музе́-и	геро́-ев
Gen.	музе́-я	геро́-я	музе́-ев	геро́-ев
Dat.	музе́-ю	геро́-ю	музе́-ям	геро́-ям
Instr.	музе́-ем	геро́-ем	музе́-ями	геро́-ями
Prep.	о музе́-е	о геро́-е	о музе́-ях	о геро́-ях

Note

(a) Nouns in **-ий** have prepositional singular **-ии**: ге́ний 'genius', о **ге́нии**.

(b) **Воробе́й** 'sparrow' is declined as follows: acc./gen. воробья́, dat. воробью́, instr. воробьём, prep. о воробье́; nom. pl. воробьи́, acc./gen. воробьёв, dat. воробья́м, instr. воробья́ми, prep. о воробья́х. Similarly, мураве́й 'ant', солове́й 'nightingale' and inanimate (acc. = nom.), репе́й 'burdock', руче́й 'stream' and stem-stressed у́лей 'bee-hive'.

(ii) Soft-sign nouns

Declension of **портфе́ль** 'briefcase' and **тесть** 'father-in-law':

	Singular		Plural	
Nom.	портфе́ль	тесть	портфе́л-и	тест-и
Acc.	портфе́ль (=nom.)	тест-я (=gen.)	портфе́л-и	тест-ей
Gen.	портфе́л-я	тест-я	портфе́л-ей	тест-ей
Dat.	портфе́л-ю	тест-ю	портфе́л-ям	тест-ям
Instr.	портфе́л-ем	тест-ем	портфе́л-ями	тест-ями
Prep.	о портфе́л-е	о тест-е	о портфе́л-ях	о тест-ях

52 The fleeting vowel

The vowel in the final syllable of many nouns which end in a hard consonant or soft sign does *not* appear in oblique cases. Vowels affected include the following:

(1) 'o': ры́нок 'market'

	Nom./Acc.	Gen.	Dat.	Instr.	Prep.
Singular	ры́нок	ры́нка	ры́нку	ры́нком	о ры́нке
Plural	ры́нки	ры́нков	ры́нкам	ры́нками	о ры́нках

Most nouns in **-ок** are similarly declined. Exceptions include **знато́к** 'connoisseur' (gen. **знатока́**), **игро́к** 'player', **уро́к** 'lesson'.

Note
Some other nouns also contain a fleeting **-o-**:
(a) Hard-ending nouns: лоб 'forehead', gen. **лба**; мох 'moss'; посо́л 'ambassador'; рот 'mouth'; сон 'sleep'; у́гол 'corner'; шов 'seam'.
(b) Soft-sign nouns: дёготь, gen. **дёгтя** 'tar'; ко́готь 'claw'; ломо́ть 'slice'; но́готь 'nail'; ого́нь 'fire'; у́голь 'coal', gen. **угля́/у́гля**.

(2) 'e': коне́ц 'end'

	Nom./Acc.	Gen.	Dat.	Instr.	Prep.
Singular	коне́ц	конца́	концу́	концо́м	о конце́
Plural	концы́	концо́в	конца́м	конца́ми	о конца́х

Most nouns in **-ец** are similarly declined. However, stressed **-é-** is retained when preceded by a double consonant: близне́ц 'twin', gen. **близнеца́**; кузне́ц 'blacksmith', gen. **кузнеца́**.

Note
(a) See **51** (1) notes (b) and (d) for the instrumental singular and genitive plural of stem-stressed nouns in **-ц**.
(b) **-ле-** becomes **-ль-** in oblique cases: па́лец 'finger', gen. **па́льца**.
(c) A fleeting vowel preceded by another vowel is replaced by **-й-** in oblique cases: бельги́ец 'Belgian', gen. **бельги́йца**; кита́ец 'Chinese', gen. **кита́йца**. Cf. заём 'loan', gen. **займа́**; за́яц 'hare', gen. **за́йца**.

Other hard and soft nouns with a fleeting -**e**- include ве́тер 'wind' (gen. **ве́тра**), за́мысел 'project', у́зел 'knot' (gen. **узла́**), хребе́т 'range of hills'; день 'day' (gen. **дня**), ка́мень 'stone', ка́шель 'cough', ко́рень 'root', ли́вень 'downpour', па́рень 'fellow', пень 'stump', реме́нь 'strap', сте́бель 'stalk'.

(3) 'ё': ковёр 'carpet'

Nouns with a fleeting **ё** include ковёр 'carpet' (gen. **ковра́**), козёл 'goat', костёр 'bonfire', котёл 'boiler'. Note that in some words **ё** is replaced by a soft sign following **л**, **н** or **р**: лёд 'ice' (gen. **льда**), конёк 'skate' (gen. **конька́**), хорёк 'ferret' (gen. **хорька́**).

53 Partitive genitive in -у/-ю

Some hard-ending masculine nouns and a few nouns in -**й** have an alternative genitive singular in -**у**/-**ю**. The nouns all denote measurable quantities, e.g. **виногра́д** 'grapes' (gen. **виногра́да/ виногра́ду**), чай 'tea' (gen. **ча́я/ча́ю**). Other nouns with a partitive genitive in -**у**/-**ю** include:

жир	fat	**са́хар**	sugar
квас	kvass	**снег**	snow
клей	glue	**суп**	soup
лук	onions	**сыр**	cheese
мёд	honey	**таба́к**	tobacco
мел	chalk	**творо́г**	cottage cheese
мех	fur	**чесно́к**	garlic
наро́д	people	**шёлк**	silk
песо́к	sand, castor sugar	**шокола́д**	chocolate
рис	rice		

Most genitives in -**у**/-**ю** appear only in quantitative expressions: кусо́к **сы́ру** 'piece of cheese', ча́шка **ча́ю** 'cup of tea'. See also **84**.

Owing to the colloquial nature of the genitives in -**у**, they are not found with nouns denoting rarer substances such as, for example, **молибде́н** 'molybdenum'.

54 Prepositional/locative singular in -ý/-ю́

(1) Locative in -ý

Some nouns have an alternative prepositional singular in stressed -ý; it is used with the prepositions **в** and **на** to denote location, but not with other prepositions that take the prepositional case (о, по, при); cf. **в порту́** 'in the port' and **о по́рте** 'about the port':

аэропо́рт	airport
бал	ball, dance
бе́рег	shore, bank
бок	side
бор	coniferous forest
борт	side (of a ship, etc.)
	на борту́ 'on board'
верх	top, summit
глаз	eye
Дон	the Don
Клин	Klin
Крым	the Crimea
лёд	ice
	(**на льду́** 'on the ice')
лес	forest
лоб	forehead
	(**на лбу́** 'on the forehead')
луг	meadow
мост	bridge
мох	moss
	(**во мху́** 'in the moss')
нос	nose, prow
плот	raft
пол	floor
полк	regiment
порт	port
пост	post
	(**на посту́** 'at one's post')
пруд	pond
рот	mouth
	(**во рту́** 'in the mouth')
сад	garden, orchard

снег	snow
тыл	the rear
у́гол	corner
	(**в/на углу́** 'in/at the corner')
шкаф	cupboard

Note

(a) Some phrases denote state: **в бреду́** 'in a delirium', **в быту́** 'in everyday life', **в жару́** 'in a fever', **в плену́** 'in captivity'.

(b) Where **в** or **на** have non-locational meanings, the noun takes the ending **-е**: знать толк в ле́се 'to understand the forest'.

(c) The ending **-е** is also used in the names of books: в «*Вишнёвом са́де*» Че́хова 'in Chekhov's *Cherry Orchard*'.

(d) Sometimes both **-е** and **-у́** are possible, the form in **-у́** being the more colloquial variant: **в о́тпуске/отпуску́** 'on holiday', **в це́хе/цеху́** 'in the workshop'.

(e) The endings **-е** and **-у́** may be differentiated semantically and phraseologically, cf. в XX ве́ке 'in the twentieth century' and Мно́го ви́дел я люде́й на своём веку́ 'I have seen a lot of people in my time'; **в ви́де** исключе́ния 'by way of an exception' and име́ть **в виду́** 'to bear in mind'; в до́ме 'in the house' and на дому́ 'on the premises'; в спаса́тельном **кру́ге** 'in a life-belt' and в семе́йном **кругу́** 'in the family circle'; труди́ться в **по́те** лица́ 'to labour by the sweat of one's brow' and весь в **поту́** 'bathed in sweat'; в **ря́де** слу́чаев 'in a number of cases' and в пе́рвом **ряду́** 'in the front row'; умере́ть во **цве́те** лет 'to die in one's prime' and дере́вья в по́лном **цвету́** 'the trees are in full bloom'; в **ча́се** лёта от Москвы́ 'an hour's flight from Moscow' and во второ́м **часу́** 'between one and two o'clock'.

(f) Note also жить в ладу́ 'to live in harmony', ку́ртка **на меху́** 'fur-lined jacket', **на ка́ждом шагу́** 'at every step'.

(2) Locative in -ю́

A few nouns in **-й** and **-ь** have a locative singular in **-ю́**: **бой** 'battle', в **бою́** 'in battle' (but о бо́е 'about the battle'). Similarly рай 'paradise', строй (стоя́ть **в строю́** 'to stand in line'). Cf. на **краю́** 'on the edge', в родно́м **краю́** 'on one's native soil', but в Краснода́рском **кра́е** 'in Krasnodar Territory', на пере́днем **кра́е** оборо́ны 'in the front line of defence', from край 'edge, territory, front line'. Хмель (a) 'hops' (b) 'inebriation' has a locative in -ю́ in meaning (b): во хмелю́ 'in his cups', cf. о хме́ле 'about hops'.

55 Special masculine plural forms

Some first-declension masculine nouns have special plural forms.

(1) Nominative plural in -á/я́

(i) Some hard-ending nouns have a nominative plural in stressed -á: а́дрес 'address', pl. **адреса́**. Similarly:

бе́рег	shore	**но́мер**	number, issue
бок	side	**обшла́г**	cuff
борт	side of ship	**о́круг**	district
бу́фер	buffer	**о́рдер**	warrant
ве́ер	fan	**о́стров**	island
век	age, century	**па́рус**	sail
ве́чер	evening	**па́спорт**	passport
глаз	eye	**пе́репел**	quail
го́лос	voice, vote	**по́езд**	train
го́род	town	**по́яс**	belt
дире́ктор	director	**профе́ссор**	professor
до́ктор	doctor	**рог**	horn
дом	house	**рука́в**	sleeve
ко́локол	bell	**сорт**	brand
лес	forest	**сто́рож**	watchman
луг	meadow	**том**	volume
ма́стер	craftsman	**че́реп**	skull

Note

(a) Some plurals in -**а** and -**ы**/-**и** are differentiated semantically: кондуктора́ 'bus-conductors', кондукторы 'electrical conductors'; корпуса́ 'corps, buildings', ко́рпусы 'torsos'; меха́ 'furs', мехи́ 'bellows'; образа́ 'icons', о́бразы 'forms'; ордена́ 'orders, decorations', о́рдены 'monastic orders'; провода́ 'electric wires', про́воды 'send-off' (no sing.); счета́ 'accounts', счёты 'abacus' (no sing.); тона́ 'colour shades', то́ны (musical) 'tones'; тормоза́ 'brakes', то́рмозы 'hindrances'; хлеба́ 'cereals', хле́бы 'loaves'; цвета́ 'colours', цветы́ 'flowers' (sing. цвето́к).

(b) Some plurals in -**ы**/-**и** are used in written styles, and their counterparts in -**á** in colloquial or technical contexts: год 'year', инспе́ктор 'inspector', инстру́ктор 'instructor', корре́ктор 'proof-reader', крéйсер 'cruiser', редáктор 'editor', цех 'work-shop'.

(ii) A few nouns ending in **-й** or **-ь** have nominative plural **-я**: край 'edge', pl. **края́** (gen. pl. **краёв**); вéксель 'bill of exchange', pl. **векселя́**. Likewise лáгерь 'camp' (but лáгери 'political camps'), тóполь 'poplar', учи́тель 'teacher' (but pl. учи́тели in the meaning 'teachers of a doctrine', e.g. учи́тели коммуни́зма 'the teachers of communism'), штáбель 'stack', штéмпель 'stamp', я́корь 'anchor'.

Note

Пéкарь 'baker', слéсарь 'metal worker' and тóкарь 'turner' have standard plurals in **-и** and alternative, colloquial plurals in **-я́** (also used in professional parlance).

(2) Nominative plural in **-ья**

(i) Stem-stressed: **стул** 'chair' (inanimate), **брат** 'brother' (animate).

Plural	Nom.	Acc.	Gen.	Dat.	Instr.	Prep.
	сту́лья	сту́лья	сту́льев	сту́льям	сту́льями	о сту́льях
	брáтья	брáтьев	брáтьев	брáтьям	брáтьями	о брáтьях

Similarly (all inanimate): брус 'beam', зуб 'cog' (cf. зуб 'tooth', pl. зу́бы, зубо́в), клин 'wedge', клок 'shred' (pl. **кло́чья, кло́чьев** 'tatters'), кол 'stake', ко́лос 'ear of corn' (pl. **коло́сья**), ком 'lump', лист 'leaf' (cf. лист 'sheet of paper', pl. **листы́, листо́в**), лоску́т 'scrap' (pl. **лоску́тья** 'rags', cf. **лоскуты́** 'scraps of paper'), о́бод 'rim' (pl. **обо́дья**), по́вод 'rein' (pl. **пово́дья**, cf. **по́воды** 'causes'), по́лоз 'runner' (pl. **поло́зья**, cf. **по́лозы** 'grass-snakes'), прут 'twig', струп 'scab', сук 'bough' (pl. **су́чья, су́чьев** or **суки́, суко́в**). Note also the plural-only form **хло́пья** 'flakes'.

(ii) End-stressed in plural.

(a) **Дéверь** 'brother-in-law', **друг** 'friend', **муж** 'husband', **сын** 'son':

Plural	Nom.	Acc./Gen.	Dat.	Instr.	Prep.
	деверья́	деверéй	деверья́м	деверья́ми	о деверья́х
	друзья́	друзéй	друзья́м	друзья́ми	о друзья́х
	мужья́	мужéй	мужья́м	мужья́ми	о мужья́х
	сыновья́	сыновéй	сыновья́м	сыновья́ми	о сыновья́х

(*But* мужи́ нау́ки 'men of science', сыны́ ро́дины 'sons of the fatherland'.)

(b) **зять** 'son-in-law, brother-in-law', **кум** 'godfather':

Plural	Nom.	Acc./Gen.	Dat.	Instr.	Prep.
	зятья́	зятьёв	зятья́м	зятья́ми	о зятья́х
	кумовья́	кумовьёв	кумовья́м	кумовья́ми	о кумовья́х

(3) Plural of nouns in -анин/-янин, e.g. англича́нин 'Englishman'

Plural	Nom.	Acc./Gen.	Dat.	Instr.	Prep.
	англича́не	англича́н	англича́нам	англича́нами	об англича́нах

Note the stress change in **граждани́н** 'citizen', pl. **гра́ждане**, **гра́ждан**.

(4) Plural of ба́рин, болга́рин, тата́рин, цыга́н

The plural of **болга́рин** 'Bulgarian' is: nom. болга́ры, acc./gen. болга́р, dat. болга́рам, instr. болга́рами, prep. о болга́рах. Similarly ба́рин 'landowner' (nom. pl. ба́ры/ба́ре), тата́рин 'Tatar', цыга́н 'gipsy' (nom. pl. цыга́не).

(5) Plural of nouns in -ёнок/-онок

Nouns in **-ёнок/-онок** have plurals in **-я́та/-а́та**: **котёнок** 'kitten'.

Plural	Nom.	Acc./Gen.	Dat.	Instr.	Prep.
	котя́та	котя́т	котя́там	котя́тами	о котя́тах

Similarly **волчо́нок** 'wolf', pl. **волча́та**, **волча́т** etc.

Note

(a) Щено́к 'puppy' has alternative plurals **щеня́та**, **щеня́т/щенки́**, **щенко́в**.

(b) Ребёнок 'child' has plural **де́ти** 'children', acc./gen. **дете́й**, dat. **де́тям**, instr. **детьми́**, prep. **о де́тях**. Colloquially, **ребя́та** is also used as a plural of ребёнок. **Ребя́та** can also mean 'the lads', cf. **девча́та** 'the girls' (also де́вушки и ребя́та 'young men and girls').

(6) Plural of сосе́д and чёрт

Сосе́д 'neighbour' and чёрт 'devil' have hard endings in the singular, soft endings in the plural: **сосе́ди**, **сосе́дей**, **сосе́дям**; **че́рти**, **черте́й**, **чертя́м**.

(7) Plural of господи́н and хозя́ин

Господи́н 'master' and хозя́ин 'owner, host' have nominative plural
-a:

Plural	Nom.	Acc./Gen.	Dat.	Instr.	Prep.
	господа́	госпо́д	господа́м	господа́ми	о господа́х
	хозя́ева	хозя́ев	хозя́евам	хозя́евами	о хозя́евах

56 Nouns whose genitive plural is identical with the nominative singular

The genitive plural of some masculine nouns is the same as the
nominative singular: глаз 'eye', погóн 'epaulette', раз 'time',
челове́к 'person' (after numerals: пять **челове́к** 'five people', cf.
нет **люде́й** 'there are no people'). Note the stress difference in
во́лос 'a hair', gen. pl. **воло́с**. Categories also include:

(1) Footwear: боти́нок 'shoe', ва́ленок 'felt boot', носо́к 'sock'
(gen. pl. also **носко́в**), сапóг 'boot', чуло́к 'stocking'.

(2) Nationalities (including some minorities in the former USSR):
башки́р 'Bashkir', буря́т 'Buryat' (gen. pl. also **буря́тов**), грузи́н
'Georgian', мадья́р 'Magyar', румы́н 'Romanian', туркме́н 'Turk-
menian' (gen. pl. also **туркме́нов**), ту́рок 'Turk'.

(3) The military: партиза́н 'partisan', солда́т 'soldier' and others.

(4) Measurements: ампе́р 'ampere', ватт 'watt', вольт 'volt', герц
'cycle', грамм 'gram' (10 **ампе́р** '10 amperes', 100 **ватт** '100 watts',
5 **вольт** '5 volts'). The zero genitive plural is used in technical and
scientific contexts and colloquial speech, while **-ов** is normal in
literary styles (Вы́пили сто **гра́ммов** тёплой во́дки (Vanshenkin)
'They drank 100 grams of warm vodka'), though here too the zero
ending is making headway.

(5) Fruits (colloquial speech only): абрико́с 'apricot', апельси́н
'orange', баклажа́н 'aubergine', помидо́р 'tomato'. In written
Russian, however, the genitive plural **-ов** is preferred for these
nouns.

57 Stress patterns in first-declension masculine nouns

There are three basic types of stress pattern in declension.

(1) Fixed stem stress

Стул 'chair', **герóй** 'hero', **автомобúль** 'car' etc.

Note
(a) With few exceptions (e.g. **дирéктор** 'manager', pl. **директорá**), nouns with medial stress have fixed stem stress in declension.
(b) Most nouns of three or more syllables have fixed stem stress throughout declension (**парохóд** 'steamer' etc.).
(c) All masculine nouns with unstressed prefixes or suffixes have fixed stem stress throughout declension (**разговóр** 'conversation', **мáльчик** 'boy' etc.).
(d) Only a limited number of monosyllabic masculine nouns have fixed stem stress throughout declension (e.g. **звук** 'sound').

(2) Fixed end-stress

(i) Hard ending:

	Nom./Acc.	Gen.	Dat.	Instr.	Prep.
Singular	стол	стол-á	стол-ý	стол-óм	о стол-é
Plural	стол-ы́	стол-óв	стол-áм	стол-áми	о стол-áх

(ii) Soft ending:

Singular	рубль	рубл-я́	рубл-ю́	рубл-ём	о рубл-é
Plural	рубл-и́	рубл-éй	рубл-я́м	рубл-я́ми	о рубл-я́х

Note
(a) This category includes many hard-ending nouns, including almost all those with the stressed suffixes: -áк/-я́к, -áч, -éж, -ёж, -úк, -úч, -ýн, -ýх: бегýн 'runner', моря́к 'sailor', платёж 'payment', рубéж 'boundary', скрипáч 'violinist', старúк 'old man' etc.
(b) Soft-ending nouns include богаты́рь 'hero', вождь 'leader', вратáрь 'goalkeeper', дождь 'rain', журáвль 'crane' (bird), календáрь 'calendar', корáбль 'ship', кремль 'kremlin', ломóть 'slice', ноль/нуль 'nought', ремéнь 'strap', секретáрь 'secretary', словáрь 'dictionary' etc.

(3) Mobile stress

(i)   Stem stress in the **singular**, end stress in the **plural**: дуб 'oak', бой 'battle'.

	Nom./Acc.	Gen.	Dat.	Instr.	Prep.
Singular	дуб	дýб-а	дýб-у	дýб-ом	о дýб-е
Plural	дуб-ы́	дуб-о́в	дуб-а́м	дуб-а́ми	о дуб-а́х
Singular	бой	бó-я	бó-ю	бó-ем	о бó-е
Plural	бо-и́	бо-ёв	бо-я́м	бо-я́ми	о бо-я́х

Note

(a)   Many nouns in the category have a prepositional-locative in -ý/ -ю́: **бой** 'battle', **круг** 'circle', **мост** 'bridge', **ряд** 'row', **сад** 'garden' etc. (see **54**).

(b)   Other nouns in the category include many with plurals in -**ья** (see **55** (2) (ii)) and in -**á**/-**я** (see **55** (1)).

(ii)   End stress in **oblique** cases of the **plural**: порт 'port', жёлудь 'acorn'.

	Nom./Acc.	Gen.	Dat.	Instr.	Prep.
Singular	порт	пóрт-а	пóрт-у	пóрт-ом	о пóрт-е
Plural	пóрт-ы	порт-о́в	порт-а́м	порт-а́ми	о порт-а́х
Singular	жёлудь	жёлуд-я	жёлуд-ю	жёлуд-ем	о жёлуд-е
Plural	жёлуд-и	желуд-е́й	желуд-я́м	желуд-я́ми	о желуд-я́х

Note

This group comprises mainly soft-sign nouns: го́лубь 'dove', гость 'guest', гусь 'goose', зверь 'wild animal', ка́мень 'stone', ко́готь 'claw', ко́рень 'root', ло́коть 'elbow', но́готь 'fingernail', па́рень 'lad', сте́бель 'stalk' (gen. pl. also **стебле́й**). Hard-ending nouns include **волк** 'wolf' and **зуб** 'tooth'.

(iii)   End stress in **oblique** cases of **singular** *and* **plural**: гвоздь 'nail'.

	Nom./Acc.	Gen.	Dat.	Instr.	Prep.
Singular	гвоздь	гвозд-я́	гвозд-ю́	гвозд-ём	о гвозд-е́
Plural	гвóзд-и	гвозд-е́й	гвозд-я́м	гвозд-я́ми	о гвозд-я́х

Likewise конь 'steed', уголь 'coal' (gen. sing. **угля́/ýгля**), червь 'worm'.

Note

For all animate nouns acc. = gen. See **47**.

58 First declension: neuter nouns in -o

(1) Declension of **боло́то** 'swamp'.

	Singular	Plural
Nom.	боло́т-**о**	боло́т-**а**
Acc.	боло́т-**о**	боло́т-**а**
Gen.	боло́т-**а**	боло́т
Dat.	боло́т-**у**	боло́т-**ам**
Instr.	боло́т-**ом**	боло́т-**ами**
Prep.	о боло́т-**е**	о боло́т-**ах**

Note

(a) Не́бо 'sky', pl. **небеса́**, gen. pl. **небе́с**, dat. pl. **небеса́м**. Likewise **чу́до** 'miracle'.

(b) Су́дно 'ship', pl. **суда́**, **судо́в** (cf. су́дно 'chamber-pot', pl. **су́дна**, **су́ден**).

(2) Buffer vowel in the genitive plural.

(i) In the 'zero' genitive plural of many nouns in -o, a 'buffer' vowel appears between two final consonants. This may be -**o**- (following **к**):

волокно́ 'fibre'   **воло́кон**

Similarly окно́ 'window', gen. pl. **о́кон**; стекло́ 'pane of glass', gen. pl. **стёкол**.

(ii) Otherwise the buffer vowel is -**e**-:

бедро́ 'hip'   **бёдер**

Others of this type include бревно́ 'log', ведро́ 'bucket', весло́ 'oar', зерно́ 'grain', кольцо́ 'ring' (gen. pl. **коле́ц**), кре́сло 'armchair' (gen. pl. **кре́сел**), крыльцо́ 'porch' (gen. pl. **крыле́ц**), письмо́ 'letter' (gen. pl. **пи́сем**), полотно́ 'canvas', пятно́ 'stain', ребро́ 'rib', ремесло́ 'trade' (gen. pl. **ремёсел**), число́ 'number', ядро́ 'nucleus'.

Note

(a) Vowel change from **e** to **ё** under stress.

(b) Не́дра, недр (pl. only) 'bowels of the earth'.

(c) Яйцо́ 'egg', pl. я́йца, яи́ц.

(d) Зло 'evil' has only one plural form, genitive plural **зол**: ме́ньшее из двух **зол** 'the lesser of two evils'.

(e) Nouns in **-ство** have no buffer vowel in the genitive plural: чу́вство 'feeling', gen. pl. **чувств**.

(3) The following nouns have nominative plural -**и**: ве́ко 'eyelid', pl. **ве́ки, век; коле́но** 'knee', pl. **коле́ни, коле́ней** (**коле́н** in combination with prepositions and comparatives, e.g. вы́ше, ни́же коле́н 'above, below the knees', до коле́н 'to the knees', встать с коле́н 'to rise from one's knees', зажа́ть мѐжду коле́н 'to grip between the knees'); **о́ко** 'eye' (archaic), pl. **о́чи, оче́й;** плечо́ 'shoulder', pl. **пле́чи, плеч;** у́хо 'ear', pl. **у́ши, уше́й.**

Note
Except for о́блако 'cloud', pl. **облака́, облако́в**, all nouns in **-ко** have nominative plural -**и**: **блю́дечко** 'saucer', pl. **блю́дечки, блю́дечек; дре́вко** 'shaft', pl. **дре́вки, дре́вков; зёрнышко** 'small grain', pl. **зёрнышки, зёрнышек** (likewise **пёрышко** 'small feather'); **колёсико** 'small wheel', pl. **колёсики, колёсиков** (likewise **ли́чико** 'small face', **пле́чико** 'small shoulder' – pl. **пле́чики** also means 'coat-hanger'); **озерко́** 'small lake', pl. **озерки́, озерко́в; очко́** 'point' (in a game), pl. **очки́, очко́в** (also 'spectacles'); **око́шко** 'small window', pl. **око́шки, око́шек; у́шко** 'small ear', pl. **у́шки, у́шек** (cf. ушко́ 'eye of a needle', pl. **ушки́, ушко́в**); **я́блоко** 'apple', pl. **я́блоки, я́блок**.

(4) Some nouns in **-о** have plural **-ья: звено́** 'link'.

Plural	Nom./Acc.	Gen.	Dat.	Instr.	Prep.
	звен-ья́	звен-ьев	звен-ьям	звен-ьями	о звен-ьях

The following nouns behave similarly:

(i) With initial stress in the plural: крыло́ 'wing', pl. **кры́лья, кры́льев; перо́** 'feather'; **ши́ло** 'awl'.

(ii) With medial stress in the plural: де́рево 'tree', pl. **дере́вья, дере́вьев; коле́но** 'joint in a pipe' (cf. коле́но 'knee', see (3) above and note that in the meaning 'bend in a river', 'generation' (in a genealogical table), 'part of a dance or song', коле́но has the plural **коле́на, коле́н**).

(iii) **Дно** 'bottom' (of a barrel), pl. **до́нья, до́ньев**.

59 First declension: nouns in -е, -ье, -ё, -ьё

(1) Declension of **мо́ре** 'sea' (likewise **по́ле** 'field'):

	Singular	Plural
Nom.	мо́р-**е**	мор-**я́**
Acc.	мо́р-**е**	мор-**я́**
Gen.	мо́р-**я**	мор-**е́й**
Dat.	мо́р-**ю**	мор-**я́м**
Instr.	мо́р-**ем**	мор-**я́ми**
Prep.	о мо́р-**е**	о мор-**я́х**

Note

(a) Nouns in **-це**, **-ще** replace **я** by **а**: thus блю́дце 'saucer', gen. sing./nom. and acc. pl. **блю́дца**. Similarly кла́дбище 'cemetery' etc.
(b) Nouns in **-ьё** (e.g. бельё 'linen') have instrumental singular **-ьём** and prepositional singular **-ьé**.
(c) Masculine augmentatives in **-ище** have nominative plural **-и**: доми́ще 'large house', pl. **доми́щи**, **доми́щ** (see **109** (2)).

(2) Nouns in **-е/-ье** and **-ё/-ьё** take a variety of endings in the genitive plural:

(i) **-ев**: боло́тце 'little swamp', **боло́тцев**. Likewise **око́нце** 'small window'.

Note

Some nouns in **-це** have alternative genitive plurals in **-ев** and zero ending: коры́тце 'small trough' (gen. pl. **коры́тцев/коры́тец**). Likewise одея́льце 'small blanket', щу́пальце 'tentacle'.

(ii) **-ей**: мо́ре 'sea', gen. pl. **море́й** (likewise по́ле 'field'); ружьё 'gun', gen. pl. **ру́жей**.

(iii) **-ий**: побере́жье 'coast', gen. pl. **побере́жий**. Likewise варе́нье 'jam', копьё 'spear' (gen. pl. **ко́пий**), ущелье 'ravine'.

(iv) **-ьев**: верхо́вье 'upper reaches', gen. pl. **верхо́вьев**. Likewise низо́вье 'lower reaches', пла́тье 'dress', подмасте́рье (m.) 'apprentice', у́стье 'river mouth'.

Note

Alternative genitive plural **верхо́вий** and **низо́вий**.

(v) **Zero ending**: блю́дце 'saucer', gen. pl. **блю́дец**. Likewise зéр-кальце 'small mirror', полотéнце 'towel', сéрдце 'heart', gen. pl. **сердéц**, as well as nouns in **-ище/-бище** (кла́дбище 'cemetery', gen. pl. **кла́дбищ**).

Note

Дéревце/деревцó 'small tree' has genitive plural **деревцо́в** or **деревéц**; **остриё** 'point', gen. pl. **остриёв**.

60 Stress patterns in the plural of neuter nouns

Stress in the plural of many neuter nouns moves as follows:

(1) From the ending on to the stem (**e** changes to **ё**): thus, **окнó** 'window'.

Plural	Nom./Acc.	Gen.	Dat.	Instr.	Prep.
	о́кна	о́кон	о́кнам	о́кнами	об о́кнах

Similarly ведрó 'bucket', pl. **вёдра, вёдер**; веслó 'oar', pl. **вёсла, вёсел**; винó 'wine', pl. **ви́на, вин**; гнездó 'nest', pl. **гнёзда, гнёзд**; зернó 'grain', pl. **зёрна, зёрен**; колесó 'wheel', pl. **колёса, колёс**; кольцó 'ring', pl. **ко́льца, колéц**; копьё 'spear', pl. **ко́пья, ко́пий**; крыльцó 'porch', pl. **кры́льца, крылéц**; лицó 'face', pl. **ли́ца, лиц**; письмó 'letter', pl. **пи́сьма, пи́сем**; пятнó 'stain', pl. **пя́тна, пя́тен**; ружьё 'gun', pl. **ру́жья, ру́жей**; стеклó 'pane', pl. **стёкла, стёкол**; числó 'number', pl. **чи́сла, чи́сел**; яйцо 'egg', pl. **я́йца, яи́ц**.

(2) From the stem on to the ending: **дéло** 'matter'.

Plural	Nom./Acc.	Gen.	Dat.	Instr.	Prep.
	дела́	дел	дела́м	дела́ми	о дела́х

Similarly зéркало 'mirror', pl. **зеркала́**; мéсто 'place', pl. **места́**, мóре 'sea', pl. **моря́, морéй**; пóле 'field', pl. **поля́, полéй**; пра́во 'right', pl. **права́**; сéрдце 'heart', pl. **сердца́, сердéц**; слóво 'word', pl. **слова́**; ста́до 'herd', pl. **стада́**; тéло 'body', pl. **тела́**.

61 Second declension: nouns in -a/-я

(1) Most second-declension nouns are feminine; some are masculine, e.g. **дéдушка** 'grandfather', **дя́дя** 'uncle'; others are of common gender, e.g. **пья́ница** 'drunkard', **рази́ня** 'gawper' (see **35**).

(2) Declension of **ка́рта** 'map', **же́нщина** 'woman':

	Singular		Plural	
Nom.	ка́рт-а	же́нщин-а	ка́рт-ы	же́нщин-ы
Acc.	ка́рт-у	же́нщин-у	ка́рт-ы	же́нщин (= gen.)
Gen.	ка́рт-ы	же́нщин-ы	карт	же́нщин
Dat.	ка́рт-е	же́нщин-е	ка́рт-ам	же́нщин-ам
Instr.	ка́рт-ой/-ою	же́нщин-ой/-ою	ка́рт-ами	же́нщин-ами
Prep.	о ка́рт-е	о же́нщин-е	о ка́рт-ах	о же́нщин-ах

Note

(a) **ы** is replaced by **и** after **г, к, х, ж, ч, ш** or **щ**; ви́лка 'fork', да́ча 'villa', gen. sing./nom. and acc. pl. ви́лки, да́чи (see **16** (1)).

(b) **о** is replaced by **е** in unstressed position after **ж, ч, ш, щ** or **ц**: у́лица 'street', instr. sing. у́лиц**ей**; кры́ша 'roof', instr. sing. кры́ш**ей** (see **16** (2)).

(c) Some nouns in -**жа**, -**ча**, -**ша** have genitive plural -**ей**: свеча́ 'candle', gen. pl. **свече́й** (but игра́ не сто́ит свеч 'the game is not worth the candle'). Likewise бахча́ 'water melon plantation', левша́ 'left-handed person', ханжа́ 'hypocrite', чу́кча 'Chukchi', ю́ноша 'youth'.

(d) The genitive plural of **мечта́** 'dream' (and of мечта́ние 'reverie') is **мечта́ний**.

(e) The instrumental singular in -**ою** (and -**ею**, see (3)) is the more 'literary' form and is commonly found in poetry.

(3) Declension of **ды́ня** 'melon' and **ня́ня** 'nurse':

	Singular		Plural	
Nom.	ды́н-я	ня́н-я	ды́н-и	ня́н-и
Acc.	ды́н-ю	ня́н-ю	ды́н-и	нянь (= gen.)
Gen.	ды́н-и	ня́н-и	дынь	нянь
Dat.	ды́н-е	ня́н-е	ды́н-ям	ня́н-ям
Instr.	ды́н-ей/-ею	ня́н-ей/-ею	ды́н-ями	ня́н-ями
Prep.	о ды́н-е	о ня́н-е	о ды́н-ях	о ня́н-ях

Note

(a) End-stressed nouns have -**ёй** in the instrumental singular: земля́ 'ground', instr. **землёй**; статья́ 'article', instr. **статьёй**.

(b) *Stem*-stressed nouns in -**ья** have genitive plural -**ий**: го́стья 'female guest', gen. pl. **го́стий**.

(c) *End*-stressed nouns in -**ья́** have genitive plural -**ей**: семья́ 'family', gen. pl. **семе́й**; судья́ 'judge', gen. pl. **суде́й/су́дей**. Similarly до́ля 'share', gen. pl. **доле́й**; дя́дя 'uncle', gen. pl. **дя́дей** (nom. pl. **дядья́**, gen. pl. **дядьёв** are also found); клешня́ 'claw' (of crustacean), gen. pl. **клешне́й**; ноздря́ 'nostril', gen. pl. **ноздре́й**; при́горшня 'handful', gen. pl. **при́горшней/ при́горшен**; простыня́ 'sheet', gen. pl. **просты́нь/ простыне́й**; ступня́ 'foot', gen. pl. **ступне́й**; тётя 'aunt', gen. pl. **тётей/тёть**.

(d) Nouns in **-ая/-ея** have genitive plural **-ай/-ей**: **ста́я** 'pack', gen. pl. **стай**; **ше́я** 'neck', gen. pl. **шей**.

(4) Buffer vowel in the genitive plural.

(i) **-o-** appears between a consonant (see, however, (4) (ii) (a)) and **-к-** (or **-к-** + consonant):

бе́лка 'squirrel'   **бе́лок**

Similarly бу́лка 'roll', gen. pl. **бу́лок**; доска́ 'board, plank', gen. pl. **досо́к**; ку́кла 'doll', gen. pl. **ку́кол**. Note also ку́хня 'kitchen', gen. pl. **ку́хонь**.

(ii) **-e-** appears:

(a) Between **ж, ч, ш** and **-к-**: ба́бочка 'butterfly', gen. pl. **ба́бочек**; ко́шка 'cat', gen. pl. **ко́шек**; ло́жка 'spoon', gen. pl. **ло́жек** etc. (but кишка́ 'intestine', gen. pl. **кишо́к**).

(b) Between pairs of consonants which do not include **к**:

сосна́ 'pine tree'   **со́сен**

Likewise две́рца 'car door', gen. pl. **две́рец**; десна́ 'gum', gen. pl. **дёсен**.

(c) In place of a soft sign: де́ньги (pl. only) 'money', gen. pl. **де́нег**; сва́дьба 'wedding', gen. pl. **сва́деб**; тюрьма́ 'prison', gen. pl. **тю́рем** (but ве́дьма 'witch', gen. pl. **ведьм**, про́сьба 'request', gen. pl. **просьб**).

(d) In place of **-й-** in diphthongs followed by **-к-**: копе́йка 'kopeck', gen. pl. **копе́ек** etc. (cf. война́ 'war', gen. pl. **войн**).

(e) Between two final consonants in the genitive plural of many nouns in **-я**: земля́ 'land', gen. pl. **земе́ль**; ка́пля 'drop', gen. pl. **ка́пель**; кро́вля 'roof', gen. pl. **кро́вель**; пе́тля 'loop', gen. pl. **пе́тель**; ца́пля 'heron', gen. pl. **ца́пель**.

Note

Most nouns in consonant + **-ня** have *no* soft sign in the genitive plural: **ба́шня** 'tower', gen. pl. **ба́шен**. Similarly **ви́шня** 'cherry', **жаро́вня** 'brazier', **колоко́льня** 'belfry', **пе́сня** 'song', **со́тня** 'hundred', **спа́льня** 'bedroom', **чере́шня** 'cherry tree', **чита́льня** 'reading room'. Note, however, **ба́рышня** 'young lady', gen. pl. **ба́рышень**; **дере́вня** 'village', gen. pl. **дереве́нь**.

(iii) **-ё-** appears in the genitive plural of a few nouns: **кочерга́** 'poker', gen. pl. **кочерёг**; **серьга́** 'ear-ring', gen. pl. **серёг**; **сестра́** 'sister', gen. pl. **сестёр**.

(iv) Some clusters, many ending in **б, в, л, м, н, п, р**, have *no* buffer vowel in the genitive plural: **бо́мба** 'bomb', gen. pl. **бомб**. Likewise **бу́ква** 'letter', **волна́** 'wave', **вы́дра** 'otter', **зе́бра** 'zebra', **игла́** 'needle', **игра́** 'game', **изба́** 'peasant hut', **и́скра** 'spark', **но́рма** 'norm', **слу́жба** 'service', **ты́ква** 'pumpkin', **у́рна** 'urn', **фо́рма** 'uniform', **ци́фра** 'figure'.

62 Stress patterns in second-declension nouns

Most nouns in stressed **-а́/-я́** undergo stress change in declension (nouns in *unstressed* **-а/-я** are immune from stress change).

(1) Stem stress in the plural, e.g. **война́** 'war'.

	Nom.	Acc.	Gen.	Dat.	Instr.	Prep.
Singular	война́	войну́	войны́	войне́	войно́й	о войне́
Plural	**во́йны**	**во́йны**	**войн**	**во́йнам**	**во́йнами**	**о во́йнах**

Similarly **волна́** 'wave' (alternative dat., instr., prep. pl. **волна́м, волна́ми, о волна́х**), **глава́** 'chapter', **заря́** 'dawn' (pl. **зо́ри, зорь**), **змея́** 'snake' (pl. **зме́и, змей**), **игра́** 'game', **красота́** 'beauty' (pl. **красо́ты** 'beauty spots'), **овца́** 'sheep' (gen. pl. **ове́ц**), **река́** 'river' (acc. sing. **реку́/ре́ку**), **сосна́** 'pine', **страна́** 'country', **струна́** 'string' (of instrument, racket) etc.

Note

е–ё mutation: **десна́** 'gum', pl. **дёсны, дёсен**; **жена́** 'wife', pl. **жёны, жён**; **звезда́** 'star', pl. **звёзды, звёзд**; **пчела́** 'bee', pl. **пчёлы, пчёл**; **сестра́** 'sister', pl. **сёстры, сестёр**.

(2) Stem stress in accusative singular and nominative/accusative plural, e.g. **рука́** 'hand, arm':

	Nom.	Acc.	Gen.	Dat.	Instr.	Prep.
Singular	рука́	**ру́ку**	руки́	руке́	руко́й	о руке́
Plural	**ру́ки**	**ру́ки**	рук	рука́м	рука́ми	о рука́х

Similarly гора́ 'mountain', доска́ 'board' (gen. pl. **досо́к**), нога́ 'foot, leg', щека́ 'cheek' (acc. sing. **щёку/щеку́**, pl. **щёки, щёк, щека́м**), борода́ 'beard' (acc. sing. **бо́роду**, pl. **бо́роды, боро́д, борода́м**), голова́ 'head', полоса́ 'strip' (acc. sing. **по́лосу/полосу́**), сторона́ 'side').

(3) Stem stress in nominative/accusative plural, e.g. **губа́** 'lip':

	Nom.	Acc.	Gen.	Dat.	Instr.	Prep.
Singular	губа́	губу́	губы́	губе́	губо́й	о губе́
Plural	**гу́бы**	**гу́бы**	губ	губа́м	губа́ми	о губа́х

Similarly волна́ 'wave' (see also (1) above) and железа́ 'gland' (pl. **же́лезы, желёз, железа́м**).

(4) Stem stress in accusative singular and all plural forms, e.g. **вода́** 'water':

	Nom.	Acc.	Gen.	Dat.	Instr.	Prep.
Singular	вода́	**во́ду**	воды́	воде́	водо́й	о воде́
Plural	**во́ды**	**во́ды**	вод	**во́дам**	**во́дами**	**о во́дах**

Similarly спина́ 'back', стена́ 'wall', цена́ 'price'.

(5) Stem stress in nominative/inanimate accusative, dative, instrumental and prepositional plural, e.g. **семья́** 'family':

	Nom.	Acc.	Gen.	Dat.	Instr.	Prep.
Singular	семья́	семью́	семьи́	семье́	семьёй	о семье́
Plural	**се́мьи**	**се́мьи**	семе́й	**се́мьям**	**се́мьями**	**о се́мьях**

Likewise свинья́ 'pig', скамья́ 'bench' (pl. **скамьи́/ска́мьи**), судья́ 'judge' (gen. pl. **суде́й/су́дей**).

(6) Stem stress in accusative singular and nominative, accusative, dative, instrumental and prepositional plural, e.g. **земля́** 'land':

	Nom.	Acc.	Gen.	Dat.	Instr.	Prep.
Singular	земля́	**зе́млю**	земли́	земле́	землёй	о земле́
Plural	**зе́мли**	**зе́мли**	земе́ль	**зе́млям**	**зе́млями**	**о зе́млях**

63 Third declension: soft-sign feminine nouns

(1) Declension of **тетра́дь** 'exercise book' and **свекро́вь** 'mother-in-law':

	Singular		Plural	
Nom.	тетра́дь	свекро́вь	тетра́д-**и**	свекро́в-**и**
Acc.	тетра́дь	свекро́вь	тетра́д-**и**	свекро́в-**ей** (= gen.)
Gen.	тетра́д-**и**	свекро́в-**и**	тетра́д-**ей**	свекро́в-**ей**
Dat.	тетра́д-**и**	свекро́в-**и**	тетра́д-**ям**	свекро́в-**ям**
Instr.	тетра́дь-**ю**	свекро́вь-**ю**	тетра́д-**ями**	свекро́в-**ями**
Prep.	о тетра́д-**и**	о свекро́в-**и**	о тетра́д-**ях**	о свекро́в-**ях**

Note

я is replaced by **а** after **ж, ч, ш, щ**: thus ночь 'night', dat., instr., prep. pl. **ноча́м, ноча́ми, о ноча́х**; likewise вещь 'thing', мышь 'mouse' etc.

(2) Declension of **мать** and **дочь**: мать 'mother' declines in the singular nom./acc. **мать** 'mother', gen./dat. **ма́тери**, instr. **ма́терью**, prep. **о ма́тери**, and in the plural nom. **ма́тери**, acc./gen. **матере́й**, dat. **матеря́м**, instr. **матеря́ми**, prep. **о матеря́х**. Similarly дочь 'daughter' (instr. pl. **дочерьми́**).

(3) The fleeting vowel **-о-**. Genitive, dative and prepositional singular and all plural forms are affected, e.g. вошь 'louse', gen., dat. sing. **вши**, instr. **во́шью**, prep. **о вши**; pl. **вши**, acc./gen. **вшей**, dat. **вшам**, instr. **вша́ми**, prep. **о вшах**.

Note

(a) Ложь 'lie' is found only in the singular (gen./dat. **лжи**, instr. **ло́жью**, prep. **о лжи**); likewise любо́вь 'love', рожь 'rye'.

(b) As a first name Любо́вь 'Lyubov' has gen./dat. **Любо́ви**, prep. **о Любо́ви**.

(c) Це́рковь 'church' has soft endings in the singular (gen./dat. **це́ркви**, instr. **це́рковью**, prep. **о це́ркви**) and nominative/accusative and genitive plural (**це́ркви, церкве́й**), but hard endings in the other oblique cases of the plural (**церква́м, церква́ми, о церква́х**).

(4) Stress changes in declension:

(i) Some nouns have prepositional singular **-и́** when governed by the prepositions **в** and **на**:

    дверь 'door'   **на двери́** 'on the door'

Likewise глубь 'depths', горсть 'handful', грязь 'mud' (**в грязи́** 'covered in mud'), кровь 'blood' (**в крови́** 'covered in blood'), мель 'shallows' (**на мели́** 'aground'), печь 'stove', пыль 'dust' (**в пыли́** 'covered in dust'), Русь 'Rus' (**на Руси́** 'in Rus'), связь 'connection' (**в связи́ с** 'in connection with'), сеть 'net', степь 'steppe', Тверь 'Tver' (**в Твери́** 'in Tver'), тень 'shadow', цепь 'chain'.

Note

(a)   *Stem* stress is used when these nouns combine with other prepositions (**о две́ри** 'about the door'), or when в and на do *not* denote location (Ему́ отказа́ли **в но́вой две́ри** 'He was refused a new door').

(b)   Глушь 'backwoods' and грудь 'chest, breast' have end stress in genitive, dative (**глуши́, груди́**) and prepositional singular (**в глуши́, в груди́**).

(ii)   Many nouns have end stress in plural oblique cases, e.g. **сеть** 'net':

Plural	Nom./Acc.	Gen.	Dat.	Instr.	Prep.
	се́ти	**сетей**	**сетя́м**	**сетя́ми**	**о сетя́х**

Likewise вещь 'thing', кость 'bone', мышь 'mouse' (acc./gen. pl. мыше́й), но́вость 'piece of news', ночь 'night', о́бласть 'oblast, province', о́чередь 'queue', печь 'stove', пло́щадь 'square', ска́терть 'tablecloth', ско́рость 'speed', смерть 'death', соль 'salt', степь 'steppe', тень 'shade', треть 'third', цепь 'chain', часть 'part', че́тверть 'quarter'.

Note

(a)   Plural вла́сти 'the authorities', gen. **власте́й**, dat. **властя́м**.

(b)   Дверь 'door' and ло́шадь 'horse' have alternative instrumental plural **дверя́ми/дверьми́** (colloquial), **лошадьми́** or **лошадя́ми**.

64   Declension of neuter nouns in -мя

Declension of **и́мя** 'name':

	Singular	Plural
Nom./Acc.	и́м-я	имен-а́
Gen.	и́мен-и	имён
Dat.	и́мен-и	имен-а́м

Instr.	и́мен-**ем**	имен-**а́ми**
Prep.	об и́мен-**и**	об имен-**а́х**

Similarly вре́мя 'time', зна́мя 'banner' (pl. **знамёна, знамён**), пле́мя 'tribe', се́мя 'seed' (gen. pl. **семя́н**), стре́мя 'stirrup' and (sing. only) бре́мя 'burden', вы́мя 'udder', пла́мя 'flames' (cf. **языки́ пла́мени** 'flames, tongues of flame'), те́мя 'temple'.

65 Declension of nouns in -ия/-ие

Declension of **ста́нция** 'station', **зда́ние** 'building':

	Singular		Plural	
Nom.	ста́нци-**я**	зда́ни-**е**	ста́нци-**и**	зда́ни-**я**
Acc.	ста́нци-**ю**	зда́ни-**е**	ста́нци-**и**	зда́ни-**я**
Gen.	ста́нци-**и**	зда́ни-**я**	ста́нций	зда́ний
Dat.	ста́нци-**и**	зда́ни-**ю**	ста́нци-**ям**	зда́ни-**ям**
Instr.	ста́нци-**ей/-ею**	зда́ни-**ем**	ста́нци-**ями**	зда́ни-**ями**
Prep.	о ста́нци-**и**	о зда́ни-**и**	о ста́нци-**ях**	о зда́ни-**ях**

66 The masculine noun путь

Путь 'way' declines as follows:

	Singular	Plural
Nom./Acc.	путь	пут-**и́**
Gen.	пут-**и́**	пут-**е́й**
Dat.	пут-**и́**	пут-**я́м**
Instr.	пут-**ём**	пут-**я́ми**
Prep.	о пут-**и́**	о пут-**я́х**

Note

Despite feminine endings in the genitive, dative and prepositional singular, путь is qualified by masculine adjectives: **Счастли́вого пути́!** 'Bon voyage!'.

67 The neuter noun дитя

Дитя 'child' declines as follows:

Nom./Acc.	дит-**я**
Gen./Dat.	дитя́т-**и**
Instr.	дитя́т-**ей**/-**ею**
Prep.	о дитя́т-**и**

Note

Дитя́ is now used only in some figurative expressions, e.g. **дитя́ ве́ка** 'child of the age', and, in some contexts, for emotional effect, e.g. Да он же ещё **дитя́!** 'Why, he's still just a child!' For practical purposes it has been replaced by ребёнок 'child'.

68 Де́ти and лю́ди

Де́ти 'children' (sing. ребёнок or дитя́) and **лю́ди** 'people' (sing. челове́к) decline in the same way:

Nom.	де́т-**и**	лю́д-**и**
Acc./Gen.	дет-**е́й**	люд-**е́й**
Dat.	де́т-**ям**	лю́д-**ям**
Instr.	деть-**ми́**	людь-**ми́**
Prep.	о де́т-**ях**	о лю́д-**ях**

69 Declension of first names

First names ending in a consonant or **-й** (e.g. Ива́н, Никола́й, Юрий) decline like first-declension nouns (see **51**), first names in **-а** and **-я** (e.g. Óльга 'Olga', Ната́лья 'Natalya') like second-declension nouns (see **61**). Patronymics (e.g. Ива́нович, Ива́новна) also decline like first- and second-declension nouns respectively.

70 Declension of surnames

(1) Surnames in **-ев, -ёв, -ин, -ов, -ын** decline partly like nouns and partly like adjectives, e.g. Тургéнев 'Turgenev':

	Masculine	Feminine	Plural
Nom.	Тургéнев	Тургéнев-**а**	Тургéнев-**ы**
Acc.	Тургéнев-**а**	Тургéнев-**у**	Тургéнев-**ых**
Gen.	Тургéнев-**а**	Тургéнев-**ой**	Тургéнев-**ых**
Dat.	Тургéнев-**у**	Тургéнев-**ой**	Тургéнев-**ым**
Instr.	Тургéнев-**ым**	Тургéнев-**ой**	Тургéнев-**ыми**
Prep.	о Тургéнев-**е**	о Тургéнев-**ой**	о Тургéнев-**ых**

Note

Foreign names in **-ин** have instrumental singular **-ом**: Чáплин 'Chaplin', instr. **Чáплином**; cf. Гéрцен 'Herzen', instr. **Гéрценом**.

(2) Surnames in **-ский, -ой** etc. decline like adjectives.

(3) Surnames in **-ко, -енко** (e.g. Громы́ко 'Gromyko', Шевчéнко 'Shevchenko') tend not to decline, though in speech they may decline like second-declension nouns in **-а** (Максимéнко, acc. Максимéн**ку**, gen. Максимéн**ки**, dat. Максимéн**ке**, instr. Максимéн**кой**, prep. о Максимéн**ке**) or like first-declension nouns in **-о**.

(4) Surnames in **-аго, -яго** (e.g. Живáго 'Zhivago'), **-ово** (e.g. Дурновó 'Durnovo'), **-их, -ых** (e.g. Чутки́х 'Chutkikh') and stressed **-кó** (Франкó 'Franko') do not decline:

> Ники́тин шагáл ря́дом с **Княжкó** (Bondarev)
> Nikitin strode along beside Knyazhko

(5) Masculine foreign surnames ending in a consonant (e.g. Шмидт 'Schmidt') decline like nouns of the first declension, but they do *not* decline at all when they refer to a woman: речь премьéр-мини́стра **Тэ́тчер** 'Prime Minister Thatcher's speech', cf.

> Это натолкну́ло Мелáнью **Цатиня́н** на мысль написáть пьéсу (*Sputnik*)
> This gave Melanya Tsatinyan the idea of writing a play

(6) Foreign surnames ending in **-е, -и, -о, -у** and in stressed **-á** and **-я** do not decline: Гарибáльди 'Garibaldi', Гёте 'Goethe', Гюгó 'Hugo', Дюмá 'Dumas', Золя́ 'Zola', Шóу 'Shaw'. However, foreign

names in unstressed -**a** and -**я** *do* decline: карти́ны **Го́йи** 'paintings by Goya', пе́сни **Окуджа́вы** 'Okudzhava's songs'. Ва́йда 'Wajda', Куроса́ва 'Kurosawa' etc. also decline. Less-familiar Japanese names such as Тана́ка 'Tanaka' do not normally decline.

71 Declension of place names

(1) Place names ending in a consonant or -**a** (Ки́ев 'Kiev', Москва́ 'Moscow') decline like nouns of the first and second declensions respectively. Hyphenated Russian place names decline in both parts: в Петропа́вловске-Камча́тском 'in Petropavlovsk-Kamchatsky'. Place names in -**ин**, -**ов**, -**ын** have instrumental -**ом** (Пу́шкин 'Pushkin', **Пу́шкином**; Ки́ров 'Kirov', **Ки́ровом**), cf.:

Держа́л у себя́ до́ма, под **Сара́товом**, мото́рную ло́дку (Trifonov)
He kept a motor boat at his home near Saratov

(2) Place names in -**ево**, -**ино**, -**ово** tend *not* to decline (о̀коло **Ре́пино** 'near Repino'), especially where the names derive from a proper name (от **Ле́рмонтово** 'from Lermontovo'). The tendency not to decline such names was consolidated by practice in the 1941–45 War, designed to avoid ambiguity in place names such as Пу́шкин 'Pushkin' and Пу́шкино 'Pushkino', which would share declension endings. Despite instances of declension in written styles (e.g. в **Пу́щине** 'in Pushchino' (*Russia Today*)), non-declension remains the recommended norm.

(3) Non-Russian place names in -**е**, -**и**, -**о**, -**у** do not decline, e.g. Ско́пье 'Skopje'; Чи́ли 'Chile'; Брно 'Brno', Ме́хико 'Mexico City'; Баку́ 'Baku'. Бангладе́ш 'Bangladesh' does not decline either: из **Бангладе́ш** 'from Bangladesh'. Та́тры 'the Tatras' declines like a plural noun (gen. Татр). Both nouns in a hyphenated compound decline where a river is involved: во **Фра́нкфурте-на-Ма́йне** 'in Frankfurt-am-Main'. Compare, however, под **Буэ̀нос-А́йресом** 'near Buenos-Aires', в **Алма́-Ате́** 'in Alma-Ata', из **Карл-Маркс-Шта́дта** 'from Karl-Marx-Stadt' (now Chemnitz).

72 Apposition in the names of publications, towns etc.

(1) Titles of books, newspapers etc. decline like nouns: в «**Пра́вде**» 'in *Pravda*'; Он чита́л «**Отцо́в и дете́й**» 'He has read *Fathers and Sons*'. If, however, the genre of the work is mentioned, the title is not declined: в **газе́те** «**Пра́вда**» 'in the newspaper *Pravda*', Он чита́л **рома́н** «**Отцы́ и де́ти**» 'He has read the novel *Fathers and Sons*'.

(2) In referring to the names of Russian towns, both го́род 'town' and the name decline (в **го́роде Москве́** 'in the city of Moscow') except:

(i) When confusion may arise, e.g. in the case of towns in -**ов** and -**ово**, where only the former declines: в **го́роде Ки́рове** 'in the town of Kirov', cf. в **го́роде Ки́рово** 'in the town of Kirovo'.

(ii) When a town has a plural name: в **го́роде Вели́кие Лу́ки** 'in the town of Velikie Luki' (if го́род is omitted, however, the town name is declined: в **Вели́ких Лу́ках** 'in Velikie Luki').

(iii) When the place-name consists of adjective + noun: в **го́роде Сове́тская Га́вань** 'in the town of Sovetskaya Gavan'.

(3) Similar criteria apply to river names: на **реке́ Днепре́** 'on the river Dnieper', but на **реке́ Се́верный Доне́ц** 'on the river Severny Donets'. 'On the Moscow river' may be rendered as на **Москве́-реке́/на реке́ Москве́**, cf. вниз по **Во́лге-реке́/вниз по реке́ Во́лге** 'down the river Volga'.

(4) The names of well-known non-Russian towns decline (except for those ending in -**е** etc., see **71** (3)), whether they stand in apposition to **го́род** or not: в **Пари́же** 'in Paris', в **го́роде Пари́же** 'in the city of Paris'. Compare, however, близ **го́рода Мэ́нстон** 'near the town of Manston' (which is unlikely to be known to Russians and is therefore left undeclined).

(5) With place-names other than those of towns and rivers it is normal to decline only the generic term: у горы́ **Казбе́к** 'by Mount Kazbek', в дере́вне **Бе́лкино** 'in the village of Belkino', на о́зере **Байка́л** 'on Lake Baikal', ре́йсы ме́жду порта́ми **Оде́сса и Новоросси́йск** 'trips between the ports of Odessa and Novorossiisk'.

(6) This also applies to foreign place names: над вулка́ном **Э́тна** 'above Mount Etna', в гра́фстве **Са́ссекс** 'in the county of Sussex',

на о́строве **Дие́го-Гарси́а** 'on the island of Diego-Garcia', из по́рта **Гды́ня** 'from the port of Gdynia', в шта́те **Алаба́ма** 'in the State of Alabama'. Where the generic term is omitted, however, the place name declines: на о́строве **Кипр** 'on the island of Cyprus', but на **Ки́пре** 'on Cyprus'. In a few cases, where the generic term and the place name are of the same gender, both may decline: в пусты́не **Саха́ре/Саха́ра** 'in the Sahara desert'.

73 Declension of alphabetisms

(1) Only those alphabetisms decline which are masculine and have the form of first-declension nouns ending in a consonant (see **40** (1) (i) (2) (3)):

> Вчера́шние солда́ты отли́чно рабо́тают на **БА́Ме** (*Russia Today*)
> Yesterday's soldiers are doing excellent work on the Baikal–Amur Railway

> Риск зарази́ться **СПИ́Дом** вы́ше у наркома́нов (*Sputnik*)
> The risk of contracting AIDS is greater in drug addicts

(2) Other alphabetisms are not declined: **ГАИ** [гаи́] (Государст-венная автомоби́льная инспе́кция) 'State Vehicle Inspectorate', **ГЭС** [гэс] (гидроэлектроста́нция) 'hydroelectric power station', **НАТО** [на́то] 'NATO', **ООН** [оо́н] (Организа́ция Объединён-ных На́ций) 'UNO', **ОТК** [о-тэ-ка́] (отде́л техни́ческого контро́ля) 'technical control department', **ЦДСА** [це-дэ-са́] (Центра́льный дом Сове́тской А́рмии и́мени М. В. Фру́нзе) 'M. V. Frunze Central Soviet Army Club', **ЭВМ** [э-вэ-э́м] (электро́нная вычисли́тельная маши́на) 'computer':

> Вы́бор **ЭВМ́** был одо́брен (*Sputnik*)
> The computer's choice was approved

> Мо́жно связа́ться с ближа́йшим посто́м **ГАЙ** (*Izvestiya*)
> You can contact the nearest traffic police control point

Note

(a) Though ГЭС (power station) and ОО́Н (UNO) end in a consonant they are of feminine gender and undeclined.

(b) **ЖЭК** [жэк] (жили́щно-эксплуатацио́нная конто́ра) 'hous-ing office', now masculine, is either left undeclined or (in colloquial styles) is declined: в **на́шем ЖЭ́Ке**. Similarly **ДОСА́АФ** [доса́ф] (Доброво́льное о́бщество соде́йствия а́рмии, авиа́ции и фло́ту СССР) 'Voluntary Association for Co-operation with the Soviet Army, Air Force and Navy' and **МИД** [мид] (Министе́рство иностра́нных дел) 'Ministry of Foreign Affairs'.

74 Declension of hyphenated noun co-ordinates

(1) The *first* element in the compound does not decline if it is:

(i) Indeclinable, a recent loan, an abbreviation or a letter of the alphabet: **а́льфа**-во́лны 'alpha-waves', **кафе́**-заку́сочная 'snack-bar', **конфере́нц**-за́л 'conference hall'.

(ii) Descriptive and qualifies the second element: **национа́л**-социали́сты 'National Socialists', **шта́б**-кварти́ра 'headquarters'.

(iii) The first component in a rank or occupation: **генера́л**-лейтена́нт 'lieutenant-general', **премье́р**-мини́стр 'prime minister'.

(iv) The first component in a measurement: **килова́тт**-ча́с 'kilowatt-hour', **во́льт**-ампе́р 'volt-ampere'.

(2) The *second* element in the compound does not decline if its function is to qualify the first: **слова́рь-ми́нимум** 'minimum vocabulary'.

(3) *Both* components decline, each being a full noun in its own right: автомоби́ль-самосва́л 'tip-up lorry', ваго́н-рестора́н 'restaurant car', дива́н-крова́ть 'divan bed', же́нщина-милиционе́р 'police-woman', заку́сочная-автома́т 'vending machine', инжене́р-строи́тель 'construction engineer', раке́та-носи́тель 'carrier-rocket'. In speech, only the *second* noun may decline in commonly-used compounds: в **ваго́не-рестора́не/ваго́н-рестора́не** 'in the restaurant car', на **дива́не-крова́ти/дива́н-крова́ти** 'on the divan bed'.

Note

In the following, only the *second* element is declined: ма́тч-турни́р 'match tournament', плащ-пала́тка 'groundsheet', яхт-клу́б 'yacht-club'.

75 Agreement of ряд, большинство etc.

(1) **Ряд**

(i) Ряд traditionally combines with a singular predicate, especially in a passive construction:

Допу́щен ряд оши́бок
A number of mistakes have been made

(ii) Ряд may combine with a plural predicate when followed by a dependent **genitive plural**, particularly when the construction involves an **animate** noun and an **active** verb:

Ряд штанги́стов **занима́ли** призовы́е места́
A number of the weight-lifters occupied medal positions

(2) **Большинство́** also traditionally takes a singular predicate:

(i) In passive constructions: Большинство́ пи́сем **доста́влено** 'Most letters have been delivered'.

(ii) Where it has no post-positive dependent form: Большинство́ **уча́ствует** в обще́ственной жи́зни 'Most participate in public life'.

(iii) Where the dependent form is in the genitive singular or is the genitive plural of an **inanimate** noun:

Большинство́ населе́ния **пострада́ло** от наводне́ния
Most of the population suffered as a result of the flood

Большинство́   телефо́нов   в   го́роде   **безмо́лвствует**
(Tendryakov)
Most telephones in the town are silent

When, however, большинство́ has a dependent form in the genitive plural of an **animate** noun, a **plural** predicate is possible:

Большинство́ уча́щихся хорошо́ **подгото́влены**
Most of the pupils are well prepared

Большинство́ роди́телей **при́няли** уча́стие
Most parents participated

Note
Other collective nouns of this type behave in similar fashion. Compare

На площа́дке перед уса́дьбой обы́чно **остана́вливается
мно́жество** авто́бусов и автомоби́лей
A multitude of buses and cars usually stop on the area in front of
the estate

and

Мно́жество люде́й пою́т э́ту пе́сню на ра́зных языка́х
A great many people sing this song in different languages

Compare also

Часть пи́сем **затеря́лась**
A number of the letters went missing

Часть уча́щихся не **яви́лись**/не **яви́лась**
A number of the pupils did not turn up

76 Constructions of the type все поверну́ли го́лову

(1) The singular of the object is regarded as the norm in constructions such as Все поверну́ли **го́лову** 'Everyone turned their
head(s)', where identical objects or parts of the body belong to or
relate to each member of a group. A plural noun is recommended
only when differentiation is essential: Все по́дняли **ру́ку** 'Everyone
raised their hand', cf. Все по́дняли **ру́ки** 'Everyone raised their
arms'. Otherwise the singular is the preferred form:

Соба́ки бежа́ли, поджа́в **хвост**
The dogs were running along with their **tails** between their legs

Все со свя́занными за **спино́й** рука́ми (Rybakov)
All with their hands tied behind their **backs**

Мама́ша, ба́бушка и па́па в кра́сных носка́х и с таки́м же
кра́сным **лицо́м** (Granin)
Mum, Gran and Dad in red socks and with similarly red **faces**

(2) However, there are signs of the alternative use of the *plural* in
modern Russian:

Склони́ли над доско́й **го́ловы** (Koluntsev)
They bent their heads over the board

Мы пожа́ли дру̀г дру́гу **ру́ки** (Rybakov)
We shook hands

Хло́пали дру̀г дру́га по **спи́нам** (Aksenov)
They were slapping each other on the back

Соба́ки с поджа́тыми **хвоста́ми** ле́зли в подворо́тни
(Rasputin)
Dogs were slinking into the gateways with their tails between
their legs

Вскри́кивали, маха́ли **ша́пками** (Trifonov)
They were screaming, waving their caps

(3) A similar alternative use of singular and plural is observed in the
case of the noun **жизнь** 'life' (though the singular is more common in
Russian, and the plural is used *far* more sparingly than in English).
Compare

Я был капита́ном «Кальма́ра» и отвеча́л за их **жизнь**
(Gagarin)
I was the captain of the 'Kalmar' and was responsible for their
lives

and

Лю́ба, Воло́дя и их това́рищи опери́ровали в полевы́х
го́спиталях, мно́гим сохрани́ли **жи́зни** (Rybakov)
Lyuba, Volodya and their comrades operated in the field
hospitals and saved many people's lives

Note
With numerals above four, only the genitive plural is possible (see
195):

Боле́знь, кото́рая уже́ унесла́ почти́ 15 ты́сяч **жи́зней**
(*Sputnik*)
A disease which has already claimed 15,000 lives

Case Usage

See **401–53** for prepositional usage.

77 The nominative

The nominative is used as follows.

(1) It denotes the subject of an action or state:

Мой брат читáет кнúгу
My brother is reading a book

Нáши дéти довóльны подáрками
Our children are pleased with the presents

(2) It may be introduced

(i) by **э́то** 'this is, these are':

| Э́то **моя́ женá** | This is my wife |
| Э́то **моú дéти** | These are my children |

(ii) by **вот** 'here is, here are, there is, there are':

| Вот **мой дом** | There is my house |
| Вот **кнúги** | Here are the books |

(3) It is used in possessive constructions:

| У меня́ [есть] **кнúга** | I have a book |
| У негó был **брат** | He had a brother |

(4) It is used in comparative constructions after **чем**:

Я стáрше, чем **моя́ сестрá**
I am older than my sister

(5) It is used in generalizing constructions after **как**:

в такúх стрáнах, как **Нигéрия**
in countries such as Nigeria

Note
The meaning of the above example is 'in countries such as Nigeria **is**'. Нигéрия is therefore *not* in apposition to стрáнах. Compare:

Наш завóд специализúруется по производству такúх издéлий, как **шúны** и **колёса**
Our factory specializes in the manufacture of products such as tyres and wheels

(6) It is used in definitions:

Москва́ — **столи́ца** Росси́и Moscow is the capital of Russia

(7) It is used in apposition to various generic terms (see **72**):

Я чита́ю рома́н «**А́нна Каре́нина**»
I am reading the novel *Anna Karenina*

78 The vocative

Vocative meanings are expressed by the nominative: **Ива́н Фёдорович!** 'Ivan Fedorovich!'. Relics of the former vocative case survive only in certain ecclesiastical terms, now used as exclamations: **Бо́же мой!** 'My God!', **Го́споди!** 'Good Lord!'. Some truncated familiar forms are used as vocatives in colloquial Russian: **мам!** 'Mum!', **Нин!** 'Nina!', **Вань!** 'Vanya!', **Коль!** 'Kolya!', **Петь!** 'Pete!' (also **дядь!** 'Uncle!' etc.).

79 The accusative

The accusative case is used as follows.

(1) It denotes the object of a transitive verb:

Он лю́бит **Ма́шу**   He loves Masha
Она́ у́чится води́ть **маши́ну**   She is learning to drive a car

Note
In colloquial Russian the verb may sometimes be 'understood': Бу́дьте добры́ (, попроси́те к телефо́ну) Зо́ю 'Can I speak to Zoya, please'.

(2) It is used in certain impersonal constructions:

Де́вочку рвёт   The girl feels sick
Дом зажгло́ мо́лнией   The house was struck by lightning
Мне жаль (жа́лко) **сестру́**   I feel sorry for my sister (for жаль + genitive, see **80** (8))
Мне бо́льно **ру́ку** (colloquial) My hand is sore

For other impersonal constructions with the accusative, see **295** (1).

(3) It denotes:

(i) Duration in time:

Всю зи́му бы́ло хо́лодно   It was cold all winter

(ii) Duration in space:

Всю доро́гу они́ шли мо́лча They walked in silence all the
way

(iii) Repetition:

Он э́то говори́л **ты́сячу** раз He has said that a thousand
times

Он боле́ет **ка́ждую весну́** He is ill every spring

(iv) Cost, weight, measure etc.:

Кни́га сто́ит **рубль** The book costs a rouble
У́голь ве́сит **то́нну** The coal weighs a ton
Он мне до́лжен **пять рубле́й** He owes me five roubles

Note

(a) For the use of the accusative after negated transitive verbs, see
87 (4).

(b) Some verbs which have traditionally governed the genitive may
take the *accusative* of animate nouns in colloquial Russian: Он
слу́шается **сестру́** 'He obeys his sister', Де́ти боя́лись **мать**
'The children were afraid of their mother', Дожида́лись **Áнну**
'They were waiting for Anna'. See also **88** (1) (ii) (a) and (2) (i).

80 The genitive: possession and relationship

The genitive case is used to denote the following:

(1) Possession:

дом **бра́та** my brother's house

(2) Relationships:

член **па́ртии** a member of the Party

(3) The whole in relation to the part:

кры́ша **до́ма** the roof of the house

(4) The agent of an action or process:

выступле́ние **арти́ста**   the artiste's performance

(5) The object of an action or process:

убо́рка **урожа́я**   the gathering in of the harvest

(6) Descriptive attributes:

час **обе́да**   lunch time
бума́га **пе́рвого со́рта**   first-grade paper

(7) The second item in a comparison:

Он моло́же **бра́та**   He is younger than his
    brother (see also **182** (1) (ii))

(8) The object of regret (constructions with **жаль**):

Мне жаль **де́нег**   I grudge the money

81 The genitive: quantity

The genitive is used with:

(1) **Ма́ло** 'few', **мно́го** 'much, many', **нема́ло** 'not a little', **немно́го** 'not much, many', **не́сколько** 'a few', **ско́лько** 'how much, many', **сто́лько** 'so much, many':

мно́го **де́нег**   a lot of money
ско́лько **лет?**   how many years?
не́сколько **челове́к**   several people

(2) **Доста́точно** 'enough', **недостава́ть** 'to be insufficient', **скопи́ть** 'to accumulate', **хвата́ть/хвати́ть** 'to be enough': **Вре́мени** хвата́ет 'There is enough time', Ему́ недостаёт **рубля́** 'He is a rouble short', доста́точно **сил** 'enough strength':

Хва́тит ли им **бензи́на** для ночны́х блужда́ний? (Trifonov)
Will they have enough petrol for their nocturnal escapades?

(3) Collective nouns:

ста́до **ове́ц**   a flock of sheep

(4) Nouns denoting measure:

литр **молока́**   a litre of milk

(5) Nouns denoting containers:

ча́шка **молока́**   a cup of milk

82 The genitive with adjectives

The following adjectives (and their short forms) govern the genitive: **досто́йный** 'worthy', **лишённый** 'lacking in', **по́лный** 'full', **чу́ждый** 'devoid':

корзи́на, по́лная **я́блок**	a basket full of apples
Он досто́ин **награ́ды**	He is worthy of an award
челове́к, чу́ждый **честолю́бия**	a man devoid of ambition
Он лишён **остроу́мия**	He is lacking in wit

83 The partitive genitive

(1) The genitive is used to denote part of a substance or liquid (Он вы́пил **молока́** 'He drank some milk') or to denote a quantity of objects (Он пое́л **я́год** 'He ate some berries'). The accusative denotes *whole* rather than part: Он вы́пил **молоко́** 'He drank **the** milk'.

(2) The partitive genitive appears only as the *object* of a verb, never as the subject, cf. Она́ налила́ гостя́м **вина́** 'She poured her guests some wine' and На столе́ есть **вино́** 'There is some wine on the table'.

(3) Except for constructions with verbs such as **хоте́ть/захоте́ть** 'to want' and **проси́ть/попроси́ть** 'to request', where either aspect may be used (Хочу́ **воды́** 'I want some water', Он про́сит **мёда** 'He asks for some honey'), most partitive constructions involve *perfective* verbs only (Она́ принесла́ **дров** 'She brought some firewood', Он доста́л **де́нег** 'He acquired some money', Он отме́рил **сати́на** 'He measured out some satin'). With many imperfectives the partitive genitive is never used: Он вы́пил **воды́** 'He drank some water' but Он пил **во́ду** 'He was drinking some water'; Он съел **хле́ба** 'He ate some bread' but Он ел **хлеб** 'He was eating some bread'.

(4) Some perfectives with the quantitative prefix **на-** also take the partitive genitive: нае́сться **я́год** 'to eat one's fill of berries',

накупи́ть **книг** 'to buy some books', нарва́ть **цвето́в** 'to pick some flowers', наруби́ть **дров** 'to chop some wood'.

(5) Containers and quantitative words also appear in partitive constructions: ло́жка **мёда** 'a spoonful of honey'.

(6) Examples of partitive genitives:

> Гри́ша привёз по её про́сьбе **овоще́й** (Trifonov)
> Grisha brought some vegetables at her request

> Налила́ ребя́там **молока́** (Rasputin)
> She poured the kids some milk

> **Де́нег** на доро́гу вы́шлю (Shukshin)
> I'll send some money for the journey

> Я тебе́ дам **успокои́тельных ка́пель** (Rybakov)
> I'll give you some tranquillizers

84 The partitive genitive in -у/-ю

(1) Some masculine nouns, mainly those which denote substances, have genitives in -а/-я and in -у/-ю, e.g. cа́хар 'sugar', **са́хара/ са́хару**; чай 'tea', **ча́я/ча́ю**. See **53**.

(2) Other nouns with two genitives include бензи́н 'petrol', виногра́д 'grapes', горо́х 'peas', кероси́н 'paraffin', кипято́к 'hot water', конья́к 'brandy', лук 'onions', мёд 'honey', мел 'chalk', песо́к 'sand', суп 'soup', сыр 'cheese', таба́к 'tobacco', творо́г 'cottage cheese', шёлк 'silk'.

(3) Genitive **-у/-ю** appears only in partitive constructions: налить **ча́ю** 'to pour some tea', таре́лка **су́пу** 'a plate of soup':

> Ба́бушка посла́ла Во́вку пощипа́ть **лу́ку** (Belov)
> Grandma sent Vovka to pick some onions

> У́тром она́ взяла́ у хозя́ев **кипятку́** (Rybakov)
> In the morning she fetched some hot water from the proprietors

> Доста́л буты́лку **коньяку́**
> He got out a bottle of brandy

(4) If quantity is *not* implied, -**а**/-**я** are used: за́пах и цвет **табака́** 'the smell and colour of tobacco', произво́дство **сы́ра** 'the production of cheese', цена́ **ча́я** 'the price of tea'.

(5) Note that -**а**/-**я** are also used if the noun denoting the substance or liquid is qualified by an adjective: стака́н **кре́пкого ча́я** 'a glass of strong tea'.

(6) The use of the partitive genitive in -**у**/-**ю** is decreasing, and -**а**/-**я** are now possible in all meanings and styles (ча́шка **ча́ю**/**ча́я** 'a cup of tea'), with the commonest nouns (e.g. са́хар 'sugar', чай 'tea') most likely to be found with a genitive in -**у**/-**ю**. However, even with such nouns the partitive in -**а**/-**я** is usually acceptable:

> Стою́ в о́череди в ка́ссу и прики́дываю: килогра́мм **са́хара**, па́чка **ча́я** ... (*Nedelya*)
> I stand in the queue to the cash-desk and calculate: a kilogram of sugar, a packet of tea ...

(7) Genitive -**у**/-**ю** is most consistently found in end-stressed diminutives: свари́ть **кофейку́** (from кофеёк) 'to boil some coffee', Хо́чешь **чайку́**? (from чаёк) 'Would you like some tea?' (others include **коньячку́** from конья́к/коньячо́к 'brandy', **лучку́** from лук/лучо́к 'onions', **сырку́** from сыр/сыро́к 'cheese', **табачку́** from таба́к/табачо́к 'tobacco').

(8) Partitive constructions involving perfective verbs and genitives in -**у**/-**ю** are also very common: доба́вить **са́хару** 'to add some sugar', завари́ть **ча́ю** 'to make some tea', пое́сть **су́пу** 'to eat some soup', положи́ть **чесноку́** 'to put in some garlic'.

(9) -**у**/-**ю** are also found with **нет**, with indefinite numerals and with measures and containers: килогра́мм **виногра́ду** 'a kilo of grapes', нет **коньяку́** 'there is no brandy', мно́го **наро́ду** 'many people', па́чка **са́хару** 'a packet of sugar', кусо́к **сы́ру** 'a piece of cheese'; -**а**/-**я** are also possible in such cases:

> Оста́лось лишь полпа́чки **ча́я** (Povolyaev)
> Only half a packet of tea remained

Only occasionally is the partitive governed by an *imperfective* verb:

> И́зредка мать набива́ла **творогу́** в ба́ночку (Rasputin)
> Now and again mother would cram some cottage cheese into a little jar

85 Genitive in -y in set phrases

(1) Genitives in -y appear in certain idioms and set phrases:

до **зарéзу** нýжно	very necessary
ни **рáзу**	not once
ни **слýху** ни **дýху**	neither sight nor sound
ни **шáгу** назáд	not a step back
с **бóку** нá бок	from side to side
с **глáзу** нá глаз	tête-à-tête
танцевáть до **упáду**	to dance till one drops
упускáть **и́з виду**	to lose sight of

(2) The genitive in -a/-я has had very little impact on such phrases, except for **без прóмаху/-a** 'unerringly' and **без разбóру/-a** 'indiscriminately'.

(3) In some causal expressions **от** combines with -a/-я (от **гóлода** 'from hunger', от **испýга** 'from fright', от **смéха** 'with laughter') and **c** with -y/-ю (умерéть **с гóлоду** 'to starve to death', кри́кнуть с **испýгу** 'to scream with fright', пры́снуть сó **смеху** 'to burst out laughing', умерéть со **стрáху** 'to die of fright'). Some forms in -y/-ю appear in spatial expressions: уйти́ **и́з дому** 'to leave home' (cf. уйти́ из дóма 'to leave the house'), вы́йти **и́з лесу** 'to emerge from the forest'.

86 Genitive and negative

(1) **Нет** 'there is not', **нé было** 'there was not' and **не бýдет** 'there will not be' combine with the genitive to denote **non-existence** or **non-availability**:

Нет **дéнег**	There is no money
Нé было **врéмени**	There was no time
Не бýдет **войны́**	There will be no war

Note
(a) Compare frequentative usage in Всё чáще **Ли́ли** не бывáет дóма (Kazakov) 'Lilya is out more and more often'.
(b) Compare constructions which involve **identification**, where the **nominative** is used: Это не **моя́ женá** 'That is not my wife', Это нé были **мои́ дéти** 'Those were not my children'.

(c) Constructions of the type: **Роди́тели** (nominative) не до́ма 'The parents are out' (for the normal **Роди́телей** нет до́ма) may be used when actual whereabouts are indicated: Они́ не до́ма, а **в гостя́х** 'They are not in, but out visiting'.

(2) The genitive is also used in possessive phrases: У меня́ **нет компью́тера** 'I have no computer', У нас **не́ было дете́й** 'We had no children', У вас **не бу́дет пробле́м** 'You will not have any problems'.

(3) Other negated verbs denoting non-availability, non-occurrence or non-appearance may be used in this construction: **Ле́звий** не име́ется 'There are no blades in stock', **Де́нег** не оста́лось 'There was no money left', **Таки́х люде́й** не существу́ет 'Such people do not exist', **Встре́чных маши́н** не попада́лось 'No oncoming vehicles were encountered'.

(4) In some negative constructions a nominative indicates the absence of *specific* objects, a genitive the absence of *all* objects of a particular type, cf. **Докуме́нтов** не сохрани́лось 'No documents were preserved' (at all) and **Докуме́нты**, о кото́рых шла речь, не сохрани́лись 'The documents in question were not preserved'.

(5) The genitive construction is also used after **не ви́дно** 'cannot be seen', **не заме́тно** 'cannot be discerned', **не слы́шно** 'cannot be heard':

Из-за ды́ма **двере́й** не ви́дно (Abramov)
You can't see the doors for the smoke

Ни **соба́ки**, ни **голосо́в** не́ было слы́шно (Trifonov)
Neither the dog nor people's voices could be heard

(6) It is also used with **не на́до, не ну́жно** etc.:

Не на́до ни **дров**, ни **угля́** (*Rabotnitsa*)
Neither firewood nor coal is necessary

Note
Compare the use of the *genitive* case in the general statement: **По́мощи** не ну́жно 'No help is required' and the *nominative* in the specific **Ва́ша по́мощь** не нужна́ '*Your* help is not required'.

(7) The genitive case is used in negative passive constructions: **Книг** не выпуска́ется 'No books are issued', **Подтвержде́ния** не полу́чено 'No confirmation has been received'.

(8) It is also used in time expressions:

И пяти минут не прошло (Orlov)
Not five minutes had passed

Мы поженились, когда мне ещё не исполнилось **восемнадцати** (*Russia Today*)
We got married when I had not yet **turned 18**

87 The genitive and accusative after negated verbs

(1) Both the genitive and the accusative can be used after a negated transitive verb:

Он не посещал **город/города**   He did not visit the town

(2) While in case of doubt it is advisable to use a genitive, there are situations where one case or the other is preferable.

(3) The **genitive** is preferred:

(i) In generalized statements:

Я не вижу **стола**
I don't see a (i.e. *any*) table

(ii) With compound negatives:

Он никогда и никому не говорил **неправды** (Trifonov)
He has never told lies to anyone

(iii) With the emphatic negative particle **ни**:

Он не прочитал **ни одной книги**
He has not read a single book

(iv) With abstract nouns: Она не скрывает **своего раздражения** 'She does not conceal her irritation'. Many set expressions are involved: не играть **роли** 'to play no part', не иметь **понятия** 'to have no idea', не иметь **права** 'not to have the right', не иметь **смысла** 'not to have any point', не обращать **внимания** 'not to pay any attention', не придавать **значения** 'not to attach significance to', не принимать **участия** 'not to take part', не производить **впечатления** 'to make no impression', не терять **времени** 'not to waste time'.

(v) With a negative gerund: не скрывая своей **радости** 'without concealing his joy', не дослушав **спора** до конца 'without hearing out the argument'.

(vi) With **это**: **Этого** я не допущу 'I won't allow that', and after negated verbs of perception: Он не знал **урока** 'He did not know the lesson', Он не понял **вопроса** 'He did not understand the question', Он не чувствовал **боли** 'he did not feel any pain'.

(4) The **accusative** is preferred:

(i) When a specific object or objects are involved:

Я не вижу **стол**
I do not see *the* table

Он не получил **письмо**
He did not receive *the* letter (cf. Он не получил **письма** 'He did not receive *a* letter')

(ii) When the object denotes a person:

Он не встретил **мою сестру**
He did not meet my sister

(iii) With 'false' negatives such as **едва не/чуть не**, 'almost', **не могу не** 'I can't help, cannot but':

Он чуть не пропустил **трамвай**
He almost missed the tram

Не могу не простить его **поведение**
I cannot but forgive his behaviour

(iv) When the noun is qualified by an instrumental predicate:

Я не считаю **эту статью** интересной
I do not consider this article interesting

(v) When a part of the sentence other than the verb is negated:

Он не **вполне** усвоил урок
He has not **completely** assimilated the lesson

Не **я** придумал новый порядок
It was not **I** who devised the new regime.

(vi) In set phrases: **палец** о палец не ударить 'not to do a stroke of work'.

(5) If none of the above criteria apply, then **either case** is usually possible. Factors which influence choice include:

(i) Word order, the accusative being preferred when the noun precedes the verb (**Идéю** онá не понялá 'She did not understand the idea') and the genitive when it follows (Онá не понялá **идéи** 'She did not understand the idea').

(ii) An accusative is often regarded as the more colloquial alternative: Я не читáл **вчерáшнюю газéту** 'I have not read yesterday's newspaper'.

(iii) Nouns in -**а** and -**я** are more prone to appear in the accusative case after a negated transitive verb than are other nouns.

(iv) When an infinitive appears between the negated verb and the object, the latter usually appears in the accusative:

Он не хотéл смотрéть **эту пьéсу**
He did not want to see this play

Я не умéю писáть **стихи́**
I can't write verse

However, the genitive is also possible:

Вы же никомý не даёте раскры́ть **рта** (Trifonov)
Why, you don't give anyone a chance to get a word in edgeways

Note
To avoid ambiguity, it is better to replace, say, Он не читáет **кни́ги** either by Он не читáет **кни́гу** 'He is not reading the book' or by Он не читáет **книг** 'He does not read books' (since it is otherwise not clear whether **кни́ги** is genitive singular or accusative plural).

(6) In cases of doubt it is advisable to use the *genitive* after a negated transitive verb:

Пригнýвшись, чтóбы не задéть головóй **потолкá** (Zalygin)
Stooping, so as not to hit his head on the ceiling

Note
Verbs which take a case other than the accusative are not affected by the negative–genitive rule: Он помогáет брáту 'He helps his brother', Он не помогáет брáту 'He does not help his brother'; Он горди́тся свои́м полкóм 'He is proud of his regiment', Он не горди́тся свои́м полкóм 'He is not proud of his regiment'.

88 Verbs that take the genitive

Verbs which govern the genitive case belong to four principal categories:

(1) Verbs of asking, waiting, seeking, achieving etc.:

(i) Verbs that take only the genitive. These include **добиваться** 'to strive for', **достигать** 'to achieve', **жаждать** 'to crave for', **желать** 'to desire', **заслуживать** 'to deserve':

добиваться	**успеха**	to strive for success
достигать	**своей цели**	to achieve one's aim
жаждать	**славы**	to crave for glory
желать	**счастья**	to desire happiness
заслуживать	**похвалы**	to deserve praise

Note
(a) The perfective **заслужить** 'to earn' takes the accusative: **заслужить доверие** 'to earn someone's confidence'.
(b) **Желать** 'to wish' is 'understood' in such phrases as **Счастливого пути!** 'Bon voyage!' and **И вам того же!** 'The same to you!'.

(ii) Verbs that take the genitive *and* the accusative. Generally speaking, such verbs take the genitive of nouns denoting general and abstract concepts, and the accusative of nouns denoting persons and specific inanimate objects. The verbs include:

(a) **Дожидаться** 'to wait until'.

Genitive	дожидаться **победы**	to wait till victory comes
Accusative	дожидаться **сестру**	to wait till one's sister comes

(b) **Ждать** 'to wait for'.

Genitive	Жду **ответа**	I am awaiting an answer
	Жду **приказа**	I am awaiting an order
	Жду **решения**	I am awaiting a decision

Ждём писем о самых интересных клубах (*Russia Today*)
We are expecting letters about the most interesting clubs

Она́ ждала́ от меня́ **комплиме́нта** (Avdeenko)
She was expecting a compliment from me

Accusative   Жду **сего́дняшнюю**   I am waiting for
                       по́чту   today's mail

Сиде́л за столо́м, занима́лся, ждал **жену́** (Grekova)
He sat at the table, worked, waited for his wife

Note
Ждать **авто́бус** No. 5 'to wait for the number 5 bus' (a particular
bus), but Жду **авто́буса** 'I am waiting for a bus' (any bus; but Жду
авто́бус is also possible, especially in spoken Russian).

(c) **Иска́ть** 'to seek, look for'.

Genitive ('to try to achieve')

иска́ть **возмо́жности**	to seek an opportunity
иска́ть **по́мощи**	to seek assistance

Accusative ('to try to find')

иска́ть **упа́вшую иго́лку**	to look for a dropped needle
иска́ть **своё ме́сто** в за́ле	to look for one's place in the hall
иска́ть **пра́вду**	to seek the truth
иска́ть **доро́гу**	to try to find the way

Note
Рабо́та is found in either case (иска́ть **рабо́ты/рабо́ту** 'to look for
work'), with the accusative (the more usual form) referring to more
specific work.

(d) **Ожида́ть** 'to wait for, expect'.

Genitive	ожида́ть **слу́чая**	to wait for an opportunity
	ожида́ть **авто́буса**	to wait for a bus (cf.
		ждать (b) note)

Втяну́л го́лову в пле́чи, бу́дто ожида́я **уда́ра** со спины́
(Gagarin)
He hunched his shoulders, as if expecting a blow from behind

Accusative	ожида́ть **ма́му**	to wait for, expect Mum

(e) **Проси́ть** 'to ask for'.

Genitive	Прошу́ **по́мощи**	I ask for assistance (also
		прошу́ о по́мощи)

Прошу́ **проще́ния**   I ask forgiveness

See **83** (3) for usage with the partitive genitive.

| Accusative | Прошу́ **де́ньги** | I ask for the money (cf. Прошу́ **де́нег** 'I ask for **some** money') |
| | Прошу́ **ма́му** откры́ть окно́ | I ask Mum to open the window |

(f) **Тре́бовать** 'to demand'.

Genitive	тре́бовать **внима́ния**	to demand attention
	тре́бовать **приба́вки**	to demand an increment
	тре́бовать **книг**	to demand some books

| Accusative | тре́бовать **свою́ кни́гу** | to demand one's book |

(g) **Хоте́ть** 'to want'.

| Genitive | Хоти́м **ми́ра** | We want peace |

See **83** (3) for usage with the partitive genitive.

| Accusative | Хочу́ **бу́лку** | I want a roll |

(2) Verbs of fearing, avoiding etc. Such verbs usually take the genitive of abstract, impersonal and inanimate nouns, but may now govern the accusative of animate nouns.

(i) **Боя́ться** 'to fear'.

| Genitive | боя́ться **темноты́** | to be afraid of the dark |
| | боя́ться **грозы́** | to be afraid of a thunderstorm |

Он боя́лся **го́рода**, не хоте́л в него́ (Rasputin)
He was afraid of the town, did not want to go there

| Accusative | боя́ться **ба́бушку** | to be afraid of grandmother |

(ii) Other verbs include дичи́ться 'to be shy of', избега́ть 'to avoid', опаса́ться 'to fear', остерега́ться 'to beware of', пуга́ться 'to be scared of', стесня́ться 'to be shy of', сторони́ться 'to shun', стыди́ться 'to be ashamed of', чужда́ться 'to avoid':

избега́ть **неприя́тностей**	to avoid trouble
избега́ть **тёщу**	to avoid one's mother-in-law
опаса́ться **осложне́ний**	to fear complications

остерега́ться **зара́зы**	to beware of an infection
пуга́ться **гро́ма**	to be scared of thunder
стесня́ться **о́бщества**	to shun society
сторони́ться **недо́брых люде́й**	to shun wicked people
стыди́ться **своего́ ви́да**	to be ashamed of one's appearance
чужда́ться **дурно́й компа́нии**	to avoid bad company

(3) Verbs of depriving etc.

| лиша́ть **роди́тельских прав** | to deprive of parental rights |
| лиша́ться **свобо́ды** | to be deprived of one's freedom |

(4) Verbs denoting conformity or non-conformity. These include держа́ться 'to adhere to', ослу́шиваться 'to disobey', приде́рживаться 'to hold to', слу́шаться 'to obey':

держа́ться **мне́ния**	to stick to one's opinion
ослу́шиваться **прика́за**	to disobey an order
приде́рживаться **то́чки зре́ния**	to hold to a point of view
слу́шаться **сове́та**	to heed advice

Note

In colloquial styles the accusative is possible with an animate object: слу́шаться **ма́тери** or **мать** 'to obey one's mother'.

Other verbs that take the genitive include **каса́ться** 'to touch, touch on' and **сто́ить** 'to be worth':

каса́ться **стола́**	to touch the table
каса́ться **вопро́са**	to touch on a question
э́то сто́ит **награ́ды**	that is worth an award

89 The dative as indirect object of a verb

The dative case denotes the indirect object of a verb, i.e. the person for whom an action is performed, the recipient or beneficiary: дава́ть де́ньги **касси́ру** 'to give the money to the cashier', звони́ть **сестре́** на рабо́ту 'to ring one's sister at work', отвеча́ть **сосе́ду** 'to answer a neighbour' (cf. отвеча́ть **на** письмо́ 'to answer a letter'), писа́ть письмо́ **бра́ту** 'to write a letter to one's brother', плати́ть **дру́гу** 'to pay one's friend', пожима́ть ру́ку **солда́ту** 'to shake the soldier's hand', посла́ть де́ньги **сы́ну** 'to send money to one's son' (note, however, use of the preposition **к** when the object sent is animate : отпра́вить дете́й **к ро́дственникам** 'to send the children to stay with relatives'), сказа́ть **отцу́** пра́вду 'to tell one's father the truth'.

90 Verbs that take the dative

Verbs which take the dative denote:

(1) Conforming, rendering assistance or other service; conversely, causing a hindrance: аккомпани́ровать 'to accompany' (music), аплоди́ровать 'to applaud', вреди́ть 'to harm', изменя́ть 'to betray', меша́ть 'to hinder', напомина́ть 'to remind', повинова́ться 'to obey', позволя́ть 'to allow', покрови́тельствовать 'to patronize', помога́ть 'to help', препя́тствовать 'to hinder', противоре́чить 'to contradict', служи́ть 'to serve', сове́товать 'to advise', соде́йствовать 'to co-operate', спосо́бствовать 'to foster', угожда́ть 'to please'.

Note
(a) Запреща́ть 'to forbid' and разреша́ть 'to permit' take the dative of the person (запреща́ть/разреша́ть **солда́там** кури́ть 'to forbid/permit the soldiers to smoke') and the accusative of an action or process (запреща́ть/разреша́ть **обго́н** 'to forbid/permit overtaking').
(b) Учи́ть 'to teach' takes the dative of the subject taught: учи́ть дете́й **му́зыке** 'to teach the children music'. Учи́ть + accusative means 'to learn': учи́ть **ру́сский язы́к** 'to learn Russian'.

(2) Attitude: ве́рить 'to believe', доверя́ть(ся) 'to trust', грози́ть 'to threaten', досажда́ть 'to annoy', зави́довать 'to envy', льстить 'to flatter', мстить 'to take vengeance on' (cf. мстить за + accusative 'to avenge someone'), надоеда́ть 'to bore', подража́ть 'to imitate', поража́ться 'to be amazed at', ра́доваться 'to rejoice at', сочу́вствовать 'to sympathize with', удивля́ться 'to be surprised at'. Note also смея́ться, улыба́ться **шу́тке** 'to laugh, smile at a joke' (but смея́ться **над** ке́м-нибудь 'to laugh at someone').

(3) Other meanings: насле́довать 'to succeed' (someone), предше́ствовать 'to precede', принадлежа́ть 'to belong to' (in the

meaning of possession; cf. принадлежа́ть **к** 'to belong to' (a group, society etc.)), равня́ться 'to equal', сле́довать 'to follow' (advice etc.).

Note

Many verbal and other nouns cognate with the above verbs also take the dative: обуче́ние **ру́сскому языку́** 'the teaching of Russian', подража́ние **ска́зке** 'imitation of a folk tale', по́мощь **же́ртвам** землетрясе́ния 'help for the victims of the earthquake', служе́ние **нау́ке** 'service to science', соде́йствие **фло́ту** 'co-operation with the navy', сочу́вствие **чужо́му го́рю** 'sympathy for others' grief', угро́за **ми́ру** 'a threat to peace'.

91 Adjectives that take the dative

Adjectives (long *and* short forms) which take the dative include:

благода́рный	grateful to
ве́рный	loyal to
знако́мый	known to
изве́стный	well known to
подо́бный	similar to
послу́шный	obedient to
прису́щий	inherent in
рад (short form only)	glad (я рад **гостя́м** 'I am glad to see the guests')
сво́йственный	characteristic of, inherent in

Предусмотри́тельность **сво́йственна** э́тому челове́ку
Prudence is inherent in this person

92 Impersonal constructions using the dative

(1) Most impersonal constructions involving the dative case denote a state of mind, feeling, inclination or attitude:

Ученику́ ве́село, гру́стно, ду́шно, жа́рко, лу́чше, ску́чно, сты́дно, тепло́, удо́бно, хо́лодно, ху́же
The pupil feels cheerful, sad, stifled, hot, better, bored, ashamed, warm, comfortable, cold, worse

(2) Some constructions involve verbs: **Брáту** кáжется, что тепло́ 'My brother thinks it is warm', **Брáту** надое́ло рабо́тать 'My brother is bored with working', **Брáту** нездоро́вится 'My brother feels off colour', **Брáту** нра́вится танцева́ть 'My brother likes dancing', **Брáту** прихо́дится мно́го рабо́тать 'My brother is obliged to work hard', **Брáту** удало́сь доста́ть де́ньги 'My brother managed to get the money', **Брáту** хоте́лось уйти́ 'My brother felt like leaving'.

(3) Note also:

(i) Constructions with reflexive verbs that denote disinclination:

> **Сестре́** не поётся, не рабо́тается, не сиди́тся
> My sister does not feel like singing, working, sitting still

(ii) The impersonal predicate **жаль** also combines with the dative: **Отцу́** жаль 'My father feels sorry' (for жаль with accusative see **79** (2) and for жаль with genitive see **80** (8)).

(4) The dative is also used in denoting age: **Сы́ну** (испо́лнилось) 20 лет 'My son is (has turned) 20'.

93 The dative as the logical subject of an infinitive

(1) A noun or pronoun in the dative case may function as the logical subject of an infinitive: Что **де́тям** де́лать? 'What are the children to do?', Не **вам** реша́ть 'It is not for you to decide', **Брáту** не́куда идти́ 'My brother has nowhere to go'.

(2) The dative can also be used to express a peremptory command: **Всем сотру́дникам** собра́ться в час! 'All employees meet at one!'

94 The instrumental of function

A noun is placed in the instrumental case to denote that the object it represents is being used to perform a function: мы́ться **горя́чей водо́й** 'to wash with hot water', писа́ть **карандашо́м** 'to write with a pencil', ре́зать **ножо́м** 'to cut with a knife', руби́ть **топоро́м** 'to chop with an axe'.

Note

(a) Analogous use of the instrumental in броса́ть **камня́ми** 'to throw stones' (at a target), говори́ть **гро́мким го́лосом** 'to speak in a loud voice', дыша́ть **кислоро́дом** 'to breathe oxygen', плати́ть **англи́йскими деньга́ми** 'to pay in English money'.

(b) Use of the instrumental of function (e.g. ре́зать **ножо́м** 'to cut with a knife') must be distinguished from **с** + instrumental ('with' in the meaning 'holding'): он сиде́л **с ножо́м** в руке́ 'he sat with a knife in his hand'.

(c) Корми́ть **ры́бой** 'to feed on (= with) fish', награжда́ть **пре́мией** 'to reward with a bonus', наполня́ть **водо́й** 'to fill with water', снабжа́ть **не́фтью** 'to supply with oil' also belong in the category 'instrumental of function'.

95 The instrumental in constructions denoting movements of the body

The instrumental is used in constructions denoting movements of the body:

(1) Дви́гать **руко́й** 'to move one's arm' (cf. дви́гать **стол** 'to move a table'), кача́ть/кива́ть **голово́й** 'to shake/nod one's head', маха́ть **руко́й** 'to wave one's hand', мига́ть **глаза́ми** 'to blink one's eyes', пожима́ть **плеча́ми** 'to shrug one's shoulders', то́пать **нога́ми** 'to stamp one's feet', щёлкать **языко́м** 'to click one's tongue'.

(2) The construction also applies to objects held with the hand (разма́хивать **па́лкой** 'to brandish a stick', хло́пать **две́рью** 'to slam a door', щёлкать **бичо́м** 'to crack a whip') and to the figurative expressions И **бро́вью** не повёл 'He did not turn a hair', шевели́ть **мозга́ми** 'to use one's brains'.

96 The instrumental in passive constructions

The instrumental is used to denote the agent in a passive construction:

Дом стро́ится **рабо́чими**	The house is being built by workers

| Горá покры́та **снéгом** | The mountain is covered with snow |
| **Вéтром** сорвáло кры́шу | The roof was torn off by the wind |

See also **359** and **360** (2) for the use of the instrumental with passive participles.

97 The instrumental in adverbial expressions

The instrumental is used to denote:

(1) The type of route covered in a journey: идти́ **бéрегом** 'to walk along the shore', éхать **лéсом** 'to ride through the forest', **мóрем** 'by sea', éхать **пóлем** 'to ride through the fields', **сухи́м путём** 'overland'. Note also идти́ **своéй доро́гой** 'to go one's own way' (fig.).

(2) Time:

(i) Parts of the day: **у́тром, днём, вéчером, но́чью** 'in the morning, daytime, evening, at night' (**глубóкой нóчью** 'at dead of night', **однáжды у́тром** 'one morning', **вечерáми** 'in the evenings', **ночáми** '(at) nights').

Note
Днём may also mean 'in the afternoon' (also rendered as во второ́й полови́не дня).

(ii) Seasons of the year: **весно́й, лéтом, óсенью, зимо́й** 'in the spring, summer, autumn, winter' (однáжды **зимо́й** 'one winter', **пóздней óсенью** 'in late autumn' etc.).

(iii) Others: **цéлыми часáми/дня́ми** 'for hours/days on end'.

(3) The **manner** in which or the **means** by which an action is performed, in terms of:

(i) Position: вверх **дном** 'upside down', вниз **головóй** 'head first', стоя́ть **спино́й** к огню́ 'to stand with one's back to the fire'.

(ii) Movement: **бегóм** 'at a run', **шáгом** 'at walking pace'.

(iii) Group activity: уéхать **семьёй** 'to leave in a family group', пéние **хóром** 'singing in chorus'.

(iv) Utterance: **други́ми слова́ми** 'in other words', петь **ба́сом** 'to sing bass', **шёпотом** 'in a whisper'.

(v) Means of transport: е́хать **по́ездом**, лете́ть **самолётом** 'to go by train, by air'.

(vi) Degree of effort: **любо́й цено́й** 'at any cost'.

(vii) Quantity: Дома́ не стро́или **ты́сячами**, как сейча́с (Rybakov) 'Houses were not built in thousands as they are now'.

(viii) Form, manner: **каки́м о́бразом?** 'in what way?', Снег па́дает на зе́млю **больши́ми хло́пьями** (Rasputin) 'The snow falls to earth in large flakes'.

98 Use of the instrumental to denote similarity

The instrumental is also used to express similarity: выть **во́лком** 'to howl like a wolf', умере́ть **геро́ем** 'to die like a hero', шипе́ть **змеёй** 'to hiss like a snake', Снег лежи́т **ковро́м** 'The snow lies like a carpet', лете́ть **стрело́й** 'to fly like an arrow', усы́ **щёточкой** 'toothbrush moustache':

> За куста́рником **тёмной стено́й** выраста́ло чернопе́сье (Abramov)
> Deciduous forest grew up beyond the bushes like a dark wall

99 Verbs that take the instrumental

Verbs that take the instrumental case denote:

(1) **Use** or **control**: владе́ть 'to own, have a command of' (a language), дирижи́ровать 'to conduct' (an orchestra), заве́довать 'to be in charge of', злоупотребля́ть 'to abuse, misuse', кома́ндовать 'to command', облада́ть 'to possess', по́льзоваться 'to use', пра́вить 'to rule', располага́ть 'to have at one's disposal', распоряжа́ться 'to manage', руководи́ть 'to run', управля́ть 'to control'.

(2) **Attitude**: восхища́ться 'to be delighted with', горди́ться 'to be proud of', грози́ть 'to threaten with', дово́льствоваться 'to be satis-

fied with', дорожи́ть 'to value', интересова́ться 'to be interested in', любова́ться 'to admire' (also на + acc.), наслажда́ться 'to delight in', обходи́ться 'to make do with', пренебрега́ть 'to disregard', увлека́ться 'to be obsessed with', хва́статься 'to boast of', щеголя́ть 'to flaunt'.

(3) **Reciprocal action**: дели́ться 'to share', обме́ниваться 'to exchange'.

(4) **Other meanings**: боле́ть 'to be sick', же́ртвовать 'to sacrifice' (cf. же́ртвовать + acc. 'to donate'), занима́ться 'to busy oneself with', изоби́ловать 'to abound in', ограни́чиваться 'to limit oneself to', отлича́ться 'to be distinguished by', па́хнуть 'to smell of', прославля́ться 'to be renowned for', рискова́ть 'to risk', страда́ть 'to suffer from' (chronically) (cf. страда́ть от 'to suffer from' (a *temporary* ailment)), торгова́ть 'to trade in'.

Note
Participial, verbal and other nouns cognate with many of the above also take the instrumental: владе́ние **до́мом** 'ownership of a house' (but владе́лец **до́ма** 'house owner'), злоупотребле́ние **вла́стью** 'abuse of power', кома́ндование **а́рмией** 'command of the army', кома́ндующий **а́рмией** 'army commander' (but команди́р **диви́зии** 'divisional commander'), руково́дство **па́ртией** 'leadership of the party' (as an action or process, cf. руково́дство **па́ртии** 'the leadership (i.e. 'the leaders') of the party', руководи́тель **гру́ппы** 'leader of the group'), торго́вля **нарко́тиками** 'drugs trade', увлече́ние **матема́тикой** 'obsession with mathematics'.

100 Adjectives that take the instrumental

These include long *and* (where available) short forms: бере́менная (**тре́тьим ребёнком**) 'pregnant' (with her third child), бога́тый 'rich in', больно́й 'sick with', го́рдый 'proud of', дово́льный 'pleased with', изве́стный 'famous for', обя́занный 'obliged':

> Свои́ми успе́хами они́ бы́ли обя́заны со́бственному трудолю́бию (Rybakov)
> They owed their success to their own industriousness

101 The instrumental of dimension

The instrumental is used to express dimension: горá **высотóй** в
1 000 мéтров 'a mountain 1,000 m high', рекá **длинóй** в стó
килóмéтров 'a river 100 km long', человéк **рóстом** в метр
вóсемьдесят 'a man one metre eighty tall'.

Note
(a) The preposition **в** may be omitted, especially in technical styles.

(b) Questions to which these are the notional answers appear in the
genitive: **какóй высотьí** горá? 'how high is the mountain?',
какóй длины́ рекá? 'how long is the river?', **какóго** он **рóста**?
'how tall is he?'

102 The instrumental as predicate

(1) The instrumental is used as predicate to the infinitive, future
tense, imperative, conditional and gerund of the verb **быть** 'to be': Я
хочý быть **врачóм** 'I want to be a doctor', éсли бы я был **врачóм**
'if I were a doctor', Когдá-нибудь вы бýдете **старикóм** 'One day
you will be an old man', Не будь **трýсом** 'Don't be a coward', Не
бýдучи **знатокóм**, не могý судíть 'Not being a connoisseur I cannot judge'.

Note
The *nominative*, not the instrumental, is used when no part of быть
is present: Онá врач 'She is a doctor'.

(2) In the *past* tense:

(i) The nominative denotes **permanent** state, occupation, nationality etc.: По профéссии он был **ботáник** 'By profession he was a
botanist', Онá былá **испáнка** (Granin) 'She was a Spaniard',
Смольянов был **сарáтовец** (Trifonov) 'Smolyanov was a native of
Saratov'.

(ii) The instrumental denotes **temporary** status: Во врéмя войны́ я
был **офицéром** 'During the war I was an officer' (the verb **быть** is
sometimes omitted: Я потерял родíтелей (когдá я был/бýдучи)
ребёнком 'I lost my parents as a child').

Note

Permanent status may *also* be denoted by the instrumental: Она́ была́ **сестро́й** Полево́го (Propp), 'She was Polevoi's sister', Пу́шкин был **велича́йшим ру́сским поэ́том/велича́йший ру́сский поэ́т** 'Pushkin was the greatest Russian poet'.

(3) Of two nouns (or noun and pronoun) linked by the verb **быть** the more specific appears in the nominative, the more general in the instrumental:

Ключо́м к успе́ху была́ гра́мотность
The key to success was literacy

В на́шем до́ме неме́цкий был **тре́тьим языко́м** (Rybakov)
In our house German was the third language

Одно́й из на́ших гла́вных пробле́м был тра́нспорт
One of our main problems was transport

Note

The subject may be an infinitive: **Учи́ться** бу́дет его́ це́лью 'His aim will be to study', Пе́рвым её побужде́нием бы́ло **помо́чь** до́чери 'Her first impulse was to help her daughter'.

(4) The rule described in (3) also applies to **явля́ться** 'to be':

Основно́й фо́рмой рабо́ты в шко́ле явля́ется уро́к (*Russia Today*)
The lesson is the basic form of work in school

(5) An instrumental predicate also appears with verbs such as **запи́сываться** 'to enrol', **рабо́тать** 'to work', **служи́ть** 'to serve':

Записа́лся **доброво́льцем**, да́ли ему́ коня́ (Rybakov)
He signed on as a volunteer, and they gave him a horse

(6) A number of verbs which denote state, appearance or manner also take an instrumental: **вы́глядеть** 'to look', **каза́ться** 'to seem', **называ́ться** 'to be called', **ока́зываться** 'to turn out to be', **остава́ться** 'to remain', **расстава́ться** 'to part', **роди́ться** 'to be born', **состоя́ть** (**чле́ном**) 'to be' (a member), **станови́ться** 'to become', **счита́ться** 'to be considered', **чу́вствовать себя́** 'to feel':

Ещё с войны́ она́ **вдово́й** оста́лась (Shcherbakov)
She had been left a war widow

Он ка́жется **о́пытным инжене́ром**
He seems to be an experienced engineer

Впервы́е в жи́зни я чу́вствую себя́ **преда́телем** (Makarov)
For the first time in my life I feel like a traitor

(7) The instrumental may also be predicate to the object of transitive verbs which denote appointment, naming, considering: Сестру́ зову́т **Та́ней** (alternatively, especially in colloquial Russian, Сестру́ зову́т **Та́ня**) 'My sister is called Tanya', назнача́ть Ивано́ва **председа́телем** 'to appoint Ivanov chairman', Мак счита́ют **снотво́рным сре́дством** 'Poppy is considered to be a soporific':

Он называ́ет Толья́тти «**эксперимента́льной лаборато́-рией**» сове́тского градострои́тельства (*Sputnik*)
He calls Togliatti 'an experimental laboratory' in Soviet town planning

103 Nouns in apposition

When two or more nouns, pronouns or modifiers refer to the same object or person they appear in the same case:

Она́ жила́ в **Москве́, столи́це** Росси́и
She lived in **Moscow, the capital** of Russia

Он знал **моего́ отца́, изве́стного хиру́рга**
He knew **my father, a famous surgeon**

Я чита́ю «**Сове́тскую Росси́ю**», **одну́** из са́мых интере́с-ных сове́тских газе́т
I am reading *Sovetskaya Rossiya*, one of the most interesting Soviet newspapers

Diminutive and augmentative nouns

104 Meanings and functions of the diminutive

(1) Diminutive suffixes not only denote smallness (**сто́лик** 'a small table'), but may also express emotional nuances such as affection (**дя́денька** 'dear uncle'), disparagement (**городи́шко** 'wretched little town'), irony (**иде́йка** 'a paltry little idea') etc. Depending on context the same diminutive phrase may convey a caring attitude (Вот тебе́ **горя́ченький су́пчик** 'Here's some nice hot soup for you' (mother to child)) or be evidence of affectation.

(2) Diminutives are used mainly in colloquial speech. Many have acquired independent meanings, e.g. **ру́чка** 'handle', 'pen'.

105 Masculine diminutives

The following diminutive suffixes may be affixed to the stems of masculine nouns.

(1) **-ец**.

-ец may express an affectionate or positive attitude (**бра́тец** from брат 'brother', **хле́бец** from хлеб 'bread'), or alternatively disparagement (**анекдо́тец** from анекдо́т 'anecdote').

(2) **-ик**.

(i) **-ик** (*never stressed*) imparts the meaning of smallness to many masculine nouns: **до́мик** from дом 'house', **ко́врик** 'mat' from ковёр 'carpet'.

(ii) Emotional nuances expressed by **-ик** include affection (**са́дик** from сад 'garden'), and irony or scorn (**анекдо́тик** from анекдо́т 'anecdote').

(iii) Diminutives with independent meanings include **мо́стик** 'captain's bridge', **но́жик** 'pen-knife' and **сто́лик** 'restaurant table'.

(3) **-ок/-ёк/-ек**.

(i) **-ок/-ёк** (*always stressed*) express affection, irony or disparagement, as well as smallness. Guttural consonants undergo mutation:

дружо́к from друг 'friend', **старичо́к** from стари́к 'old man', **пастушо́к** from пасту́х 'shepherd'.

(ii) Other diminutives in -**ок** include **городо́к** from го́род 'town', **лесо́к** from лес 'forest' etc. **Дурачо́к** from дура́к 'fool' and **женишо́к** from жени́х 'fiancé, bridegroom' express irony.

(iii) Nouns in -**ь** and -**й** take the suffix -**ёк**: **огонёк** from ого́нь 'fire, light' (Нет ли у вас **огонька́**? 'Do you happen to have a light?'), **чаёк** from чай 'tea' (Хоти́те **чайку́**? 'Have some tea?').

(iv) Nouns with independent meanings include **волосо́к** 'filament', **глазо́к** 'peephole', **значо́к** 'badge', **конёк** 'skate', **кружо́к** 'circle, club', **молото́к** 'hammer', **носо́к** 'sock, toe of shoe or stocking', **язычо́к** 'tongue of shoe, clapper of bell'.

Note

(a)   Second-stage diminutives can be formed: друг 'friend', дружо́к, **дружо́чек**.

(b)   Diminutives in unstressed -**ек** include **челове́чек** from челове́к 'person'.

(4) -**чик**.

(i) -**чик** (*never stressed*) is affixed mainly to nouns ending in:

(a) -**л**/-**ль** (**автомоби́льчик** from автомоби́ль 'car', **журна́льчик** from журна́л 'journal').

(b) -**н** (**карма́нчик** from карма́н 'pocket').

(c) -**р** (**забо́рчик** from забо́р 'fence').

(d) -**й** (**трамва́йчик** from трамва́й 'tram').

(e) -**ф** (**шка́фчик** from шкаф 'cupboard').

(ii) The suffix may also express affection: **дива́нчик** from дива́н 'couch'. Forms with independent meanings include **колоко́льчик** 'bluebell' from ко́локол 'bell'.

(5) Examples of masculine diminutives expressing:

(i) Smallness:

На корме́ поблёскивал **мото́рчик** (Nagibin)
In the stern glinted a small engine

(ii) Animosity:

Я приду́мывал но́вый **вопро́сец** похлёстче (Gagarin)
I was devising a more scathing question

(iii) Irony:

А муж счита́ет, что уже́ отве́тил на э́тот вопро́с, наде́в
кольцо́ на **па́льчик** свое́й супру́ги
Whereas the husband thinks he has already answered this
question by placing a ring on his wife's dear little finger

(iv) Disparagement:

Сыно́к профе́ссора. Чи́стенький тако́й **пижо́нчик**
(Yakhontov)
A professor's pampered brat. A young fop, pure as the driven
snow

106 Feminine diminutives

(1) **-ица**.

(i) The suffix **-ица** bears the stress in diminutives derived from
nouns in stressed **-а́**, **-я́** and in **-ь**: **вещи́ца** from вещь 'thing' (cf.
про́сьбица from про́сьба 'request').

(ii) Second-stage diminutives in **-ичка** are also formed: вода́
'water', води́ца, **води́чка** (both have the positive nuance typical of
diminutives based on the names of food and drink); сестра́ 'sister',
сестри́ца, **сестри́чка** (cf., from Russian folk-tale, **Лиси́чка-
Сестри́чка** 'Sister Fox').

(2) **-ка**.

(i) The suffix may denote smallness (**крова́тка** 'cot' from крова́ть
'bed') as well as affection (**до́чка** from дочь 'daughter') or irony
(**иде́йка** from иде́я 'idea').

(ii) The stress in diminutives in **-ка** derived from end-stressed
nouns falls on the syllable preceding **-ка**: **голо́вка** from голова́
'head'. Some diminutives are based on genitive plurals with the
vowel **-е-**: пе́сня 'song', gen. pl. пе́сен, dim. **пе́сенка**; семья́ 'family',
gen. pl. семе́й, dim. **семе́йка**.

(iii) Guttural consonants and **ц** undergo mutation: **кни́жка** from кни́га 'book', **ре́чка** from река́ 'river', **му́шка** from му́ха 'fly', **страни́чка** from страни́ца 'page'.

(iv) The following have independent meanings: **голо́вка** 'head of a nail' (also **боеголо́вка** 'war-head'), **доро́жка** 'path', **ёлка** 'Christmas tree', **кры́шка** 'lid', **маши́нка** 'typewriter', **но́жка** 'leg of chair, table', **пли́тка** 'bar' (of chocolate), **площа́дка** 'stair landing, playground, launch pad', **пти́чка** 'tick', **ру́чка** 'arm of a chair', **се́тка** 'tennis net', **спи́нка** 'back of a chair', **стре́лка** 'clock-hand', **тру́бка** 'telephone receiver, pipe'.

(v) Second-stage diminutives in **-очка** are formed as follows: мину́та 'minute', мину́тка, **мину́точка** (Подожди́те **мину́точку!** 'Wait a sec!').

(vi) Nouns with a double consonant + **-a** form **first-stage** diminutives in **-очка**: звезда́ 'star', **звёздочка** 'small star, asterisk'; ка́рта 'card, map', **ка́рточка** 'greetings card' (but игла́ 'needle', **иго́лка**, **иго́лочка**).

107   Neuter diminutives

(1)   **-ико**.

This suffix is used with very few nouns: **колёсико** from колесо́ 'wheel', **ли́чико** from лицо́ 'face', **пле́чико** from плечо́ 'shoulder' (pl. **пле́чики** also 'coat-hanger').

(2)   **-ко**.

Stress is unpredictable in diminutives with this ending, cf. **ведёрко** from ведро́ 'bucket', **озерко́** from о́зеро 'lake'. **К** and **ц** mutate to **ч**: **о́блачко** from о́блако 'cloud', **яи́чко** from яйцо́ 'egg'.

(3)   **-цо/-це; -ецо**.

The suffixes **-цо/-це** appear after a single consonant, **-ецо** after a double consonant: **зе́ркальце** from зе́ркало 'mirror', **письмецо́** from письмо́ 'letter'. Stress is as in the source noun except for **словцо́** from сло́во 'word' and **де́ревце/деревцо́** from де́рево 'tree'.

108 Other diminutive suffixes

(1) **-ашка** expresses slight disparagement or endearment, depending on context: **мордáшка** from мóрда 'mug' (face), **старикáшка** from старúк 'old man'.

(2) **-ишко** (inanimate)/**-ишка** (animate) express disparagement or irony: **ворúшка** from вор 'thief', **домúшко** from дом 'house':

У меня́ дóма **коньячúшко** есть (Shukshin)
I've got a nice little bottle of brandy at home (nuance of affection)

(3) **-онка/-ёнка** express disparagement: **книжóнка** from кнúга 'book', **лошадёнка** from лóшадь 'horse' (however, **сестрёнка** from сестрá 'sister' denotes affection).

(4) **-ушка/-юшка** and **-енька/-онька** express affection: **дóченька** from дочь 'daughter', **избýшка** from избá 'hut'.

(5) **-ышек**, **-ышко**: **кóлышек** 'tent-peg' from кол 'stake', **гóрлышко** 'neck of bottle' from гóрло 'throat', **зёрнышко** from зернó 'grain'.

109 Augmentative suffixes

The suffixes **-ина**, **-ище** and **-ища** are attached to the stems of nouns to denote largeness. Augmentatives may also express emotive nuances: **идиóтина** 'a blithering idiot'.

(1) **-ина**.

(i) **-ина** is affixed to the stems of masculine and feminine nouns: **зверúна** (from зверь) 'an enormous beast', **лáпина** (from лáпа) 'a massive paw'.

(ii) The suffix is stressed if attached to the stem of a noun which has mobile stress in declension (**домúна** 'a vast house') and is unstressed if attached to the stem of a noun which has fixed stress in declension (**рýбина** 'a large fish').

(iii) Gutturals undergo mutation: **дурачúна** (from дурáк) 'a great fool', **оплеýшина** (from оплеýха) 'a hefty slap in the face'.

(2) -ище/-ища.

(i) These suffixes are far more productive than -ина. -ище is affixed to the stems of masculine and neuter nouns, -ища to those of feminine nouns: **арбу́зище** (from арбу́з) 'an enormous melon', **бороди́ща** (from борода́) 'a massive beard'.

(ii) Stress position depends on the same principles as those described for -ина: **велика́нище** (from велика́н) (fixed stress in declension) 'an enormous giant', **голоси́ще** (from го́лос) (mobile stress in declension) 'a mighty voice'.

(iii) Guttural consonants undergo mutation: **волчи́ще** (from волк) 'a large wolf', **ручи́ща** (from рука́) 'a mighty hand'.

The Pronoun

(1) The personal pronouns **я** 'I', **ты** 'you' (informal), **он** 'he, it', **она́** 'she, it', **оно́** 'it', **мы** 'we', **вы** 'you' (formal and plural), **они́** 'they' decline as follows:

Nom.		я	ты	он	он-**а́**	он-**о́**
Acc./Gen.		мен-**я́**	теб-**я́**	его́	её	его́
Dat.		мн-**е**	теб-**е́**	ему́	ей	ему́
Instr.		мн-**ой**	тоб-**о́й**	им	ей/е́ю	им
Prep.	обо мн-**е**		о теб-**е́**	о нём	о ней	о нём

Nom.		м-**ы**	в-**ы**	он-**и́**
Acc./Gen.		н-**ас**	в-**ас**	их
Dat.		н-**ам**	в-**ам**	им
Instr.		н-**а́ми**	в-**а́ми**	и́ми
Prep.	о н-**ас**		о в-**ас**	о них

Note

(a) Я and ты have alternative instrumental forms: **мно́ю** and **тобо́ю**, used in verse and in some colloquial registers, are also found in passive constructions (Это сде́лано **мно́ю/мной** 'That was done by me').

(b) **Его́**, the accusative/genitive of **он/оно́**, is pronounced [jɪˈvo].

(c)   The alternative instrumental form of она́ (**е́ю**) is preferred to **ей** in educated speech and is particularly important in passive constructions, avoiding possible confusion with the dative:

Револю́цией перестро́йку мо́жно назва́ть в си́лу ради-ка́льности поста́вленных **е́ю** це́лей (*Izvestiya*)
Restructuring can be called a revolution by virtue of the radical nature of the goals set **by it**

(**Ей** would imply a dative meaning: 'the goals set **for** it'.)

(2)   The oblique cases of **он**, **она́**, **оно́**, **они́** take initial **н**- when governed by a preposition: от **него́** 'from him', к **ней** 'to her', с **ни́ми** 'with them' etc. However, some *compound* prepositions take a third-person pronoun *without* initial **н**-. They include:

(i)   A number of derivative prepositions governing the dative: благодаря́ **им** 'thanks to them', **ему́** навстре́чу 'to meet him', на зло **ей** 'to spite her'. Others include **вопреки́** 'contrary to', **напереко́р** 'counter to', **подо́бно** 'similar to', **согла́сно** 'in accordance with'.

(ii)   Some which take the genitive: **внѐ** 'outside', **в отноше́нии** 'in relation to'. **Внутрѝ** 'inside' takes alternative forms with or without н-: внутрѝ **их**/**них** 'inside them'.

Note
When a declined form of the third-person plural pronoun combines with a declined form of **все** 'all', a pronoun with initial **н**- is the norm: смея́ться над все́ми **ни́ми** 'to laugh at all of them'. У/от неё 'She has/from her' has an alternative form **у/от ней**, used nowadays mainly in verse.

111 Use of personal instead of possessive pronouns

(1)   Personal pronouns are more usual than possessive pronouns in referring to parts of the body, articles of clothing, location etc.: Он пожа́л **мне** ру́ку 'He shook **my** hand', Он пришёл **ко мне** в ко́мнату 'He came to **my** room', Пла́тье **у неё** всё испа́чкано '**Her** dress is all stained'. The reflexive pronoun (see **117**) is used similarly: Он лёг **у себя́** в ко́мнате 'He lay down in **his** room' etc.

(2) Note also the idioms: **мне** пришло́ в го́лову 'it occurred to me' (lit. 'came into **my** head'), Красота́ зда́ния бро́силась **ему́** в глаза́ 'He was struck by the beauty of the building'.

112 Use of the nominative pronoun with э́то

In contrast to English, nominative pronouns are used in such phrases as Э́то **я** 'It's me', Э́то **он** 'It's him', Э́то **мы** 'It's us' etc.

113 The pronoun я

(1) **Я** 'I' combines with first-person singular forms of the present and future of verbs: я **чита́ю** 'I read', я **прочита́ю** 'I shall read', я **бу́ду чита́ть** 'I shall be reading'. The gender of predicative adjectives, of other pronouns and of past verbs depends on the sex of the speaker:

> Я дово́лен, я оди́н, я пришёл
> I am pleased, I am alone, I have arrived (of a **male** speaker)

> Я дово́льна, я одна́, я пришла́
> I am pleased, I am alone, I have arrived (of a **female** speaker)

(2) Compare also the oblique cases: Оста́вьте меня́ **одного́** 'Leave me by myself' (of a male), Оста́вьте меня́ **одну́** 'Leave me by myself' (of a female).

Note

(a) 'You and I' is rendered as **мы с ва́ми**, 'he and I' as **мы с ним** etc. (also, in relevant contexts, though less usually, 'you and ourselves', 'he and ourselves').

(b) **Я** as a noun may be qualified by neuter modifiers: **моё второ́е я** 'my alter ego'.

(c) **Я** is often omitted in everyday speech (**Начну́** сейча́с! 'I'll begin at once!') and in official applications and announcements (**Прошу́** предоста́вить мне о́тпуск 'I apply to be granted leave'). In spoken Russian, pronouns in general are often omitted, since present and future verb forms alone are sufficient to express person and number (i.e. **пишу́** is first-person singular, **пишешь** second-person singular and so on), while past tense forms indicate gender and number. Thus, **Вы писáли? Да, я писáл** 'Did you write?', 'Yes, I wrote' could be rendered as **Вы писáли? Да, писáл** or **Писáли? Писáл**, depending on the degree of familiarity of the speech mode.

114 The pronoun мы

(1) **Мы** 'we' combines with first-person plural forms of the present or future tense of a verb (мы **говорим** 'we speak'), with plural forms of the past tense (мы **говорили** 'we were speaking'), and with plural adjectives and pronouns: Мы **одни** 'we are alone'.

(2) **Мы** can also be used to refer to the whole of a social or other group, or all society etc.: Я подчёркиваю слóво «**мы**», ибо имéю в видý всё óбщество в цéлом 'I stress the word "we" since I have in mind society as a whole'.

(3) **Мы** also expresses the royal 'we' (**мы**, всероссийский император 'we, Emperor of all the Russias'), the authorial 'we' (**Мы** пришли к слéдующим вы́водам 'We (i.e. I) have come to the following conclusions') and the jocular paternal 'we' used by doctors (Ну, сегóдня **нам** лýчше? 'Well, are we better today?'). **Мы** may also convey a nuance of mockery (**Мы** улыбáемся! 'So we're smiling!') or contempt (Видáли **мы** таки́х! 'We've seen your type before!').

115 The pronouns ты and вы

(1) Ты

(i) **Ты** 'you' (familiar) takes second-person singular forms of the present and future tenses of a verb (ты **говоришь** 'you speak' etc.). Like **я**, **ты** is of common gender: Ты **один** 'You are alone' (to a male), Ты **одна** 'You are alone' (to a female).

(ii) **Ты** is used in addressing a relation, a friend, a colleague of similar age and status, a child, God, nature, oneself, an animal etc. While **ты** is generally acknowledged as the 'familiar' form, older people are likely to restrict its use to a circle of close friends and colleagues, whereas young people are usually quicker to address members of their own age group as **ты**.

(iii) **Ты** may also be used in conveying generalized information or instruction (cf. English 'you'), as in the following guidance for correct breathing in singing: **Ты** набира́ешь по́лную грудь во́здуха, а пото́м ма̀ло-пома́лу выпуска́ешь его́ изо рта 'You fill your lungs with air and then expel it little by little through your mouth'.

(2) Вы

(i) **Вы** is used to address any group of more than one person, or an adult who is not a relation, friend or colleague of similar age and status. When writing to someone, **Вы** is usually spelt with a capital letter.

(ii) **Вы** combines with plural forms of the verb, whether the pronoun represents an individual or a group: вы **чита́ете**, вы **чита́ли** 'you read, were reading'. When reference is to one person, the pronoun combines with the *singular* forms of long adjectives (Вы **тако́й до́брый** (to a male), Вы **така́я до́брая** (to a female) 'You are so kind', Я счита́ю вас **у́мным** (to a male)/**у́мной** (to a female) 'I consider you clever'), but with the *plural* forms of short adjectives and participles: Вы **пра́вы** 'You are right'.

(3) Ты or вы

Usage may depend on social status, age difference, education and context of situation (e.g. teachers may address each other as **вы** in the presence of pupils or students but as **ты** in their absence). Any transition from **вы** to **ты** is normally initiated by the senior in age or rank. **Вы** is used as a mark of respect to adult strangers, and by academic staff to students and (desirably, though many school teachers prefer to use **ты**) to senior pupils. Subordinates have traditionally used the formal **вы** to their superiors, but have been addressed by them with the familiar **ты**. This practice is still widespread, despite condemnation in official circles of its perpetuation in, for example, the armed forces, the health service and industry.

116 The third-person pronouns (он, онá, онó, они́)

(1) **Он, онá** may replace nouns denoting persons *or* things of masculine and feminine gender respectively:

Где **брат**?	Вот **он**	Where is my brother?	There he is
Где **стол**?	Вот **он**	Where is the table?	There it is
Где **моя́ сестра́**?	Вот **онá**	Where is my sister?	There she is
Где **кни́га**?	Вот **онá**	Where is the book?	There it is

(2) **Онó** replaces neuter nouns:

Где **кре́сло**?	Вот **онó**	Where is the armchair?	There it is

(3) **Они́** replaces plural nouns denoting persons or things:

Где **ма́льчики**?	Вот **они́**	Where are the boys?	There they are
Где **кни́ги**?	Вот **они́**	Where are the books?	There they are
Где **кре́сла**?	Вот **они́**	Where are the armchairs?	There they are

(4) **Они́** may be used when the plural noun it replaces has been mentioned: Что де́лают **маляры́**? **Они́** кра́сят дом 'What are the painters doing?' 'They are painting the house'. In impersonal constructions, however, the third-person plural of the verb is used *without* a pronoun: Здесь **стро́ят** общежи́тие 'They (identity unspecified) are building a hostel here' (or 'A hostel is being built here'). This is in marked contrast with English, in which the pronoun 'they' is used in both personal *and* impersonal constructions. Note also the phrases: Здесь **не ку́рят** 'No smoking', **говоря́т** 'they say, it is said' etc.

(5) Verbs of yearning (**скуча́ть** 'to miss', **тоскова́ть** 'to yearn' etc.) and the verbs **стреля́ть** 'to shoot' and **ударя́ть** 'to strike' take the preposition **по** + the **prepositional** case of first- and second-person pronouns (Скуча́ли по **вас** 'They missed you', Стреля́ли по **нас** 'They were firing at us') and *either* the dative *or* the prepositional of third-person pronouns (Скуча́ли по **нему́**/по **нём** 'He was missed'). Such verbs take по + the *dative* of nouns (e.g. скуча́ть по **му́жу** 'to miss one's husband').

(6) 'He and Sergei/she and Sergei' etc. may be rendered as **они́** с Серге́ем (also, in context, 'they and Sergei').

(7) The instrumental case of a third-person pronoun may be the equivalent of English 'one': Он стал вратарём, потому́ что реши́л **им** стать (Makarov) 'He became a goalkeeper because he had made up his mind to become **one**'.

117 The reflexive pronoun себя

(1) The reflexive pronoun **себя** declines as follows:

Nom.	—
Acc./Gen.	себ-**я**
Dat.	себ-**é**
Instr.	соб-**óй**/соб-**óю**
Prep.	о себ-**é**

(2) The reflexive pronoun refers back to the subject of the clause or, more exactly, to the subject or agent of the nearest verb or adjective (it therefore has no nominative case, since it cannot *itself* be a subject). The same form is used for all persons (Онá довóльна **собóй** 'She is pleased with herself', Мы довóльны **собóй** 'We are pleased with ourselves' etc.), there being no differentiation between singular and plural or between the genders.

(3) **Себя** expresses more varied relationships than -**ся**, -**сь** (see also **285** and **286**), e.g. the indirect object (Онá купúла **себé** кнúгу 'She bought herself a book') and government by preposition (Он смóтрит **на себя** в зéркало 'He looks at himself in the mirror', Онú разговáривают **мèжду собóй** 'They are talking among themselves').

(4) Считáть **себя** гéнием means 'to consider oneself a genius', считáться гéнием 'to be considered a genius' (cf. лишáть **себя** 'to deprive oneself' and лишáться 'to be deprived').

(5) Some verbs combine with себя on a seemingly arbitrary basis: вестú **себя** 'to behave', представлять **собóй** 'to represent, be', чýвствовать **себя** 'to feel'.

(6) Ambiguity may arise when there are two verbs in a sentence: Мать велéла сыну налúть себé чáю (мать is the subject of the sentence, сын is the logical subject of налúть). The sentence should be taken to mean 'The mother told her son to pour **himself** some tea', but the following can be used to avoid confusion: Мать велéла, чтóбы сын налúл **себé** чáю 'The mother told her son to pour **himself** some tea', cf. Мать велéла, чтóбы сын налúл **ей** чáю 'The mother told her son to pour **her** some tea'.

(7) Russian is more consistent than English in the use of reflexive pronouns: Он разложúл перед **собóй** кáрту 'He spread out the

map in front of **him**', Она́ закры́ла за **собо́й** дверь 'She closed the door behind **her**', Возьми́те меня́ с **собо́й** 'Take me with **you**'.

(8) The reflexive pronoun appears in a number of set phrases: так **себе́** 'so-so', Он хоро́ш **собо́й** 'He is good-looking', само **собо́й** разуме́ется 'it goes without saying'.

(9) A reflexive pronoun may combine for emphasis with the emphatic pronoun **сам**: — Я тебя́ не понима́ю. — — Я **сам себя́** не понима́ю! 'I don't understand you'. 'I don't understand myself!' (see **131** (1)).

118 The possessive pronouns мой, твой, наш, ваш

(1) The possessive pronoun **мой** declines as follows:

	Masculine	Feminine	Neuter	Plural
Nom.	мой	мо-**я́**	мо-**ё**	мо-**и́**
Acc.	мой/мо-**его́**	мо-**ю́**	мо-**ё**	мо-**и́**/мо-**и́х**
Gen.	мо-**его́**	мо-**е́й**	мо-**его́**	мо-**и́х**
Dat.	мо-**ему́**	мо-**е́й**	мо-**ему́**	мо-**и́м**
Instr.	мо-**и́м**	мо-**е́й**/-**е́ю**	мо-**и́м**	мо-**и́ми**
Prep.	о мо-**ём**	о мо-**е́й**	о мо-**ём**	о мо-**и́х**

Note
Твой 'your' (familiar) declines like **мой**.

(2) The possessive pronoun **наш** declines as follows:

	Masculine	Feminine	Neuter	Plural
Nom.	наш	на́ш-**а**	на́ш-**е**	на́ш-**и**
Acc.	наш/на́ш-**его**	на́ш-**у**	на́ш-**е**	на́ш-**и**/на́ш-**их**
Gen.	на́ш-**его**	на́ш-**ей**	на́ш-**его**	на́ш-**их**
Dat.	на́ш-**ему**	на́ш-**ей**	на́ш-**ему**	на́ш-**им**
Instr.	на́ш-**им**	на́ш-**ей**/-**ею**	на́ш-**им**	на́ш-**ими**
Prep.	о на́ш-**ем**	о на́ш-**ей**	о на́ш-**ем**	о на́ш-**их**

Note
(a) **Ваш** 'your' declines like **наш**.
(b) Like **мы** and **вы** (see **113** note (a)), **наш** and **ваш** can form compounds with other pronouns or nouns: **ва́ша с па́пой** маши́на 'yours and Dad's car', **наш с тобо́й** дом 'our house' (i.e. yours and mine).
(c) The colloquial phrase **наш брат** means 'people like us': Зна́ю, что нере́дко руга́ют **на́шего бра́та** за рва́чество (*Russia Today*) 'I know that our sort are often cursed for self-seeking'.

(d) Phrases of the type **на́ша** те́ма 'our theme' (i.e. 'the present topic') are used by authors and lecturers (cf. **114** (3)).

(e) The use of possessive instead of personal pronouns is characteristic of casual speech: Он сде́лал бо́льше **моего́** (= бо́льше, чем я) 'He did more than me'.

(f) **Ваш** is spelt with a capital letter in correspondence.

119 The possessive pronouns его́, её, их

Его́ 'his', **её** 'her', **их** 'their' are invariable:

его́ сестра́	his sister
её кни́ги	her books
их брат	their brother
Я зна́ю **его́** сестру́	I know his sister
Я дово́лен **её** бра́том	I am pleased with her brother

Note

(a) **н**- is never affixed to the third-person possessives: cf. письмо́ от **него́** (personal pronoun) 'a letter from him' and письмо́ от **его́** (possessive pronoun) бра́та 'a letter from his brother' (see **110** (2)).

(b) **Его́** is pronounced [jɪˈvo]. See also **110** (1) note (b).

120 The reflexive possessive pronoun свой, своя́, своё, свои́

(1) The reflexive possessive pronoun **свой** declines like **мой** (see **118** (1)).

(2) Like **себя́**, **свой** refers back to noun and pronoun subjects of any gender and either number (see **117** (2): Я по́мню **свою́** шко́лу 'I remember my school', Ты по́мнишь **свою́** шко́лу 'You remember your school', Де́ти по́мнят **свою́** шко́лу 'The children remember their school'.

(3) In clauses which have a first- or second-person subject, **свой** can be used as an *alternative* to мой, твой, наш and ваш (Я говорю́ о **свое́й/мое́й** рабо́те 'I am talking about my work', Ты продаёшь **свой/твой** дом 'You are selling your house', Мы мо́ем **свою́/на́шу** маши́ну 'We are washing our car'), though **свой** is commoner.

(4) Where there is a third-person subject, however, care must be taken to distinguish between **свой** and the possessive pronouns **его**, **её**, **их** (see **119**), when rendering 'his', 'her', 'their', in order to avoid ambiguity:

Он дово́лен **свои́м** ученико́м
He is pleased with **his** (own) pupil

Он не лю́бит Джо́на, но он дово́лен **его́** ученика́ми
He does not like John, but he is pleased with **his** (John's) pupils

Note that in English 'his' is used in both examples, and context is relied upon to differentiate meaning. Russian **её** 'her' and **их** 'their' are similarly distinguished from свой:

Орло́вы лю́бят **свои́х** дете́й
The Orlovs love **their** children

Ивано́вы поги́бли в катастро́фе, и Орло́вы усынови́ли **их** дете́й
The Ivanovs died in an accident and the Orlovs adopted their children

(5) It is important to remember to use the reflexive possessive pronoun even when it is distanced from the subject:

Он, пра́вда, никому́ не даёт **своего́** а́дреса (Trifonov)
It is true that he does not give **his** address to anyone

Он был свиде́телем собы́тий **своего́** вре́мени
He was a witness of the events of **his** time

(6) **Свой** cannot qualify the *subject* of a clause in this type of construction:

Он говори́т, что **его́** друг бо́лен
He says that **his** friend (subject of new clause) is ill

Врач и **её** помо́щник совеща́ются
The doctor and **her** assistant (joint subjects) are consulting

(7) In a sentence with two verbs, **свой** refers back to the subject of the nearer of the two, cf:

Реда́ктор попроси́л журнали́ста прочита́ть **свою́** статью́
The editor asked the journalist to read his (the journalist's) article

and

Реда́ктор попроси́л журнали́ста прочита́ть **его́** статью́
The editor asked the journalist to read his (the editor's) article

To avoid possible ambiguity, an alternative construction can be used:

Реда́ктор попроси́л журнали́ста, что̀бы он прочита́л его́ статью́
The editor asked the journalist to read his (the editor's) article

Note

When ownership is obvious from the context, Russian usually dispenses with a possessive pronoun: Я **мо́ю** ру́ки 'I am washing **my** hands' (it is clear whose hands are being washed – mine), Он потеря́л **програ́мму** 'He has lost **his** (or 'the') programme'.

Па́рень опуска́ет **ру́ки**, **го́лову**, закрыва́ет **глаза́** (Rasputin)
The lad lowers his hands, hangs his head, closes his eyes

(8) Свой appears in the *nominative* case in phrases that denote possession: У меня́ **своя́** маши́на 'I have my own car', У нас **свой** дом 'We have our own house' etc. Note: **Своя́** руба́шка бли́же к те́лу 'Charity begins at home', Он у нас **свой** челове́к 'He is one of us'.

121 Declension of the interrogative/relative pronouns

Кто 'who', **что** 'what', **како́й** 'what' (adjective), **кото́рый** 'which' and **чей** 'whose' function as both interrogative and relative pronouns. **Како́й** and **кото́рый** decline like hard-ending adjectives (see **145** and **146** (3) note (b)). **Кто, что** and **чей** decline as follows:

			Masculine	Feminine	Neuter	Plural
Nom.	кт-о	чт-о	чей	чь-я	чь-ё	чь-и
Acc.	к-ого́	чт-о	чей/чь-его́	чь-ю	чь-ё	чь-и/чь-их
Gen.	к-ого́	ч-его́	чь-его́	чь-ей	чь-его́	чь-их
Dat.	к-ому́	ч-ему́	чь-ему́	чь-ей	чь-ему́	чь-им
Instr.	к-ем	ч-ем	чь-им	чь-ей/-е́ю	чь-им	чь-и́ми
Prep.	о к-ом	о ч-ём	о чь-ём	о чь-ей	о чь-ём	о чь-их

122 Кто, что, какой, который, чей as interrogative pronouns

(1) Кто

(i) **Кто** 'who' is used in both direct questions (**Кто** э́тот мужчи́на? 'Who is that man?', О **ком** вы говори́те? 'Who are you talking about?') and indirect questions (Он спроси́л, **кому́** вы даёте уро́ки 'He asked whom you give lessons to').

(ii) **Кто** takes a masculine predicate even when only females are involved: Кто **вы́шел** за́муж? 'Who (in a group of women) got married?' However, feminine agreement is possible if the subject contains a reference to a female exponent of an activity: Кто из **лы́жниц** пришла́ пе́рвой? 'Which of the skiers (female) came in first?'.

(iii) Russian is consistent in using **кто** for people: Кто́ у вас роди́лся? Ма́льчик и́ли де́вочка? '**What** is it, a boy or a girl?', **Кем** ты хо́чешь быть? '**What** do you want to be?', cf.:

А **кем** мы ста́нем тепе́рь: друзья́ми и́ли врага́ми? (Gagarin)
And **what** will we become now, friends or enemies?

(iv) **Кто** may be amplified to **кто тако́й/така́я/таки́е?**: Кто тако́й э́тот па́рень? 'Who is this fellow?', Кто така́я э́та де́вушка? 'Who is that girl?', Кто таки́е э́ти молоды́е лю́ди? 'Who are these young people?', Кто вы **тако́й**? (to a male)/Кто вы **така́я**? (to a female) 'Who are you?'

(2) Что

Что 'what' is used to ask about the identity of a thing or an animal (**Что** э́то — волк и́ли соба́ка? 'What is that, a wolf or a dog?') or the nature of an action (**Что** он де́лает? 'What is he doing?'). **Что** may be expanded to **что тако́е?** (Что э́то **тако́е**? 'What is that?') or be extended by a genitive adjective (Что **но́вого**? 'What's new?', Что же тут **оби́дного**? 'What's so offensive about that?').

(3) Како́й

Како́й means 'what, what kind of'?: **Како́й** у него́ го́лос? 'What kind of a voice does he have?', **Каку́ю** кни́гу вы чита́ете? 'What

book are you reading?'. **Что за** may be used as a synonym of какой:
Что сегодня **за** погода? (= Какая сегодня погода?) 'What is the
weather like today?'.

(4) Который

(i) **Который?** means 'which?' (in a sequence) and appears in the
phrases **Который** час? 'What's the time?', В **котором** часу? 'At
what time?' (now largely replaced in the speech of young people by
Сколько времени? and Во сколько?). **Который** can also mean
'umpteenth': **Который** раз спрашиваю 'I am asking for the
umpteenth time'.

(ii) However, **какой** is now more commonly used in questions, the
answers to which contain an ordinal numeral: **Какой** ряд? 'Which
row?' **Пятый** 'Five'.

(5) Чей

Чей means 'whose?': **Чей** это дом? 'Whose house is that?', **Чью**
дачу вы покупаете? 'Whose country cottage are you buying?'.

123 Который, какой, чей, кто and что as relative pronouns

(1) Который

(i) **Который** 'who, which' is used with animate and inanimate noun
antecedents (кто and что are normally used as relatives to *pronoun*
antecedents; see (4) and (5) below).

(ii) **Который** agrees with its antecedent in gender and number, but
its *case* depends on the grammar of the relative clause:

Я познакомился с молодым **человеком, за которого** она
вышла замуж
I made the acquaintance of the young man (whom) she married

Он вошёл в **комнату, которая** находилась рядом с кухней
He went into the room which was next to the kitchen

(iii) The genitive forms **которого** (masculine and neuter), **которой**
(feminine), **которых** (plural) mean 'whose', and *follow* the noun:

Вот **студент**, работу **которого** я проверяю
There is the student whose work I am correcting

Про́дали **маши́ну**, владе́льцы **кото́рой** обанкро́тились
They have sold the car whose owners have gone bankrupt

Нельзя́ не жале́ть **дете́й**, роди́тели **кото́рых** поги́бли во
вре́мя блока́ды
You cannot but pity the children whose parents perished during
the blockade

(2) Како́й

Unlike **кото́рый**, which relates to specific objects and persons,
како́й relates to things and persons of a particular *type*, cf.:

Вокру́г ви́дишь переме́ны, **каки́е** возмо́жны то́лько здесь
All around you can see changes **of a kind which** are possible
only here

and

Вокру́г ви́дишь переме́ны, **кото́рые** возмо́жны то́лько
здесь
All around you can see changes **which** are possible only here

Compare

Тако́е выраже́ние отча́яния, **како́е** быва́ет у люде́й
то́лько перед сме́ртью (Simonov)
The **kind of** expression of despair that people have only at
death's door

(3) Чей

The use of **чей** as a relative is a mark of a bookish or poetic style:
писа́тель, **чью** кни́гу ты изуча́ешь . . . 'the writer whose book you
are studying . . .'. Normal usage is: писа́тель, кни́гу **кото́рого** ты
изуча́ешь . . . .

(4) Кто

(i) **Кто** functions as relative pronoun to **тот** (**тот, кто** 'he, the one
who'), **те** (**те, кто** 'those who'), **никто́** 'nobody' (**никто́, кто** 'no one
who'), **все** 'everybody' (**все, кто** 'everyone who'), **пе́рвый** 'the first'
(**пе́рвый, кто** пришёл 'the first to come'), **еди́нственный** 'only'
(Он же **еди́нственный, кто** на нас постоя́нно жа́луется 'He is
the only one who constantly complains about us').

(ii) **Кто** takes a masculine singular predicate: тот, кто **реши́л** зада́чу 'he who solved the problem'. ('She who' may be rendered as **та** (же́нщина), **кото́рая**: **Та, кото́рая** полне́е, оде́та с больши́м вку́сом (Zalygin) 'The one who is plumper is dressed with consummate taste'.)

(iii) When, however, there is a *plural* antecedent (**все** or **те**), **кто** may take *either* a singular *or* a plural verb: Все, кто **пришёл/ пришли́** на собра́ние, голосова́ли за меня́ 'Everyone who came to the meeting voted for me', cf.:

Среди́ тех, кто **оста́лся**, был Ива́н Ка́рлович, наш сосе́д (Rybakov)
Among those who remained was Ivan Karlovich, our neighbour

and

Те из нас, кто **чита́ли** стихотворе́ние, бы́ли в восто́рге
Those of us who read the poem were delighted

(iv) **Тот, кто** may be abbreviated to **кто**, with **тот** transferring to the beginning of a separate clause: Кто э́то ви́дел, **тот** не забу́дет 'Anyone who has seen that will not forget it'.

(5) Что

(i) **Что** may function as relative pronoun to a full noun, e.g.:

Пришло́сь прибе́гнуть к по́мощи пионе́ров моско́вских **школ, что** нахо́дятся по сосе́дству (*Yunyi naturalist*)
He had to enlist the aid of Pioneers from Moscow **schools which** are in the vicinity

but **кото́рый** should be regarded as the norm (see (1) (i) above).

(ii) **Что** as a relative pronoun is used mainly with:

(a) **Всё** 'everything':

Я скажу́ вам **всё, что** зна́ю   I'll tell you all I know

(b) Substantivized adjectives such as **гла́вное** 'the main thing', **пе́рвое** 'the first thing':

Пе́рвое, что броса́ется в глаза́ — а́втовокза́л
The first thing that strikes you is the bus station

(c) **To** 'that':

> **То, что** он сказа́л, удиви́ло меня́
> **What** (lit. 'that which') he said surprised me

> Случи́лось **то, чего́** ника́к не ожида́л Григо́рий (Sholo-khov)
> **Something** happened **that** Grigory had in no way anticipated

> **В том, что** вы говори́те, есть до́ля пра́вды
> There's a measure of truth **in what** you say

> Я не согла́сен **с тем, что** он сказа́л
> I do not agree **with what** he said

Variants of **то, что** thus function as links between clauses:

> Учи́тельницу огорчи́ло **то, что** де́ти не хоте́ли её слу́шать
> The teacher was upset by **the fact that** the children did not want to listen to her

> Мы принима́ем **то, от чего́** вы отказа́лись
> We accept **what** you refused

The construction is particularly important when the verb in the main clause governs an oblique case or prepositional phrase:

> Он горди́тся **тем, что** он ру́сский
> He is proud **of being** Russian

> Начало́сь **с того́, что** Ко́лька о́тнял у меня́ кни́жку (Soloukhin)
> It all began **with** Kolka **taking away** my book

То, что may be abbreviated to **что** for special emphasis, **то** transferring to the beginning of a separate clause:

> **Что** нам про́сто ка́жется, **то** на́шим пре́дкам пото́м да му́кой доста́лось
> **What** seems simple to us was achieved through the sweat and toil of our ancestors

Что also functions as relative pronoun to a whole clause:

> Он не приходи́л на ве́чер, **что** меня́ удиви́ло
> He did not come to the party, **which** surprised me (i.e. the fact that he did not come surprised me, *not* any particular noun)

124 Other functions of the interrogative/relative pronouns

(1) **Какой** can also be used as an exclamation (**Какой** позо́р! 'What a disgrace!') and, with negatives, can express quantity (**Каки́х** то́лько пода́рков ему́ не накупи́ли! 'And the **presents** they bought him!').

(2) **Кто** appears:

(i) In the phrase **не кто ино́й** 'none other than': Э́то был **не кто ино́й**, как мой брат 'It was none other than my brother'.

(ii) In concessive constructions: С **кем** ни говори́, все настро́ены легкомы́сленно 'Whoever you speak to is in a carefree mood'.

(iii) In the meaning 'some ... others' (also rendered as одни́ ... други́е): **Кто** за, **кто** про́тив 'Some are for, others are against'.

(iv) In the reduplicated pronoun **кто-кто́**: **Кому́-кому́**, а ему́-то грех бы́ло не реаги́ровать (Zalygin) 'For him of all people it was sinful not to react'.

(3) **Что** appears:

(i) In the phrase **не что ино́е, как** 'nothing but': Э́то **не что ино́е, как** вымога́тельство 'That is nothing but extortion'.

(ii) In concessive constructions: **Что** бы он ни де́лал, он не забыва́л свои́х друзе́й 'Whatever he did, he never forgot his friends'.

(iii) In quantitative contexts: **Чего́** там то́лько не́ было 'There was everything imaginable there'.

(iv) In the reduplicated pronoun **что-что́**: ... Уж **что-что́**, а э́то никто́ у неё не отни́мет (Zalygin) 'That of all things no one will take away from her'.

125 Declension of the demonstrative pronouns э́тот, тот, тако́й, сей and э́кий

Тако́й declines like a hard-ending adjective (see **146** (3) note (b)).
Э́тот, **тот** and **сей** decline as follows:

	Masculine	Feminine	Neuter	Plural
Nom.	э́тот	э́т-а	э́т-о	э́т-и
Acc.	э́тот/э́т-ого	э́т-у	э́т-о	э́т-и/э́т-их
Gen.	э́т-ого	э́т-ой	э́т-ого	э́т-их
Dat.	э́т-ому	э́т-ой	э́т-ому	э́т-им
Instr.	э́т-им	э́т-ой/-ою	э́т-им	э́т-ими
Prep.	об э́т-ом	об э́т-ой	об э́т-ом	об э́т-их

	Masculine	Feminine	Neuter	Plural
Nom.	тот	т-а	т-о	т-е
Acc.	тот/т-ого́	т-у	т-о	т-е/т-ех
Gen.	т-ого́	т-ой	т-ого́	т-ех
Dat.	т-ому́	т-ой	т-ому́	т-ем
Instr.	т-ем	т-ой/т-о́ю	т-ем	т-е́ми
Prep.	о т-ом	о т-ой	о т-ом	о т-ех

	Masculine	Feminine	Neuter	Plural
Nom.	сей	си-я́	си-е́	си-и́
Acc.	сей/с-его́	си-ю́	си-е́	си-и́/с-их
Gen.	с-его́	с-ей	с-его́	с-их
Dat.	с-ему́	с-ей	с-ему́	с-им
Instr.	с-им	с-ей/с-е́ю	с-им	с-и́ми
Prep.	о с-ём	о с-ей	о с-ём	о с-их

Note

(a) Except for usage in certain set phrases (see **129** (1)), **сей** is regarded as archaic and is used for purposes of irony.

(b) **Э́кий** declines as follows: m. nom. э́кий, acc. э́кий/э́коего, gen. э́коего, dat. э́коему, instr. э́ким, prep. об э́ком; f. nom. э́кая, acc. э́кую, gen. э́кой, dat. э́кой, instr. э́кой/-ою, prep. об э́кой; neut. э́кое, oblique cases as masculine; pl. nom. э́кие, acc. э́кие/э́ких, gen. э́ких, dat. э́ким, instr. э́кими, prep. об э́ких. It is found mainly in conversational registers.

126 The demonstrative pronouns этот and тот

(1) Этот/тот

(i) **Этот** 'this' refers to something close to hand, **тот** 'that' to something further removed:

Это дерево такое же большое, как и **то**
This tree is just as big as that one

(ii) **Это** is used in the meaning 'this, that is', 'these, those are': **Это** мой дом 'This is my house', **Это** мои дети 'Those are my children'. Verbs agree with the noun, *not* with это: Это **были** мои книги 'Those were my books', Это **была** его жена 'That was his wife'.

Note
Что вы хотите **этим** сказать? 'What do you mean by **that**?'

(iii) It is necessary to distinguish between

Этот дом	This house
Эта картина	This picture
Это окно	This window
Эти книги	These books

and

Это дом	This **is** a house
Это картина	This **is** a picture
Это окно	This **is** a window
Это книги	These **are** books

(2) Тот

(i) **Тот** is sometimes used where English might use a definite article, especially when the pronoun is part of the antecedent to a relative clause:

Он часто говорил в **той** холодной манере, в какой начал разговор с Серпилиным (Simonov)
He often spoke in **the** cold manner with which he had begun his conversation with Serpilin

Я смотрел в **ту** сторону, откуда должна была появиться лодка
I was looking in **the** direction from which the boat was expected to appear

(ii) **Тот** can also mean, 'he, she, the latter':

О приéзде брáтьев Лйза узнáла от Áнки. **Та** прибежáла к тётке, как тóлько пришлá телегрáмма (Abramov)
Liza learnt of her brothers' arrival from Anka. **She** (Anka) came running to her aunt as soon as the telegram arrived

Note
The use of **онá** instead of **та** in this example would imply that the first-named (Liza) had come running. **Тот** thus has an important role to play in avoiding ambiguity.

(iii) **Тот** is used as a pronoun antecedent to a relative pronoun:

Аркáдий пожáл однúм плечóм, не **тем, на котóром** лежáла рукá Ирýнчика (Zalygin)
Arkady shrugged one shoulder, not **the one** on which Irunchik's arm lay

(iv) **Не тот** means 'the wrong' (cf. непрáвильный 'incorrect'): Он взял **не ту** кнúгу 'He took the wrong book'.

(v) **Тот же** (or **тот же сáмый**) means 'the same':

Гостúница оказáлась **той же**, в котóрой останáвливались прéжде (Yakhontov)
The hotel turned out to be **the (same) one** they had stayed in before

Note
(a) **Тот же** can also mean 'just the same as': Ведь нéнависть — **та же** любóвь, тóлько с обрáтным знáком (Zalygin) 'After all hatred is **just the same as** love, but from the reverse side'.
(b) В однó и **то же** врéмя 'at one and the same time'.

(vi) **То** combines with the conjunction **что**:

Онá привыкла **к томý, что** мужчúны на неё заглядываются (Rybakov)
She was used to men feasting their eyes on her

It also appears in many time phrases: в **то** врéмя, как 'while', с **тех** пор 'since then', до **тех** пор 'until then', пóсле **тогó** как 'after', до **тогó** как 'before' (see also **466**).

127 Constructions of the type приме́р тому́

Приме́р, **причи́на** and some other abstract nouns combine with the dative of the pronoun **то** (and occasionally **э́то**):

Приме́ром **тому́** явля́ется выступле́ние арти́ста
The artiste's performance is an example of this

Причи́ной **тому́** явля́ется его́ упря́мство
His obstinacy is the cause of this

Да и фильм даёт нагля́дное **тому́** свиде́тельство
And in fact the film bears graphic witness to this

Приме́ров **э́тому** мо́жно привести́ мно́го (*Izvestiya*)
One can quote many examples of this

Note
(a) These nouns normally combine with the *genitive* of a dependent *noun*: приме́р **му́жества** 'an example of courage', причи́на **несча́стного слу́чая** 'the cause of the accident' (note also the use of the genitive *pronoun* where **причи́на** is defined by a prepositional phrase: Причи́на **э́того** в демографи́ческом взры́ве 'The cause of this is the population explosion').
(b) The dative reflexive pronoun appears in the expression знать **себе́** це́ну 'to know one's worth'.

128 The demonstrative pronoun тако́й

(1) **Тако́й** 'such' combines with long adjectives: Пого́да **така́я** хоро́шая (or **так** хороша́) 'The weather is so fine'.

(2) It can have a generalizing meaning: **Таки́х** ма́рок, **каки́е** он собира́ет, о́чень ма́ло 'There are very few stamps **of the kind that** he collects' (cf. **123** (2) 'како́й').

Note
В **тако́м** слу́чае 'in **that** case', Зада́м **тако́й** вопро́с 'I shall ask **the following** question', при **таки́х** обстоя́тельствах 'in **the** circumstances'.

(3) **Тако́й же** means 'the same, the same kind as': Ты **тако́й же**, как и все молоды́е лю́ди твоего́ во́зраста 'You're just like all young people of your age'.

Note

Же is absent in the negative: Она́ не **така́я, как** была́ в де́тстве 'She's not **the same as** she was in her childhood'.

129 The pronouns сей and э́кий

(1) **Сей** appears mainly in set phrases: по **сей** день 'to this very day', ни с того́ ни с **сего́** 'for no particular reason', **сию́** мину́ту 'this instant' (Иди́ сюда́ **сию́** мину́ту! 'Come here this instant!'), до **сих** пор 'hitherto' etc.

> На **сей** раз в турни́ре не уча́ствовал наш сильне́йший тенниси́ст (*Sputnik*)
> This time round our best tennis player did not take part in the championships

(2) **Э́кий** 'what a' is a very colloquial form: Э́кий шалу́н 'What a rogue' (cf. also э́такий: э́такая неуда́ча 'such a disaster').

130 Declension of the determinative pronouns сам, са́мый, весь, вся́кий, ка́ждый, вся́ческий

Ка́ждый and **са́мый** are declined like hard-ending adjectives, **вся́кий** and **вся́ческий** like **ру́сский** (see **146** (3)). **Сам** and **весь** decline as follows:

	Masculine	Feminine	Neuter	Plural
Nom.	сам	сам-а́	сам-о́	са́м-и
Acc.	сам/сам-ого́	сам-у́/сам-оё	сам-о́	са́м-и/сам-и́х
Gen.	сам-ого́	сам-о́й	сам-ого́	сам-и́х
Dat.	сам-ому́	сам-о́й	сам-ому́	сам-и́м
Instr.	сам-и́м	сам-о́й/-о́ю	сам-и́м	сам-и́ми
Prep.	о сам-о́м	о сам-о́й	о сам-о́м	о сам-и́х

Note

(a) The accusative feminine **самоё** is the traditional literary form, but **саму́** is now found in all styles. **Самоё**, though obsolescent and 'bookish', is still common with the reflexive pronoun **себя**: уничтожа́ть **само́ё себя** 'to destroy oneself'.

(b) Unlike **сам**, the oblique cases of which take *end stress* (**самого́** etc.), **са́мый** is *stem stressed* throughout declension (**са́мого** etc.)

	Masculine	Feminine	Neuter	Plural
Nom.	весь	вс-**я**	вс-**ё**	вс-**е**
Acc.	весь/вс-**его́**	вс-**ю**	вс-**ё**	вс-**е**/вс-**ех**
Gen.	вс-**его́**	вс-**ей**	вс-**его́**	вс-**ех**
Dat.	вс-**ему́**	вс-**ей**	вс-**ему́**	вс-**ем**
Instr.	вс-**ем**	вс-**ей**/-**е́ю**	вс-**ем**	вс-**е́ми**
Prep.	обо вс-**ём**	обо вс-**ей**	обо вс-**ём**	обо вс-**ех**

131 Сам and са́мый

(1) Сам

(i) **Сам** is an emphatic pronoun: Я **сам** э́то сде́лаю 'I shall do it myself', Она́ **сама́** вста́ла 'She got up by herself'.

(ii) **Сам** may precede or follow a noun: Спроси́те учи́теля **самого́/самого́** учи́теля 'Ask the teacher himself'. Note gender distinction in Я пе́редал письмо́ тебе́ **самому́** 'I passed the letter on to you personally' (to a male), Я пе́редал письмо́ тебе́ **само́й** 'I passed the letter on to you personally' (to a female).

(iii) **Сам** can also add emphasis to the reflexive pronoun **себя́**: Вы гу́бите **самого́/саму́/сами́х** себя́ 'You are ruining yourself/ yourselves'. It can also qualify *inanimate* nouns:

Сам зако́н заставля́ет алиме́нтщиков идти́ на обма́н (*Nedelya*)
The law **itself** compels alimony payers to resort to deception

Note
Сам agrees with other pronouns which stand in apposition to it: **Ей** надое́ло **само́й** носи́ть бельё в пра́чечную 'She is sick of taking the washing to the laundry **herself**'.

(2) Са́мый

(i) **Са́мый** indicates precise location: Он подошёл к **са́мому** обры́ву 'He went right up to the precipice', в **са́мом** це́нтре го́рода 'in the very centre of the city'. Note also По́езд идёт до **са́мой** Москвы́ 'The train goes all the way to Moscow', с **са́мого** нача́ла 'from the very beginning' (for **са́мый** in superlative meaning, see also **185**).

(ii) **Тот са́мый** means 'the very': Он купи́л **ту са́мую** кни́гу, кото́рую вы рекомендова́ли 'He bought **the very** book you recommended'. **Тот же са́мый** means 'the same': У нас **те же** (**са́мые**) интере́сы 'We have **the same** interests'.

132 Весь, це́лый, вся́кий, ка́ждый, любо́й, вся́ческий

(1) Весь/це́лый

Весь means 'all, the whole' etc.: **весь** мир 'the whole world', Мы е́здили по **всей** стране́ 'We travelled all over the country', **все** рабо́чие 'all (the) workers'. **Це́лый** means 'a whole, whole', cf. Он съел **це́лое** я́блоко 'He ate **a whole** apple' and Он съел **всё** я́блоко 'He ate **the whole** apple', Голода́ли **це́лые** се́мьи 'Whole families starved' and **Все** се́мьи голода́ли 'All the families starved'. **Всё** also means 'everything' (**всё, что** я зна́ю 'everything I know'), while **все** can mean 'everyone', and takes a *plural* verb or adjective (Все **голосу́ют** 'Everyone votes'). Note the phrases **все** они́, **все** мы etc. 'all of them, all of us'.

(2) Вся́кий/ка́ждый/любо́й/вся́ческий

(i) **Вся́кий** means 'all kinds of': Он торгу́ет **вся́кими** това́рами 'He trades in all kinds of goods', **Вся́кое** (adjectival noun) быва́ет 'All kinds of things happen'. In combination with the preposition **без**, it may be rendered as 'any': без **вся́кого** сомне́ния 'without any doubt', без **вся́кого** труда́ 'without any trouble'. Note also во **вся́ком** слу́чае 'in any case, at any rate' (cf. the precautionary на **вся́кий** слу́чай 'just in case').

(ii) By comparison with **ка́ждый**, **вся́кий** expresses *totality* (**вся́кий** раз 'each and every time', Вся́кому ребёнку нужна́ ла́ска '**Every** child needs affection'), while **ка́ждый** emphasizes *each one individually* (**ка́ждый** раз 'every time', Ка́ждый из ученико́в получи́л по кни́ге 'Each of the pupils received a book'). **Ка́ждый** is also used with numerals and with plural-only nouns:

ка́ждые два дня 'every two days', **ка́ждые** су́тки 'every twenty-four hours', **ка́ждые** че́тверть часа́ 'every quarter of an hour'.

(iii) **Любо́й** has a strong nuance of *selectivity*: Запиши́ **любо́е** число́ ме́ньше 50 'Write down **any** number less than 50'. Купи́те газе́ту в **любо́м** кио́ске 'Buy the newspaper at any (but not every) kiosk'.

(iv) **Вся́ческий** is a synonym of **вся́кий** in the meaning 'all kinds of'.

133 The negative pronouns никто́, ничто́, никако́й, ниче́й. The negative particle не

(1) **Никто́** 'no one', **ничто́** 'nothing', **никако́й** 'none (whatsoever)', **ниче́й** 'nobody's' decline, respectively, like **кто**, **что**, **како́й** and **чей** (see **121**).

(2) The negative particle **не** appears between a negative pronoun and the predicate: Никто́ **не** рабо́тает 'No one works'.

134 Никто́

(1) **Никто́** means 'no one, nobody, not anybody':

Никто́ не пришёл	No one has come
Он **никого́** не лю́бит	He doesn't like anybody
Она́ **никому́** не ве́рит	She doesn't believe anyone
Мы **нике́м** не дово́льны	We are not pleased with anyone

Note

The presence of **нет** or **нельзя́** renders **не** superfluous: Никого́ **нет** 'No one's here', Никому́ **нельзя́** входи́ть 'No one may enter'.

(2) **Никто́** takes a masculine predicate even when reference is exclusively to females (cf. **122** (1) (ii)), unless a feminine noun appears as part of the subject: Никто́ из учени́ц, да́же **Зо́я**, не нашла́сь что сказа́ть 'None of the pupils, **not even Zoya**, could think of anything to say'.

(3) While English reverts to positive after the first negative, e.g. 'No one **ever** says **anything** to **anyone**', Russian can accumulate negatives: **Никто́ никогда́ ничего́ не** говори́т **никому́**.

(4) In prepositional constructions the prepositions appear between **ни** and the oblique form of **кто**:

Она́ **ни с кем** не игра́ет
She doesn't play with anyone

Он **ни на ком** не собира́ется жени́ться
He doesn't mean to marry anyone

В до́ме **ни у кого́ ни от кого́** нет секре́тов (Rybakov)
No one in the house has any secrets from anyone

(5) 'Hardly anyone' is rendered as **почти́ никто́**.

135 Ничто́

(1) **Ничто́** can act as a subject to adjectives (**Ничто́** не ве́чно 'Nothing is eternal') and to *transitive* verbs (**Ничто́** не интересу́ет его́ 'Nothing interests him'). With intransitive verbs, however, **ничего́** is preferred: С ва́ми **ничего́** не случи́тся 'Nothing will happen to you'.

(2) The same rules of grammatical government and 'accumulation of negatives' apply to **ничто́** as to **никто́** (see **134**):

Он **ничего́ не** де́лает
He does nothing

Я **ниче́м не** дово́лен
I am not satisfied with anything

Никто́ никогда́ ничему́ не ве́рит
No one ever believes anything

Prepositions appear between **ни** and the relevant form of **что**:

Никогда́ и **ни о чём** она́ Никола́я Демья́новича не проси́ла (Trifonov)
She had never asked Nikolay Demyanovich for anything

(3) **Не** is omitted in certain set phrases: уйти́ **ни с чем** 'to come away empty-handed', поги́бнуть **ни за что** 'to die for nothing', Но э́то бы́ло **ни к чему́** сейча́с (Zalygin) 'But this was irrelevant at the moment'.

(4) 'Hardly anything' is rendered as **почти́ ничего́/почти́ ничто́**.

Note the idioms: **Ничего́!** 'Never mind!', Муж у неё **ничего́** 'Her husband is not a bad chap', **ни за что** на све́те 'not for anything in the world', **Ничего́ не** поде́лаешь 'It can't be helped'.

136 Никако́й and ничей

(1) **Никако́й** 'none' is used mainly for emphasis: Нет **никако́й** наде́жды 'There is no hope at all', **Никаки́е** угро́зы не мо́гут сломи́ть наш дух 'No threats can break our spirit', Мы **ни перед каки́ми** тру́дностями не остано́вимся 'We shall not baulk at any difficulties'.

(2) **Ничей** means 'nobody's':

И де́душка то́же понима́л, что **ничьему́** реше́нию, кро́ме со́бственного, Ио́сиф не подчини́тся (Rybakov)
And grandfather also realized that Joseph would bow to no one's decision but his own

Вы не де́йствуете **ни в чьих** интере́сах
You are acting in nobody's interest

Note
(a) Prepositions appear between **ни** and the relevant form of **како́й** or **чей**.
(b) The particle **не** is omitted when **ничей** is used predicatively: Э́тот дом ничей 'This house isn't anybody's'.

137 The 'potential' negative pronouns не́кого, не́чего

(1) The 'potential' negative, both in English and in Russian, involves a negative + infinitive construction: Не́чего **де́лать** 'There is nothing to do' (cf. Мы **ничего́** не де́лаем 'We are not doing anything').

(2) Only oblique forms of **кто** and **что** appear in the construction (**не́кого, не́кому, не́кем, не́ [о] ком; не́чего, не́чему, не́чем, не́ [о] чем**). (**Не́кто** and **не́что** mean, respectively, 'someone' and 'something'; see **140**.)

The case of the pronoun is determined by the infinitive: thus **писа́ть** (+ instr. case) 'to write with' (**Не́чем** писа́ть 'There is nothing to write with'); **спроси́ть** (+ acc. case) 'to ask' (**Не́кого** спроси́ть 'There is no one to ask').

(3) The construction comprises the following components:

не́ (always stressed) + relevant case of pronoun + infinitive

Не́чем писа́ть	There is nothing to write **with**
Не́кому писа́ть	There is no one to write **to**

(4) There are two variants of the construction:

(i) The impersonal:

Не́чего де́лать	There is nothing to do
Не́кого посла́ть	There is no one to send

(ii) The personal:

Мне не́чего де́лать	I have nothing to do (the logical subject of an infinitive appears in the dative, cf. **93** (1))

Не́чего **мне** боя́ться, за ава́рию я не отве́тчик (Tendryakov)
I have nothing to fear, I am not responsible for the accident

Ленингра́д! Тума́н и сы́рость! **Лю́дям** не́чем дыша́ть (Rybakov)
Leningrad! Fog and damp! People have nothing to breathe

(5) In prepositional constructions the preposition appears between **не́** and the pronoun:

Ему́ **не́ к кому** обрати́ться за по́мощью
He has no one to turn to for aid

Ей **не́ в чем** признава́ться (Rybakov)
She has nothing to confess to

(6) The construction may also be used in the past and future: Мне не́чем **бы́ло** писа́ть 'I had nothing to write with', Мне не́чем **бу́дет** писа́ть 'I won't have anything to write with':

Кома́нде **не́ с кем** бы́ло игра́ть (Vanshenkin)
The team had nobody to play against

(7) The *positive* equivalent of the construction involves present **есть**, past **бы́ло**, future **бу́дет**: **Есть** чем горди́ться 'There is something to be proud of' (cf. **Не́чем** горди́ться 'There is nothing to be proud of'):

Ребя́т оста́вить **бы́ло** с кем — как раз в э́то вре́мя прибежа́ла А́нка но́вое пла́тье пока́зывать (Abramov)
There **was** someone to leave the children with – Anka came running up at that very moment to show her new dress

Note

Idiomatic usage in **Не́чего** (**не́зачем**) обижа́ться 'There's no point in taking offence', **не́чего** и говори́ть 'needless to say', от **не́чего** де́лать 'for want of something to do', **Не́ за что** 'Don't mention it'.

(8) In all the above examples, the case of the pronoun is determined by the infinitive: **Кого́** посла́ть? **Не́кого** посла́ть 'Whom to send? There is no one to send'.

However, in phrases of the type 'There is no one to drive the car, look after the children', 'no one' is the logical *subject* of the verb and therefore appears in the dative (see (4) (ii) above):

Не́кому о нём забо́титься (Rybakov)
There is no one to care for him

Поря́док навести́ **не́кому** (Rybakov)
There is no one to establish order

До́ма **не́кому** объясни́ть ма́льчику уро́ки
There is no one at home to explain the homework to the boy

---

138 The indefinite pronouns кто́-то, кто́-нибудь, кто́-либо; что́-то, что́-нибудь, что́-либо; како́й-то, како́й-нибудь, како́й-либо; че́й-то, че́й-нибудь, че́й-либо

The particles -**то**, -**нибудь** and -**либо** can be attached to **кто**, **что**, **како́й**, **чей** to form indefinite pronouns (for declension, see **121**; note that they can also be attached to **где**, **как**, **куда́**, **когда́**, **почему́**, see **395**).

(1) -то

(i) Кто́-то.

(a) **Кто́-то** 'someone' denotes one particular person whose identity, however, is unknown to or has been forgotten by the speaker. Since reference is to a definite event, **кто́-то** tends to be confined almost exclusively to the past or present tense (for use with the future, however, see (iv) below): **Кто́-то** стучи́т в дверь 'Someone is knocking on the door' (i.e. a definite person, but the speaker does not know who it is), **Кто́-то** позвони́л из шко́лы 'Someone rang from the school' (again, a definite person, but identity unknown (or possibly forgotten by the person who took the call)), Она́ помога́ла **кому́-то** перейти́ доро́гу 'She was helping someone to cross the road' etc.

(b) **Кто́-то** can also be extended by an adjective: кто́-то **высо́кий** 'someone tall'.

(c) **Кто́-то** takes a masculine predicate even when reference is to a female: Кто́-то звони́л. **Это была́ кака́я-то де́вушка** 'Someone rang. It was some girl or other'.

(ii) Что́-то.

(a) **Что́-то** 'something' likewise denotes a definite object or thing, details of which are unknown to the speaker: Он **что́-то** сказа́л, но я не расслы́шал, что и́менно 'He said something, but I did not catch exactly what it was', Она́ **что́-то** жуёт 'She is chewing something' (but the speaker does not know what it is), Он **чём-то** недово́лен 'He is displeased about something', cf.:

> На́дю **о чём-то** спроси́л Михаи́л, она́ **что́-то** отве́тила — всё шёпотом (Rasputin)
> Mikhail asked Nadya about **something**, she gave **some answer or other** – all in a whisper

(b) **Что́-то** can also be extended by a neuter adjective: Он бормота́л что́-то **непоня́тное** 'He was mumbling something incomprehensible'. Note also Это сто́ит рубль **с чём-то** 'It costs something over a rouble'.

(iii) Како́й-то and чей-то.

(a) **Како́й-то** and **чей-то** are used in similar fashion to кто́-то and что́-то: Он изуча́ет **како́й-то** язы́к 'He is studying some (definite but unspecified) language or other', Она проверяла **чью-то** тетрадь 'She was correcting someone's exercise book'.

(b) **Какой-то** may sometimes render English 'a': Вас спрашивала **какая-то** девушка 'A girl (some girl or other) was asking for you'.

(iv) Forms with -**то** may be used in the future, but only if the identity of the person or thing referred to is already known: Я подарю тебе **что-то** ко дню рождения 'I shall give you something for your birthday' (meaning that I have already decided **what** to give. If I still have to make the choice, **что-нибудь** must be used).

(2) -нибудь

(i) Unlike forms in -**то**, forms in -**нибудь** do not imply a particular person or thing, but someone or something indefinite, or one of an unspecified number, still to be decided or selected:

Я счастливее здесь, чем в каком-нибудь другом месте
I am happier here than anywhere else

The hypothetical nature of forms in -**нибудь** accounts for their usage in **questions**, in the **future**, after **imperatives** and in **conditional** and **subjunctive** constructions:

(a) Questions:

— Ты **в кого-нибудь** влюбился? (Nikolaev)
'Have you fallen in love with **someone**?'

— Коля! **Что-нибудь** случилось? (Yakhontov)
Kolya! Has **anything** (or **something**) happened?

(b) Future:

Он придумает **какое-нибудь** неотложное дело (Koluntsev)
He is bound to think up **some** urgent business **or other**

(c) Imperative:

— Расскажите ещё **о чём-нибудь**, — попросила она ободряюще.
— О чём же?
— О чём хотите (Nosov)
'Tell me about **something** else', she asked encouragingly.
'About what, then?'
'About anything you like'

(d) Conditional and subjunctive.

Conditional:

> Ра́зве **кто́-нибудь** в э́том слу́чае поступи́л бы ина́че? (Kuleshov)
> Do you really think **anyone** would have behaved differently in the circumstances?

Subjunctive:

> Он хо́чет, что̀бы **кто́-нибудь** ему́ помо́г
> He wants **someone** to help him

(ii) **-нибудь** is also used, irrespective of tense, when reference is to different people or things on different occasions. Thus, Я ча́сто приглаша́ю **кого́-нибудь** сде́лать докла́д, 'I often invite **someone** to give a talk' (different speakers on different occasions), Я всегда́ дарю́ ей **что́-нибудь** ко дню рожде́ния 'I always give her **something** for her birthday' (a different present on each birthday), cf.:

> У нас в отде́ле всегда́ **кто́-нибудь** висе́л на телефо́не (Avdeenko)
> In our department **someone** (i.e. different people on different occasions) was always on the phone

> Чу́дик облада́л одно́й осо́бенностью: с ним постоя́нно **что́-нибудь** случа́лось (Shukshin)
> Chudik had a peculiarity: **something** was always happening to him

> — Дядь, проведи́те на стадио́н, — проси́л я **како́го-нибудь** до́брого мужчи́ну … (Makarov)
> 'Mister, take me into the stadium with you', I would ask **some kind man or other**

> Когда́ на́до бы́ло перенести́ из скла́да **что́-нибудь** тяжёлое, то помога́л Кузьма́ (Rasputin)
> Whenever **something** heavy had to be moved from the warehouse, Kuzma would help

(iii) **Како́й-нибудь** can also denote:

(a) Approximation:

> За **каки́х-нибудь** 70–80 лет на гра́ни исчезнове́ния оказа́лось 600 ви́дов млекопита́ющих (*Selskaya zhizn*)

Over a period of **some** 70–80 years 600 species of mammals have found themselves on the verge of extinction

(b) Inferior quality:

Дам тебе́ не **како́й-нибудь** уче́бник, а хоро́ший
I won't give you just **any old** textbook, but a good one

(3) -либо

Forms in -**либо** are similar in meaning to those in -**нибудь**, but imply an even greater degree of indefiniteness ('anyone, anything you care to name' etc.), functioning sometimes as a 'bookish' alternative to forms in -**нибудь**:

— Коне́чно, ты прав, — сказа́ла она́. — Меня́ть **что́-либо** по́здно (Zalygin)
'You're right, of course', she said, 'It's too late to change **anything whatsoever**'

И происхо́дит э́то . . . без **како́й-либо** волоки́ты (*Nedelya*)
And this happens . . . without **any** red tape **at all**

Ра́зве любо́вь к свое́й кома́нде оскорбля́ет **чье́-либо** досто́инство (Makarov)
Does love for one's team really offend **anyone's** dignity

See also **395** (3).

139 The indefinite pronouns **ко̀е-кто́, ко̀е-что́, ко̀е-како́й**

(1) **Ко̀е-кто́, ко̀е-что́** and **ко̀е-како́й** decline like **кто, что** and **како́й** respectively (see **121** and **146** (3) note (b)). Note that ко̀е- does *not* decline. Though both **ко̀е-кто́** and **ко̀е-что́** take singular predicates, they have plural meaning (**ко̀е-кто́** 'one or two people', **ко̀е-что́** 'a thing or two'):

Ко̀е-кто́ на За́паде зада́лся це́лью за́ново «переписа́ть» исто́рию второ́й мирово́й войны́ (*Russia Today*)
One or two people in the West have set themselves the task of 'rewriting' the history of the Second World War

На́до **ко̀е к кому́** забежа́ть
I need to pop in to see **a couple of people**

Кòе на чтó смотрéли сквòзь пáльцы (Rybakov)
Some things they turned a blind eye to

(2) As the examples show, prepositions appear between **кòе** and the oblique case form. In constructions with **кòе-какóй**, however, prepositions may precede or follow **кòе**:

Он обратѝлся ко мне **кòе с каки́ми** (or **с кòе-каки́ми**) предложéниями
He approached me with **a number of** proposals

140 Нéкто, нéчто

Нéкто 'someone, a certain' appears only in the nominative (**нéкто** Ивáнóв 'one Ivanov') and **нéчто** 'something' only in the nominative/accusative. The pronouns are usually qualified, e.g. **нéкто** в бéлых перчáтках 'someone in white gloves', **нéчто** подóбное 'something similar'.

141 Нéкоторый

Нéкоторый declines like a hard adjective. It appears in a number of set phrases (в/до **нéкоторой** стéпени 'to a certain extent', **нéкоторое** врéмя 'a certain time', с **нéкоторого** врéмени 'for some time now'), but usually takes plural form (**нéкоторые** 'some, certain'). By comparison with **нéсколько** it is selective rather than merely quantitative:

У неё в грýппе **нéсколько** инострáнных студéнтов; **нéкоторые** из них блестя́щие языковéды
There are **a few** foreign students in her group; **some** of them are brilliant linguists

142 Нéкий

(1) The indefinite pronoun **нéкий** declines as follows:

	Masculine	Feminine	Neuter	Plural
Nom.	нéк-ий	нéк-ая	нéк-ое	нéк-ие
Acc.	нéк-ий/нéк-оего	нéк-ую	нéк-ое	нéк-ие/нéк-оих or нéк-их
Gen.	нéк-оего	нéко-ей/нéк-ой	нéк-оего	нéк-оих/нéк-их
Dat.	нéк-оему	нéк-оей/нéк-ой	нéк-оему	нéк-оим/нéк-им
Instr.	нéк-оим/нéк-им	нéк-оей/нéк-ой	нéк-оим/нéк-им	нéк-оими/нéк-ими
Prep.	о нéк-оем	о нéк-оей	о нéк-оем	о нéк-оих/нéк-их

(2) The pronoun's main function is to qualify surnames: **нéкий** Брáгин 'a certain Bragin'.

(3) The contracted forms **нéким, нéкой, нéких, нéкими** are now preferred by many users of the language: У **нéкой** Ивáновой нет пáспорта 'A certain Ivanova has no passport'. However, the longer forms are still found:

Дом принадлежáл **нéкоему** Кислы́х (Granin)
The house belonged to a certain Kislykh

ссылáясь на **нéкоего** представи́теля в ООН (*Pravda*)
with reference to a certain representative at the UNO

143 Other parts of speech which can also function as pronouns

Some other parts of speech can also function as pronouns. They include:

(1) **Дáнный** 'present': в **дáнный** момéнт 'at the present moment'.

(2) **Оди́н**:

(i) 'A (certain)': К вам заходи́л **оди́н** студéнт 'A student called to see you'.

(ii) 'The same': Они́ учи́лись в **однóй** шкóле 'They went to the same school'.

(3)   The reciprocal pronoun **дру̀г дру́га** 'each other', the first part of which is invariable, while the second part is governed by the verb or adjective. Only singular forms are involved, never plural:

Они́ лю́бят **дру̀г дру́га** (Uvarova)
They love each other

Они́ сигна́лили **дру̀г дру́гу** фонаря́ми (Aytmatov)
They were signalling to each other with lanterns

Prepositions appear centrally, between **дру̀г** and the declined form: Они́ се́ли на свои́ крова́ти **дру̀г про̀тив дру́га** (Yakhontov) 'They sat down opposite each other on their beds'. This does not apply, however, to some secondary prepositions: **вблизѝ** дру̀г дру́га 'near each other', **благодаря́ дру̀г дру́гу** 'thanks to each other', **вопреки́** дру̀г дру́гу 'contrary to each other', **навстре́чу** дру̀г дру́гу 'to meet each other'.

Дру̀г дру́га also functions as a possessive: Зна́ли о сне́жном челове́ке по расска́зам **дру̀г дру́га** (Povolyaev) 'They knew of the yeti from each other's stories'.

The Adjective

144 Introduction

(1) Adjectives may be attributive, either preceding the noun (e.g. 'The **black** cat purred') or following it and separated from it by a comma ('A cat, **wet** with the rain, sat on the step'). Adjectives may also be predicative, following the noun and linked to it by a verb: 'The cat **is wet**'.

(2) Adjectives also have comparative forms ('My car is **newer** than yours') and superlative forms ('His house is the **oldest** in the street').

(3) Most adjectives in Russian have *two* forms, a long (attributive) form (e.g. **красивый, красивая, красивое, красивые** 'beautiful') and a short (predicative) form (e.g. **красив, красива, красиво, красивы** 'am, is, are beautiful'). This is also true of comparatives.

Note
Subsequently, 'is, are' are used to designate the short form.

The Long Form of the Adjective

145 The long adjective: hard endings

(1) Most long adjectives in Russian have **hard** endings, that is, the first vowel of the ending is **a, o** or **ы**, e.g.

Masculine	Feminine	Neuter	Plural
нóв-**ый**	нóв-**ая**	нóв-**ое**	нóв-**ые** 'new'

(2) Hard-ending adjectives decline as follows:

	Masculine	Feminine	Neuter	Plural
Nom.	нóв-**ый**	нóв-**ая**	нóв-**ое**	нóв-**ые**
Acc.	нóв-**ый**/нóв-**ого**	нóв-**ую**	нóв-**ое**	нóв-**ые**/нóв-**ых**
Gen.	нóв-**ого**	нóв-**ой**	нóв-**ого**	нóв-**ых**
Dat.	нóв-**ому**	нóв-**ой**	нóв-**ому**	нóв-**ым**
Instr.	нóв-**ым**	нóв-**ой**/нóв-**ою**	нóв-**ым**	нóв-**ыми**
Prep.	о нóв-**ом**	о нóв-**ой**	о нóв-**ом**	о нóв-**ых**

Note

(a) The instrumental feminine form in **-ою** survives mainly in poetry.

(b) End-stressed adjectives (e.g. **молодóй**) decline like **нóвый** except in the masculine nominative singular and inanimate accusative singular, which have the ending **-óй**.

(c) **-го** in adjectival endings is pronounced [вə] ([во] under stress).

146 'Mixed' declension

(1) The 'mixed' declension involves adjectives whose final consonant is a guttural (**г**, **к** or **х**), a palatal sibilant (**ж**, **ч**, **ш** or **щ**) or **ц**.

(2) Endings are determined by the spelling rules (see **16** (1) and (2)):

(i) **и** replaces **ы** after **г**, **к**, **х**, **ж**, **ч**, **ш** and **щ**;

(ii) unstressed **о** is replaced by **е** after **ж**, **ч**, **ш**, **щ** and **ц**.

(3) Declension of **рýсский** 'Russian':

	Masculine	Feminine	Neuter	Plural
Nom.	рýсск-**ий**	рýсск-**ая**	рýсск-**ое**	рýсск-**ие**
Acc.	рýсск-**ий**/рýсск-**ого**	рýсск-**ую**	рýсск-**ое**	рýсск-**ие**/рýсск-**их**
Gen.	рýсск-**ого**	рýсск-**ой**	рýсск-**ого**	рýсск-**их**
Dat.	рýсск-**ому**	рýсск-**ой**	рýсск-**ому**	рýсск-**им**
Instr.	рýсск-**им**	рýсск-**ой**/-**ою**	рýсск-**им**	рýсск-**ими**
Prep.	о рýсск-**ом**	о рýсск-**ой**	о рýсск-**ом**	о рýсск-**их**

Note

(a) Adjectives in **-гий** and **-хий** (e.g. **дóлгий** 'long', **тúхий** 'quiet') decline like **рýсский**.

(b) End-stressed adjectives have **-ой** in the masculine nominative singular and inanimate accusative singular, e.g. **другóй** 'other', **какóй** 'which', **сухóй** 'dry'.

(4) Declension of **хорóший** 'good':

	Masculine	Feminine	Neuter	Plural
Nom.	хорóш-**ий**	хорóш-**ая**	хорóш-**ее**	хорóш-**ие**
Acc.	хорóш-**ий**/-**его**	хорóш-**ую**	хорóш-**ее**	хорóш-**ие**/хорóш-**их**
Gen.	хорóш-**его**	хорóш-**ей**	хорóш-**его**	хорóш-**их**
Dat.	хорóш-**ему**	хорóш-**ей**	хорóш-**ему**	хорóш-**им**
Instr.	хорóш-**им**	хорóш-**ей**/-**ею**	хорóш-**им**	хорóш-**ими**
Prep.	о хорóш-**ем**	о хорóш-**ей**	о хорóш-**ем**	о хорóш-**их**

Note

(a) Adjectives in **-жий** (e.g. **свéжий** 'fresh'), **-чий** (e.g. **горя́чий** 'hot') and **-щий** (e.g. **настоя́щий** 'real') decline like **хорóший**.

(b) Adjectives in **-цый** (e.g. **кýцый** 'dock-tailed') decline like **хорóший** except in the masculine nominative singular and inanimate accusative singular, which end in **-ый**, the masculine and neuter instrumental singular (**кýцым**) and the whole of the plural (**кýцые, кýцых** etc.). See 2 (ii) above.

(5) Declension of **большóй** 'big':

	Masculine	Feminine	Neuter	Plural
Nom.	больш-**óй**	больш-**áя**	больш-**óе**	больш-**ие**
Acc.	больш-**óй**/-**óго**	больш-**ýю**	больш-**óе**	больш-**ие**/больш-**их**
Gen.	больш-**óго**	больш-**óй**	больш-**óго**	больш-**их**
Dat.	больш-**óму**	больш-**óй**	больш-**óму**	больш-**им**
Instr.	больш-**им**	больш-**óй**/-**óю**	больш-**им**	больш-**ими**
Prep.	о больш-**óм**	о больш-**óй**	о больш-**óм**	о больш-**их**

Note

Чужóй 'someone else's' declines like **большóй**.

147 Soft-ending adjectives

(1) Soft-ending adjectives comprise some thirty adjectives in **-ний** and the adjective **кáрий** 'hazel' (eye colour).

Declension of **послéдний** 'last':

	Masculine	Feminine	Neuter	Plural
Nom.	послéдн-**ий**	послéдн-**яя**	послéдн-**ее**	послéдн-**ие**
Acc.	послéдн-**ий**/-**его**	послéдн-**юю**	послéдн-**ее**	послéдн-**ие**/послéдн-**их**
Gen.	послéдн-**его**	послéдн-**ей**	послéдн-**его**	послéдн-**их**

	Masculine	Feminine	Neuter	Plural
Dat.	послéдн-ему	послéдн-ей	послéдн-ему	послéдн-им
Instr.	послéдн-им	послéдн-ей/-ею	послéдн-им	послéдн-ими
Prep.	о послéдн-ем	о послéдн-ей	о послéдн-ем	о послéдн-их

(2) Adjectives in **-ний** subdivide into those which express:

(i) **Time**: весéнний 'spring', вечéрний 'evening', всегдáшний 'customary', вчерáшний 'yesterday's', дáвний 'long-standing', давнишний 'of long standing', дрéвний 'ancient', зáвтрашний 'tomorrow's', зимний 'winter', лéтний 'summer', недáвний 'recent', нынешний 'present-day', осéнний 'autumn', пóздний 'late', прéжний 'former', прошлогóдний 'last year's', рáнний 'early', сегóдняшний 'today's', суббóтний 'Saturday's', тепéрешний 'present-day', тогдáшний 'of that time', ýтренний 'morning'.

(ii) **Location**: бл`ижний 'near', вéрхний 'upper, top', внéшний 'external', внýтренний 'internal', дáльний 'far', домáшний 'domestic', зáдний 'back', здéшний 'of this place', крáйний 'extreme', нижний 'lower, bottom', передний 'front', сосéдний 'neighbouring, next', тáмошний 'of that place'.

Note

(a) **Ближний** and **дáльний** express relative distance: **ближний** ýгол 'the near corner', **дáльний** ýгол 'the far (*not* 'the distant') corner', **Ближний** Востóк 'the Near East', **Дáльний** Востóк 'the Far East'. Note that the counterpart to **дáльний** рóдственник 'distant relative' is **рóдственник** 'relative' or **близкий** рóдственник 'close relative'.

(b) **Послéдний** 'last' and **срéдний** 'middle' can refer to both time and space.

(c) Some soft endings relate only to compound adjectives: **новогóдний** 'new year' (cf. годовóй 'annual' from год 'year'), **односторóнний** 'unilateral'.

(iii) **Others**: дочéрний 'daughter's, daughterly', замýжняя 'married' (of a woman), искренний 'sincere', лишний 'superfluous', порóжний 'empty', синий (dark) 'blue', сынóвний 'filial'.

148 Formation of adjectives from nouns: the suffixes -н-, -ск- and -ов-/-ев-

(1) Unlike English, in which most nouns can also function as adjectives (e.g. 'steel' (noun) becomes 'steel' (adjective) in '**steel** bridge'), adjectives in Russian derive from nouns mainly through suffixation.

(2) The commonest suffix is -**н**-: thus, **чáйный** from чай 'tea' (чáйная чáшка 'tea cup'), **кóмнатный** from кóмната 'room' (кóмнатная температýра 'room temperature'), **мéстный** from мéсто 'place' (мéстный наркóз 'local anaesthetic'). **Г, к, х, ц** and **л** undergo mutation before suffix -**н**-:

г : ж	юг 'south'	ю́жный 'southern'
к : ч	рекá 'river'	речнóй 'river' (adjective)
х : ш	вóздух 'air'	воздýшный 'air' (adjective)
ц : ч	ýлица 'street'	ýличный 'street' (adjective)
л : ль	шкóла 'school'	шкóльный 'school' (adjective)

(3) The suffix -**ск**- is associated mainly with adjectives derived from the names of:

(i) People, thus : **мужскóй** 'male', **граждáнский** 'civic' etc.

Note
Adjectives from some animate nouns have the suffix -**еск**-, e.g. **человéческий** 'human' from человéк 'human'. Adjectives derived from some proper names take the infix -**ов**-: **гóрьковский** from Гóрький 'Gorky'.

(ii) Towns, rivers etc. (note also **городскóй** from гóрод 'town', **сéльский** from селó 'village'): **донскóй** from Дон 'the Don', **москóвский** from Москвá 'Moscow'.

Note
(a) Some town names ending in a vowel have adjectives in -**инский**: **алма-атúнский** from Алмá-Атá 'Alma Ata', **бакúнский** from Бакý 'Baku', **я́лтинский** from Я́лта 'Yalta' (note also **кубúнский** 'Cuban', cf. **кубáнский** from **Кубáнь** 'the (river) Kuban').
(b) Adjectival stress differs in some cases from noun stress: **астрахáнский** from А́страхань 'Astrakhan', **новгорóдский** from Нóвгород 'Novgorod'.

(c) Consonant mutation occurs in adjectives derived from the names of some towns, rivers, mountain ranges etc.: **во́лжский** from Во́лга 'the Volga', **пра́жский** from Пра́га 'Prague', **ри́жский** from Ри́га 'Riga', **ура́льский** from Ура́л 'the Urals'.

(iii) Nationalities and languages: **ру́сский** 'Russian', **по́льский** 'Polish', including more recent formations such as **зимбабви́йский** 'Zimbabwean'. Note that **латви́йский** 'Latvian', referring to the whole population of Latvia, is distinguished from **латы́шский** 'Latvian' (from **латы́ш** 'a Latvian'), referring to the indigenous population only.

(iv) Organizations: **заводско́й** from заво́д 'factory', **комсомо́ль-ский** from комсомо́л 'the Komsomol', **на́товский** from НА́ТО 'NATO' etc.

(v) Months: **октя́брьский** 'October' etc. Note the absence of a soft sign in **янва́рский** 'January' and the infix -ов- in **а́вгустовский** 'August', **ма́ртовский** 'March'.

(4) The suffix -ов-/-ев- is used to form adjectives from the names of many trees (e.g. **бу́ковый** from бук 'beech'), fruits and vegetables (e.g. **оре́ховый** from оре́х 'nut'), growing areas (e.g. **полево́й** from по́ле 'field'), metals and alloys (e.g. **ци́нковый** from цинк 'zinc'), certain other substances (e.g. **рези́новый** from рези́на 'rubber'), animals (e.g. **слоно́вый** from слон 'elephant'), suits of cards (e.g. **пи́ковый** from пи́ки 'spades'), colours (e.g. **ро́зовый** 'pink' from ро́за 'rose') and other nouns (e.g. **звуково́й** from звук 'sound', **ра́ковый** from рак 'cancer' etc.).

149 Adjectival endings with specific meanings

Some adjectival endings have specific meanings. These include:

(1) -ивый, -ливый, -чивый

Adjectives with these endings denote characteristics: **лени́вый** 'lazy', **терпели́вый** 'patient', **разгово́рчивый** 'talkative' etc.

(2) -мый

Adjectives with this ending denote potential qualities (cf. English -ble): **преодолимый** 'surmountable', **растворимый** 'soluble'. Such adjectives are of participial derivation (see also **344**).

(3) -атый

Adjectives with this ending denote possession of the object denoted by the root noun: **пернатый** 'feathered', **рогатый** 'horned'.

(4) -астый

Adjectives with this ending denote possession of a prominent physical feature: **грудастый** 'busty', **скуластый** 'high-cheek-boned' etc.

(5) -истый

Adjectives with this ending denote abundance of the feature denoted by the root noun: **тенистый** 'shady'. They can also denote similarity: **золотистый** 'golden' (of colour etc.) (cf. золотой '(made of) gold').

(6) -чий

Adjectives with this ending denote various states: **висячий** 'hanging' (**висячий** мост 'suspension bridge'), **сидячий** 'sedentary' etc. The adjectives are of participial origin.

150 Nouns with more than one adjective

Nouns with two or more derivative adjectives subdivide as follows:

(1) Different meanings of the same noun are involved. Thus, мир 'world' has the adjective **мировой** (мировая война 'world war'), while мир 'peace' has the adjective **мирный** (мирный договор 'peace treaty').

(2) The adjectival endings express different qualities or properties of a noun. Thus, both **дружеский** 'friendly' and **дружный** 'con-

certed, harmonious' derive from друг 'friend', as does the official
дрýжественный (Переговóры проходи́ли в дрýжественной
обстанóвке 'The talks were held in a cordial atmosphere').

151 Possessive adjectives

Possessive adjectives fall into two categories:

(1) The type **вóлчий** 'wolf's'.

(i) **Вóлчий** is declined as follows:

	Masculine	Feminine	Neuter	Plural
Nom.	вóлчий	вóлчь-я	вóлчь-е	вóлчь-и
Acc.	вóлчий/вóлчь-его	вóлчь-ю	вóлчь-е	вóлчь-и/-их
Gen.	вóлчь-его	вóлчь-ей	вóлчь-его	вóлчь-их
Dat.	вóлчь-ему	вóлчь-ей	вóлчь-ему	вóлчь-им
Instr.	вóлчь-им	вóлчь-ей/-ею	вóлчь-им	вóлчь-ими
Prep.	о вóлчь-ем	о вóлчь-ей	о вóлчь-ем	о вóлчь-их

(ii) Most adjectives in this category derive from the names of
animals, birds, fish etc.: **ли́сий** 'fox's', **ры́бий** 'fish's' and so on. Some
derive from the names of human beings. Consonant mutation
operates as follows:

г : ж	бог	бóжий 'god's'
д : ж	медвéдь	медвéжий 'bear's'
к : ч	собáка	собáчий 'dog's'
	охóтник	охóтничий 'hunter's'
х : ш	черепáха	черепáший 'tortoise's'
ц : ч	овцá	овéчий 'sheep's'
	деви́ца	дéвичий 'maiden' (e.g. дéвичья фами́лия 'maiden name')

(iii) A number of the adjectives appear in set phrases: волк в
овéчьей шкýре 'wolf in sheep's clothing', вид с **пти́чьего** полёта
'bird's eye view'.

Note
Трéтий 'third' also declines like **вóлчий**.

(2) The type **мáмин** 'Mum's'.

(i) **Мáмин** declines as follows, combining adjective and noun
endings:

	Masculine	Feminine	Neuter	Plural
Nom.	ма́мин	ма́мин-**а**	ма́мин-**о**	ма́мин-**ы**
Acc.	ма́мин/ма́мин-**ого**	ма́мин-**у**	ма́мин-**о**	ма́мин-**ы**/-**ых**
Gen.	ма́мин-**ого**	ма́мин-**ой**	ма́мин-**ого**	ма́мин-**ых**
Dat.	ма́мин-**у**	ма́мин-**ой**	ма́мин-**у**	ма́мин-**ым**
Instr.	ма́мин-**ым**	ма́мин-**ой**/-**ою**	ма́мин-**ым**	ма́мин-**ыми**
Prep.	о ма́мин-**ом**	о ма́мин-**ой**	о ма́мин-**ом**	о ма́мин-**ых**

(ii) Possessive adjectives of this type are formed by adding the suffixes **-ин**, **-нин** or **-ов** to the stems of nouns (ма́ма 'Mum' etc.): **ба́бушкин** 'grandma's', **бра́тнин** 'brother's', **де́дов** 'granddad's', **дя́дин** 'uncle's', **же́нин** 'wife's', **ки́син/ко́шкин** 'pussy's', **ма́мин** 'Mum's', **му́жнин** 'husband's', **ня́нин** 'nanny's', **отцо́в/па́пин** 'Dad's', **сестрин** 'sister's', **тётин** 'auntie's'. They are used mainly within the family circle:

> От **ма́миных** за́втраков он реши́л бежа́ть (Tendryakov)
> He decided to escape from Mum's breakfasts

(iii) They also derive from the familiar forms of first names: **Ко́лин** 'Kolya's':

> Я счита́ю, что **Ната́шина** ма́ма права́ (*Rabotnitsa*)
> I consider that Natasha's Mum is right

(iv) The endings also appear in phrases deriving from mythology, the Bible etc. (**ахилле́сова** пята́ 'Achilles' heel'), geographical terms (**Бе́рингов** проли́в 'Bering Straits'), other phrases (**крокоди́ловы** слёзы 'crocodile tears') etc.

(v) Some forms in **-ин**, mostly denoting animals, have acquired long adjectival endings and decline like **но́вый**: **лебеди́ный** 'swan's', **лошади́ный** 'horse's' (**лебеди́ная** пе́сня 'swan song', **лошади́ная** си́ла 'horse power').

152 Diminutive adjectives in -енький/-онький

(1) Most diminutive adjectives end in **-енький** (e.g. **но́венький** from но́вый 'new') and (after gutturals) **-онький** (**высо́конький** from высо́кий, **лёгонький** from лёгкий 'light, easy', **ти́хонький** from ти́хий 'quiet'). The stress falls on the syllable preceding **-енький/-онький**.

(2) Diminutive adjectives may express smallness: **бле́дненькое
ли́чико** 'a pale little face', А́лька передёрнула **у́зенькими
плеча́ми** (Koluntsev) 'A spasm convulsed Alka's narrow little
shoulders'.

(3) Like diminutive nouns (see **104–108**), diminutive adjectives
may also express emotive nuances of sympathy, scorn etc.:
моло́денький студе́нтик 'a nice young student', **глу́пенький**
мальчо́нка 'a stupid little kid'.

(4) Diminutive endings may also impart a meaning of intensity to an
adjective: e.g. **про́стенький** 'very plain', **чи́стенький** ма́льчик
'spotlessly clean little boy', cf.:

> Михаи́л принёс две **холо́дненькие** буты́лки моско́вского
> пивка́ (Abramov)
> Mikhail brought two **ice-cold** bottles of Moscow beer

153 Diminutive adjectives in -оватый/-еватый

(1) The diminutive suffix **-оват(ый)/-еват(ый)** denotes incom-
pleteness: **дорогова́тый** 'rather dear', **кислова́тый** 'rather sour',
синева́тый 'bluish'.

Note
These diminutives cannot be formed from all adjectives. Thus, they
are formed from ста́рый 'old' and глу́пый 'stupid' (старова́тый,
глупова́тый), but not from their opposites молодо́й 'young' and
у́мный 'clever'.

(2) Such diminutives may acquire an evaluative nuance: **дорого-
ва́тая кварти́ра** 'a rather expensive apartment', **холоднова́тая
пого́да** 'weather somewhat on the cold side'.

(3) Maximum colloquial expressiveness is achieved by the addition
of **-енький**: **глухова́тенький** 'somewhat hard of hearing'.

154 Indeclinable adjectives

(1) Most indeclinable adjectives are loan words and *follow* the
noun. Some denote colour (e.g. **ха́ки** 'khaki'):

Два но́вых пла́тья: откры́тое, **беж** … и цве́та **бордо́**
(Zalygin)
Two new dresses, an open-necked beige … and a deep red

(2) Others denote:

(i) Food and drink:

кóфе **мóкко** mocha coffee

(ii) Styles of clothing:

пальто́ **демисезо́н**	spring or autumn coat
брю́ки **клёш**	bell-bottom trousers
пальто́ **регла́н**	Raglan coat

(iii) Languages (these adjectives *precede* the noun):

ко́ми заи́мствования	Komi loans
урду́ язы́к	Urdu
хи́нди язы́к	Hindi

Compare, however, язы́к **эспера́нто** 'Esperanto'.

(iv) Various other meanings:

вес **бру́тто**	gross weight
вес **не́тто**	net weight
часы́ **пик**	rush hour

155 Attributive use of the long adjective

(1) The long adjective usually precedes the noun and agrees with it in gender, case and number:

	'new house' Masculine		'new book' Feminine		'new armchair' Neuter	
Nom.	но́в-**ый**	дом	но́в-**ая**	кни́га	но́в-**ое**	кре́сло
Acc.	но́в-**ый**	дом	но́в-**ую**	кни́гу	но́в-**ое**	кре́сло
Gen.	но́в-**ого**	до́ма	но́в-**ой**	кни́ги	но́в-**ого**	кре́сла
Dat.	но́в-**ому**	до́му	но́в-**ой**	кни́ге	но́в-**ому**	кре́слу
Instr.	но́в-**ым**	до́мом	но́в-**ой/-ою**	кни́гой	но́в-**ым**	кре́слом
Prep. о	но́в-**ом**	до́ме	о но́в-**ой**	кни́ге	о но́в-**ом**	кре́сле

Plural

Nom.	нóв-**ые** домá	нóв-**ые**	кни́ги	нóв-**ые**	крéсла
Acc.	нóв-**ые** домá	нóв-**ые**	кни́ги	нóв-**ые**	крéсла
Gen.	нóв-**ых** домóв	нóв-**ых**	книг	нóв-**ых**	крéсел
Dat.	нóв-**ым** домáм	нóв-**ым**	кни́гам	нóв-**ым**	крéслам
Instr.	нóв-**ыми** домáми	нóв-**ыми**	кни́гами	нóв-**ыми**	крéслами
Prep.	о нóв-**ых** домáх	о нóв-**ых**	кни́гах	о нóв-**ых**	крéслах

Note

(a) The animate accusative/genitive rule is applied: Знáю **нóвого учи́теля, нóвых учителéй** 'I know the new teacher, the new teachers' (see **47**).

(b) An adjective or pronoun qualifying a masculine animate noun in **-а/-я** takes masculine endings, while the noun takes feminine endings: Я знáю **вáшего дя́дю** 'I know your uncle', дом **вáшего дя́ди** 'your uncle's house', Вéрю **вáшему дя́де** 'I trust your uncle', Я довóлен **вáшим дя́дей** 'I am pleased with your uncle', о **вáшем дя́де** 'about your uncle'.

(2) The long adjective may also follow the noun, separated from it by a comma and agreeing with it in gender, case and number:

Он лежáл на **травé, мóкрой** от росы́
He was lying on the grass, (which was) wet with the dew

Note

In certain contexts (e.g. in restaurant menus, with generic nouns) the long attributive adjective may follow the noun: кóфе **натурáльный** 'real coffee', Тури́зм — дéло **полéзное** 'Tourism is a healthy pursuit'.

156 Use of the long adjective with predicative meaning

(1) In predicative position, the long adjective denotes characteristics which are inherent in or completely identified with the noun (cf. the predicative *short* form (see **166–174**)), e.g.

Э́та кóмната — **большáя**
This room is **large** (is **a large one**)

(2) When linked to the noun by the past or future tense of the verb **быть**, the long predicative adjective appears:

(i) In the nominative case (the more *colloquial* variant):

Лес был **тёплый и спокойный** (Aksenov)
The forest was warm and serene

И я буду тогда **старая, некрасивая**, в морщинках (Kovaleva)
And by that time I shall be old, ugly, wrinkled

(ii) In the instrumental case (more typical of *written* styles):

Перестройка была **нелёгкой**, но она произошла (Kovaleva)
Restructuring was not easy, but it occurred

— Буду я когда-нибудь **богатым**? (Rubina)
'Will I ever be rich?'

(3) When linked to the noun by the conditional, subjunctive, infinitive or imperative mood of the verb **быть**, the instrumental case of the adjective is the norm:

Если бы он был **высоким**, он поступил бы в милицию
If he were tall he would join the police

Главное, чтобы эти встречи были **регулярными**
The main thing is that these meetings should be regular

Эти догадки могут быть **правильными** или **ошибочными** (Rybakov)
These conjectures may be right or wrong

Будь всегда **вежливым**!
Always be polite!

(4) After other verbs which take a predicate (**выглядеть** 'to look', **казаться** 'to seem', **притворяться** 'to pretend', **чувствовать** себя 'to feel' etc.), the adjective also appears in the instrumental case:

Улицы выглядели **грязными**
The streets looked dirty

Мой расчёт оказался **точным** (Nikolaev)
My calculation turned out to be accurate

Она́ всегда́ остаётся **споко́йной**
She always stays calm

Я чу́вствовал себя́ перед ним **винова́тым** (Bogomolov)
I felt I owed him an apology

(5) An adjectival complement to intransitive and transitive verbs also appears in the instrumental:

Он на́чал **пе́рвым**
He began first

Он оста́вил сейф **откры́тым**
He left the safe open

Я никогда́ не ви́дел её **тако́й краси́вой** (Kazakov)
I had never seen her looking so lovely

157 Some uses of singular and plural adjectives

(1) A plural adjective is used to qualify two or more singular nouns if it relates to all the nouns named:

Маргари́та с гро́хотом бро́сила **желе́зные** сово́к и лопа́тку (Rubina)
With a clatter Margarita threw down an iron trowel and spade

Note
A *singular* adjective or pronoun may be used, however, if it is obvious that it relates to all the nouns named. The adjective or pronoun in such circumstances agrees with the first of the nouns: написа́ть **свою́** фами́лию, и́мя и о́тчество 'to write one's surname, first name and patronymic'.

(2) A singular adjective is also used if it relates only to the *first* of the nouns named: **ка́менный** дом и гара́ж 'a stone house and a garage' (cf. **ка́менные** дом и гара́ж 'a stone house and (a stone) garage').

(3) Phrases comprising numeral and noun are qualified by a plural adjective: **ка́ждые** два дня 'every two days'. Adjectives which fulfil an emphatic role (e.g. **до́брый**, **по́лный**, **це́лый**) appear in the genitive plural: **по́лных** три ме́сяца 'a full three months', **це́лых** две таре́лки 'two whole plates' (cf. also опозда́л на **це́лых** полчаса́ 'he was a whole half hour late').

(4) Singular adjectives and nouns are used in the following phrases: **в ра́зное вре́мя** 'at various times', **вся́кого ро́да** 'all kinds of' (**вся́кого ро́да** това́ры 'all kinds of goods'), **ра́зного ро́да** 'of various kinds'.

158 Adjectival nouns

(1) An adjectival noun has the form of an adjective but functions as a noun (**бе́лые** 'the Whites').

(2) Most adjectival nouns result from the omission of a word that can be understood from the context, e.g. **столо́вая** (ко́мната) 'dining room'.

(3) Adjectival nouns decline like adjectives (**в ва́нной** (from ва́нная) 'in the bathroom'), behave like adjectives when governed by numerals (**два моро́женых** 'two ice-creams' (see **194** (2) (v))) and can themselves be qualified by adjectives: **ру́сское моро́женое** 'Russian ice-cream'.

(4) Most **masculine** adjectival nouns denote people: **рядово́й** 'private soldier', **учёный** 'scientist', **часово́й** 'sentry' etc.

(5) **Feminine** adjectival nouns denote:

(i) Lines: **крива́я** 'curve', **пряма́я** 'straight line' (ли́ния 'line' understood).

(ii) Rooms and other accommodation: **заку́сочная** 'snack-bar', **кладова́я** 'store-room', **пра́чечная** 'laundry', **убо́рная** 'lavatory'.

(6) **Neuter** adjectival nouns denote:

(i) The names of dishes: **пе́рвое** 'first course', **сла́дкое** 'sweet' etc. (блю́до 'dish' understood).

(ii) Time: **про́шлое** 'the past', **настоя́щее** 'the present', **бу́дущее** 'the future' (вре́мя 'time' understood).

(iii) Abstracts: **ста́рое и но́вое** 'the old and the new'.

(iv) Classes of animal: **живо́тное** 'animal', **млекопита́ющее** 'mammal', **насеко́мое** 'insect', (существо́ 'being' understood).

(v) Grammatical terms: **прилага́тельное** 'adjective', **существи́-тельное** 'noun', **числи́тельное** 'numeral' (**и́мя** 'noun, nomen' understood).

(7) **Plural** adjectival nouns denote money: **нали́чные** 'cash', **свёрхуро́чные** 'overtime', **чаевы́е** 'gratuities' (cf. **де́ньги** 'money').

Note

(a) Many adjectival nouns are formed on a seemingly *ad hoc* basis: Она́ поступи́ла в **архитекту́рный** (институ́т) 'She has enrolled at the school of architecture'. Note also **борза́я** (соба́ка) 'borzoi', **выходно́й** (день) 'day off', **сбо́рная** (кома́нда) 'combined team, international team' etc.

(b) Some adjectival nouns function *only* as nouns (**вселе́нная** 'the universe', **запята́я** 'comma', **мостова́я** 'roadway'), whereas others function as nouns or adjectives (cf. **рабо́чий** 'worker' and **рабо́чий** день 'working day' etc.).

The Short Form of the Adjective

159 Endings of the short form of the adjective

(1) Most adjectives have long forms and short forms (compare, however, **160**).

(2) The short form derives from the long form by the removal of the whole of the masculine ending and the final vowel of the feminine, neuter and plural endings, e.g. **суро́вый** 'severe':

	Long form	Short form
Masculine	суро́в-**ый**	суро́в
Feminine	суро́в-**ая**	суро́в-**а**
Neuter	суро́в-**ое**	суро́в-**о**
Plural	суро́в-**ые**	суро́в-**ы**

See also **161** on the use of buffer vowels.

160 Adjectives which have long forms only

(1) Some adjectives which denote **inherent characteristics** have long forms only. They include:

(i) Adjectives of colour (except for **си́ний** 'blue').

(ii) Adjectives with the suffix **-ск-**, e.g. **ру́сский** 'Russian'.

Note

Many adjectives in **-ический**, e.g. **драмати́ческий** 'dramatic', have synonyms in **-ичный**, e.g. **драмати́чный**, which *do* have short forms.

(iii) Adjectives in **-ний** (except for **и́скренний** 'sincere' and **си́ний** 'blue').

(iv) Adjectives of time (e.g. **ме́сячный** 'month's') and place (e.g. **ме́стный** 'local').

(v) Adjectives which denote materials or substances: **деревя́нный** 'wooden', **желе́зный** 'iron' etc.

(vi) Possessive adjectives of the type **во́лчий** 'wolf's' (see **151** (1)).

(vii) Ordinal numerals: **пе́рвый** 'first', **второ́й** 'second' etc.

(2) Some adjectives have short forms in certain meanings only. For example, **глухо́й** has short forms in the meaning 'deaf', but not in the meanings 'blank' (**глуха́я** стена́ 'blank wall'), 'remote' (**глуха́я** прови́нция 'remote province') and 'voiceless' (**глухо́й** согла́сный 'voiceless consonant'). **Ви́дный** has a short form in the meaning 'visible' (see **161** (1)) but not in the meaning 'prominent'.

161 The buffer vowels -е-, -о- and -ё- in the masculine short form

A buffer vowel is introduced between two or more final consonants in the *masculine* short form of many adjectives.

(1) The commonest of the buffer vowels is **-е-**:

Long-form masculine		Short forms
ва́жный	'important'	**ва́жен**, важна́, ва́жно, важны́/ва́жны
ви́дный	'visible'	**ви́ден**, видна́, ви́дно, видны́
голо́дный	'hungry'	**го́лоден**, голодна́, го́лодно, голодны́/го́лодны

Long-form masculine		Short forms
дли́нный	'long'	**дли́нен**, длинна́, дли́нно, длинны́/дли́нны
слы́шный	'audible'	**слы́шен**, слышна́, слы́шно, слышны́/слы́шны

Compare:

> Сейча́с зага́р не **мо́ден** (Koluntsev)
> Now a suntan is not fashionable

The buffer vowel -**e**- may replace a soft sign or the semi-consonant **й**:

больно́й	sick	**бо́лен**, больна́, больно́, больны́
дово́льный	pleased	**дово́лен**, дово́льна, дово́льно, дово́льны
споко́йный	calm	**споко́ен**, споко́йна, споко́йно, споко́йны

(2) The buffer vowel -**o**- splits clusters of consonants ending in **к**, **г**:

до́лгий	long	**до́лог**, долга́, до́лго, до́лги
лёгкий	light, easy	**лёгок**, легка́, легко́, легки́
у́зкий	narrow	**у́зок**, узка́, у́зко, узки́/у́зки

> — По мое́й статье́ преде́льный срок доста́точно **до́лог** (Koluntsev)
> 'The maximum term for my offence is fairly long'

Note

However, -**e**- replaces a *soft sign* in such clusters: го́рький 'bitter', short form **го́рек**. It also appears in unstressed position between **ж**, **ч**, **ш** and **к**: тя́жкий 'severe', short form **тя́жек**.

The following adjectives also take -**o**-:

злой	wicked	**зол**, зла, зло, злы
по́лный	full	**по́лон**, полна́, полно́, полны́
смешно́й	funny	**смешо́н**, смешна́, смешно́, смешны́

(3) The buffer vowel -**ё**- affects a small number of adjectives:

о́стрый	sharp, sharp-witted	**остёр**, остра́, остро́, остры́

си́льный	strong	**силён**, сильна́, си́льно, сильны́
у́мный	clever	**умён**, умна́, умно́, умны́
хи́трый	cunning	**хитёр**, хитра́, хитро́, хитры́

Note

Some adjectives with a stem ending in more than one consonant do *not* take a buffer vowel in the masculine short form. They include бо́дрый 'cheerful' (**бодр**), до́брый 'kind' (**добр**), го́рдый 'proud' (**горд**), мёртвый 'dead' (**мёртв**), пёстрый 'multicoloured' (**пёстр**).

162 Some special short forms

The following short forms should be specially noted.

(1) Большо́й big : **вели́к, велика́, велико́, велики́**.

(2) Досто́йный worthy : **досто́ин, досто́йна, досто́йно, досто́йны**.

(3) И́скренний sincere : **и́скренен, и́скренна, и́скренне** (the commoner alternative)/**и́скренно, и́скренни/и́скренны**.

(4) Ма́ленький small : **мал, мала́, мало́, малы́**.

(5) Си́ний blue : **синь, синя́, си́не, си́ни**.

(6) Солёный salted : **со́лон, солона́, со́лоно, солоны́/со́лоны**.

Note

(a) **Рад, ра́да, ра́до, ра́ды** 'glad' has no long form (however, ра́достный means 'glad, joyful': ра́достное собы́тие 'a joyful event').

(b) Како́в, какова́, каково́, каковы́ are used predicatively in the meaning 'what, what kind of' (**Какова́** сме́ртность от ра́ка? 'What is the mortality rate from cancer?') and тако́в, такова́, таково́, таковы́ in the meaning 'such' (**Таково́** на́ше мне́ние 'Such is our opinion'). However, **как** and **так** are used to modify short adjectives: Он **так** добр/Она́ **так** добра́ 'He is so kind/She is so kind'.

(c) For meanings of **вели́к** and **мал**, see **169**.

163 Masculine short forms of adjectives in -енный

(1) The masculine short form of adjectives in unstressed -**енный** ends in -**ен**, e.g. бессмы́сленный 'senseless', short form **бессмы́слен**:

Разгово́р был **бессмы́слен** (Trifonov)
The conversation was senseless

(2) Adjectives in stressed -**е́нный** have masculine short forms in -**е́нен**, e.g. открове́нный 'candid', short form **открове́нен**:

А взгляд его́, пожа́луй, сли́шком **открове́нен** (Koluntsev)
But I suppose his glance is too frank

Note
(a) Some adjectives in unstressed -**енный** have alternative masculine short forms in -**ен** and -**енен**, e.g. есте́ственный 'natural', **есте́ствен/есте́ственен**, the form in -**ен** usually being preferred.
(b) Some 'high style' adjectives in -**е́нный** have masculine short forms in -**ё́н**, e.g. благослове́нный 'blessed':

Благослове́н ма́стер, дости́гший верши́ны мастерства́ (*Sovetskii ekran*)
Blessed is the craftsman who has achieved the summit of craftsmanship

164 Stress patterns

(1) Very many adjectival short forms have fixed stem stress throughout:

краси́в краси́ва краси́во краси́вы (is, are) 'beautiful'

(2) Short forms with mobile stress subdivide into the following:

(i) End stress in feminine, neuter and plural:

хоро́ш хороша́ хорошо́ хороши́ (is, are) 'good'

Similarly **бо́лен** 'ill', **горя́ч** 'hot', **лёгок** 'light, easy', **по́лон** 'full', **смешо́н** 'funny', **тяжёл** 'heavy', **умён** 'clever'.

Note

Some adjectives of this type (e.g. свеж 'fresh') have alternative end or stem stress in the plural (свежи́/све́жи); others (e.g. широ́кий 'wide') have alternative end or stem stress in the neuter *and* plural (широ́ко ог широко́, широки́/широ́ки).

(ii)   End stress in the feminine:

> **жив   жива́   жи́во   жи́вы**   (is, are) 'alive'

Similarly **цел** 'whole' and, with alternative *end* stress in the plural, **бле́ден** 'pale', **го́лоден** 'hungry', **мил** 'dear', **слы́шен** 'audible', **строг** 'strict'.

(iii)   End stress in the feminine and plural:

> **ви́ден   видна́   ви́дно   видны́**   (is, are) 'visible'

Similarly **силён** 'strong'.

165   Divergence in stress between masculine, neuter and plural long and short forms

(1)   A handful of adjectives switch from medial or end stress in the long form to initial stress in the masculine, neuter and plural short forms, with end stress in the feminine: весёлый 'merry', **ве́сел, весела́, ве́село, ве́селы**; голо́дный 'hungry', **го́лоден, голодна́, го́лодно, го́лодны/голодны́**; дешёвый 'cheap', **дёшев, дешева́, дёшево, дёшевы**; дорого́й 'dear', **до́рог, дорога́, до́рого, до́роги**; коро́ткий 'short', **ко́роток, коротка́, ко́ротко, ко́ротки/коротки́**; молодо́й 'young', **мо́лод, молода́, мо́лодо, мо́лоды**.

(2)   Счастли́вый 'happy' has initial stress in all short forms: **сча́стлив, сча́стлива, сча́стливо, сча́стливы**.

166   The short form: usage. Introductory comments

(1)   Both long and short forms may be used predicatively (see **156**).

(2)   However, there is usually a distinction in meaning, the long form denoting inherent permanent characteristics (Он **злой** 'He is wicked') and the short form relating to temporary states (Он

го́лоден 'He is hungry') or to specific contexts or circumstances (Он
прав 'He is right' (i.e. about a particular matter)).

(3) Usage depends to a considerable extent on the capacity or
incapacity of a particular adjective to denote both permanent and
temporary states. Thus, Он **больно́й** 'He is (chronically) sick' may
be contrasted with Он **бо́лен** 'He is (temporarily) ill'. In adjectives,
however, where no such distinction is possible, long and short forms
are virtually synonymous: Он у́мный/Он умён 'He is clever'.

(4) The difference between the two forms of the adjective may be
stylistic, the short form reflecting a more 'bookish' style:

Психоло́гия ли́чности о́чень **сложна́**
The psychology of the personality is very complex

and the long form being the 'colloquial' variant:

Психоло́гия ли́чности о́чень **сло́жная**

167 Use of the short form to denote temporary state

While the long form implies *complete identification* of the quality
expressed by the adjective with the person or thing it qualifies, the
short form indicates a temporary state or condition, cf.

Река́ **бу́рная**
The river is a turbulent one (an inherent characteristic)

and

Сего́дня река́ **споко́йна**
Today the river is calm (the short form denoting a temporary
state)

Similarly Он о́чень **весёлый, бо́дрый** 'He is very jolly, cheerful'
(i.e. by nature), but Ты был **бодр** и **ве́сел** и шути́л всю доро́гу
(Koluntsev) 'You were cheerful and jolly and joked the whole way',
where the short forms refer to a person's mood *on a particular
occasion*.

168 Short forms: pairs of opposites

Many short forms comprise pairs of opposites and describe alternative states: hungry/full, healthy/ill etc.:

(1) **го́лоден, голодна́, го́лодно, голодны́/го́лодны** (is, are) hungry
сыт, сыта́, сы́то, сы́ты (is, are) full, replete

(2) **здоро́в, здоро́ва, здоро́во, здоро́вы** (is, are) healthy
бо́лен, больна́, больно́, больны́ (is, are) sick

Note

(a) Unlike **здоро́в** and **бо́лен**, which denote *temporary* states, Он **здоро́вый** 'He has a strong constitution' denotes an *inherent* characteristic and Он **больно́й** 'He is chronically sick, an invalid' denotes a chronic state.

(b) The colloquial forms **здоро́в, здорова́, здорово́, здоровы́** mean 'strong, good at': Ему́ удало́сь наконе́ц вы́толкнуть её. — Ну, **здорова́**! (Shukshin) 'He finally managed to shove her out. "Gosh, she's strong!"'

(3) **сча́стлив, сча́стлива, сча́стливо, сча́стливы** (is, are) happy
несча́стен, несча́стна, несча́стно, несча́стны (is, are) unhappy

(4) **жив, жива́, жи́во, жи́вы** (is, are) alive
мёртв, мертва́, мёртво, мёртвы (is, are) dead

Note

Он **живо́й** means 'he is lively' (an *inherent* characteristic).

(5) **прав, права́, пра́во, пра́вы** (is, are) right
непра́в, неправа́, непра́во, непра́вы (is, are) wrong

Compare На́ше де́ло **пра́вое** 'Our cause is just'.

Note

Она́ **хоро́шая** 'she is good' but Она́ **хороша́ (собо́й/собо́ю)** 'She is good-looking'; Он — **плохо́й** 'He is bad' but Он **плох (здоро́вьем)** 'He is poorly'.

169 Adjectives of dimension

The short form of an adjective of dimension relates the dimension to a particular set of circumstances, while the long form completely identifies the dimension with the noun it qualifies, cf.

(a) Эта ко́мната **больша́я**
     This room is big/a big one

(b) Эта ко́мната **велика́**
     This room is **too** big (i.e. for a particular purpose)

     Этот пиджа́к **широ́к**
     This jacket is too big (for a particular person)

     Пла́тье ей **мало́**
     The dress is too small for her

Compare Ю́бка **длинна́** 'The skirt is too long', Рукава́ **коротки́** 'The sleeves are too short', Дверь **низка́** 'The door is too low', Костю́м **свобо́ден** 'The suit is too loose-fitting', Сапоги́ **тесны́** 'The boots are too tight', Брю́ки **узки́** 'The trousers are too tight', Но́ша **тяжела́** для ребёнка 'The burden is too heavy for the child' (cf. Но́ша **тяжёлая** 'The burden is a heavy one').

Note
(a) The idea of excess may be reinforced by the adverb **сли́шком** 'too': Не **сли́шком** ли вы **мо́лоды** для нас? (Rubina) 'Don't you think you are too young for us?'
(b) The short form of adjectives of dimension can also be used *without* a relative nuance: **Широ́к** круг интере́сов у на́ших чита́телей (*Yunyi naturalist*) 'Our readers' range of interests **is broad**'.

170 Delimitation of meaning by the oblique case of a noun or pronoun

(1) When the meaning of a predicative adjective is 'delimited' by the oblique case of a noun or pronoun, the short form must be used. Compare

Какое имеет значение, **симпати́чен** он **ей** и́ли нет? (Koluntsev)
What does it matter if she likes him or not?

where the quality denoted by **симпати́чен** is valid only for *her* (**ей**), with

Он о́чень **симпати́чный**
He is very good-looking/attractive

where the *long* form denotes an inherent trait.

(2) The short form can be 'delimited' by any of the oblique cases.

(i) Genitive:

Авто́бус по́лон **наро́ду**
The bus is full **of people**

Note
Он по́лный means 'He is over-weight'.

(ii) Dative:

Я **вам** благода́рен
I am grateful **to you**

(iii) Instrumental:

Я дово́лен **ва́ми**
I am pleased **with you**

Э́тот край бога́т **не́фтью** и **пушни́ной** (*Sputnik*)
This territory is rich **in oil and furs**

171 Delimitation by a prepositional phrase

(1) The short form is also used when the quality expressed by the adjective is delimited by a **prepositional phrase**. Thus, while either long or short form may be used in

Ле́кция была́ **интере́сная/интере́сна**
The lecture was interesting

the short form *must* be used in

Лéкция былá интерéсна **по фóрме**
The lecture was interesting in form

since the adjective is 'delimited' by the phrase **по фóрме**. Compare:

Мы **безорýжны** перед мóщью совремéнной рàдиоап-
паратýры (*Izvestiya*)
We are powerless in the face of the might of modern radio tech-
nology

Рáньше онá былá **равнодýшна** к лы́жам (Koluntsev)
She used to be indifferent to skiing

(2)   Common prepositional phrases include **глух на** (лéвое ýхо)
'deaf in' (the left ear), **готóв к** 'ready for', **готóв на** + acc. 'ready for'
(in the meaning 'desperate'), **добр к** 'kind to', **знакóм с** + instr.
'familiar with', **похóж на** + acc. 'similar to', **сердúт на** + acc. 'angry
with', **силён в** (математике) 'good at' (mathematics), **склóнен к**
'inclined to', **слеп на** (прáвый глаз) 'blind in' (the right eye), **соглáсен на** (услóвия) 'agreeing to' (conditions), **соглáсен с** 'in agreement with', **спосóбен к** 'good at', **спосóбен на** (обмáн) 'capable of'
(deception), **характéрен для** 'characteristic of', **хром на** (прáвую
нóгу) 'lame in' (the right leg).

Note
Used predicatively, the long forms of some of these adjectives
denote inherent characteristics: Онá **дóбрая** 'She is kind', Он
сúльный 'He is strong', Он **спосóбный** 'He is a capable person'.

172   Delimitation by a subordinate clause or an infinitive

The short form predicative is also used when the adjective is delimited:

(1)   By a subordinate clause:

Я **счáстлив**, что вас встречáю
I am happy to meet you

(2)   By an infinitive, either:

(i) *with* чтобы

> Он достаточно **умён, чтобы понять**, где раскаяние, а где игра (Koluntsev)
> He is intelligent enough to understand where remorse ends and play-acting begins

or:

(ii) *without* чтобы

> — Ты не **способен понять**, чего мне стоило прийти сюда (Koluntsev)
> You are incapable of understanding what it has cost me to come here

173 The short form as predicate to infinitives, verbal nouns and nouns with certain qualifiers

The short form is also used as predicate to the following.

(1) Infinitives and verbal nouns:

> Пить/Употребление наркотиков **вредно**
> Drinking/Use of drugs is **harmful**

(2) Nouns qualified by **всякий/каждый** 'each, every', **какой?** 'what kind of?', **любой** 'any', **такой** 'such' etc.:

> Любой совет **полезен**
> Any advice is useful

> **Такого рода** комплименты **бессмысленны**
> Compliments of that kind are meaningless

174 The short form in generalized statements

The short form appears in many generalized sayings, proverbs etc.:

Жизнь **трудна**	Life is hard
Любовь **слепа**	Love is blind

175 Position of the short form of the adjective

The short form of the adjective normally follows the noun:

Все вели́кие и́стины **просты́**   All great truths are simple

but may, for greater emphasis or expressiveness, precede it (see **484** (1) (i)):

Изве́стна зави́симость доро́жных происше́ствий от во́зраста шофёра (*Sovetskaya Rossiya*)
The connection between road accidents and the age of the driver **is well known**

The Comparative Degree of the Adjective

176 The comparative degree. Introductory comments

Most English adjectives have either

   a comparative in -er (e.g. '*harder*')

or

   a comparative with 'more' (e.g. '*more comfortable*').

By contrast, most Russian adjectives have two comparatives, each with a specific function.

177 The attributive comparative with бо́лее

(1) The attributive form of almost all comparatives comprises бо́лее + long adjective, e.g. **бо́лее краси́вый** дом 'a more beautiful house'.

(2) **Бо́лее** is *invariable*, while the adjective agrees with the noun it qualifies:

(i) In gender and number:

   бо́лее краси́вый дом   a more beautiful house

бо́лее краси́вая	де́вушка	a more beautiful girl
бо́лее краси́вое	де́рево	a more beautiful tree
бо́лее краси́вые	де́ти	more beautiful children

(ii) In case:

Нет **бо́лее краси́вого са́да**
There is no more beautiful garden

Он подошёл к **бо́лее краси́вой де́вушке**
He went up to the more beautiful girl

(3) Comparatives with **бо́лее** may also be used predicatively:

Перви́чные па̀рторганиза́ции ста́ли **бо́лее кру́пными**
(*Pravda*)
The primary Party organizations have become larger

However, predicative forms in **-ee** or **-e** should be regarded as the norm (see **179–181**).

(4) **Ме́нее** 'less' is used to form a 'reverse' comparative:

Э́то **ме́нее краси́вый** дом   This is a less beautiful house

178 One-word attributive comparatives

Six adjectives have attributive comparatives consisting of one word:

хоро́ший 'good'	**лу́чший** 'better'
плохо́й 'bad'	**ху́дший** 'worse'
ста́рый 'old'	**ста́рший** 'older, senior'
молодо́й 'young'	**мла́дший** 'younger, junior'
большо́й 'big'	**бо́льший** 'bigger'
ма́ленький 'small'	**ме́ньший** 'smaller'

Note

(a) Ста́рший and мла́дший are used only with animate nouns and collectives, and usually imply seniority and juniority: **мла́дший/ ста́рший** сын 'younger/elder son', **мла́дший/ста́рший** класс 'junior/senior class', **мла́дший/ста́рший** лейтена́нт 'junior/ senior lieutenant' etc. The context may be amplified to resolve possible ambiguity: ста́рший **по во́зрасту/по служе́бному положе́нию** 'older **in years**/senior **in rank**', мла́дший **по** во́зрасту/по до́лжности 'younger **in years**/junior **in position**'. For inanimate nouns, **бо́лее ста́рый** is used:

На эстра́де стоя́ло ста́рое пиани́но и лежа́ла ещё **бо́лее ста́рая** шта́нга (Kuleshov)
On the stage were an old piano and an even older lifting weight

(b) **Мла́дший** and **ста́рший** can also mean 'youngest' and 'eldest', **лу́чший** and **ху́дший** 'best' and 'worst' (see **185** (3) notes (a) and (b)).

(c) Some forms of **большо́й** 'big' and **бо́льший** 'bigger' are distinguished only by stress: **больша́я** часть 'a large part', **бо́льшая** часть 'the greater part' etc.

179 Predicative comparative forms in -ee

(1) The predicative comparative of most adjectives is formed by adding the ending **-ee** to the stem of the adjective:

краси́в-ее	(is, are) more beautiful
удо́бн-ее	(is, are) more comfortable

(2) Comparatives in **-ee** are invariable, that is, they are used as predicates to nouns of any gender and either number:

сад **краси́вее**	the garden is more beautiful
карти́на **краси́вее**	the picture is more beautiful
де́рево **краси́вее**	the tree is more beautiful
цветы́ **краси́вее**	the flowers are more beautiful

(3) Adjectives which have end-stressed **-а́** in the feminine short form have end stress **-е́е** in the comparative (see **164** (2)):

нове́е	(is, are) newer
сложне́е	(is, are) more complex
тяжеле́е	(is, are) heavier

Note
Здорове́е, (is, are) 'healthier', despite feminine short form здоро́ва.

(4) An alternative comparative form in **-ей** is confined mainly to conversational styles, verse and the more casual prose styles:

Клу́бы де́лают жизнь свои́х чле́нов **поле́зней** (*Sputnik*)
The clubs make the lives of their members more useful

(5) The following types of adjective either have *no* comparative short forms or have forms which are very rarely used:

(i) Adjectives which denote concepts which cannot be manifested to a greater or lesser degree, e.g. **босо́й** 'barefoot', **бра́тский** 'fraternal', **деревя́нный** 'wooden'.

(ii) Adjectives of colour.

(iii) Some others, e.g. **вне́шний** 'external', **го́рдый** 'proud'.

(6) Some adjectives with no short-form comparative (e.g. **драмати́ческий** 'dramatic') have synonyms which *do* have short forms (**драмати́чнее** 'is, are more dramatic', from **драмати́чный**).

(7) If an adjective *does* have a short-form comparative, the use of its long form in predicative meaning is regarded as 'bookish' (Э́та кни́га **бо́лее поле́зная** 'The book is more useful' (**поле́знее** is the preferred form)) and may distinguish high style (Показа́тели **бо́лее высо́кие** 'Indices are higher') from neutral style (Дом **вы́ше** 'The house is taller'. See **180**(1)).

180 Comparative short forms in -e

(1) The final consonants of some adjectives undergo mutation in the comparative short form (note, however, that in some adjectives with suffix **-к-** it is the *preceding* consonant that mutates, e.g. гла́дкий: гла́же). The resultant comparatives end in a single unstressed **-е**:

| **в : вл** | дешёвый | cheap | деше́вле | (is, are) cheaper |

(However, но́вый 'new', comparative **нове́е** (is, are) 'newer'.)

г : ж	дорого́й	dear	доро́же	(is, are) dearer
	стро́гий	strict	стро́же	(is, are) stricter
	туго́й	tight	ту́же	(is, are) tighter

д : ж	гла́дкий	smooth	гла́же	(is, are) smoother
	молодо́й	young	моло́же	(is, are) younger
	ре́дкий	rare	ре́же	(is, are) rarer
	твёрдый	hard	твёрже	(is, are) harder

(However, худо́й 'thin', comparative **худе́е** 'is, are thinner'.)

Note

'Is, are younger' is also rendered as **мла́дше**, mainly in a family context: cf. Она́ **мла́дше/моло́же** сестры́ 'She is younger than her sister' and Она́ **моло́же** нача́льника 'She is younger than the boss'.

з : ж	бли́зкий	near	бли́же	(is, are) nearer
	ни́зкий	low	ни́же	(is, are) lower
	у́зкий	narrow	у́же	(is, are) narrower
к : ч	гро́мкий	loud	гро́мче	(is, are) louder
	жа́ркий	hot	жа́рче	(is, are) hotter
	кре́пкий	strong	кре́пче	(is, are) stronger
	лёгкий	light, easy	ле́гче	(is, are) lighter, easier
	ме́лкий	shallow	ме́льче	(is, are) shallower
	мя́гкий	soft	мя́гче	(is, are) softer
	ре́зкий	sharp	ре́зче	(is, are) sharper
с : ш	высо́кий	high	вы́ше	(is, are) higher
ск : щ	пло́ский	flat	пло́ще	(is, are) flatter
ст : щ	густо́й	thick	гу́ще	(is, are) thicker
	просто́й	simple	про́ще	(is, are) simpler
	то́лстый	thick	то́лще	(is, are) thicker
	ча́стый	frequent	ча́ще	(is, are) more frequent
	чи́стый	clean	чи́ще	(is, are) cleaner
т : ч	бога́тый	rich	бога́че	(is, are) richer
	коро́ткий	short	коро́че	(is, are) shorter
	круто́й	steep	кру́че	(is, are) steeper

(However, свято́й 'holy', comparative **святе́е** 'is, are holier'.)

х : ш	сухо́й	dry	су́ше	(is, are) drier
	ти́хий	quiet	ти́ше	(is, are) quieter

Note

(a) Though го́рький 'bitter' has the short-form comparative **го́рче**, **бо́лее го́рький** (is, are) 'more bitter' is normally used in both attributive and predicative meanings.

(b) Adjectives which have no short-form comparative or a little-used comparative also form the predicate with **бо́лее** : **ве́тхий** 'ancient', **го́рдый** 'proud', **зы́бкий** 'shaky', **ли́пкий** 'sticky', **ста́рый** 'old' (of objects) etc.

(2) Irregular short forms include a number which end in **-ше**:

большо́й	big	бо́льше	(is, are) bigger
до́лгий	long	до́льше	(is, are) longer
ма́ленький	small	ме́ньше	(is, are) smaller
ста́рый	old	ста́рше	(is, are) older
то́нкий	thin	то́ньше	(is, are) thinner
хоро́ший	good	лу́чше	(is, are) better

Объём това́рного хле́ба был на 40% **бо́льше**
The volume of marketable grain was 40 per cent greater

Note
Да́льше 'further' and **ра́ньше** 'earlier' are used only as adverbs.

(3) Other irregular short forms end in -**же**, -**ще**, -**е** :

глубо́кий	deep	глу́бже	(is, are) deeper
плохо́й	bad	ху́же	(is, are) worse
по́здний	late	по́зже	(is, are) later (also **поздне́е**)
сла́дкий	sweet	сла́ще	(is, are) sweeter
широ́кий	wide	ши́ре	(is, are) wider

Note
Unlike **поздне́е**, **по́зже** (here used as an adverb) also has an absolute meaning : Опера́цию ребя́та провели́ то́чно — ска́жет **по́зже** гла́вный гео́лог (*Komsomolskaya pravda*) '"The lads carried out the operation precisely", the chief geologist was to say later' (i.e. afterwards).

181 The short-form comparative in predicative meaning

The short-form comparative's main function is predicative :

Его́ го́лос **гро́мче**
His voice is **louder**

Моя́ маши́на была́ **нове́е**
My car **was newer**

Её воспомина́ния бу́дут **интере́снее**
Her reminiscences **will be more interesting**

Живы́е цветы́ ста́ли ещё **свеже́е**
The live flowers **became fresher still**

182 Constructions with the comparative

(1) Than

'Than' is rendered in one of the following ways:

(i) By **чем**, preceded by a comma. Both items for comparison must be in the same case :

Я вы́ше, **чем** он
I am taller than he is

У меня́ бо́лее све́тлые глаза́, **чем** у вас
I have lighter eyes than you do

or:

(ii) By the genitive of comparison. This construction is possible only when the first item for comparison is in the *nominative* case:

Я вы́ше **его́**
I am taller than he is

Я ста́рше **свое́й** сестры́
I am older than my sister

Note
Only the **чем** construction is possible with attributive adjectives:

Это бо́лее краси́вый дом, **чем** наш
This is a more attractive house than ours

and when the second item for comparison has the form of a third-person possessive pronoun (его́, её, их)

Мой дом краси́вее, **чем** его́
My house is more beautiful than his

(2) Quantification of a difference

A difference is quantified in one of the following ways:

(i) By the preposition **на** + accusative case :

Он ста́рше меня́ **на три го́да**
He is three years older than me

(ii) (Less usually) with an instrumental :

Он тремя́ года́ми ста́рше меня́
He is three years older than me

(3) Expression of comparison through a multiple

Comparison may also be expressed through a multiple (constructions with **в** + accusative):

Он в два ра́за (вдво́е) ста́рше меня́
He is twice as old as I am

(4) The 'gradational' comparative

Constructions of the type 'the bigger the better' are rendered by **чем . . ., тем**:

Чем бо́льше, **тем** лу́чше
The bigger the better

Note
Тем лу́чше 'So much the better'.

(5) The expression of 'much' + comparative

'Much' in combination with a comparative is expressed by **намно́го, гора́здо, куда́** or **мно́го**:

Его́ рабо́та **намно́го** лу́чше/**гора́здо** лу́чше, чем моя́
His work is much better than mine

(6) As . . . as possible

'As . . . as possible' is rendered by **как мо́жно** + comparative:

Купи́ буты́лку **как мо́жно бо́лее дешёвого** вина́
Buy a bottle of the cheapest wine you can get

Note
This construction, however, is commoner with *adverbs* than with adjectives, in combination with which it can sound somewhat stilted (cf. also use of the *short* form in: Купи́ вина́ **подеше́вле** 'Buy some cheaper wine'. See **183** (2).

(7) Repeated comparatives (e.g. 'smaller and smaller')

Repeated comparatives normally combine with **всё**:

Всё бли́же и бли́же роково́й моме́нт (Makarov)
The fateful moment gets nearer and nearer

Note

Unlike English, Russian may omit the second comparative: всё бли́же 'nearer and nearer'. However, the repetition of the comparative lends greater expressiveness. Cf. **всё бо́льшее** (и бо́льшее) призна́ние 'greater and greater recognition'.

183 The short-form comparative in attributive meaning

(1) In colloquial registers the short-form comparative is sometimes used attributively:

У тебя́ нет челове́ка **бли́же** (Aksenov)
There is no person closer to you

(2) This is particularly common with short forms prefixed **по-**:

Покажи́те пла́тье **подеше́вле**
Show me a slightly cheaper dress

184 Other functions of the short-form comparative

(1) Short-form comparatives can function as introductory words:

Интере́снее говори́ть, чем слу́шать
It is more interesting to speak than to listen

(2) Many short-form comparatives also function as adverbs (see **398**):

Он е́дет **быстре́е**   He is driving faster
Она́ рабо́тает **бо́льше**   She works harder

Вожа́к всё **ни́же и ни́же** опуска́л го́лову к земле́ (Astafev)
The leader of the herd hung his head lower and lower to the ground

Note

In such cases the distinction between comparative adjective and comparative adverb is syntactic only, cf.: Эта книга **интереснее**, чем та 'This book is **more interesting** (adjective) than that one' and Эта книга написана **интереснее**, чем та 'This book is written **in a more interesting way** (adverb) than that one'.

(3) Short-form comparatives are also used impersonally: **ветренее** 'it is windier', **прохладнее** 'it is cooler', **светлее** 'it is lighter', **темнее** 'it is darker', **теплее** 'it is warmer', **холоднее** 'it is colder'.

Note

Adverbs of the type **более внимательно** 'more attentively' (for standard внимательнее) are rarely used.

The Superlative Degree of the Adjective

185 The superlative degree with са́мый

(1) The superlative degree is formed by combining **са́мый** with the positive adjective:

са́мый	краси́вый дом	the most beautiful house
са́мая	краси́вая маши́на	the most beautiful car
са́мое	краси́вое зда́ние	the most beautiful building
са́мые	краси́вые де́ти	the most beautiful children

(2) **Са́мый** agrees with the adjective and noun in gender, number and case:

Он провёл пять лет в одно́м из **са́мых краси́вых европе́йских** городо́в
He spent five years in one of the most beautiful European cities

Она́ живёт в **са́мом большо́м** до́ме на на́шей у́лице
She lives in the largest house in our street

(3) **Са́мый** also combines with the comparatives лу́чший and ху́дший:

са́мые лу́чшие пожела́ния
the very best wishes

са́мое ху́дшее, что мо́жно себе́ предста́вить
the worst thing one can imagine

Note

(a) **Лу́чший** and **ху́дший** (see **178** note (b)) also function as superlatives in their own right: **лу́чшая** из же́нщин 'the best of women'; в **ху́дшем** слу́чае 'in the worst case, if the worst comes to the worst'.

(b) **Ста́рший** and **мла́дший** may also function as comparatives or superlatives: **ста́рший** брат 'elder/eldest brother', **мла́дшая** сестра́ 'younger/youngest sister'. Outside the family or other hierarchy, however, 'youngest' and 'oldest' are rendered as **са́мый ста́рый, са́мый молодо́й**:

Ма́слов — кста́ти, **са́мый молодо́й** из полковы́х нача́льников (Bogomolov)
Maslov, incidentally, is the youngest of the regimental commanders (cf. са́мый **мла́дший** 'the most **junior**')

(c) The phrases **са́мое бо́льшее** 'at most', **са́мое ме́ньшее** 'at the very least': **са́мое бо́льшее** 30 челове́к '30 people at most'.

(4) Superlatives with **са́мый** may also express an extreme manifestation of the quality denoted by the adjective:

Са́мые широ́кие круги́ учёных
The very widest circles of scientists

186 Вы́сший and ни́зший

Вы́сший and **ни́зший** are used mainly in technical and set expressions: **вы́сший/ни́зший балл** 'top/bottom mark', **вы́сший/ни́зший сорт** 'superior/inferior brand', **вы́сшая матема́тика** 'higher mathematics', **вы́сшее уче́бное заведе́ние** 'higher teaching establishment', в **вы́сшей сте́пени** 'to the highest degree'.

Note

'Highest' and 'lowest' in the literal sense are rendered as **са́мый высо́кий/ни́зкий**: **са́мый высо́кий/ни́зкий** потоло́к 'the highest/lowest ceiling'.

187 The superlative in -ейший and -айший

(1) Superlatives in **-ейший** are formed from a limited range of adjectives, mainly with monosyllabic roots: **важнейший** 'most important', **крупнейший** 'largest, very large', **малейший** 'slightest', **новейший** 'latest, most recent', **сильнейший** 'strongest', **сложнейший** 'most complex':

Нет ни малейшего сомнения
There is not the slightest doubt

Новейшие достижения науки
The latest achievements of science

Чистейший вздор
The most arrant nonsense

(2) However, a number of superlatives derive from roots of more than one syllable: **выгоднейший** 'most favourable', **интереснейший** 'most interesting' etc.

(3) The ending **-айший** is affixed to stems ending in a guttural, following mutation of **г** to **ж** (**строжайший** from строгий 'strict', **дражайший** from дорогой 'dear'), **к** to **ч** (**высочайший** from высокий 'high', **кратчайший** from краткий 'short', **легчайший** from лёгкий 'light', **мельчайший** from мелкий 'small', **редчайший** from редкий 'rare') and **х** to **ш** (**тишайший** from тихий 'quiet'). Note also **ближайший** 'nearest' from близкий 'near'.

(4) Most superlatives in **-ейший** and **-айший** express an extreme manifestation of the quality denoted by the adjective:

Вернейшее средство
A **most reliable** remedy

С помощью лазеров проводятся **тончайшие** операции (*Russia Today*)
The **most delicate** of operations are carried out with the help of lasers

(5) However, forms in **-ейший** and **-айший** may also be true superlatives:

Ближайшая остановка
The nearest stop

Велича́йший поэ́т
The greatest poet (or 'A very great poet')

Кратча́йшее расстоя́ние
The shortest distance

Note
Дальне́йший 'further' has comparative, not superlative, meaning.

(6) Forms in **-ейший/-айший** are often characteristic of high style:
cf. **глубоча́йшие** мы́сли 'the most profound thoughts' and **са́мые
глубо́кие** сква́жины 'the deepest bore-holes' (neutral style).

188 The superlative with наибо́лее

The superlative with **наибо́лее** is characteristic of a 'bookish' style.
Наибо́лее is indeclinable and combines mainly with adjectives with
roots of more than one syllable (**наибо́лее вероя́тный** исхо́д 'the
most likely outcome', **наибо́лее влия́тельный** челове́к 'the most
influential person', **наибо́лее жела́тельный** результа́т 'the most
desirable result') and with a number of adjectives with monosyllabic
roots (**наибо́лее то́чный** 'the most accurate' etc.).
    Note also **наиме́нее** 'the least': **наиме́нее то́чный** ме́тод 'the
least accurate method'.

189 Other superlatives

(1) Other superlatives include **наибо́льший** 'the greatest',
наивы́сший 'the highest', **наилу́чший** 'the very best', **наиме́ньший**
'the smallest'. These forms are characteristic of newspaper style:
наибо́льшая вы́года 'the greatest benefit', **наилу́чшее** реше́ние
'the best solution', **наиме́ньший** риск 'the smallest risk'.

(2) The prefix пре- is used to form colloquial superlatives of the
type **преспоко́йный** 'as cool as a cucumber'.

The Numeral

Cardinal, Collective and Indefinite Numerals

190 The cardinal numeral

The cardinal numerals are as follows:

0	ноль/нуль		
1	оди́н, одна́, одно́; одни́	50	пятьдеся́т
2	два/две	60	шестьдеся́т
3	три	70	се́мьдесят
4	четы́ре	80	во́семьдесят
5	пять	90	девяно́сто
6	шесть	100	сто
7	семь	200	две́сти
8	во́семь	300	три́ста
9	де́вять	400	четы́реста
10	де́сять	500	пятьсо́т
11	оди́ннадцать	600	шестьсо́т
12	двена́дцать	700	семьсо́т
13	трина́дцать	800	восемьсо́т
14	четы́рнадцать	900	девятьсо́т
15	пятна́дцать	1,000	ты́сяча
16	шестна́дцать	2,000	две ты́сячи
17	семна́дцать	5,000	пять ты́сяч

18 восемнáдцать	1,000,000 миллиóн
19 девятнáдцать	2,000,000 два миллиóна
20 двáдцать	5,000,000 пять миллиóнов
30 трúдцать	1,000,000,000 миллиáрд/биллиóн
40 сóрок	1,000,000,000,000 триллиóн

Note

(a) Each of the numerals 5–20 and 30 ends in a soft sign. The construction of the numerals 11–19 is based on the model **одúн-на-дцать** 'eleven' (lit. one-on-ten) etc., that of 20 and 30 on the model **двá-дцать** and **трú-дцать** (lit. two tens and three tens), **-дцать** being a contraction of **дéсять** 'ten'. Of the numerals 11–19, only **одúннадцать** 'eleven' and **четы́рнадцать** 'fourteen' are *not* stressed on the penultimate **a**.

(b) **Пятьдеся́т** and **шестьдеся́т** have end stress, **сéмьдесят** and **вóсемьдесят** initial stress. All four numerals have a soft sign in the middle, but not at the end.

(c) 300–900 subdivide formally into **трúста** 'three hundred', **четы́реста** 'four hundred' (**три, четы́ре** + gen. sing. of **сто**) and **пятьсóт** 'five hundred' through to **девятьсóт** 'nine hundred' (**пять** etc. + gen. pl. of **сто**). The form **двéсти** 'two hundred' is a residue of the dual number.

(d) Compound numerals are formed by placing simple numerals in sequence: **двáдцать четы́ре** 'twenty-four', **шестьсóт пятьдеся́т два** 'six hundred and fifty-two', **сóрок четы́ре ты́сячи семьсóт девянóсто одúн** 'forty-four thousand seven hundred and ninety-one' etc.

(e) The inversion of numeral and dependent noun indicates approximation: **лет пять** 'about five years'. Prepositions are placed between inverted noun and numeral: **лет через пять** 'in about five years' time'.

191 Declension of cardinal numerals

The cardinal numerals decline as follows.

(1) Ноль/нуль 'nought, zero, nil'

Ноль/нуль declines like a masculine soft-sign noun with end stress in declension (see **57** (2) (ii)).

(2) Один/одна́/одно́/одни́ 'one'

Один/одна́/одно́/одни́ decline like э́тот but with stressed endings, cf. **125**:

	Masculine	Feminine	Neuter	Plural
Nom.	оди́н	одн-**а́**	одн-**о́**	одн-**и́**
Acc.	оди́н/одн-**ого́**	одн-**у́**	одн-**о́**	одн-**и́**/одн-**и́х**
Gen.	одн-**ого́**	одн-**о́й**	одн-**ого́**	одн-**и́х**
Dat.	одн-**ому́**	одн-**о́й**	одн-**ому́**	одн-**и́м**
Instr.	одн-**и́м**	одн-**о́й**/-**о́ю**	одн-**и́м**	одн-**и́ми**
Prep.	об одн-**о́м**	об одн-**о́й**	об одн-**о́м**	об одн-**и́х**

(3) Полтора́ (m. and n.)/полторы́ (f.) 'one and a half'

There is only one oblique case form: **полу́тора**, the genitive, dative, instrumental and prepositional of полтора́ *and* полторы́.

(4) Два (m. and n.)/две (f.) 'two', три 'three', четы́ре 'four'

Nom.	дв-**а**/дв-**е**	тр-**и**	четы́р-**е**
Acc.	дв-**а**, дв-**е**/дв-**ух**	тр-**и**/тр-**ёх**	четы́р-**е**/четы́р-**ёх**
Gen.	дв-**ух**	тр-**ёх**	четыр-**ёх**
Dat.	дв-**ум**	тр-**ём**	четыр-**ём**
Instr.	дв-**умя́**	тр-**емя́**	четырь-**мя́**
Prep.	о дв-**ух**	о тр-**ёх**	о четыр-**ёх**

(5) О́ба (m. and n.)/о́бе (f.) 'both'

Nom.	о́б-**а**	о́б-**е**
Acc.	о́б-**а**/обо́-**их**	о́б-**е**/обе́-**их**
Gen.	обо́-**их**	обе́-**их**
Dat.	обо́-**им**	обе́-**им**
Instr.	обо́-**ими**	обе́-**ими**
Prep.	об обо́-**их**	об обе́-**их**

Note the phrase де́ти **обо́его** по́ла 'children of both sexes'.

(6) Пять 'five' (declension of numerals ending in a soft sign)

Nom./Acc.	пять	шесть	семь
Gen./Dat.	пят-**и́**	шест-**и́**	сем-**и́**

Instr.	пять-**ю**	шесть-**ю**	семь-**ю**
Prep.	о пят-**и**	о шест-**и**	о сем-**и**

Nom./Acc.	в**о́**семь	два́дцать
Gen./Dat.	восьм-**и́**	двадцат-**и́**
Instr.	восьм-**ю́**/восемь-**ю́**	двадцать-**ю́**
Prep.	о восьм-**и́**	о двадцат-**и́**

Note

(a) 5–20 and 30 decline like soft-sign feminine nouns, 5–10, 20 and 30 with end stress in declension, 11–19 with medial stress in declension.

(b) Instrumental восьмью́ is characteristic of colloquial styles, восемью́ of written styles.

(7) 50–80

Each of the numerals 50–80 declines like *two* feminine soft-sign nouns. The stress in oblique cases falls on the second syllable:

Nom./Acc.	пятьдес**я́**т	шестьдес**я́**т
Gen./Dat.	пят**и́**десят-**и**	шест**и́**десят-**и**
Instr.	пять**ю́**десять-**ю**	шесть**ю́**десять-**ю**
Prep.	о пят**и́**десят-**и**	о шест**и́**десят-**и**

Nom./Acc.	с**е́**мьдесят	в**о́**семьдесят
Gen./Dat.	сем**и́**десят-**и**	восьм**и́**десят-**и**
Instr.	семь**ю́**десять-**ю**	восьмь**ю́**десять-**ю**
Prep.	о сем**и́**десят-**и**	о восьм**и́**десят-**и**

(8) С**о́**рок 'forty', девян**о́**сто 'ninety', сто 'hundred'

Each of these numerals has one oblique case ending only: -**а**.

Nom./Acc.	с**о́**рок	девян**о́**ст-**о**	ст-**о**
Gen./Dat./Instr.	сорок-**а́**	девян**о́**ст-**а**	ст-**а**
Prep.	о сорок-**а́**	о девян**о́**ст-**а**	о ст-**а**

(9) 200–900

Nom.	дв**е́**ст-**и**	тр**и́**ст-**а**	пятьс**о́**т
Acc.	дв**е́**ст-**и**	тр**и́**ст-**а**	пятьс**о́**т
Gen.	двухс**о́**т	трёхс**о́**т	пятис**о́**т

Dat.	двумст-а́м	трёмст-а́м	пятист-а́м
Instr.	двумяст-а́ми	тремяст-а́ми	пятьюст-а́ми
Prep.	о двухст-а́х	о трёхст-ах	о пятист-а́х

(10) Ты́сяча 'thousand', миллио́н 'million', миллиа́рд 'thousand million', биллио́н 'billion', триллио́н 'trillion'.

Ты́сяча 'thousand' declines like second-declension да́ча 'country cottage', миллио́н, миллиа́рд, биллио́н and триллио́н like hard-ending masculine nouns of the first declension. However, ты́сяча has two forms of the instrumental: ты́сячью and ты́сячей (see 197 note (a)). The numerals also appear in multiples: две ты́сячи 'two thousand', пять ты́сяч 'five thousand', две́сти пятьдеся́т одна́ ты́сяча '251,000', четы́ре миллио́на 'four million', шестьдеся́т миллио́нов 'sixty million', два́дцать два миллиа́рда 'twenty-two thousand million' and so on.

For declension of compound numerals see **198**.

192 Ноль/нуль. Meanings and usage

(1) **Ноль/нуль** 'nought, zero, nil' governs the genitive case of singular and plural nouns.

(2) The two forms are often stylistically and phraseologically differentiated. Thus:

(i) **Нуль** tends to be used in mathematics, in technical terminology and in indicating temperature:

нуль гра́дусов Це́льсия	zero degrees Celsius
ни́же нуля́	below zero

(ii) **Ноль** is used:

(a) In colloquial contexts:

Игра́ ко́нчилась со счётом 5:0 (пять:**ноль**)
The game ended 5:0

Её телефо́н: 231–00–45 (две́сти три́дцать оди́н **ноль ноль** со́рок пять)
Her telephone number is 231 00 45

(Also, in colloquial contexts, ноль **гра́дусов** 'zero degrees'.)

(b) In decimals (see **205** (1)).

(c) In giving precise indications of the time:

ше́сть **ноль-ноль**
six hundred hours (six o'clock precisely)

(iii) Either numeral may be used to indicate the figure 0, though **нуль** is preferred in technical registers.

(iv) **Нуль** is used in the phrases начина́ть с **нуля́** 'to start from scratch' and своди́ться к **нулю́** 'to come to nothing', **ноль** in **ноль внима́ния** 'no attention whatsoever'. Either is possible in стри́жка под **ноль/нуль** 'a close haircut'.

193 The numeral оди́н, одна́, одно́, одни́

(1) The numeral 1 agrees with the noun in gender, number and case:

оди́н сто́л 'one table'	**одно́** окно́ 'one window'
одна́ ка́рта 'one map'	**одни́** часы́ 'one clock'

Он по́днял шта́нгу **одно́й** руко́й
He lifted the weight with one hand

Note

(a) The numeral is omitted in some time expressions: ча́с дня 'one o'clock in the afternoon'.

(b) In counting, **ра́з** usually replaces **оди́н**: Ра́з … два́ … три́ … 'One … two … three …'.

(c) The animate accusative/genitive rule applies: Ви́жу **одного́** ма́льчика 'I see one boy'.

(2) The agreement of compound numerals ending in **оди́н, одна́, одно́** is as follows:

(i) They take a singular noun: со́рок оди́н **сту́л** 'forty-one **chairs**', cf.:

Бы́л де́нь её рожде́ния, и я принёс **два́дцать одну́ свечу́** (Gagarin)
It was her birthday and I brought twenty-one candles

(ii) They take a singular predicate:

В э́том году́ **был заде́ржан во́семьдесят оди́н наруши́тель**
пра́вил пожа́рной безопа́сности в лесу́ (*Russia Today*)
This year eighty-one people have been arrested for breaches of
forest fire safety precautions

В про́шлом году́ **поги́б 271 челове́к** (*Nedelya*)
271 people died last year

21 депута́т **голосова́л** за предложе́ние
21 delegates voted for the proposal

(iii) Long adjectives and participles also appear in the singular:

Всего́ у Чо́сера два́дцать **оди́н расска́з, изло́женный**
просты́м языко́м (*Propp*)
Chaucer has twenty-one tales in all, told in simple language

(iv) However, *relative pronouns* normally appear in the plural:

Два́дцать оди́н ма́льчик, **кото́рые** бежа́ли по у́лице
Twenty-one boys who were running down the street

(3) The plural form **одни́** is used with plural-only nouns (see **49**):
одни́ са́нки 'one sledge', **одни́** носи́лки 'one stretcher' (also
два́дцать одни́ са́нки, носи́лки 'twenty-one sledges, stretchers').

Note
Compare also the colloquial **одни́** сли́вки 'one cream' (= one
portion, packet of cream), heard in shops and buffets.

(4) Other meanings of **оди́н, одна́, одно́, одни́** include:

(i) 'Alone, by oneself': Она́ **одна́** 'She is all by herself', Ему́ ску́чно
одному́ 'He is bored by himself'.

Note
Compare the use of the nominative in Я был **оди́н** 'I was alone' and
the use of the instrumental in Я был **одни́м** из его́ друзе́й 'I was
one of his friends'.

(ii) 'Only, nothing but': Я **оди́н** (**одна́**) зна́ю 'Only I know/I alone
know':

— Наве́рное, о́стров. Тут **одни́** острова́ (*Gagarin*)
'It's probably an island. There are nothing but islands here'

(iii) 'A', 'a certain', 'some': У меня́ есть оди́н знако́мый, кото́рый роди́лся в СССР 'I have a friend who was born in the USSR', **Одни́** мои́ знако́мые неда́вно перее́хали в другой го́род 'Some of my friends recently moved to another town'.

(iv) 'The same': Мы учи́лись в **одно́й** шко́ле 'We went to the same school'.

(v) **Одни́** ... **други́е** ... **тре́тьи** render 'some ... others ... others still': **Одни́** молча́т, **други́е** красне́ют, **тре́тьи** возмуща́ются 'Some are silent, others blush, others still get indignant'.

Note

In some cases, potential ambiguity can be resolved only by context: Здесь растёт **одна́** ель 'One fir-tree grows here' or 'Only fir-trees grow here'.

See also **143** (2).

---

194   Полтора́/полторы́; два/две, три, четы́ре; о́ба/о́бе

The numerals **полтора́/полторы́; два/две, три, четы́ре; о́ба/о́бе** take the genitive singular of the noun, when the numerals themselves are in the nominative or inanimate accusative (for usage after *declined* forms of these numerals, see **196**).

(1) **Полтора́** (m. and n.)/**полторы́** (f.) 'one and a half':

полтора́ **часа́**   an hour and a half
полторы́ **мину́ты**   a minute and a half

(i) Other numerals which include a half are expressed as follows: два **с полови́ной** часа́ 'two and a half hours', пять **с полови́ной** часо́в 'five and a half hours' etc.

(ii) Полтора́- also appears in the compound numeral **полтора́ста** '150' (oblique case полу́тораста).

(2) **Два** (m. and n.)/**две** (f.) 'two', **три** 'three', **четы́ре** 'four' (nom. and inan. acc.):

два **ма́льчика**	'two boys'	три **сту́ла**	'three chairs'
два **окна́**	'two windows'	четы́ре **стра́ны**'four countries'
две **го́ры**	'two mountains'		

(i) **Ряд** 'row', **час** 'hour', **шаг** 'step', **шар** 'sphere, globe' have *end* stress in the genitive singular after два, три, четы́ре: два **часа́** 'two o'clock', два **шара́** 'two globes', три **ряда́** 'three rows', четы́ре **шага́** 'four steps' (cf. *stem* stress with other forms: о́коло **ча́са** 'about an hour').

(ii) The accusative plural of the noun is used as an alternative to the genitive singular in certain set expressions: отпусти́ть на все четы́ре **стороны́/сто́роны** 'to give complete freedom of movement'.

(iii) Nouns governed by the numerals **два/две, три, четы́ре** appear in the genitive *plural* if the noun *precedes* the numeral and is linked to it by a form of the verb 'to be' or other copula: **Стака́нов** бы́ло то́лько два (Rasputin) 'There were only two glasses'. Compare use with 1: **Больни́ц** в го́роде **две**, а **шко́л** то́лько **одна́** 'There are two hospitals in the town, and only one school'.

(iv) Compound numerals ending in **два/две, три, четы́ре** also take the genitive singular of the noun when the numerals themselves are in the nominative or inanimate accusative case:

со́рок два **рубля́**	forty-two roubles
пятьдеся́т две **копе́йки**	fifty-two kopecks
сто три **окна́**	one hundred and three windows
девяно́сто четы́ре **челове́ка**	ninety-four people

(v) **Два/две, три, четы́ре** take the *genitive plural* of an adjective qualifying a masculine or neuter noun and the *nominative* plural of an adjective qualifying a feminine noun:

два **больши́х** стака́на/окна́	two large glasses/windows
три **бе́дные** де́вушки	three poor girls

Note

(a) A *genitive* plural adjective is preferred with a feminine noun after 2–4 when there is a stress difference between the genitive singular and nominative plural of the noun (три **высо́ких** горы́ 'three high mountains' (cf. nom. pl. **го́ры**)), when a distributive phrase is governed by the preposition **по** (по три **спе́лых** гру́ши 'three ripe pears each') and in fractions and decimals (see **205** (1)).

(b) Pre-positive adjectives appear in the *nominative* plural: **ка́ждые** три мину́ты 'every three minutes', **после́дние** два дня 'the last two days'. See, however, **157** (3).

(c) Adjectival nouns behave like adjectives after 2–4: два **учёных** 'two scientists', три **гости́ные** 'three living-rooms', четы́ре **живо́тных** 'four animals'. See **158**.

(3) **О́ба** (m. and n.)/**о́бе** (f.) 'both':

(i) **о́ба/о́бе** behave like **два/две** 'two', taking a genitive singular noun and a plural adjective:

о́ба **кру́глых стола́/окна́**	both round tables/windows
о́бе **кру́глые таре́лки**	both round plates

(ii) **о́ба** may also denote a male–female pair: И ста́ли они́ **о́ба** смотре́ть друг на дру́га ... Не вы́держала она́ его́ взгля́да (Shcherbakov) 'And they both began looking at each other, ... she could not withstand his gaze'.

Note

(a) Accusative plural сто́роны is possible as an alternative to genitive singular стороны́ in the phrase в о́бе стороны́/сто́роны: переводи́ть в о́бе стороны́/сто́роны 'to translate both ways'.

(b) Два **ряда́** 'two rows' but о́ба **ря́да** 'both rows'.

195 Numerals five and above

The nominative and accusative of the numerals 5–999 take the *genitive plural* of the adjective and noun:

пять **рубле́й**	five roubles
во́семь **часо́в**	eight o'clock, eight hours
пятна́дцать **мину́т**	fifteen minutes
два́дцать **ва́жных пи́сем**	twenty important letters
со́рок пять **дней**	forty-five days
се́мьдесят **школ**	seventy schools
сто семь **грамм/гра́ммов**	one hundred and seven grams
три́ста **просто́рных ко́мнат**	three hundred spacious rooms

Note

(a) See **193** (2) (i) and **194** (2) (iv) for usage after compound numerals ending in 1–4.

(b) 5–999 take the genitive plural **человéк**, not людéй: семь **человéк** 'seven people' (if the noun is qualified by an adjective, however, **людéй** is preferred: пять незнакóмых **людéй** (or **лиц** or **человéк**) 'five unknown people'). Cf. also dat. пятú **человéкам** 'to five people', instr. с пятью́ **человéками** 'with five people', etc.

196 Agreement of oblique cases of numerals полторá/ полторы́ to 999 with oblique plural forms of nouns

(1) Declined numerals from $1\frac{1}{2}$ to 999 combine with nouns and adjectives in the same case of the *plural*:

(i) Genitive

óколо **полу́тора часóв**	about an hour and a half
бóльше **трёх дней**	more than three days

(ii) Dative

Онá у́чит **трём языкáм**
She teaches three languages

Он обратúлся к **четырёмстáм нóвым избирáтелям**
He addressed four hundred new voters

(iii) Instrumental

Кудá онá моглá дéться с **четырьмя́ детьмú**? (Rybakov)
Where could she have got to with four children?

Он обещáл огранúчиться **десятью́ сигарéтами** в день (Avdeenko)
He promised to confine himself to ten cigarettes a day

(iv) Prepositional

В **двух шагáх** от кáмня стоя́л человéк (Gagarin)
At two paces from the stone stood a man

в **пяти́десяти ю́жных** города́х
in fifty southern towns

(2) The **animate accusative/genitive rule** (see **47**) applies to the numerals 2–4 and to 'both', the numeral appearing in the genitive (**двух, трёх, четырёх; обо́их/обе́их**), adjectives and nouns in the genitive *plural*:

> Она́ приняла́ на ку́рсы **трёх молоды́х студе́нтов**
> She accepted three young students on to the course

> Она́ пригласи́ла **четырёх медсестёр**
> She invited four nurses

> Она́ лю́бит **обо́их бра́тьев** и **обе́их сестёр**
> She loves both her brothers and both her sisters

Note
(a) The animate accusative/genitive rule does *not* apply to *compound* numerals ending in **два/две, три** or **четы́ре**: Она́ приняла́ на ку́рсы **два́дцать три студе́нта** 'She accepted twenty-three students on to the course'.
(b) Application of the animate accusative/genitive rule varies where animals, birds, quasi-animates etc. are concerned: Он пойма́л **двух пти́чек** (or **две пти́чки**) 'He caught two small birds', Он принёс **двух ку́кол** (or **две ку́клы**) 'He brought two dolls' (cf. alternative accusative forms of существо́ 'being': **двух суще́ств** or **два существа́**).
(c) The animate accusative/genitive rule does *not* apply to the numerals 5–999: я встре́тил **пять/со́рок/сто** моряко́в 'I met five/forty/a hundred sailors'.

197 Ты́сяча 'thousand', миллио́н 'million', миллиа́рд 'a thousand million', биллио́н 'billion', триллио́н 'trillion'

Ты́сяча (pronounced ты́ща in colloquial speech), **миллио́н** and **миллиа́рд** etc. take the *genitive plural* of the noun, regardless of their own case (see, however, note (a) below):

> ты́сяча **рубле́й**
> a thousand roubles

с **тремя́ ты́сячами рубле́й**
with three thousand roubles

забо́титься о **миллио́нах дете́й**
to care for millions of children

Ассигнова́ния равня́ются **семи́ миллиа́рдам до́лларов**
Subsidies amount to seven thousand million dollars

Note

(a) In its capacity as a noun of quantity, **ты́сяча** has instrumental **ты́сячей** + genitive plural (с ты́сячей **друзе́й** 'with a thousand friends'), while in its capacity as a numeral it has instrumental **ты́сячью** + instrumental plural: **с ты́сячью рабо́чими** 'with a thousand workers'. **Ты́сячей** is regarded as the more literary form, **ты́сячью** as the more colloquial. While **ты́сячей** is the preferred instrumental in its function as a noun of quantity, **ты́сячью** is making inroads in this area also. In combination with одно́й, however, **ты́сячей** is always used: с одно́й **ты́сячей** солда́т 'with one thousand soldiers'.

(b) Ты́сяча, миллио́н, миллиа́рд take genitive plural **челове́к**: ты́сяча **челове́к** 'a thousand people'. However, **люде́й** is preferred when qualified by an adjective (ты́сяча **че́стных** люде́й 'a thousand honest people') and with **ты́сячи** 'thousands' (ты́сячи люде́й 'thousands of people') (emphasizing mass rather than precise quantity).

(c) **Ты́сяча** may be written in figures as '1.000', '1000', or '1 000' (commas are reserved for decimals, see **205** (1)).

(d) **Ты́сяча** observes feminine singular agreement: Пятьдеся́т одна́ ты́сяча из них **больна́** наркома́нией (*Izvestiya*) 'Fifty-one thousand of them are addicted to drugs'.

198 Declension of compound numerals

(1) In **written** Russian, all parts of a compound numeral are declined, the noun agreeing with the final element of the compound:

К тремста́м тридцати́ шести́ часа́м приба́вить ещё сто шестьдеся́т четы́ре (Koluntsev)
Add another one hundred and sixty-four hours **to three hundred and thirty-six**

довольствоваться **двадцатью одним рублём**
to make do with **twenty-one roubles**

(2) In colloquial speech, however, it is common to decline either:

(i) the **final elements** of the numeral only:

представители **пятьдесят одной** страны
representatives of **fifty-one countries** (cf. written norm
пятидесяти одной страны)

с четыреста **пятью́десятью двумя́ рубля́ми**
with four hundred and fifty-two roubles (cf. written norm с
четырьмя́ста́ми . . .)

с шестьсот семьдесят **семью́ иллюстра́циями**
with six hundred and seventy-seven illustrations (cf. written
norm с шестьюста́ми семью́десятью . . .)

or:

(ii) the **first and final** elements only:

с **пятью́ ты́сячами** пятьсот семьдесят **четырьмя́ рубля́ми**
with five thousand five hundred and seventy-four roubles (cf.
written norm с пятью́ ты́сячами пятьюста́ми семью́-
десятью четырьмя́ рубля́ми)

199 Cardinals as numerical 'labels'

(1) Cardinal numerals are widely used as indeclinable numerical
'labels' in addresses, both with но́мер 'number':

в кварти́ре но́мер **два́дцать семь**
in flat number 27

and without но́мер

Мичу́рина, **два́дцать семь**, кварти́ра **восемна́дцать** (Shukshin)
Flat 18, 27 Michurin Street

Она́ занима́ется у подру́ги в до́ме **четы́рнадцать**
(Trifonov)
She is studying at her friend's house at number 14

(2) Cardinal numerals are also used with series of air/spacecraft (Салю́т-4 (**четы́ре**) 'Salyut-4', ТУ-104 (**сто четы́ре**) 'TU-104', ИЛ-62 (**шестьдеся́т два**) 'IL-62'), with the names of major international events, where the cardinal numeral denotes the year of occurrence (Олимпиа́да-88 (**во́семьдесят во́семь**) 'the 1988 Olympics'), with the names of airports (Шереме́тьево-**оди́н** 'Sheremetevo-1'), flight numbers (рейс **сто три́дцать семь** 'flight number 137'), ticket numbers (**два́дцать четы́ре ты́сячи сто се́мьдесят** (ticket number) '24170') and receipt numbers (**семна́дцать два́дцать пять** '1725'). Telephone numbers are read in one group of three digits and two groups of two: **сто пятьдеся́т во́семь двена́дцать ноль четы́ре** (158-12-04).

Note
In other contexts (e.g. the numbers of trains, carriages, seats) the more colloquial **ordinal** is the norm: **восьмо́й** ваго́н 'carriage number 8', три́дцать **пя́тое** ме́сто 'seat number 35', се́мьдесят **второ́й** по́езд 'train number 72'. Compare **двадца́тый** ряд, середи́на 'row 20, centre', в **пя́той** пала́те 'in ward 5' (rooms are numbered with cardinals or ordinals: ко́мната **пя́тая/пять** 'room 5').

(3) Numerals may be left undeclined in measuring speed: е́хать со ско́ростью **три́дцать** км/ч (киломе́тров в час) 'to travel at a speed of thirty kilometres per hour' (or **тридцати́ киломе́тров в час** or **в три́дцать киломе́тров в час**).

200 Collective numerals

(1) The collective numerals:

(i) Constitute a series from 2 to 10: **дво́е** 'two', **тро́е** 'three', **че́тверо** 'four', **пя́теро** 'five', **ше́стеро** 'six', **се́меро** 'seven', **во́сьмеро** 'eight', **де́вятеро** 'nine', **де́сятеро** 'ten'. Collectives above **се́меро** 'seven' are little used now. The collectives decline as follows (**се́меро, во́сьмеро, де́вятеро** decline like **ше́стеро**):

Nom.	дво́-е	тро́-е	че́твер-о
Acc.	дво́-е/-и́х	тро́-е/-и́х	че́твер-о/-ы́х
Gen.	дво-и́х	тро-и́х	четвер-ы́х
Dat.	дво-и́м	тро-и́м	четвер-ы́м

| Instr. | дво-**и́ми** | тро-**и́ми** | четвер-**ы́ми** |
| Prep. | о дво-**и́х** | о тро-**и́х** | о четвер-**ы́х** |

Nom.	пя́тер-**о**	ше́стер-**о**
Acc.	пя́тер-**о**/-**ы́х**	ше́стер-**о**/-**ы́х**
Gen.	пятер-**ы́х**	шестер-**ы́х**
Dat.	пятер-**ы́м**	шестер-**ы́м**
Instr.	пятер-**ы́ми**	шестер-**ы́ми**
Prep.	о пятер-**ы́х**	о шестер-**ы́х**

(ii) They take the genitive plural of adjectives and nouns when they themselves are in the nominative/inanimate accusative.

(2) Collective numerals are used in four main constructions:

(i) With nouns used only in the plural (see **49**). This applies especially to **дво́е** 'two', **тро́е** 'three' and **че́тверо** 'four', which, unlike the cardinal numerals **два**, **три**, **четы́ре**, govern genitive *plural* forms:

дво́е **часо́в**	two clocks
тро́е **носи́лок**	three stretchers
тро́е **похоро́н**	three funerals

Через че́тверо **су́ток** по́езд бу́дет в Москве́ (Trifonov)
In four days' time the train will be in Moscow

Above four, collective numerals are the norm with plural-only nouns:

| **пя́теро** сане́й | five sledges |
| **ше́стеро** воро́т | six gates |

and cardinals a colloquial variant (пять сане́й etc.)

Note

(a) The collectives can be used with 'paired' objects (e.g. дво́е **лыж** 'two pairs of skis', тро́е **но́жниц** 'three pairs of scissors'), but constructions with па́ра 'pair' are preferred: **три па́ры** но́жниц etc.

(b) Compare also the colloquial **дво́е сли́вок** 'two creams' (= portions, packets of cream), heard in shops and buffets, **дво́е щей** 'two cabbage soups', **тро́е духо́в** 'three types *or* bottles of perfume' etc.

(c) Collectives cannot appear in compound numerals. Thus, **день**, not **су́тки**, is used in rendering '22 days' (**два́дцать два дня**). Paraphrases with **шту́ка** 'item', **коли́чество** 'quantity' and

па́ра 'pair' are also found: Про́дано пятьсо́т со́рок три **шту́ки** са́нок or Про́даны са́нки **в коли́честве** пятисо́т сорока́ трёх 'Five hundred and forty-three sledges have been sold', со́рок три **па́ры** сане́й/часо́в '43 sledges/clocks'.

(d) *Cardinal* numerals, *not* collectives, are used with the *oblique cases* of plural-only nouns: на **четырёх** (not *четверы́х) са́нках 'on four sledges'.

(ii) The collectives can be used with *animate masculine nouns*: дво́е друзе́й (= два дру́га) 'two friends', тро́е ма́льчиков (= три ма́льчика) 'three boys'. As with animate forms in general (see below), the use of the collective numeral emphasizes the cohesiveness of the group, by contrast with the individualizing nature of the cardinals. Usage is particularly common:

(a) With nouns in -а/-я (e.g. мужчи́на, судья́, ю́ноша) (**пя́теро мужчи́н** 'five men', **тро́е суде́й** 'three judges', **дво́е ю́ношей** 'two youths'), including nouns of common gender (**дво́е сиро́т** 'two orphans' (две сиро́ты is preferred, however, if both orphans are female)).

(b) With **лю́ди** 'people' and **лицо́** 'person': **тро́е люде́й** 'three people', **пя́теро незнако́мых лиц** 'five strangers'.

(c) With adjectival nouns: **дво́е прохо́жих** 'two passers-by', **тро́е больны́х** 'three patients', **че́тверо знако́мых** 'four acquaintances', **се́меро отдыха́ющих** 'seven holiday-makers'.

Note that either cardinals *or* collectives may be used in oblique cases:

> Он вы́грузил в Берёзове **шестеры́х** (or **шесть**) пассажи́ров (Zalygin)
> He off-loaded six passengers in Berezovo

The use of collective numerals with *feminine* animate nouns (e.g. че́тверо же́нщин 'four women') is a mark of substandard colloquial Russian, cf. standard **четы́ре же́нщины**.

The collectives are not normally used with nouns denoting high rank: thus **два мини́стра** 'two ministers' rather than дво́е мини́стров; similarly, **два профе́ссора** 'two professors', **четы́ре генера́ла** 'four generals'.

(iii) The collectives are used with **де́ти** 'children': **дво́е дете́й** 'two children', **тро́е дете́й** 'three children', **че́тверо дете́й** 'four children', **пя́теро дете́й** 'five children' (colloquially also два ребёнка 'two children' etc.). The series rarely proceeds beyond **се́меро** 'seven', cf.

Супру́ги Ники́тины, у кото́рых **се́меро** дете́й (*Sputnik*)
The Nikitins, who have seven children

and

Она́ вспомина́ет свою́ мать, у кото́рой бы́ло **де́вять** дете́й (*Russia Today*)
She recalls her mother, who had nine children

In oblique cases, either cardinal or collective numerals may be used, cf.

Мать **четырёх** дете́й ... (Rybakov)
The mother of four children

and

Пятеры́х дете́й вы́растила (Trifonov)
She raised five children

Note

The collective numerals are also used:

(a) With **ребя́та**: **пя́теро** ребя́т 'five kids', с пятеры́ми/пятью́ ребя́тами 'with five kids', cf. У него́ пя́теро **ребяти́шек** (Shukshin) 'He has five kiddies'.

(b) With вну́ки 'grandchildren': За столо́м — **че́тверо дете́й** и **тро́е вну́ков** (Kovaleva) 'At the table are four children and three grandchildren'.

(c) With **близнецы́**: **тро́е/че́тверо** близнецо́в 'triplets/quadruplets'.

(d) Colloquially, with the young of animals: **тро́е щеня́т/три щенка́** 'three puppies'.

(iv) The collective numerals are also used when an animate noun is absent from the construction: Нас бы́ло **дво́е** 'There were two of us', **Тро́е** стоя́ли на углу́ 'Three people were standing on the corner', Эти **пя́теро** оста́лись 'These five stayed', Мы **тро́е** протестова́ли 'We three protested', Ко́мната на **трои́х** 'A room for three'. Reference is to:

(a) Groups of males:

Их **шéстеро** прòтив нáших **тройх** (*Russia Today*)
Their six against our three (in an ice-hockey match)

(b) Females:

Их **чéтверо**; все онѝ машинѝстки высóкого клáсса
There are four of them; they are all first-class typists

(c) Mixed company:

Нас **чéтверо**: мой приятель с дéвушкой, Лѝля и я (Kazakov)
There are four of us: my friend and his girl-friend, Lilya and I

(v) The collectives are also used in some idioms: есть, рабóтать за **тройх**, 'to eat, work enough for three' etc., **на свойх двойх** (colloquial) 'on foot'.

201 Indefinite numerals

(1) Indefinite numerals include **достáточно** 'enough', **мáло** 'few', **мнóго** 'many, much', **немáло** 'not a few', **немнóго** 'not many, a few', **нéсколько** 'several', **скóлько** 'how many', **стóлько** 'so many'.

(2) All the indefinite numerals may govern the genitive singular and plural: достáточно **продýктов** 'sufficient provisions', мáло **солдáт** 'not many soldiers' мнóго **врéмени** 'much time', скóлько **сáхару**? 'how much sugar?', стóлько **дéнег** 'so much money'.

(3) **Стóлько** and **скóлько** often relate to each other, standing in adjacent clauses:

Старáйтесь давáть хомякý **стóлько** кóрма, **скóлько** он в состоянии съесть (*Yunyi naturalist*)
Try to give the hamster as much food as it is able to eat

(4) **Нéсколько, скóлько, стóлько** take genitive plural человéк (**нéсколько человéк** 'a few people'), while **мáло, мнóго, немáло, немнóго** take genitive plural людéй (**мнóго людéй** 'many people' etc.).

Note

Скóлько людéй is used in emotive contexts: **Скóлько людéй** получѝли в послéдние гóды нóвые квартѝры! 'How many people have received new apartments in recent years!', cf. the matter-of-fact Ско́лько челове́к поги́бло? 'How many people died?'

(5) **Не́сколько** is distinguished from the 'selective' pronoun **не́которые** 'some, certain' (see also **141**). Compare В за́ле сиде́ло **не́сколько пассажи́ров** 'In the hall sat several passengers' and **Не́которые** из них бы́ли недово́льны 'Some of them were dissatisfied'.

(6) **Не́сколько**, **ско́лько** and **сто́лько** decline like plural adjectives, agreeing with oblique cases of plural nouns:

> Мо́жно одновреме́нно соедини́ться с **не́сколькими або-не́нтами** (*Izvestiya*)
> It is possible to link up with several subscribers simultaneously

(7) **Ма́ло** implies negative quantity (У него́ **ма́ло** де́нег 'He has not got much money'), while **немно́го** can imply negative *or* positive (У него́ **немно́го** де́нег 'He has not got much money' (negative)/ 'He does have a little money' (positive)). Since **ма́ло** does not decline, paraphrase is sometimes necessary: в ре́дких слу́чаях 'in a few cases', с о́чень ма́леньким коли́чеством муки́ 'with very little flour' etc.

(8) **Мно́го** (or **мно́гое**, pl. **мно́гие**) declines both in the singular (**Мно́гое** бы́ло скры́то от меня́ 'Much was concealed from me', Я **мно́гому** научи́лся у него́ 'I learnt a lot from him') and in the plural (**Мно́гие** так ду́мают 'Many people think that', У **мно́гих** рек пра́вый бе́рег вы́ше ле́вого 'The right bank of many rivers is higher than the left').

Note

(a) While **мно́го** means 'a lot' and is often used with passive or static verbs (На собра́нии бы́ло **мно́го** учителе́й 'There were a lot of teachers at the meeting'), **мно́гие** implies 'not all, a considerable proportion', and is more common with verbs which denote action on the part of the subject (**Мно́гие** учителя́ голосова́ли за предложе́ние 'Many teachers voted for the proposal'). **Мно́го** is commoner with inanimate nouns, unless the intention is to individualize, cf. Снесено́ **мно́го** зда́ний 'Many buildings have been demolished' and **Мно́гие** дома́ восстано́влены в пре́жнем сти́ле 'Many houses have been restored in their original style', **Мно́гие** берёзы уже́ без ли́стьев 'Many birches are already without leaves'.

(b) The animate accusative/genitive rule is not normally applied to indefinite numerals: thus, Я встре́тил **не́сколько** (rather than не́скольких) студе́нтов.

202 Agreement of the predicate with a subject which contains a numeral

(1) It is difficult to formulate hard and fast rules for the agreement of a verb predicate with a subject which contains a numeral. In some instances the predicate appears in the *singular*, in others it appears in the *plural*.

(2) Factors which affect choice include word order, with a preference for the *singular* when the verb *precedes* the noun:

Его́ **опереди́ло** не́сколько лы́жников
He was overtaken by several skiers

and for the *plural* when the verb *follows* the noun:

Не́сколько лы́жников **опереди́ли** его́
Several skiers overtook him

(3) **Мно́го** and **ма́ло** almost invariably take a *singular* predicate: Там **бы́ло** ма́ло наро́ду 'There were not many people there', Во вре́мя пожа́ра **поги́бло** мно́го книг 'Many books perished during the fire'.

(4) With cardinal and collective numerals, **не́сколько** 'several' and **ско́лько** 'how much', the choice of a *singular* or *plural* predicate depends on a number of factors. Prime among these is the nature of the verb predicate.

(i) If this denotes state (**быть** 'to be', **существова́ть** 'to exist' etc.), then a *singular* predicate is preferred:

У неё **бы́ло** три бра́та
She had three brothers

Нас **бы́ло** дво́е
There were two of us

Нам **предстои́т** не́сколько тру́дных встреч с роди́телями
We face a number of difficult meetings with parents

(ii) A *singular* is also preferred with verbs which do not denote
action on the part of the subject:

В бою́ **поги́бло** со́рок солда́т
Forty soldiers perished in the battle

Во вре́мя налёта **уби́то** две же́нщины
Two women were killed during the raid

Издаётся 80 журна́лов
80 journals are published

Зарегистри́ровано бо́лее 130 ты́сяч люде́й (*Izvestiya*)
More than 130,000 people have been registered

in expressions of time

Ей ско́ро **испо́лнится** два́дцать лет
She will soon be twenty

Прошло́ три го́да
Three years have passed

До прихо́да почто́вого авто́буса **остава́лось** часа́ полтора́
(Abramov)
About an hour and a half remained to the arrival of the post bus

in expressing approximate quantity

Кварти́ры **получа́ет** о̀коло трёхсот семе́й
About three hundred families receive apartments

and where a distributive phrase in **по** functions as subject (see also
448):

У ка́ждой две́ри **стоя́ло** по солда́ту
At each door stood a soldier

(iii) A *plural* predicate will be used, however, if the numeral phrase
is qualified by a demonstrative or other plural form (Э́ти пять лет
прошли́ незаме́тно 'These five years have passed by impercept-
ibly', Э́ти три до́ма **про́даны** неда́вно 'These three houses have
been sold recently'), or by a relative clause (cf. Со́рок мину́т
истекло́ 'Forty minutes have expired' and Со́рок мину́т, о

кото́рых вы проси́ли, истекли́ 'The forty minutes that you requested have expired').

(iv) A *plural* predicate is also preferred if the verb denotes action on the part of the subject:

Вошли́ тро́е в шине́лях
Three people came in wearing greatcoats

Не́сколько челове́к **ки́нулись** вслед бежа́вшему (Nikitin)
Several people dashed off after the running man

Note also use with fractions and decimals: В движе́нии за сохране́ние национа́льной самобы́тности и охра́ну приро́ды **уча́ствуют** соотве́тственно 3,5 и 3,1 проце́нта (*Komsomolskaya pravda*) '3.5 and 3.1 per cent respectively participate in the movement for the preservation of national identity and nature conservation'. Compare the use of the *plural* of an *active* verb in Сейча́с по̀лгорода **хо́дят** в таки́х шмо́тках (*Komsomolskaya pravda*) 'Now half the town wears such gear' and the use of the *singular* of a *passive reflexive* verb in По̀лдо́ма **ремонти́руется** 'Half the house is being repaired'.

(v) A *plural* predicate is especially common where attention is drawn to separate activity on the part of individual members of a subject group:

Со́рок демонстра́нтов **разошли́сь**
The forty demonstrators dispersed

Его́ три сестры́ **вы́шли** за́муж
His three sisters got married

Note
This factor may affect even indefinite numerals like **мно́го**: Мно́го фаши́стских самолётов **бомби́ли** испа́нский го́род Ге́рника 'Many Fascist aircraft bombed the Spanish town of Guernica'.

(vi) A *plural* predicate is also used with **о́ба/о́бе**: О́ба сы́на **верну́лись** 'Both sons returned'.

(vii) The *plural* is normal if the predicate is a *short adjective*:

Не́сколько стате́й в э́том сбо́рнике **интере́сны**
Several articles in this collection are interesting

Ordinal Numerals

203 Formation of ordinal numerals

Apart from **пе́рвый** 'first' and **второ́й** 'second', ordinal numerals derive from cardinals (see **190**). They are as follows:

1st	пе́рвый	51st	пятьдеся́т пе́рвый
2nd	второ́й	60th	шестидеся́тый
3rd	тре́тий	61st	шестьдеся́т пе́рвый
4th	четвёртый	70th	семидеся́тый
5th	пя́тый	71st	се́мьдесят пе́рвый
6th	шесто́й	80th	восьмидеся́тый
7th	седьмо́й	81st	во́семьдесят пе́рвый
8th	восьмо́й	90th	девяно́стый
9th	девя́тый	91st	девяно́сто пе́рвый
10th	деся́тый	100th	со́тый
11th	оди́ннадцатый	200th	двухсо́тый
12th	двена́дцатый	300th	трёхсо́тый
13th	трина́дцатый	400th	четырёхсо́тый
14th	четы́рнадцатый	500th	пятисо́тый
15th	пятна́дцатый	600th	шестисо́тый
16th	шестна́дцатый	700th	семисо́тый
17th	семна́дцатый	800th	восьмисо́тый
18th	восемна́дцатый	900th	девятисо́тый
19th	девятна́дцатый	1000th	ты́сячный
20th	двадца́тый	1001st	ты́сяча пе́рвый
21st	два́дцать пе́рвый	1002nd	ты́сяча второ́й
22nd	два́дцать второ́й	2000th	двухты́сячный
30th	тридца́тый	3000th	трёхты́сячный
31st	три́дцать пе́рвый	5000th	пятиты́сячный
40th	сороково́й	1,000,000th	миллио́нный
41st	со́рок пе́рвый	10,000,000th	десятймиллио́нный
50th	пятидеся́тый		

Note

(a) Ordinal numbers decline like hard adjectives in **-ый/-о́й**, except for **тре́тий** (see **151** (1) note).

(b) **Девя́тый** 'ninth', **деся́тый** 'tenth', **двадца́тый** 'twentieth',

тридца́тый 'thirtieth' have medial stress, cf. the initially-stressed cardinals from which they derive.

(c) Note the central **-и-** in 50th to 80th: **пятидеся́тый** 'fiftieth' etc.

(d) In abbreviations, the final letter of the ending is used (**1-я** пятиле́тка 'the first five-year plan', **3-й** день 'the third day', **20-е** го́ды 'the twenties'), unless the penultimate letter of the ending is a consonant, in which case the final *two* letters are used (**5-го** ря́да 'of row 5').

(e) In compounds, only the final component has the form of an ordinal and declines: пятьсо́т **четвёртый** биле́т 'the five hundred **and fourth** ticket', в два́дцать **пе́рвом** ряду́ 'in row 21'.

(f) Roman numerals are used in denoting centuries (в **XX** (двадца́том) ве́ке 'in the 20th century'), Communist Party congresses (**XXII** (два́дцать второ́й) съезд 'XXII Congress'), major international events (e.g. sessions of the General Assembly of the UNO), international congresses (**VII** (седьмо́й) Конгре́сс МАПРЯ́Л 'the VII Congress of MAPRYAL') and monarchs (Пётр I (Пе́рвый) 'Peter the First').

204 Ordinal numerals: usage

(1) Like adjectives, ordinal numerals agree in gender, case and number with the noun they qualify:

в пя́том ряду́ in row five

(2) For use in time expressions see **206**.

(3) Ordinals are used with pages, chapters, TV channels etc.:

уро́к **пятидеся́тый**	lesson **fifty**
на страни́це **семна́дцатой**	on page **seventeen**
в **три́дцать седьмо́й** главе́	in chapter **thirty-seven**
по **второ́й** програ́мме	on channel **two**

and to denote clothes and footwear sizes

ту́фли **три́дцать четвёртого** разме́ра
size **thirty-four** shoes

See also **199** (2) note.

(4) Ordinals cannot be extended by a superlative, as they can in English. Instead, prepositional phrases with **по** are used:

втора́я река́ **по длине́**	the second **longest** river
тре́тий го́род **по величине́**	the third **largest** town

Special Functions of Numerals

205 Cardinals and ordinals in fractions and decimals

(1) Both cardinals and ordinals are used in **fractions** and **decimals**. In Russian *commas* are used instead of decimal points:

(i) Fractions

одна́ **пя́тая** (часть or до́ля understood)	one-fifth
две **пя́тых**	two-fifths
пять **восьмы́х**	five-eighths

Note the use of the genitive plural of the ordinal after 2–4 (cf. **194** (2) (v) note (a)).

(ii) Decimals

0,1 (одна́ деся́тая/ноль це́лых и одна́ деся́тая)   0.1 *or* 1/10

0,05 (пять со́тых/ноль це́лых и пять со́тых)   0.05

1,375 (одна́ це́лая и три́ста се́мьдесят пять   1.375
  ты́сячных)

2,4 (две це́лых и четы́ре деся́тых/два и четы́ре   2.4
  деся́тых)

57,365 (пятьдеся́т семь це́лых, три́ста   57.365
  шестьдеся́т пять ты́сячных)

Note

(a) 1, 2 and compounds take the gender of a following noun: два́дцать **оди́н** и одна́ деся́тая ме́тра '21.1 metres', **две** и четы́ре деся́тых то́нны '2.4 tons'.

(b) Decimals/fractions are followed by the genitive singular of the noun:

12,5% (двена́дцать и пять деся́тых **проце́нта**)
12.5% (twelve point five per cent)

even if the decimal or fraction is declined:

Су́мма равня́ется пяти́ седьмы́м **насле́дства**
The sum equals five-sevenths of the inheritance

(c) Треть 'a third', че́тверть 'a quarter' and полови́на 'a half' are commonly used instead of fractions: две **тре́ти**/две **тре́тьих** 'two-thirds', три **че́тверти**/три **четвёртых** 'three-quarters', три с **че́твертью** 'three and a quarter', два **и пять деся́тых** проце́нта/два **с полови́ной** проце́нта 'two and a half per cent'.

(d) Temperatures are read as follows: три́дцать шесть и шесть '36.6' (normal body temperature).

(2) По̀л- combines with the genitive singular of many nouns to denote half of something: по̀лго́да 'six months', по̀лме́тра 'half a metre', по̀лчаса́ 'half an hour'.

Note
(i) A hyphen separates по̀л- from the noun component when the latter begins with an л or a vowel or has proper-noun status: по̀л-ли́тра 'half a litre', по̀л-я́блока 'half an apple', по̀л-Варша́вы 'half Warsaw'.

(ii) In oblique cases по̀л- becomes полу-, while the noun component declines in the usual way:

Nom./Acc.	по̀лчас-а́
Gen.	получа́с-а
Dat.	получа́с-у
Instr.	получа́с-ом
Prep.	о получа́с-е

(iii) In colloquial speech, -y- is omitted in the declension of some compounds: в по̀л[у]стака́не воды́ 'in half a glass of water', бо́лее по̀л[у]миллио́на 'more than half a million'. The better-established of these oral forms have found their way into the written language as alternatives to forms with полу-: Ему́ нет и по̀лго́да/полуго́да 'He is not even six months old'. По̀л- also appears in certain set phrases:

на полпути 'half-way', **на полставки** 'on half-pay', **к полпервого** 'by half past twelve' etc.

(iv) Compounds in пол- are qualified by plural adjectives (**первые полчаса** 'the first half-hour'), while oblique cases are qualified by singular adjectives (после **первого** полугода 'after the first six months').

(v) **Полу-** is also used as an adjective and noun prefix: **полукруг** 'semicircle', **полуфинал** 'semi-final', **получасовой** 'half-hour' (adjective), **полушарие** 'hemisphere'.

206 Telling the time

(1) Numerals are used to answer the questions **который час?**/ **сколько времени?** 'what is the time?' and **в котором часу?/во сколько?** 'at what time?'

(i) On the hour, the question **Который час?/Сколько времени?** 'What is the time?' is answered as

час, два часа, три часа, четыре часа, пять часов
one, two, three, four, five o'clock

up to **двенадцать часов** 'twelve o'clock'.

(ii) The 24-hour clock may be used in official contexts: **семнадцать часов** 'five p.m.' Otherwise one distinguishes (apart from двенадцать часов ночи 'twelve o'clock at night' and двенадцать часов дня 'twelve noon'):

час/два часа/три часа **ночи**	one/two/three o'clock **in the morning**
четыре часа through to одиннадцать часов **утра**	four o'clock through to eleven o'clock **in the morning**
час/два часа/три часа/ четыре часа/пять часов **дня**	one/two/three/four/five o'clock **in the afternoon**
шесть часов through to одиннадцать часов **вечера**	six o'clock through to eleven o'clock **in the evening**

Note
(a) **Четыре часа ночи** 'four a.m.' and пять часов **вечера** 'five p.m.' are also found.

(b) **Пóлдень** 'midday', **пóлночь** 'midnight'.

(c) Approximation is expressed by the preposition òколо: òколо двух часóв 'about two o'clock', òколо полýночи 'about midnight', òколо девятú вéчера 'about nine p.m.'

(iii) Between the hour and half-hour, the time is rendered as 'five, ten minutes' etc. of the *next* hour (expressed as an ordinal numeral):

пять минýт		five	
дéсять минýт		ten	
чéтверть	шестóго	quarter	past **five**
двáдцать минýт		twenty	
двáдцать пять минýт		twenty-five	
половúна		half	

(Literally, 'five minutes of the sixth', 'ten minutes of the sixth' etc.)

Note

(a) In spoken Russian **половúна** can be replaced by **пол-: пòлпéрвого** 'half past twelve', **пòлдевя́того** 'half past eight'.

(b) Минýт may be omitted in multiples of five (**двáдцать пять (минýт)** шестóго 'twenty-five (minutes) past five'); otherwise минýты/минýт must be included (**две минýты** трéтьего 'two minutes past two').

(c) Ordinal numerals are used to denote unspecified times between hours: **вторóй час** 'between one and two' (usually closer to one than two), **начáло пя́того** 'just after four' (lit. 'the beginning of the fifth') etc.:

Кудá ж уходúть? **Вторóй час**. На метрó опоздáла (Trifonov)
'What's the hurry? It's **past one**. You've missed the last train on the Underground'

(iv) After the half-hour the time is rendered as 'without five, ten minutes' etc. one (o'clock), two (o'clock), three (o'clock), the hours being expressed as *cardinal* numerals:

без двадцатú пятú (минýт)		25 (minutes) to	
без двадцатú (минýт)		20 (minutes) to	
без чéтверти	четьíре	quarter to	**four**
без десятú (минýт)		ten (minutes) to	
без пятú (минýт)		five (minutes) to	
без двух минýт		two minutes to	

(Literally 'without 25 minutes four' etc.)

Note

Neuter agreement in **бы́ло** три часа́/де́сять мину́т пе́рвого/полови́на шесто́го/без пяти́ мину́т три 'it was three o'clock/ten past twelve/half past five/five to three' etc.

(2) **В кото́ром часу́?/во ско́лько?** 'at what time?'

(i) The construction **в** + accusative case is used up to the half-hour:

в час дня	at 1 p.m.
в пять мину́т шесто́го	at five past five

(ii) After the half-hour, however, **в** is omitted:

без че́тверти семь	at quarter to seven
без десяти́ два	at ten to two

It is also omitted when the time phrase is governed by another preposition or a comparative:

Втору́ю то́ню мы зака́нчиваем **о̀коло двух часо́в** но́чи (Nikolaev)
We complete the second haul **at about 2 o'clock** in the morning

Он ложи́лся всегда́ **не по́зже оди́ннадцати** (Yakhontov)
He always went to bed **no later than 11 o'clock**

(iii) **В** + prepositional case is used to denote unspecified times between hours (**в нача́ле** седьмо́го 'at just gone six', **во второ́м часу́** 'between one and two'):

Одна́ко **в оди́ннадцатом часу́** он сам занерви́чал (Trifonov)
However, **after it had gone ten** he began to get the jitters himself

and for times on the half-hour:

В полови́не пе́рвого (colloquially в по̀лпе́рвого) но́чи тёща побежа́ла на Со́кол, к метро́ — встреча́ть (Trifonov)
At half past midnight mother-in-law rushed off to Sokol to meet them off the Underground

Note

The time may be given, both colloquially and in official contexts, using cardinals only: в три пятна́дцать 'at three fifteen', cf.:

Телевизио́нный репорта́ж по второ́й програ́мме смотри́те в **семна́дцать часо́в два́дцать пять мину́т** (radio)
Watch TV coverage on channel 2 at 5.25 p.m.

207 Giving the date

(1) The questions **Како́е (бы́ло, бу́дет) число́?** 'What is (was, will be) the date?' are answered by an ordinal numeral in the neuter nominative and the name of a month in the genitive:

Сего́дня **пе́рвое февраля́**   Today it is 1 February

Вчера́ **бы́ло два́дцать пя́тое** Yesterday was 25 March
ма́рта

Ско́ро бу́дет **семна́дцатое**   Soon it will be 17 June
ию́ня

(2) The question **Како́го числа́?** 'On what date?' is answered by a genitive:

Междунаро́дный же́нский день — **восьмо́го ма́рта**
International Women's Day is **on 8 March**

(3) The question Како́й год? 'Which year is it?' is answered as follows: Сейча́с **двухты́сячный год** 'Now it is **the year 2000**' etc.

(4) The question **В како́м году́?** 'in which year?' is answered as follows:

в ты́сяча девятисо́том году́	in 1900
в ты́сяча девятьсо́т пятидеся́том году́	in 1950
в двухты́сячном году́	in the year 2000
в две ты́сячи пятна́дцатом году́	in 2015

Note

(a) Only the final component of the numeral declines (see **203** note (e)).

(b) If any detail other than the year itself is added, the year appears in the genitive case:

в ма́е ты́сяча девятьсо́т девяно́сто **восьмо́го го́да**
in May **1998**

в воскресе́нье тре́тьего сентября́ ты́сяча девятьсо́т три́дцать **девя́того го́да**
on Sunday 3 September 1939

(c) Plural forms may be involved: **В 1957–1963 года́х** во всех респу́бликах появи́лись зако́ны об охра́не приро́ды (*Izves-*

tiya) 'Over the period **1957–1963** laws on nature conservation appeared in all republics'.

(d) Note the use of **г.** (singular) and **гг.** (plural) in abbreviations: **в 1995 г.** 'in 1995', **в 1957–1963 гг.** 'in 1957–63'.

(e) In denoting decades, **в** is used with the accusative *or* prepositional case: **В пятидеся́тые го́ды/пятидеся́тых года́х** XX ве́ка 'In the 1950s'. Compare: В 90-х года́х в Япо́нии плани́руют вы́пустить но́вую семью́ компью́теров (*Nedelya*) 'The Japanese are planning to manufacture a new family of computers **in the 90s**' (see also **429** (2) (ii) note (c)).

208 Age

(1) The question **Ско́лько вам (ему́, ей** etc.) **лет?** 'How old are you (is he, she etc.)?' is answered as follows:

Ему́ **два́дцать оди́н год**   He is twenty-one
Ей **со́рок два го́да**   She is forty-two
Мне **восемна́дцать лет**   I am eighteen

Ребёнку ещё **нет двух лет** (ещё не испо́лнилось два го́да/ двух лет)
The child is not yet two (has not had its second birthday)

The numeral may be used alone in more relaxed speech: Мне два́дцать пять (лет) 'I am 25'. Note also the following:

«На́шей Ле́ночке **четвёртый год**» (*Russia Today*)
'Our Lenochka is **in her fourth year**'

Га́лке **шёл 17-й год** (Rasputin)
Galka was **in her seventeenth year**

Ему́ **уже́ за со́рок** or Ему́ **40 с чём-то**
He is **in his forties**

Ей ещё **нет двадцати́**
She is in her **late teens**

(2) To answer the question **В како́м во́зрасте?/Ско́льких лет?** 'At what age?' it is possible to use **в** + accusative:

Он у́мер **в се́мьдесят лет**   He died at the age of 70

Alternatively, a genitive construction may be used:

Он у́мер (в во́зрасте) семи́десяти лет
He died at the age of 70

209 Quantitative nouns

Quantitative nouns include:

(1) The series **едини́ца** 'one', **дво́йка** 'two', **тро́йка** 'three', **четвёрка** 'four', **пятёрка** 'five', **шестёрка** 'six', **семёрка** 'seven', **восьмёрка** 'eight', **девя́тка** 'nine', **деся́тка** 'ten'. Their functions are as follows:

(i) The first five of the nouns figure in the five-point marking scale: **едини́ца** 'fail', **дво́йка** 'two' (unsatisfactory), **тро́йка** 'three' (satisfactory), **четвёрка** 'four' (good), **пятёрка** 'five' (very good). Colloquially, cardinal numerals can also be used: **учи́ться на пять** 'to get very good marks'.

(ii) The series can denote playing cards (**семёрка бубён, пик** 'seven of diamonds, spades', **деся́тка черве́й, треф** 'ten of hearts, clubs') as well as the numbers of buses etc. (Он прие́хал **на девя́тке** 'He arrived on the no. 9').

(iii) They also denote various other groups or objects consisting of several units: **тро́йка** 'sleigh drawn by three horses', 'three-piece suit', 'three-man commission'; **четвёрка** 'a rowing four'; **пятёрка** 'five-rouble note'; **деся́тка** 'ten-rouble note' etc.

(2) The series **пято́к** 'a five', **деся́ток** 'a ten' (also **полтора́ деся́тка** 'fifteen', **два деся́тка** 'a score'), **со́тня** 'a hundred' (**не́сколько со́тен** 'several hundreds'): **пято́к** яиц 'five eggs', **деся́ток** сигаре́т 'ten cigarettes', **деся́тки** люде́й 'dozens of people', продава́ть я́йца **со́тнями** 'to sell eggs in hundreds' etc.

210 Numerals in arithmetic

Numerals are used in operating the four arithmetical processes (**четы́ре арифмети́ческих де́йствия**):

(1) Multiplication (Умножéние).

одúножды три —	три	once three is three
двáжды три —	шесть	two threes are six
трúжды три —	дéвять	three threes are nine
четы́режды три —	двенáдцать	four threes are twelve
пя́тью три —	пятнáдцать	five threes are fifteen
шéстью три —	восемнáдцать	six threes are eighteen
вóсемью три —	двáдцать четы́ре	eight threes are twenty-four etc.

Note

Stress in **пя́тью**, **шéстью** etc. differs from the normal end stress of the instrumental пятью́, шестью́.

(2) Division (Делéние):

двáдцать вóсемь (разделúть) на четы́ре — бýдет семь
twenty-eight divided by four is seven

(3) Addition (Сложéние):

$$\left.\begin{array}{l}\text{к пятú прибáвить два — бýдет семь}\\\text{сложúть пять с двумя́ — бýдет семь}\\\text{пять плюс два — бýдет семь}\\\text{пять да два — семь}\end{array}\right\}\quad\text{five plus two is seven}$$

(4) Subtraction (Вычитáние):

$$\left.\begin{array}{l}\text{(вы́честь) два из пятú — бýдет три}\\\text{пять мúнус два — бýдет три}\end{array}\right\}\quad\begin{array}{l}\text{five minus two}\\\text{is three}\end{array}$$

Note

Два **в квадрáте** — четы́ре 'The square of two is four', Два **в кýбе** — вóсемь 'Two cubed is eight', **Кóрень квадрáтный** из четырёх — два 'The square root of four is two'.

211 Numerals in compound nouns and adjectives

(1) With the exception of 1, 90, 100 and 1000 (see (2) below), numeral components of compound nouns and adjectives appear in the *genitive* case of the cardinal:

двухлéтний	two year old
пятилéтка	five-year plan

сорокапя́тка (colloquial)   forty-five (gramophone record)

двадцатипятимину́тная па́уза   a 25-minute break

Note

A number of more abstract or technical terms take **дву-/тре-/четверо-** instead of **двух-/трёх-/четырёх-**: **дву**сло́жный 'disyllabic', **дву**сторо́нний 'bilateral', **дву**язы́чный 'bilingual' (note also **двою́**родный брат 'cousin'); **тре**уго́льник 'triangle'; **четверо**но́гий 'quadruped'.

(2) 1, 90, 100 and 1000 assume the forms **одно-, девяносто-, сто-** and **тысяче-** in compound nouns and numerals:

одноэта́жный дом   single-storey house
девяно́стомину́тная игра́   a ninety-minute game
сто́метро́вка   hundred metres race
стопятидесятиле́тие   one hundred and fiftieth anniversary
тысячеле́тие   millennium

The Verb

Conjugation

212 Infinitive-preterite stem and present-future stem

(1) Each Russian verb has:

(i) An *infinitive* (*infinitive–preterite*) *stem*, from which the past tense, the future imperfective, past participles and most perfective gerunds are formed.

(ii) A *present–future stem*, from which the present tense, the future perfective, the imperative, present participles, imperfective gerunds and some perfective gerunds are formed.

In some verbs the two stems coincide, in others they differ.

(2) The present–future stem of a verb is derived by removing the last two letters of the third-person plural of the verb:

Infinitive	Third-person plural	Present-future stem
понима́ть 'to understand'	**понима́-ют**	**понима́-**
говори́ть 'to say'	**говор-я́т**	**говор-**
сказа́ть 'to tell'	**ска́ж-ут**	**скаж-**

213 The conjugation of the verb

Each Russian verb conjugates in accordance with one of two patterns: the first (or **-e-**) conjugation and the second (or **-и-/-я-**) conjugation. The following endings are added to the present-future stems of verbs:

First-conjugation endings	Second-conjugation endings
-ю	**-ю**
-ешь	**-ишь**
-ет	**-ит**
-ем	**-им**
-ете	**-ите**
-ют	**-ят**

Note

(a) In first-conjugation verbs **y** replaces **ю** after a consonant (except after **л** and **р** in certain verbs, for example, verbs in **-оть**, **слать** 'to send' and **стлать** 'to spread').

(b) **ё** replaces **e** under stress.

(c) **y** and **a** replace **ю** and **я** respectively after **ж, ч, ш** or **щ** (see **16** (1)).

214 The first conjugation

(1) The first conjugation contains:

(i) Most verbs in **-ать/-ять**.

(ii) Many verbs in **-еть**.

(iii) All verbs with a monosyllabic infinitive in **-ить**, **почи́ть**, compounds of **-шиби́ть**.

(iv) All verbs in **-оть, -уть, -ыть, -сть, -зть, -ти, -чь**.

(2) First-conjugation verbs subdivide into:

(i) Those with stems ending in **vowels**.

(ii) Those with stems ending in **consonants**.

215 First-conjugation verbs with stems ending in a vowel

First-conjugation verbs with vowel stems comprise most verbs of the first conjugation in **-ать/-ять** (including all verbs in **-авать, -евать, -ивать, -овать, -увать, -ывать**), many in **-еть** and some in **-ить, -уть, -ыть**.

(1) Verbs in -ать/-ять

знать	**гуля́ть**
'to know'	'to stroll'
я	зна́-**ю**	гуля́-**ю**
ты	зна́-**ешь**	гуля́-**ешь**
он	зна́-**ет**	гуля́-**ет**
мы	зна́-**ем**	гуля́-**ем**
вы	зна́-**ете**	гуля́-**ете**
они́	зна́-**ют**	гуля́-**ют**

Note

(a) Most vowel stems in **-ать/-ять** conjugate like **знать** and **гуля́ть**. See, however, verbs in **-авать** and **-овать/-евать** ((2) and (3) below) and note that *stem*-stressed verbs in **-ять** lose **я** in conjugation (**се́ять** 'to sow': я се́ю, ты се́ешь), except for **ка́шлять** 'to cough', я ка́шляю, ты ка́шляешь.

(b) **Смея́ться** 'to laugh' conjugates смею́сь, смеёшься, смеётся, смеёмся, смеётесь, смею́тся.

(2) Verbs in -ава́ть

дава́ть
'to give'

я да-**ю́**
ты да-**ёшь**
он да-**ёт**
мы да-**ём**
вы да-**ёте**
они́ да-**ю́т**

Note

Compounds of **дава́ть**, **-знава́ть** (e.g. **узнава́ть** 'to recognize') and **-става́ть** (e.g. **встава́ть** 'to get up') conjugate like **дава́ть**.

(3) Verbs in -овать/-евать

голосова́ть	кова́ть	плева́ть
'to vote'	'to forge'	'to spit'
я голосу́-**ю**	ку-**ю́**	плю-**ю́**
ты голосу́-**ешь**	ку-**ёшь**	плю-**ёшь**
он голосу́-**ет**	ку-**ёт**	плю-**ёт**
мы голосу́-**ем**	ку-**ём**	плю-**ём**
вы голосу́-**ете**	ку-**ёте**	плю-**ёте**
они́ голосу́-**ют**	ку-**ю́т**	плю-**ю́т**

Note

(a) All verbs in **-овать** with more than two syllables conjugate like **голосова́ть** (some are stem stressed, e.g. **тре́бовать** 'to demand', тре́бую, тре́буешь).

(b) Note the conjugation of the following:

воева́ть 'to wage war'	вою́ю, вою́ешь
горева́ть 'to grieve'	горю́ю, горю́ешь
жева́ть 'to chew'	жую́, жуёшь
клева́ть 'to peck'	клюю́, клюёшь
снова́ть 'to dart'	сную́, снуёшь
сова́ть 'to thrust'	сую́, суёшь

(c) **Застрева́ть** 'to get stuck', **затева́ть** 'to undertake', **здоро́ваться** 'to greet', **зева́ть** 'to yawn', **подозрева́ть** 'to suspect', **преодолева́ть** 'to overcome' and secondary imperfectives in -дева́ть, -пева́ть, -спева́ть conjugate like **знать**.

(4) Verbs in -еть

красне́ть
'to blush'

я красне́-**ю**
ты красне́-**ешь**
он красне́-**ет**
мы красне́-**ем**
вы красне́-**ете**
они́ красне́-**ют**

Note

(a) Verbs in **-еть** which are derived from adjectives (e.g. **худе́ть** 'to slim' from **худо́й** 'slim') and nouns (e.g. **сироте́ть** 'to be orphaned' from **сирота́** 'an orphan') conjugate like **краснéть**, as do **владéть** 'to own', **греть** 'to heat', **жалéть** 'to pity', **зреть** 'to ripen', **имéть** 'to have', **млеть** 'to grow numb', **преодолéть** 'to overcome', **сметь** 'to dare', **спеть** 'to ripen', **тлеть** 'to decay', **умéть** 'to know how to'.

(b) **Петь** 'to sing' conjugates пою́, поёшь, поёт, поём, поёте, пою́т.

(5) Verbs in -ить

бить 'to strike'	**брить** 'to shave'	**гнить** 'to rot'
я бь-**ю́**	брé-**ю**	гни-**ю́**
ты бь-**ёшь**	брé-**ешь**	гни-**ёшь**
он бь-**ёт**	брé-**ет**	гни-**ёт**
мы бь-**ём**	брé-**ем**	гни-**ём**
вы бь-**ёте**	брé-**ете**	гни-**ёте**
они́ бь-**ю́т**	брé-**ют**	гни-**ю́т**

Note

(a) **Вить** 'to weave', **лить** 'to pour', **пить** 'to drink' and **шить** 'to sew' conjugate like бить (with 'zero vowel' in the present-future stem).

(b) **Почи́ть** 'to rest' conjugates like гнить, but with stress on -**й**-: почи́ю, почи́ешь.

(6) Verbs in -ыть

мыть 'to wash'	
я мó-**ю**	мы мó-**ем**
ты мó-**ешь**	вы мó-**ете**
он мó-**ет**	они́ мó-**ют**

Similarly **выть** 'to howl', **крыть** 'to roof', **ныть** 'to gnaw' and **рыть** 'to dig'.

(7) Verbs in -уть

Дуть 'to blow': ду́ю, ду́ешь, ду́ет, ду́ем, ду́ете, ду́ют. Likewise **обу́ть** 'to put shoes on someone' and **разу́ть** 'to take shoes off someone'.

216 First-conjugation verbs with consonant stems I

(1) Present-future and infinitive stems coincide

(i) Verbs in **-ать**, e.g. **ждать** 'to wait':

> я жд-**у**
> ты жд-**ёшь**
> он жд-**ёт**
> мы жд-**ём**
> вы жд-**ёте**
> они́ жд-**ут**

Similarly:

врать 'to lie'	вру, врёшь
жа́ждать 'to thirst for'	жа́жду, жа́ждешь
жрать 'to devour'	жру, жрёшь
ора́ть 'to yell'	ору́, орёшь
рвать 'to tear'	рву, рвёшь
ржать 'to neigh'	ржу, ржёшь
соса́ть 'to suck'	сосу́, сосёшь
стона́ть 'to groan'	стону́, сто́нешь
ткать 'to weave'	тку, ткёшь

Note
The absence of guttural/sibilant mutation in the conjugation of **ткать** is abnormal, cf. mutation in **лгать** 'to lie': **лгу, лжёшь, лжёт, лжём, лжёте, лгут**.

(ii) Verbs in **-(н)уть**:

> **гнуть** 'to bend'   гну, гнёшь

Likewise all other verbs in **-нуть** (some with stem stress (**мёрзнуть** 'to freeze': мёрзну, мёрзнешь) and a few with mobile stress, see **219** (3) (iv).

(iii) Verbs in **-оть**:

> **коло́ть** 'to chop'   колю́, ко́лешь, ко́лют

Likewise all other verbs in **-оть**: **боро́ться** 'to struggle', **моло́ть** 'to grind' (мелю́, ме́лешь), **поло́ть** 'to weed', **поро́ть** 'to rip'.

(2) Present-future stem and infinitive stem differ

(i) Through the presence of a mobile vowel in conjugation:

брать 'to take'	беру́, берёшь (likewise **драть** 'to flay')
звать 'to call'	зову́, зовёшь
стлать 'to spread'	стелю́, сте́лешь, сте́лют

(ii) **-в-** appears in conjugation:

жить 'to live'	живу́, живёшь
плыть 'to swim'	плыву́, плывёшь (likewise **слыть** 'to have the reputation of being')

(iii) **-д-** appears in conjugation:

быть 'to be'	бу́ду, бу́дешь
е́хать 'to travel'	е́ду, е́дешь

(iv) **-м-** or **-н-** appears in conjugation:

взять 'to take'	возьму́, возьмёшь
деть 'to put'	де́ну, де́нешь
жать 'to press'	жму, жмёшь
жать 'to reap'	жну, жнёшь
застря́ть 'to get stuck'	застря́ну, застря́нешь
мять 'to crumple'	мну, мнёшь
нача́ть 'to begin'	начну́, начнёшь
поня́ть 'to understand'	пойму́, поймёшь
распя́ть 'to crucify'	распну́, распнёшь
снять 'to take off'	сниму́, сни́мешь
стать 'to become'	ста́ну, ста́нешь
стыть 'to go cold'	сты́ну, сты́нешь

Note

Compounds of **-нять** with prefixes ending in a vowel (except for **приня́ть** 'to accept': приму́, при́мешь) conjugate like **поня́ть** 'to understand'; those with prefixes ending in a consonant conjugate like **снять** 'to take off'.

(v) Mobile vowel lost in conjugation (verbs in **-ереть**):

тере́ть 'to rub'	тру, трёшь (likewise compounds of -мереть, -переть)

(vi) Others (**реве́ть, слать** and compounds of -**шиби́ть**)

ошиби́ться 'to err'   ошибу́сь, ошибёшься
реве́ть 'to roar'   реву́, ревёшь
слать 'to send'   шлю, шлёшь, шлют

217 First-conjugation verbs with consonant stems II: verbs in -ать with consonant mutation throughout conjugation

(1) Verbs of this type:

(i) Undergo consonant mutation throughout conjugation.

(ii) Switch stress from the ending to the *stem* after the first-person singular, except for:

(a) **Алка́ть** 'to crave', **колеба́ться** 'to hesitate', **колыха́ть** 'to sway', which have stem stress *throughout* conjugation.

(b) Verbs with stem stress in the infinitive, e.g. **ма́зать** 'to daub'.

(2) The following consonant mutations operate:

д : ж	т :ч	т : щ	з : ж	с : ш
глода́ть	шепта́ть	клевета́ть	вяза́ть	писа́ть
'to gnaw'	'to whisper'	'to slander'	'to tie'	'to write'
я глож-у́	шепч-у́	клевещ-у́	вяж-у́	пиш-у́
ты гло́ж-ешь	ше́пч-ешь	клеве́щ-ешь	вя́ж-ешь	пи́ш-ешь
он гло́ж-ет	ше́пч-ет	клеве́щ-ет	вя́ж-ет	пи́ш-ет
мы гло́ж-ем	ше́пч-ем	клеве́щ-ем	вя́ж-ем	пи́ш-ем
вы гло́ж-ете	ше́пч-ете	клеве́щ-ете	вя́ж-ете	пи́ш-ете
они́ гло́ж-ут	ше́пч-ут	клеве́щ-ут	вя́ж-ут	пи́ш-ут

г : ж	к : ч	х : ш	ск : щ	б : бл/м : мл/
				п : пл
дви́гать	пла́кать	маха́ть	иска́ть	дрема́ть
'to move'	'to weep'	'to wave'	'to seek'	'to doze'
я дви́ж-у	пла́ч-у	маш-у́	ищ-у́	дремл-ю́
ты дви́ж-ешь	пла́ч-ешь	ма́ш-ешь	и́щ-ешь	дре́мл-ешь
он дви́ж-ет	пла́ч-ет	ма́ш-ет	и́щ-ет	дре́мл-ет
мы дви́ж-ем	пла́ч-ем	ма́ш-ем	и́щ-ем	дре́мл-ем
вы дви́ж-ете	пла́ч-ете	ма́ш-ете	и́щ-ете	дре́мл-ете
они́ дви́ж-ут	пла́ч-ут	ма́ш-ут	и́щ-ут	дре́мл-ют

Note

(a) Дви́гать 'to move' conjugates дви́жу, дви́жешь in figurative meanings (Им **дви́жет** самолю́бие 'He is motivated by self-esteem') and in technical contexts (Пружи́на **дви́жет** механи́зм 'A spring activates the mechanism'), but дви́гаю, дви́гаешь in literal meaning (Он **дви́гает** ме́бель 'He moves the furniture'). Note also the distinction between По́езд **дви́гается** 'The train moves off' and По́езд **дви́жется** 'The train is in motion'.

(b) Other verbs of this type include **алка́ть** 'to crave for' (а́лчу, а́лчешь), **бормота́ть** 'to murmur' (бормочу́, бормо́чешь), **бры́згать** 'to spray, sprinkle' (бры́зжу, бры́зжешь in intransitive meanings (Фонта́н **бры́зжет** 'The fountain plays'); бры́згаю, бры́згаешь in transitive meanings (Он **бры́згает** во́лосы духа́ми 'He sprays his hair with perfume')), **грохота́ть** 'to rumble' (грохочу́, грохо́чет), **каза́ться** 'to seem' (кажу́сь, ка́жешься) (likewise compounds of -каза́ть), **ка́пать** 'to drip' (ка́плю, ка́плешь; also ка́паю, -аешь), **клокота́ть** 'to gurgle' (клоко́чет), **колыха́ть** 'to sway' (колы́шу, колы́шешь), **лепета́ть** 'to babble' (лепечу́, лепе́чешь), **лиза́ть** 'to lick' (лижу́, ли́жешь), **ма́зать** 'to daub' (ма́жу, ма́жешь), **мета́ть** 'to throw' (мечу́, ме́чешь), **мурлы́кать** 'to purr' (мурлы́чу, мурлы́чешь; also мурлы́каю, -аешь), **паха́ть** 'to plough' (пашу́, па́шешь), **плеска́ть** 'to splash' (плещу́, пле́щешь), **пляса́ть** 'to dance' (пляшу́, пля́шешь), **полоска́ть** 'to rinse' (полощу́, поло́щешь), **пря́тать** 'to hide' (пря́чу, пря́чешь), **ре́зать** 'to cut' (ре́жу, ре́жешь), **ропта́ть** 'to grumble' (ропщу́, ро́пщешь), **ры́скать** 'to rove' (ры́щу, ры́щешь), **скака́ть** 'to gallop' (скачу́, ска́чешь), **скрежета́ть** 'to grind' (скрежещу́, скрежжещешь), **сы́пать** 'to sprinkle' (сы́плю, сы́плешь), **теса́ть** 'to hew' (тешу́, те́шешь), **топта́ть** 'to trample' (топчу́, то́пчешь), **трепа́ть** 'to tousle' (треплю́, тре́плешь), **трепета́ть** 'to tremble' (трепещу́, трепе́щешь), **ты́кать** 'to prod' (ты́чу, ты́чешь), **хлопота́ть** 'to busy oneself' (хлопочу́, хлопо́чешь), **чеса́ть** 'to scratch' (чешу́, че́шешь), **щебета́ть** 'to twitter' (щебечу́, щебе́чешь), **щекота́ть** 'to tickle' (щекочу́, щеко́чешь), **щипа́ть** 'to pinch' (щиплю́, щи́плешь).

218 First-conjugation verbs with consonant stems III: verbs in -ти, -сть/-зть, -чь

(1) Verbs in -ти

Verbs in -**ти** subdivide in accordance with the following stem consonants:

-б-	-д-	-з-
грести́	**идти́**	**везти́**
'to row'	'to go'	'to convey'
я греб-**у́**	ид-**у́**	вез-**у́**
ты греб-**ёшь**	ид-**ёшь**	вез-**ёшь**
он греб-**ёт**	ид-**ёт**	вез-**ёт**
мы греб-**ём**	ид-**ём**	вез-**ём**
вы греб-**ёте**	ид-**ёте**	вез-**ёте**
они́ греб-**у́т**	ид-**у́т**	вез-**у́т**

-с-	-т-	-ст-
нести́	**мести́**	**расти́**
'to carry'	'to sweep'	'to grow'
нес-**у́**	мет-**у́**	раст-**у́**
нес-**ёшь**	мет-**ёшь**	раст-**ёшь**
нес-**ёт**	мет-**ёт**	раст-**ёт**
нес-**ём**	мет-**ём**	раст-**ём**
нес-**ёте**	мет-**ёте**	раст-**ёте**
нес-**у́т**	мет-**у́т**	раст-**у́т**

Other verbs include:

блюсти́ 'to conserve'	блюду́, блюдёшь
брести́ 'to wander'	бреду́, бредёшь
вести́ 'to lead'	веду́, ведёшь
обрести́ 'to acquire'	обрету́, обретёшь
пасти́ 'to tend'	пасу́, пасёшь
плести́ 'to plait'	плету́, плетёшь
ползти́ 'to crawl'	ползу́, ползёшь
скрести́ 'to scour, claw'	скребу́, скребёшь
трясти́ 'to shake'	трясу́, трясёшь
цвести́ 'to flower'	цвету́, цветёшь

(2) Verbs in -сть/-зть

Verbs in **-сть/-зть** subdivide in accordance with the following stem consonants:

-д- **класть** 'to place'	-н- **клясть** 'to curse'	-т- **честь** 'to consider'	-з- **лезть** 'to climb'
я клад-**у́**	клян-**у́**	чт-**у**	ле́з-**у**
ты клад-**ёшь**	клян-**ёшь**	чт-**ёшь**	ле́з-**ешь**
он клад-**ёт**	клян-**ёт**	чт-**ёт**	ле́з-**ет**
мы клад-**ём**	клян-**ём**	чт-**ём**	ле́з-**ем**
вы клад-**ёте**	клян-**ёте**	чт-**ёте**	ле́з-**ете**
они́ клад-**у́т**	клян-**у́т**	чт-**ут**	ле́з-**ут**

Other verbs include the following:

грызть 'to gnaw'	грызу́, грызёшь
красть 'to steal'	краду́, крадёшь
пасть 'to fall'	паду́, падёшь
сесть 'to sit down'	ся́ду, ся́дешь

Note

Честь 'to consider' is now obsolete as an independent verb, but appears as a component of compound prefixed verbs such as уче́сть 'to take into account'.

(3) Verbs in -чь

Verbs in **-чь** subdivide into **г**-stems (with mutation to **ж** before **е/ё**) and **к**-stems (with mutation to **ч** before **е/ё**).

-г- **бере́чь** 'to look after'	-к- **печь** 'to bake'
я берег-**у́**	пек-**у́**
ты береж-**ёшь**	печ-**ёшь**
он береж-**ёт**	печ-**ёт**
мы береж-**ём**	печ-**ём**
вы береж-**ёте**	печ-**ёте**
они́ берег-**у́т**	пек-**у́т**

Other verbs include the following:

влечь 'to pull, draw'	влеку́, влечёшь, влеку́т
жечь 'to burn'	жгу, жжёшь, жгут
лечь 'to lie down'	ля́гу, ля́жешь, ля́гут
мочь 'to be able'	могу́, мо́жешь, мо́гут
напря́чь 'to strain'	напрягу́, напряжёшь, напрягу́т (similarly other compounds of -**прячь**)
пренебре́чь 'to disdain'	пренебрегу́, пренебрежёшь, пренебрегу́т
сечь 'to cut'	секу́, сечёшь, секу́т
стричь 'to cut' (hair)	стригу́, стрижёшь, стригу́т
течь 'to flow'	течёт, теку́т

Note

Дости́чь (= **дости́гнуть**) 'to achieve': дости́гну, дости́гнешь. Both infinitives are standard forms. **Дости́чь** has a colloquial nuance and is commoner in the press; **дости́гнуть** is regarded as more 'bookish'.

219 Mobile stress in the conjugation of first-conjugation verbs

(1) Stress change in the conjugation of verbs of more than one syllable usually involves a shift of stress from the *ending* in the first-person singular to the *stem* in the other forms of the present tense or future perfective: **я пишу́** 'I write', **ты пи́шешь** 'you write'; **я приму́** 'I shall accept', **ты при́мешь** 'you will accept' etc.

(2) Verbs with stem-stressed infinitives (e.g. **пря́тать** 'to hide') are not subject to stress change in conjugation.

(3) Stress change takes place in the conjugation of the following types of first-conjugation verbs with *consonant* stems:

(i) Verbs in -**ать** with end stress in the infinitive and consonant mutation throughout conjugation (see **217**). Note that **алка́ть**, **колеба́ть[ся]** and **колыха́ть** take stem stress *throughout* conjugation.

(ii) **Стлать** 'to spread' (see **216** (2) (i)) and **стона́ть** 'to groan' (see **216** (1) (i)).

(iii) Verbs in **-оть** (see **216**) (1) (iii)).

(iv) Compounds of **-глянуть**, e.g. **заглянуть** 'to peep in' (загляну́, загля́нешь), **обману́ть** 'to deceive', **тону́ть** 'to drown', **тяну́ть** 'to pull' (see **216** (1) (ii)).

(v) **Приня́ть** 'to accept' and compounds of **-нять** with prefixes ending in a consonant (see **216** (2) (iv) note).

(vi) **Мочь** 'to be able' (see **218** (3)).

220 Second conjugation: present-future stems

(1) The present-future stems of verbs in the second conjugation end in a *consonant* (with very few exceptions, which include **бо-я́ться** 'to fear', **сто́-ить** 'to cost', **сто-я́ть** 'to stand', **стро́-ить** 'to build').

(2) Second-conjugation verbs include:

(i) All verbs in **-ить** (except for those with monosyllabic infinitives (see **215** (5), **216** (2) (ii)), **почи́ть** 'to rest' and compounds of **-шиби́ть** (see **216** (2) (vi)).

(ii) Many verbs in **-еть**.

(iii) Some verbs in **-ать**.

(iv) Two verbs in **-ять**: **боя́ться** 'to fear', **стоя́ть** 'to stand'.

221 Present-future endings in the second conjugation

Second-conjugation verbs conjugate as follows:

Verbs in **-ить** **говори́ть** 'to speak'	Verbs in **-еть** **смотре́ть** 'to look'	Verbs in **-ать** **стуча́ть** 'to knock'	Verbs in **-ять** **стоя́ть** 'to stand'
я говор-**ю́**	смотр-**ю́**	стуч-**у́**	сто-**ю́**
ты говор-**и́шь**	смо́тр-**ишь**	стуч-**и́шь**	сто-**и́шь**
он говор-**и́т**	смо́тр-**ит**	стуч-**и́т**	сто-**и́т**
мы говор-**и́м**	смо́тр-**им**	стуч-**и́м**	сто-**и́м**
вы говор-**и́те**	смо́тр-**ите**	стуч-**и́те**	сто-**и́те**
они́ говор-**я́т**	смо́тр-**ят**	стуч-**а́т**	сто-**я́т**

(1) **ю** is replaced by **у** and **я** by **а** after **ж, ч, ш** or **щ** (see **16** (1)).

(2) Second-conjugation verbs in **-еть** include many verbs which denote sounds, and some others: **вертéть** 'to spin' (верчý, вéртишь), **вúдеть** 'to see' (вúжу, вúдишь), **висéть** 'to hang' (вишý, висúшь), **глядéть** 'to glance' (гляжý, глядúшь), **горéть** 'to burn' (горю́, горúшь), **гремéть** 'to thunder' (гремлю́, гремúшь), **гудéть** 'to buzz' (гудúт), **звенéть** 'to ring' (звеню́, звенúшь), **кипéть** 'to boil' (киплю́, кипúшь), **летéть** 'to fly' (лечý, летúшь), **свистéть** 'to whistle' (свищý, свистúшь), **сидéть** 'to sit' (сижý, сидúшь), **скрипéть** 'to creak' (скриплю́, скрипúшь), **смотрéть** 'to look' (смотрю́, смóтришь), **терпéть** 'to endure' (терплю́, тéрпишь), **храпéть** 'to snore' (храплю́, храпúшь), **хрипéть** 'to wheeze' (хриплю́, хрипúшь), **шипéть** 'to hiss' (шиплю́, шипúшь), **шумéть** 'to make a noise' (шумлю́, шумúшь). For consonant changes see **222** and for stress changes see **223**.

(3) Second-conjugation verbs in **-ать** include:

(i) Many verbs associated with sound, with stems ending in **ж, ч, ш** or **щ**: **бренчáть** 'to strum' (бренчý, бренчúшь); likewise **визжáть** 'to scream, squeal', **ворчáть** 'to growl', **дребезжáть** 'to jingle' (third person only), **жужжáть** 'to buzz', **звучáть** 'to sound' (third person only), **кричáть** 'to shout', **молчáть** 'to be silent', **мычáть** 'to moo, bellow', **пищáть** 'to squeak', **рычáть** 'to roar', **слы́шать** 'to hear', **стучáть** 'to knock', **трещáть** 'to crackle'.

(ii) A number of other verbs: **гнать** 'to drive' (гоню́, гóнишь), **держáть** 'to hold' (держý, дéржишь), **дрожáть** 'to tremble' (дрожý, дрожúшь), **дышáть** 'to breathe' (дышý, ды́шишь), **лежáть** 'to lie' (лежý, лежúшь), **спать** 'to sleep' (сплю, спишь).

(4) **Боя́ться** 'to fear' conjugates бою́сь, бойшься.

222 Consonant change in the conjugation of second-conjugation verbs

A consistent feature of the second conjugation is the mutation of the consonant in the first-person singular of the present tense and future perfective of verbs in **-ить** and **-еть**. This is regular for all second-conjugation verbs with stems ending in **-б-, -в-, -д-, -з-, -с-, -т-, -ф-** (verbs in **-ить** only), **-м-, -п-** and **-ст-** (verbs in **-ить** *and* **-еть**).

б : бл	в : вл	д : ж	з : ж
люби́ть	**ста́вить**	**гла́дить**	**ла́зить**
'to love'	'to stand'	'to iron'	'to climb'
я люблю́	ста́влю	гла́жу	ла́жу
ты лю́бишь	ста́вишь	гла́дишь	ла́зишь
он лю́бит	ста́вит	гла́дит	ла́зит
мы лю́бим	ста́вим	гла́дим	ла́зим
вы лю́бите	ста́вите	гла́дите	ла́зите
они́ лю́бят	ста́вят	гла́дят	ла́зят

с : ш	т : ч	ф : фл
проси́ть	**плати́ть**	**графи́ть**
'to ask'	'to pay'	'to rule' (paper)
я прошу́	плачу́	графлю́
ты про́сишь …	пла́тишь …	графи́шь …

	м : мл		п : пл	
	корми́ть	**шуме́ть**	**топи́ть**	**храпе́ть**
	'to feed'	'to make a noise'	'to heat'	'to snore'
	я кормлю́	шумлю́	топлю́	храплю́
	ты ко́рмишь …	шуми́шь …	то́пишь …	храпи́шь …

	ст : щ	
	мстить	**свисте́ть**
	'to avenge'	'to whistle'
	мщу	свищу́
	мстишь …	свисти́шь …

Note

The mutation **т : щ** affects only certain perfective verbs (e.g. **прекрати́ть** 'to cease' (прекращу́, прекрати́шь).

For other verbs affected by consonant changes see **221** (2) and **223** (3) (i), (ii).

223 Stress change in the second conjugation

(1) Many second-conjugation verbs with end-stressed infinitives shift stress from the ending in the first-person singular to the stem in

the rest of the conjugation, e.g. **кури́ть** 'to smoke' (курю́, ку́ришь, ку́рит). Verbs with *stem*-stressed infinitives (e.g. **ве́рить** 'to believe') do not undergo stress change in conjugation.

(2) Verbs in -**ить**, -**еть** and -**ать** which undergo stress change in conjugation include the following types:

вари́ть	**смотре́ть**	**держа́ть**
'to boil'	'to look'	'to hold'
я варю́	смотрю́	держу́
ты ва́ришь	смо́тришь	де́ржишь
он ва́рит	смо́трит	де́ржит
мы ва́рим	смо́трим	де́ржим
вы ва́рите	смо́трите	де́ржите
они́ ва́рят	смо́трят	де́ржат

(3) Other verbs which undergo stress change include the following (those which also undergo *consonant* change (see **222**) are indicated with an asterisk):

(i) Verbs in -**ить**:

бро`ди́ть	'to wander'	**лови́ть**	'to catch'
буди́ть	'to awaken'	compounds of -**ложи́ть** 'to lay'
води́ть	'to lead'	**люби́ть**	'to like'
вози́ть	'to convey'	**мани́ть**	'to entice'
вскочи́ть	'to jump up'	compounds of -**мени́ть** 'to change'
гаси́ть	'to cancel'	**моли́ть**	'to pray'
грузи́ть	'to load'	**молоти́ть**	'to thresh'
дави́ть	'to press, crush'	**мочи́ть**	'to wet'
дари́ть	'to present'	**носи́ть**	'to carry'
дели́ть	'to share'	**пили́ть**	'to saw'
дразни́ть	'to tease'	**плати́ть**	'to pay'
дружи́ть	'to be friends'	**получи́ть**	'to receive'
души́ть	'to stifle'	**провали́ться**	'to fail'
жени́ться	'to marry'	**проглоти́ть**	'to swallow'
заблуди́ться	'to get lost'	**проси́ть**	'to request'
кати́ть	'to roll'	**простуди́ться**	'to catch cold'
клони́ть	'to incline'	**пусти́ть**	'to let go'
колоти́ть	'to hammer'	**руби́ть**	'to chop'
копи́ть	'to accumulate'	**свети́ть**	'to shine'
корми́ть	'to feed'	**серди́ть**	'to anger'
коси́ть	'to scythe'	**служи́ть**	'to serve'
крести́ть	'to christen'	compounds of **-станови́ть**
купи́ть	'to buy'	**ступи́ть**	'to step'
лепи́ть	'to mould, sculpt'	**суди́ть**	'to judge'
лечи́ть	'to give treatment'	**суши́ть**	'to dry'

тащи́ть	'to drag'	**хвали́ть**	'to praise'
*топи́ть	'to heat'	**ходи́ть*	'to go, walk'
*торопи́ть	'to hasten'	**хорони́ть**	'to bury'
точи́ть	'to sharpen'	**цени́ть**	'to value'
*труди́ться	'to labour'	**черти́ть*	'to draw'
туши́ть	'to extinguish'	**шути́ть*	'to joke'
урони́ть	'to drop'	**яви́ть*	'to display'
учи́ть	'to teach'		

Note

Коси́ть 'to squint' has fixed end stress in conjugation.

Some verbs have alternative stress in conjugation:

до́ит or дои́т	'milks'
зу́брит or зубри́т	'swats'
кро́шит or кроши́т	'crumbles'
кру́жит or кружи́т	'circles'
по́ит or пои́т	'waters'

(ii) Verbs in **-еть**:

*верте́ть 'to spin'	я верчу́	ты ве́ртишь
смотре́ть 'to look'	я смотрю́	ты смо́тришь
*терпе́ть 'to endure'	я терплю́	ты те́рпишь

(iii) Verbs in **-ать**:

гнать 'to drive'	я гоню́	ты го́нишь
держа́ть 'to hold'	я держу́	ты де́ржишь
дыша́ть 'to breathe'	я дышу́	ты ды́шишь

224 Irregular verbs

A number of verbs conform to none of the above patterns, or combine elements of both conjugations. They include

бежа́ть	**есть**	**хоте́ть**	**дать**
'to run'	'to eat'	'to want'	'to give'
я бегу́	ем	хочу́	дам
ты бежи́шь	ешь	хо́чешь	дашь
он бежи́т	ест	хо́чет	даст
мы бежи́м	еди́м	хоти́м	дади́м

| вы бежи́те | еди́те | хоти́те | дади́те |
| они́ бегу́т | едя́т | хотя́т | даду́т |

as well as **чтить** 'to honour' (чту, чтишь, чтит, чтим, чти́те, чтут/ чтят).

225 Deficiencies in the conjugation of certain verbs

(1) The following verbs have no first-person singular: **затми́ть** 'to eclipse', **очути́ться** 'to find oneself', **победи́ть** 'to win', **убеди́ть** 'to convince', **чуди́ть** 'to behave eccentrically'. However, paraphrases can be used: **могу́ очути́ться** 'I may find myself', **я смогу́ победи́ть** 'I shall win', **мне уда́стся его́ убеди́ть** 'I shall convince him', **я не ду́маю чуди́ть** 'I have no intention of behaving eccentrically'. A paraphrase (e.g. **говорю́ де́рзости**) is also required for the first-person singular of **дерзи́ть** 'to be impertinent' (since **держу́**, as the first-person singular of **держа́ть** 'to hold', is not available).

(2) Some doubt remains about the first-person singular of **пылесо́-сить** (colloquial) 'to hoover'; **пылесо́шу** is recorded, but the para-phrase **убира́ю пылесо́сом** 'I hoover' is often preferred.

(3) Some verbs have no first- or second-person singular or plural. They include **звуча́ть** 'to sound', **зна́чить** 'to mean' ('I mean', 'you mean' etc. are rendered as **хочу́ сказа́ть**, **хо́чешь сказа́ть**), **означа́ть** 'to signify', **течь** 'to flow'.

(4) The first and second persons of some other verbs (e.g. **горе́ть** 'to burn', **кипе́ть** 'to boil') appear in figurative meanings only: **горю́** жела́нием уе́хать 'I am burning with a desire to leave', **киплю́** негодова́нием 'I am boiling with indignation'.

(5) **Ку́шать** 'to eat' should not be used in the first-person singular or plural, while in the second-person singular and plural it can sound cloying, and the third-person forms are addressed mainly to children. 'To eat' is best rendered by the verb **есть** (see **224**), except in the imperative, where **ку́шай!**, **ку́шайте!** are preferred. (Note, however, a mother's strict instruction to her child: **Ешь** всё по поря́дку! 'Eat everything in the right order!' See **229** (2).)

(6) **Слыха́ть** 'to hear' is used only in the infinitive and past tense (there are, however, no such restrictions on **слы́шать** 'to hear').

(7) **Мочь** 'to be able' and **хотеть** 'to want' are not normally found in the imperfective future. Instead, the perfectives **смочь, захотеть** are used, or, in the case of **мочь**, the paraphrase **быть в состоянии** 'to be capable of'.

226 The verb 'to be'

(1) The verb **быть** 'to be' has no present tense in Russian:

Я ру́сский	I am Russian
Э́то мой муж	This is my husband

(2) A dash may be used for emphasis:

Я ру́сский, а он — нет	I am Russian and he is not

A dash also appears in definitions:

Москва́ — столи́ца России	Moscow is the capital of Russia

(3) 'It is' has no equivalent in many impersonal expressions:

Интере́сно слу́шать ра́дио	It is interesting to listen to the radio
Темне́ет	It is getting dark
Хо́лодно	It is cold

(4) The declarative '**there is/are**' either has no equivalent in Russian or may be rendered by a dash:

На стене́ — карти́на	There is a picture on the wall

Alternatively, На стене́ **есть** карти́на. See (5).

(5) **Есть**, a relic of a former verb conjugation, may be used for emphasis. **Есть** is particularly common:

(i) In questions (and positive answers to questions):

— Папиро́сы **есть**?
— **Есть!**
'Are there any cigarettes?'
'Yes, there are'

(ii)   In contexts where the verb is heavily emphasized:

— Кем же ты хо́чешь быть?
— Кем **есть** — рядовы́м матро́сом
'What do you want to be, then?'
'What I **am**, an ordinary rating'

— Ну́жно справедли́вое реше́ние
— На́ше реше́ние **и есть** справедли́вое
'We need an equitable solution'
'Our solution **is** equitable'

Зако́н **есть** зако́н
The law is the law

(iii)   When 'to be' means 'to exist':

Есть таки́е лю́ди, кото́рые не лю́бят икры́
There are people who do not like caviar

(iv)   **Есть** is also found in definitions:

Пряма́я ли́ния **есть** кратча́йшее расстоя́ние мѐжду двумя́
то́чками
A straight line is the shortest distance between two points

(6)   In the press and other official contexts the verb **явля́ться** 'to be'
also appears in definitions (for case usage see **102** (3) and (4)):

Це́лью перегово́ров **явля́ется** подписа́ние догово́ра
The aim of the talks is the signing of a treaty

Равнопра́вие **явля́ется** осно́вой на́шего о́бщества
Equality is the basis of our society

(7)   To point something out, **вот** is used, the equivalent of English
'here is, are; there is, are':

Вот моя́ тетра́дь
Here is/there is my exercise book

(8)   A more specific verb is often used as an equivalent of 'to be':

Наступа́ет па́уза	There **is** a pause
Раздаю́тся аплодисме́нты	There **is** applause
сиде́ть в тюрьме́	**to be** in prison
служи́ть в а́рмии	**to be** in the army
состоя́ть чле́ном	**to be** a member

стоя́ть на я́коре	**to be** at anchor
Простира́ются леса́	There **are** forests
учи́ться в университе́те	**to be** at university

(9) **Быва́ть** denotes repetition or frequency:

Я ча́сто **быва́ю** в Москве́
I am often in Moscow

В на́шем рестора́не **быва́ют** грибы́
You can sometimes get mushrooms in our restaurant

227 Formation of the imperative

(1) The *familiar* imperative is used in issuing commands to persons one normally addresses as **ты** (see **115**). The *formal* imperative, which is used in addressing people whom one would normally address as **вы** (see **115**), is made by adding **-те** to the familiar imperative.

(2) The familiar imperative is formed from imperfective and perfective verbs by adding **-й**, **-и** or **-ь** to the present-future stem (see **212**).

(i) Imperative in -й

The letter **-й(те)** is added to present-future stems ending in a vowel.

Infinitive	Third-person plural	Stem	Imperative
петь	**по-ю́т**	**по-**	**по́й(те)**
постро́ить	**постро́-ят**	**постро́-**	**постро́й(те)**
рабо́тать	**рабо́та-ют**	**рабо́та-**	**рабо́тай(те)**

Note

(a) The imperatives of **дава́ть** 'to give' and compounds of **-дава́ть** **-знава́ть** and **-става́ть** are as follows: **дава́й(те)** 'give', **встава́й(те)** 'get up'.

(b) **Бить** 'to hit' has the imperative **бей(те)**; **вить** 'to weave', **лить** 'to pour', **пить** 'to drink', **шить** 'to sew' form their imperatives in the same way.

(c) Perfective compounds in **-éхать** (e.g. **приéхать**) have the same imperative as imperfective compounds in **-езжáть** (e.g. **приезжáть**): **приезжáй(те)**! 'come!'

(ii) Imperative in -и

The letter **-и(те)** is added to the present-future stem of verbs with *final* or *mobile* stress in conjugation and with a present-future stem ending in a *consonant*.

(a) Final stress throughout conjugation:

Infinitive	Third-person plural	Stem	Imperative
вестú	**вед-ýт**	**вед-**	**ведú(те)**
взять	**возь-мýт**	**возьм-**	**возьмú(те)**
говорúть	**говор-я́т**	**говор-**	**говорú(те)**

(b) Mobile stress in conjugation:

держáть	**дéрж-ат**	**дéрж-**	**держú(те)**
получúть	**полýч-ат**	**полýч-**	**получú(те)**
шептáть	**шéпч-ут**	**шéпч-**	**шепчú(те)**

(iii) Imperative in -ь

A soft sign is added to the present-future stem of verbs which are *stem-stressed throughout conjugation* and whose present-future stem ends in a *single* consonant.

вéрить	**вéр-ят**	**вéр-**	**верь(те)**
зажáрить	**зажáр-ят**	**зажáр-**	**зажáрь(те)**
мáзать	**мáж-ут**	**мáж-**	**мажь(те)**
плáкать	**плáч-ут**	**плáч-**	**плачь(те)**
постáвить	**постáв-ят**	**постáв-**	**постáвь(те)**

Note

(a) Apart from many stem-stressed second-conjugation verbs (**знакóмить** 'to acquaint' (imper. **знакóмь**), **мнóжить** 'to multiply' (imper. **мнóжь**) etc.), this category contains a number of first-conjugation verbs with consonant stems and stress on the stem throughout conjugation: **быть** 'to be' (imper. **будь**), **деть** 'to put' (imper. **день**), **лезть** 'to climb' (imper. **лезь**), **мáзать** 'to daub' (imper. **мажь**), **пря́тать** 'to hide' (imper.

прячь), ре́зать 'to cut' (imper. режь), сесть 'to sit down' (imper. сядь), стать 'to stand' (imper. стань). Note лечь 'to lie down', imper. ляг – a soft sign may not appear after a guttural consonant.

(b) Stem-stressed по́мнить 'to remember' has imperative по́мни, since the stem ends in *two* consonants.

(c) The third-person imperative is expressed by the particle пусть and the third-person singular or plural of the present tense or perfective future: пусть (она́) пи́шет 'let her write', пусть (они́) приду́т 'let them come'.

228 Stress in the imperative

With the exception of a number of monosyllabic imperatives, where the stress necessarily falls on the single syllable (жди! 'wait!', пой! 'sing!', не сме́йся! 'don't laugh!'), stress in the imperative falls on the same syllable as in the first-person singular.

Infinitive	First-person singular	Imperative
гнать	гоню́	гони́!
дыша́ть	дышу́	дыши́!
звать	зову́	зови́!
писа́ть	пишу́	пиши́!
получи́ть	получу́	получи́!
сказа́ть	скажу́	скажи́!
смотре́ть	смотрю́	смотри́!

229 Verbs with no imperative or a little-used imperative

(1) Ви́деть 'to see' and слы́шать 'to hear' do not have imperatives. However, слу́шай! 'listen!' and смотри́! 'look!' are commonly used.

(2) Есть 'to eat' has the imperative ешь! However, it is usually replaced by the imperative of ку́шать, since the latter has a courteous nuance absent in the rather familiar ешь! (see 225 (5)).

230 Formation of the past tense

(1) The past tense of verbs with infinitives in **-ть** and **-сть** is formed by replacing **-ть** or **-сть** by **-л** to give the masculine past:

курить	он курил	'he was smoking'
писать	он писал	'he was writing'
сказать	он сказал	'he said'
упасть	он упал	'he fell'
покраснеть	он покраснел	'he blushed'

(2) The feminine, neuter and plural are formed by adding **-a**, **-o** and **-и** respectively to the masculine:

он писал/упал	(masculine)
она писала/упала	(feminine)
оно писало/упало	(neuter)
мы, вы, они писали/упали	(plural)

(3) The past agrees with the subject of the verb in *number* (singular or plural) and *gender* (masculine, feminine or neuter):

я **писал**	I was writing (male subject)
я **писала**	I was writing (female subject)
ты **писал**	you were writing (male subject)
ты **писала**	you were writing (female subject)
он **писал**	he was writing
она **писала**	she was writing
оно **писало**	it was writing
мы, вы, они **писали**	we, you, they were writing

Note
Учесть 'to take into account', past учёл, учла, учло, учли (similarly other compounds of -честь).

231 Verbs with no -л in the masculine past tense

Some types of verb have no **-л** in the masculine past tense.

(1) Verbs in -ереть

тереть 'to rub': **тёр** тёрла тёрло тёрли

Similarly **запере́ть** 'to lock' (он за́пер/она́ заперла́/они́ за́перли 'he/she/they locked'), **умере́ть** 'to die' (он у́мер/она́ умерла́/они́ у́мерли 'he/she/they died').

(2) Verbs in -ну-

The suffix **-ну-** is optional in the masculine past of *imperfective* stem-stressed verbs which indicate a change in state:

   га́снуть 'to be extinguished': **гас/га́снул** га́сла га́сло га́сли

Similarly:

вя́знуть	'to stick fast'	**кре́пнуть**	'to get stronger'
ги́бнуть	'to perish'	**ме́ркнуть**	'to grow dim'
гло́хнуть	'to go deaf'	**па́хнуть**	'to smell'
до́хнуть	'to die' (of animals)	**сле́пнуть**	'to go blind'
ки́снуть	'to turn sour'	**со́хнуть**	'to become dry'

Note

(a) Some imperfectives in **-нуть** are now often replaced by secondary imperfectives:

га́снуть	**погаса́ть**	'to be extinguished'
ги́бнуть	**погиба́ть**	'to perish'
мёрзнуть	**замерза́ть**	'to freeze'
со́хнуть	**просыха́ть**	'to become dry'
ту́хнуть	**потуха́ть**	'to be extinguished'

(b) Stem-stressed *perfective* verbs in **-нуть** which indicate a change in state (**замёрзнуть** 'to freeze', **привы́кнуть** 'to get used to' etc.) do *not* have optional **-ну-** in the masculine past: он **замёрз**, **привы́к** etc.

(c) Verbs in **-ну-** which denote instantaneous actions (e.g. **пры́г-нуть** 'to jump') retain the suffix in all past forms: он **пры́гнул** 'he jumped'.

(3) Verbs in -ти

Verbs in **-ти** (except for those with present-future stems in **-д** and **-т**, e.g. **вести́** 'to lead', past **вёл**, вела́, вело́, вели́; **мести́** 'to sweep', past **мёл**, мела́, мело́, мели́).

б-stems	з-stems	с-stems	ст-stems
грести́	**везти́**	**нести́**	**расти́**
'to row'	'to convey'	'to carry'	'to grow'

грёб	вёз	нёс	рос
гребла́	везла́	несла́	росла́
гребло́	везло́	несло́	росло́
гребли́	везли́	несли́	росли́

Note

Пасти́ 'to tend, graze' (past **пас, пасла́**), **ползти́** 'to crawl' (**полз, ползла́**), **скрести́** 'to scour, claw' (**скрёб, скребла́**), трясти́ 'to shake' (**тряс, трясла́**).

(4) Verbs in -зть

These include **грызть** 'to gnaw' (past **грыз, гры́зла, гры́зло, гры́зли**) and **лезть** 'to climb'.

(5) Verbs in -чь

г-stems	**к**-stems
бере́чь	**печь**
'to look after'	'to bake'

берёг	пёк
берегла́	пекла́
берегло́	пекло́
берегли́	пекли́

The past of other verbs in -**чь** is as follows:

влечь 'to pull, draw'	влёк, влекла́, влекло́, влекли́
дости́чь 'to achieve'	дости́г, дости́гла, дости́гло, дости́гли
жечь 'to burn'	жёг, жгла, жгло, жгли
лечь 'to lie down'	лёг, легла́, легло́, легли́
мочь 'to be able'	мог, могла́, могло́, могли́
напря́чь 'to strain'	напря́г, напрягла́, напрягло́, напрягли́
пренебре́чь 'to disdain'	пренебрёг, -брегла́, -брегло́, -брегли́
сечь 'to cut'	сёк, секла́, секло́, секли́
стере́чь 'to guard'	стерёг, стерегла́, стерегло́, стерегли́
стричь 'to cut' (hair)	стриг, стри́гла, стри́гло, стри́гли
течь 'to flow'	тёк, текла́, текло́, текли́

(6) Compounds of -шибить

Perfective compounds of -**шибить** (e.g. **ушибить** 'to bruise') have past tense -шиб, -шибла, -шибло, -шибли.

232 Mobile stress in the past tense of verbs

Most past-tense forms from verbs in -**ть** have the same stress as the infinitive. There are, however, a number of verbs which have:

(1) End stress in the feminine past

Most of them are monosyllabic verbs and their prefixed derivatives:

(i) Unprefixed verbs

> **быть** 'to be': был **была** было были

Similarly **брать/взять** 'to take', **вить** 'to twine', **гнать** 'to drive', **дать** 'to give', **драть** 'to flay', **ждать** 'to wait', **жить** 'to live', **звать** 'to call', **лить** 'to pour', **пить** 'to drink', **плыть** 'to swim', **рвать** 'to tear', **слыть** 'to have the reputation of being', **спать** 'to sleep', **ткать** 'to weave'.

Note

(a) **Дать** 'to give' has alternative neuter stress да́ло or дало́.

(b) **Не** is stressed when combined with the masculine, neuter and plural past forms of **быть** (**не́** был, не была́, **не́** было, **не́** были) and *may* be stressed when combined with the masculine, neuter and plural forms of the verbs **жить** and **дать**: не́ жил, не жила́, не́ жило, не́ жили **or** не жи́л, не жила́, не жи́ло, не жи́ли; не́ дал, не дала́, не́ дало, не́ дали **or** не да́л, не дала́, не да́ло, не да́ли.

(ii) Prefixed verbs

(a) **Собра́ть** 'to collect': собра́л, **собрала́**, собра́ло, собра́ли.

Similarly **взорва́ть** 'to blow up', **добы́ть** 'to acquire', **избра́ть** 'to elect', **разда́ть** 'to distribute', **сдать** 'to surrender', **снять** 'to take off', **убра́ть** 'to clear away' etc.

(b) **Заня́ть** 'to occupy': за́нял, **заняла́**, за́няло, за́няли.

Similarly **заперéть** 'to lock' (зáпер, заперлá), **начáть** 'to begin', **отперéть** 'to unlock', **поднять** 'to pick up', **понять** 'to understand', **принять** 'to accept', **умерéть** 'to die' (ýмер, умерлá) etc.

Note
Задáть 'to set' has alternative stem and prefix stress in the masculine, neuter and plural past: зáдал, задалá, зáдало, зáдали, **or** задáл, задалá, задáло, задáли. Similarly **налить** 'to pour', **обнять** 'to embrace', **отдáть** 'to give back', **поднять** 'to raise', **полить** 'to water', **продáть** 'to sell', **прожить** 'to live, spend' (a certain time), **создáть** 'to create' etc. **Передáть** 'to hand over' has the past forms пéредал, передалá, пéредало, пéредали.

(2) End stress in the feminine, neuter and plural

This affects:

(i) A number of reflexive verbs, e.g.

собрáться 'to assemble': собрáлся, **собралáсь, собралóсь, собралúсь**

Similarly **брáться/взяться** 'to get down to', **дождáться** 'to wait until', **оторвáться** 'to be torn away from', **создáться** 'to be created', **удáться** 'to succeed' (план удáлся 'the plan succeeded', мне удалóсь 'I succeeded').

(ii) All verbs in -**ти**:

блюстú 'to conserve'	блюл, блюлá, блюлó, блюлú
брестú 'to wander'	брёл, брелá, брелó брелú
везтú 'to convey'	вёз, везлá, везлó, везлú
вестú 'to lead'	вёл, велá, велó, велú
грестú 'to row'	грёб, греблá, греблó, греблú
идтú 'to go'	шёл, шла, шло, шли
местú 'to sweep'	мёл, мелá, мелó, мелú
нестú 'to carry'	нёс, неслá, неслó, неслú
обрестú 'to acquire'	обрёл, обрелá, обрелó, обрелú
пастú 'to tend'	пас, паслá, паслó, паслú
плестú 'to weave'	плёл, плелá, плелó, плелú
ползтú 'to crawl'	полз, ползлá, ползлó, ползлú
растú 'to grow'	рос, рослá, рослó, рослú
скрестú 'to scour'	скрёб, скреблá, скреблó, скреблú
трястú 'to shake'	тряс, тряслá, тряслó, трясли
цвестú 'to flower'	цвёл, цвелá, цвелó, цвелú

(iii) Most verbs in -**чь** (see **231** (5)).

(3) Reflexive endings stressed throughout

нача́ться 'to begin': **начался́, начала́сь, начало́сь, начали́сь**

Similarly **заня́ться** 'to occupy oneself' (with alternative masculine заня́лся).

233 Formation of the future (imperfective and perfective)

(1) The imperfective future

The compound future (imperfective) consists of the relevant form of the future tense of **быть** and the imperfective infinitive:

я **бу́ду** отдыха́ть	I shall rest
ты **бу́дешь** отдыха́ть	you will rest
он, она́, оно́ **бу́дет** отдыха́ть	he, she, it will rest
мы **бу́дем** отдыха́ть	we shall rest
вы **бу́дете** отдыха́ть	you will rest
они́ **бу́дут** отдыха́ть	they will rest

Note

(a) **Бу́ду** is also used as a future in its own right: Ле́том он **бу́дет** в Санкт-Петербу́рге 'In the summer he will be in St Petersburg'.

(b) In some contexts it implies suspicion (Вы кто **бу́дете**? 'Who might you be?'), approximation (Ему́ **бу́дет** 50 лет 'He must be about 50') and is used in arithmetic (ше́стью шесть **бу́дет** 36 'six sixes are 36' (see **210**)).

(2) The perfective future

The perfective future is expressed by conjugating a perfective verb. The same endings are used as those used with imperfective verbs in rendering the present tense:

я **пишу́**	(impf.)	письмо́	'I am writing a letter'
я **напишу́**	(pf.)	письмо́	'I shall write a letter'
она́ **чита́ет**	(impf.)	статью́	'she is reading the article'
она́ **прочита́ет**	(pf.)	статью́	'she will read the article'

See **215–223** for conjugation patterns, **238–253** for the formation of aspects and **263–268** for differentiation of imperfective and perfective usage in the future.

234 The buffer vowel -o- in conjugation

In many verbs the vowel -o- appears between a prefix ending in a consonant and a verb form which begins with two or more consonants or with a consonant + soft sign. This may affect:

(1) *All* perfective forms:

Infinitive	Past	Future	Imperative
соврáть 'to lie'	соврáл	совру́	соври́(те)
отослáть 'to send away'	отослáл	отошлю́	отошли́(те)

(2) The **future, imperative** and **feminine, neuter** and **plural past**:

сжечь 'to burn'	сжёг	сожгу́	сожги́(те)
	сожглá		
	сожглó		
	сожгли́		

(3) The **infinitive** and **past tense** only:

разобрáть	'to discern'	разобрáл	разберу́	разбери́(те)
отозвáть	'to recall'	отозвáл	отзову́	отзови́(те)
разогнáть	'to disperse'	разогнáл	разгоню́	разгони́(те)

(4) The **future** and **imperative** only:

сжать	'to compress'	сжал	сожму́	сожми́(те)
отперéть	'to unlock'	óтпер	отопру́	отопри́(те)

(5) The **future** only (compounds of -бить, -вить, -лить, -пить, -шить):

разби́ть	'to smash'	разби́л	разобью́	разбéй(те)
сшить	'to sew'	сшил	сошью́	сшей(те)

Aspect

235 The aspect. Introductory comments

(1) The Russian verb system is dominated by the concept of **aspect**.

(2) Most Russian verbs have *two* aspects, an **imperfective** and a **perfective**, formally differentiated in one of the following ways:

(i) By prefixation: imperfective писа́ть/perfective **на**писа́ть.

(ii) By internal modification: imperfective забыва́ть/perfective забы́ть 'to forget'; imperfective пуска́ть/perfective пусти́ть 'to let go'.

(iii) By derivation from entirely different roots: imperfective **говори́ть**/perfective **сказа́ть** 'to say'.

(iv) In a few instances, by stress: imperfective **насыпа́ть**/perfective **насы́пать** 'to pour'; imperfective **среза́ть**/perfective **сре́зать** 'to cut down'.

Note
Where aspect is differentiated by stress, the imperfectives are conjugated like **знать** and the perfectives like first-conjugation verbs with consonant stems (type II; see **217**).

(3) *Both* aspects are used in the past and future, the imperative and the infinitive. However, only the *imperfective* is used in the present tense.

(4) Most verbs thus have five finite forms, e.g. imperfective **пить**/perfective **вы́пить** 'to drink':

	Past	Present	Future
Impf.	я пил	я пью	я бу́ду пить
Pf.	я вы́пил	—	я вы́пью

(5) The fundamental distinction between the aspects is that the **imperfective**:

(i) focuses on **an action in progress**.

Он **пил/пьёт/бу́дет пить** молоко́
He **was, is, will be drinking** milk

(ii) denotes **frequency** of occurrence:

Он ча́сто **пил, пьёт, бу́дет пить** молоко́
He often **drank, drinks, will drink** milk

The **perfective**, by contrast, emphasizes **successful completion and result**:

| Я **вы́пил** молоко́ | I **have drunk** the milk |
| Я **вы́пью** молоко́ | I **shall drink** the milk |

(Note, as a *result*, there is, will be no milk left.)

Note

The perfective past can render *both* perfect *and* pluperfect tenses. Thus, он написа́л письмо́ can mean, in context, either 'I **have** written a letter' or 'I **had** written a letter'.

(6) The aspects may also distinguish attempted action (imperfective) from successfully completed action (perfective). Compare

Он **угова́ривал** (impf.) меня́ оста́ться
He **tried to persuade** me to stay

Он **уговори́л** (pf.) меня́ оста́ться
He **persuaded** me to stay

Note
Aspectival usage is dealt with in **255–283**.

236 Verbs with one aspect only

(1) While most verbs have two aspects, some have an imperfective only:

госпо́дствовать	'to dominate'
зави́сеть	'to depend'
изоби́ловать	'to abound'
наблюда́ть	'to observe'
находи́ться	'to be situated'
нужда́ться	'to need'
отрица́ть	'to deny'
повинова́ться	'to obey'
подлежа́ть	'to be subject to'
полага́ть	'to assume'
предви́деть	'to foresee'
предстоя́ть	'to be imminent'
предчу́вствовать	'to have a premonition'
преоблада́ть	'to prevail'
пресле́довать	'to persecute'
принадлежа́ть	'to belong'

противоре́чить	'to contradict'
содержа́ть	'to contain'
состоя́ть	'to consist'
сочу́вствовать	'to sympathize'
сто́ить	'to cost'
уча́ствовать	'to participate'

Note

Утвержда́ть has no perfective in the meaning 'to affirm' but has perfective **утверди́ть** in the meaning 'to fix, establish'.

(2) Other verbs are perfective only (many though not all of these denote precipitate action):

воспря́нуть	'to cheer up'
встрепену́ться	'to start' (with surprise)
гря́нуть	'to burst out, ring out'
очути́ться	'to find oneself'
понадобиться	'to be needed, come in handy'
хлы́нуть	'to gush'

237 Bi-aspectual verbs

(1) Some verbs are bi-aspectual, that is, imperfective and perfective are represented by one verb form (though some also have alternative imperfectives: **образова́ть** (imperfective and perfective) 'to form', alternative imperfective **образо́вывать**). There are many bi-aspectuals in **-овать** and **-изировать**.

(2) Among the commonest bi-aspectuals are **атакова́ть** 'to attack', **веле́ть** 'to order, bid', **возде́йствовать** 'to have an effect on', **гармонизи́ровать** 'to harmonize', **жени́ться** 'to marry' (of a man marrying a woman – the perfective **пожени́ться** is used only when both partners are joint subjects of the verb: Они́ пожени́лись 'They got married'), **испо́льзовать** 'to use', **иссле́довать** 'to research', **казни́ть** 'to execute', **коллективизи́ровать** 'to collectivize', **конфискова́ть** 'to confiscate', **крести́ть** 'to christen' (alternative perfective **окрести́ть**), **минова́ть** 'to pass by', **насле́довать** 'to inherit' (alternative perfective **унасле́довать**), **обеща́ть** 'to promise' (alternative perfective **пообеща́ть**), **обору́довать** 'to equip', **ра́нить** 'to wound', **роди́ться** 'to be born' (alternative imperfective **рожда́ться**), **сочета́ть** 'to combine'.

(3) Thus, for example, **исслéдую** can mean both 'I research' and 'I shall/will research'. Ambiguity may be resolved by contrastive adverbs, as follows:

Положéние **постепéнно** стабилизи́руется
The situation is gradually stabilizing

Положéние **скóро** стабилизи́руется
The situation will soon stabilize

Note

Imperfective **бежáть** 'to run' is also perfective in the meaning 'to escape'; imperfective **привéтствовать** 'to greet' is also perfective in the past tense; in the past tense, bi-aspectual **организовáть** 'to organize' (imperfective also **организóвывать**) is perfective only.

238 Formation of the aspects

Most pairs of verbal aspects arise in one of the following ways:

(1) Through the addition of a **prefix** to the imperfective to make the perfective:

читáть (impf.)   **про**читáть (pf.)   'to read'

(2) Through **internal modification** involving:

(i) The insertion of a syllable into the stem infinitive:

завязáть (pf.)   завя́**зыв**ать (impf.)   'to tie'

сосредотóчить (pf.) сосредотó**чив**ать (impf.) 'to concentrate'

разби́ть (pf.)   разби**вá**ть (impf.)   'to smash'

(ii) A change in conjugation, an *imperfective* first-conjugation verb in **-а-/-я-** being paired with a *perfective* second-conjugation verb in **-и-/-е-**:

бросáть (impf.)   брóсить (pf.)   'to throw'
загорáть (impf.)   загорéть (pf.)   'to acquire a
                                             tan'

239 Formation of the perfective by prefixation

(1) An imperfective verb may become perfective through the addition of a **prefix**:

писа́ть (impf.)   **на**писа́ть (pf.)   'to write'

(2) The conjugation of a perfective verb gives it **future** meaning:

Я **напишу́** э́то письмо́
I **shall write** this letter (= get it written)

(3) While the choice of perfective prefixes appears in most cases to be arbitrary, some prefixes are associated with particular meanings; for example, **на-** is associated with verbs of printing, writing and drawing (**на**печа́тать, **на**писа́ть, **на**рисова́ть), **у-** with verbs of perception (**у**ви́деть, **у**зна́ть, **у**слы́шать), and so on.

(4) All common prefixes (except for **в-** and **до-**) participate in the process of perfectivization:

Imperfective	Perfective	
кипяти́ть	**вс**кипяти́ть	to boil
учи́ть	**вы́**учить	to learn
плати́ть	**за**плати́ть	to pay
купа́ть	**ис**купа́ть	to bathe
писа́ть	**на**писа́ть	to write
сироте́ть	**о**сироте́ть	to be orphaned
редакти́ровать	**от**редакти́ровать	to edit
ночева́ть	**пере**ночева́ть	to spend the night
смотре́ть	**по**смотре́ть	to look
ждать	**подо**жда́ть	to wait
грози́ть	**при**грози́ть	to threaten
чита́ть	**про**чита́ть	to read
буди́ть	**раз**буди́ть	to awaken
петь	**с**петь	to sing
ви́деть	**у**ви́деть	to see

240 Functions of the perfective prefixes

(1) The perfective prefixes tend to be semantically neutral, that is, they change the *aspect* of a verb but *not* its meaning. Thus, both

буди́ть and **разбуди́ть** mean 'to awaken', but **буди́ть** describes the progress of the action, without any reference to result, whereas the perfective **разбуди́ть** stresses the result:

Я его́ **буди́л, буди́л** и, наконе́ц, **разбуди́л**
I tried and tried to wake him, and finally woke him

(2) The *imperfective* verb describes:

(i) A past, present or future action in progress:

Он **учи́л** уро́к/**у́чит** уро́к/**бу́дет учи́ть** уро́к
He **was learning/is learning/will be learning** the lesson

(ii) Repeated actions:

Она́ **плати́ла/пла́тит/бу́дет плати́ть** регуля́рно
She **paid/pays/will pay** regularly

(3) The *perfective* focuses on the *completion* of a single action in the past or future. Usually, a result is implied:

Она́ **написа́ла** письмо́
She has written a letter (it is ready to send)

Она́ **прочита́ла** кни́гу
She has read the book (now *you* can read it, or it can be returned to the library)

Она́ **запла́тит** за электри́чество
She will pay the electricity (the account will be settled)

(4) Often the perfective denotes the *culmination of a process*:

Она́ **пригото́вила** у́жин   She cooked dinner

In this example the culmination of the action, expressed by the perfective **пригото́вила**, will have been preceded by a process of indeterminate length (она́ **гото́вила** у́жин 'she **was cooking** dinner'), the completion of which is denoted by the perfective.

241 Semantic differentiation of aspects

In some verbs it is possible to detect at least a minor measure of semantic differentiation between imperfective and perfective. Thus, the imperfective past of **ви́деть** 'to see' contains a nuance ('to associate with')

> **Я ви́дел** его́ вчера́   I saw him yesterday

which the perfective **уви́деть** contains in the future, but *not* in the past. Compare

> **Я уви́дел** его́ вчера́
> I caught sight of him (but *not* 'saw, associated with him') yesterday

and

> **Я уви́жу** его́ за́втра
> I shall see him (i.e. 'meet, associate with him') tomorrow
>
> **Я уви́жу** его́, как то́лько он войдёт
> I shall catch sight of him as soon as he comes in

242 Submeanings of perfectives

Apart from the resultative meaning (see **240** (3)), the perfective has a number of submeanings.

(1) **The inceptive**, denoting the beginning of an action. This meaning is often conveyed by the prefix **за-**:

заболе́ть	to fall ill
заговори́ть	to start speaking
закури́ть	to light up
замолча́ть	to fall silent
запе́ть	to burst into song
запла́кать	to burst into tears
засмея́ться	to burst out laughing
зацвести́	to blossom

Note

(a) Only some of these verbs have imperfectives: **заболева́ть, заку́ривать, запева́ть, зацвета́ть**. Where a verb has no imperfective, a paraphrase may be possible: **залива́ться сме́хом** 'to burst out laughing', **облива́ться слеза́ми** 'to burst into tears'.

(b) The meaning of inception also adheres to the perfective aspects of unidirectional verbs of motion (он **пошёл** 'he set out') (see also **326**) and to the perfectives **полюби́ть, понра́виться**: Вы лю́бите литерату́ру? Да, я **полюби́л** её ещё в шко́ле (Vasilenko) 'Do you like literature?' 'Yes, I **took a liking to it** when still at school'. Compare Вам **понра́вится** фильм 'You **will like** the film'.

(c) Inception can also be expressed by the prefixes **вз-/вс-** and **раз-/рас-**: **встрево́житься** 'to get alarmed', **рассерди́ться** 'to get angry'.

(2) The **instantaneous** or **semelfactive** submeaning:

Он **услы́шал** мой го́лос
He heard, caught the sound of my voice

Note
Instantaneous meanings are often expressed by perfectives with the suffix **-ну-**:

Он **чи́ркнул** спи́чкой   He struck a match

Other semelfactives include **кри́кнуть** 'to shout', **махну́ть** 'to wave', **плю́нуть** 'to spit' etc.

(3) The submeaning of **limited duration** (prefix **по-**):

поговори́ть   to have a chat
посиде́ть   to sit for a while
поспа́ть   to have a nap

Note
(a) **По-** can impart the meaning of limited duration to verbs which form their 'neutral' perfectives with other prefixes:

написа́ть (neutral pf.)   **по**писа́ть 'to write for a while'
запла́кать (neutral pf.)   **по**пла́кать 'to cry for a while'

(b) See **249** for imperfective submeanings.

243 Formation of verbal aspects by internal modification

Many aspectival pairs are created as the result of internal modification, in particular through suffixation. This may involve:

(1) The insertion of a syllable into a perfective infinitive to form the imperfective. This is the commonest method of forming aspectival pairs:

переписа́ть (pf.)   перепи́сывать (impf.)   'to copy'

(2) The pairing of a first-conjugation imperfective in -a-/-я- with a second-conjugation perfective in -и-/-e-: impf. позволя́ть/pf. позво́лить 'to allow'; impf. реша́ть/pf. реши́ть 'to decide'; impf. загора́ть/pf. загоре́ть 'to acquire a tan'.

244 The formation of imperfectives from prefixed first-conjugation verbs

(1) This occurs when a prefix other than the 'neutral' perfective prefix is added to an imperfective first-conjugation verb, changing not only its *aspect* but also its *meaning*.

(2) Thus, the neutral perfective of писа́ть 'to write' (changing its aspect only, *not* its meaning) is написа́ть. But other prefixes may combine with писа́ть, changing aspect **and** meaning:

записа́ть	to note down
переписа́ть	to copy
подписа́ть	to sign

and so on, each newly formed verb being a perfective *with a new meaning*.

(3) Imperfectives of such verbs are formed by inserting the suffix -ыв- before the final syllable of the infinitive, with stress falling on to the syllable preceding the suffix. In this way new sets of aspectival pairs are established:

записа́ть (pf.)   запи́сывать (impf.)   'to note down'
подписа́ть (pf.)   подпи́сывать (impf.)   'to sign'

(4) This method of forming 'secondary imperfectives' from compounds of first-conjugation verbs is an important word-formatory device which is used with many verbs, e.g.

вяза́ть 'to tie'   → связа́ть (neutral pf.) 'to tie'
    ↓
развяза́ть (pf. with new   → развя́зывать (impf.) 'to untie'
meaning: 'to untie')

(5) Of two adjacent vowels in a compound perfective, the second is replaced by -ива- in the imperfective: pf. отта́ять 'to thaw out' impf. отта́ивать (there are exceptions, e.g. pf. зате́ять 'to undertake', impf. затева́ть).

245 Vowel mutation in secondary imperfective verbs

(1) The vowel **e** becomes **ё** under stress in the secondary imperfective, thus (based on root verb **чеса́ть** 'to scratch'):

причеса́ться (pf.)/причёсываться (impf.)   'to comb one's hair'

Similarly,

завоева́ть (pf.)/завоёвывать (impf.)   'to conquer'

(2) In similar circumstances, **o** becomes **a** in the secondary imperfective:

зарабо́тать (pf.)/зараба́тывать (impf.)   'to earn'
раскопа́ть (pf.)/раска́пывать (impf.)   'to excavate'

Note

The **o** : **a** mutation does *not* affect verbs in -овать: pf. образова́ть 'to form', impf. образо́вывать.

246 Secondary imperfectives based on second-conjugation verbs

(1) A process similar to that described in **244** is used to form secondary imperfectives from second-conjugation verbs, but with the following differences:

(i) The suffix **-ив-** is used instead of **-ыв-**.

(ii) Consonant mutation operates, e.g. **с** : **ш** in

кра́сить (impf.)   → окра́сить (neutral pf.) 'to paint'
        ↓
перекра́сить (pf. with new → перекра́шивать (impf.
meaning 'to repaint')   'to repaint')

Note that **o** mutates to **a** in stressed position:

рассмотре́ть (pf.)/рассма́тривать (impf.)   'to scrutinize'

приговори́ть (pf.)/приговáривать (impf.)   'to sentence'

Similarly pf. заподо́зрить 'to suspect', impf. заподáзривать; pf. зако́нчить 'to conclude', impf. закáнчивать; pf. оспо́рить 'to

dispute', impf. оспа́ривать; подгото́вить 'to prepare, train', impf.
подгота́вливать; pf. приспосо́бить 'to adapt', impf.
приспоса́бливать.

Note

(a) In some secondary imperfectives, **o** and **a** are stylistically
differentiated, **o** being characteristic of literary style, **a** of a more
conversational style: thus pf. сосредото́чить 'to concentrate'/
impf. сосредото́чивать or сосредота́чивать. Similarly, pf.
обусло́вить, 'to condition', impf. обусло́вливать/
обусла́вливать.

(b) Some imperfectives retain **o**: pf. опоро́чить 'to discredit', impf.
опоро́чивать; pf. отсро́чить 'to defer', impf. отсро́чивать; pf.
подыто́жить, 'to sum up', impf. подыто́живать; pf.
приуро́чить 'to time', impf. приуро́чивать; pf. уполномо́чить
'to authorize', impf. уполномо́чивать; pf. упро́чить 'to con-
solidate', impf. упро́чивать.

(2) Of two adjacent vowels in a compound perfective, the second is
replaced by -ива- in the imperfective. The mutation **o : a** operates
(pf. успоко́ить 'to reassure', impf. успока́ивать):

pf. прикле́ить 'to stick to'   impf. прикле́**ива**ть
pf. устро́ить 'to arrange'   impf. устра́**ива**ть

247 Consonant mutation in secondary imperfectives based on second-conjugation verbs

Standard consonant mutations are observed in deriving secondary
imperfectives from second-conjugation perfective verbs.

б : бл	приспосо́бить 'to adapt'	impf. приспоса́**бл**ивать
в : вл	вы́здороветь 'to recover'	impf. выздора́**вл**ивать
д : ж	проследи́ть 'to track'	impf. просле́**ж**ивать
з : ж	заморо́зить 'to freeze'	impf. замора́**ж**ивать
м : мл	вскорми́ть 'to rear'	impf. вска́р**мл**ивать
п : пл	затопи́ть 'to heat'	impf. зата́**пл**ивать
с : ш	взве́сить 'to weigh'	impf. взве́**ш**ивать
ст : щ	вы́растить 'to grow'	impf. выра́**щ**ивать
т : ч	оплати́ть 'to pay'	impf. опла́**ч**ивать

Note

(a) Absence of mutation in pf. захвати́ть 'to seize', impf. захва́тывать, pf. проглоти́ть 'to swallow', impf. прогла́тывать, pf. сбро́сить 'to drop, throw down', impf. сбра́сывать.

(b) 'Reverse mutation' (**ч : к**) in pf. вы́скочить 'to jump out', impf. выска́кивать, pf. перекрича́ть 'to shout down', impf. перекри́кивать.

248 Secondary imperfectives based on monosyllabic verbs

(1) Secondary imperfectives derive from the compound prefixed perfectives of many monosyllabic verbs by the insertion of the suffix **-ва-** after the root vowel of the perfective. Thus:

бить (impf)
↓
         → поби́ть (neutral pf.) 'to hit'

заби́ть (pf. with new meaning   → забива́ть (impf.) 'to score'
  'to score')

Similarly,

pf. зажи́ть 'to heal'	impf. зажива́ть
pf. наде́ть 'to put on'	impf. надева́ть
pf. нали́ть 'to pour'	impf. налива́ть
pf. откры́ть 'to open'	impf. открыва́ть

Note

The initial consonant of the syllable inserted into compounds of monosyllabic verbs in the formation of secondary imperfectives is often identical with that which appears in the first-person singular of the conjugation of the stem verb.

Perfective	Imperfective	First-person singular of stem verb
заже́чь 'to ignite'	зажига́ть	жгу (from жечь 'to burn')
пересе́чь 'to intersect'	пересека́ть	секу́ (from сечь 'to cut')
сгрести́ 'to rake together'	сгреба́ть	гребу́ (from грести́ 'to row')
сжать 'to compress'	сжима́ть	жму (from жать 'to squeeze')
уче́сть 'to take into consideration'	учи́тывать	чту (from честь 'to consider')

Note also pf. разъéсть 'to corrode', impf. разъедáть (cf. -д- in, for example, едá 'food').

(2) The suffix -ы- or -и- is inserted between two initial consonants in the stem verb to form the imperfective:

pf. вы́звать 'to call out, cause'	impf. вызывáть
pf. вы́рвать 'to tear out'	impf. вырывáть
pf. отослáть 'to send away'	impf. отсылáть
pf. собрáть 'to collect'	impf. собирáть

249 Submeanings of some prefixed imperfectives

Some imperfective verbs with the prefixes **пере-**, **по-** or **при-** have the following submeanings, as distinct from the standard imperfective meanings of duration and frequency:

(1) Reflexives with the prefix **пере-** denote joint action (mostly imperfective only): **перепи́сываться** 'to correspond', **перестýкиваться** 'to communicate by knocking', **перешёптываться** 'to exchange whispers'.

Note

Some verbs of this type have perfectives: **переглáдываться** (impf.)/**переглянýться** (pf.) 'to exchange glances', **переми́гиваться** (impf.)/**перемигнýться** (pf.) 'to wink at each other'.

(2) Verbs in **по-** with the iterative ending **-ивать/-ывать** denote the intermittent performance of a short-lived action, e.g. **посви́стывать** 'to whistle every now and again'. The mutations е:ё and о:а operate: **поблёскивать** 'to glint' (cf. блестéть 'to shine'), **посмáтривать** 'to steal glances at' (cf. смотрéть 'to look'). Compare

Головá у меня́ **побáливает**
I keep getting headaches

Шпиль **поблёскивает** на сóлнце
The spire glints in the sun

Мáслов флегмати́чно **позёвывал** (Yakhontov)
Maslov kept yawning in a phlegmatic sort of way

Бéрежно, **постáнывая** и **покря́хтывая**, он опускáется вниз (Rasputin)
He descends cautiously, groaning and wheezing intermittently

Note
(a) Verbs in this category have no perfective.
(b) Other verbs of this type include **погла́живать** from **гла́дить** 'to stroke', **подёргивать** from **дёргать** 'to tug', **пока́шливать** from **ка́шлять** 'to cough', **пома́ргивать** from **морга́ть** 'to blink', **поси́живать** from **сиде́ть** 'to sit', **посту́кивать** from **стуча́ть** 'to knock', **почи́тывать** from **чита́ть** 'to read'.

(3) Verbs in **при-** with the suffix **-ва-** or **-ива-/-ыва-** may denote actions accompanying other actions: **припева́ть** 'to sing along', **припля́сывать** 'to skip up and down', **прито́пывать** 'to stamp one's feet' (e.g. in time to music).

Note
Verbs in this category have no perfectives.

250 The differentiation of aspects by conjugation

(1) Many aspectival pairs consist of a first-conjugation imperfective in **-ать/-ять** and a second-conjugation perfective in **-ить** (or **-еть**). This affects:

(i) A number of unprefixed verbs (imperfectives first):

броса́ть	бро́сить	'to throw'
конча́ть	ко́нчить	'to finish'
лиша́ть	лиши́ть	'to deprive'
реша́ть	реши́ть	'to decide, resolve'

(ii) More especially, prefixed verbs:

включа́ть	включи́ть	'to switch on'
выполня́ть	вы́полнить	'to fulfil'
выступа́ть	вы́ступить	'to appear, perform'
загора́ть	загоре́ть	'to get sun-tanned'

Note
Покупа́ть, купи́ть 'to buy' (prefixed imperfective/**un**prefixed perfective).

(2) In many pairs the imperfective has *end* stress and the perfective *stem* stress: доверя́ть, дове́рить 'to trust'; измеря́ть, изме́рить 'to measure'; наруша́ть, нару́шить 'to disrupt'; позволя́ть, позво́-лить 'to allow'; улучша́ть, улу́чшить 'to improve' etc.

(3)   The usual consonant mutations apply to many verbs of this type:

б : бл	pf. употреби́ть 'to use'	impf. употребля́ть
в : вл	pf. оста́вить 'to leave'	impf. оставля́ть
д : ж	pf. заряди́ть 'to load'	impf. заряжа́ть
д : жд	pf. награди́ть 'to reward'	impf. награжда́ть
з : ж	pf. отрази́ть 'to reflect'	impf. отража́ть
п : пл	pf. прикрепи́ть 'to attach, fasten'	impf. прикрепля́ть
с : ш	pf. пригласи́ть 'to invite'	impf. приглаша́ть
ст : ск	pf. пусти́ть 'to let go'	impf. пуска́ть
ст : щ	pf. угости́ть 'to treat'	impf. угоща́ть
т : ч	pf. заме́тить 'to notice'	impf. замеча́ть
т : щ	pf. запрети́ть 'to ban'	impf. запреща́ть

Note

(a) Double perfectivization (imperfective first) in **ве́шать, пове́-сить** 'to hang', **куса́ть, укуси́ть** 'to bite', **роня́ть, урони́ть** 'to drop', **сажа́ть, посади́ть** 'to seat' and **стреля́ть, вы́стрелить** 'to shoot'.

(b) Some prefixed derivatives of **меня́ть** 'to change' are imperfective, with a perfective in **-менить: заменя́ть/замени́ть** 'to replace', **изменя́ть/измени́ть** 'to alter', **отменя́ть/отмени́ть** 'to cancel'. Others acquire perfective meaning, with an imperfective in **-менивать: обме́нивать/обменя́ть** 'to exchange', **разме́нивать/разменя́ть** 'to change' (money to smaller denominations).

251 Aspectival pairs with different roots

The verbs in some aspectival pairs derive from different roots. These include (imperfective first) the following:

бить	уда́рить	'to strike'
брать	взять	'to take'
говори́ть	сказа́ть	'to say'
класть	положи́ть	'to put, place'
лови́ть	пойма́ть	'to catch'

252 Verbs which are reflexive in the imperfective aspect only

Some verbs are reflexive in the imperfective aspect only. These include:

(1) Some verbs of sitting, lying and standing:

ложи́ться	лечь	to lie down
переса́живаться	пересе́сть	to change seats, trains etc.
приса́живаться	присе́сть	to sit down for a while
сади́ться	сесть	to sit down
станови́ться	стать	to (go and) stand

(2) **Ло́паться/ло́пнуть** 'to burst, snap' and **ру́шиться/ру́хнуть** 'to collapse'.

253 Compounds of -ложить

Some perfective compounds of **-ложить** have imperfectives in **-кла́дывать**, while others have imperfectives in **-лага́ть**. Those with imperfectives in **-кла́дывать** have a more literal meaning (**прокла́дывать**, проложи́ть доро́гу 'to lay a road'); those with imperfectives in **-лага́ть** are more abstract (**предлага́ть**, предложи́ть 'to propose'). The distinction is well marked in verbs which have both types of imperfective, with differing meanings: **вкла́дывать**, вложи́ть письмо́ в конве́рт 'to place a letter into an envelope', **влага́ть**, вложи́ть ду́шу во что́-нибудь 'to put one's heart into something'.

254 Meanings of verbal prefixes

Prefixes are important elements in Russian word formation. As many as sixteen prefixes may be attached to certain root verbs, each prefix imparting a different meaning: thus **вяза́ть** 'to tie', **завяза́ть** 'to knot', **отвяза́ть от** 'to untie from', **привяза́ть к** 'to tie to' and so on. Most prefixes are associated with particular prepositions as follows.

Prefix	Preposition		Meaning
в-	**в**	+ acc.	into
вы-	**из**	+ gen.	out of
до-	**до**	+ gen.	as far as
за-	**за**	+ acc.	behind
из-	**из**	+ gen.	out of
на-	**на**	+ acc.	on to

Prefix	Preposition		Meaning
от-	**от**	+ gen.	detaching
пере-	**через**	+ acc.	across
под-	**к**	+ dat.	approach
	под	+ acc.	under
при-	**к**	+ dat.	attaching
с-	**с**	+ gen.	down from
	с	+ instr.	together with

Note

(a) Prefixed verbs in some meanings also have non-prepositional government, or government through other prepositions.

(b) Prefixes also impart meanings to parts of speech other than verbs: cf. **перелётный** 'migratory', **приложéние** 'supplement', **съезд** 'congress' etc.

(c) Some prefixes have alternative spellings (**вз-/вс-; из-/ис-; раз-/рас-**), **вс-**, **ис-** and **рас-** combining with stems which begin with unvoiced consonants (**к, п, с, т, ф, х, ц, ч, ш, щ**), **вз-**, **из-** and **раз-** combining with other stems.

(d) Compare also prefixes with verbs of motion (see **331**).

(e) Imperfectives are listed first in aspectual pairs.

(1) В(о)-

(i) Direction into:

включáть/включи́ть в спи́сок	to include in a list
вмéшиваться/вмешáться в спор	to interfere in an argument

(ii) Movement upwards (mainly with verbs of motion, e.g. **влезáть/влезть** на дéрево 'to climb a tree'):

вставáть/встать из-за столá	to get up from a table

(2) Вз(о)-/вс-; воз-/вос

(i) Movement upwards:

взбирáться/взобрáться нá гору	to climb a hill

(ii) Disruption:

взрывáть/взорвáть мост	to blow up a bridge

(3) Вы-

(i) Movement out of:

вырыва́ть/вы́рвать страни́цу из дневника́
to tear a page out of a diary

(ii) Achievement through the action of the root verb:

выпра́шивать/вы́просить о́тпуск
to get leave on request

(iii) Exhaustiveness of action (reflexive verbs):

выска́зываться/вы́сказаться
to have one's say

высыпа́ться/вы́спаться
to have a good sleep

Note
As a perfective prefix, **вы-** is always stressed; as an imperfective prefix it is stressed only in **вы́глядеть** 'to look'.

(4) До-

(i) Completion of action already begun:

дожива́ть/дожи́ть до ста́рости
to live to a ripe old age

допи́сывать/дописа́ть письмо́
to finish writing a letter

(ii) Achievement of hard-won result:

догова́риваться/договори́ться
to come to an agreement

дозва́ниваться/дозвони́ться (к) дру́гу
to get through to one's friend

(5) За-

(i) Movement behind:

закла́дывать/заложи́ть ру́ки за́ спину
to put one's hands behind one's back

(ii) Process covering an area:

засáживать/засадить сад дерéвьями
to plant a garden with trees

(iii) Absorption in an action (often detrimental (reflexives)):

засиживаться/засидéться в гостя́х
to outstay one's welcome

зачи́тываться/зачитáться
to get absorbed in reading

(iv) Acquisition:

завоёвывать/завоевáть	to conquer
зарабáтывать/зарабóтать	to earn
захвáтывать/захвати́ть	to seize

(v) Fastening, securing:

завя́зывать/завязáть гáлстук	to fasten a tie
закрывáть/закрыть	to close
застёгивать/застегнýть пальтó	to fasten a coat

(vi) To spoil by excess:

закáрмливать/закорми́ть щенкá	to overfeed a puppy

(6) Из(о)-/-ис

(i) Extraction, selection:

избирáть/избрáть	to elect
исключáть/исключи́ть	to exclude, expel

(ii) Action affecting whole area:

изорвáть (pf. only) рубáшку to tear a shirt all over

(7) На-

(i) Action directed on to:

нажимáть/нажáть (на) кнóпку
to press a button

накле́ивать/накле́ить ма́рку на конве́рт
to stick a stamp on an envelope

(ii) Action performed to point of satisfaction:

наеда́ться/нае́сться	to eat one's fill
насмотре́ться (pf. only)	to have a good look

(iii) Quantity, accumulation:

наруба́ть/наруби́ть дров	to chop some firewood
нарва́ть (pf. only) **цвето́в**	to pick some flowers

(8) Над(о)-

(i) Superimposition:

надстра́ивать/надстро́ить эта́ж
to add a storey

(ii) Detaching part of surface:

надку́сывать/надкуси́ть гру́шу
to take a bite out of a pear

(9) Недо- (opposite of 13 (v))

Shortfall:

недовыполня́ть/ недовы́полнить но́рму
to underfulfil one's norm

недооце́нивать/ недооцени́ть
to underrate

(10) О-/об-/обо-

(i) Action affecting many:

опра́шивать/опроси́ть студе́нтов
to canvas student opinion

(ii) Detailed comprehensive action:

обсужда́ть/обсуди́ть	to discuss
осма́тривать/осмотре́ть	to examine

(iii) Action directed over whole area:

окле́ивать/окле́ить сте́ны обо́ями	to wall-paper
окружа́ть/окружи́ть	to surround

(iv) Error:

огова́риваться/ оговори́ться	to make a slip of the tongue
ошиба́ться/ошиби́ться	to make a mistake

(v) Endowment with/acquisition of a quality or state:

облегча́ть/облегчи́ть	to lighten, relieve
оглуша́ть/оглуши́ть	to deafen

Note

In some verbs the prefix appears only in the perfective: **вдове́ть/ овдове́ть** 'to be widowed', **сле́пнуть/осле́пнуть** 'to go blind'.

(vi) Outdoing:

обгоня́ть/обогна́ть	to overtake
обы́грывать/обыгра́ть	to outplay

(vii) Deception:

обма́нывать/обману́ть	to deceive
обсчи́тывать/обсчита́ть покупа́теля	to short-change a customer

(11) Обез-/обес-

Deprival (bookish styles):

обесце́нивать/обесце́нить	to devalue

(12) От(о)-

(i) Moving, receding a certain distance:

отстава́ть/отста́ть от други́х
to lag behind the others

отступа́ть/отступи́ть
to retreat, digress

(ii) Detachment:

отруба́ть/отруби́ть ве́тку от де́рева
to lop a branch off a tree

отрыва́ть/оторва́ть листо́к
to tear off a sheet

(iii) Reversal of action:

отвыка́ть/отвы́кнуть от куре́ния
to get out of the habit of smoking

отменя́ть/отмени́ть
to cancel

(13) Пере-

(i) Movement across:

перепры́гивать/перепры́гнуть (через) кана́ву
to jump across a ditch

переставля́ть/переста́вить ме́бель
to move furniture round

(ii) Redoing:

перекра́шивать/перекра́сить
to repaint

переодева́ться/переоде́ться
to change one's clothes

(iii) Division:

перепи́ливать/перепили́ть
to saw through

(iv) Action affecting many objects:

пересма́тривать/пересмотре́ть все фи́льмы
to see all the films

(v) Excess:

перегружа́ть/перегрузи́ть маши́ну
to overload a vehicle

(vi) Reciprocal action:

перепи́сываться (impf. only)
to correspond

(vii) Outdoing:

перекри́кивать/перекрича́ть толпу́
to shout down a crowd

(14) Под(о)-

(i) Movement or position under:

подкла́дывать/подложи́ть поду́шку под го́лову
to place a pillow under one's head

подпи́сывать/подписа́ть
to sign

(ii) Approach:

пододвига́ть/пододви́нуть стул к стене́
to move a chair up to the wall

(iii) Addition of substance or material:

подсыпа́ть/подсы́пать са́хару в чай
to add some sugar to one's tea

(iv) Furtive, underhand action:

подде́лывать/подде́лать
to forge, counterfeit

подслу́шивать/подслу́шать
to eavesdrop

(v) Supplementary action:

подви́нчивать/подвинти́ть кран немно́го
to tighten up a tap

(15) Пре- (mainly in bookish styles)

(i) Transformation:

преобразо́вывать/ преобразова́ть
to transform

(ii) Termination:

прекраща́ть/прекрати́ть
to curtail

(iii) Excess:

преувели́чивать/ преувели́чить
to exaggerate

превыша́ть/превы́сить
to exceed

(16) Пред(о)-

Anticipation:

предви́деть (impf. only)
to foresee

предполага́ть/предположи́ть
to presume

предупрежда́ть/предупреди́ть
to warn, prevent

(17) При-

(i) Approach, arrival:

приближа́ться/прибли́зиться
to approach

приземля́ться/приземли́ться
to land

(ii) Attachment:

привя́зывать/привяза́ть соба́ку к де́реву
to tie a dog to a tree

прикрепля́ть/прикрепи́ть фотогра́фию к бла́нку
to attach, pin a photograph to a form

(iii) Addition:

прибавля́ть/приба́вить
to add

припи́сывать/приписа́ть не́сколько строк
to add a few lines

(iv) Limited action:

привстава́ть/привста́ть
to half rise

приоткрыва́ть/приоткры́ть дверь
to open a door slightly

(v) Accustoming:

привыка́ть/привы́кнуть к дисципли́не
to get used to discipline

(18) Про-

(i) Through, past:

пропуска́ть/пропусти́ть
to miss, let past

просма́тривать/просмотре́ть
to look through

(ii) Harmful error:

пролива́ть/проли́ть	to spill
просыпа́ть/проспа́ть	to oversleep, sleep in

(19) Раз(о)-/рас-

(i) Separation, dispersal, disintegration, distribution:

раздвига́ть/раздви́нуть занаве́ски
to part the curtains

размеща́ть/размести́ть раке́ты
to deploy missiles

распи́ливать/распили́ть ствол
to saw up a tree trunk

(ii) Reversal of an action:

развя́зывать/развяза́ть	to untie
раздева́ться/разде́ться	to get undressed
разду́мывать/разду́мать	to change one's mind

(20) С(о)-

(i) Removal:

сверга́ть/све́ргнуть самодержа́вие
to overthrow an autocracy

снима́ть/снять пальто́
to take off one's coat

(ii) Descent:

спуска́ться/спусти́ться на морско́е дно
to descend to the sea bed

(iii) Joining:

скрепля́ть/скрепи́ть	to staple together
скла́дывать/сложи́ть	to fold

(iv) Joint feeling or action:

сочу́вствовать (impf. only)   to sympathize

(21) У-

(i) Removal:

удаля́ть/удали́ть о́пухоль   to remove a tumour

(ii) Imparting a quality:

улучша́ть/улу́чшить	to improve
упроща́ть/упрости́ть	to simplify

255 The imperfective and perfective aspects

See also **235**.

(1) The imperfective

(i) The imperfective may describe an action:

(a) In progress:

Он за́втракал (impf.)   He was having breakfast

(b) Progressing towards the completion of a goal, represented by a perfective:

Он до́лго **вспомина́л** (impf.) мою́ фами́лию, и наконе́ц **вспо́мнил** (pf.) её
He took a long time to recall my name, and finally he **did** recall it

(ii) Imperfectives may describe a number of actions occurring simultaneously or in an indeterminate order:

Говори́ли (impf.) мы сра́зу, **перебива́ли** (impf.) дру̀г дру́га, **смея́лись** (impf.) (Shukshin)
We were all speaking at once, interrupting each other, laughing

Note

(a) The imperfective here does not *move* events, but describes actions as they *develop*, focusing on *circumstances* rather than completion. The imperfective therefore tends to be associated with conjunctions which imply development or continuity of action: **по ме́ре того́ как** 'in proportion as', **чем ... тем**, 'the ... the' (with comparatives), **в то вре́мя как/пока́** 'while' etc. Compare

В то вре́мя пока́ он **собира́лся** (impf.), я **успе́ла** (pf.) **убра́ть** (pf.) всю посу́ду в шкаф
While he was getting ready I managed to clear all the crockery away into the cupboard

Here the completed action ('I managed to clear all the crockery away into the cupboard' (pf.)) is set against the background of an action in progress ('while he was getting ready' (impf.)).

(b) In the following example two processes are seen developing in parallel and are therefore rendered by imperfectives:

И чем бо́льше Коси́хин его́ **слу́шал** (impf.), тем грустне́е ему́ **станови́лось** (impf.) (Yakhontov)
And the more Kosikhin listened to him, the sadder he became

(iii) The idea of continuity of action can be reinforced by an adverb which either:

(a) Emphasizes action in progress:

Он расска́зывал (impf.) **подро́бно**
He related his story in detail

or:

(b) Denotes the passage of time, thus underlining the durative meaning:

> Он чита́л (impf.) «*Войну́ и мир*» **три часа́**
> He read *War and Peace* for three hours

Attention here is drawn to the *time* involved in the action, *not* its completion or result; hence the use of the *imperfective* aspect.

Note

For frequentative meanings see **256** (2) (ii), **257** (3), **266**, **269** (2), **274**, **276** (2) (i).

(2) The perfective aspect

(i) Unlike the imperfective, the perfective emphasizes **result**:

> Он **дал** (pf.) ученика́м по уче́бнику
> He **gave** each pupil a textbook (as a result, they have a copy, can prepare their homework, take a full part in the class work etc.)

(ii) The perfective **moves** events, advances the action step by step, unlike the imperfective, which describes an action in progress:

> Воше́дший **снял** (pf. 1) плащ, **сел** (pf. 2) за стол и **по́днял** (pf. 3) дневни́к
> The man who had come in **removed** his coat, **sat down** at the table and **picked up** the diary

Here emphasis is laid on the completion in sequence of a series of actions: perfective 1 is completed before perfective 2 takes place, perfective 2 is completed before perfective 3 takes place, and so on, each perfective moving events a stage further.

(iii) Verbs of different aspect may coexist in the same sentence, the imperfectives **describing the scene** and the perfectives **advancing the action**:

> Она́ **сняла́** (pf.) пальто́, **стоя́ла** (impf.) спино́й ко мне и **шелесте́ла** (impf.) бума́гами (Kazakov)
> She took off her coat and stood with her back to me, rustling the papers

(iv) An imperfective describing an action in progress can be succeeded by a perfective which denotes successful completion of that action:

Он до́лго **догоня́л** (impf.) меня́ и, наконе́ц, **догна́л** (pf.)
He chased me for a long time and finally caught me up

This exemplifies the comparison which has been made between the use of imperfectives and the filming of a scene, and between the use of some perfectives and a **snapshot**.

(v) The perfective tends to combine with conjunctions which imply the completion or the suddenness of an action (**до того́ как** 'before', **как то́лько** 'as soon as', **по́сле того́ как** 'after' etc.), and with adverbs which imply immediacy or unexpectedness (**внеза́пно** 'suddenly', **сра́зу** 'immediately', **чуть не** 'almost, within an ace of' etc.).

(vi) Unlike the imperfective past, which is totally rooted in past time, the perfective may have implications for the present. This occurs when a **present state** results from a past perfective action or process (the so-called 'pure perfect'):

Я **забы́л** (pf.)	I have forgotten, I **forget**
Он **опозда́л** (pf.)	He **is late** (but has arrived; cf. Он опа́здывает (impf.) 'He is late' (and has not yet arrived))
Я **привы́к** к э́тому (pf.)	I **am used** to this
Он **у́мер** (pf.)	He **is dead** (has died)

256 Aspect in the present tense

(1) The present tense has only one form, the imperfective.

(2) The present tense is used:

(i) To denote actions in progress:

Сейча́с я **пишу́** письмо́
At the moment I am writing a letter

(ii) To denote habitual actions:

По воскресе́ньям он **ло́вит** ры́бу в реке́
On Sundays he fishes in the river

(iii) To make general statements:

Земля́ **враща́ется** вокру́г Со́лнца
The Earth revolves around the Sun

(iv) To denote capabilities and qualities:

Зо́лото не **ржа́веет**
Gold does not tarnish

Note

Except for verbs of motion (see **315–325**), the present tense does not distinguish durative from habitual actions, thus: Я **чита́ю** кни́гу 'I **am reading/read** a book'.

(v) To express intention to perform an action in the not distant future. The verb involved is often a simple or compound verb of motion in the first-person singular or plural:

Сего́дня ве́чером **иду́** в кино́
I am going to the cinema this evening

Бу́дущей зимо́й **уезжа́ем** за грани́цу
We are going abroad next winter

Note

Other verbs found in this meaning include **возвраща́ться** 'to return', **встреча́ть** 'to meet', **начина́ть** 'to begin' etc.

(vi) As a 'historic present'. The use of the present tense with past meaning brings the action more graphically before the mind's eye of the reader or listener. It is a device commonly found in literary works and is much more widely used in Russian than in English:

Приходи́л он к нам ча́сто. **Сиди́т**, быва́ло, и **расска́зывает**
He would often come to see us. He **would sit** and **tell** us stories

(vii) To describe an action or state that *began* in the past and *continues* into the present (the 'continuous present'):

Я **рабо́таю** здесь с про́шлого го́да
I **have been working/have worked** here since last year

Note

The use of the past tense in such contexts would be rendered by an English pluperfect: Она́ **была́** за́мужем уже́ 10 лет 'She **had been** married for ten years'.

(viii) In reported speech (see also **265**).

(a) In reporting a statement, the same tense is used as in direct speech. Thus the statement **Я люблю́** её 'I love her' is reported as:

Я сказа́л, что **люблю́** её
I said I loved her

or

Он сказа́л, что **лю́бит** её
He said he loved her

(b) This contrasts with English, where a past tense in the main clause ('he said') generates a past tense in the subordinate clause: 'He said he *loved* her'. To use a past tense here in Russian would imply that the direct statement had contained a past tense. Thus, Он сказа́л, что **люби́л** её means 'He said he **had loved** her/**used to love** her'.

(c) The construction extends to reported knowing, asking, hoping etc., and can be introduced by **ду́мать** 'to think', **знать** 'to know', **наде́яться** 'to hope', **обеща́ть** 'to promise', **спроси́ть** 'to ask' etc.:

Ей каза́лось, что ма́льчик **спит**
She thought the child **was asleep**

Он писа́л, что **прово́дит** ле́то в Волгогра́де
He wrote that he **was spending** the summer in Volgograd

(d) The same principles of tense sequence apply, though *less rigidly*, to verbs of perception, cf. use of the *present* tense in

Шу́рка слы́шал, как в темноте́ **бе́гает** ёж (Vasilev)
Shurka heard a hedgehog running about in the dark

and the *past* tense in

Слы́шно бы́ло, как **мурлы́кал** Ку́стик (Belov)
You could hear Kustik purring

Бы́ло ви́дно, что он не **боя́лся** холо́дной воды́ (Fadeev)
It was obvious that he was not afraid of cold water

In such contexts, the present tense is said to be more 'vivid' than the past.

257 Aspect in the past tense

(1) The durative meaning

(i) Past durative meanings, that is, descriptions of actions as they develop, are invariably rendered by the **imperfective** aspect:

Мы **составля́ли** (impf.) телегра́мму в Москву́
We **were composing** a telegram to send to Moscow

(ii) Passage of time may be indicated by an appropriate adverb or adverbial phrase:

Че́тверть ве́ка он собира́л (impf.) всё, что относи́лось (impf.) к исто́рии кра́я (Granin)
He spent **a quarter of a century** collecting everything that related to the history of the area

(2) Endeavour contrasted with successful completion

(i) An action in progress (impf.) can be contrasted with its successful completion (pf.):

Мы до́лго **реша́ли** (impf.) зада́чу — и наконе́ц **реши́ли** (pf.) её
We **spent a long time solving** the task and finally **solved it**

(ii) The imperfective denotes an *attempt* which may either:

(a) Fail:

Он **убежда́л** (impf.) меня́, что без согла́сия роди́телей мы всё равно́ не смо́жем быть сча́стливы (*Russia Today*)
He **tried to convince me** that we could not be happy anyway without our parents' consent

(b) Succeed, achievement being expressed by a perfective:

Я **пробива́лся** (impf.) к нему́ ро́вно неде́лю и наконе́ц **проби́лся** (pf.)
I spent exactly a week **trying to force my way** into his office, and finally **succeeded in doing so**

(iii) Some aspectival pairs consist of *imperfectives* which denote attempt to achieve and *perfectives* which denote successful achievement:

Imperfective		Perfective	
добива́ться	'to try to achieve'	**доби́ться**	'to achieve'
дока́зывать	'to contend'	**доказа́ть**	'to prove'
лови́ть	'to try to catch'	**пойма́ть**	'to catch'
реша́ть	'to tackle'	**реши́ть**	'to solve'
сдава́ть	'to take' (an examination)	**сдать**	'to pass' (an examination)
уверя́ть	'to try to assure'	**уве́рить**	'to assure'
угова́ривать	'to try to persuade'	**уговори́ть**	'to persuade'

(3)   Repeated actions in the past

(i)   Repeated actions are normally expressed by the **imperfective**:

Он **звони́л** (impf.) нам по вечера́м
He used to ring us in the evenings

Быва́ло is sometimes added to emphasize repetition:

Он, **быва́ло**, звони́л (impf.) нам по вечера́м
He was in the habit of ringing us in the evenings

(ii) Frequency may also be stressed by an adverb or adverbial phrase of time: **всегда́** 'always', **иногда́** 'sometimes', **никогда́** 'never', **раз в неде́лю** 'twice a week', **ча́сто** 'often':

Пото́м он **ча́ще всего́**, не разогрева́я, съеда́л (impf.) оста́в-ленный ма́терью обе́д (Vanshenkin)
Then, **more often than not**, he would eat the lunch left by his mother, without heating it up

Note
Secondary imperfectives (here, **съеда́ть**) are often preferred to *primary* imperfectives (cf. **есть** 'to eat') in frequentative constructions, in view of the durative connotations which adhere to primaries, cf. Он **сиде́л** (primary impf.) над статьёй не ме́нее трёх часо́в 'He **pored** over the article for no less than three hours', a reference to one durative action, and Он **проси́живал** (secondary impf.) над статьёй не ме́нее трёх часо́в 'He **would pore** over the article for not less than three hours at a time', a reference to a **series** of actions.

(iii) When reference is made to the **number of times** an action occurs:

(a) The **imperfective** is preferred when the actions are repeated at irregular and spaced-out intervals:

Три ра́за они́ **покида́ли** (impf.) борт ста́нции и **выходи́ли** (impf.) в откры́тый ко́смос (*Russia Today*)
Three times they left the space station and walked in space

Не́сколько раз я **прогоня́л** (impf.) его́. Он **сади́лся** (impf.) в отдале́нии, немно́го **пережида́л** (impf.) и сно́ва **бежа́л** (impf.) за мной (Kazakov)
Several times I chased him away. He would sit down at a distance, bide his time and run after me again

(b) The **perfective** is preferred when a series of identical actions, repeated in swift succession, can be interpreted as **components of one multiple action**:

Вы́лез (pf.) из-под кры́ши кру́пный воробе́й, **чири́кнул** (pf.) **два́жды** и улете́л (pf.) (Belov)
A large sparrow emerged from under the eaves, **chirped twice** and flew off

Прибли́зившись к нему́, она́ доста́ла (pf.) из су́мочки пистоле́т и **три ра́за вы́стрелила** (pf.) в упо́р
Approaching him she took a pistol from her bag and **fired three times** at point-blank range

Note
The imperfective is preferred for verbs of *beginning*, however, even when a number of actions occur in swift succession:

Он **начина́л** (impf.) письмо́ **раз двена́дцать**, рвал (impf.) листы́, изне́рвничался (pf.), испсихова́лся (pf.) (Shukshin)
He began the letter about a dozen times, kept tearing up the sheets, got all hot and bothered, almost went out of his mind

258 Use of the imperfective past to express a 'statement of fact'

— Вы **звони́ли** (impf.) ему́?	'Have you rung him?'
— Да, **звони́л** (impf.)	'Yes, I have'
— Я где́-то **ви́дел** (impf.) вас	'I have seen you somewhere'

— Вы **читáли** (impf.) «*Цемéнт*»? 'Have you read *Cement*?'
— Да, **читáл** (impf.)   'Yes, I have'

(1) The imperfective is used in the above examples to denote an action in isolation, with no emphasis on its completion or non-completion, the circumstances in which it occurred, or other detail. The statements and responses show that a phone call has been made, that two people have met before, that *Cement* is one of the books read by a particular person. These are bald statements of fact, with no fleshing-out of the context and no stress on the achievement of a result. This 'submeaning' of the imperfective is known as **констатáция фáкта** 'statement of fact'. It is particularly common in the past tense and is usually set in the vaguest of contexts:

— Э́тот человéк вам знакóм?
'Do you know that man?'
— Да, я однáжды **встречáл** (impf.) егó
'Yes, I met him once'

(2) The 'statement of fact' is common:

(i) In the imprecise context of an interrogative or in a situation where, for example, a check is being made to see whether a particular action has been carried out:

Вы **провéтривали** (impf.) кóмнату?
Have you aired the room?

(ii) In enquiring about someone's whereabouts:

Вы не **вúдели** (impf.) Лéну?
Have you seen Lena?

(iii) In delivering a reminder:

Но ведь я **говорúл** (impf.) вам об э́том!
But I told you about this!

(3) As the context is firmed up, however, or a result emphasized, the perfective comes into contention. Compare:

(i) Use of the *imperfective* in:

Я **писáл** (impf.) ей	I wrote to her
Я **расскáзывал** (impf.) вам об э́том	I told you about that
Я **звонúл** (impf.) емý	I have rung him

Мы уже́ **встреча́лись** (impf.)   We have already met
Я **чита́л** (impf.) «*Чапа́ева*» в шко́ле   I read *Chapaev* at
  school

(ii) Use of the *perfective* as the context is filled in:

Я написа́л (pf.) ей **письмо́**
I wrote her **a letter**

Я **то́лько что** сказа́л (pf.) вам об э́том
I have **only just** told you about this

Я позвони́л (pf.) ему́, **что̀бы напо́мнить ему́** о ве́чере
I rang him to **remind him about the party**

Я встре́тил (pf.) его́ **в про́шлом году́ на Чёрном мо́ре**
I met him **last year on the Black Sea**

(4) It will be clear from the above examples that the imperfective is preferred where a fact is placed in a contextual vacuum, and that the perfective is preferred when the context is filled in, in terms of **what** action was carried out, **when**, **where** or **for what purpose**, or if the result or completion of an action is stressed. Thus, the question — Вы **прочита́ли** (pf.) «*Накану́не*»? can be rendered as 'Have you **finished** *On the Eve*? – completion of the action is important since, say, the person asking the question is waiting to read the novel. The answer to this question might be **Прочита́л** (pf.), возьми́те, пожа́луйста 'Yes, I have; here you are'. The perfective would also be used if someone had been *told* to read the novel: Вы **прочита́ли** (pf.) «*Накану́не*»? '**Did you read** *On the Eve*?' (i.e. as you were told to).

259 Use of the imperfective past to denote an action and its reverse

(1) The imperfective past may be used to denote an action and its reverse:

Она́ **брала́** (impf.) кни́гу в библиоте́ке
She had a book out of the library (*and has now returned it*)

Similarly, **открыва́л** (impf.) can mean 'opened **and closed again**':

У меня́ в ко́мнате так хо́лодно сего́дня. Наве́рное, кто́-то **открыва́л** (impf.) здесь **окно́**
It is so cold in my room today. Someone has probably **had the window open** in here

The implication of this example is that the window has been opened but is now shut again. By contrast, Кто́-то **откры́л** (pf.) окно́ means that the window is still open 'Someone has opened the window', or refers to the single act of opening 'Someone opened the window'.

(2) Other imperfective past forms of this type include:

включа́л	'switched on' (and off again)
встава́л	'got up' (and sat or lay down again)
выключа́л	'switched off' (and on again)
дава́л	'gave' (and received back again)
закрыва́л	'closed' (and opened again)
клал	'put down' (and took up again)
ложи́лся	'lay down' (and got up again)
надева́л	'put on' (and took off again)
поднима́лся	'ascended' (and came down again)
спуска́лся	'descended' (and went up again):

Он **встава́л** (impf.) но́чью
He got up in the night (and went back to bed again)

Ребёнок **просыпа́лся** (impf.), но сейча́с он опя́ть спит
The child woke up, but now he is asleep again

(3) In fact, the imperfective past of *any* verb denoting an action which has an opposite action may be used in this way:

Оди́н из них **по́днял** (pf.) ру́ку. Их ли́ца понра́вились мне, и я останови́лся. Тот, кто **поднима́л** (impf.) ру́ку, просу́нул в маши́ну сму́глое лицо́ (Strugatskys)
One of them **raised his arm**. I liked the look of them and stopped. The one who **had raised his arm** thrust a dark-skinned face through the car window

Here, the perfective denotes a *one-way* action (**по́днял** ру́ку 'raised his arm') and the imperfective a *two-way* action, the action and its reverse (**поднима́л** ру́ку 'raised his arm **and lowered it again**').

260 Aspectival usage when emphasis is on the identity of the person performing the action

(1) If we examine the examples

Кто мыл (impf.) посу́ду?   Who washed the dishes?
Кто убира́л (impf.) ко́мнату?   Who tidied the room?

then it is clear that the washing up has been done and the room tidied. Emphasis centres *not* on the *action*, but on the identity of the person who *performed* it. In such circumstances the *imperfective* is preferred:

Та́ня, э́то ты **разбира́ла** (impf.) кни́ги в шкафу́?
Tanya, was it you who sorted the books in the cupboard?

Use of the imperfective may also imply that something (usually untoward) happened while the action was being carried out (e.g. papers were mislaid).

Вы не зна́ете, кто **открыва́л** (impf.) окно́? На подоко́н-нике лежа́ли мо́и бума́ги.
Do you know who opened the window? My papers were lying on the window-sill.

(2) The *perfective* is preferred, however:

(i) When the **quality** of the action is stressed:

Кто **так хорошо́** убра́л (pf.) кни́ги в шкаф?
Who made such a good job of tidying the books into the cupboard?

or when the result is specially emphasized:

В ко́мнате так чи́сто. Интере́сно, кто **убра́л** (pf) её?
The room is beautifully clean. I wonder who tidied it?

(ii) When the verb denotes 'discovery':

Кто **изобрёл** (pf.) ра́дио?
Who invented radio?

Кто **откры́л** (pf.) Аме́рику?
Who discovered America?

Кто **нашёл** (pf.) ключи́?
Who found the keys?

(iii) When the action involved is not deliberate or has an untoward result:

> **Кто разби́л** (pf.) ча́шку?
> Who broke the cup?

(3) The imperfective is also used when attention is directed to the **place** or **time** of an action rather than to the action itself:

> Где вы **покупа́ли** (impf.) «Вече́рку»?
> Where did you buy the evening paper?

> — Я показа́л (pf.) ему́ чертёж
> 'I showed him the blueprint'
> — Когда́ ты **пока́зывал** (impf.)?
> 'When did you show it to him?'

In these examples the questioner is interested in the place and time of the actions, **not** in their completion, which is in any case clear from the context (as in the first example) or explicitly stated (as in the second).

261 Use of the imperfective past to denote a forthcoming event

The imperfective past is used to indicate that an action was due to take place:

> По́езд **отходи́л** (impf.) в пять часо́в
> The train **was due to leave** at five o'clock

> Он мно́го рабо́тал, потому́ что в воскресе́нье **выступа́л** (impf.) перед большо́й аудито́рией
> He worked hard, because on Sunday he **was to appear** in front of a large audience

262 Negated verbs in the past

(1) Both aspects may be used to indicate non-performance of an action in the past, but while the negative imperfective indicates that

the action **did not take place at all**, the negative perfective indicates that it took place but **was not successful**, thus:

Он не **реша́л** (impf.) зада́чу
He **did not** do the sum (perhaps because he was off school)

Он не **реши́л** (pf.) зада́чу
He **could not** do the sum (he tried but failed)

(2) The aspects may similarly be used to distinguish an action which has not yet begun (impf.) from one which has begun but is not yet completed (pf.):

Я ещё не **чита́л** (impf.) э́ту статью́
I haven't **read** this article yet

Я ещё не **прочита́л** (pf.) э́ту статью́
I haven't **finished** this article yet

(3) The imperfective past is also used to negate a statement or supposition expressed by a perfective:

— Почему́ вы ушли́ из ци́рка, почему́ вас **уво́лили**? (pf.)
— Меня́ не **увольня́ли** (impf.), я ушла́ сама́ (*Ogonek*)
'Why did you leave the circus, why were you dismissed?'
'I was not dismissed, I left of my own accord'

(4) The imperfective past is also used to denote the continuation of a negative state:

Он до́лго **не соглаша́лся** со мной (impf.)
He **took a long time to agree** with me

(5) The **perfective** past is used when an expected event did not take place:

Меня́ никто́ не **встре́тил** (pf.)
No one met me (despite, for example, a promise or understanding that someone would)

Compare Меня́ никто́ не **встреча́л** (impf.), 'No one met me' — a simple statement of fact with no implication that the reverse was expected.

Мы не **посмотре́ли** (pf.) фильм
We **didn't see** the film (though, for example, it is just the kind of film we might have been expected to see)

Compare Мы не **смотре́ли** (impf.) фильм 'We **haven't seen** the film'.

(6) The perfective past is also used when an expected or desired result has not yet materialized:

Он ещё не **пришёл** (pf.)
He has not arrived yet.

263 Aspect in the future

(1) The imperfective future focuses on the progress of an action, while the perfective future stresses expected result or successful attainment. Compare the two future forms, the first imperfective and the second perfective, in the following example:

Бу́ду **чита́ть** (impf.) статью, наде́юсь, что **прочита́ю** (pf.)
I shall **read/be reading** the article and hope I shall **get it finished**

(2) The imperfective is used when emphasis is placed on the way in which an action is carried out, *not* on its result or successful implementation:

Как бы **бу́дете отправля́ть** (impf.) кни́ги, просто́й или заказно́й бандеро́лью?
How will you be sending the books, as ordinary printed matter or registered?

(3) A perfective future may refer to a completed action within the framework of an action in progress, e.g.

Когда́ я **бу́ду проходи́ть** (impf.) ми́мо апте́ки, **куплю́** (pf.) табле́тки от ка́шля
When I pass the chemist's I shall buy some cough drops

Note
(a) Perfectives often appear in sequence, each perfective advancing the action a stage further: Я **свяжу́сь** (pf.) со свои́ми друзья́ми, всё **узна́ю** (pf.), и **позвоню́** (pf.) (Soloukhin) 'I shall contact my friends, get all the facts and give you a ring'.
(b) A negated perfective future may be used to denote the impossibility of an action: Раскалённое желе́зо го́лой руко́й **не возьмёшь** 'You cannot take hold of red-hot iron with your bare hands'.

264 The 'logical' future

Unlike English, where the future tense is not used after conjunctions such as 'after', 'as soon as', 'before', 'until', 'when' etc., Russian uses an imperfective or perfective future to express future meaning in such contexts:

Когда́ вы **бу́дете ремонти́ровать** (impf.) маши́ну, не забу́дьте (pf.) поменя́ть све́чи
When you **are overhauling** the car, don't forget to change the plugs

Как то́лько он **придёт** (pf.), поста́вим (pf.) ча́йник
As soon as he **arrives** we shall put the kettle on

265 The future in reported speech

An imperfective or perfective future in **direct** speech

— В э́том году́ я не **бу́ду отдыха́ть**
'This year I won't be having a holiday'

— Я **приду́,** е́сли **успе́ю**
'I shall come if I have time'

is expressed as a future in **reported** speech:

Он сказа́л, что в э́том году́ не **бу́дет отдыха́ть**
He said he **wouldn't** be having a holiday this year

Она́ обеща́ла, что **придёт**, е́сли **успе́ет**
She promised she **would** come if she **had** time

Compare **256** (2) (viii).

266 Use of the future to express repeated actions

(1) Repeated actions in the future are usually expressed using the imperfective aspect:

Ле́том я **бу́ду** регуля́рно **загора́ть** (impf.)
In summer I shall sun-bathe regularly

(2) A perfective future may be used to stress the sequential nature of actions:

> Когда́ пито́мцы **окре́пнут** (pf.), их выпуска́ют (impf.) в тайгу́ (*Sputnik*)
> When our small charges (baby sable) **grow strong enough** they are released into the taiga

The use of two imperfectives in this example would imply that the actions occur simultaneously, that the sable are released while they are still in the process of growing strong. The perfective (**окре́пнут**) shows that the actions are sequential: first the sable get strong, then they are released. Compare

> У меня́ был кро́хотный но́мер с телеви́зором, кото́рый **включа́лся** (impf.), когда́ в автома́т **опу́стишь** (pf.) сто ие́н (Granin)
> I had a tiny room with a television set which switched on when one inserted one hundred yen

In this example, too, the perfective (**опу́стишь**) indicates that the actions are sequential (first the money is inserted, then the set switches on), *not* simultaneous.

(3) The 'historic perfective future' may be used for graphic effect in past frequentative contexts, in literary and other written styles, to denote repeated quick movements:

> Она́ то **вздохнёт** (pf.), то **о́хнет** (pf.)
> She would now sigh, now moan

Быва́ло serves to stress the past frequentative nature of the action:

> **Быва́ло**, он загля́нет (pf.) к нам
> He was in the habit of looking in to see us

(4) The perfective future can also appear in frequentative contexts in combination with temporal adverbs such as **всегда́** 'always':

> Он вам **всегда́** помо́жет (pf.)
> He will always give you a hand

Note
The meaning of the perfective future in such contexts is 'potential' rather than frequentative, since its use does not imply a repeated action (cf. genuine repetition in Ка́ждый день она́ **бу́дет** ему́

помога́ть (impf.) 'She will help him every day'), but rather constant readiness to perform an action if the need should arise, the element of repetition being expressed in terms of one typical action.

267 The perfective future in warnings

In colloquial Russian the first-person singular of the perfective future may be used to express a warning:

Я тебе́ **поспо́рю**! (pf.)
I'll give you argue!

Я тебе́ **погуля́ю**! (pf.)
I'll give you gallivanting around!

268 Aspect in questions

(1) Questions about intended actions are more often than not couched in the imperfective:

Что вы **бу́дете де́лать**? (impf.)
What are you going to do?

Что вы **бу́дете зака́зывать**? (impf.)
What are you going to order?

Вы **бу́дете пить** (impf.) чай и́ли ко́фе?
Will you have tea or coffee?

unless special emphasis is laid on successful completion:

Вы **найдёте** (pf.) э́тот дом?
Will you find the house?

(2) Answers, however, can be in either aspect, depending on the context:

Я бу́ду **дочи́тывать** (impf.) кни́гу/**дочита́ю** (pf.) кни́гу
I **shall be finishing off** the book/shall **get** the book **finished**

Я бу́ду **пить** (impf.) ко́фе/**вы́пью** (pf.) ча́шечку ко́фе
I **shall have** coffee/**have** a small cup of coffee

Compare

> — Ла́дно, я уйду́. А ты что **бу́дешь де́лать** (impf.)?
> — **Уложу́** (pf.) Светла́нку спать, а пото́м **бу́ду реве́ть**
> (impf.) (Zalygin)
> 'All right, I'll leave. And what are you going to do?'
> 'I shall put Svetlanka to bed and then cry my eyes out'

(3) The answer to the question Что вы бу́дете зака́зывать? 'What are you going to order?' is likely to be perfective, however, since the *result* of the action is of particular importance (the diner will presumably get the dish he or she orders):

> **Я возьму́** (pf.) бульо́н
> I will have clear soup

Note

In colloquial Russian *negative* forms of the verb are frequently used in making requests: Вы на сле́дующей **не схо́дите**? (impf.) 'Are you getting off at the next stop?' Quite often the perfective future is used: Вы не **ска́жете** (pf.), ско́лько сейча́с вре́мени? 'You couldn't tell me the time, could you?'; Вы не **разреши́те** (pf.) позвони́ть от вас? 'Would you mind if I used your phone?'

269 Some uses of the imperfective imperative

The imperfective imperative is used to express:

(1) General injunctions:

> **Береги́те** (impf.) приро́ду!
> Conserve nature!

(2) Frequentative instructions:

> **Всегда́ относи́** (impf.) кни́ги в срок
> Always return your books on time

(3) Instructions to continue an action:

> **Пиши́те** (impf.) да́льше!
> Carry on writing!

270 Use of the imperative in the context of a single action

(1) The **perfective** imperative is used to order the implementation of a single action:

Закро́йте (pf.) окно́!
Shut the window!

Note

The addition of the particle **-ка** adds a nuance of familiarity to the command: Запиши́-ка! (pf.) 'Do jot it down!'

(2) The negated **imperfective** imperative is used to **forbid** an action:

Не **закрыва́йте** (impf.) окно́!   **Don't shut** the window!

(3) Both aspects can appear in one sentence, the imperfective forbidding and the perfective ordering an action:

Éсли всё же что́-то загоре́лось, **не теря́йтесь** (impf.), **постара́йтесь** (pf.) сохрани́ть хладнокро́вие (*Rabotnitsa*)
If something really has caught fire, **don't panic**, **try** to retain your composure

(4) If a perfective imperative has been ineffectual, then an imperfective may be used to impart a sense of urgency:

Запиши́ (pf.) мой телефо́н.... **Запи́сывай** (impf.), пожа́луйста, я о́чень тороплю́сь!
Make a note of my telephone number. ... **Would you mind writing it down**, please, I am in a terrible hurry!

271 Use of the imperative to exhort and invite

(1) The imperfective imperative is also used:

(i) In exhortations:

— **Встава́й** (impf.), сказа́ла она́   'Do get up', she said

(ii) In expressing wishes:

Поправля́йтесь! (impf.)   Get well soon!

(iii) In conveying an invitation, in social or other conventional situations:

Проходи́те (impf.), пожа́луйста!
Pass down the aircraft, please! (air-hostess to passengers)

Бери́те! (impf.)	Take one/some!
Клади́те (impf.) cа́хар!	Have some sugar!
Раздева́йтесь!(impf.)	Take off your hat and coat!
Сади́тесь! (impf.)	Sit down!
Снима́йте (impf.) пальто́!	Take off your coat!

(2) In a more formal or professional relationship, however, the **perfective** may be preferred:

Нюра, **сними́** (pf.) с больно́го пижа́му, хладнокро́вно сказа́ла Ве́ра Ива́новна (Aksenov)
'Nyura, remove the patient's pyjamas', said Vera Ivanovna coolly (doctor to nurse)

«Я тебе́ покажу́ фанта́зию! **Сядь** (pf.) как сле́дует!» (Trifonov)
'I'll give you imagination! Sit properly!' (mother to child)

Note

(a) The first-person plural of an imperfective or perfective verb may also be used to express wishes or appeals: **бу́дем наде́яться** (impf.), что 'let's hope that', **Попро́буем** (pf.) 'Let's have a go'. The addition of **дава́й/дава́йте** lends emphasis: **Дава́йте** бу́дем чита́ть (impf.) Пу́шкина! 'Let's read Pushkin!', **Дава́й** сыгра́ем! (pf.) 'Let's have a game!'

(b) The negative optative is usually expressed by an imperfective: Не **бу́дем зажига́ть** (impf.) све́та, ла́дно? — сказа́ла она́ (Kazakov) '"Do you mind if we leave the light off?" she said', **Не бу́дем преувели́чивать** (impf.) 'Let's not exaggerate', Дава́йте **не бу́дем спо́рить** (impf.) 'Let's not argue'.

272 A command arising naturally from context

The imperfective imperative is preferred when an instruction is the expected norm in particular circumstances. For example, a student at an examination knows the procedure: he selects a slip of paper with a question on it, prepares his answer and is invited to speak. The examiner's instructions are therefore expressed in the imperfective:

Берите (impf.) билет! **Отвечайте!** (impf.)
Take a slip! Answer!

Similarly, standard recommendations and requests from a shop assistant will be in the imperfective:

Платите (impf.) в кассу!　　　Pay at the cash-desk!

while non-predictable statements will be in the perfective:

Возьмите (pf.) эту кофточку! Она вам идёт
Take this blouse! It suits you

273 Negative commands/warnings

(1) A negative command usually appears in the imperfective aspect (see **270** (2)). When the imperative implies a **warning**, however, rather than a command, tempered with a nuance of apprehension that the action might occur inadvertently, then the **perfective** is preferred:

Не заболей! (pf.)	Mind you don't fall ill!
Не поскользнись! (pf.)	Mind you don't slip!
Не пролей (pf.) молоко!	Mind you don't spill the milk!
Не простудись! (pf.)	Mind you don't catch a cold!
Не уроните (pf.) вазу!	Mind you don't drop the vase!

Note
(a) These commands forbid actions which would not normally be performed deliberately, but might occur inadvertently or as the result of carelessness. It is in these circumstances that the negative perfective imperative is used, sometimes combined with смотри(те)! 'mind!':

Смотри, не забудь! (pf.)	Mind you don't forget!
Смотри, не обрежься! (pf.)	Mind you don't cut yourself!
Смотри, не опоздай! (pf.)	Mind you're not late!
Смотри, не упади! (pf.)	Mind you don't fall!

(b) Other perfective verbs whose negative imperatives may be used to express warnings include **испа́чкаться** 'to get dirty', **опроки́нуть** 'to overturn, capsize', **потеря́ться** 'to get lost', **промахну́ться** 'to miss the target', **проспа́ть** 'to oversleep'. Compare «Умоля́ю, девчо́нки, **не зарази́тесь** (pf.), бу́дьте осторо́жнее!» (*Rabotnitsa*) 'I implore you, girls, don't get infected, be more careful!'

(2) The imperfective is used, however, when reference is to a protracted period rather than a single occurrence:

Смотри́ **не забыва́й** (impf.) нас!
Mind you don't forget us!

274 Use of the perfective imperative with repeated actions

While a repeated action is usually associated with an imperfective imperative (See **269** (2).), the perfective is used when reference is made to the number of times an action is repeated in swift succession (cf. **257** (3) (iii) (b)):

Прослу́шайте (pf.) плёнку **два ра́за/не́сколько раз**
Listen to the tape twice/several times

275 Use of the future and the infinitive to express peremptory commands

(1) Future perfectives may be used to express categorical commands:

Пойдёшь к ма́ме, **возьмёшь** у неё ключи́ от шка́фа и **принесёшь** посу́ду
You will go to mother, get the keys of the cupboard from her and bring the crockery

(2) A strict imperative may also be rendered by use of the infinitive:

Сиде́ть сми́рно!   Sit quietly!

276 Aspect in the infinitive. Introductory comments

(1) The perfective infinitive is used to denote the completion of a single action:

Мне на́до **позвони́ть** (pf.) домо́й
I need to ring home

(2) The imperfective infinitive denotes:

(i) A repeated action:

Их на́до **корми́ть** (impf.) три ра́за в день
They have to be fed three times a day

(ii) A continuous action:

Помогли́ ей **воспи́тывать** (impf.) де́вочку
They helped her to bring up the little girl

(3) An imperfective infinitive may simply name an action, with no implication of result or completion, while the perfective stresses intention to achieve a result. Compare

Мне сего́дня ну́жно **разбира́ть** (impf.) кни́ги
I must **spend some time sorting out** the books today

and

Мне сего́дня ну́жно **разобра́ть** (pf.) кни́ги
I must **get the books sorted out** today

277 Use of the infinitive to denote habitual actions

(1) The imperfective infinitive combines with verbs and other forms that imply habitual processes, tendencies, preferences etc.:

Ры́бка **научи́лась** открыва́ть (impf.) холоди́льник (*Yunyi naturalist*)
Rybka (an otter) learned how to open the fridge

Я **привы́к** встава́ть (impf.) ра́но   I am used to rising early
Он **уме́ет** рисова́ть (impf.)   He knows how to draw

(2) Other words that combine with an imperfective infinitive include **надое́сть** 'to be bored with', **отвы́кнуть** 'to get out of the habit of', **предпочита́ть** 'to prefer', **привы́чка** 'habit', **разучи́ться** 'to forget how to' (Я разучи́лся игра́ть (impf.) на пиани́но 'I have forgotten how to play the piano').

(3) Though **люби́ть** 'to like' almost invariably combines with the imperfective infinitive, the perfective is possible in the meaning of 'intermittent repetition'. Compare

Он лю́бит **отдыха́ть** (impf.) в саду́
He likes to relax in the garden

Он лю́бит **отдохну́ть** (pf.) в саду́
He likes relaxing in the garden now and then

Note

Боя́ться 'to fear' is used with the perfective infinitive when it expresses apprehension that something might happen inadvertently: Бою́сь **заблуди́ться** 'I am afraid of getting lost'. In the case of deliberate actions, use of aspect depends on context, cf.: Бою́сь **купа́ться** (impf.) в о́зере 'I am scared of bathing in the lake' and Бою́сь **призна́ться** (pf.) 'I am afraid to confess'.

(4) The perfective infinitive also appears in a frequentative context when the element of frequency relates to another word in the sentence, and *not* to the infinitive. Thus, in

Я всегда́ рад **помо́чь** (pf.) тебе́
I am always glad to help you

the meaning of frequency expressed by **всегда́** 'always' is 'absorbed' by the adjective **рад** 'glad'. The construction: adverb of frequency + adjective or verb + *perfective* infinitive reflects standard practice:

Вы всегда́ мо́жете (impf.) **взять** (pf.) у меня́ слова́рь
You can always get a dictionary from me

Иногда́ мне удава́лось (impf.) **подста́вить** (pf.) ему́ но́жку (Granin)
Sometimes I succeeded in tripping him up

Его́ неоднокра́тно пыта́лись (impf.) **отпугну́ть** (pf.) (*Izvestiya*)
Several times they had tried to scare it (a tiger) off

278 Use of the imperfective infinitive after verbs of beginning, continuing and concluding

The imperfective infinitive is mandatory after:

(1) Verbs of beginning:

начина́ть/нача́ть	to begin
принима́ться/приня́ться	to get down to
стать (pf. only)	to begin

Они́ приняли́сь **выдвига́ть** (impf.) я́щики (Nagibin)
They set to work pulling out the drawers

(2) Verbs of continuing:

продолжа́ть	to continue

Он продолжа́л **укла́дываться** (impf.)
He continued packing

Note
Perfective **продо́лжить** usually takes a direct object, *not* an infinitive: **продо́лжить** прове́рку 'to continue the check'.

(3) Verbs of concluding:

броса́ть/бро́сить	'to give up'
конча́ть/ко́нчить	'to finish'
перестава́ть/переста́ть	'to cease'
прекраща́ть/прекрати́ть	'to desist'

Ли́дия Миха́йловна переста́ла **приглаша́ть** (impf.) меня́ за стол (Rasputin)
Lidia Mikhailovna stopped inviting me for meals

279 Inadvisable and advisable actions

(1) The imperfective infinitive combines with adverbs, impersonal expressions and other words which imply the inadvisability or deny the necessity of an action: **бесполе́зно** 'it's useless', **вре́дно** 'it is harmful', **доста́точно** 'that's enough', **заче́м**? 'why?', **не на́до** 'you should not', **не ну́жно** 'it is not necessary', **не сле́дует** 'you ought

not to', **не стóит** 'there is no point in', **нéчего** 'there is no point', **смешнó** 'it is ridiculous', **сты́дно** 'it is disgraceful':

Да и зачéм **менять** (impf.) кýзов? (*Sputnik*)
And anyway, why change the bodywork?

Не нýжно **вызывáть** (impf.) врачá
There is no need to call the doctor

В кáждый дом **заходить** (impf.) нет смы́сла (Rasputin)
There's no point in calling into every house

Нехорошó **обижáть** (impf.) старикá (Nagibin)
It's not nice to hurt an old man's feelings

Note
Не дóлжен combines with the imperfective infinitive to denote inadvisability (Вы не должны́ **подавáть** (impf.) заявлéние 'You shouldn't apply') and with the perfective infinitive to denote supposition (Он не дóлжен **опоздáть** (pf.) 'He is not likely to be late') (see also **313** (1)).

(2) **Perfective** infinitives may be used to denote advisability:

Не слéдует ли **послáть** (pf.) поздравлéние?
Don't you think we should send our congratulations?

Почемý не **спросить**?(pf.)   Why not ask?

(3) **Нельзя** combines with the imperfective infinitive in the meaning of inadmissibility and the perfective in the meaning of impossibility:

Нельзя́ **входить** (impf.)
You can't go in (i.e. it is forbidden)

Нельзя́ **войти** (pf.)
You can't get in (because, for example, the door is locked)

280 A request to perform/not to perform an action

(1) A **perfective** infinitive is used after a verb denoting a request or intention to perform a single completed action:

Онá попросила меня **уйти** (pf.)   She asked me to leave
Он обещáл **помóчь** (pf.) мне   He promised to help me

Other verbs denoting request or intention include реша́ть/реши́ть 'to decide', сове́товать/посове́товать 'to advise', убежда́ть/убеди́ть 'to convince', угова́ривать/уговори́ть 'to persuade'.

(2) An **imperfective** infinitive is used, however, if **не** appears between the verb and the infinitive:

> Она́ реши́ла **не уходи́ть** (impf.)
> She decided not to go away

> Он обеща́л **не приглаша́ть** (impf.) Та́ню на ве́чер
> He promised not to invite Tanya to the party

Note

(a) A negated **perfective** infinitive in such contexts expresses, not a request or undertaking to abstain from certain actions, but apprehension that an undesired action might inadvertently take place: Стара́юсь не **сде́лать** (pf.) оши́бок 'I am trying not to make any mistakes'.

(b) Verbs such as **отгова́ривать/отговори́ть** 'to dissuade' and **разду́мывать/разду́мать** 'to change one's mind' contain a built-in negative meaning and combine with an imperfective infinitive:

> Он отговори́л меня́ **спра́шивать** (impf.)
> He dissuaded me from asking

> Он разду́мал **е́хать** (impf.)
> He changed his mind about going (decided not to go)

281 Use of the infinitive after не хочу́

(1) Infinitives of either aspect are used after **не хочу́** 'I don't want to', **нет жела́ния** 'I have no wish to', **я не ду́маю** 'I do not mean to', the imperfective being preferred after a categorical negative:

> Я и не ду́мал **отка́зываться** (impf.)
> I didn't dream of refusing

Note

The imperfective infinitive is virtually compulsory after the impersonal reflexive **не хоте́ться**: Домо́й **уходи́ть** (impf.) не хо́чется (Abramov) 'We don't feel like going home'.

(2) The use of a *perfective* infinitive after **не хочу́** etc. may denote that an action *has* taken place, but *unintentionally*:

Я не хоте́л его́ **оби́деть** (pf.)
I did not mean to offend him

282 Use of the infinitive with пора́

(1) In the meaning 'it is time to', **пора́** combines with the **imperfective** infinitive:

Пора́ **начина́ть** (impf.)   It is time to begin

(2) In the meaning 'it is necessary to' it combines with the **perfective** infinitive:

Но ведь пора́ **поня́ть** (pf.), что чу́да не бу́дет (*Nedelya*)
It is high time we realized that there isn't going to be any miracle

283 Use of infinitives after verbs of motion

(1) The imperfective infinitive is used after verbs of motion to describe actions involving processes:

Со́ня пошла́ **ста́вить** (impf.) ча́йник (Grekova)
Sonya went to put on the kettle

Она́ ведёт ребёнка в поликли́нику **проверя́ть** (impf.) зре́ние
She is taking the child to the polyclinic to have his eyes tested

(2) If, however, result is emphasized rather than process, then the perfective is preferred:

Пошёл **почини́ть** (pf.) часы́
He has gone to get the clock mended

Reflexive Verbs

284 Reflexive verbs: conjugation

In conjugating a reflexive verb, the ending -ся is affixed to verb forms ending in a consonant or the semi-consonant -й, and to all active participles; -сь is affixed to forms ending in a vowel. The reflexive verb is thus conjugated as follows:

мы́ться	**верну́ться**
'to wash'	'to return'
я мо́юсь	верну́сь
ты мо́ешься	вернёшься
он мо́ется	вернётся
мы мо́емся	вернёмся
вы мо́етесь	вернётесь
они́ мо́ются	верну́тся

Past tense
мы́лся, мы́лась   верну́лся, верну́лась
мы́лось, мы́лись   верну́лось, верну́лись

Imperative
мо́йся, мо́йтесь   верни́сь, верни́тесь

For active participles, see **340** (2) and **342** (2).

285 The 'true' reflexive

(1) The number of 'true' reflexives, in which the agent 'turns the action back' upon himself or herself, is relatively small. The category contains a number of verbs which relate to personal grooming:

бри́ться/по-	to shave (oneself)
гото́виться/при-	to get ready, prepare oneself
гримирова́ться/за-	to put on make-up
завива́ться/зави́ться	to have one's hair waved
кра́ситься/вы́-, по-	to dye one's hair
накра́ситься/на-	to make up one's face
купа́ться/вы́-, ис-	to bathe (oneself)

мы́ться/по-, вы́-	to wash (oneself)
обува́ться/обу́ться	to put on one's shoes
одева́ться/оде́ться	to dress oneself
переодева́ться/переоде́ться	to change (one's clothes)
причёсываться/причеса́ться	to do one's hair, have one's hair done
пу́дриться/на-, по-	to powder one's face
раздева́ться/разде́ться	to get undressed
разува́ться/разу́ться	to take off one's shoes
умыва́ться/умы́ться	to wash one's hands and face

(2) Other 'true' reflexives include the following:

(i) **Броса́ться/бро́ситься** 'to rush', **защища́ться/защити́ться** 'to defend oneself', **поднима́ться/подня́ться** 'to ascend', **прислоня́ться/прислони́ться** 'to lean', **спуска́ться/спусти́ться** 'to descend'.

(ii) A number of verbs which are reflexive only in the **imperfective**:

ложи́ться/лечь	to lie down
переса́живаться/пересе́сть	to change places, trains etc.
сади́ться/сесть	to sit down
станови́ться/стать	to (go and) stand

Note

Уса́живаться/усе́сться 'to settle down' is reflexive in both aspects.

286 Semi-reflexive verbs

Semi-reflexive verbs describe an action which the agent performs **for** rather than to himself or herself: **запаса́ться/запасти́сь** 'to stock up with', **укла́дываться/уложи́ться** 'to pack' etc.

287 Intransitive reflexives

A reflexive ending may transform a transitive into an intransitive verb. Compare transitive **возвраща́ть**

Он возвраща́ет кни́гу в библиоте́ку
He returns the book to the library

with intransitive **возвращаться** in

Он **возвращается** домой
He returns home

Other examples include:

Земля **вращается**	The Earth rotates
Колесо **вертится**	The wheel spins
Война **кончается**/ **кончилась**	The war ends/ended
Стул **ломается**/**сломался**	The chair breaks/broke
Дом **находится** на берегу	The house is situated on the shore
Фильм **начинается**/ **начался**	The film begins/began
Урок **продолжается**	The lesson continues
Болезнь **распространяется**/**распространилась**	The disease is spreading/spread
Положение **улучшается**/ **улучшилось**	The situation improves/ improved

Note

(a) All the verbs in the above list can be used transitively without the reflexive endings: Учитель **вращает** глобус 'The teacher rotates the globe' etc.

(b) While English uses many verbs both transitively *and* intransitively ('She *grows* tulips'/'Tulips *grow*'; 'She *stops* the bus'/'The bus *stops*'), Russian always distinguishes transitive from intransitive, either by using different verbs (Она **выращивает** тюльпаны/Тюльпаны **растут**) or by affixing a reflexive ending to convert a transitive into an intransitive verb (Она **останавливает** автобус/Автобус **останавливается**).

288 Reflexive verbs with passive meaning

(1) Reflexive suffixes impart **passive** meaning to many imperfective transitive verbs. There is usually a third-person subject:

Как это **делается**?
How is that done?

Соната **исполняется** (оркéстром)
The sonata is performed (by an orchestra)

(2) The possibility of indicating the **agent** of an action (usually in the form of an instrumental) distinguishes the passive from the intransitive construction. Compare:

Passive:

Книги **возвращаются** в библиотéку **учениками**
The books **are returned** to the library **by the pupils**

Intransitive:

Они **возвращаются** домóй
They return home

Likewise, Колёса движутся **водóй** 'The wheels are moved by water power' (passive), Толпá движется по улице 'The crowd moves down the street' (intransitive).

Note
In general, only **imperfective** verbs function as reflexive passives: Проéкт **обсуждáлся** министрами 'The project was being discussed by the ministers', Как **пишется** э́то слóво? 'How is this word spelt?' The **perfective** passive is normally rendered by a participle (see **359** (3)).

289 Reciprocal meanings

(1) A small number of reflexives denote reciprocal or joint action:

Они чáсто **встречáются**	They often meet
Мы **собирáемся**	We gather
Скóро **увидимся**	We shall see each other soon

(2) Others include:

делиться/по-	to share
здорóваться/по-	to say hello
мириться/по-, при-	to make it up
обнимáться/обняться	to embrace
объединяться/объединиться	to amalgamate
прощáться/проститься	to say goodbye

сове́товаться/по-	to take advice
совеща́ться (impf. only)	to consult
срабо́таться (pf. only)	to achieve a working relation-ship
усла́вливаться/усло́виться	to agree
целова́ться/по-	to kiss

(3) **C** + instrumental may combine with such verbs:

Дели́ться **с ке́м-нибудь** куско́м хле́ба
To share a crust of bread with someone

Совеща́ться **со специали́стами**
To consult experts

in which case the **subject** of the verb may be singular

Я здоро́ваюсь/проща́юсь с ним
I say hello/goodbye to him

or plural

Мы срабо́тались с ни́ми
We developed a good working relationship with them

In the absence of **c** + instrumental, however, the subject is always plural:

Друзья́ обняли́сь	The friends embraced
Враги́ помири́лись	The enemies made it up

(4) Some reciprocal reflexives denote conflict and dispute:

Он со все́ми **брани́тся**   He quarrels with everyone

Other verbs include: **би́ться** 'to fight', **боро́ться/по-** 'to struggle', **руга́ться/по-** 'to abuse one another', **ссо́риться/по-** 'to quarrel'.

(5) Reflexive verbs of motion with the prefixes **раз-** and **c-** (**разбега́ться/разбежа́ться** 'to disperse', **слета́ться/слете́ться** 'to congregate' (of birds) etc.) also express joint action (see **331**).

Note
See **143** (3) (constructions with **дру̀г дру́га** 'each other').

290 Reflexive verbs which express feelings and attitudes

A number of reflexive verbs express or reflect feelings and attitudes. They may be subdivided into:

(1) Those which appear only as reflexives: **боя́ться** + gen. 'to fear', **горди́ться** + instr. 'to be proud of', **любова́ться/по-** + instr./**на** + acc. 'to admire', **надея́ться на** + acc. 'to hope for, rely on', **наслажда́ться** + instr. 'to revel in', **нра́виться/по-** + dat. 'to please', **опаса́ться** + gen. 'to fear', **распла́каться** (pf. only) 'to burst into tears', **рассмея́ться** (pf. only) 'to burst out laughing', **смея́ться/за-** + dat./**над** + instr. 'to laugh', **сомнева́ться/усомни́ться в** + prep. 'to doubt', **улыба́ться/улыбну́ться** 'to smile'.

(2) Those which, shorn of their reflexive endings, can be used as transitive verbs in their own right: **беспоко́иться/по-** 'to worry', **весели́ться/по-** 'to enjoy oneself', **волнова́ться/вз-** 'to get excited', **восхища́ться/восхити́ться** + instr. 'to be delighted', **печа́литься/о-** 'to grieve' **признава́ться/призна́ться в** + prep. 'to confess to', **пуга́ться/ис-** + gen. 'to be frightened', **ра́доваться/об-** + dat. 'to rejoice', **расстра́иваться/расстро́иться** 'to get distraught, upset', **серди́ться/рас- на** + acc. 'to get angry', **удивля́ться/удиви́ться** + dat. 'to be surprised'. Compare

Э́то меня́ **беспоко́ит**　　　That concerns me

and

Я **беспоко́юсь**　　　I am worried

291 Intense or purposeful action

The following reflexive verbs denote intense or purposeful action: **добива́ться/доби́ться** + gen. 'to achieve', **принима́ться/приня́ться за** + acc. 'to tackle', **проси́ться/по-** 'to apply', **пыта́ться/по-** 'to attempt', **стара́ться/по-** 'to try', **стреми́ться** (impf. only) 'to strive', **стуча́ться/по-** 'to knock' (hoping to be admitted), **труди́ться/по-** 'to labour'.

292 Reflexive verbs that emphasize thoroughness

(1) A number of reflexive verbs, mostly prefixed **вы-**, **до-** or **на-**, emphasize thorough completion of an action: **высыпа́ться/ вы́спаться** 'to have a good sleep', **доу́чиваться/доучи́ться** 'to complete one's studies', **наеда́ться/нае́сться** 'to eat one's fill', **напива́ться/напи́ться** 'to slake one's thirst/get drunk', **насмотре́ться** (pf. only) 'to look one's fill' etc.

(2) Reflexive verbs in **за-** denote absorption in an activity: **заду́мываться/заду́маться** 'to be lost in thought', **засма́триваться/ засмотре́ться** 'to be absorbed in looking at something' etc.

293 Reflexive verbs that denote potential to perform an action

Some reflexives denote that the subject has the potential to perform some, usually harmful, action:

Коро́вы **бода́ются**	Cows butt
Крапи́ва **жжётся**	Nettles sting
Соба́ки **куса́ются**	Dogs bite
Ко́шки **цара́паются**	Cats scratch

Impersonal Constructions

294 Use of impersonal constructions to denote natural processes

(1) The third-person singulars of some verbs denote climatic or other natural processes:

Вечере́ет	Evening is drawing in
Моро́зит	Frost is in the air
Света́ет	Dawn is breaking
Сквози́т	There is a draught
Смерка́ется ра́но	It gets dark early
Темне́ет	It is getting dark

(2) In the past tense, the neuter is used:

Вечере́ло　　　　　Evening was drawing in

295 Impersonal constructions with an animate accusative or dative

Impersonal verbs may denote physical state, inclination or urge, the person affected appearing:

(1) In the accusative case:

Петра́ **зноби́т**	Petr feels shivery
Меня́ ко сну **кло́нит**	I feel drowsy
Ната́шу **лихора́дит**	Natasha feels feverish
Больно́го **рвёт**	The patient vomits (Его́ **вы́рвало** 'He threw up')
Ма́шу **тошни́т**	Masha feels sick (Ма́шу **стошни́ло** 'Masha vomited')
Нас **тяну́ло** дру́г к дру́гу (Gagarin)	We felt drawn to each other

Меня́ **зуди́ло** посмотре́ть, как они́ отнесу́тся к моему́ появле́нию (Rasputin)
I was itching to see how they would react to my appearance

(2) In the dative case (with a reflexive verb):

Мне **нездоро́вится**	I am feeling off colour
Ей не **рабо́тается**	She doesn't feel like working
Ему́ не **спи́тся**	He doesn't feel sleepy
Мне **хо́чется** пить	I feel thirsty

Про́бовал чита́ть, **не чита́лось**, лёг на крова́ть, кури́л (Trifonov)
He tried to read but **wasn't in the mood for reading**, lay down on the bed, smoked

296 Impersonal constructions involving an external force

(1) In some impersonal constructions the object of a verb (usually in the neuter past tense) appears in the **accusative** and its inanimate

agent, often a natural phenomenon or external force, in the **instrumental**:

Да́чу **зажгло́ мо́лнией**	The country cottage was struck by lightning
Подва́л **за́лило водо́й**	The cellar was flooded
Избу́ **занесло́ сне́гом**	The hut was snow-bound
Его́ **уби́ло электри́чеством**	He was electrocuted
Труп **унесло́ реко́й**	The body was carried away by the river
Засы́пало песко́м сква́жины (Trifonov)	The bore-holes got clogged with sand

Note

(a) The agent of the action is not always indicated: Вчера́ на стро́йке **задави́ло** челове́ка 'A man was run over at the building-site yesterday', Ло́дку **кача́ло** 'The boat was pitching and tossing', За́ борт **смы́ло** судово́го по́вара (Gagarin) 'The ship's cook was washed overboard'.

(b) An alternative construction is also possible, with the natural or other phenomenon in the nominative, as the subject of the action: Его́ **уби́ла мо́лния** 'He was struck by lightning'.

(2) The incidents in this type of construction are **accidental**. Compare:

(i) Use of the third-person **plural** for **intentional** occurrences:

Его́ **уби́ли** в рукопа́шном бою́
He was killed in hand-to-hand fighting

(ii) Use of the third-person neuter **singular** for **accidental** occurrences:

Его́ **уби́ло** в перестре́лке	He was killed in a skirmish

297 Expression of other meanings (chance, sufficiency etc.)

Some impersonal constructions are concerned with chance, success, sufficiency/insufficiency, the person affected appearing in the **dative**:

(1) The verb denotes chance, luck, success:

Мне **везёт** в ка́рты
I am lucky at cards

Мне **повезло́**
I am in luck, have been lucky

Ученику́ **удало́сь** реши́ть зада́чу
The pupil succeeded in solving the problem

Отцу́ **довело́сь** побыва́ть на собра́нии
My father had occasion to attend a meeting

Note also **Вы́шло** ина́че 'It turned out differently', where no per-sonal involvement is expressed, and Что **случи́лось/произошло́?**
'What has happened?', where the person affected may appear in a prepositional phrase: Что случи́лось **с ним**? 'What has happened to him?' (cf. У вас что́-то **с телефо́ном** 'Something's wrong with your telephone').

(2) The verb denotes sufficiency/insufficiency, the quantifiable item appearing in the **genitive** case:

Бра́ту **недостаёт о́пыта**	My brother lacks experience
Ему́ всегда́ **не хвата́ет де́нег**	He is always short of money
Хва́тит бензи́ну	There will be enough petrol

Note
Э́того нам ещё не **хвата́ло**! 'That's the last straw!'

298 Constructions with the second-person singular

(1) Impersonal meanings can be expressed using the second-person singular of a verb (the equivalent of English 'one' or 'you'):

Ко всему́ **привыка́ешь**
You/one can get used to anything

Там не **уви́дишь** на́ших фи́льмов, не **прочтёшь** на́ших книг (*Russia Today*)
You won't see our films or read our books there (in the West)

(2) The second-person singular pronoun may be added for emphasis:

И то́лько при усло́вии, е́сли **ты** бу́дешь кури́ть и пить — **ты** бу́дешь по́льзоваться успе́хом. Е́сли же **ты** не накра́шена и не ра́дуешься пло́ским шу́точкам, ми́мо **тебя́** прохо́дят, как ми́мо пусто́го ме́ста (*Russia Today*) And you'll only get anywhere if you smoke and drink. But if you don't wear make-up or laugh at their pathetic jokes, they'll cut you dead

299 Constructions with the third-person plural

(1) The third-person plural is used (*without a pronoun*) to denote action taken by 'the authorities' or other third parties:

Говоря́т, что . . .	They say that . . .
Меня́ **задержа́ли**	I was arrested
Его́ **награди́ли**	He was decorated
Про́сят не кури́ть	You are requested not to smoke

Note
Как тебя́ **зову́т**? 'What is your name?'

(2) Use of the plural may be purely conventional, as in the following examples, in which the subject of the action could be interpreted as singular:

Тебя́ **ждут**
Someone is/Some people are waiting for you

Вас **про́сят** к телефо́ну
You are wanted on the phone

Тебя́ **спра́шивают**
Someone's asking for you

Note
The following example draws a clear distinction between the second-person singular, which identifies with the **individual**, and the third-person plural, which identifies with **authority**:

Са́мое ужа́сное во всех шко́лах, так э́то то, что **сиди́шь** и **трясёшься**, что **тебя́ спро́сят**, и **поста́вят**, наприме́р, тро́йку и́ли дво́йку (*Russia Today*)
The worst thing in any school is sitting there trembling at the prospect of being asked a question and getting a bare pass or a fail

The Passive Voice

300 The passive voice. Introductory comments

(1) In a passive construction, the *natural object* of an action becomes the *grammatical subject*. Compare English:

(i) 'They hate *him*' (active construction, with '*him*' the natural object of the verb).

(ii) '*He* is hated by them' (passive construction in which '*he*' has become the grammatical subject while remaining the natural object).

(2) Russian expresses passive meaning through reflexive verbs, the third-person plural, participles (see **359** and **360** (2)) and word order (see **478** (2) (i)).

301 The passive expressed by imperfective reflexive verbs

(1) The passive may be expressed by an imperfective reflexive verb:

Здесь **ловились** (impf.) селёдка и рéдкая рыба — кутýм (Lebedev)
Herring and a rare species, the kutum, **were fished for** here

(2) The agent of the action may be represented by an **instrumental**

Смéта составляется **бухгáлтером**
The estimate is being prepared **by an accountant**

or omitted

По рáдио **передавáлась** нóвая пьéса
A new play **was being broadcast** on the radio

Óбувь снимáлась у вхóда в храм (Granin)
Footwear was removed at the entrance to the temple

Note

A reflexive verb with an animate subject is often either a 'true' reflexive (Он **мóется** 'He is having a wash' (not *'He is being washed', which should be rendered as Егó мóют)) or denotes joint action (Пассажúры **собирáются** 'The passengers congregate'). However, reflexive passives with animate subjects appear in examples such as Герóи **награждáются** госудáрством 'Heroes **are rewarded** by the state'.

302 Passive meaning expressed by third-person plural verbs

The use of a third-person plural instead of a reflexive passive emphasizes the involvement of a human agent. Compare use of the reflexive in

Магазúн **открывáется**   The shop opens

with the third-person plural, with its emphasis on human agency:

И вдруг он слы́шит, что **дверь открывáют**. Но э́то ещё не пáрень, э́то проводни́ца (Rasputin)
And suddenly he hears the door **being opened**. But it's not the boy back yet, it's the guard

303 Perfective reflexives with passive meaning

Perfective passives are normally expressed by a participle (see **359** and **360** (2) (ii)). However, passives may also be expressed by perfective reflexives that denote:

(1) Covering:

Верши́ны **покры́лись** снéгом
The peaks became covered in snow

Note
This sentence describes an *action*. Compare the use of a participle to describe a state: Верши́ны **покры́ты** снéгом 'The peaks **are covered** in snow'.

(2) Filling:

Таз **напóлнился** водóй
The basin filled with water

(3) Illuminating:

Поля́ **освети́лись** пóздним сóлнцем
The fields were illuminated by the late sun

(4)   Others, for example 'replacing', 'creating', 'breaking':

> Её пре́жняя ра́дость **смени́лась** чу́вством кра́йнего раздраже́ния
> Her former joy yielded to a feeling of extreme irritation

> **Создало́сь** сло́жное положе́ние
> A complex situation developed

> **Разби́лся** стул
> A chair got smashed

Note

Animate instrumentals are excluded from such constructions. They are possible only with a passive participle (see **359**), cf.:

> Кружо́к **созда́лся/был со́здан**
> The club was set up

> Кружо́к **был со́здан** (but not *созда́лся) **ученика́ми**
> The club was set up by the **pupils**

The Conditional and Subjunctive Moods

304 The conditional mood. Introductory comments

(1)   If we compare the sentences

   (i)   If he *wakes* his wife she *will be* angry

   (ii)   If he *woke* his wife she *would be* angry

then it is clear that the situation described in (i) *may* occur, while the situation described in (ii) is *hypothetical*. The implication of statements of type (ii) is that the opposite situation obtains, e.g.

> If I *knew* (the implication is that I do *not* know), I *would tell* you

(2)   In the above examples, (i) is rendered in Russian by a verb in the future

> Éсли он **разбу́дит** жену́, она́ рассе́рдится

while the two examples under (ii) are rendered by the **conditional mood**:

Éсли бы он **разбуди́л** жену́, она́ **рассерди́лась бы**
Éсли бы я знал, я **сказа́л бы** вам

305 Formation of the conditional

A conditional construction comprises:

(i) A conditional clause (**éсли бы** + past tense of the verb).

(ii) A main clause (past tense of the verb + **бы**):

Éсли бы у меня́ **была́** путёвка, я **отдыха́л бы** в Крыму́
If I had a holiday voucher **I would** spend my vacation in the Crimea

Note

(a) Alternatively, the main clause may precede the conditional:

Я пошёл бы, éсли бы меня́ **пригласи́ли**
I would go if they **invited** me

(b) Conditionals can also have **pluperfect** meanings. Thus, the sentence under (a) could also be rendered as 'I **would have gone if** they **had invited** me'.

(c) In the main clause, **бы** may precede the verb:

Я бы помо́г вам, éсли бы вы меня́ попроси́ли
I would help you if you asked me (or **I would have helped** you if you had asked me)

(d) The conjunction **то** 'then' may introduce a main clause that follows the conditional clause:

Éсли бы она́ родила́сь в на́ше вре́мя, **то** ста́ла бы арти́ст-кой, и́ли ди́ктором, и́ли стюарде́ссой (*Russia Today*)
If she had been born in our time **then** she would have become a performer, or an announcer, or an air hostess

(e) Sometimes the **éсли** clause is omitted. The implication of such statements is 'this is what I would do if I had my way', as in the following example:

Я бы запрети́л шко́льникам появля́ться в обще́ственных места́х в како́й-либо ино́й оде́жде, кро́ме шко́льной фо́рмы (*Rabotnitsa*)
I would ban school-children from appearing in public places other than in school uniform

(f)   The conditional is used with either aspect, but is commoner with the perfective.

306   Use of (1) the imperative and (2) the preposition без to express conditional meanings

(1)   The **singular imperative** may be used colloquially with conditional meaning:

Доведи́сь мне (= е́сли бы мне **довело́сь**) встре́титься с ним ра́ньше, все **бы́ло бы** ина́че
If I had chanced to meet him earlier everything would have been different

Note
The singular imperative can also replace **е́сли** + future tense:

Разгори́сь (= Е́сли разгори́тся) а́томный пожа́р — и ока́жутся бессмы́сленными уси́лия люде́й до́брой во́ли (Lebedev)
If an atomic holocaust **breaks out**, the efforts of people of goodwill will be pointless

(2)   A prepositional phrase with **без** 'without' may also have conditional meaning:

Без Лю́бы (= Е́сли бы не Лю́ба), я бы не получи́л вы́сшего образова́ния (Rybakov)
Had it not been for Lyuba I would not have received a higher education

307   Use of the particle бы to express desire

(1)   The past tense + **бы** can be used to express desire on the part of the subject:

За́втра я с удово́льствием **пошёл бы** в теа́тр
I would very much **like to go** to the theatre tomorrow

(2)   The phrase **хоте́л бы** 'I would like to' is commonly used in this meaning:

Я хотéл бы пойти́ в кино́
I **would like** to go to the cinema

Note

(a) Note the expression of desire in constructions of the type **Скорéй бы пришло́** лéто! 'Roll on summer!', **Поéхать бы** домо́й! 'Oh, to go home!'

(b) Past tense + **бы** is also used to express a mild injunction: **Помогли́ бы** ей 'You might give her a hand'. This is much less peremptory than the imperative: **Помоги́те** ей! 'Help her!'

308 Use of the subjunctive to express wish or desire

(1) In translating the sentences

(i) **I want to vote**
(ii) **I want you to vote**

the infinitive in (i), in which the subject is the **same** for both verbs, is rendered by a Russian **infinitive**

Я хочу́ голосова́ть

while the infinitive in (ii), in which the subjects of the two verbs are **different**

I want
you to vote

is rendered in Russian by a **subjunctive** (**что́бы** + past tense):

Я хочу́, что́бы вы голосова́ли

Compare

Он не хо́чет, что́бы я танцева́л с Тама́рой (Nikolaev)
He **does not want me to dance** with Tamara

Note

Что́бы is *never* used with the present or future tense, only with the *past*.

(2) Other words denoting desirability or undesirability may also appear in the main clause: **ва́жно** 'it is important', **жела́тельно** 'it is desirable', **за то** 'in favour of', **лу́чше** 'it is better', **наста́ивать/**

настоя́ть 'to insist', **про̀тив того́** 'against', **тре́бовать/по-** 'to demand':

> **Гла́вное**, что̀бы спорт служи́л де́лу ми́ра (Kuleshov)
> **The main thing** is that sport should serve the cause of peace

> Он **настоя́л (на том)**, что̀бы я подписа́лся
> He **insisted** I sign

> Я не **про̀тив того́, что̀бы** он брал на себя́ часть хлопо́т на ку́хне (*Russia Today*)
> **I do not object to his taking on** some of the kitchen chores

> Никто́ не **тре́бует**, что̀бы де́вушка сиде́ла одна́ взаперти́ (*Rabotnitsa*)
> No one **demands** that a girl should remain locked up in seclusion

Note

(a) Desirability may also be implied by constructions with **сказа́ть** 'to tell' (Мне мой прие́мный оте́ц **сказа́л, что̀б я запо́мнил** ме́сто, где ру́кописи зако́паны (*Izvestiya*) 'My foster father **told me to remember** where the manuscripts are buried', **Скажи́те** ва̀шему Ви́тьке, что̀бы он **за мной не ходи́л** (Rasputin) '**Tell** your Vitka **to stop following me around**') and **предупреди́ть** 'to warn' (Я **предупреди́л** его́, что̀бы он **не уходи́л** 'I warned him **not to go away**').

(b) The idiomatic use of **что̀бы** + past tense to issue a warning: **Что̀бы я э́того бо́льше не слы̀шал!** 'Don't ever let me hear you say that again!'

(c) In colloquial contexts, **хоте́ть** may combine with a future verb: Хоти́те, я вам **скажу́** 'Would you like me to tell you?'

309 The subjunctive of purposeful endeavour

(1) If we compare

   (i) **Я хочу́, что̀бы он пришёл**
       I want him to come

   (ii) **Я добива́юсь того́, что̀бы он пришёл**
        I am trying to get him to come

then the wish that he should come, expressed in (i) by the verb **хочу́**, finds its counterpart in (ii) in purposeful endeavour (**добива́юсь**) to achieve the desired aim.

(2) Other words involved in this type of construction include **де́лать всё, что́бы** 'to do everything to ensure that', **забо́титься о том, что́бы** 'to take care that', **следи́ть за тем, что́бы** 'to see to it that', **смотре́ть, что́бы** 'to mind that', **стреми́ться к тому́, что́бы** 'to strive':

> **Забо́титься о то́м, что́бы** вы не проспа́ли, бу́дет ЭВМ́ телефо́нной ста́нции (*Izvestiya*)
> The computer at the telephone exchange **will see to it that** you do not sleep in

> **Смотри́, что́б** Куту́зов тебя́ не пойма́л (Yakhontov)
> **Mind** Kutuzov doesn't catch you

Note

Добива́ться/доби́ться is used with the *subjunctive* to denote intent to achieve a purpose (Мы **добива́емся того́, что́бы** она́ согласи́лась 'We are trying to get her to agree') and with the *indicative* to denote achievement (В конце́ концо́в председа́тель **доби́лся того́, что** она́ **согласи́лась** (Rasputin) 'The chairman eventually got her to agree').

310 Purpose clauses

A purpose clause describes an action which is taken with the aim of achieving a desired result. The result clause is introduced:

(1) By **что́бы** + **infinitive** if both clauses have the **same** subject:

> Он встал, **что́бы откры́ть окно́**
> He got up **in order to open the window**

> Я позвоню́ бра́ту, **что́бы напо́мнить** ему́ о ве́чере
> I shall ring my brother **in order to remind him of the party**

(2) By **что́бы** + the **past tense** (the **subjunctive of purpose**) if the two clauses have **different** subjects:

> Он встал, **что́бы она́ могла́ сесть**
> He got up **so that she could sit down**

> Я позвоню́ бра́ту, **что́бы он знал**, что я прие́хал
> I shall ring my brother, **so that he knows** I have arrived

Человéк снял лы́жи, **чтóбы онú не мешáли** емý ползтú
(Nagibin)
The man removed his skis, **so that they should not prevent him**
from crawling

311 The expression of hypothesis

(1) If we compare the sentences

  (i) I have not met *the man who swam the Channel*
  (ii) I have never met *a man who has not heard of Leo Tolstoy*

then it is clear that (i) refers to *an actual person* (the man who swam
the Channel), while (ii) is dealing with *a hypothetical situation* (an
imaginary person who has not heard of Leo Tolstoy).

  (i) is expressed in Russian using the **indicative**:

Я не встречáл человéка, **котóрый переплы́л** Ла-Мáнш
I have not met the man who swam the Channel

  (ii) is expressed using the **subjunctive of hypothesis** (past tense +
бы):

Я не встречáл человéка, **котóрый бы не слыхáл** о
Толстóм
I have never met a man who has not heard of Tolstoy

Compare

Нет óтрасли промы́шленности, для котóрой освоéние
космúческого прострáнства **не оказáлось бы** полéзным
(*Izvestiya*)
There is no industry which **has not benefited** from the conquest
of space

(2) A similar distinction is made in constructions with **слýчай**
between:

(i) Incidents which *did* occur, where the indicative is used:

Скóлько у нас бы́ло **слýчаев, когдá снимáли** с машúн
стёкла (*Literaturnaya gazeta*)
There have been umpteen **cases of** car wind-screens **being
removed**

(ii) Incidents which did *not* occur, where the subjunctive is used:

Нé было слýчая, **чтòбы он заблудѝлся** (Kazakov)
There was not a single instance **of his getting lost**

(3) The same principle applies to constructions with verbs of perception and statement: **вѝдеть** 'to see', **замéтить** 'to notice', **пòмнить** 'to remember', **сказáть** 'to say', **слы́шать** 'to hear' etc.

(i) The indicative is used to refer to an actual occurrence:

Вѝжу, **как онѝ игрáют** в футбóл
I see **them playing** football

(ii) The subjunctive indicates that the subject did not witness or recall the incident and may doubt whether it in fact occurred:

Не пòмню, **чтòбы онá** хоть раз **взялá** кóрку хлéба (Rasputin)
I do not recall **her** even once **taking** a crust of bread

Я не замéтил, **чтòбы он упáл в òбморок**
I did not notice **him fainting**

Use of the indicative here would constitute an acknowledgement that the incident occurred – but that the subject did not witness it:

Я не замéтил, **что он упáл в òбморок**
I did not notice **that he had fainted**

Note

(a) Hypotheses may also be introduced by the phrase **не то, чтòбы**,

И он **не то чтòбы был** недовóлен жѝзнью, считáл себя́ неудáчником (Tendryakov)
It is not that he was dissatisfied with life, he just considered himself unlucky

or by negated verbs which imply an unreal situation:

Дня ведь не проходѝло, **чтòбы онá не похвалѝла** невéстку (Zalygin)
Never a day passed **without her praising** her daughter-in-law

(b) **Боя́ться** 'to fear' combines either with the indicative (Боюсь, **что он провáлится** 'I am afraid he will fail', Боюсь, **что он не придёт** 'I am afraid he won't come') or a subjunctive (note 'illogical' negative): Бою́сь, **что̀бы он не провали́лся** 'I am afraid he may fail'.

312 Concessive constructions

(1) The particle **бы** also appears in concessive constructions (English 'whoever', 'whatever' etc.):

кто/что/как/где/куда́/како́й/ско́лько + бы + ни + past tense

Чего́ бы э́то мне ни сто́ило, на каки́е бы же́ртвы **ни пришло́сь** пойти́ — а своего́ добью́сь (*Rabotnitsa*)
Whatever it costs, whatever sacrifices I may be called upon to make, I shall achieve my goal

Я ви́дел, что черепа́хам пло́хо в нево́ле, **ка́к бы я ни стара́лся** хорошо́ за ни́ми уха́живать (*Yunyi naturalist*)
I saw that the tortoises were ill at ease in captivity, **however much I might try** to look after them properly

(2) **Бы** may be omitted, in reference to an actual incident:

Ско́лько Но́сов **ни тряс** приёмник, го́лос ди́ктора не зазвуча́л вновь (Povolyaev)
However much Nosov **shook** the receiver, the announcer's voice remained silent

Как я **ни боро́лся** за её здоро́вье, всё напра́сно (*Yunyi naturalist*)
No matter how much I fought to restore her to health, it was all in vain

(3) The future may be used to denote that all instances are covered:

Каку́ю газе́ту **ни откро́ешь** — всю́ду разгово́р о же́нщине (*Russia Today*)
Whichever paper you open, the talk is only of women

Note the set phrases

во что бы то ни ста́ло	at any cost
как бы то ни́ было	however that might be
как э́то ни парадокса́льно	paradoxical as it may seem
как э́то ни стра́нно	strange as it may seem

Лы́жник **во что бы то ни ста́ло** хоте́л продолжа́ть свой
мучи́тельный путь (Nagibin)
The skier was determined to continue his agonizing journey
come what may

Constructions Expressing Obligation, Necessity, Possibility or Potential

313 The expression of obligation and necessity

Obligation and necessity can be expressed in the following ways:

(1) До́лжен + infinitive

(i) **До́лжен, должна́, должно́, должны́** have the endings of short-
form adjectives and agree with the subject in gender and number:

я, ты, он **до́лжен**	'I, you, he must' (masculine subject)
я, ты, она́ **должна́**	'I, you, she must' (feminine subject)
оно́ **должно́**	'it must'
мы, вы, они́ **должны́**	'we, you, they must'

(ii) They also combine with past and future forms of **быть**:

я, ты, он до́лжен **был**	'I, you, he had to' (masculine subject)
я, ты, она́ должна́ **была́**	'I, you, she had to' (feminine subject)
оно́ должно́ **бы́ло**	'it had to'
мы, вы, они́ должны́ **бы́ли**	'we, you, they had to'
я до́лжен/должна́ **бу́ду**	'I shall have to'
ты до́лжен/должна́ **бу́дешь**	'you will have to'
он до́лжен **бу́дет**	'he will have to'
она́ должна́ **бу́дет**	'she will have to'
оно́ должно́ **бу́дет**	'it will have to'
мы должны́ **бу́дем**	'we shall have to'
вы должны́ **бу́дете**	'you will have to'
они́ должны́ **бу́дут**	'they will have to'

(iii) **До́лжен** expresses moral necessity:

Ка́ждый челове́к **до́лжен** труди́ться
Every person must work

(iv) It is also used to express other modal concepts, the equivalents of 'should', 'ought to', 'is supposed to', 'is due to' etc.:

Цéны **должны́** быть ги́бкими (*Literaturnaya gazeta*)
Prices **should** be flexible

В разли́чных стра́нах ми́ра храня́тся великоле́пные па́мятники культу́ре, и мы **должны́** знать о них (*Nedelya*)
Splendid monuments to culture are preserved in various countries of the world, and we **ought to** know about them

Пыта́юсь буты́лки из-под минера́льной воды́ сдать, а пункт хоть и **до́лжен** рабо́тать, но не рабо́тает (*Nedelya*)
I try to hand in some empty mineral-water bottles, but the collection point is not working, though it **is supposed to** be

По́езд **до́лжен** прийти́ в час дня
The train is **due** in at 1 p.m.

Note

(a) Past and future usage:

Сейча́с Мансу́ров **до́лжен был** подойти́ к ней, обня́ть её (Zalygin)
Now Mansurov **should have** come up to her and embraced her

Она́ **должна́ бу́дет** помо́чь ма́тери
She **will have to** help her mother

(b) The use of **должно́ быть**, in parenthesis, to denote supposition:
Она́, **должно́ быть**, заболе́ла 'She must have fallen ill'; Он, **должно́ быть**, не по́нял 'He can't have understood'.

(2) Ну́жно, на́до

(i) **Ну́жно, на́до** refer to necessity:

Ему́ **ну́жно/на́до бы́ло** преждевре́менно уйти́ на пе́нсию по сла́бости здоро́вья
He **had to** retire early due to ill health

(ii) They can also express the meaning 'ought to':

Больно́му **на́до бы́ло** сде́лать перелива́ние кро́ви
The patient **ought to have** had a blood transfusion

(iii) Compare **не ну́жно** 'it is not necessary' and **не на́до** 'one should not':

Не ну́жно запира́ть дверь
It is **not necessary** to lock the door

Не на́до запира́ть дверь
You **should not** lock the door

(3) Сто́ит, сле́дует, прийти́сь, вы́нужден, обя́зан

(i) **Сто́ит** refers to recommended action:

Сто́ит посмотре́ть э́тот фильм
It is worth seeing this film

(ii) **Сле́дует** is more categorical:

Не сле́дует так поступа́ть
One shouldn't behave like that

(iii) **Прийти́сь** implies reluctant acceptance of necessity:

Ему́ **пришло́сь** бежа́ть всю доро́гу
He had to run all the way

(iv) **Вы́нужден** means 'forced', **обя́зан** means 'obliged':

Пило́т **был вы́нужден** посади́ть самолёт в пусты́не
The pilot was forced to land the aircraft in the desert

Врач **обя́зана** помо́чь больно́му
The doctor is obliged to help the patient

314 The expression of possibility or potential

Possibility or potential may be expressed in the following ways:

(1) Мочь, смочь 'to be able'

Я **могу́/смогу́** приня́ть ва́ше приглаше́ние
I **can/shall be able** to accept your invitation

Note
(a) A distinction is made between **мочь** 'to be (physically) able' and
уме́ть 'to be able, know how to'. Compare Я **уме́ю** пла́вать 'I
can/know how to swim' and Сего́дня я не **могу́** пла́вать: у
меня́ рука́ боли́т 'I can't swim today: I have a sore arm'.

(b) The imperfective future of **мочь** is rarely, if ever, used. Instead, the future of **быть в состоянии** + the infinitive is preferred (see **225** (7)).

(c) **Мочь** can also be the equivalent of English 'may', 'might', 'could have', 'might have':

Мне **мо́гут** возрази́ть: лу́чше по кооперати́вной цене́, чем вообще́ отсу́тствие това́ра в магази́не (*Literaturnaya gazeta*)
People **may** object: better at the co-operative price, than the unavailability of the product in the shops

В ка́ссе **мо́гут** быть биле́ты
There **might be** tickets at the box-office

Как он **мог** отве́тить ина́че?
What other answer **could he have** given?

Е́сли она́ реши́лась на э́то, зна́чит, **могла́** реши́ться и на друго́е (Zalygin)
If she made this decision, she **might** equally well **have** made a different decision

(2) Мо́жно/нельзя́, (не)возмо́жно

(i) **Мо́жно** and **нельзя́** can denote:

(a) Permission/prohibition:

— **Мо́жно** сюда́ сесть?
— Нет, **нельзя́**
'May I sit here?'
'No, you may not'

Note
Нельзя́ ли is used to express a very polite request: **Нельзя́ ли** сюда́ сесть? 'Please, may I sit here?' (cf. 'neutral' **Мо́жно ли?**). Conversely, it may express irritation: **Нельзя́ ли** поти́ше?! 'Couldn't you be a little quieter?!'

(b) Possibility/impossibility:

Кислоро́д **мо́жно** получи́ть из воды́
Oxygen can be extracted from water

Нельзя́ согласи́ться с ним
One cannot agree with him

Note

(a) **Мо́жно** is often used with interrogative words: На како́м авто́бусе **мо́жно** дое́хать до це́нтра? 'Which bus do I take for the city centre?'

(b) See **279** (3) for the aspect of the infinitive with **нельзя́**. Note that the imperfective infinitive may be used with **нельзя́** in the meaning of impossibility in a **frequentative** context: **Нельзя́** мыть маши́ну ка́ждый день 'It is impossible to wash the car every day'.

(ii) **Возмо́жно/невозмо́жно** denote only possibility or impossibility (*not* permission/prohibition):

Возмо́жно/мо́жно поста́вить то́чный диа́гноз
It is possible to make a precise diagnosis

Невозмо́жно/нельзя́ реши́ть э́ту зада́чу
It is impossible to solve this problem

Verbs of Motion

315 Unidirectional and multidirectional verbs of motion

Each of fourteen types of motion are represented in Russian by two **imperfective** verbs.

(1) One denotes **movement in one direction** (unidirectional verbs):

Я **иду́** на заво́д   I **am on my way** to the factory
Я **шёл** на заво́д   I **was on my way** to the factory

(2) The other denotes **movement in more than one direction, movement in general, habitual action, return journeys** (multidirectional verbs):

Ка́ждый день он **хо́дит** в шко́лу
He **goes** to school every day

Она́ **хо́дит** по ко́мнате
She **is walking up and down** the room

Он **хо́дит** с па́лкой
He **walks** with a stick

Она́ **ходи́ла** в кино́
She **went** to the cinema

316 Conjugation of verbs of motion

The fourteen pairs of imperfective non-prefixed verbs are conjugated as follows (unidirectional first):

(1)	**идти́**	иду́, идёшь, идёт, идём, идёте, иду́т	'to go,
	ходи́ть	хожу́, хо́дишь, хо́дит etc.	walk'
(2)	**е́хать**	е́ду, е́дешь, е́дет, е́дем, е́дете, е́дут	'to travel,
	е́здить	е́зжу, е́здишь, е́здит etc.	ride'
(3)	**бежа́ть**	бегу́, бежи́шь, бежи́т, бежи́м, бежи́те, бегу́т	'to run'
	бе́гать	бе́гаю, бе́гаешь, бе́гает etc.	
(4)	**лете́ть**	лечу́, лети́шь, лети́т etc.	'to fly'
	лета́ть	лета́ю, лета́ешь, лета́ет etc.	
(5)	**плыть**	плыву́, плывёшь, плывёт etc.	'to swim,
	пла́вать	пла́ваю, пла́ваешь, пла́вает etc.	float'
(6)	**нести́**	несу́, несёшь, несёт etc.	'to carry'
	носи́ть	ношу́, но́сишь, но́сит etc.	
(7)	**вести́**	веду́, ведёшь, ведёт etc.	'to lead'
	води́ть	вожу́, во́дишь, во́дит etc.	
(8)	**везти́**	везу́, везёшь, везёт etc.	'to convey,
	вози́ть	вожу́, во́зишь, во́зит etc.	transport'
(9)	**лезть**	ле́зу, ле́зешь, ле́зет etc.	'to climb'
	ла́зить	ла́жу, ла́зишь, ла́зит etc.	
(10)	**ползти́**	ползу́, ползёшь, ползёт etc.	'to crawl'
	по́лзать	по́лзаю, по́лзаешь, по́лзает etc.	
(11)	**тащи́ть**	тащу́, та́щишь, та́щит etc.	'to drag'
	таска́ть	таска́ю, таска́ешь, таска́ет etc.	
(12)	**гнать**	гоню́, го́нишь, го́нит etc.	'to drive,
	гоня́ть	гоня́ю, гоня́ешь, гоня́ет etc.	chase'
(13)	**кати́ть**	качу́, ка́тишь, ка́тит etc.	'to roll'
	ката́ть	ката́ю, ката́ешь, ката́ет etc.	
(14)	**брести́**	бреду́, бредёшь, бредёт etc.	'to wander'
	броди́ть	брожу́, бро́дишь, бро́дит etc.	

Note

There are grounds for excluding **брести́/броди́ть** from the series, since the two verbs differ somewhat in meaning: **брести́** 'to walk along slowly, with difficulty', **броди́ть** 'to wander aimlessly'. **Броди́ть** differs from other multidirectional verbs in that it cannot denote motion towards a destination. However, the two verbs have traditionally been treated as verbs of motion, and are accordingly dealt with in this section.

317 Imperatives of verbs of motion

Imperatives of verbs of motion are formed according to the rules formulated in **227**:

беги́!	run!
веди́!	lead!
иди́!	go!
неси́!	carry!

Note

Поезжа́й! 'Go!', the imperative of **пое́хать**, is used for single positive commands (**Поезжа́й** по́ездом! 'Go by train!'), **е́зди!** for frequentative commands and **Не** е́зди! for negative commands (**Не е́зди** авто́бусом! 'Don't go by bus').

318 Past tense of verbs of motion

(1) Verbs of motion in **-ать/-ять/-еть/-ить** have past tense forms in -л: **ходи́л, лете́л** etc.

(2) The past tenses of other verbs of motion are as follows:

брести́:	брёл, брела́, брело́, брели́
везти́:	вёз, везла́, везло́, везли́
вести́:	вёл, вела́, вело́, вели́
идти́:	шёл, шла, шло, шли
лезть:	лез, ле́зла, ле́зло, ле́зли
нести́:	нёс, несла́, несло́, несли́

319 'To go': идти́/ходи́ть and е́хать/е́здить

(1) 'To go' on foot is rendered in Russian as **идти́/ходи́ть**:

Она́ **идёт** в шко́лу
She **is going (is walking, is on her way)** to school

Она́ **хо́дит** в шко́лу
She **goes (walks)** to school

(2) 'To go' by some form of transport is rendered as **éхать/éздить**:

Она́ **éдет** в шко́лу
She **is going (is riding, travelling, driving)** to school

Она́ **éздит** в шко́лу авто́бусом
She **goes (travels)** to school by bus

(3) Thus, 'I am going to town' can be rendered as

Я **иду́** в го́род
'I am going to town' (on foot)

Я **éду** в го́род
'I am going to town' (by some form of transport)

Substantial trips normally imply the use of **éхать/éздить**: Я **éду** во Фра́нцию 'I am going to France'.

Note
Идти́/ходи́ть is used with trains (По́езд **идёт** 'The train is travelling along'), with ships, as an alternative to **плыть** 'to sail', and with road vehicles, as an alternative to **éхать** (Маши́на **идёт/éдет** по доро́ге 'The car **is driving** along the road').

320 Functions of unidirectional verbs of motion

(1) Unidirectional verbs of motion denote movement in one particular direction, usually on one occasion:

Не́которое вре́мя мы **шли** мо́лча (Nikolaev)
For a time we **walked along** in silence

Три дня и три но́чи нас **везли́** в ареста́нтском ваго́не (Gagarin)
For three days and nights **we were transported** in a convict truck

often with a named destination:

Е́дем в го́род
We are driving to **town**

От пьедеста́ла до **раздева́лки** его́ несу́т на рука́х (Khrutsky)

They carry him shoulder-high from the rostrum to the changing-room

(2) The movement is not necessarily in a straight line:

Он шёл **зигза́гами** к до́му
He was **zigzagging** towards the house

but in all instances the verb advances the subject or object along a line of progression:

Он **плыл** про̀тив ве́тра и был слабе́е нас (Nikolaev)
He **was swimming** against the current and was weaker than we were

Шу́рка до́лго **шёл** ле́сом, унося́ ежа́ пода́льше от жилья́ (Vasilev)
Shurka **walked** through the forest for a long while, carrying the hedgehog further and further away from human habitation

(3) The destination or direction of the movement may be:

(i) unspecified, as in the last example,

(ii) specified, as in

К зали́ву шли через па́рк (Yakhontov)
They walked through the park **towards the bay**

(iii) more generally specified, e.g. in terms of points of the compass:

По́езд шёл **на восто́к**
The train was on its way **east**

Note
The future of unidirectional verbs is far less common than the present and past: Когда́ мы **бу́дем идти́** мѝмо кинотеа́тра, мы ку́пим биле́ты на за́втра 'When we **are passing** the cinema, we shall buy tickets for tomorrow', **Бу́дем вести́** по о́череди 'We shall take it in turns to drive'.

321 Unidirectional verbs in frequentative contexts

(1) Unidirectional verbs usually describe movement in progress on one occasion:

Он **идёт, шёл** в шко́лу   He **is, was going** to school

while habitual actions are usually the province of the multidirectional verb (see **322** (3)).

(2) Unidirectional verbs are, however, used to express repeated actions:

(i) Where **movement in one direction** is particularly stressed:

Я иду́ на рабо́ту це́лых полчаса́
I **take** a whole half-hour **to get** to work

(Compare Ка́ждый день я **хожу́** на рабо́ту 'Every day I **go** to work' (and back).)

Обы́чно я **иду́** с рабо́ты пешко́м, а на рабо́ту **е́ду** на автобусе
I usually **walk home** from work but **go to work** on the bus

Пи́сьма 5–6 дней **иду́т** отсю́да в Росси́ю
Letters **take** 5–6 days **to get** from here to Russia

Note
A unidirectional verb is also used in Ка́ждый день **летя́т** пи́сьма из страны́ в страну́ 'Every day letters **wing their way** from country to country' (since each individual letter progresses *in one direction only*).

Когда́ я **иду́** на рабо́ту, я всегда́ покупа́ю газе́ту
When I **am on my way** to work, I always buy a newspaper

О́сенью журавли́ **летя́т** на юг
In the autumn the cranes fly south (*one-way* (*though repeated*) *flight* within the given time-span (о́сенью))

Ка́ждое у́тро в 8.45 **иду́** на автобусную остано́вку
Every morning at 8.45 **I walk** to the bus-stop (but not back again!)

(ii) Where reference is to actions or processes occurring **in sequence**:

Ка́ждое у́тро встаю́, за́втракаю и **иду́** на автобусную остано́вку
Every morning I get up, have breakfast and **go** to the bus-stop

Ка́ждый год, как то́лько наступа́ет ле́то, я **е́ду** на мо́ре
Every year, as soon as summer comes, **I am off** to the sea-side

(Compare Ка́ждый год **е́зжу** на мо́ре 'Every year I go to the sea-side' (and back).)

322 Functions of multidirectional verbs of motion

As their name implies, multidirectional verbs denote **movement in more than one direction**. Meanings may be subdivided as follows:

(1) They denote the action in general, a capacity to perform it, to perform it in a particular way, to know how to perform it, to like performing it and so on:

Я хорошо́ **бе́гаю** на конька́х
I **skate** well

Челове́к **хо́дит** на двух нога́х
Man **walks** upright

Истреби́тели **лета́ют** бы́стро
Fighter-planes **fly** fast

Multidirectional infinitives frequently combine with verbs such as **люби́ть** 'to like', **предпочита́ть** 'to prefer', **уме́ть** 'to know how to', **учи́ться** 'to learn how to' etc.:

Девча́та лю́бят **ходи́ть** в ро́щу за цвета́ми (Nikolaev)
The girls like **going** to the grove for flowers

Он предпочита́ет **ходи́ть** пешко́м, она́ **е́здит** в авто́бусе йли в трамва́е (Kovaleva)
He prefers **to walk**, she **goes** by bus or tram

А ты меня́ нау́чишь так **ла́зить**? . . . спроси́л мальчи́шка (Povolyaev)
'And will you teach me **to climb** like that?', asked the boy

Я уме́ю **води́ть** маши́ну
I know how **to drive** a car

(2) They denote movement **in various directions**, up and down, round and round, to and fro, backwards and forwards, and so on:

Всё своё внима́ние сосредото́чил на проти́внике, кото́рый **гоня́лся** за ним по ри́нгу (Salnikov)
He concentrated all his attention on his opponent, who **was chasing him round** the ring

В сара́е **лета́ли** белогру́дые ла́сточки (Belov)
White-breasted swallows **were flying about** in the shed

А стару́хи до по́здней но́чи **по́лзали** по кла́дбищу, втыка́ли обра́тно кресты́ (Rasputin)
And the old women **crawled round** the cemetery until late at night, sticking the crosses back in the ground

Никола́й Ива́нович стал **ходи́ть** по ко́мнате (Proskurin)
Nikolai Ivanovich began to **walk up and down** the room

(3) They denote habitual action, expressed as return journeys:

По воскресе́ньям мы **бу́дем е́здить** за́ город
On Sundays we shall drive into the country

Авто́бусы **ходи́ли** в са́мые да́льние сёла (Rybakov)
The buses **would go** to the most remote villages

Я **хожу́** в це́рковь
I go to church

323 Use of the past tense of a multidirectional verb to denote a single return journey

(1) The past tense (but **never** the present or future) of a multi-directional verb can be used to denote a single return journey:

На про́шлой неде́ле она́ **е́здила** в Ло́ндон
Last week she **went** to London (and back)

Она́ неда́вно **вози́ла** дете́й в Нью-Йорк
Recently she **took** the children to New York (and back)

(Compare Она́ **отвезла́** дете́й в Нью-Йорк 'She took the children to New York' (and returned alone).)

Не обраща́йте на него́ внима́ния, — говори́т она́ Кузьме́. — Он опя́ть в рестора́н **ходи́л** (Rasputin)
'Pay no attention to him', she says to Kuzma. 'He's **been** to the restaurant again'

Пока́ я **бе́гал** за фо̀тоаппара́том к маши́не, оле́нь ушёл
By the time I **had run** to the car for my camera the deer had gone

Note

In this example **бе́гал** denotes running to the car *and back*. The use of the unidirectional **бежа́л** would imply that the deer escaped while the subject *was still running* towards the car.

(2) Sentences which refer to a return journey may also report what happened at the point of destination, between the outward and return legs of the trip:

Ходи́л с отцо́м в зоопа́рк и там **ката́лся** на ма́ленькой лоша́дке (Belov)
I **went** with my father to the zoo, where I **had a ride** on a little horse

Note

This sentence comprises three actions: (a) went to the zoo, (b) rode on a little horse while there (c) came home again, (a) and (c) being represented by the verb **ходи́л**.

(3) The multidirectional verb is also used in interrogative and negative sentences which refer to return trips:

Ты **ходи́л** в шко́лу сего́дня?
Have you been/Did you go to school today?

Сего́дня я **не ходи́л** в шко́лу
I **haven't been/I didn't go** to school today

324 The verbs нести́, носи́ть; вести́, води́ть; везти́, вози́ть

Нести́, носи́ть; вести́, води́ть; везти́, вози́ть may all mean 'to take':

(1) **Нести́, носи́ть** means 'to take (on foot), carry':

Он **несёт** кни́гу в библиоте́ку
He **is taking** the book to the library (on foot)

Она́ **носи́ла** малю́тку по ко́мнате
She **was carrying** the baby up and down the room

(2) **Вести́, води́ть** means 'to take, lead' (persons or animals):

Она́ **вела́** дете́й в шко́лу
She **was taking** the children to school (on foot)

Она́ **води́ла** дете́й в цирк
She **took** the children to the circus

Note
Вести́/води́ть also means 'to drive' (a vehicle).

(3) **Везти́, вози́ть** means 'to take, drive, convey' (in a vehicle):

Авто́бус **во́зит** тури́стов по А́нглии
The bus **is taking** the tourists round England

Она́ **везёт** ребёнка в коля́ске
She **is wheeling** the child in a pram

Note
(a) While **нести́/носи́ть**, **вести́/води́ть** and **везти́/вози́ть** denote the *specific* purpose of a journey, **брать/взять** 'to take' does not. Compare **Веди́те** дете́й в зооса́д 'Take the children to the zoo' (the specific reason for the outing) and **Возьми́те** меня́ с собо́й 'Take me with you' (the person addressed is going anyway).
(b) A similar principle distinguishes **нести́/носи́ть** from **везти́/вози́ть** in contexts which involve travelling. Thus, a passenger in a train who is taking a picture to an exhibition may say — **Везу́** карти́ну на вы́ставку в Москву́, while of the briefcase he happens to be carrying he will say — **Несу́** портфе́ль, since it is *not* the object of his journey to transport the briefcase, which is simply an item of personal equipment.

325 Translation of 'to drive'

The verb 'to drive' can be rendered as follows:

(1) **Éхать/éздить** 'to drive, travel':

Я **éду** в го́род
I **am driving** to town

(2) **Везти́/вози́ть** 'to drive, convey, transport':

Я вёз бага́ж на ста́нцию
I **was driving** the luggage to the station

(3) **Вести́/води́ть** 'to drive' (a vehicle):

Я учу́сь **води́ть** маши́ну
I am learning **to drive**

Note

Гнать/гоня́ть ста́до 'to drive' (a herd).

326 Perfectives of unidirectional verbs

(1) The perfective infinitives of unidirectional verbs are formed with the prefix **по-**:

идти́/**пойти́**	'to go'	е́хать/**по-**	'to travel'
лете́ть/**по-**	'to fly'	бежа́ть/**по-**	'to run' etc.

Note

Only **идти́** undergoes modification (to **-йти́**) in the formation of the perfective.

(2) The perfectives of unidirectional verbs denote the beginning of movement, setting off for a destination etc.:

Он **пошёл** на по́чту
He **has gone** to the post office

(Compare Он **ходи́л** на по́чту 'He went/has been to the post office' (implying a return journey).)

Она́ **пое́хала** за грани́цу
She **has gone** abroad

(Compare Она́ **е́здила** за грани́цу 'She went/has been abroad' (and has returned).)

Он **понёс** кни́гу в библиоте́ку
He **has taken** the book to the library (and is not back yet)

Note

(a) English '**went**' can refer to one-way journeys ('He **went** to China last week'), rendered by the perfective of a unidirectional verb:

На про́шлой неде́ле он **пое́хал** в Кита́й

or to return trips ('I **went** on holiday to France last year'), rendered by a Russian multidirectional verb:

В про́шлом году́ я **е́здил** на кани́кулы во Фра́нцию

(b) Note the contrast between durative **шёл** and perfective **пошёл** in the following example: Он кру́то поверну́лся и **пошёл** навстре́чу проти́внику, кото́рый **шёл** на него́ уже́ без улы́бки (Salnikov) 'He turned sharply and **set off** towards his opponent, who **was bearing down** on him, no longer with a smile on his face'.

(3) The future of unidirectional perfectives can be used independently (Я **пойду́** с тобо́й 'I shall go with you') or with the future perfective of another verb:

— **Пойду́ покурю́**, — говорю́ я (Kazakov)
'I'll go and have a smoke', I say

(4) The unidirectional perfective may indicate a new phase of an action already in progress (e.g. a change in tempo):

Они́ шли ме́дленно, пото́м **пошли́** быстре́е
They were walking along slowly, then **quickened their pace**

Плове́ц почу́вствовал уста́лость и **поплы́л** ме́дленнее
The swimmer felt tired and **began to swim** more slowly

(5) An English phrase may translate a unidirectional perfective:

Мы оттолкну́лись от ба́кена и **поплы́ли** к бе́регу (Nikolaev)
We pushed off from the buoy and **struck out** for the shore

Он шёл по бе́регу, но **побежа́л**, уви́дев меня́
He was walking along the shore but **broke into a run** on catching sight of me

327 Special meanings of пойти́

Пойти́ can mean:

(1) 'To start walking' of a toddler:

Он **пошёл** с десяти́ ме́сяцев
He **started walking** at ten months

(2) 'To start school' of an infant:

Ми́ша в э́том году́ **пошёл** в шко́лу
Misha **started** school this year

Note also the 'illogical' use of the past in **Я пошёл!** 'I'm off!',
Пое́хали! Let's go!' etc.

328 Не пошёл and не ходи́л

(1) **Не ходи́л** denotes that a journey did not take place:

Вчера́ мы никуда́ **не ходи́ли**
We didn't go anywhere yesterday

(2) **Не пошёл** implies an intention unfulfilled:

Вчера́ мы никуда́ **не пошли́**
We didn't go anywhere yesterday (though we had planned to)

329 Perfectives of multidirectional verbs

(1) The perfectives of multidirectional verbs are also formed with
the prefix **по-**:

ходи́ть/**по-** 'to walk'   е́здить/**по-** 'to travel' etc.

(2) They denote an action of short duration in the past or future:

Он **полета́л** над го́родом и опусти́лся
He **circled** the town **for a while** and then landed

Оста́лось два ра́унда. **Походи́** немно́го, пото́м укро́йся
полоте́нцем и сиди́ здесь, жди меня́ (Salnikov)
There are two rounds left. **Walk around for a bit**, then wrap
yourself in a towel, sit here and wait for me

330 Figurative and idiomatic uses of verbs of motion

Verbs of motion have a number of figurative or idiomatic meanings. In most cases only one of a pair (either the unidirectional or the multidirectional) can be used in a particular figurative sense: the usual differential criteria between unidirectional and multidirectional do *not* apply when the verbs are used figuratively.

(1) Only **unidirectional** verbs can be used in the following:

(i) **Идёт** война, уро́к, фильм
     A war, a lesson, a film **is on**

     Э́та шля́па вам **идёт**
     This hat **suits** you

     Страна́ **идёт** к социали́зму
     The country is **moving** towards socialism

     Идти́ про̀тив во́ли большинства́
     To go against the will of the majority

     Идёт дождь, снег
     It is raining, snowing

     Иду́т часы́
     The clock **is going**

Note
Часы́ **хо́дят** is possible in certain contexts: Часы́ **давно́** не хо́дят 'The clock has not gone **for a long time**'.

(ii) **вести́** войну́   **to wage** war
      вести́ дневни́к   **to keep** a diary
      вести́ перепи́ску   **to carry on** a correspondence
      Доро́га **ведёт** в лес   The road **leads** to the forest
      Ложь к добру́ **не ведёт**   No good **can come of** lying

(iii) **нести́** отве́тственность **to bear** the responsibility
       нести́ поте́ри   **to bear** losses
       нести́ наказа́ние   **to undergo** punishment

(iv) А́кции **летя́т** вниз   Shares **are plummeting**
      Вре́мя **лети́т**   Time **flies**

(v)   **лезть** в дра́ку   **to get into** a brawl

(vi) Ему́ **везёт/повезло́**   He **is lucky/is in luck**

Повезло́, что отыска́ли льди́ну толщино́й 47 см. (Lebedev)
We were lucky enough to find an ice-floe 47 cm thick

(vii) Дни **бегу́т**; Кровь **бежи́т** The days **fly past**; Blood **flows**

(viii) Тролле́йбус **ползёт**, как черепа́ха
The trolley-bus **is crawling along** at a snail's pace

(2) Only **multidirectional** verbs are used in the following:

(i) **носи́ть** зва́ние, и́мя   **to bear** a title, a name
носи́ть отпеча́ток   **to bear** the imprint
носи́ть оде́жду   **to wear** clothes (habitually: cf.
Он **но́сит** шля́пу 'He wears a
hat' and Он **в шля́пе** 'He is
wearing a hat')

(ii) **води́ть** за́ нос   **to lead** up the garden path

(iii) **хо́дит** слух/**хо́дят** слу́хи
rumour **has it**/rumours **are rife** (also, though less commonly,
иду́т слу́хи)

(iv) **ката́ться** на конька́х   **to skate**
ката́ться на велосипе́де **to go** for a cycle ride
ката́ться на ло́дке   **to go** for a row

331 Compound verbs of motion

(1) All simple verbs of motion combine with up to fifteen different
prefixes to form compound aspectual pairs, multidirectional verbs
forming the basis of the imperfectives and unidirectional verbs the
basis of the perfectives (see **332** for modified verb stems).

(2) These prefixed imperfective/perfective aspectual pairs lack the
unidirectional/multidirectional dichotomy of the simple verbs.

(3) Most compound verbs of motion are intransitive and are linked
to the following noun by a preposition (see (4)).

(4) Prefixed compounds of **-ходи́ть/-йти́**, for example, are as
follows:

Imperfective	Perfective	Preposition	Meaning
входи́ть	войти́	в + acc.	to enter
всходи́ть	взойти́	на + acc.	to go up on to
выходи́ть	вы́йти	из + gen.	to go out of
доходи́ть	дойти́	до + gen.	to go as far as
заходи́ть	зайти́	к + dat.	to call on someone
		в/на + acc.	to call in at a place
		в + acc.	to go a long way into
находи́ть	найти́	+ acc.	to find
обходи́ть	обойти́	вокру̀г + gen.	to go round
		+ acc.	to inspect/avoid
отходи́ть	отойти́	от + gen.	to move away from
переходи́ть	перейти́	через + acc.	to cross
		+ acc.	
подходи́ть	подойти́	к + dat.	to go up to
приходи́ть	прийти́	к + dat.	to come to see a person
		в/на + acc.	to come to/arrive at a place
проходи́ть	пройти́	мѝмо + gen.	to pass
		+ acc.	to cover (a distance)
расходи́ться	разойти́сь	по + dat	to disperse to (separate destinations)
сходи́ть	сойти́	с + gen.	to come down from, step off
сходи́ться	сойти́сь	с + instr.	to come together with
уходи́ть	уйти́	от + gen.	to leave a person
		из/с + gen	to leave a place

Note

(a) Alternative usage may be determined by context: Она́ вы́шла в коридо́р/на у́лицу 'She came out **into** the corridor/**on to** the street', Он ушёл **на рабо́ту** 'He left **for** work', Они́ пришли́ **от дире́ктора** 'They have come **from** the manager', Она́ сошла́ **на перро́н** 'She got down **on to** the platform' etc.

(b) The choice of preposition with **заходи́ть/зайти́** and **приходи́ть/прийти́** depends on the type of location involved: Он пришёл **в шко́лу/на заво́д** 'He arrived **at the school/factory**' (cf. Он ушёл **из шко́лы/с рабо́ты** 'He left **school/work**'). See **408** and **412**.

(c) Some compounds in **на-** take **на** + acc.: **нае́хать на де́рево** 'to run into a tree'.

(d) Prefix and prepositional usage is similar to but not identical with usage with other verbs (see **254**).

332 Stems of compound verbs of motion

Prefixes are added to the following stems to make imperfective and perfective compounds. Stems which differ in form from the simple verbs of motion (for meanings, see **316**) are in **bold** type:

Imperfective	Perfective
-ходи́ть	**-йти́**
-езжа́ть	-е́хать
-бега́ть	-бежа́ть
-лета́ть	-лете́ть
-леза́ть	-лезть
-плыва́ть	-плыть
-полза́ть	-ползти́
-носи́ть	-нести́
-води́ть	-вести́
-вози́ть	-везти́
-та́скивать	-тащи́ть
-гоня́ть	-гнать
-ка́тывать	-кати́ть
-бреда́ть	-брести́

Note

The stems **-бега́ть** and **-полза́ть** differ from the simple verbs of motion **бе́гать** 'to run' and **по́лзать** 'to crawl' only in stress.

333 Spelling rules in the formation of compound verbs of motion

(1) For **вз-/-вс-**, **раз-/рас-**, see **16** (4).

(2) The vowel '**o**' is inserted between a consonant and -**йти**:

войти́ (impf. входи́ть)   to enter (future **войду́**; past **вошёл**)

Likewise **взойти́** 'to ascend', **обойти́** 'to go round', **отойти́** 'to move away from', **подойти́** 'to go up to', **разойти́сь** 'to disperse', **сойти́** 'to descend', **сойти́сь** 'to come together'.

(3) A hard sign is inserted between a prefix ending in a consonant and all forms based on the infinitive stems **-езжа́ть/-е́хать**:

въезжа́ть, въе́хать   to drive in etc.

334 Prefixed verbs of motion

The following examples illustrate the use of compound verbs of motion (for examples with **-ходи́ть/-йти́** see **331** (4)):

(1) **К** подно́жью раке́ты **подъезжа́ет** авто́бус (*Russia Today*)
A bus **draws up to** the base of the rocket

(2) Де́ти **выбега́ют из** мо́ря на пляж (Muraveva)
The children **run out of** the sea on to the beach

(3) Их объединя́ет одна́ о́бщая цель — они́ должны́ **доплы́ть до бе́рега** (*Russia Today*)
They are united by a common aim – they must **reach** the shore

(4) Ко́нонов **отпо́лз** в у́гол пала́тки (Belov)
Kononov **crawled off** into the corner of the tent

(5) Мяч **залете́л на** кры́шу
The ball **sailed away on to** the roof

(6) Она́ **перелезла через** забо́р
She **climbed over** the fence

(7) **Разбреда́лись по** вла́жному ле́су (Vanshenkin)
They **were wandering off through** the damp forest

(8) Мяч **перекати́лся через** ли́нию
The ball **rolled over** the line

(9) **Вы́тащили** лётчика **из** горя́щего самолёта
They **dragged** the pilot **out** of the burning aircraft

(10) Мото́ры их катеро́в сверхмо́щные, рыбинспе́кторам не **догна́ть** (*Izvestiya*)
The engines of their launches are high-powered, the fisheries inspectors haven't a hope of **catching up with** them

(11) **Перенёс** телефо́н **на** тахту́ (Avdeenko)
He **carried** the telephone **over** to the divan

(12) — Вот, матро́са тебе́ **привёл**, — сказа́л Куту́зов
(Yakhontov)
'Look, I have **brought** you a sailor', said Kutuzov

(13) Куту́зов сообщи́л: я́хты уже́ **привезли́** (Yakhontov)
Kutuzov reported that the yachts **had** already **been
delivered**

335 Use of the imperfective past of a compound verb of motion to denote an action and its reverse

(1) The past tense of the imperfective aspect of a compound verb of motion can denote the action and its reverse (see also **259**): Он **приходи́л** 'He came' (and has now gone away again), Он **уезжа́л** 'He went away' (and has now returned).

(2) The prefixes most frequently involved are **в-/вы-**, **за-**, **под-**, **при-/у-**:

Ка́к-то она́ **приводи́ла** свои́х дете́й на рентге́н (Aksenov)
She **had** once **brought** her children for an X-ray

Каки́е краси́вые цветы́! Кто́-то, **должно́ быть**, **входи́л** в ко́мнату без меня́
What beautiful flowers! Someone **must have been** into the room when I was out

Же́нщина, кото́рая то́лько что **подходи́ла к** кио́ску за газе́той, изве́стная актри́са
The woman who **has just been up to** the kiosk for a newspaper is a famous actress

336 Figurative and idiomatic uses of compound verbs of motion

Many compound verbs of motion have figurative or idiomatic meanings. The following list contains only a representative sample:

(1) Compounds in -ходи́ть, -йти́

входи́ть/войти́ в мо́ду	to come into fashion
выходи́ть/вы́йти из стро́я	to break down
доходи́ть/дойти́ до слёз	to be reduced to tears
заходи́ть/зайти́ сли́шком далеко́	to go too far
переходи́ть/перейти́ к друго́й те́ме	to switch to a different topic
подходи́ть/подойти́	to be suitable
приходи́ть/прийти́ в го́лову (кому́-нибудь)	to occur (to someone)
проходи́ть/пройти́	to pass (e.g. вре́мя, боль прохо́дит 'time, pain passes')
расходи́ться/разойти́сь во мне́ниях	not to see eye to eye
сходи́ть/сойти́ с ума́	to go mad
сходи́ться/сойти́сь во мне́ниях	to see eye to eye

(2) Compounds in -води́ть, -вести́

вводи́ть/ввести́ в обраще́ние	to bring into circulation
выводи́ть/вы́вести из терпе́ния	to exasperate
доводи́ть/довести́ до конца́	to put the finishing touches to
заводи́ть/завести́ часы́	to wind up a watch
наводи́ть/навести́ спра́вки	to make enquiries
отводи́ть/отвести́ ду́шу	to unburden one's soul
переводи́ть/перевести́	to translate
подводи́ть/подвести́ дру́га	to let a friend down
приводи́ть/привести́ к	to lead to
проводи́ть/провести́ вре́мя	to spend time
разводи́ть/развести́	to breed (livestock)
разводи́ться/развести́сь	to get divorced
своди́ть/свести́ к ми́нимуму	to reduce to a minimum

(3) Compounds in -носи́ть, -нести́

вноси́ть/внести́ вклад	to make a contribution
выноси́ть/вы́нести пригово́р	to pass sentence
доноси́ть/донести́ на + асс.	to denounce
заноси́ть/занести́	to record, register
наноси́ть/нанести́ пораже́ние	to inflict a defeat
переноси́ть/перенести́ зи́му	to survive the winter
приноси́ть/принести́ по́льзу	to bring benefit

337 Perfectives in c- based on multidirectional verbs

(1) Multidirectional verbs combine with the prefix **c-** to form perfectives: **сбе́гать, сходи́ть, съе́здить** etc. They do not have imperfectives.

(2) Such verbs denote the performance of an action and its result, usually within a limited period of time:

> Ни́кон **сходи́л** (pf.) за дрова́ми, затопи́л ма́ленькую пе́чку (Abramov)
> Nikon **went to fetch** some firewood and lit the small stove

Note

Compounds with **c-** are preferred to the simple unprefixed multi-directional verb (e.g. он ходи́л, он е́здил):

(a)   where sequential actions are involved:

> **Съе́здил** (pf.) за кни́гами и **сел** занима́ться
> He **went to fetch** the books and sat down to study

(b)   where a time element is involved:

> Он **сходи́л** (pf.) за газе́той **за 10 мину́т**
> He **took 10 minutes to fetch** the newspaper

(3) Unlike the simple unprefixed multidirectional verb, which can describe single return journeys in the past tense only (see **323**), per-fectives in **c-** can also express this meaning in the future, the infinitive and the imperative:

> Да и ле́гче, пожа́луй, **на Луну́ слета́ть** (pf.), чем приду́мать тако́й вездехо́д (Abramov)

I do believe it would be easier **to fly to the Moon and back** than devise a cross-country vehicle like that

Сходи (pf.) к Ма́йе и переда́й ей, чтббы она́ подошла́ за́втра пòсле игры́ к газе́тному кибску (Trifonov)
Pop over to Maya's and tell her to come to the newspaper kiosk after the game tomorrow

Note
It is important to distinguish perfectives **сходи́ть, слета́ть, сбе́гать** from imperfectives **сходи́ть**/perfective **сойти́** 'to go down', **слета́ть**/perfective **слете́ть** 'to fly down' and **сбега́ть**/perfective **сбежа́ть** 'to run down'.

338 Perfectives in за-, из- and на- based on multidirectional verbs

За-, **из-** and **на-** also combine with multidirectional verbs to form compound perfectives (such verbs do not have imperfectives):

(1) За- (in the meaning 'beginning of an action')

Он в волне́нии **заходи́л** (pf.) по кбмнате
He **began walking about** the room in agitation

(2) Из- (in the meaning 'to cover the whole area')

Он **изъе́здил** (pf.) всю страну́
He **has travelled the length and breadth** of the country

Он **избе́гал** (pf.) весь сад
He **covered every inch** of the garden

(3) На- (in the meaning of time or distance covered)

Э́тот шофёр **нае́здил** (pf.) 100 000 км.
This driver **has clocked** 100,000 km.

Лётчик **налета́л** (pf.) 1000 часбв
The pilot **has clocked** 1000 hours

Note

It is important to distinguish perfective **заходи́ть** from imperfective **заходи́ть**/perfective **зайти́** 'to drop in' and perfective **избега́ть** from imperfective **избега́ть**/perfective **избежа́ть** 'to avoid'.

Participles

339 Participles. Introductory comments

There are five verbal participles in Russian. The active participles, the imperfective passive and the long-form perfective passive decline like long adjectives and agree in case, gender and number with the nouns they qualify, while the short-form perfective passive functions like a short adjective:

the present active	**чита́ющий**	'who is reading'
the past active (imperfective)	**чита́вший**	'who was reading'
the past active (perfective)	**прочита́вший**	'who read'
the imperfective passive	**чита́емый**	'which is read'
the perfective passive (short form)	**прочи́тан**	'has been read'
the perfective passive (long form)	**прочи́танный**	'which has been read'

Note

The participles are confined mainly to written styles, except for those used as adjectives and nouns and the perfective passive short form.

340 Present active participle. Formation

(1) The present active participle is formed by replacing the final -**т** of the third-person plural of the present tense by the endings -**щий** (m.), -**щая** (f.), -**щее** (n.), -**щие** (pl.):

бегу́т	бегу́щий	-ая	-ее	-ие	'who is, are running'
крича́т	крича́щий	-ая	-ее	-ие	'who is, are shouting'
танцу́ют	танцу́ющий	-ая	-ее	-ие	'who is, are dancing'
чита́ют	чита́ющий	-ая	-ее	-ие	'who is, are reading'

(2) In the case of reflexive verbs, -**ся** is used throughout:

смею́тся	смею́щийся	-аяся	-ееся	-иеся	'who is, are laughing'

341 Stress in the present active participle

(1) The stress in present active participles formed from **first-conjugation** verbs is usually as in the third-person plural:

понима́ть	понима́ют	**понима́ющий**	'who understands'
тону́ть	то́нут	**то́нущий**	'who drowns/is drowning'
иска́ть	и́щут	**и́щущий**	'who looks for/is looking for'
течь	теку́т	**теку́щий**	'which flows/is flowing'

Note
There are a few exceptions to this rule, e.g. **могу́щий** from мо́гут, third-person plural of мочь 'to be able'.

(2) The stress in participles from **second-conjugation** verbs is usually the same as that of the **infinitive**:

буди́ть	бу́дят	**будя́щий**	'who wakes, is waking'
води́ть	во́дят	**водя́щий**	'who leads'
кати́ть	ка́тят	**катя́щий**	'who is rolling'

(3) However, a number of participles from second-conjugation verbs have the same stress as the third-person plural: **ды́шащий** from дыша́ть 'to breathe', **ле́чащий** from лечи́ть 'to treat' (medically), **лю́бящий** from люби́ть 'to love', **ру́бящий** from руби́ть 'to chop', **су́шащий** from суши́ть 'to dry', **те́рпящий** from терпе́ть 'to endure', **ту́шащий** from туши́ть 'to extinguish'.

(4) A number of participles have alternative stress: **ва́рящий/варя́щий** from вари́ть 'to boil', **го́нящий/гоня́щий** from гнать 'to drive', **де́лящий/деля́щий** from дели́ть 'to share', **су́дящий/судя́щий** from суди́ть 'to judge', **у́чащий/уча́щий** from учи́ть 'to teach', **хва́лящий/хваля́щий** from хвали́ть 'to praise', **шу́тящий/шутя́щий** from шути́ть 'to joke'.

342 The past active participle. Formation

(1) The past active participle is formed from imperfective and perfective verbs by replacing the -л of the masculine past tense by -вший (m.), -вшая (f.), -вшее (n.), -вшие (pl.):

| писа́л | писа́вший | -вшая | -вшее | -вшие | 'who was, were writing' |
| написа́л | написа́вший | -вшая | -вшее | -вшие | 'who wrote' |

(2) In reflexive verbs, the suffix **-ся** is used throughout:

> смея́вший**ся**   'who laughed, was laughing'

(3) If the masculine past does not end in -л, the endings **-ший**, **-шая**, **-шее**, **-шие** are added to it to make the participle:

замёрз	замёрзший	-шая	-шее	-шие	'who, which froze'
привы́к	привы́кший	-шая	-шее	-шие	'who got used to'
у́мер	уме́рший	-шая	-шее	-шие	'who died'

Note

(a) Unprefixed verbs with the suffix **-ну-**, e.g. **га́снуть** 'to go out' (past гас/га́снул), **ги́бнуть** 'to perish', **па́хнуть** 'to smell', and the prefixed verb **исче́знуть** 'to disappear' (past исче́з) form the past participle with the suffix **-вш-**: **га́снувший**, **ги́бнувший, исче́знувший, па́хнувший**.

(b) Дости́гнуть 'to achieve' (past дости́г) has alternative participles: **дости́гший/дости́гнувший**. Likewise compounds of -вергнуть, e.g. **подве́ргший/подве́ргнувший** from подве́ргнуть 'to subject' (past подве́рг) and **вто́ргшийся/вто́ргнувшийся** from вто́ргнуться 'to invade' (past вто́ргся). **Воскре́сший** from воскре́снуть 'to rise again' (past воскре́с) is commoner than **воскре́снувший**.

(4) Verbs in **-ти** with a present-future stem in **-т-** or **-д-** have participles based on stems ending in these consonants:

идти́, past шёл	ше́дший	-шая	-шее	-шие	'who was, were going'
вести́, past вёл	ве́дший	-шая	-шее	-шие	'who was, were leading'
цвести́, past цвёл	цве́тший	-шая	-шее	-шие	'which was, were blooming'

Note

Произойти́ 'to occur' has alternative participles **происше́дший** and **произоше́дший**.

343 Stress in the past active participle

Stress is as in the masculine past, with the exception of **уме́рший** 'who died' (cf. past у́мер).

344 The imperfective passive participle. Formation

(1) The imperfective passive participle is formed by adding adjectival endings to the first-person plural of an imperfective **transitive** verb:

First-
person
plural

Participle				
лю́бим	**люби́мый** -ая	-ое	-ые	'who, which is, are loved'
це́ним	**цени́мый** -ая	-ое	-ые	'who, which is, are valued'
чита́ем	**чита́емый** -ая	-ое	-ые	'which is, are read'

(2) Many unprefixed transitive verbs (e.g. **жева́ть** 'to chew', **копа́ть** 'to dig') do not form the participle. However, participles can be made from most prefixed transitive secondary imperfectives and verbs in **-овать**:

испы́тываемый -ая	-ое	-ые	'which is, are (being) tested'
сжига́емый -ая	-ое	-ые	'which is, are (being) burnt'
тре́буемый -ая	-ое	-ые	'which is, are (being) demanded'
устра́иваемый -ая	-ое	-ые	'which is, are (being) arranged'

(3) Participles from transitive verbs in -ава́ть are as follows: **дава́емый** 'which is given/being given', **признава́емый** 'which is acknowledged' etc.

Note

(a) The participle is also formed from a limited number of **intransitive** or **semi-transitive** verbs. Some of these take the dative: **предше́ствовать** 'to precede' (**предше́ствуемый**), **угрожа́ть** 'to threaten' (**угрожа́емый**). Others take the instrumental: **кома́ндовать** 'to command' (**кома́ндуемый**), **прене-**

брега́ть 'to scorn, take no heed of' (**пренебрега́емый**), **руководи́ть** 'to run' (**руководи́мый**), **управля́ть** 'to manage, guide' (**управля́емый**). The series also includes **обита́емый** 'inhabited' (from intransitive **обита́ть**).

(b) Among verbs in -**ти**, only **вести́** 'to lead' (**ведо́мый** (**ведо́мый** самолёт 'wing-man' (in an aircraft formation))) and **нести́** 'to carry' (**несо́мый**) form imperfective passive participles (see **346** (2)).

345 Stress in the imperfective passive participle

Stress in imperfective passive participles derived from **first-conjugation** verbs is as in the first-person plural: **испо́льзуемый** 'which is used'. In participles derived from **second-conjugation** verbs the stress falls on -**и**-: **гони́мый** 'which is driven', from **гнать** 'to drive' (except for verbs with stem stress throughout: **слы́шимый** from слы́шать 'to hear').

346 Verbs which have no imperfective passive participle

Many verbs have no imperfective passive participle. These include the following:

(1) Verbs in -**ереть**, -**зть**, -**оть**, -**сть**,-**уть**, -**чь**.

(2) Verbs in -**ти** (except for **вести́** 'to lead' and **нести́** 'to carry' (see **344** (3) note (b)).

(3) Very many monosyllabic verbs, including **бить** 'to strike', **брать** 'to take', **брить** 'to shave', **есть** 'to eat', **жать** 'to press', **ждать** 'to wait for', **звать** 'to call', **знать** 'to know', **лить** 'to pour', **мыть** 'to wash', **петь** 'to sing', **пить** 'to drink', **рвать** 'to tear', **ткать** 'to weave', **шить** 'to sew'.

(4) First-conjugation consonant-stem verbs of the type **вяза́ть** 'to tie', **писа́ть** 'to write', **пря́тать** 'to hide'. However, **иска́ть** 'to seek' has the participle **иско́мый** (**иско́мая** величина́ 'unknown quantity') and **колеба́ть** 'to shake' has **коле́блемый** 'which is being shaken'. See **217**.

(5) Many second-conjugation verbs: **благодари́ть** 'to thank', **буди́ть** 'to awaken', **гла́дить** 'to iron', **гото́вить** 'to prepare', **держа́ть** 'to hold', **жа́рить** 'to fry', **корми́ть** 'to feed', **кра́сить** 'to paint', **лечи́ть** 'to treat' (medically), **находи́ть** 'to find', **плати́ть** 'to pay', **по́ртить** 'to spoil', **руби́ть** 'to chop', **смотре́ть** 'to watch', **ста́вить** 'to stand', **стро́ить** 'to build', **суши́ть** 'to dry', **тра́тить** 'to spend', **туши́ть** 'to extinguish', **учи́ть** 'to teach, learn', **чи́стить** 'to clean'.

347 Formation of passive participles from secondary imperfectives whose primaries have no participle

Most imperfective passive participles derive from prefixed verbs. They include synonyms or cognates of a number of unprefixed verbs which have no participle (see **346**). Thus, the verb **есть** 'to eat' has no participle, whereas its synonym, the secondary imperfective **съеда́ть**, *does* have a participle: **съеда́емый** 'which is eaten'. Compare

жева́ть	= разжёвывать	**разжёвываемый**	'which is chewed'
жечь	= сжига́ть	**сжига́емый**	'which is burnt'
пить	= выпива́ть	**выпива́емый**	'which is drunk'
плати́ть	= опла́чивать	**опла́чиваемый**	'who is paid'
тере́ть	= растира́ть	**растира́емый**	'which is rubbed'

348 The perfective passive participle. Introductory comments

(1) The perfective passive participle has a **short** (predicative) form and a **long** (attributive) form. It is derived only from verbs which are (i) *perfective* and (ii) *transitive*.

(2) Most perfective passive participles contain the suffix -**н**-/-**ен**-, while a minority contain the suffix -**т**-.

349 Formation (infinitives in -ать/-ять)

(1) The masculine short form of the participle derives from infinitives in -**ать** and -**ять** (except for a number of monosyllabic

roots, see **357** (5)) by replacing **-ть** by **-н**, to give endings **-ан/-ян**. The syllable immediately preceding **-ан**, **-ян** bears the stress:

задержа́ть	**заде́ржан**	'has been arrested'
избра́ть	**и́збран**	'has been elected'
написа́ть	**напи́сан**	'has been written'

Note

The perfective prefix **вы́-** is always stressed: **вы́игран** 'has been won'.

(2) **-е-** is liable to mutate to **-ё-** under stress:

завоева́ть **завоёван**	'has been conquered'
причеса́ть **причёсан**	'has had his hair done'

(3) The feminine, neuter and plural forms are derived from the masculine by the addition of **-а, -о, -ы**:

напи́сан	напи́сана	напи́сано	напи́саны
заде́ржан	заде́ржана	заде́ржано	заде́ржаны

350 Stress in the participles from дать and its compounds

(1) The short forms of the perfective passive participle of the verb **дать** 'to give' have end stress in the feminine, neuter and plural:

дан дана́ дано́ даны́

Им дана́ власть
Authority has been given to them

Similarly **сдать** 'to hand over'.

(2) The short forms of other compounds of **дать** (e.g. **изда́ть** 'to publish') have prefix stress except in the end-stressed feminine (where prefix stress is, however, also allowable):

и́здан издана́ и́здано и́зданы   'has, have been published'

Similarly **отда́ть** 'to return', **переда́ть** 'to convey' (**пе́редан, передана́**), **пода́ть** 'to serve', **прида́ть** 'to impart', **прода́ть** 'to sell', **разда́ть** 'to distribute' (**ро́здан, раздана́, ро́здано, ро́зданы**), **созда́ть** 'to create'.

351 Formation of the long-form (attributive) participle from verbs in -ать/-ять

Long-form participles are made from verbs in **-ать/-ять** by adding **-ный**, **-ная**, **-ное**, **-ные** to the masculine short form:

	Masculine	Feminine	Neuter	Plural
напи́сан	**напи́санный**	**напи́санная**	**напи́санное**	**напи́санные**

'written'

352 Formation of the short-form participle from second-conjugation verbs in -ить/-еть

The masculine short form of the participle is derived from second-conjugation infinitives in **-ить/-еть** by replacing the infinitive ending by **-ен** or **-ён**:

(1) **-ен**

(i) Verbs with **fixed stem stress** or **mobile stress** in conjugation take the ending **-ен**.

(a) Fixed stem stress in conjugation: **запо́лнить** 'to fill in', **прове́рить** 'to check':

Бланк **запо́лнен**	The form has been filled in
Счёт **прове́рен**	The account has been checked

(b) Mobile stress in conjugation: **осмотре́ть** 'to examine' (**осмотрю́**, **осмо́тришь**), **получи́ть** 'to receive' (**получу́**, **полу́чишь**):

Больно́й **осмо́трен**	The patient has been examined
Докла́д **полу́чен**	The report has been received

(ii) The feminine, neuter and plural forms derive from the masculine by the addition of **-а**, **-о** and **-ы**: запо́лнен, запо́лнена, запо́лнено, запо́лнены.

Анке́та **запо́лнена**   The questionnaire **has been completed**

Note

Принуждён from **прину́дить** 'to compel'.

(2) -ён

(i) Verbs with **fixed end stress** in conjugation take the masculine short-form ending **-ён**: **реши́ть** 'to decide' (**решу́**, **реши́шь**), **включи́ть** 'to switch' (**включу́**, **включи́шь**):

Вопро́с **решён** The question has been decided
Телеви́зор **включён** The TV has been switched on/is on

(ii) The feminine, neuter and plural endings are **end stressed**: решён, решена́, решено́, решены́:

Пробле́ма **решена́** The problem has been solved

Note
A few verbs with *mobile* stress in conjugation take *end* stress in the participle:

измени́ть: изменён **-ена́ -ено́ -ены́** 'has, have been changed'

Likewise **осуждён** from осуди́ть 'to condemn', **оценён** from оцени́ть 'to estimate', **разделён** from раздели́ть 'to divide', **склонён** from склони́ть 'to incline' (cf. **скло́нен**, **скло́нна** (adjective) 'is inclined').

353 Consonant mutation in participles from second-conjugation infinitives in -ить/-еть

The following consonant changes operate in the formation of perfective passive participles from second-conjugation verbs in **-ить/-еть** (for stress rules see **352**):

б : бл	сруби́ть	сру́блен	has been felled
	употреби́ть	употреблён	has been used
в : вл	доста́вить	доста́влен	has been delivered
	удиви́ть	удивлён	is surprised

Note
Dual mutation in умерщвлён from умертви́ть 'to mortify'.

м : мл	офо́рмить	офо́рмлен	has been designed
п : пл	купи́ть	ку́плен	has been bought
	прикрепи́ть	прикреплён	is pinned to

ф : фл	разграфи́ть	разграфлён	is ruled (with lines)
д : ж	заряди́ть	заря́жен/заряжён	is loaded
	оби́деть	оби́жен	is offended

Note

The participle from уви́деть 'to see' is уви́ден.

| д : жд | освободи́ть | освобождён | has been liberated |

Note

-жд- also appears in the imperfective infinitive (**освобожда́ть**) and the verbal noun (**освобожде́ние** 'liberation'). Other verbs which undergo this mutation are mainly abstract and, like **освободи́ть**, have fixed end stress in conjugation: **подтверди́ть** 'to confirm', **убеди́ть** 'to convince' etc.

| з : ж | загрузи́ть | загру́жен/загружён | is laden |
| | изобрази́ть | изображён | is depicted |

Note

The mutation does not operate in some participles: **вонзён** from вонзи́ть 'to plunge', **пронзён** from пронзи́ть 'to transfix'.

| с : ш | пригласи́ть | приглашён | has been invited |
| | скоси́ть | ско́шен | has been mown |

Note

One or two participles do not undergo mutation: **обезле́сен** from обезле́сить 'to deforest'.

ст : щ	запусти́ть	запу́щен	has been launched
	прости́ть	прощён	has been forgiven
т : ч	оплати́ть	опла́чен	has been paid, settled
т : щ	сократить	сокращён	has been curtailed

Note

-щ- also appears in the first-person singular (**сокращу́**), the imperfective infinitive (**сокраща́ть**) and the verbal noun (**сокраще́ние** 'curtailment'). Other verbs of this type, mainly abstract and with fixed end stress in conjugation, include **запрети́ть** 'to ban'.

354 Formation of the long-form (attributive) participle from second-conjugation verbs in -ить/-еть

Long-form participles from second-conjugation verbs in **-ить/-еть** are derived by adding **-ный, -ная, -ное, -ные** to the masculine short form:

Masculine	Feminine	Neuter	Plural	
запо́лненный	запо́лненная	запо́лненное	запо́лненные	'completed'
включённый	включённая	включённое	включённые	'switched on'

355 Formation of perfective passive participles (short form) from verbs in -ти, -чь, -зть, -сть

The masculine short form of perfective passive participles from verbs in **-ти, -зть, -сть** and **-чь** is derived by replacing the final **-т** of the third-person singular of the conjugation of the verb by **-н**:

Infinitive		Third-person singular	Participle			
перевести́	to translate	переведёт	**переведён**	-ена́	-ено́	-ены́
подмести́	to sweep	подметёт	**подметён**	-ена́	-ено́	-ены́
спасти́	to save	спасёт	**спасён**	-ена́	-ено́	-ены́
испе́чь	to bake	испечёт	**испечён**	-ена́	-ено́	-ены́
обже́чь	to scorch	обожжёт	**обожжён**	-ена́	-ено́	-ены́
разгры́зть	to gnaw	разгрызёт	**разгры́зен**	-ена	-ено	-ены
укра́сть	to steal	украдёт	**укра́ден**	-ена	-ено	-ены

Note

(a) The participles from **найти́** 'to find' and **пройти́** 'to cover' (a distance) are, respectively, **на́йден** and **про́йден**.

(b) **Дости́чь** 'to achieve' has no participle. However, a participle is formed from its synonym **дости́гнуть**: **дости́гнут**. See **357** (2).

(c) Stem stress in participles from some verbs in **-зть/-сть**.

(d) For participles formed from compounds of **-клясть**, see **357** (5) note (a).

(e) **Съесть** 'to eat' has the participle **съе́ден**.

356 Long-form participles from verbs in -ти, -чь, зть, -сть

The long form of participles from verbs in -**ти**, -**чь**, -**зть** and -**сть** is made by adding -**ный**, -**ная**, -**ное**, -**ные** to the short-form masculine, e.g. **переведён**:

Masculine	Feminine	Neuter	Plural
переведённый	**переведённая**	**переведённое**	**переведённые** 'translated'

357 Perfective passive participles in -т

The masculine short form of the participle of certain categories of verb is made by removing the soft sign of the infinitive: **открыть** 'to open', participle **открыт**. The feminine, neuter and plural forms derive from the masculine by the addition of the endings -**а**, -**о**, -**ы**. The following types of verb are involved:

(1) Verbs in -**оть** (note stress change in participle):

   смоло́ть 'to grind'   **смо́лот, -а, -о, -ы**

(2) Verbs in -**уть** (note stress change in participle):

   протяну́ть 'to stretch out'   **протя́нут, -а, -о, -ы**

Note

е is liable to mutate to **ё** under stress: заверну́ть 'to wrap', **завёрнут**; застегну́ть 'to fasten', **застёгнут**.

(3) Verbs in -**ыть**:

   забы́ть 'to forget'   **забы́т, -а, -о, -ы**

(4) Compounds of **бить, вить, лить, пить, шить**:

   вы́шить 'to embroider'   **вы́шит, -а, -о, -ы**
   разби́ть 'to smash'   **разби́т, -а, -о, -ы**

Note

(a) Зали́ть 'to flood': **за́лит, залита́, за́лито, за́литы** (likewise **проли́ть** 'to spill': **про́лит** etc.).

(b) Разви́ть 'to develop': **ра́звит/разви́т, развита́, ра́звито/разви́то, ра́звиты/разви́ты**.

(5) Verbs which introduce 'н' or 'м' in conjugation (**взять** 'to take', compounds of **деть** 'to put', **жать** 'to press', **клясть** 'to curse' and **-нять**, **начáть** 'to begin', **распя́ть** 'to crucify'):

Infinitive		First-person singular	Participle
взять	'to take'	возьму́	**взят, -á, -о, -ы**
заня́ть	'to occupy'	займу́	**зáнят,-á, -о, -ы**
начáть	'to begin'	начну́	**нáчат -á, -о, -ы**
одéть	'to dress'	одéну	**одéт, -а, -о, -ы**
распя́ть	'to crucify'	распну́	**распя́т, -а, -о, -ы**
сжать	'to compress'	сожму́	**сжат, -а, -о, -ы**
сжать	to reap'	сожну́	**сжат, -а, -о, -ы**
смять	'to crumple'	сомну́	**смят, -а, -о, -ы**

Note

(a) Прокля́сть 'to curse', first-person singular прокляну́, participle **прóклят, -á, -о, -ы**. Compare *stem* stress in the adjective **прокля́тый** 'wretched'.

(b) Participles from all compounds of **-нять** have the same stress pattern as **зáнят** (except **снят, снятá, сня́то, сня́ты** from **снять** 'to take off').

(6) Verbs in **-ереть** (note loss of second **-е-** in formation of participle):

запере́ть	'to lock'	**зáперт, -á, -о, -ы**
стере́ть	'to erase'	**стёрт, -а, -о, -ы**

(7) Others:

вы́брить	'to shave'	**вы́брит, -а, -о, -ы**
спеть	'to sing'	**спет, -а, -о, -ы**
прожи́ть	to spend' (time)	**прóжит, прожитá, прóжито, прóжиты**

358 The long form of participles in -т

The long-form participle is formed by adding full adjectival endings to the masculine short form in -т, e.g. **одéт**:

Masculine	Feminine	Neuter	Plural	
одéтый	**одéтая**	**одéтое**	**одéтые**	'dressed'

Note

Compare the participles **развитый** (ско́рость, **ра́звитая** теплово́зом 'speed developed by a diesel locomotive') and **разви́тый** (**разви́тая** пружи́на 'uncoiled spring'), and the adjective **развито́й** (**развита́я** промы́шленность 'highly-developed industry').

359 Functions of short-form participles

(1) Only passive participles have short forms. Active participles have long forms only.

(2) The short form of the imperfective passive participle is rarely used:

Э́тот писа́тель все́ми **люби́м, уважа́ем**
This writer is loved and respected by everyone

A reflexive verb or third-person plural is preferred instead:

Прое́кты **финанси́руются** госуда́рством
Projects are financed by the state

Э́того писа́теля **лю́бят и уважа́ют**
This writer is loved and respected

(3) The short form of the **perfective** passive participle is very much used. It functions as predicate to the noun, with which it agrees in gender and number, and denotes:

(i) The completion of an action:

Война́ **объя́влена**	War has been declared
Флаг **по́днят**	The flag has been hoisted
Письмо́ **подпи́сано**	The letter has been signed

(ii) The existence of a state:

Дверь **заперта́**	The door is locked
Телеви́зор **включён**	The television is on

Note

(a) The participle may precede or follow the noun:

Укрощены́ не́которые опа́сные боле́зни (*Russia Today*)
Certain dangerous diseases **have been curbed**

О́стров **превращён** в зака́зник (Lebedev)
The island **has been converted** into a nature reserve

(b) It may also combine with forms of the verb **быть**:

Он то́лько что **был разбу́жен** гро́мким го́лосом Солоу́хи
(Povolyaev)
He **had** just been **awakened** by Souloukha's loud voice

(Likewise Он **бу́дет разбу́жен** 'He will be awakened', Он **был бы
разбу́жен** 'He would be/would have been awakened', Рабо́ты
должны́ **быть напеча́таны** 'The essays have to be typed'.)

(c) The agent of the action may be rendered by an instrumental:

Письмо́ подпи́сано **мини́стром**
The letter is signed by a minister

360 Functions of long-form participles

Long-form participles, both active and passive, replace relative
clauses beginning with **кото́рый** 'who', 'which'.

(1) Active participles

Active participles relate to and qualify nouns which are the subject
of an action or state. A comma appears between the noun and the
following participle which qualifies it.

(i) The **present** active participle denotes an action which is
simultaneous with the action or state denoted by the main verb:

Вы́ставки, **расска́зывающие** о предупрежде́нии несча́ст-
ных слу́чаев, всегда́ вызыва́ют большо́й интере́с
Exhibitions **which describe** accident prevention always arouse
great interest

Note
The main verb may denote present *or* past action: Я **ви́дел/ви́жу**
соба́ку, бегу́щую по бе́регу 'I saw/see a dog running along the
shore'.

(ii) The **imperfective past** active participle denotes an action
simultaneous with the action of a main verb in the *past tense*:

Же́нщина, **продава́вшая** я́блоки, подошла́ к прохо́жему
The woman **who was selling** apples approached a passer-by

(iii) The **perfective past** active participle denotes an action completed *prior to* the action of the main verb:

Медве́дя прогна́л рабо́чий, **прибежа́вший** на бе́рег с заря́женным ружьём
The bear was chased off by a worker **who had come running** on to the shore with a loaded gun

(2) Passive participles

Passive participles relate to and qualify nouns which are the natural **object** of the action denoted by the participle.

(i) The **imperfective** passive denotes an action which is simultaneous with the action of the main verb. The main verb may be in the present, past or future tense of either aspect. A *comma* appears between the noun and the participle which qualifies it:

Он писа́л статью́	о **предме́те,**	
Он написа́л статью́	о **предме́те,**	
Он пи́шет статью́	о **предме́те,**	**изуча́емом** все́ми
Он бу́дет писа́ть статью́	о **предме́те,**	ученика́ми
Он напи́шет статью́	о **предме́те,**	

('He was writing/wrote/is writing/will be writing/will write an article about a subject **studied** by all pupils'.)

Note
The meaning expressed by the participle may be durative:

програ́мма, **передава́емая** по ра́дио
a programme **being broadcast** on the radio

or habitual:

пе́сни, **люби́мые** наро́дом
songs loved by the people

(ii) The **perfective** passive participle denotes an action completed prior to the action of the main verb. A *comma* appears between the noun and the following participle which qualifies it:

Пересма́тривается програ́мма, **одо́бренная** мини́страми
A programme **approved** by the ministers is being revised

В прода́жу поступи́ла ма́рка, **вы́пущенная** в Финля́ндии
A stamp **issued** in Finland has gone on sale

361 Agreement of long-form participle and noun

(1) The long-form participle agrees with the noun it qualifies in gender, number and case. It differs in this respect from the relative pronoun **кото́рый**, which agrees with the noun in gender and number but *not* in case (the case of **кото́рый** being determined by the function it fulfils in the relative clause it introduces. See **123** (1) (ii).).

(i) Present active participle

Я зна́ю **ма́льчика, пи́шущего** письмо́
I know **the boy (who is) writing** the letter

(ii) Past active participle

Я помога́ю **ученика́м, провали́вшимся** на экза́мене
I am helping **the pupils who failed** the examination

(iii) Imperfective passive participle

Э́то — **де́вочка, люби́мая** все́ми
That is **the girl liked** by everyone

(iv) Perfective passive

Он пи́шет статью́ о **ю́ношах, нака́занных** за хулига́нство
He is writing an article about **the youths punished** for hooliganism

(2) Long participles may *precede* the noun:

(i) If the participle is the noun's only qualifier and functions as an adjective:

спя́щий ребёнок	A sleeping child
замёрзшее о́зеро	A frozen lake
Разва́лины **разбомблённых** городо́в (Granin)	The ruins of bombed towns

Note

In some cases the participle may be qualified by an adverb:

хорошо́ опла́чиваемые рабо́чие
well-paid workers

вновь вы́шедший рома́н
a novel which has recently come out

(ii) A pronoun or noun may appear between the participle and the noun it qualifies:

спасённые **им** де́вочки   the girls rescued **by him**

(iii) It is also possible, especially in literary and journalistic styles, for circumstantial detail to appear between the participle and the noun:

Соше́дшие **с по́езда** немно́гие пассажи́ры разошли́сь
(Nosov)
The few passengers who had alighted **from the train** dispersed

передава́емые **по телеви́зору** прогно́зы пого́ды
weather forecasts transmitted **on TV**

Дви́гался конве́йер уви́денных **в ра́зное вре́мя** люде́й
(Gagarin)
A panorama of people he had seen **at various times** passed before him

362 Participial synonymy

(1) The imperfective passive participle may be synonymous with the present active participle of the corresponding reflexive verb:

слова́, **употребля́емые/употребля́ющиеся** в ре́чи
the words **used** in a speech

(2) The active participle is used if the verb (e.g. **стро́ить** 'to build') has no passive participle:

стро́ящееся зда́ние   a building **under construction**

(3) A 'true' reflexive cannot be used with passive meaning, however. Thus, одева́ющийся can only mean 'who is dressing' (but not *'who is being dressed').

(4) Where both types of participle are available, the passive participle is used when the *agent* is named:

словá, **употребля́емые** (not *употребля́ющиеся) орáтором в публи́чной ре́чи
words **used** by an orator in a public speech

363 Participles as adjectives and nouns

Many participles are also used as adjectives or nouns.

(1) Present active

(i) Adjectives:

блестя́щий	brilliant
веду́щий	leading
выдаю́щийся	outstanding
далеко́ иду́щий	far-reaching
подходя́щий	suitable
сле́дующий	next, following
соотве́тствующий	appropriate
теку́щий	current

(ii) Nouns:

куря́щий	smoker
начина́ющий	beginner
непью́щий	tee-totaller
трудя́щийся	worker
уча́щийся	pupil, student

(2) Past active

(i) Adjective:

бы́вший	former

(ii) Nouns:

пострада́вший	a casualty
сумасше́дший	a madman
уме́рший	the deceased
уцеле́вший	a survivor

(3) Imperfective passive

вообража́емый	imaginary
люби́мый	favourite
терпи́мый	tolerable
уважа́емый	respected

Note

Many have negative prefixes, cf. English equivalents in -ble:

невыноси́мый	unbearable
незабыва́емый	unforgettable
необходи́мый	indispensable

A number derive from perfective stems

незамени́мый	irreplaceable
(не)излечи́мый	(in)curable
неоспори́мый	indisputable
непобеди́мый	invincible
(не)совмести́мый	(in)compatible

or intransitive verbs

незави́симый	independent

A few are used as nouns:

обвиня́емый	the accused
содержи́мое	contents (of a receptacle)

(4) Perfective passive

заключённый	convict

364 Participial adjectives

(1) A number of long adjectives of participial origin differ from long-form participles:

(i) In having no prefix.

(ii) In having one -**н**- instead of two:

варёное яйцо́	a boiled egg
жа́реная карто́шка	fried potatoes
кра́шеный пол	a painted floor
(не)пи́саный зако́н	a(n) (un)written law
сушёные фру́кты	dried fruit

Note

(a) Adjectives based on second-conjugation verbs in **-ить** with mobile stress in conjugation tend to have suffix **-ён-**.

(b) If circumstantial detail is added, *participles* must be used: **ра́ненный** в но́гу солда́т 'a soldier wounded in the leg' (cf. ра́неный солда́т 'wounded soldier'), **сва́ренное** в кастрю́льке яйцо́ 'an egg boiled in a saucepan' (cf. варёное яйцо́ 'boiled egg').

(2) Some of the adjectives have the suffix **-т-**:

кры́тый ры́нок	covered market
небри́тое лицо́	unshaven face

К обе́ду мы яви́лись в **мя́той** оде́жде (Nikolaev)
We appeared for lunch in crumpled clothing

(3) Others function as adjectival nouns: **кра́деное** 'stolen goods'.

365 Distinction between short-form adjectives and short-form participles

Certain short adjectives differ from short-form participles in having the suffix **-нн-** in their feminine, neuter and plural forms by contrast with **-н-** in the participle:

озабо́чен, озабо́ченна, озабо́ченно, озабо́ченны (adjective)
озабо́чен, озабо́чена, озабо́чено, озабо́чены (participle)

Compare

Глаза́ его́ бы́ли **озабо́ченны** (adj.)
His eyes were troubled

and

Она́ была́ **озабо́чена** (part.) отъе́здом ма́тери
She was upset by her mother's departure

Likewise Егó речь былá **сдéржанна** (adj.) 'His speech was restrained', but Водá былá **сдéржана** (part.) плотúной 'The water was contained by a dam'. A similar distinction is made between **образóван, -а, -о, -ы** 'has been formed' (part.) and **образóван, -нна, -нно, -нны** 'educated' (adj.), **ограничен, -а, -о, -ы** 'limited' (part.) and **ограничен, -нна, -нно, -нны** 'hide-bound' (adj.), **рассéян, -а, -о, -ы** 'dispersed' (part.) and **рассéян, -нна, -нно, -нны** 'absent-minded' (adj.).

366   Impersonal function of short-form participles

(1) The neuter short forms of the perfective passive participles of certain verbs can be used impersonally:

— Здесь **зáнято**?	Is this place occupied?
За всё **заплáчено**	Everything has been paid for
В вагóне бы́ло биткóм **набúто**	The carriage was packed
В зáле **накýрено**	The hall is smoke-filled
Кýшать **пóдано**	Dinner is served
С доскú **стёрто**	The board has been cleaned
С вéчера не **ýбрано** бы́ло со столá (Rasputin)	The table had not been cleared since the previous evening
Вам **откáзано** в прóсьбе	Your request has been refused

(2) Imperfective participles of this type are found in colloquial speech (mainly in the negative):

Давнó **не тóплено**
The heating has not been on for a long time

Compare Пол **не мыт** 'The floor has not been washed', Бельё **не глáжено** 'The washing has not been ironed'.

Note
Impersonal usage in **Прикáзано** остáться 'We have been instructed to stay', Комý э́то **скáзано**? 'How many times do I have to tell you?', and the phrase **Скáзано — сдéлано** 'No sooner said than done'.

Gerunds

367 The gerund. Introductory comments

(1) Gerunds (or 'verbal adverbs') are *indeclinable* forms of the verb that substitute for co-ordinate or adverbial clauses in 'and', 'when', 'since', 'by', 'without' etc.

(2) Gerunds, like active participles, have English equivalents in '-ing', but participles are adjectival in form, agree in gender, case and number with the noun they qualify and replace relative clauses in **кото́рый** (see **360**), while gerunds are invariable. Compare the use of the *participle* in

the **weeping** boy (= the boy **who is weeping**): **пла́чущий** ма́льчик

with the use of the *gerund* in

he sits **weeping** (= **and weeps**): он сиди́т, **пла́ча**

(3) There are imperfective and perfective gerunds.

368 Formation of the imperfective gerund

Most imperfective gerunds are formed by adding -**я** (-**а** after **ж, ч, ш** or **щ**) to the present-tense stem of the verb (see **212**):

говоря́т	говор-	**говоря́**	'speaking'
ды́шат	дыш-	**дыша́**	'breathing'
несу́т	нес-	**неся́**	'carrying'
пла́чут	плач-	**пла́ча**	'weeping'
тре́буют	требу-	**тре́буя**	'demanding'
чита́ют	чита-	**чита́я**	'reading'

Note

(a) **Дава́ть** and compounds, compounds of -**знава́ть**, -**става́ть** form gerunds as follows: **встава́я** 'rising', **дава́я** 'giving':

— Извини́те, у меня́ дела́, — сказа́л Неша́тов, **встава́я** со сту́ла (Grekova)

'Excuse me, I have something to attend to', said Neshatov, **getting up** from his chair

(b) The gerund from **маха́ть** 'to wave' has alternative forms: **маха́я** and **маша́**. Similarly **бры́згать**, **бры́зжа** 'playing' (of a fountain), **бры́згая** 'sprinkling' (water on ironing etc.). **Ка́пать** 'to drip' has **ка́пая**, **сы́пать** 'to strew' has **сы́пля**.

(c) Быть has the gerund **бу́дучи** 'being':

Он прие́хал в Ло́ндон давно́, ещё **бу́дучи** солда́том
He arrived in London long ago **when he was** still a soldier

(d) **Е́дучи** from е́хать is sometimes found in poetic or folk speech; **припева́ючи** is used in the phrase жить **припева́ючи** 'to live in clover'.

(e) Imperfective gerunds from reflexive verbs take the ending **-сь**: **жа́луясь** from жа́ловаться 'to complain'.

369 Stress in the imperfective gerund

Stress in the gerund is normally as in the first-person singular:

голосова́ть	'to vote'	голосу́ю	'I vote'	**голосу́я**	'voting'
держа́ть	'to hold'	держу́	'I hold'	**держа́**	'holding'
кури́ть	'to smoke'	курю́	'I smoke'	**куря́**	'smoking'
смотре́ть	'to look'	смотрю́	'I look'	**смотря́**	'looking'
шепта́ть	'to whisper'	шепчу́	'I whisper'	**шепча́**	'whispering'

Note

Гля́дя 'looking', **лёжа** 'lying', **си́дя** 'sitting' and **сто́я** 'standing' have *stem* stress despite *end* stress in conjugation: Бараба́нов, **сто́я** на одно́м коле́не, дошнуро́вывал бу́тсы (Vanshenkin) 'Barabanov was kneeling to finish lacing his boots'.

370 Verbs with no imperfective gerund

Many verbs have no imperfective gerund. These include the following:

(1) **Бежа́ть** 'to run', **бить** 'to strike', **вить** 'to twine', **врать** 'to lie', **гнить** 'to rot', **драть** 'to flay', **есть** 'to eat', **е́хать** 'to travel' (see, how-

ever, **368** note (d)), **жа́ждать** 'to hunger for', **жать** 'to press', **ждать** 'to wait', **лгать** 'to lie', **лезть** 'to climb', **лить** 'to pour', **мять** 'to crumple', **петь** 'to sing', **пить** 'to drink', **рвать** 'to tear', **слать** 'to send', **стона́ть** 'to groan', **ткать** 'to weave', **хоте́ть** 'to want', **шить** 'to sew'.

Note

Gerunds from some other verbs are rarely used: **беря́** from брать 'to take', **гоня́** from гнать 'to drive', **зовя́** from звать 'to call', **плывя́** from плыть 'to swim'. **Нося́** from носи́ть 'to carry' and **ходя́** from ходи́ть 'to go' are rarely found; cf., however, compound **принося́** 'bringing' etc.

(2) First-conjugation consonant-stem verbs with **с : ш**, **з : ж** mutation (e.g. **писа́ть** 'to write', **ре́зать** 'to cut', see **217** (2)).

(3) Verbs in **-чь**.

(4) Verbs in **-ереть**.

(5) Verbs with the suffix **-ну-** (**га́снуть** 'to go out' etc.).

371 Compensation for the lack of an imperfective gerund

(1) If a primary verb has no imperfective gerund it is often possible to form one from its synonym. Thus, **мочь** 'to be able' has no gerund, but **быть в состоя́нии** 'to be capable of' does: **бу́дучи в состоя́нии** 'being able to'. Likewise, **хоте́ть** 'to want' has no gerund, but **жела́ть** 'to wish' does (**жела́я** 'wishing, wanting'):

> **Жела́я** скоре́е уе́хать, он торопи́лся зако́нчить рабо́ту
> **Wishing** to get away as soon as possible he hastened to finish his work

(2) Other primaries with no gerund have a synonymous secondary imperfective from which a gerund may be formed:

Primary verb	Secondary imperfective	Gerund	
есть	съеда́ть	**съеда́я**	'eating'
éхать	проезжа́ть	**проезжа́я**	'travelling'
ждать	ожида́ть	**ожида́я**	'waiting'

жечь	сжига́ть	**сжига́я**	'burning'
петь	распева́ть	**распева́я**	'singing'
пить	выпива́ть	**выпива́я**	'drinking'
рвать	разрыва́ть	**разрыва́я**	'tearing up'
слать	посыла́ть	**посыла́я**	'sending'
тереть	вытира́ть	**вытира́я**	'wiping'

Ко́стя Пимурзя́ весь извёлся, **ожида́я** нас (Nikolaev)
Kostya Pimurzya suffered agonies waiting for us

372 The perfective gerund: formation (verbs in -ть, -сть (д-stems))

(1) The perfective gerund is formed from verbs in **-ть** by replacing the perfective infinitive ending by **-в**:

написа́в	having read
постро́ив	having built
промо́кнув	having got soaked

(2) Likewise gerunds from verbs in **-сть** (д-stems only: **присе́сть** 'to sit down for a while', **укра́сть** 'to steal', **упа́сть** 'to fall'):

присе́в	having sat down for a while

373 Reflexive perfective gerunds

Reflexive perfective gerunds have the ending **-вшись**:

верну́вшись	having returned
умы́вшись	having washed

Note

Оперши́сь from **опере́ться** 'to lean on' (cf. figurative usage: **опере́вшись** на инициати́ву масс 'relying on the initiative of the masses'); similarly **вто́ргшись** 'having invaded' from вто́ргнуться, **вы́тершись** 'having dried oneself', **заперши́сь** 'having locked oneself in'.

374 Perfective gerunds with alternative forms in -я/-а

(1) Some perfective gerunds have alternative forms in -в and -я/-а, the forms in -в generally being preferred in written styles:

| заме́тив/заме́тя | having noticed |
| уви́дев/уви́дя | having seen |

(2) The forms in -я-/a are common with reflexive verbs: **возвратя́сь/возврати́вшись** (**верну́вшись**) 'having returned', **встре́тясь/встре́тившись** 'having met', **прищу́рясь/прищу́рившись** 'screwing up one's eyes':

Я ждал, **прислоня́сь** к стене́ (Granin)
I waited, **leaning** against a wall

375 Gerunds from perfective verbs in -ти and -сть

Gerunds from most perfective verbs in -ти and (except for д-stems, see **372**) -сть are formed by replacing the final two letters of the third-person plural of the verb by -я:

| пройд-у́т | **пройд-я́** | 'having passed' |
| сойд-у́т | **сойд-я́** | 'having descended' |

Likewise **изобретя́** 'having invented' from изобрести́, **подметя́** 'having swept' from подмести́, **принеся́** 'having brought' from принести́, **разбредя́сь** 'having wandered off in different directions' from разбрести́сь (cf. also **учтя́** 'having taken into consideration' from уче́сть):

Принеся́ самова́р и завари́в чай, Да́рья наконе́ц заговори́ла (Rasputin)
Having brought in the samovar and made the tea Darya finally began to speak

Note
Compounds of грести́, пасти́, расти́ and цвести́ have perfective gerunds in -ши: **вы́росши** 'having grown up' from вы́расти, **расцве́тши** 'having blossomed' from расцвести́, **сгрёбши** 'having raked together' from сгрести́, **спа́сши** 'having saved' from спасти́.

376 Gerunds from perfective verbs in -чь and -зть

Gerunds from perfective verbs in **-чь** and **-зть** are formed by adding **-ши** to the masculine past tense of the verb: **вы́лезши** 'having climbed out' from вы́лезть, **испёкши** 'having baked' from испе́чь, **сжёгши** 'having burnt' from сжечь.

377 Functions of the gerunds

Gerunds replace co-ordinate clauses or adverbial clauses of time, manner, cause, condition etc. They are found mainly in written Russian, co-ordinate or adverbial clauses (enclosed in parentheses in the following examples) being preferred in speech.

(1) Imperfective gerunds

The imperfective gerund denotes an action which is simultaneous to the action of the main verb. Either the two actions run in parallel or one interrupts the other. The following meanings are conveyed by the gerund:

Он сиди́т, **чита́я**
He sits **reading** (= and reads)

Он бежи́т, тяжело́ **дыша́**
He is running along, **breathing** (= and breathes) heavily.

Чита́я, запи́сываю незнако́мые слова́
When reading (= when I read) I make a note of words I do not know

Поднима́ясь по ле́стнице, она́ упа́ла
While going up (= when/while/as she was going up) the stairs, she fell

Занима́ясь аэро́бикой, укреплю́ здоро́вье
By doing aerobics (= if I do) I shall improve my fitness

Боя́сь грозы́, я поспеши́л домо́й
Fearing (= since I feared) a thunderstorm I hurried home

Я шёл, **не встреча́я** ни души́
I walked along **without meeting** (= and did not meet) a soul

(2) Perfective gerunds

(i) The perfective gerund describes an action which is completed prior to the action denoted by the main verb:

Написа́в письмо́, он лёг спать
Having written (= when, after he had written) the letter he went to bed

Не поня́в вопро́са, она́ растеря́лась
Not having understood (= since she had not understood) the question she got confused

Примени́в но́вый ме́тод, брига́да смо́жет перевы́полнить но́рму
By using (= if it uses) the new method, the work-team will be able to over-fulfil its norm

(ii) The perfective gerund may also denote a state resulting from the completion of an action:

Он сиде́л, **вы́тянув** но́ги
He sat, **stretching out** (= having stretched out) his legs

Note
Care must be taken to resolve English ambiguity in rendering verb forms in -ing. Compare

Stepping (= **as** she was stepping) off the pavement she tripped and fell
Сходя́ (imperfective gerund) с тротуа́ра, она́ споткну́лась и упа́ла

and

Stepping (= **having** stepped) off the pavement she crossed the road
Сойдя́ (perfective gerund) с тротуа́ра, она́ перешла́ доро́гу

378 Special features of constructions with gerunds

Certain features are characteristic of constructions with gerunds:

(1) The subject of the gerund and the subject of the main clause are the same:

Верну́вшись домо́й, **он поста́вил** самова́р
Having returned home he put on the samovar

Возвраща́ясь домо́й, **я попа́л** под дождь
While returning home I got caught in the rain

Note

(a) In this example the main clause could *not* be replaced by the synonymous Меня́ засти́г дождь 'I got caught in the rain', since this would involve a change in subject.

(b) The gerund is not normally used in conjunction with an impersonal phrase; thus one should write *not* ***Подходя́** к ле́су, мне ста́ло хо́лодно, but Когда́ я подходи́л к ле́су, мне ста́ло хо́лодно 'As I approached the forest I felt cold'. Impersonal constructions involving *infinitives* may, however, sometimes combine with gerunds: Выполня́я э́то упражне́ние, **мо́жно по́льзоваться** словарём 'When doing this exercise you may use a dictionary'. (Note, however, that an alternative rendering: Выполня́я э́то упражне́ние, обраща́й-тесь к словарю́ 'When doing this exercise, consult the diction-ary', observes the principle of identity of subject in both clauses.)

(c) A gerund should be avoided when the subject of the main clause appears in a passive construction, since in such cases the *grammatical* subject of the main clause is not the *logical* subject. Thus По́сле того́ как он переле́з (rather than переле́зши) через забо́р, он был заде́ржан сторожа́ми 'Having climbed over the fence, he was detained by guards'.

(2) A comma separates the main clause from the clause in which the gerund appears:

Он **говори́л**, **стара́ясь** сохраня́ть хладнокро́вие
He spoke, trying to retain his composure

Прочита́в письмо́, он **спря́тал** его в я́щик
Having read the letter he hid it in a drawer

(3) The verb in the main clause may be in any tense and either aspect:

Возвраща́ясь с заво́да, я **встреча́л/встре́тил/встреча́ю/бу́ду** (ча́сто) **встреча́ть/встре́чу** И́ру
When returning from the factory **I used to meet/met/meet/will** (often) **meet/will meet** Ira

Верну́вшись домо́й, он **ста́вил/поста́вил/ста́вит/бу́дет ста́вить/поста́вит самова́р**
Returning home, **he used to put on/put on/puts on/will put on the samovar**

Compare

Он **просыпа́лся** по утра́м и, **откры́в** фо́рточку, **начина́л** в ри́тме разма́хивать рука́ми (Trofimov)
He **would wake up** in the morning and, **opening** the casement window, **begin** rhythmically to swing his arms

Note
The use of the perfective gerund **откры́в** shows that the actions of opening the window and swinging the arms were sequential (imperfective **открыва́я** would suggest that they were simultaneous).

379 Reversal of the sequence of actions expressed by main verb and gerund

Occasionally the action denoted by the verb in the main clause *precedes* that denoted by the gerund:

Он вы́шел, **хло́пнув** две́рью   He went out, slamming the door

This construction should *not*, however, be regarded as the norm.

380 Gerunds as other parts of speech

Some gerunds or former gerunds also function as other parts of speech, in particular prepositions and adverbs.

(1) **Imperfective**:

благодаря́	thanks to (+ dat.; cf. **благодаря́** as gerund + acc.)
исключа́я	excluding, except for
кра́дучись	stealthily
мо́лча	silently

не счита́я	not counting
не теря́я вре́мени	without delay
су́дя по	judging by (cf. gerund **судя́**)

Note

(a) Some phrases are compounded with the gerund **говоря́**: **открове́нно говоря́** 'frankly speaking', **стро́го говоря́** 'strictly speaking', **не говоря́ уже́** 'let alone, to say nothing of' etc.:

О́бщество предоставля́ет им библиоте́ки, музе́и, **не говоря́ уже́** о теа́трах и кино́ (Kovaleva)
Society puts at their disposal libraries and museums, to say nothing of theatres and cinemas

(b) Other phrases include отвеча́ть не **заду́мываясь** 'to answer without hesitation', говори́ть **заика́ясь** 'to stammer', не **поклада́я** рук 'tirelessly', не **спеша́** 'unhurriedly', **не́хотя** 'reluctantly'.

(2) **Perfective** (mainly in set phrases involving gerunds in -**я**/-**а**; see **374**):

слу́шать **рази́ня** рот	to listen open-mouthed
сказа́ть **положа́** ру́ку на́ сердце	to say hand on heart
рабо́тать **спустя́** рукава́	to work in a slipshod fashion
согласи́ться **скрепя́** се́рдце	to agree reluctantly
сиде́ть **сложа́** ру́ки	to sit twiddling one's thumbs

Note also the preposition **спустя́**: неде́лю **спустя́** 'a week later'. See **439** (2) (i).

The Adverb

381 Introductory comments

(1) Adverbs are indeclinable forms that modify verbs ('he writes *well*'), adjectives ('*surprisingly* good'), other adverbs ('*extremely* quickly') or nouns ('reading *aloud*').

(2) They answer questions such as '**where**?', '**when**?', '**how**?', '**why**?', '**for what purpose**?', '**to what extent**?'

(3) A feature of Russian adverbs is that they all derive from other parts of speech (though in the case of most primary adverbs (**так** 'thus', **там** 'there', **тогда́** 'then' etc.) the principle of their formation is no longer clear).

(4) The most productive types of adverb are those which derive from **adjectives**. They also derive from **nouns, verbs, numerals** and **pronouns**.

382 Adverbs derived from adjectives

(1) Adverbs in -o/-e

(i) Most adverbs derived from descriptive adjectives are identical with the neuter adjectival short form in **-o/-e** (see **159, 161, 164**):

Long adjective	Adverb
высо́кий 'high'	высоко́ 'high up'
гла́дкий 'smooth'	гла́дко 'smoothly'
краси́вый 'beautiful'	краси́во 'beautifully'
вне́шний 'external'	вне́шне 'externally'
и́скренний 'sincere'	и́скренне 'sincerely'
кра́йний 'extreme'	кра́йне 'extremely'

(ii) In some cases, however, there is a difference in stress, cf. больно́ (neuter short adjective) 'is sick' and бо́льно (adverb) 'painfully, it hurts'; мало́ (neuter short adjective) 'too small' and ма́ло (adverb) 'not much'.

Note

(a) Soft-ending adjectives да́вний 'long-standing', по́здний 'late' and ра́нний 'early' have hard-ending adverbs давно́ 'long ago', по́здно 'late, it is (too) late', ра́но 'early, it is (too) early'. Note that whereas ра́нний has double **н**, ра́но has only one.

(b) Adverbs in -о/-е also derive from participles: неожи́данно 'unexpectedly' from неожи́данный, угрожа́юще 'threateningly' from угрожа́ющий.

(2) Adverbs based on по- + dative singular of the adjective

Adverbs of manner of the type **по-** + the dative masculine/neuter singular of the adjective derive from adjectives in -ый/-ий/-ой which have no adverb in -о/-е (e.g. друго́й 'different', но́вый 'new', пре́жний 'former'):

по-друго́му	in a different way
по-настоя́щему	in a proper fashion
по-но́вому	in a new way
по-пре́жнему	as before
по-ра́зному	in various ways

(3) Adverbs in -и

(i) Adverbs from adjectives in -ский/-цкий (mostly adverbs of manner) take the ending -и: thus бра́тски 'fraternally', дура́цки 'foolishly, in a foolish way', логи́чески 'logically' etc.

(ii) Those with animate connotations, including all which denote nationality, may take the prefix **по-**: ко́фе по-туре́цки 'coffee

Turkish style', **по-ле́нински** 'after the style of Lenin', **по-ру́сски** 'in Russian, in the Russian style'.

(iii) In some contexts, prefixed and unprefixed variants are synonymous: **бра́тски/по-бра́тски** похло́пать по плечу́ 'to slap on the shoulder in a brotherly fashion', **геро́йски/по-геро́йски** вести́ себя́ 'to behave in a heroic way', **де́тски/по-де́тски** дове́рчивый 'as trusting as a child':

> В Но́вый год осо́бенно серде́чно и **по-дру́жески/ дру́жески** мы вспомина́ем со́тни имён знако́мых люде́й (*Turist*)
> At New Year we recall, in a particularly cordial and friendly way, the names of hundreds of acquaintances

(iv) In most cases, however, choice is dictated by usage: **дру́жески** подмигну́ть 'to wink in a friendly manner', **зве́рски** голо́дный 'ravenously hungry', **по-де́тски** оби́делся 'he took childish offence'.

Note
(a) While forms with **по-** answer the implied question **подо́бно кому́/чему́?** 'similar to whom/what?', forms without **по-** answer the questions **как/каки́м о́бразом?** 'how/in what way?'
(b) Adverbs in **-ически** cannot combine with **по-**.

(4) Adverbs in -ьи

Adverbs from adjectives of the type **во́лчий** 'wolf's' (see **151** (1)) take the ending **-ьи**, and are prefixed **по-**: Он **по-медве́жьи** неуклю́ж 'He is as clumsy as a bear', Он **по-соба́чьи** пре́дан своему́ хозя́ину 'He displays a dog-like devotion to his master'.

(5) Adverbs based on preposition + the oblique case of an adjective

(i) Most adverbs of this type consist of a preposition + the fossilized oblique case of a short adjective, run together to form a single word (e.g. **с** + old genitive *****пра́ва** = **спра́ва** 'on, from the right'). The adverbs denote variously location, time, manner and extent:

вско́ре	soon
(раздева́ться) **догола́**	(to strip oneself) naked
(вытира́ть) **до́суха**	(to rub) dry

издалека́	from a distance
сле́ва	on, from the left
сно́ва	again

(ii) A smaller number of adverbs consist of the preposition **в** + the feminine accusative of a long adjective:

вплотну́ю	right up close to
вручну́ю	by hand
(лете́ть) вслепу́ю	(to fly) blind

383 Adverbs derived from nouns

(1) Adverbs based on the oblique cases of nouns

(i) Many adverbs have the form of the **instrumental singular** of a noun. The adverbs denote location or manner:

верхо́м	on horseback
да́ром	free, for nothing
ря́дом	next door, adjacent
шёпотом	in a whisper

Note

(a) End stress in the adverb **круго́м** 'around' and stem stress in the instrumental of the noun **круг** (**кру́гом**) and in the phrase голова́ идёт **кру́гом** 'my head is spinning'.

(b) Some adverbs derive from no-longer extant nouns: **о́птом** 'wholesale', **о́щупью** 'gropingly', **пешко́м** 'on foot', **укра́дкой** 'furtively'.

(c) Instrumentals are also used to denote the time of day and the season of the year (see **97** (2) (i), (ii)).

(ii) Other adverbs derived from nouns include **вчера́** 'yesterday' (also **позавчера́** 'the day before yesterday'), **до́ма** 'at home', **домо́й** 'home(wards)', **за́втра** 'tomorrow' (also **послеза́втра** 'the day after tomorrow'), **о́чень** 'very, very much' (Я **о́чень** люблю́ моро́женое 'I am very fond of ice-cream'), **сего́дня** 'today'.

(2) Adverbs based on preposition–noun phrases

(i) The preposition appears as a separate word in some phrases (**в прида́чу** 'into the bargain', **на днях** 'the other day', **на ходу́** 'while on the move'), but in most cases preposition and noun are run together. The prepositions **в, на, по** + dative, **с** + genitive are particularly common in this type of formation. All oblique cases are represented:

(a) Accusative:

вслух	aloud
наоборо́т	on the contrary

(b) Genitive:

и́здали	from afar
све́рху	from above

(c) Dative:

кста́ти	apropos
побли́зости	in the vicinity

(d) Instrumental:

сли́шком	too

(e) Prepositional:

вме́сте	together

(ii) Some adverbs appear in pairs, one denoting location and the other destination or goal:

вдали́/вдаль	in/into the distance
внизу́/вниз	downstairs (location/direction)
внутри́/внутрь	inside (location/direction)
впереди́/вперёд	in front/forwards
за грани́цей/за грани́цу	abroad (location/direction)
наверху́/наве́рх	upstairs (location/direction)

Note
Compare **за́мужем за** + instrumental 'married to' and **выходи́ть/вы́йти за́муж за** + accusative 'to get married' (of a woman).

(iii) Some prepositional phrases involve *two* nouns:

бок о́ бок	cheek by jowl
вре́мя от вре́мени	from time to time
лицо́м к лицу́	face to face

384   Adverbs derived from verbs

Some adverbs are based on imperfective gerunds (see also **380** (1)):

кра́дучись	stealthily
не́хотя	reluctantly

Others are based on perfective gerunds, often as part of an adverbial phrase:

сломя́ го́лову	at breakneck speed

See also **380** (2).

385   Adverbs derived from numerals

Adverbs derived from numerals include the series

вдвоём/втроём/вчетверо́м. . .
two/three/four together . . .

во-пе́рвых/во-вторы́х/в-тре́тьих. . .
in the first/second/third place . . .

одна́жды/два́жды/три́жды. . .
once/twice/thrice . . .

as well as **впервы́е** 'for the first time', **наедине́** 'in private, alone (with)', and the phrase **оди́н на оди́н** 'tête-à-tête'.

386   Adverbs derived from pronouns

A number of adverbs are based on:

(i)   The demonstrative pronouns **э́тот** 'this', **тот** 'that', **сей** 'this':

зате́м	afterwards
пото́м	then, afterwards
поэ́тому	for that reason, therefore
сейча́с	now
с тех пор/до тех пор/до сих пор	since then/until then/hitherto

Note

(a) **Потóм** and **затéм** are synonymous in referring to sequential actions, though **потóм** is commoner: Куплю́ билéт, **потóм/ затéм** зайду́ к прия́телю 'I shall buy a ticket, **then** call on a friend'. **Потóм** is also used in the meaning 'afterwards, in a little while': Я сдéлаю э́то **потóм** 'I'll do that later'. In colloquial registers it can be governed by a preposition (отложи́ть **на потóм** 'to put off until afterwards') and can also be used colloquially in the meaning 'besides': Не хочу́ я éхать, **а потóм** у меня́ и врéмени нет 'I don't want to go, and besides I don't have any time'. **Затéм** can also denote purpose: Поговори́м, ведь я **затéм** и пришёл 'Let's talk, after all that's the reason I have come', Я пришёл (**затéм**), чтòбы поговори́ть 'I have come (in order) to have a chat'.

(b) **Тепéрь** 'now' is more limited in meaning and usage than **сейчáс**, which can refer to the past and future, as well as to the present: О чём они́ говори́ли **сейчáс**? 'What were they talking about **just now?**', Я бу́ду с вáми **сейчáс** 'I'll be with you **in a minute**', Что вы дéлаете **сейчáс/тепéрь**? 'What are you doing **now?**'

(ii) The pronoun **что** 'what': **зачéм?** 'for what purpose?', **почему́?** 'why?' Compare

Зачéм включи́ли свет? — Чтòбы мóжно бы́ло читáть
Why have you switched on the light? So as to be able to read (purpose)

and

.**Почему́** включи́ли свет? — Ужé темнó
Why have you switched on the light? Because it's dark (cause)

(iii) The possessive pronouns **мой, твой, свой, наш, ваш**:

по-мóему/по-твóему	in my opinion/in your opinion (familiar)
по-нáшему/по-вáшему	in our opinion/in your opinion (formal)

Note

(a) The difference in stress between **по-мóему**, **по-твóему**, and the dative case of the possessive pronouns (**моему́, твоему́**).

(b) 'In his/her/their opinion' are rendered as **по егó/её/их мнéнию**.

(c) **По-своему** means 'in one's own way': Он всё делает **по-своему** 'He does everything in his own way'.

(iv) **Весь** 'all':

везде́/всю́ду; отовсю́ду	everywhere; from everywhere
весьма́	extremely
совсе́м	quite

Note

Compare Э́то **не совсе́м** пра́вда 'That's **not quite** true' and Э́то **совсе́м не** пра́вда 'That's **not at all** true'.

387   Primary spatial adverbs

(1) **Где** 'where', **здесь** 'here' and **там** 'there' denote location:

Где вы рабо́таете?	Where do you work?
Я рабо́таю **здесь**; Он рабо́тает **там**	I work here; He works there

Note

Тут 'here' is more colloquial than **здесь** and can also have a temporal meaning, e.g. **Тут** расска́зчик замолча́л 'Here the narrator fell silent'.

(2) **Куда́** 'where' (to), **сюда́** 'here' and **туда́** 'there' indicate direction:

Куда́ вы идёте?	Where are you going?
Иди́те **сюда́**!	Come here!
Туда́ идёт авто́бус но́мер пять	The number 5 bus goes there

(3) **Отку́да** 'from where', **отсю́да** 'from here' and **отту́да** 'from there' indicate withdrawal:

Отку́да он пришёл?	Where has he come from?

Note

Отку́да вы зна́ете? '**How** do you know?'

388 Primary adverbs of time

(1) Тогда́ 'then'

Тогда́ 'then, at that time' must be differentiated from **пото́м/зате́м** 'then, afterwards'. Compare

> **Тогда́** я жил на се́вере
> I lived in the north **then**/at that time

and

> Снача́ла ду́май, **пото́м** говори́
> First think, **then** speak

(2) Когда́/как 'when/as'

(i) **Когда́** or **в то вре́мя как** are preferred to **как** in rendering 'as' (= 'when') in clauses of time:

> **Когда́/в то вре́мя как** я шёл по доро́ге, я встре́тил ста́рого знако́мого
> **As** I was walking down the road I met an old acquaintance

(ii) However, **как** is used with verbs of perception (**ви́деть** 'to see', **слу́шать** 'to listen', **слы́шать** 'to hear', **смотре́ть** 'to watch'):

> Смо́трим, **как** де́ти игра́ют
> We watch the children playing

> Я слу́шаю, **как** она́ поёт
> I listen to her singing

(iii) **Ждать** 'to wait' and **люби́ть** 'to like' govern object clauses introduced by **когда́**:

> Жду, **когда́** вы ко́нчите
> I am waiting for you to finish

> Люблю́, **когда́** ты поёшь наро́дные пе́сни
> I like you to sing folk songs

Note

For constructions with **слу́чай** 'case' see **311** (2).

(3) Как/как вдруг 'when suddenly/than'

(i) **Как** (ог **как вдруг**) is used to introduce a sudden or unexpected action, often interrupting another action:

Я как раз гла́дил брю́ки, **как вдруг** пога́с свет
I was just ironing my trousers **when suddenly** the light went out

(ii) The main clause in such constructions is often introduced by a negative:

Не прошёл он и десяти́ шаго́в, **как** разда́лся вы́стрел
He had not taken ten paces **when** a shot rang out

(iii) Frequently the verb (**не**) **успе́ть** or the conjunction **едва́** is involved in such constructions:

Не (ог **Едва́**) **успе́л** я нажа́ть кно́пку, **как** дверь распахну́-
лась
I had not had time (had hardly had time) to press the button when the door flew open

Едва́ я вы́шел на у́лицу, **как** пошёл си́льный дождь
Hardly had I gone out on to the street **than** it began raining heavily

Note
See also **466–467** for further examples of adverbial clauses of time.

389 Уже́, уже́ не

(1) **Уже́** 'already' is far commoner in Russian than 'already' in English, which often has no equivalent in indicating the early implementation or completion of an action:

Он пришёл **уже́** вчера́
He arrived yesterday/as early as yesterday

(2) **Уже́** is particularly important in clarifying tense sequence:

Демонстра́нты **уже́** разбежа́лись, когда́ прие́хала опера-
ти́вная маши́на
The demonstrators **had already** dispersed when the squad car arrived

Note

Without **ужé** the above sentence means 'The demonstrators dispersed **when** the squad car arrived'.

(3) **Ужé не** (or **бóльше не**) means 'no longer, not any more': Он **ужé не/бóльше не** рабóтает здесь 'He doesn't work here any more'.

Note

Ужé нет replaces **ужé не** in the absence of a predicate: Он рабóтает здесь? **Ужé нет** 'Does he work here? Not any more'.

390 Ещё, ещё не

(1) **Ещё** 'still/yet', **ещё не** 'not yet' can be used with temporal meaning:

Ребёнок **ещё** (or **всё ещё**) спит
The child is still asleep

Ещё дéвочкой онá лишúлась мáтери
She lost her mother when she was only a little girl

Онá **ещё не** пришлá
She hasn't arrived yet

Note

Ещё нет replaces **ещё не** in the absence of a predicate: Онá пришлá? **Ещё нет** 'Has she arrived?' 'Not yet'.

(2) **Ещё** can also mean 'additional', compare:

Дай **ещё** чáшку чáю
Give me another (= an additional) cup of tea

and

Дай **другýю** чáшку
Give me another (= a different) cup

(3) It can also be synonymous with **ужé** in a temporal context:

Он уéхал **ещё/ужé** на прóшлой недéле
He left last week

Note

(a) The use of **ещё** with comparatives, as an adverb of degree: **ещё** лу́чше 'still/even better'.

(b) **Ещё раз** 'once more', referring to a repeated action (but not a repeated state): Я позвоню́ **ещё раз** 'I'll ring again'. Compare **сно́ва**, which may denote resumption rather than repetition: По̀сле боле́зни он **сно́ва** стал ходи́ть в кино́ 'After his illness he has begun going to the cinema again'. **Опя́ть** may be used as a synonym of **сно́ва** (**Сно́ва/опя́ть** пошёл дождь 'It began raining again'), but may also have emotional overtones, sometimes expressing irritation (**Опя́ть** по́езд опа́здывает! 'The train is late again!').

391 The temporal adverbs до́лго, давно́ and неда́вно

(1) **До́лго** denotes a definite but unspecified period of time:

Он **до́лго** одева́ется
He takes a long time to dress

(2) **Давно́** 'for a long time' (it also means 'a long time ago') implies an unfinished action or process:

Он **давно́** рабо́тает здесь
He has been working here for a long time (and still is)

Он **давно́** жил там
He **had** been living there for a long time

Note

(a) Cf. **256** (2) (vii).

(b) The use of the 'continuous present' does *not* extend to *negative* verbs: Я **давно́ не лета́л** 'I have not/had not flown for a long time'.

(3) **Неда́вно** refers to a recent event

Он у́мер **неда́вно**
He died **recently**

while (**в/за**) **после́днее вре́мя** 'recently, of late' refers to a process or state extending over a period of time. Absence of a preposition represents more colloquial usage:

После́днее вре́мя не́ было дождя́
There hasn't been any rain **recently**

392 Primary adverbs of manner and extent

(1) **Как** and **так** may denote:

(i) Manner:

Вот **как** на́до писа́ть!   That's **how** to write!
На́до вести́ себя́ **так**   You should behave **like that**

Note

(a) **Как** also combines with the verb **люби́ть** 'to like' in expressing manner: Люблю́, **как** ты гото́вишь еду́ 'I like the way you cook'.

(b) **Не так** may mean 'wrongly': Вы **не так** меня́ете про́бку 'You're not changing the fuse the right way' (cf. непра́вильно 'incorrectly').

(ii) Degree or extent:

Как хорошо́ она́ игра́ет!   How well she plays!
Я **так** мно́го ходи́л, что   I have walked so much that
устал   I am tired

(2) In comparisons, the particle **же** usually follows **так**:

Он **так же** умён, **как** я   He is just as clever as I am

but this does not occur in a negative comparison

Он **не так** умён, **как** я   He is not as clever as I am

When two qualities relate to the same person, the particle **и** is used for emphasis:

Он **так же** умён, **как и**   He is as clever as he is kind
добр

(3) **Как**? is used as the equivalent of English 'what?' in establishing personal and other detail:

Как твоё и́мя?/твоё о́тчество?/твоя́ фами́лия?
What is your first name?/your patronymic?/your surname?

Как тебя́ зову́т?
What is your name?

Как ваш а́дрес?
What is your address?

Note also the phrase **Как** э́то по-ру́сски? 'What is the Russian for that?'

393 Interrelating adverbs

Interrelating adverbs

там, где
туда́, куда́
туда́, отку́да
тогда́, когда́
так, как etc.

may be used when no specific referent of place, time or manner is named:

Я рабо́таю **там, где** он рабо́тал ра́ньше
I work **where** (lit. 'there, where') he used to work

По́мню, как побежа́ли мы **туда́, куда́** нас вела́ густа́я толпа́ люде́й (Grekova)
I recall how we ran **to where** a dense crowd of people led us

Люба́я рабо́та то́лько **тогда́** увлека́ет, **когда́** ты в ней уже́ каки́е-то та́йны откры́л (*Yunyi naturalist*)
A job only becomes absorbing **when** you have discovered some of its secrets

Он поступи́л **так, как** я ему́ веле́л
He acted **as** I told him to

394 То́же, та́кже

(1) Both **то́же** and **та́кже** mean 'also, as well, too'. **То́же** may be regarded as the more colloquial variant, **та́кже** as the more official:

Он **тóже/тáкже** поéдет   He will go **too**
Мы **тóже/тáкже** соглáсны   We **also** agree

Note

(a) **Тóже/тáкже не** means 'not ... either': Он **тóже/тáкже** не поéдет 'He won't go **either**'.

(b) See **472** (9) for **тóже** as a particle.

(2) **Тóже** is preferred in contexts which express identification with an action, state or attribute already referred to:

Вы зáняты? Я **тóже**
Are you busy? **So am** I

— Я óчень хочý пойтú на концéрт
'I am very keen to go to the concert'
— Онá **тóже** хóчет пойтú
'She wants to go **too**'

У стены́ стоя́л бéлый стол и четы́ре стýла, **тóже** бéлых
A white table and four chairs, **also** white, stood by the wall

(3) **Тáкже** is preferred when providing additional or supplementary information (in the meaning **крòме тогó, ещё и** 'apart from that, in addition'):

Я нáчал, крòме книг, читáть **тáкже** и журнáльные статьú
I began to read magazine articles **as well as** books

Он óчень хитёр, не хýже брáта; но он **тáкже** óчень талáнтлив
He is very cunning, no less so than his brother; but he is **also** very talented

Существýют **тáкже** стереотúпы маскулúнности и феминúнности (*Nedelya*)
There **also** exist stereotypes of masculinity and femininity

(4) **Тáкже** is particularly common with the conjunction **а**:

Речь шла в основнóм о проблéмах двусторóнних отношéний, **а тáкже** о положéнии в Ливáне
It was basically a question of problems of bilateral relations, **and also** the situation in the Lebanon

Note
A never combines with **тóже**.

(5) Compare the contrasting usage of **тóже** and **тáкже** in the following:

Он **тóже** вы́разил готóвность помóчь
He **also** expressed his willingness to help (emulating **someone else's** willingness to help)

Он **тáкже** вы́разил готóвность помóчь
He **also** expressed his willingness to help (in addition to other action **he had agreed to take**)

395 Indefinite adverbs (adverbs in -то, -нибудь, -либо and кòе-)

Adverbs in **-то**, **-нибудь** and **-либо** are adverbial counterparts to the indefinite pronouns (see **138**). They include:

гдé-то	somewhere	**гдé-нибудь**	somewhere, anywhere
кудá-то	somewhere (direction)	**кудá-нибудь**	somewhere, anywhere (direction)
кáк-то	somehow	**кáк-нибудь**	somehow, anyhow
когдá-то	once, at one time	**когдá-нибудь**	at any time, ever
почемý-то	for some reason	**почемý-нибудь**	for some, any reason

All the adverbs can also combine with **-либо**. **Кòе-** combines with **где, как, когдá** and **кудá**.

(1) Adverbs in -то

Гдé-то/кудá-то denote a particular but unidentified place, **когдá-то** a particular but unidentified time, **почемý-то** a particular but unidentified cause. The adverbs relate predominantly to the past or present tense:

Вор пря́чется **гдé-то** поблúзости
The thief is hiding **somewhere** nearby

Он кáк-то спрáвился с задáчей
Somehow he coped with the task

— Это мой друг, игра́ли **когда́-то** в футбо́л (Vanshenkin)
'That is my friend, we used to play football **at one time**'

Тре́тий пассажи́р то́же есть, но, ви́дно, **куда́-то** вы́шел (Rasputin)
There is a third passenger too, but he must have gone out **somewhere**

Он **почему́-то** недово́лен на́шим реше́нием
For some reason he is displeased with our decision

(2) Adverbs in -нибудь

Adverbs in -**нибудь** are used:

(i) In **questions**:

Вы **когда́-нибудь** отдыха́ли на Чёрном мо́ре?
Have you **ever** holidayed on the Black Sea?

(ii) In the **future**, implying a choice still to be made:

Через го́дик **куда́-нибудь** переберу́сь: в Ха́рьков, Ки́ев, Днепропетро́вск (Rybakov)
In a year or so I shall move **somewhere**: to Kharkov, Kiev, Dnepropetrovsk

(iii) After **imperatives**:

Загляни́ ко мне **когда́-нибудь**
Pop in to see me **some time**

(iv) In referring to **different** circumstances on different occasions, irrespective of tense:

По воскресе́ньям мы всегда́ е́здим **куда́-нибудь** на маши́не
We always go for a drive somewhere on Sundays (different places on different occasions)

(v) In contexts where the adverb implies inferior quality:

Я стал коммуни́стом. И не **где́-нибудь**, а в Средизе́мном мо́ре (*Russia Today*)
I have become a Communist. And not **any old where**, but in the Mediterranean

(3) Adverbs in -либо

Adverbs in -**либо** express an even greater degree of indefiniteness than adverbs in -**нибудь**. They denote 'anywhere' (at any place you like to name), 'ever' (at any time you like to name) etc.:

Э́то была́ сильне́йшая кома́нда, кото́рая **когда́-либо** выи́грывала чемпиона́ты ми́ра (*Sputnik*)
It was the strongest team that had **ever** won world championships

(4) Adverbs in кòe-

(i) **Кòe-гдé** means 'in various places':

Кòe-гдé в на́шем го́роде проводи́лись демонстра́ции
Demonstrations were held **in various localities** in our town

(ii) **Кòe-кáк** means 'with great difficulty'

Мы **кòe-кáк** добрали́сь домо́й
Somehow we struggled home

or 'carelessly'

Рабо́та сде́лана **кòe-кáк**
The work has been done **any old how**

Note
Кòe-когда́ means 'occasionally', **кòe-куда́** 'to a particular place'.

396 The negative adverbs нигдé, никуда́, ниоткýда, никогда́, никáк, нискóлько

(1) Negative adverbs are formed by affixing **ни-** to the adverbs **где** 'where', **как** 'how', **когда́** 'when', **куда́** 'where to', **откýда** 'from where', **скóлько** 'how much':

нигдé	'nowhere'	никуда́	'nowhere' (direction)
никáк	'in no way'	ниоткýда	'from nowhere'
никогда́	'never'	нискóлько	'not at all'

Note
'Hardly ever' is rendered as **почти́ никогда́**, 'hardly anywhere' as **почти́ нигдé** etc.

(2) Like negative pronouns (see **133**), negative adverbs combine with the particles **не/нет**:

Он **нигде́ не** рабо́тает	He does not work anywhere
Он **никуда́ не** идёт	He isn't going anywhere
Ниотку́да нет пи́сем	There are no letters from anywhere
Она́ **никогда́ не** лжёт	She never tells lies
Она́ **ника́к не** реаги́ровала	She did not react at all
Я **ниско́лько не** оби́делся	I wasn't at all offended

Note

Нельзя́ also combines directly with a negative adverb: **Ника́к нельзя́** согласи́ться с ним 'One can in no way agree with him'.

(3) It is possible to accumulate negatives within one sentence:

Никто́ никогда́ никуда́ не е́здит
No one ever goes anywhere

Де́ти **никогда́ ничего́ не** узна́ют о них (Zalygin)
The children will never learn anything about them

Note

Ни ра́зу 'not once' and **не раз** 'more than once'. Compare:

Он **ни ра́зу** не прибра́л в ко́мнате у А́ндерсена (Paustovsky)
Not once did he tidy Andersen's room

and

О недоста́тках **не раз** уже́ писа́лось
These shortcomings have been written about **more than once**

397 The negative adverbs не́где, не́куда, не́когда, не́откуда, не́зачем

(1) Like the 'potential' negative pronouns (see **137**), the 'potential' negative adverbs appear in infinitive constructions: **(Нам) не́где** жить 'There is nowhere (for us) to live'. The series comprises

не́где	'there is nowhere to'
не́зачем	'there is no point'

не́когда	'there is no time to'
не́куда	'there is nowhere to' (direction)
не́откуда	'there is no place from where'

Note

Не́когда can also mean 'once, at one time'.

(2) There are two variants of the construction:

(i) The **impersonal**:

Утере́ться бы́ло не́чем, переоде́ться **не́где** (Vanshenkin)
There was nothing to dry oneself on and nowhere to change

Копа́ть моги́лу бы́ло **не́когда** и **не́зачем** (Rybakov)
There was no time to dig a grave and no point in doing so

(ii) The **personal**, with the logical subject appearing in the dative case (see **93**):

Ему́ не́где рабо́тать	He has nowhere to work
Ей не́когда бы́ло разгова́ривать	She had no time to converse
Нам не́куда бу́дет е́хать	We shall have nowhere to go

Note

As with the 'potential' negative pronouns, there is a positive counterpart to this construction involving **есть** (present tense), **бы́ло** (past) and **бу́дет** (future), e.g.

Éсть/бы́ло/бу́дет куда́ пойти́
There is/was/will be somewhere to go

398 Comparative adverbs

(1) The comparatives of adverbs in **-o/-e** are identical with short-form comparative adjectives (see **179** and **180**):

Всё **сильне́е** и **глу́бже** осознаём духо́вное родство́ с други́ми наро́дами (Kostomarov)
We are **more and more intensively** and **profoundly** conscious of our spiritual kinship with other nations

Note

Adverbs with more than two syllables have an alternative comparative in **бо́лее**: **вы́годнее/бо́лее вы́годно** 'more beneficially', cf. **ме́нее вы́годно** 'less beneficially'. The form with **бо́лее** is the *norm* for comparatives of adverbs other than those in **-о/-е: бо́лее логи́чески** 'more logically' (cf. **ме́нее лочи́чески** 'less logically').

(2) Comparative adverbs appear in the same types of construction as comparative adjectives (see **182**), i.e. constructions:

(i) With **чем** 'than':

Но сильне́й, **чем** заво́д, люби́л Пётр Телепнёв свой сад (Trifonov)
But Petr Telepnev loved his garden more **than** the factory

(ii) With the **genitive**:

Тре́нер ча́ще **други́х слов** употребля́ет сло́во «рабо́та» (Salnikov)
The trainer uses the word 'work' more often **than** other words

(iii) With **гора́здо** 'much' (also **мно́го, намно́го, куда́**):

Он верну́лся домо́й **гора́здо** по́зже
He returned home **much** later

(iv) With **чем . . . тем** 'the . . . the':

Чем бо́льше я отдыха́л от футбо́ла, **тем** сильне́е хоте́лось игра́ть
The more I rested from football **the** more I wanted to play

(v) With the prefix **по-** 'a little':

Но́чью капита́н **поту́же** затя́гивался ремнём (Gagarin)
At night the captain would tighten his belt **a little**

(vi) With instrumental or **на** + accusative in quantifying a difference:

Я верну́лся **на пять мину́т/пятью́ мину́тами** ра́ньше, чем ожида́л
I arrived **five minutes** earlier than I had expected

(vii) With **как мо́жно** 'as . . . as possible':

Мы е́хали **как мо́жно** ме́дленнее
We were driving **as** slowly **as possible**

399 Variant forms of some comparative adverbs

Some comparative adverbs have variant forms:

(1) Бо́льше/бо́лее 'more'; ме́ньше/ме́нее 'less'

(i) These may be differentiated stylistically, the comparatives in -**ше** belonging to the 'neutral' register and those in -**ee** to a more 'bookish' style (**бо́льше/бо́лее тридцати́** 'more than thirty').

(ii) Only **бо́льше/ме́ньше** are used to denote extent or degree: Он лю́бит дочь **бо́льше** (*not* бо́лее), чем сы́на 'He loves his daughter more than (he loves) his son'.

(iii) **Бо́лее** and **ме́нее** are mainly used in the formation of long comparative adjectives and adverbs (see **177** and **398** (1) note), and in a number of set phrases: **бо́лее и́ли ме́нее** 'more or less', **бо́лее того́** 'furthermore' etc.

(2) Да́льше/да́лее 'further'

Apart from its spatial meaning, **да́льше** 'further' also implies subsequent action (А **да́льше** что случи́лось? 'And what happened next?') or encouragement (Ну — **да́льше**! 'Well, go on!'). **Да́лее** is limited mainly to the phrase **и так да́лее** (**и т.д.**) 'and so on'.

400 The superlative adverb

(1) A superlative adverb consists of a comparative adverb in -**e** or -**ee** + **всего́** (for **internal** comparison) or **всех** (for **external** comparison):

Я рабо́таю лу́чше **всего́** ве́чером
I work best of all in the evening (i.e. compared with other times)

Я рабо́таю лу́чше **всех** ве́чером
I work best in the evening (i.e. compared with other people)

Compare

Мы все старе́ли, А́да Ефи́мовна — **ме́ньше всех** (Grekova)
We were all ageing, Ada Efimovna **least of all** (= **less than anyone**)

(2) **Наибо́лее** can also be used in the formation of superlative adverbs (**наибо́лее свобо́дно** 'most freely, fluently' (cf. **наиме́нее свобо́дно** 'least fluently'), and this is the *norm* with adverbs which do not end in **-о/-е**, e.g. **наибо́лее логи́чески** 'most logically'.

The Preposition

401 Introductory comments

(1) A preposition is a part of speech which expresses the relationship of one word to another: колóдец **без** водьı 'a well without water', добр **к** дéтям 'kind to children', прьıгнуть **через** забóр 'to jump over the fence'.

(2) Each Russian preposition governs a noun or pronoun in an oblique case. Some prepositions govern two or even three cases.

(3) Prepositions may be subdivided as follows:

(i) Primary: **в** 'in', **до** 'as far as', **на** 'on' etc.

(ii) Adverbial: **близ** 'near', **вдоль** 'along' etc.

(iii) Prepositions derived from nouns (e.g. **в пóльзу** 'in favour of', **насчёт** 'on account of') and from verbs (**благодаря** 'thanks to' etc.).

402 Primary prepositions and cases

The primaries (central meanings only) can be arranged in a grid, as follows.

Preposition	Acc.	Gen.	Dat.	Instr.	Prep.
(1) **без**		'without'			
(2) **в**	'into'				'in'

Preposition	Acc.	Gen.	Dat.	Instr.	Prep.
(3) **для**		'for'			
(4) **до**		'as far as'			
(5) **за**	'behind' (motion)			'behind'	
(6) **из**		'out of'			
(7) **из-за**		'from behind'			
(8) **из-под**		'from under'			
(9) **к**			'towards'		
(10) **крòме**		'except for'			
(11) **мèжду**				'between'	
(12) **на**	'on to'				'on'
(13) **над**				'above'	
(14) **о**	'against'				'about'
(15) **от**		'from'			
(16) **перед**				'in front of'	
(17) **по**	'up to'		'along'		'after'
(18) **под**	'under' (motion)			'under'	
(19) **при**					'in the presence of'
(20) **про**	'about'				
(21) **ра́ди**		'for the sake of'			
(22) **с**	'approximately'	'down from'		'with'	
(23) **у**		'at'			
(24) **через**	'across'				

Note

(a) Though not strictly speaking primary prepositions, **из-за** and **из-под** are usually included in the series.

(b) See **419** (1) (i) *Note* for **мèжду** + *genitive* case.

(c) **о** is written as **об** before words beginning with **а, э, и, о** or **у** (e.g. **об Áнглии** 'about England') and as **обо** in combinations such as **обо всём** 'about everything' and **обо мне** 'about me'.

403 Repetition of prepositions

The repetition of prepositions is optional, compare:

В Москве́ и не́которых други́х города́х. . . (*Izvestiya*)
In Moscow and certain other cities . . .

and

Он был **в** пижа́ме и **в** дома́шних ту́флях (Zalygin)
He was wearing pyjamas and slippers

except where two or more items governed by the same preposition
appear in different clauses, when repetition is mandatory:

Я наде́ялся не то́лько **на** неё, **но** и **на** него́
I relied not only on her, but also on him

404 The buffer vowel -о

Primary prepositions which end in a consonant acquire a final **-о**
when followed by certain clusters of consonants. These subdivide as
follows:

(1) Clusters which affect many prepositions:

(i) **Вр-** (mainly вре́мя 'time'): во вре́мя 'during', ко вре́мени 'by
the time', со вре́мени 'since the time'.

(ii) **Вс-** (mainly declined forms of весь 'all'): во всём 'in everything',
изо всех сил 'with all one's might' (but из всех мои́х друзе́й 'of all
my friends'), обо всём 'about everything', со всех концо́в 'from all
parts' (над, перед, от are not affected).

(iii) **Вт-** (mainly вто́рник 'Tuesday' and второ́й 'second'): во
вто́рник 'on Tuesday', ко вто́рнику 'by Tuesday', со вто́рника
'since Tuesday'; во второ́м 'in the second', со второ́го 'since the
second'.

(iv) **Дн-** (mainly oblique cases of день 'day' and дно 'bottom'): ко
дню 'for the day', со/с днём 'with the day', со дня 'since the day', изо
дня в день 'daily, constantly'; ко дну 'to the bottom'.

(v) **Мн-** (mainly oblique cases of я 'I' and мно́го/мно́гие 'many'): во мне 'in me', ко мне 'to me', надо мной 'above me', передо мной 'in front of me', подо мной 'below me', со мной 'with me', обо мне 'about me'; во мно́гом 'in many ways', со мно́гими 'with many people' (*but* из мно́гих 'of many people', от мно́гих 'from many people').

(2) Clusters that affect only certain prepositions; the cluster often repeats the final consonant of the preposition or its unvoiced/ voiced/mutated counterpart: во Владивосто́ке 'in Vladivostok', во рту 'in the mouth', во фло́те 'in the navy', во Фра́нции 'in France', во МХА́Те 'in the Moscow Arts' Theatre'; со зло́сти 'out of malice', со ско́ростью 'at a speed', со среды́ 'since Wednesday', со стола́ 'from the table', со шта́том 'with a staff'; подо льдом 'under the ice' etc.

Note
Also во Вьетна́ме 'in Vietnam', во избежа́ние 'in avoidance of', во и́мя 'in the name of'.

405 Stress in primary prepositions

(1) Prepositions are usually unstressed; however, some primaries, in particular **за, на, по, под** and, to a lesser extent, **до, из** and **о/об**, take the stress when combined with certain nouns and numerals. Many such combinations are characteristic of colloquial registers.

(2) The types of noun involved include parts of the body (e.g. голова́ 'head'), geographical features (бе́рег 'shore'), other locations (го́род 'town'), time words (год 'year') and some others (вид 'view'). All nouns and numerals involved are monosyllables or have *initial* stress in the declined form.

(3) The commonest case involved is the accusative, but others are also found.

(4) Among the commonest combinations are the following:

(i) **До** + genitive: до́ дому 'as far as home', (с утра́) до́ ночи (from morning) 'till night', до́ смерти (испуга́лся) (was scared) 'to death'.

(ii) **За** + accusative: за́ борт 'overboard' (direction), за́ волосы 'by the hair', за́ год 'in a year', за́ голову 'by the head', за́ город 'into the country', зá гóру 'beyond the mountain' (direction), зá два (гóда), две (недéли), три (гóда), пять, шесть, семь, восемь, девять, десять, сто (лет) 'in two (years/weeks), three, five, six, seven, eight, nine, ten, a hundred' (years), зá день 'in a day', зá зиму 'during the winter', зá кóсу/кóсы 'by the plait/plaits', зá лето 'during the summer', зá мóре 'beyond the sea' (direction), зá нóгу/нóги 'by the leg/legs', зá нос 'by the nose', зá ночь 'during the night', зá плечи 'by the shoulders', зá пóлночь 'beyond midnight', зá рéку 'beyond the river' (direction), зá рýку/рýки 'by the hand/hands', зá спину 'behind the back' (direction), (держáться) зá стену (to hold) 'on to the wall', зá угол 'round the corner' (direction), зá ýхо/ýши 'by the ear/ears', (ущипнýть) зá щеку (to pinch) 'on the cheek'.

Note

Alternative noun/numeral stress is found in за вóлосы, гóлову, два/две, три, пять, шесть, семь, вóсемь, дéвять, дéсять, сто, лéто, мóре, плéчи.

(iii) **За** + instrumental: зá гóродом 'in the country' (cf. за гóродом 'beyond the town'), зá мóрем (or за мóрем) 'overseas', зá ýхом 'behind the ear'.

(iv) **Из** + genitive: úз виду 'from sight', úз дому 'out of the house' (one's own house, cf. из дóма 'out of someone else's house', e.g. из дóма Сáши 'from Sasha's house'), úз лесу 'from the forest' (also из лéса), úз носу 'from the nose' (also из нóса).

(v) **На** + accusative: нá берег 'on to the shore', нá бок 'on to one's side', нá борт 'on board' (direction), (спустúть) нá воду (to launch) 'on to the water' (cf. смотрéть на вóду/нá воду 'to look at the water'), нá год 'for a year', нá гóлову 'on to the head', нá гóру 'onto the hill', нá два (numerals behave as with за + accusative (see (ii) above)), нá день 'for a day', нá дом 'to the premises' (but смотрéть на дом 'to look at the house'), нá зиму 'for the winter', нá лето 'for the summer', нá мóре 'to the sea', нá нóгу/нóги 'on to the leg/legs, foot/feet', нá нос 'on to the nose', нá ночь 'for the night', нá пол 'on to the floor', нá рéку 'to the river', нá рýку/рýки 'into the arm/arms', нá спину 'on to the back', нá стену 'on to the wall', (шептáть) нá ухо (to whisper) 'into the ear' (cf. нацепúть на ýхо 'to attach to the ear').

Note

The following take alternative noun/numeral stress: на бéрег, гóлову, два (and other numerals), лéто, мóре, рéку, стéну.

(vi) **На** + prepositional: нá мóре/на мóре 'on the sea, at the seaside'.

(vii) **О/об** + accusative: (бóк) ó бок '(side) by side', óб пол/об пóл 'against the floor', (рукá) óб руку (hand) 'in hand'.

(viii) **По** + accusative: пó два/двé, двóе, три, трóе, стó 'two, three, a hundred each' (with alternative numeral stress: по двá 'two each' etc.).

(ix) **По** + dative: пó лесу/по лéсу 'through the forest', пó морю/по мóрю 'over the sea', пó полю/по пóлю 'over the field'.

(x) **Под** + accusative: пóд воду/под вóду 'under the water' (direction), пóд гору 'downhill', пóд ноги 'under one's feet' (direction), пóд руку/руки 'by the arm/arms'.

(xi) **Под** + instrumental: пóд боком/под бóком 'close at hand'.

(xii) **При** смерти 'at death's door'.

Note
Alternative stress is possible in many literal contexts, while idioms retain prepositional stress: лезть нá стену/на стéну 'to climb up on to the wall', but лезть нá стену (fig.) 'to go berserk'. Compare положá руку нá сердце 'hand on heart' and жáловаться на сéрдце 'to complain of heart trouble'.

406 Adverbial prepositions

Adverbial prepositions take the following forms.

(1) One-word prepositions (all + genitive unless otherwise indicated): близ 'near', вблизи 'close to', вглубь 'into the depths of', вдоль 'along', взамéн 'in exchange for', вмéсто 'instead of', внè 'outside', внутри 'inside' (location), внутрь 'inside' (direction), вóзле 'close to', вокрýг 'around', вопреки + dative 'contrary to', впереди 'in front of', врóде 'like', мùмо 'past', навстрéчу + dative 'towards', наканýне 'on the eve of', наперекóр + dative 'counter to', напрóтив 'opposite', óколо 'near', относùтельно 'with regard to', пóдле 'by the side of', подóбно + dative 'similar to', позади 'behind', поперёк 'across, athwart', пòсле 'after', посреди 'in the midst of', прòтив 'opposite', сверх 'above', свỳше 'more than', сзàди

'behind', сквозь + accusative 'through', согласно + dative 'according to', среди 'among'.

(2) Compounds involving a primary preposition: вблизи от 'close to', вдали от 'far from', вместе с + instrumental 'together with', вплоть до 'right up to', вслед за + instrumental 'after', независимо от 'irrespective of', рядом с + instrumental 'next to', согласно с + instrumental 'in accordance with'.

407 Prepositions derived from nouns and verbs

(1) Compound prepositions derived from nouns comprise:

(i) One-word prepositions (all + genitive): порядка 'of the order of', посредством 'by means of', путём 'by dint of'.

(ii) Those that combine with one primary preposition (all + genitive): в виде 'in the form of', ввиду 'in view of', в интересах 'in the interests of', в качестве 'in the capacity of', в направлении 'in the direction of', во время 'during', в пользу 'in favour of', в продолжение 'in the course of', в результате 'as a result of', в силу 'by force of', вследствие 'in consequence of', в сторону 'in the direction of', в течение 'during the course of', в ходе 'during the course of', в целях 'for the purpose of', за счёт 'at the expense of', на протяжении 'during', с целью 'with the object of'.

(iii) Those that combine with two primaries: в зависимости от 'depending on', в отличие от 'unlike', в связи с + instrumental 'in connection with', по направлению к 'in the direction of', по отношению к 'in relation to', по сравнению с + instrumental 'by comparison with'.

(2) Most prepositions derived from verbs are based on gerunds: благодаря + dative 'thanks to', включая + accusative 'including', начиная с + genitive 'beginning with', несмотря на + accusative 'despite', не считая + genitive 'not counting', спустя + accusative 'after', судя по + dative 'judging by'. See also **380**.

Note
Спустя may follow or precede the noun: две недели **спустя**/ **спустя** две недели 'two weeks later'.

Spatial Prepositions

408 В and на + prepositional/accusative, из/с + genitive

(1) В/на + prepositional

(i) The central meaning of **в** + prepositional is 'in, inside':

Игру́шки **в я́щике**   The toys are **in the drawer**

(ii) The central meaning of **на** + prepositional is 'on, on top of':

Кни́ги **на по́лке**   The books are **on the shelf**

(2) В/на + accusative

В and **на** + accusative are used to denote, respectively, direction **into** or **on to**:

Я кладу́ игру́шки **в я́щик**   I put the toys **in(to) the drawer**
Я ста́влю кни́ги **на по́лку** I stand the books **on(to) the shelf**

(3) Из/с + genitive

Из 'out of' and **с** 'down from' + genitive denote withdrawal. They are the 'opposites', respectively, of **в** and **на**:

Я вынима́ю игру́шки
   из я́щика   I take the toys **out of the drawer**
Я беру́ кни́ги **с по́лки**   I take the books **off the shelf**

Note

(a) The oppositions **в/из** and **на/с** are consistently observed, though there are exceptions: Я лежу́ **в посте́ли** 'I am lying in bed' but Я встаю́ **с посте́ли** 'I get out of bed' (**из посте́ли** is used with verbs prefixed **вы-**: Он **вы́скочил из посте́ли** 'He leapt out of bed'). For other exceptions, see **411** (2).

(b) Nouns which normally combine with **из**, e.g. **из го́рода** 'from the town', combine with **с** when qualified by **весь**: **со всего́ го́рода** 'from all over the town' (the meaning is 'from the whole area' not 'from inside', cf. **со всех концо́в** 'from all parts', **со всех сторо́н** 'from all sides').

(c) **B** also combines with the prepositional case of nouns denoting articles of clothing etc.: Он **в боти́нках** 'He is wearing shoes', Она́ **в бе́лом пла́тье** 'She is wearing a white dress', Он **в очка́х** 'He is wearing glasses' (cf. **носи́ть** 'to wear habitually').

(d) **B** and **на** + accusative are used after nouns such as биле́т and дверь: **биле́т в теа́тр/на о́перу/на по́езд** 'a theatre/opera/ train ticket', **дверь в ко́мнату** 'the door to the room'. Compare **вид на мо́ре** 'a view of the sea'.

409 The use of в and на with geographical terminology and the names of organizations, buildings and parts of buildings

With certain categories of noun the distinction between **в** and **на** is not always clear cut.

(1) Countries

(i) **B** is used for almost all countries: **в Великобрита́нии** 'in Great Britain', **в Росси́и** 'in Russia'.

(ii) **Ha** is used with some states which are also islands: **на Ку́бе** 'in Cuba'. Note also **на ро́дине** 'in the homeland', **на Руси́** 'in Rus' (but **в дре́вней Руси́** 'in ancient Rus') and **на чужби́не** 'in a foreign land'.

(2) Republics and other territories in the former USSR

(i) The names of former Soviet Republics and other major territories take **в**: **в Арме́нии** 'in Armenia', **в Сиби́ри** 'in Siberia'.

(ii) Note, however, **на Украи́не** 'in Ukraine' (but **в За́падной Украи́не** 'in Western Ukraine') and the use of **на** with areas ending in -**щина**: **на Днепро́вщине** 'in the area of the Dnieper'.

(3) Natural features and climatic zones

(i) **В Áрктике** 'in the Arctic', **в пусты́не** 'in the desert', **в степи́** 'in the steppe', **в тайге́** 'in the taiga'.

(ii) **На возвы́шенности** 'in the highlands', **на лугу́** 'in a meadow', **на ни́зменности** 'in the lowlands', **на по́люсе** 'at the Pole', **на** поля́не 'in a glade', **на про́секе** 'in a forest cutting', **на равни́не** 'in the plain', **на целине́** 'in the virgin soil'.

(4) Mountain ranges

(i) **В** is used with plural **го́ры** 'mountains' (**в гора́х** 'in the mountains') and with ranges that have plural names: **в А́льпах** 'in the Alps', **в А́ндах** 'in the Andes', **в Карпа́тах** 'in the Carpathians' etc. (Exceptions include **на Балка́нах** 'in the Balkans' and **на Ле́нинских гора́х** 'on the Lenin Hills'.)

(ii) **На** is used with ranges that have singular names: **на Алта́е/Кавка́зе/Пами́ре/Ура́ле** 'in the Altai/Caucasus/Pamirs/Urals'. (**Тянь-Ша́нь** 'Tien-Shan' is used with either **в** or **на**: **в/на Тянь-Ша́не**.)

Note

В replaces **на** when the noun is qualified by an adjective: **в Восто́чном Пами́ре** 'in the Eastern Pamirs' (except for Кавка́з 'Caucasus': **на Восто́чном Кавка́зе** 'in the Eastern Caucasus').

(5) Islands, archipelagoes, peninsulas

(i) **На** is the norm: **на Аля́ске** 'in Alaska', **на Гава́йях** 'in Hawaii', **на Ки́пре** 'in Cyprus', **на Ко́рсике** 'in Corsica', **на Кри́те** 'on Crete', **на Ма́льте** 'in Malta', **на Таймы́ре** 'on the Taimyr peninsula', **на Я́ве** 'in Java'.

(ii) However, **в** is used in **в Крыму́** 'in the Crimea' and with islands ending in -ия: **в Гренла́ндии** 'in Greenland', **в Сарди́нии** 'in Sardinia', **в Сици́лии** 'in Sicily' (cf. **на о́строве** Сарди́ния/Сици́лия 'on the island of Sardinia, Sicily' etc).

(6) Points of the compass

На is used with points of the compass: **на восто́ке/за́паде/ю́ге/се́вере** 'in the east/west/south/north', **на ю́го-восто́ке/се́веро-за́паде** 'in the south-east/north-west'. Political **на За́паде** 'in the West' (i.e. 'in Western countries') is distinguished from geographical **на за́паде** 'in the west'. Compare **на Бли́жнем/Да́льнем Восто́ке** 'in the Near/Far East'.

(7) Towns

(i) Town names, many parts of towns and most regions of Moscow combine with **в**: **в Москве́** 'in Moscow'; **в переу́лке** 'in a side-street', **в при́городе** 'in a suburb'; **в Оста́нкино** 'in Ostankino', **в Черёмушках** 'in Cheremushki'.

(ii) **На** is used as follows:

(a) **На окра́ине** 'in the outskirts', **на пло́щади** 'in the square', **на у́лице** 'in the street' (**в** is possible only when narrowness is emphasized: **в у́зких у́лицах** 'in the narrow streets'). Note **в/на скве́ре** 'in the small public garden'.

(b) With some Moscow regions: **на Арба́те** 'in the Arbat', **на Пре́сне** 'in Presnya', **на Со́коле** 'in Sokol'.

(8) Buildings (and parts of buildings), areas and workplaces

(i) Most names of buildings and organizations take **в**: **в апте́ке** 'at the chemist's shop', **в аэропорту́** 'at the airport', **в колхо́зе** 'at the collective farm', **в ци́рке** 'at the circus', **в шко́ле** 'at the school' etc.

(ii) Combinations with **на** relate especially to areas historically associated with open spaces or complexes of buildings rather than single structures. Thus, both **по́чта** 'post office' and **ста́нция** 'station' take **на** by association with the pre-Revolutionary **почто́вая ста́нция** 'relay station', an area with stables, administrative offices and sleeping accommodation, where travellers could obtain fresh horses. Combinations with **на** include the following:

(a) **На аэродро́ме** 'at the aerodrome', **на ба́зе** 'at the base', **на вокза́ле** 'at the main station', **на вы́ставке** 'at the exhibition', **на да́че** 'at the country cottage', **на заво́де** 'at the plant', **на по́чте** 'at the post office', **на почта́мте** 'at the main post office', **на предприя́тии** 'at the enterprise', **на ры́нке** 'at the market', **на скла́де** 'at the warehouse', **на спорти́вной площа́дке** 'at the sports ground', **на стадио́не** 'at the stadium', **на ста́нции** 'at the station', **на строи́тельстве/стро́йке** 'at the building site', **на фа́брике** 'at the factory', **на фе́рме** 'at the farm', **на я́рмарке** 'at the trade fair'.

(b) Certain parts of buildings and organizations: **на балко́не** 'on (theatr. 'in') the balcony', **на галёрке** 'in the gallery' (theatr.), **на**

ка́федре 'in the (university) department', **на факульте́те** 'in the faculty', **на чердаке́** 'in the attic', **на я́русе** 'in the circle' (theatr.).

Note

В до́ме 'in the house', but **на дому́** 'on the premises, at home': Он зараба́тывает и **на дому́** 'He earns extra money at home' (cf. Зака́з доста́влен **на́ дом** 'The order has been delivered to the door'). Compare also в теа́тре 'in the theatre' and Рабо́таю **на теа́тре/ра́дио/телеви́дении** 'I work in the theatre/in radio/on TV' (professional parlance).

(9) Miscellaneous

На де́реве 'in a tree', **на корме́** 'in the stern', **на носу́** 'in the prow', **на ре́йде** 'in the roads' (of a harbour), **на сковороде́** 'in a frying-pan'.

410 Nouns which may be used with в and на, but with different meanings

Many nouns may be used with either **в** or **на**, with negligible difference in meaning: **в/на кварти́ре** 'in the flat', **в/на коню́шне** 'in the stable', **в/на ку́хне** 'in the kitchen', **в/на фло́те** 'in the navy' etc.

Other nouns combine with в and на, but with a *difference* in meaning.

(1) Авто́бус (and other vehicles)

(i) **В авто́бусе** 'in the bus' is used if there is emphasis on the vehicle as a scene of activity: Уро́ки я вы́учила **в авто́бусе/в по́езде/в метро́** 'I did my homework in the bus/the train/on the underground'.

(ii) **На** is preferred when emphasis is on travel (though either preposition *may* be used): две остано́вки **на метро́** до Арба́та 'two stops on the underground to the Arbat'. Only **на** is possible with the names of ships: **на парохо́де** 'on the steamer'. Public transport vehicles may appear in the instrumental case, as an alternative to a prepositional construction: доéхать **трамвáем** 'to get there by tram', достáвить груз **самолётом/парохóдом** 'to deliver a load by aircraft/by steamer'. However, this does not apply to **велосипéд** 'bicycle', **лóдка** 'boat', **метрó** 'underground', **мотоцúкл** 'motorcycle', **таксú** 'taxi', which appear only with prepositions (éхать **на велосипéде/на таксú** 'to ride a bicycle/go by taxi' etc.).

(2) Вóздух

(i) **В вóздухе** means 'up in the air, pervading the air': Самолёт **в вóздухе** 'The aircraft is up in the air', **В вóздухе** повúс зáпах табакá 'The smell of tobacco hung in the air'.

(ii) **На вóздухе** means 'out in the open air': **на свéжем/открытом вóздухе** 'in the fresh/the open air'. Compare the use of **на** in other outdoor contexts: Знáмя колышется **на ветру** 'The flag flutters in the breeze', сидéть **на сóлнце** 'to sit in the sun' etc.

(3) Высотá/глубинá

(i) **В** is used in the absence of quantification: **в прозрáчной высотé** 'in the translucent heights', **в морскóй глубинé/в океáнских глубúнах** 'in the ocean depths'. Note also **в глубинé** зáла 'at the back of the hall', **в глубинé** лéса 'in the depths of the forest', **в глубинé** сáда 'at the bottom of the garden'.

(ii) **На** is used when quantification is stated or implied: **на высотé** двух киломéтров/**на этой высотé** 'at a height of two kilometres/at this height', **на глубинé** трёх сантимéтров 'at a depth of three centimetres'.

(4) Глазá

(i) **В** is used in contexts of emotion or opinion: выражéние страдáния **в глазáх** 'an expression of suffering in the eyes', Какúм болвáном я выглядел **в её глазáх** 'What an idiot I appeared in her eyes'.

(ii) **На** denotes:

(a) 'On the surface': Контáктные лúнзы остаются **на глазáх** мéсяцами 'Contact lenses stay in the eyes for months on end'.

(b) 'Swiftly/in the presence of': Города́ рожда́ются **на на́ших глаза́х** 'Towns spring up before our very eyes'.

Note
Either preposition may be used in the context of tears: **В/на глаза́х** показа́лись слёзы 'Tears appeared in her eyes'.

(5) Гора́

В го́ру means 'uphill': идти́ **в го́ру** 'to go uphill'. **На́ гору** refers to a specific hill or mountain: забра́ться **на́ гору** 'to climb a mountain'.

Note the mining term **на-гора́** 'to the surface'.

(6) Двор

(i) **Во дворе́** 'in the yard' refers to an area surrounded by houses or a fence: **Во дворе́** бы́ло две покры́шки 'There were two tyre covers in the yard'.

(ii) **На дворе́** denotes:

(a) A specific kind of yard: **на ко́нном дворе́** 'in the stable yard'.

(b) 'Outside': **На дворе́** зима́ 'It is winter outside'.

(7) Ме́сто

(i) **В ме́сте** is used to denote:

(a) Part of a whole: Кни́га по́рвана **в одно́м ме́сте** 'The book is torn in one place'.

(b) A three-dimensional area: **в тёмном ме́сте** 'in a dark place'.

(c) 'Together': всё собра́ть **в одно́м ме́сте** 'to collect everything in one place'.

(d) 'The same': Мы всегда́ встреча́лись **в одно́м ме́сте** 'We always met in the same place'.

(e) A locality: **в чуде́сном ме́сте** 'in a delightful spot'.

Note
В is also used in certain adjectival combinations: **в друго́м ме́сте** 'somewhere else', **в ра́зных места́х** 'in various places'.

(ii) **На ме́сте** is used to denote:

(a) 'The proper place': Все ве́щи **на ме́сте** 'Everything is in its proper place'.

(b) Immobility: стоя́ть **на ме́сте** 'to stand still'.

(c) Possession: Я сижу́ **на твоём ме́сте** 'I am sitting in your place'.

(d) Former whereabouts: Де́ньги лежа́т **на пре́жнем ме́сте** 'The money is lying where it was'.

(e) Replacement: **На ме́сте** пустыре́й вы́росли жилы́е кварта́лы 'Blocks of flats have sprung up in place of waste ground'.

(f) Flat areas: **на ро́вном ме́сте** 'on a level stretch of ground'.

(g) Preferred conduct: **на ва́шем ме́сте** 'if I were you'.

(h) Scale of priorities: **На второ́м ме́сте** — жили́щные усло́вия 'Housing conditions are in second place'.

Note
На места́х 'in the provinces': Пе́рвый тур прово́дится **на места́х** 'The first round is being held in the provinces'.

(8) Мо́ре

(i) **В мо́ре** denotes:

(a) Activity or location beneath the surface: Эти ры́бы во́дятся **в Чёрном мо́ре** 'These fish are found in the Black Sea'.

(b) Out at sea, on a voyage etc.: Кора́бль уже́ давно́ **в мо́ре** 'The ship has been under way for some time'; compare also **в откры́том мо́ре** 'in the open sea'.

(ii) **На мо́ре** denotes activity or location on the surface of the sea (приключе́ния на су́ше и **на мо́ре** 'adventures on land and sea') or on the seashore (Ялта нахо́дится **на Чёрном мо́ре** 'Yalta is on the Black Sea').

(9) Не́бо

Either preposition is used to denote the location of natural phenomena (огро́мное со́лнце **в/на чи́стом не́бе** 'an enormous sun in the clear sky'), while **в** is preferred for birds, aircraft, sounds etc.

(Ва́ря уви́дела **в не́бе** два вертолёта 'Varya saw two helicopters in the sky', **В не́бе** послы́шался ро́кот 'A low rumble was heard in the sky').

(10) Окно́

(i) **В окне́** means 'visible at the window': **В окне́** показа́лась его́ голова́ 'His head appeared at the window'.

(ii) **На окне́** means 'on the window/the window-sill': **На окне́** стоя́ли цветы́ 'There were flowers on the window-sill'. Note also **На о́кнах** ро́зовые занаве́ски 'There are pink curtains at the windows'.

(11) По́ле

(i) **В по́ле** means 'out in the fields': В дере́вне пу́сто, все **в по́ле** 'The village is deserted, everyone is out in the fields'.

(ii) **На по́ле** denotes a specific area or plot: **На по́ле** стоя́л тра́ктор 'In the field stood a tractor', **На поля́х** рабо́тали лю́ди 'People were working in the fields', **на карто́фельном по́ле** 'in a potato field', **на по́ле бо́я** 'on the battle field', **на лётном по́ле** 'on the flying field', **на футбо́льном по́ле** 'on the football field'.

Note
На поля́х also means 'in the margin'.

(12) Разве́дка

В разве́дке refers to military intelligence, **на разве́дке** to prospecting: Он рабо́тает **на разве́дке** не́фти 'He works in oil prospecting'.

(13) Рука́/ру́ки

(i) **В руке́/рука́х** means 'in the hand/hands': У Арсе́ния **в рука́х** аво́ська 'Arseny is holding a string-bag'.

(ii) **На руке́/рука́х** means 'in the arm(s)': **На одно́й руке́** у неё ребёнок 'She has a child in one arm', Она́ подошла́ с Ви́тькой **на рука́х** 'She came up with Vitka in her arms'.

Note
Кни́га **на рука́х** 'The (library) book is out', У него́ семья́ **на рука́х** 'He has a family to support'.

(14) Свет

(i) **В свéте** means 'in the light/bathed in light': **В жёлтом свéте** фонарéй толпи́лись дéвушки 'The girls crowded in the yellow light of the lanterns'. Note also figurative usage: **в свéте** нóвых откры́тий 'in the light of recent discoveries'.

(ii) **На свéте** means 'in the world': Скóлько ви́дов слонóв **на свéте**? 'How many species of elephant are there in the world?'. **На свету́** is used when something is examined: Онá осмáтривала одéжду **на свету́** 'She was examining the clothes in the light'.

(15) Селó

В селé means 'in a village', **на селé** 'in country areas': роль интеллигéнции **на селé** 'the intelligentsia's role in country areas'.

(16) Середи́на

В or **на** are used to denote the centre of an area: Трáктор **в/на середи́не** пóля 'The tractor is in the middle of the field'. **В середи́не** denotes enclosure, 'in between': **в середи́не** толпы́ 'in the middle of a crowd'.

(17) Сту́дия

В is used for an artist's studio, and for radio and recording studios (**в рàдиосту́дии/в сту́дии** звỳкозáписи), whereas **на** is used with film studios (Фильм дубли́рован **на кѝносту́дии** 'The film has been dubbed at the film studio').

(18) Суд

В судé means 'in the court-room': **В судé** сегóдня многолю́дно 'The court-room is crowded today'; **в/на судé** 'at the trial'.

(19) Ýхо

Нá ухо is the norm: шепну́ть **нá ухо** 'to whisper in someone's ear'. **В ýхо** may be used to emphasize directed sound: шепну́ть пря́мо **в ýхо** 'to whisper directly into someone's ear'.

(20) Шáхта

В шáхте means 'down the mine', **на шáхте** 'at the mine/colliery'.

411 Special uses of c + genitive

(1) The nouns enumerated in **410** combine with:

(i) **В/на** + accusative to denote direction:

Шахтёр спустился **в шáхту**
The miner went down the mine

Онá подхватила ребёнка **нá руки**
She gathered the child up in her arms

(ii) **Из/с** + genitive to denote withdrawal:

Монéта выпала **из её рук**
The coin fell from her hands

Он упáл **с большóй высоты́**
He fell from a great height

(2) Some nouns combine only with **c** + genitive to denote withdrawal, even where location is expressed by **в** + prepositional: cf.

Самолёт **в вóздухе**
The aircraft is in the air

Самолёт **с** (*not* из!) вóздуха замéтил тéрпящих бéдствие
The aircraft spotted the victims of the disaster from the air

Compare also

с горы́	downhill
со дворá	from the yard
с мóря	from the sea
с нéба	from the sky
с пóля/полéй	from the field/fields

412 Uses of в and на when the dependent noun denotes an activity, event

(1) **На** combines with the prepositional of nouns which denote activities or events: **на войне** 'at the war', **на концерте** 'at a concert', **на матче** 'at a match', **на работе** 'at work', **на свадьбе** 'at a wedding', **на собрании** 'at a meeting', **на уроке** 'at the lesson'.

(2) **На** + accusative/**с** + genitive denote, respectively, movement towards and withdrawal from these activities, thus

Иду **на работу**	I am going to work
Иду домой **с работы**	I am going home from work

Note
В combines with nouns that denote a performance (a) if the performer is the subject of the verb (петь **в опере** 'to sing in an opera') and (b) in references to the *content* of a work (**В этой опере** много красивых арий 'There are many beautiful arias in this opera').

413 В and на: extension of the spatial meanings

A number of meanings of **в** and **на** can be regarded as extensions of the spatial meanings.

(1) В + prepositional

(i) 'Covered in':

Пальцы у меня **в царапинах**
My fingers are covered in scratches

(ii) Distance:

В километре от ГЭС — большое озеро
A large lake is situated a kilometre from the power station

Он живёт **в пяти минутах ходьбы** от станции
He lives five minutes' walk from the station

Note
'At what distance?' is rendered as **на каком расстоянии**? (See **415** (2) for **за** + accusative in the meaning of distance.)

(iii) A group to which the subject belongs:

Он **в гостя́х**	He is on a visit
остава́ться **в живы́х**	to survive

Note

The idea of plurality in phrases of this type is often an abstraction, since **в гостя́х**, for example, can be used even if the subject is the only guest (cf. also идти́ **в го́сти** 'to go visiting').

(iv) Various physical states:

в её прису́тствии	in her presence (cf. в её **отсу́тствие** 'in her absence')
в пути́	*en route*
в хоро́шем состоя́нии	in good condition

(v) Various mental states:

Он **в восто́рге**	He is delighted
Она́ **в хоро́шем настрое́нии**	She is in a good mood

Note

The phrase **в са́мом де́ле** implies confirmation (Он говори́т, что он кита́ец, и **в са́мом де́ле** он кита́ец 'He says he is Chinese, and he **really is** Chinese'), while **на са́мом де́ле** implies contrast (на вид таки́е ми́лые, а **на са́мом де́ле** злы́е 'seemingly so nice, but **in fact** spiteful').

(2) На + prepositional

На + prepositional is used in a number of phrases:

ката́ться **на конька́х**	to skate
ходи́ть **на лы́жах**	to ski
рука́ **на пе́ревязи**	an arm in a sling

including some which denote state:

на во́ле/свобо́де	at liberty
быть **на пе́нсии**	to be on a pension, retired
на второ́й/тре́тьей ско́рости	in second, third gear
на ра́нней ста́дии	at an early stage

Prepositions that Denote the Position of an Object in Relation to Another Object (Behind, in Front of, Below, on Top of etc.), or Movement to or from that Position

414 За + instrumental/accusative, из-за + genitive

(1) За + instrumental

(i) **За** + instrumental means 'behind, on the other side of, beyond' etc.:

за до́мом	behind the house
за мосто́м	on the other side of the bridge
за реко́й	beyond the river

Note

Сза́ди and **позади́** + genitive are synonymous with **за** + instrumental in the meaning 'behind': **сза́ди, позади́** до́ма 'behind the house'. **Сза́ди меня́** 'behind me' lacks the idea of close proximity that adheres to **за мной**.

(ii) The following phrases are particularly common:

за бо́ртом	overboard
за́ городом	in the suburbs, in the country
за грани́цей	abroad
за две́рью	behind, outside the door
за окно́м	outside the window (from the inside), inside the window (from the outside)
за рулём	at the wheel
за столо́м	at the table (also **за обе́дом** 'at lunch' etc.)
за угло́м	round the corner

Note also **за́мужем** 'married' (of a woman): Она́ **за́мужем** за ру́сским 'She is married to a Russian'.

(2) За + accusative

За + accusative is used to denote movement to these positions:

пое́хать	**за́ город**	to drive out of town
е́хать	**за грани́цу**	to go abroad

спря́таться	**за дверь**	to hide behind the door
сесть	**за стол**	to sit down at the table
зайти́	**за́ угол**	to go round the corner

Note also **за́муж**: Она́ вы́шла **за́муж** за актёра 'She married an actor'.

(3) Из-за + genitive

Из-за + genitive denotes withdrawal from these positions:

Он верну́лся	**из-за грани́цы**	He returned from abroad
Она́ вста́ла	**из-за стола́**	She got up from the table
Они́ показа́лись	**из-за угла́**	They appeared round the corner

415 За + instrumental/accusative: extension of the spatial meanings

Other spatial meanings of **за** are as follows:

(1) За + instrumental

(i) Sequence:

Самолёты взлете́ли **оди́н за други́м**
The aircraft took off one after the other

(ii) An object followed or pursued:

гна́ться	**за мячо́м**	to chase the ball
охо́титься	**за ти́гром**	to hunt a tiger (for the zoo, cf. охо́титься **на** ти́гра 'to hunt (to kill) a tiger')
сле́довать	**за экскурсово́дом**	to follow the guide

(iii) Occupation with an activity:

проводи́ть ве́чер **за игро́й** to spend the evening playing

(2) За + accusative

За + accusative may denote distance from a point:

За пять киломе́тров отсю́да сего́дня сва́дьба
There is a wedding today five kilometres from here

Note

В пяти́ киломе́трах could also be used here (see **413** (1) (ii)), but only **за** is possible:

(a) When movement to a goal is implied:

> бежа́ть **за во́семь киломе́тров** домо́й
> to run eight kilometres home

(b) When **за** combines with **до** to distinguish two spatial points:

> **За** пятьсо́т ме́тров **до** фи́ниша подтяну́лся англича́нин
> Five hundred metres from the finish the Englishman rallied

(c) When distance is expressed in terms of **дверь** 'door', **дом** 'house', **кварта́л** 'block':

> За два до́ма до э́того угла́ в 20-е го́ды бы́ло общежи́тие (Panova)
> There was a hostel two doors down from this corner in the 1920s

---

416 Перед + instrumental, впереди́ + genitive

---

(1) **Перед** means 'in front of':

> **перед до́мом**   in front of the house

Note

(a) Unlike **за**, **перед** cannot take the accusative to denote movement to a position, cf. Он пове́сил пальто́ **за дверь** 'He hung the coat behind the door', but Он поста́вил ми́ску **перед собо́й** 'He put the bowl in front of him'.

(b) Note figurative usage: **Перед на́ми** больша́я зада́ча 'A major task faces us'.

(2) **Впереди́** + genitive 'in front of, ahead of' is usually associated with animate nouns or moving objects: е́хать **впереди́ авто́буса** 'to drive ahead of the bus'. Unlike **перед**, it does not imply closeness: Де́ти бежа́ли **далеко́ впереди́ взро́слых** 'The children were running far ahead of the adults'.

417   Под + instrumental/accusative, из-под + genitive

(1)   Под + instrumental

(i)   The central meaning of **под** is 'under':

пла́вать **под водо́й**	to swim under water
стоя́ть **под мосто́м**	to stand under the bridge
под мы́шкой	under one's arm
по́ле **под ро́жью**	a field under rye

Note the phrases

под но́сом, под руко́й	near by, close at hand
под горо́й	at the bottom of the hill
под дождём	in the rain
под потолко́м	from the ceiling (Ла́мпы вися́т **под потолко́м** 'The lamps hang from the ceiling')

(ii)   **Под** also denotes proximity to towns:

бой **под Москво́й**	the battles near Moscow

(iii)   **Под угло́м** means 'at an angle':

У́лица выходи́ла **под угло́м** к трамва́йной остано́вке
The street went off at an angle to the tram stop

(iv)   **Под** is also used figuratively: **под аре́стом, влия́нием, давле́нием, контро́лем, угро́зой** 'under arrest, the influence, pressure, control, threat', cf.:

Экпериме́нты прово́дятся **под руково́дством** учёных
The experiments are carried out under the guidance of scientists

Note
Что вы понима́ете **под э́тим сло́вом**? 'What do you understand **by** this word?'

(2)   Под + accusative

Под + the accusative denotes:

(i) Movement to a position underneath something:

Они се́ли **под де́рево**	They sat down under a tree
Он спря́тал ру́ки **под стол**	He hid his hands under the table

Compare also the phrases

спуска́ться **по́д гору** (= с горы́)	to go downhill
Она́ попа́ла **под дождь**	She got caught in the rain
обрабо́тать по́ле **под пшени́цу**	to put a field under wheat

(ii) Movement to a position near (a town):

Мы перее́хали **под Санкт-Петербу́рг**	We moved to near St Petersburg

(iii) Transfer to a state:

ста́вить **под угро́зу**	to place under threat

(3) Из-под + genitive

(i) **Из-под** means 'from underneath, from near' (a town):

Он вы́лез **из-под стола́**	He climbed out from under the table
Он верну́лся **из-под Росто́ва**	He has returned from near Rostov

(ii) It is also used figuratively:

Маши́на вы́шла **из-под контро́ля**	The car went out of control
Она́ вы́шла **из-под его́ влия́ния**	She escaped from his influence

418 Над + instrumental, пове́рх + genitive

(1) **Над** means 'over, above':

над голово́й
overhead

Самолёт лети́т над го́родом
The aircraft is flying over the town

над у́ровнем мо́ря
above sea level

Note
(a) Unlike **под** (see **417** (2) (i)), **над** does *not* take the accusative to denote movement to a position: Пове́сили ла́мпу **над столо́м** 'They hung the lamp over the table'.
(b) **Над** is also used figuratively: побе́да **над** фаши́змом 'victory over Fascism', рабо́тать **над рома́ном** 'to work on a novel', сжа́литься **над сирото́й** 'to take pity on an orphan', смея́ться **над дурако́м** 'to laugh at a fool', суд **над Э́йхманом** 'the trial of Eichmann'.

(2) **Пове́рх** means 'over, over the top of, on top of': смотре́ть **пове́рх очко́в** 'to look over the top of one's spectacles', Он наде́л сви́тер **пове́рх руба́шки** 'He put his sweater on over his shirt'.

419 Мѐжду + instrumental, среди́, посреди́, напро́тив, про̀тив, вдо̀ль, внѐ, внутри́, вну̀трь, вокру̀г, ми́мо + genitive

(1) Мѐжду/среди́

(i) **Мѐжду** means 'between'

мѐжду магази́ном и доро́гой
between the shop and the road

Мѐжду дома́ми есть забо́р
There is a fence between the houses

мѐжду на́ми
between you and me

Note
Мѐжду governs the instrumental singular and the instrumental or (less frequently) *genitive* plural (**мѐжду дере́вьями/дере́вьев** 'between the trees'); the genitive is found mainly in poetic speech and idiomatic phrases (**мѐжду двух огне́й** 'between the devil and the deep blue sea', чита́ть **мѐжду строк** 'to read between the lines').

(ii) **Среди́/посреди́** means 'in the middle' (of an area):

Среди́/посреди́ по́ля стоя́ло не́сколько кусто́в
In the middle of the field stood several bushes

Note

Среди (but *not* посреди) can also mean 'among, surrounded by':

Среди дере́вьев сто́ит дом   A house stands among the trees

(2) Напро́тив/про̀тив

Напро́тив/про̀тив mean 'opposite', combining with verbs of state *and* movement:

Я живу́ **напро́тив/про̀тив заво́да**
I live opposite the factory

Кре́сло поста́влю **напро́тив/про̀тив** телеви́зора
I shall put the chair opposite the TV set

Note

Про̀тив (but not **напро́тив**) also has the meaning 'against, opposed to': идти́ **про̀тив ве́тра** 'to walk into the wind', плыть **про̀тив тече́ния** 'to swim against the current', **про̀тив часово́й стре́лки** 'anti-clockwise'.

(3) Вдо̀ль, внѐ, внутри́, внѝтрь, вокру̀г, ми́мо

(i) **Вдо̀ль** means 'along, alongside':

идти́ **вдо̀ль шоссе́**
to walk alongside the highway (cf. е́хать **по** шоссе́ 'to drive **along** the highway')

Вдо̀ль забо́ра поса́жены дере́вья
Trees are planted along(side) the fence

Note

See also **424** (1) (d) for **вдо̀ль** in the meaning 'along the surface of'.

(ii) **Внѐ** means 'outside':

Часть дня он прово́дит **внѐ до́ма**
He spends part of the day outside the house

Note

Figurative usage: **внѐ опа́сности, о́череди** 'out of danger, out of turn'.

(iii) **Внутри́** and its directional counterpart **внѝтрь** mean 'inside':

внутри́ го́рода   inside the town

проника́ть **внутрь** помеще́ния	to penetrate inside the building

(iv) **Вокру̀г** means 'round':

Земля́ враща́ется **вокру̀г** свое́й о́си	the Earth rotates round its axis
Они́ сиде́ли **вокру̀г стола́**	They sat round the table

(v) **Мѝмо** means 'past':

идти́ **мѝмо до́ма**	to go past the house

Prepositions that Denote Spatial Closeness to an Object, Movement Towards or Away from an Object, or Distance from an Object

420 У + genitive, к + dative, от + genitive

(1) **У** + genitive case

(i) The central meaning of **у** + genitive is 'at, by, near' an object:

останови́ться **у са́мой две́ри**	to stop right by the door
сиде́ть **у окна́**	to sit by the window

Note

(a) For prepositions denoting proximity to a *person*, see **421**.
(b) Figurative usage: быть **у вла́сти** 'to be in power'.

(ii) **У** also means 'at the house of, with, at' (the doctor's etc.):

Она́ отдыха́ет **у сестры́** в дере́вне
She is relaxing at her sister's place in the country

Сего́дня Са́ша был **у врача́**
Today Sasha was at the doctor's
у нас
at our place, in our country

(2) **K** + dative case

(i) **K** is used in the meaning 'towards' (a place), 'to see' (a person):

Я побежа́л **к вы́ходу**	I ran towards the exit
Она́ идёт **к го́роду**	She is going towards the town (cf. идти́ **по направле́нию к го́роду, в направле́нии** го́рода/к го́роду 'to walk in the direction of the town')
Он пошёл **к врачу́**	He has gone to see the doctor

Note

(a) Он пришёл **к вла́сти** 'He came to power', путь **к сча́стью** 'the path to happiness'.

(b) Идти́ **навстре́чу дру́гу** 'to go to meet a friend', and figurative usage: идти́ **навстре́чу всем опа́сностям** 'to face up to all kinds of dangers'.

(ii) **K** can also denote bodily attitude:

Я стоя́л бо́ком **к мосту́**	I stood sideways on to the bridge
Он сиде́л спино́й **ко мне**	He sat with his back to me

(3) От + genitive case

The central meaning of **от** is 'away from':

Он шёл **от реки́**	He was walking away from the river (cf. Он шёл **со стороны́** реки́ 'He was walking from the direction of the river')
Она́ ушла́ **от му́жа**	She left her husband

421 Близ, бли́зко от, во́зле, недалеко́ от, неподалёку от, о́коло, по́дле + genitive; бли́зко к, бли́же к + dative; ря́дом с + instrumental

Of these prepositions, по́дле 'beside' is rarely used, while **близ**, **во́зле** and **о́коло** 'near, close to' are commonly used to denote proximity to a person or an object:

близ/во́зле/о́коло до́ма   near the house

Note

(a) **Во́зле** may imply *greater* proximity: Он живёт **во́зле нас** 'He lives very near us'. Additional emphasis may be imparted by the pronoun **са́мый**: во́зле **са́мого ле́са** 'hard by the forest'.

(b) **Около** 'near' expresses a greater degree of proximity than **недалекó от** 'not far from'. **Неподалёку** is more colloquial than **недалекó**.

(c) **Блúзко от** 'close to' is used to denote passage at close quarters, as well as close location: Птúца пролетéла **блúзко от негó** 'The bird flew past very close to him'.

(d) **Рядом с** means 'next to, next door to': Дом **рядом с** пáрком 'The house is next to the park'.

(e) **Блúзко/блúже к** denote direction towards: Он подошёл **блúзко/блúже к дóму** 'He went up close/closer to the house'.

(f) For **под** + instrumental/accusative and **из-под** + genitive in meaning of proximity see **417** (1) (ii), (2) (ii), (3) (i).

422   При + prepositional

При + prepositional:

(i) combines with the following nouns in the meaning of proximity: **вход/въезд** 'entrance', **выход** 'exit', **дорóга** 'road':

Дáча стояла **при дорóге**
The country cottage stood at the roadside

повéсить объявлéние **при вхóде**
to hang a notice at the entrance

постáвить часовы́х **при въéзде** в туннéль
to post sentries at the entrance to the tunnel

(ii) combines with the names of the sites of battles: бúтва **при Сталингрáде** 'the battle of Stalingrad' (cf. бой **за Великобритáнию** 'the Battle of Britain').

(iii) denotes attachment: **При университéте** есть поликлúника 'There is a polyclinic attached to the university', прáчечная **при общежúтии** 'a laundry attached to the residence'.

423   Вдалú от, далекó от, подáльше от + genitive

Both **вдалú от** and **далекó от** mean 'far from': вдалú/далекó **от роднóго гóрода** 'far from one's home town'. However, **вдалú от**

never denotes movement: Он отошёл **далеко́ от** (but not вдали́
от) дере́вни 'He moved far away from the village'. ((**По)да́льше от**,
however, is used in such contexts: Сел **пода́льше от** окна́ 'He sat
down a little further away from the window'.)

See also **413** (1) (ii) and **415** (2) (**в** + prepositional, **за** +
accusative, **на** + prepositional in the meaning of distance).

Prepositions that Denote Along, Across, Through a Spatial Area

424   По + dative; через, сквозь + accusative; поперёк, вглубь, вдоль + genitive

(1) **По** means 'over the surface/along/up/down' etc.:

идти́ **по бе́регу**
to walk along the shore

плыть вверх **по тече́нию**
to sail upstream

Ка́пли дождя́ стека́ют **по стеклу́**
Raindrops stream down the pane

По коридо́ру мать прошла́ на ку́хню
Mother proceeded down the corridor to the kitchen

Note

(a) Movement may be in more than one direction: ката́ться **по
      кру́гу** 'to skate in a circle', Меня́ вози́ли **по всей Болга́рии**
      'I was driven all over Bulgaria'.
(b) The distinction between **идти́** по у́лице 'to walk down the
      street' and **ходи́ть** по у́лице 'to walk up and down the street'
      (see also **320** and **322** (2)).
(c) **По** may also denote location at or movement to various points
      in space: Пе́репись населе́ния провели́ **по всем населён-
      ным пу́нктам** 'The census was carried out throughout all
      populated areas', Весь день я ходи́л **по магази́нам** 'I spent all
      day walking round the shops'.
(d) In combination with **доро́га** 'road', **у́лица** 'street' and nouns
      that denote other lines of progress (**бе́рег** 'shore', **опу́шка**

'outskirts' etc.), **по** + dative is synonymous with the instrumental or **вдóль** + genitive: идти́ **по бéрегу/бéрегом/вдòль бéрега**.

(e) Either **по** or **чéрез** may be used to denote movement across an inhabited area: проéхать **по всей Москвé/чéрез всю Москву́** 'to travel right across Moscow' (**чéрез** implies crossing and emerging from the other side of the city).

(2) The central meaning of **чéрез** is 'through', 'across', 'from one side to the other' (often with a verb prefixed **пере-**: **перебежáть** чéрез дорóгу 'to run across the road'), 'over', 'via':

В шкóлу мы ходи́ли **чéрез лес**
We used to go to school through the forest

Он перелéз **чéрез забóр**
He climbed over the fence

éхать в Ки́ев **чéрез Москву́**
to travel to Kiev via Moscow

мост **чéрез рéку**
a bridge over the river

Note

(a) **Чéрез** implies a direction or destination and therefore does not combine with verbs such as **броди́ть** 'to roam', **гуля́ть** 'to stroll', **по** + dative being preferred: мы гуля́ли **пó лесу** 'we were strolling through the forest'.

(b) **Чéрез** may also denote:

  (i) A spatial interval: **Чéрез два дóма** живёт её дочь 'Her daughter lives two doors down', Киломéтров **чéрез пять** нашли́ скалу́ 'Some five kilometres on they found the rock'.

  (ii) A recurrent interval: **чéрез прáвильные промежу́тки** 'at regular intervals', спотыкáться **чéрез кáждые два шагá** 'to stumble at every two paces', печáтать **чéрез стрóчку** 'to type double-spaced'.

  (iii) An intermediary: разговáривать **чéрез перевóдчика** 'to converse through an interpreter'.

(3) **Сквòзь** implies difficulty of accomplishment, resistance etc.:

смотрéть **сквòзь щель**
to peer through a crack

Сквозь крышу протекала вода
Water was leaking through the roof

пробираться **сквозь толпу**
to push one's way through
the crowd

Note

(a) **Через** in such contexts implies less resistance in passing through: Лучи солнца проникали **сквозь/через** листву 'The rays of the sun were penetrating/passing through the foliage'.

(b) Only **сквозь** (*not* через) is possible with a noun that denotes a climatic feature: Солнце пробивалось **сквозь метель/туман/тучу** 'The sun was forcing its way through the snow storm/mist/cloud'.

(c) Figurative usage: смотреть **сквозь пальцы** на что-нибудь 'to turn a blind eye to something'.

(4) **Поперёк** means 'transversely across, athwart, crosswise':

лечь **поперёк постели**
to lie across the bed

Грузовик стоял **поперёк дороги** и тормозил движение
The lorry was blocking the road, impeding the traffic

(5) **Вглубь** means 'deep into':

вглубь лесов	into the heart of the forest
вглубь материка	inland

Prepositions that Denote Spatial Limit

425 До + genitive, по + accusative

(1) **До** + genitive means 'as far as': Автобус идёт только **до Арбата** 'The bus only goes as far as the Arbat'.

(2) **По** + accusative denotes the limit of an action or process, up to and including a point in space represented by:

(i) A part of the body:

обнажённая **по локоть** рука
an arm bared to the elbow

Он вошёл в воду **по пояс**
He waded into the water up to his waist

(ii) Other spatial points:

дома, **по окна** занесённые снегом
houses buried up to the windows in snow

Note the idioms занят **по горло** 'up to one's eyes in work', сыт **по горло** 'fed up to the back teeth', влюбляться **по уши** 'to fall madly in love', **по уши** в долгах 'up to the ears in debt'.

Temporal Prepositions

426 Telling the time

The question **В котором часу?/Во сколько?** 'At what time?' is answered as follows:

(1) By **в** + accusative on the hour and up to the half-hour:

в час/два часа. . .	at one o'clock/two o'clock . . .
в пять минут шестого	at five past five
в полдень/в полночь	at midday/midnight

(2) By **в** + prepositional on the half-hour:

в половине первого	at half past twelve (colloquially **в полпервого**)

(3) By **без** + genitive after the half-hour:

без пяти пять	at five to five

Note

(a) **В** + prepositional and **около** are used to denote approximate time: **в восьмом часу** 'between seven and eight', **в начале девятого** 'just after eight', **около двух часов** 'at about two o'clock'.

(b) In colloquial Russian, prepositions may be juxtaposed: До какого часа вы работаете сегодня? **До без** четверти во́семь 'What time do you work until today?' 'Until a quarter to eight'.

(c) **В** + accusative is usual in phrases with **миг/мгнове́ние** (в **после́дний миг/в после́днее мгнове́ние** 'at the last instant'), **мину́та** (в **после́днюю мину́ту** 'at the last minute', **в после́дние мину́ты** 'in the final minutes'), **моме́нт** (в **после́дний моме́нт** 'at the last moment') and **час** (в **по́здний час** 'at a late hour').

(d) However, **на** + prepositional is used in sporting contexts: **На шесто́й мину́те** сове́тская кома́нда откры́ла счёт 'The Soviet team opened the score in the sixth minute', **на пе́рвых/ после́дних мину́тах** ма́тча 'in the opening, closing minutes of the match'. Compare similar usage in chess: Па́ртия заверши́лась **на 16-м ходу́** 'The game finished at the 16th move'.

See **206** for a detailed account of how to tell the time.

427 Days

(1) **В** combines with the accusative of **день** and the days of the week:

в како́й день/в каки́е дни?	on what day/on what days?
в понеде́льник, во вто́рник	on Monday, on Tuesday
в сре́ду, в четве́рг, в пя́тницу	on Wednesday, Thursday, Friday
в суббо́ту, в воскресе́нье	on Saturday, Sunday
в э́тот, про́шлый, бу́дущий понеде́льник	this, last, next Monday

(2) While **в** is used with days qualified by **пе́рвый** (в **пе́рвый день/ в пе́рвые су́тки** 'on the first day'), **на** + accusative is used with ordinal numerals above **пе́рвый** (**на тре́тий день/тре́тьи су́тки** 'on the third day', **на второ́й день** по́сле отъе́зда 'on the second day after leaving'), and with **друго́й, сле́дующий: на друго́й/ сле́дующий** день 'on the next day' (cf. **в** друго́й день 'on **another** day').

(3) **По** combines with the dative plural to denote recurrent points in time: **по среда́м** 'on Wednesdays', **по суббо́там у́тром** 'on Saturday mornings'.

Note

(a) **День** itself is used in this meaning only in certain phrases: **по чётным/нечётным дням** 'on even/odd days' etc.

(b) An alternative construction with **в** + accusative plural is possible in certain combinations: **по будням/в будни** 'on weekdays', **по выходным дням/в выходные дни** 'on days off', **по праздникам/в праздники** 'on holidays'. In some expressions only **в** + accusative is possible: **в обычные дни** 'on normal days'.

(c) **По** + dative plural also indicates temporal continuity: **по целым часам/дням** 'for hours/days on end' (also **целыми днями/часами**).

428 Parts of a day

(1) Nouns that denote part of a day (**утро** 'morning' etc.) usually appear in the instrumental: **утром** 'in the morning' etc. (but **пять часов утра** 'five o'clock in the morning'; see **97** (2) (i)) and **206** (1) (ii).

(2) However, **в** + accusative is used with nouns denoting parts of a day which are qualified by pronouns or adjectives (including **первый** 'first'): **в первый/последний вечер** 'on the first/the last evening', **в ту ночь** 'that night', **в это воскресное утро** 'on that Sunday morning'.

(3) When nouns which denote part of a day are qualified by **другой/следующий** or ordinals above **первый**, however, they combine with **на** + accusative: **на следующий вечер/следующую ночь/другое утро/третье утро** 'on the next evening/the next night/the next morning/the third morning'.

(4) **По** + dative plural denotes recurrent points in time: по **вечерам/ночам/утрам** 'in the evenings/at nights/in the mornings'; **по ночам** он не спит 'he doesn't sleep at nights'.

Note

В сумерки/сумерках 'at dusk', but **на восходе** 'at sunrise', **на закате** 'at sunset', **на заре/рассвете** 'at dawn'.

429 Weeks, months, years and centuries

(1) **На** combines with the prepositional of **неде́ля** 'week':

на э́той, про́шлой,   this, last, next week
бу́дущей неде́ле

(2) **В** combines with the prepositional of:

(i) **Ме́сяц** 'month' and the names of calendar months:

в январе́, феврале́,   in January, February, March . . .
ма́рте. . .
в э́том, про́шлом,   this, last, next month
бу́дущем ме́сяце

Note

(a) All names of months are masculine and are spelt with a small
    letter. The six months from **сентя́брь** 'September' through to
    февра́ль 'February' take end stress in declension: **в сентябре́**
    'in September' etc. The other six, from **март** to **а́вгуст**, have
    fixed stress in declension.

(b) 'This March, last April, next December' are rendered as **в
    ма́рте э́того го́да, в апре́ле про́шлого го́да, в декабре́
    бу́дущего го́да**.

(c) The use of **на** + prepositional in contexts relating to pregnancy:
    Он оста́вил её **на седьмо́м ме́сяце** бере́менности 'He
    abandoned her in the seventh month of her pregnancy'.

(d) The use of consecutive dates in **ночь с 11-го на 12-е января́**
    'the night of 11 January'.

(ii) **Год** 'year':

в э́том, про́шлом,   this, last, next year
бу́дущем году́
в ты́сяча девятьсо́т   in 1998
девяно́сто восьмо́м году́
в двухты́сячном году́   in the year 2000

Note

(a) **В сле́дующем году́** is also used, especially with a reference
    point in the past: **В сле́дующем году́** овладе́ли ча́стью
    Финля́ндии 'In the following year they captured part of
    Finland'.

(b) The prepositional case is also used with years in the plural: **в 1920–1921 года́х** 'in 1920–1921'.

(c) With decades, the accusative is preferred for processes extending over a period: **В 1960-е го́ды** здесь продава́лись ру́сские кни́ги 'Russian books were sold here in the 1960s'. The prepositional is preferred for an event occurring at a point within a decade: Магази́н закры́лся **в 1970-х года́х** 'The shop closed in the 1970s'.

(iii) **Век/столе́тие** 'century' and **тысячеле́тие** 'millennium':

в э́том, про́шлом, бу́дущем ве́ке/столе́тии	this, last, next century
в XX (двадца́том) ве́ке	in the twentieth century
в пе́рвом тысячеле́тии	in the first millennium

Note

(a) When qualified by modifiers other than э́тот, про́шлый, бу́дущий, **в** combines with the accusative of **неде́ля, ме́сяц, год**: в пе́рвую, после́днюю неде́лю 'in the first, the last week', **в пе́рвые неде́ли** о́сени 'in the first weeks of autumn', **в пе́рвый ме́сяц** ку́рса 'in the first month of the course', **в пе́рвый/после́дний год** войны́ 'in the first/last year of the war', **в год** рожде́ния 'in the year of my birth', **в послевое́нные го́ды** 'in the post-war years'. (This also applies to the seasons, cf. о́сенью, зимо́й 'in the autumn, winter' but **в ту о́сень** 'that autumn', **в тру́дную зи́му** 'in a difficult winter'.)

(b) With ordinal numerals above **пе́рвый, на** + accusative is the norm: **на четвёртый ме́сяц** 'in the fourth month', **на втору́ю неде́лю** 'in the second week', **на четвёртый год** 'in the fourth year' (but **на четвёртом году́** перестро́йки 'in the fourth year of restructuring', where reference is to a stage in a process).

430 General time words

В governs the accusative case of nouns which denote time in general or an indefinite period of time (**век** 'age', **вре́мя** 'time', **эпо́ха** 'epoch' etc.):

в а́томный век/сре́дние века́	in the atomic age/the middle ages

в ми́рное вре́мя	in peace time
во времена́ Петра́ I	during the time of Peter I
в пери́од социали́зма	under socialism
в зи́мнюю по́ру	in winter time
в зи́мний сезо́н	in the winter season (also в зи́мнем сезо́не)
в старину́	in the old days
в тече́ние	during the course of
в на́шу эпо́ху	in our era

Note

(a) **Во вре́мя** is used with activities/events (**во вре́мя уро́ка** 'during the lesson'), but *not* with words of time. **В тече́ние** can be used with either, thus: Репорта́жи бу́дем передава́ть **в тече́ние** всей конфере́нции 'We shall be transmitting reports **throughout** the whole conference', **в тече́ние** сле́дующих не́скольких неде́ль 'during the next few weeks'.

(b) **Во времена́** is used for the distant past: **во времена́** крепостно́го пра́ва 'during serfdom', **во времена́** Шекспи́ра (= при Шекспи́ре/при жи́зни Шекспи́ра) 'in Shakespeare's time' (see **442** (2) for **при** in temporal meaning). **Во времена́** is preferred to **при** when the events are distant in time *and* (from a Russian viewpoint) location. Compare Росси́я европеизи́ровалась **при Петре́ Пе́рвом/во времена́ Петра́ Пе́рвого** 'Russia was Europeanized in the reign of Peter the First' (an event distant in time) and **Во времена́ Петра́ Пе́рвого** А́нглия была́ вели́кой морско́й держа́вой 'Britain was a great naval power during the time of Peter the First' (a historical fact distant in time *and* location).

(c) **В хо́де** is common in scientific and journalistic literature, combining with a noun that denotes a process: **в хо́де обсужде́ния** (= в проце́ссе обсужде́ния/при обсужде́нии) 'during the discussion'.

(d) **За** + accusative denotes the period during which an event occurs or events occur: Он встреча́л **за э́то вре́мя** не бо́лее 60 други́х автомоби́лей 'During this period he encountered no more than 60 other cars'.

(e) **На протяже́нии** is used with longish periods of time: **на протяже́нии не́скольких веко́в** 'over the course of several centuries'.

431 Nouns that denote stages in a process

В is used in temporal meaning with the prepositional case of:

(1) The nouns **про́шлое** 'past', **настоя́щее** 'present', **бу́дущее** 'future':

в про́шлом, настоя́щем, бу́дущем	in the past, present, future

(2) The nouns **коне́ц** 'end', **нача́ло** 'beginning', **середи́на** 'middle':

в нача́ле, середи́не, конце́	at the beginning, in the middle, at the end

Note the phrase **в конце́ концо́в** 'eventually/in the end'.

(3) Nouns that denote stages in life:

в младе́нчестве, де́тстве	in babyhood, childhood
в мо́лодости, ста́рости	in youth, old age
в глубо́кой ста́рости	at a ripe old age (but **на ста́рости лет** 'in old age')

Note

(a) **В во́зрасте** 'at an age': Приуча́ться к ко́фе **в её во́зрасте** нежела́тельно 'It is undesirable to get used to drinking coffee at her age'. 'At my age' may be rendered as **в моём во́зрасте/в мои́ го́ды**. 'At the age of seven' is expressed as follows: **в во́зрасте семи́ лет/в семиле́тнем во́зрасте/в семь лет/ семи́ лет**.

(b) Use of **на** in Он **на 76-м году́** потеря́л зре́ние 'He lost his sight in his 76th year', **на 6-м деся́тке** 'in one's fifties', **на моём веку́** 'in my lifetime'.

(4) Nouns that denote a stage in an activity or event:

в антра́кте, в переры́ве	in the interval, at break-time
в тре́тьем пери́оде	in the third period (ice-hockey)
во второ́м та́йме	in the second half
в после́днем ту́ре соревнова́ния	in the final round of a competition

432 The weather

B + accusative is used to describe the weather:

в плоху́ю пого́ду
in bad weather

Самолёты **в тума́н** прико́ваны к земле́
In fog the aircraft are grounded

Note

Во вре́мя can also be used in more general meanings (**во вре́мя метёли** 'during the snowstorm'), cf. **в** + accusative with its implications of time and circumstance (**В мете́ль** они́ сби́лись с пути́ 'They lost their way in the snowstorm'). Nouns such as **жара́** 'heat', **пого́да** 'weather', **хо́лод** 'cold' combine only with **в** + accusative.

433 Festivals

The names of many festivals combine with **в** or **на** + accusative: **в/на Но́вый год** 'at New Year', **в/на ноя́брьские пра́здники** 'at the November festivities'. **В** is commoner (**в Пра́здник** Побе́ды 'at the Victory Festival', **в нового́дний пра́здник** 'at the new year festival'), but **на** persists with religious festivals (**на Па́сху** 'at Easter', **на Рождество́** 'at Christmas').

The Use of Prepositions to Denote Action in Relation to Various Time Limits

434 The use of с + genitive, до + genitive/по + accusative to denote terminal points in time

(1) **С** + genitive denotes 'since/from' a point in time:

С суббо́ты мы вме́сте	We have been together **since Saturday**
с да́вних пор	since time immemorial
с тех пор	since then

(Начина́я) **с апре́ля** Ве́нгрия перейдёт на ле́тнее вре́мя
(With effect) from April Hungary will switch to summer time

Note

Со вре́мени, со дня, с моме́нта etc. combine with nouns that denote the names of activities or events:

Два десятиле́тия прошло́ **со вре́мени побе́ды**
Two decades have passed **since the victory**

со дня новосе́лья
since the house-warming

с моме́нта получе́ния ва́шего письма́
since receipt of your letter

Note also **со времён: со времён Ива́на III** 'since the time of Ivan III'.

(2) **До** means 'until':

ждать **до ве́чера**	to wait until evening
Я бу́ду здесь (вплоть) **до пяти́ часо́в**	I shall be here (right up) until five o'clock
до сих пор	up till now, hitherto

Note

'Not until' is rendered by **то́лько** 'only': **то́лько** по́сле полу́ночи 'not until after midnight'.

(3) **По** + accusative means 'up to and including': **по шесто́е** ма́я (ог **до** шесто́го ма́я **включи́тельно**) 'up to and including 6 May'.

С and **до/по** denote the terminal limits of an action:

Он отдыха́ет **с 26 ма́рта до пе́рвого апре́ля**
He is on holiday from 26 March to 1 April (reporting back on 1 April)

Он отдыха́ет **с 26 ма́рта по пе́рвое апре́ля**
He is on holiday from 26 March to 1 April inclusive (reporting back on 2 April)

Note the phrases **со дня на́ день** 'any day now', **с мину́ты на мину́ту** 'any minute now', **с ча́су на ча́с** 'any time now'.

435 Use of к + dative and под+ accusative to denote temporal approach

(1) **K** + dative means 'by':

| к концу́ неде́ли | by the end of the week |
| к понеде́льнику | by Monday |

(2) **Под** + accusative denotes:

(i) 'Towards, approaching' a time, in combination with **ве́чер** 'evening', **воскресе́нье** 'Sunday', **пра́здник** 'festival', **ста́рость** 'old age', **у́тро** 'morning' etc.:

Он верну́лся **под ве́чер**	He returned towards evening
под коне́ц сентября́	towards the end of September
Я встал **под у́тро**	I got up in the early hours

(ii) 'On the eve of' a holiday or festival (a synonym of **накану́не** + genitive):

| под Но́вый год | on New Year's Eve |

436 Use of в/за + accusative to denote the time taken to complete an action

Both **в** and **за** + accusative denote the time taken to complete an action:

Они́ обеща́ли вы́полнить но́рму, не **в пять лет**, а **в четы́ре го́да**
They promised to fulfil their norm not in five years, but in four

Он окра́сил ку́хню **за четы́ре дня**
He painted the kitchen in four days

Note

(a) If the *duration* of an action is emphasized, *not* its completion, the accusative is used *without* a preposition: Он чита́л рома́н **четы́ре часа́** 'He read the novel for four hours'. Compare Он прочита́л рома́н **за/в четы́ре дня** 'He read the novel **in** four days'.

(b) **За** is sometimes preferred to **в** in order to avoid possible ambiguity: Он соста́вил докла́д **за три часа́** 'He compiled the report in three hours' (**в три часа́** could mean 'at three o'clock').

(c) **За** is also usually preferred when the time appears excessive in relation to the task: В элѐктросва́рке **и за полго́да** не разберёшься! (Kochetov) 'You won't get the hang of arc-welding even in six months!'.

(d) **В** appears in the phrases: **в два счёта** 'in two shakes', **в мгнове́ние о́ка** 'in the twinkling of an eye', **в счи́танные мину́ты** 'in a few brief minutes'.

437 Use of в + accusative to denote the period during which an action occurs a stated number of times

В combines with the accusative of a time word to denote the period during which an action occurs a stated number of times:

Он е́здит на Ку́бу **4 ра́за**   He goes to Cuba 4 times a year
в год

438 Use of на + accusative to denote the time for which something has been arranged

На + accusative denotes the time for which an event has been arranged:

Собра́ние назна́чено **на седьмо́е ма́рта**
The meeting has been arranged for 7 March

Отложи́ть **на бу́дущую неде́лю**
To postpone to next week

Note

(a) Other verbs which appear in the construction include **заказа́ть (на сре́ду)** 'to order' (for Wednesday), **перенести́ (на четве́рг)** 'to carry over' (till Thursday).

(b) The elliptical construction **На деся́тое** биле́тов уже́ нет 'There are no tickets left for the tenth'.

439 Use of prepositions to denote sequence in time (before, after etc.)

(1) Prepositions denoting precedence in time

(i) **До** means (any time) 'before':

до войны́   before the war

(ii) **До** also combines with **за** + accusative where one event precedes another by a stated time interval:

Прове́рили мото́ры **за час до вы́лета**
They checked the engines an hour before take-off

Note also the adverb **задо́лго: задо́лго до** войны́ 'long before the war'.

(iii) **Перед** means '*just* before':

перед сном   before going to bed
переоде́ться **перед у́жином**   to change for (just before)
                                        dinner

Note
(a) The noun can be qualified by **са́мый**: перед **са́мым** отъе́здом 'just prior to departure'.
(b) The comparative **ра́ньше** is restricted to usage with animate nouns and nouns that denote deadlines: Он пришёл **ра́ньше меня́**, **ра́ньше вре́мени** 'He arrived before me, ahead of time'.

(iv) **Наза́д** + accusative 'ago' is now more commonly used than the pronoun + adverb formation **тому́ наза́д**: неде́лю (тому́) **наза́д** 'a week ago'.

(2) Prepositions denoting subsequent action

(i) **По́сле, через**

По́сле means 'after' an event (**по́сле заня́тий** 'after lessons'), while **через** is used with words of **time** to denote 'after the expiry of/in/ later', with reference to the past, present or future:

Начнём **через час**   We shall begin in an hour's time
Мы на́чали **через час**   We began an hour later

Note
(a) The preposition must not be separated from its noun: **ме́нее, чем че́рез час** 'in less than an hour's time' (or 'less than an hour later').
(b) **По истече́нии** 'on expiry of' is synonymous with **че́рез** in this meaning. Compare **спустя́**, which combines mainly with past tense verbs: Он у́мер **спустя́ ме́сяц/ме́сяц спустя́** 'He died a month later'.
(c) **По́сле** replaces **че́рез** when the time word is extended by a genitive: **че́рез год** 'after a year', but **по́сле** го́да разлу́ки 'after a year's separation'.

Both **че́рез** *and* **по́сле** are used in constructions which denote the temporal relationship of sequential events:

Че́рез во́семь дней по́сле Рождества́ на́ши на́чали наступле́ние
Our lads went on the offensive eight days after Christmas

Note
(a) **Че́рез** is *optional* in such contexts (cf. **за . . . до** (1) (ii) above, where **за** is *compulsory*).
(b) **Спустя́** may replace **че́рез** in such constructions: **спустя́ 8 дней/8 дней спустя́ по́сле** Рождества́.

Че́рез is also used to denote a recurrent temporal interval:

Парохо́д остана́вливается здесь **че́рез раз**
The steamer stops here every other time

Авто́бусы хо́дят **че́рез ка́ждые де́сять мину́т**
The buses run every ten minutes

(ii) **По + prepositional**

По + prepositional is synonymous with **по́сле** in official and scientific styles, in combination with verbal and some other abstract nouns:

по возвраще́нии (= **по́сле возвраще́ния**) домо́й
on returning home
по оконча́нии университе́та
on graduating

по получе́нии письма́	on receipt of the letter
по прие́зде	on arrival
по его́ сме́рти	on his death

(iii) **За + instrumental**

За + instrumental denotes sequence in time:

год за го́дом, день за днём   year after year, day after day

(iv) **В + accusative**

В + ordinal numeral + **раз** defines an event's place in a series:

Она́ голосу́ет **в пе́рвый раз**
She is voting for the first time

(v) **На + accusative**

На + accusative is used to denote the time subsequent to the **completion** of an action:

Он **на́ год** пое́хал за грани́цу
He has gone abroad for a year

Она́ пря́тала **на ле́то** зи́мние ве́щи
She would put her winter things away for the summer

Он встал с посте́ли **на 5 мину́т**
He got out of bed for 5 minutes

Note
(a) The accusative *without* a preposition denotes the time spent *performing* an action. Compare:

Он шёл в шко́лу **10 мину́т**
He took 10 minutes to get to school

  and

Он выключа́ет свет **на 10 мину́т**
He puts the light out for 10 minutes

  where the 10 minutes *follow the completion* of the action of putting out the light, and the result (darkness) is effective throughout that time.

(b) The accusative without a preposition is therefore used with durative verbs (**Я три неде́ли отдыха́л** в Я́лте 'I holidayed in Yalta for three weeks' (time and action coincide)), while **на** + accusative is used with verbs that denote completed actions (Пья́ниц **сажа́ют в ка́меру на́ ночь** 'Drunks are put in a cell for the night' (the time is subsequent to the completion of the action)).

Note also the adverb **надо́лго**: Она́ уе́хала **надо́лго** 'She went away for a long time'.

440 Temporal prepositional phrases as attributes to nouns: за + accusative, от + genitive

(1) **За** + accusative is used to denote a journal publication date:

«*Мета́лл*» **за апре́ль э́того го́да**   the journal *Metall* for this April

(2) **От** + genitive denotes the date of a document:

письмо́ **от пе́рвого а́вгуста**   a letter of 1 August

441 Positioning an event within a time span: среди + genitive, ме́жду + instrumental

Среди́ denotes 'in the middle of': **среди́ но́чи** 'in the middle of the night' (note also **средь бе́ла дня** 'in broad daylight'). **Ме́жду** positions an event between two other events: **ме́жду двумя́ во́йнами** 'between two wars', он отдыха́л **ме́жду обе́дом и у́жином** 'he relaxed between lunch and dinner'.

442 Coincidence in time: при + prepositional

При is used in a number of contexts denoting coincidence in time:

(1) 'In the presence of':

при свиде́телях   in the presence of witnesses

(2) 'In the (life-)time of', 'during' (see **430** note (b)):

| при жи́зни А́ни | in Anya's lifetime |
| при Ста́лине | in Stalin's time, under Stalin |

(3) It governs:

(i) The nouns **вид, звук, мысль, сло́во/слова́**:

при ви́де Петро́ва (= **когда́** я уви́дел Петро́ва)
at the sight of Petrov (= **when** I saw Petrov)

при зву́ке звонка́
at the sound of the bell

Он содрогну́лся **при одно́й мы́сли** о пораже́нии
He shuddered at the mere thought of defeat

При э́тих слова́х она́ побледне́ла
She grew pale at these words

(ii) Nouns that denote a source of light:

Он чита́л **при све́те ла́мпы/при ла́мпе**
He was reading by the light of a lamp

(iii) The noun **возмо́жность** 'opportunity':

при ка́ждой/пе́рвой возмо́жности
at every/the first opportunity

(iv) Nouns denoting various types of state or circumstance:

при таки́х обстоя́тельствах
in the circumstances

при температу́ре три́дцать гра́дусов
at a temperature of thirty degrees

(v) Verbal and some other abstract nouns:

При взлёте у́ровень шу́мов достига́л 112 деци́бел
On (= during) take-off engine noise reached 112 decibels

При перево́зке ме́бели бы́ло разби́то не́сколько сту́льев
Several chairs were broken during the move

(vi) Nouns that denote a social order:

при социали́зме   under socialism

| при советской власти | under Soviet power |
| при э́том режи́ме | under this regime |

Note
При́ смерти 'at death's door'.

Other Meanings

443 Prepositions with causal meaning

The following prepositions are used to denote the cause of an action or state:

(1) **Из-за** + genitive/**благодаря́** + dative

Из-за and **благодаря́** are used when the cause of an action is *external* to the subject, **из-за** being preferred when the outcome is unfavourable and **благодаря́** when it is favourable:

По́езд опозда́л **из-за тума́на**
The train was late because of the fog

Я провали́лся **из-за тебя́**
I failed because of you

Благодаря́ вам я вы́жил
Thanks to you I survived

Note
The distinction between **из-за** and **благодаря́** is sometimes blurred, **благодаря́** being used on occasion as a synonym of **из-за**, in particular when the outcome is neutral from the subject's point of view.

(2) **От** + genitive in the meaning 'physical cause'

Phrases with **от** + genitive denote the physical cause of a state or process:

доро́га, мо́края **от дождя́**	a road wet with rain
боль **от ожо́га**	pain from a burn
Он у́мер **от ра́ка**	He died of cancer

(3) От/из + genitive in the meaning 'emotional cause'

Both **от** and **из** combine with nouns of feeling which provoke a reaction on the part of the subject:

(i) Phrases with **от** imply an **involuntary or spontaneous reaction**:

Он запла́кал **от ра́дости**	He wept **with joy**
Она́ дрожи́т **от стра́ха**	She is trembling **with fear**
Он покрасне́л **от стыда́**	He blushed **with shame**

(ii) Phrases with **из** denote that the feeling experienced motivates a **deliberate action** on the part of the subject:

уби́йство **из ре́вности**	murder **motivated by jealousy**
Он солга́л **из стра́ха**	He lied **out of fear**
Он отказа́лся **из упря́мства**	He refused **out of obstinacy**

(4) От/с + genitive

(i) **С** + genitive expresses causal meanings similar to those expressed by **от**. Often the prepositions are interchangeable when the dependent noun denotes:

(a) A feeling: пла́кать **от стра́ха/со стра́ха/со стра́ху** 'to weep with fear'.

(b) A physical sensation or state: умере́ть **от го́лода/с го́лоду** 'to starve to death'.

Note

In such examples the phrases in **с** incline towards the *colloquial*.

(ii) **С** + genitive is common in figurative usage: умира́ть **со ску́ки/со́ смеху** 'to die of boredom/laughing'.

(iii) It also appears in certain set expressions:

уста́ть **с доро́ги**	to get tired from the journey
с непривы́чки	due to lack of practice
ни с того́ ни с сего́	for no particular reason

(5) По + dative

Phrases with **по** + dative case express causal meaning:

(i) When the dependent noun itself is causal (**причи́на** 'cause' etc.):

По како́му по́воду вы об э́том вспо́мнили?	What made you think of that?
по како́й причи́не?	for what reason?
по фина́нсовым соображе́ниям	for financial considerations

(ii) When the dependent noun denotes handicaps or drawbacks associated with:

(a) Ill-health:

по боле́зни
due to sickness

По сла́бости здоро́вья он почти́ не покида́ет го́рода
Because of poor health he hardly leaves the town

(b) Age or inexperience:

Сын **по мо́лодости** не понима́ет её
Her son does not understand her because of his youth

Нигде́ уже́ не рабо́тал **по ста́рости**
He had stopped working altogether owing to old age

(c) Negative character traits:

Ма́льчик э́то сде́лал **по глу́пости**
The boy did this out of stupidity

Note
Из-за would be used, however, if there was a change in subject:

Из-за его́ глу́пости пострада́ли его́ друзья́
His friends suffered because of his stupidity

(d) Error, ignorance:

По вине́ води́теля происхо́дит 8 из 10 ава́рий	Eight out of ten road accidents are caused by driver error
по оши́бке, недосмо́тру	by mistake, due to an oversight

Note also брак **по расчёту** 'marriage of convenience'.

(6) За + instrumental

(i) The spatial origins of the causal meanings of **за** + instrumental are evident in examples such as **За стеной** не ви́дно 'You can see nothing for the wall' (lit. 'behind the wall').

(ii) **За** also combines with nouns that denote:

(a) Absence:

> Лаборато́рия не рабо́тает **за неиме́нием** лабора́нта
> The laboratory is not functioning for want of a laboratory assistant

> Его́ оправда́ли **за отсу́тствием** ули́к
> He was acquitted for lack of evidence

(b) Worthlessness:

> бро́сить **за него́дностью**
> to discard as worthless

> Про́дали **за ненадобностью**
> It was sold as surplus to requirements

Note also the compound causal prepositions **в результа́те** 'as a result of' and **всле́дствие** 'in consequence of'. Both take the genitive case.

444 Prepositions that denote the object of feelings and attitudes

(1) K + dative

K is used to denote the object of many feelings and attitudes:

Она́ **ве́жлива**	**ко** всем	She is **polite**	to everyone
Он **добр**	**к** живо́тным	He is **kind**	to animals
интере́с	**к** этимоло́гии	**interest**	in etymology
любо́вь	**к** ро́дине	**love**	for the homeland
относи́ться	**к**	to **relate to, to**	**treat** (someone)
презре́ние	**к** врагу́	**scorn**	for an enemy

Note

C + instrumental is used in certain combinations: Ла́ра **ве́жлива со все́ми** 'Lara is polite to everyone' (cf. ве́жлива ко всем, above), Я была́ с **ва́ми груба́** 'I was rude to you', Суд был **строг с**

подсуди́мыми 'The court was hard on the defendants'. Compare
обраща́ться с + instrumental 'to treat'.

(2) На + accusative

На + accusative denotes the object of anger and similar emotions:

Он **негодова́л**	**на** неё	He was indignant	with her
Я **оби́делся**	**на** его́ слова́	I took offence	at his words
Он **серди́т/зол на** меня́		He is angry	with me
Я **таи́ла**	**на** неё мно́го обид	I nursed many grudges	against her

(3) Перед + instrumental

Phrases with **перед** denote the object of feelings of guilt, duty, responsibility, fear, embarrassment, ingratiation, defiance etc.:

Я **винова́т**	**перед** ва́ми	I owe you an apology
долг	**перед** ро́диной	duty to the homeland
заи́скивать	**перед** нача́льником	to ingratiate oneself with the boss
Он **извини́лся перед** ни́ми		He apologized to them
Отвеча́ю	**перед** роди́телями	I am responsible to the parents
страх	**перед** сме́ртью	fear of death
Ему́ **сты́дно**	**перед** сами́м собо́й	He is ashamed of himself

(4) По + dative

Phrases in **по** + dative denote the object of yearning, grieving etc.:

скуча́ть	**по** де́тям	to miss the children
тоска́	**по** ро́дине	homesickness
Она́ **в тра́уре**	**по** му́жу	She is in mourning for her husband

(First- and second-person pronouns appear in the *prepositional* case after such verbs: скуча́ли **по нас, вас** 'they missed us, you'. Third-person pronouns appear in the dative or prepositional.)

Note
The compound prepositions **в отноше́нии** + genitive, **по отноше́нию к**: щепети́льный **в отноше́нии** свои́х обя́занностей/**по отноше́нию** к свои́м обя́занностям 'punctilious **with respect to** his obligations'.

445 Prepositions that denote extent

Some prepositions denote extent in its various forms: the dimensions of an object, quantitative difference and so on.

(1) В + accusative

В + accusative is used to quantify a dimension:

(i) In terms of objects:

кабели толщиной **в руку**   cables the thickness of one's arm

(ii) In terms of conventional units of measurement:

река глубиной	**в три метра**	a river	three metres deep
гора высотой	**в тысячу метров**	a mountain	1000 metres high
площадь шириной	**в пятьдесят метров**	a square	50 metres wide

Note

(a) The dimension word appears in the instrumental in such constructions, but questions about dimension are posed in the genitive: **Какого он роста?** 'How tall is he?'

(b) The dimension word can be omitted altogether where it is obvious which dimension is meant: турбина (мощностью) **в двести тысяч киловатт** 'a 200,000-kilowatt turbine', места (стоимостью) **в три рубля** 'three-rouble seats'.

(c) Conversely, **в** may be omitted where the dimension word is retained, especially in journalistic, colloquial and technical styles: гора высотой **(в) пять тысяч метров** 'a mountain 5,000 metres high'.

В + accusative is also used in comparative constructions with **раз**:

Его дом **в три раза** больше моего
His house is three times bigger than mine

(2) В + prepositional

(i) **В** governs the prepositional of nouns that denote extent, scale etc.:

в крупном масштабе	on a large scale
в какой-то мере	in some measure

Приро́да изу́чена **в тако́й сте́пени**, что неожи́данности вря́д ли возмо́жны
Nature has been studied to such a degree that surprises are hardly possible

(ii) In some constructions with **сте́пень**, **в** and **до** are synonymous: **в/до не́которой сте́пени** 'to a certain extent', **в/до тако́й сте́пени** 'to such a degree', but **в** is preferred in the lower and comparative ranges: **в ма́лой сте́пени** 'to a small extent', **в бо́льшей сте́пени** 'to a greater extent', **в ра́зной сте́пени** 'to varying degrees'.

(3) До + genitive

(i) The central meaning of **до** is 'limit' or 'extent':

роди́тели, име́ющие **челове́к детей**	**до пяти́**	parents having up to five children
накури́ваться	**до тошноты́**	to smoke to the point of nausea
доводи́ть	**до слёз**	to reduce to tears

Note also the set expressions

Он промо́к **ни́тки**	**до косте́й/до после́дней**	He got soaked to the skin
Он эгои́ст	**до мо́зга косте́й**	He is an egoist to the core
вы́пить всё	**до после́дней ка́пли**	to drain to the last drop
танцева́ть	**до упа́ду**	to dance till you drop

(ii) **До** also combines with **сте́пень** (see (2) (ii) above).

(4) За + accusative

The preposition is used in constructions that denote excess:

Моро́з уже́	**за три́дцать**	There are already over thirty degrees of frost
Бы́ло	**за́ полночь**	It was past midnight
Ему́	**за со́рок**	He is over forty
Давле́ние перевали́ло атмосфе́р	**за́ сто**	The pressure exceeded 100 atmospheres

(5) На + accusative

На + accusative case denotes quantification:

(i) With comparatives (see also **182** (2) (i)):

> Он **на три го́да** ста́рше   He is three years older than me
> меня́

(ii) In terms of:

(a) Percentages and fractions:

> Земля́ **на три че́тверти**   The Earth is three-quarters
> океа́н   ocean

> выполня́ть но́рму **на сто**   to fulfil one's norm by 105%
> **пять** проце́нтов

(b) Ratio/distribution:

> **На ка́ждые три кварти́ры** должно́ быть два телефо́на
> There should be two telephones to every three apartments

(c) Monetary value:

> штрафова́ть **на 5 рубле́й**   to fine 5 roubles
> **на рубль** ма́рок   a rouble's worth of stamps

(d) Scholastic achievement:

> учи́ться **на кру́глые**   to get straight As
> **пятёрки**

(e) Projection through space:

> бег   **на ты́сячу ме́тров**   1000 metres race
> Сосна́ простира́ется **на полтора́ста**   The pines extend for 150
> **киломе́тров**   kilometres
> Кричи́т   **на весь двор**   He shouts so loud as to be
>   heard over the whole
>   yard

(6) Òколо + genitive

Òколо denotes approximation:

> **òколо ме́тра**   about a metre
> **òколо рубля́**   about a rouble
> **òколо двух неде́ль**   about two weeks

Note

Unlike **c** + accusative (see (7)), **о̀коло** combines only with nouns that denote units of measurement.

(7) C + accusative

C + accusative expresses many types of approximation (cf. (6)):

Он про́жил там	**с ме́сяц**	He spent about a month there
Он ро́стом	**с сестру́**	He is about the same height as his sister
ми́на величино́й	**с таре́лку**	a mine about the size of a plate

446 Prepositions that denote purpose

Many prepositional phrases denote the purpose for which an action is performed or for which an object is designed:

(1) B +accusative

B + accusative appears in a number of phrases which denote the purpose of an action:

Он вы́ступил	**в защи́ту** свои́х прав	He spoke up in defence of his rights
Я по́днял о́бе руки́	**в знак** примире́ния	I raised both arms as a token of reconciliation
Посади́ли де́рево	**в па́мять** о Ле́нине	They planted a tree in memory of Lenin
Устро́или приём	**в честь** отца́	They arranged a reception in honour of father

(2) Для + genitive 'meant for/designed for'

па́пка	**для бума́г**	a file for documents
общежи́тие	**для студе́нтов**	a residence for students

Note

(a) **Для** can also govern a verbal noun: Учёные собрали́сь **для обсужде́ния** ря́да вопро́сов (= что̀бы обсуди́ть ряд вопро́сов) 'The scientists gathered for a discussion of a number of questions'.

(b) The set phrases **для ве́рности** 'just to make sure', **для ви́да** 'for the sake of appearances', **для разнообра́зия** 'for a change'.

(3) За + accusative

За + accusative denotes the object of struggle, competition etc.:

боро́ться	**за** незави́симость	to struggle for independence
соревнова́ться урожа́и	**за** высо́кие	to compete for high-yield harvests

(4) За + instrumental in the meaning 'for/to fetch'

идти́	**за водо́й**	to go	for water
Я зашёл	**за свои́м дру́гом**	I called	for my friend
о́чередь	**за хле́бом**	a queue	for bread

Note usage in abstract contexts: Он обрати́лся ко мне **за сове́том/по́мощью** 'He turned to me for advice/help'.

(5) На + accusative

На + accusative denotes:

(i) A profession aspired to (constructions with **учи́ться**):

учи́ться **на** инжене́ра — to study to be an engineer

(ii) A quality, the presence/evaluation of which is the object of testing:

испы́тывать но́вый шлем **на про́чность** — to test a new helmet for strength

(iii) The purpose of a precautionary measure (constructions with **слу́чай**):

Она́ взяла́ с собо́й зо́нтик **на слу́чай дождя́** — She took an umbrella with her in case of rain

Note

На вся́кий слу́чай 'just in case/to be on the safe side':

> Спусти́лся в овра́г, **на вся́кий слу́чай** с ножо́м в руке́ (Aitmatov)
> He descended into the gully with a knife in his hand, just to be on the safe side

(6) О + prepositional

О + prepositional can denote the purpose of a request or plea:

крик, призы́в о по́мощи	a cry, an appeal for help
про́сьба о деньга́х	a request for money

(7) По + dative (constructions with **де́ло/дела́** 'business')

> Éду в го́род **по де́лу/дела́м** I am going to town on business

(8) Под + accusative

Под + accusative denotes the function for which an area is designated:

> Да́ли зе́млю **под огоро́ды**
> They allocated land for market gardens

> ко́мнаты, отведённые **под музе́й**
> rooms ear-marked for a museum

Note also **в интере́сах** 'in the interests of' and **в це́лях** 'for the purpose of' (both + genitive): **в це́лях** повыше́ния производи́тельности труда́ 'for the purpose of increasing labour productivity' (cf. **с це́лью** 'with the aim of', which normally combines with a verbal noun or an infinitive).

447 Concessive meanings expressed by prepositions

(1) **Несмотря́ на** + accusative 'despite' is the commonest of the concessive prepositions:

> **Несмотря́ на** плоху́ю пого́ду, они́ игра́ли в те́ннис
> Despite the bad weather, they played tennis

(2) **Вопреки** + dative 'contrary to', **невзирая на** + accusative 'despite, regardless of', **наперекор** + dative 'in defiance of' relate to more official styles: **вопреки приказу** 'contrary to orders'.

(3) **При** may also be used with concessive meaning, especially in combination with **весь** 'all':

При всём своём таланте он не годится в министры
For all his talent he is not cut out to be a minister

При всём желании не могу вам помочь
Much as I would like to I cannot help you

448   По + dative/accusative in distributive meaning

In distributive meanings **по** combines:

(1) With the dative of singular nouns:

Он дал ученикам **по учебнику**
He gave the pupils a book each

В 25% семей было **по одному ребёнку**
25% of families had one child each

(2) With the accusative of two, three and four (also 200, 300 and 400):

Мы выпили **по две чашки** We drank two cups each

(3) With the dative *or* accusative of other numerals, the dependent noun appearing in the *genitive plural*:

Нам дали **по пяти/по пять тетрадей**
They gave us five exercise books each

Note
The accusative, formerly confined mainly to colloquial styles, is now freely used in written styles also:

За столами сидело **по десять студентов**
At each of the tables sat ten students

Работают **по семь часов** в день
They work seven hours a day

(4) Indefinite numerals are found in either case:

Эти слова́ име́ют **по не́сколько/не́скольку** значе́ний
These words have several meanings each

Note
A distributive phrase in **по** may function as:

(a) The subject

По о́бе стороны́ пара́дной име́лось **по балко́ну**
There was a balcony at either side of the front door

(b) The object:

Сжима́л в ка́ждой руке́ **по пистоле́ту**
He gripped a pistol in each hand

(c) A temporal expression:

Остана́вливаются два по́езда в су́тки, ка́ждый **стои́т по три мину́ты**
Two trains a day stop here, each for three minutes at a time

(d) An attribute:

Четы́ре биле́та **по два́дцать копе́ек**
Four tickets at twenty kopecks each

Note the colloquial phrase **По чём**? 'how much?' (each): По чём я́блоки? 'How much are apples?' (each).

Other Important Meanings Expressed by Prepositions

449 Prepositions that take the accusative

(1) В

В + accusative denotes:

(i) The target of throwing, knocking, shooting etc. (see also **451** (2) (iv)):

Он бро́сил	**в меня́** поду́шку	He threw a pillow	**at me**
Он вы́стрелил	**в цель**	He fired	**at the target**
Он ра́нен	**в го́лову**	He is wounded	**in the head**

стуча́ть	в дверь	to knock	**on the door**
Он уда́рил меня́	в че́люсть	He punched me	**on the jaw**

(ii) A game (constructions with **игра́ть**; see also **453** (2) (i)):

игра́ть в футбо́л/пря́тки   to play football/hide and seek

(iii) The object of belief/infatuation:

ве́рить **в социали́зм**	to believe in socialism
Он влюби́лся **в медсестру́**	He fell in love with a nurse

(iv) An object looked/shouted into or through:

Он **в бино́кль** рассма́тривает ре́ку
He examines the river through binoculars

смотре́ть на себя́	**в зе́ркало**	to look at oneself in the mirror
смотре́ть	**в окно́**	to look out of the window
кри́кнуть	**в мегафо́н**	to shout through a megaphone

(v) A professional or other group (note that what appears to be the nominative plural in these constructions is historically an *accusative*):

Он не годи́тся	**в музыка́нты**	He is not cut out to be a musician
идти́	**в го́сти**	to go visiting
произвести́	**в офице́ры**	to commission

Note that the idea of plurality is lost in many such expressions: Он годи́тся ей в отцы́ 'He is old enough to be her father'.

(2) За

Constructions with **за** involve:

(i) Thanking, paying, rewarding, punishing for:

меда́ль	**за отва́гу**	a medal	**for bravery**
Его́ наказа́ли	**за оши́бку**	He was punished	**for the mistake**
Она́ пла́тит ему́	**за молоко́**	She pays him	**for the milk**
продава́ть	**за 100 рубле́й**	to sell	**for 100 roubles**
спаси́бо	**за сове́т**	thanks	**for the advice**

(ii) Identifying, evaluating as:

Он вы́дал себя́ **за специали́ста**
He passed himself off **as an expert**

Принима́ли её **за мою́ де́вушку**
They took her **for my girl friend**

Он слывёт **за знатока́**
He passes **for a connoisseur**

(iii) Seizing, holding, leading by:

Я взял И́нку **за́ руку**	I took Inka **by the hand**
Он схвати́лся **за́ голову**	He clutched **his head**

(iv) Feelings experienced on behalf of someone else:

Она́ бои́тся **за меня́**	She is afraid **for me**
Я рад **за тебя́**	I am glad **for you**

(v) The meaning 'in favour of':

Я голосова́л **за вас**	I voted for you
пить **за здоро́вье** отца́	to drink father's health

Note
Что за in the meaning **како́й** does not affect the case of the dependent noun: Что за **му́ка**! 'What torment!', Что э́то за **друзья́**? 'What kind of friends are those?', Что за **кни́гу** она́ купи́ла? 'What kind of book did she buy?'

(3) На

(i) **На** has many literal and figurative meanings which denote various forms of direction, allocation, expenditure etc.:

жа́ловаться на пита́ние	to complain of the food
зака́з на пла́тье	an order for a dress
лес на постро́йку	timber for building
мо́да/спрос на иностра́нные маши́ны	fashion/demand for foreign cars
наде́яться на успе́х/на бра́та	to hope for success/rely on one's brother
обменя́ть кварти́ру **на** да́чу	to exchange a flat for a country cottage

обращáть внимáние на совéт	to pay attention to advice
окáзывать давлéние на когó-нибудь	to put pressure on someone
охóтиться на вóлка	to hunt a wolf
прáво на óтдых	the right to relaxation
производи́ть впечатлéние на дрýга	to make an impression on a friend
рабóтать на семью́	to work for one's family
рецéпт на лекáрство	a prescription for medicine
смотрéть на кáрту	to look at a map
трáтить врéмя на пустяки́/ дéньги на конфéты	to spend time on trifles/money on sweets
что на обéд?	what's for lunch?

(ii) The main verb or adjective may denote resolve:

Он **готóв на** всё	He is prepared to go to any lengths
идти́ на риск	to take a risk

Note

Готóв на implies desperate resolve, **готóв к** only preparedness.

(iii) The main verb, adjective or noun may express reaction:

отвечáть на вопрóс	to answer a question
реáкция на кри́тику	reaction to criticism

(4) О

О + accusative denotes the object of collision, friction, pressure etc.:

Вóлны **разбивáются о** ри́фы	The waves smash against the reefs
Онá **споткну́лась о** кáмень	She tripped over a stone
Он **удáрился ногóй о** стул	He struck his leg against a chair

(5) Под

Под + accusative implies:

(i) 'Support' for the dependent noun (usually **рукá** or **рýки**):

Егó поддéрживали **пóд руки**
They were supporting him by the arms

Они́ прогу́ливаются **по́д руку**
They are strolling about arm in arm

(ii) 'Accompaniment':

| танцева́ть **под орке́стр** | to dance to an orchestra |
| Она́ се́ла **под бу́рные аплодисме́нты** | She sat down to tumultuous applause |

(iii) 'Imitation', 'adaptation to style' etc.:

Он пел **под Шаля́пина**
He sang in imitation of Shalyapin

комо́д **под кра́сное де́рево**
an imitation mahogany sideboard

стри́чься **под ма́льчика**
to have one's hair cut like a boy's

450 Prepositions that take the genitive

(1) Для

Для can have a comparative/relative meaning:

Тепло́ **для ноября́**   It is warm for November

(2) Из

Из denotes source:

Э́то я узна́л	**из газе́т**	I learnt that from the papers
Он	**из рабо́чей семьи́**	He is from a working-class family
посу́да	**из гли́ны**	crockery made of clay
Оди́н	**из нас** помо́жет	One of us will help
Со́лнце состои́т	**из водоро́да и ге́лия**	The sun consists of hydrogen and helium

(3) Из-под

Из-под denotes the former content of a container:

бутылка **из-под молока**   a milk bottle/empty milk bottle

Compare бутылка **молока** 'a bottle of milk'.

(4) От

(i) **От** appears in contexts involving protection, evasion, riddance etc.:

возде́рживаться	**от** голосова́ния	to abstain from voting
защища́ть го́род	**от** врага́	to defend the town against an enemy
избавля́ться	**от** привы́чки	to get rid of a habit
Она́ **отказа́лась**	**от** обе́да	She refused lunch

(ii) This also applies in curative contexts:

лека́рство	**от ка́шля**	cough medicine
лечи́ть ма́льчика	**от дифтери́та**	to treat the boy for diphtheria

(5) С

С + genitive is used:

(i) With verbs of beginning:

Их дру́жба **начала́сь с дра́ки**   Their friendship began with a fight

(ii) To indicate the spelling of initial letters:

писа́ть сло́во **с большо́й/ма́лой бу́квы**
to spell a word with a capital/a small letter

Note
Через is used with *non*-initial letters: Сло́во 'парашю́т' пи́шется **через ю**' 'The word парашю́т is spelt with a ю'.

(iii) To denote 'permission':

Приезжа́йте ещё — то́лько **с разреше́ния роди́телей**
Come again, but with your parents' permission

(6) У

У denotes the person from whom something is bought, borrowed, stolen, from whom lessons are taken, of whom a request is made etc.:

Берý	**у негó** урóки	I take lessons from him
заказáть костю́м	**у портнóго**	to order a suit from a tailor
Он занимáет	**у них** дéньги	He borrows money from them
Я купи́л дом	**у дя́ди**	I bought the house from my uncle
Я мнóгому научи́лся	**у э́того пáрня**	I learnt a lot from this chap
Я попроси́л	**у негó** рýчку	I asked him for a pen
Спроси́те дорóгу	**у милиционéра**	Ask a policeman the way
У меня́ укрáли часы́		I had my watch stolen

Note

(a) **От** is used, however, when the subject is a passive recipient (Я получи́л письмó **от отцá** 'I received a letter from my father') and **с** + genitive in contexts denoting the exaction of due payment, tax etc. (собирáть налóг **с чáстников** 'to collect tax from private owners', Скóлько **с меня́**? 'How much do I owe you?').

(b) **Узнáть** 'to learn/find out' combines with either **от** or **у**: Это я узнáл **от/у неё** 'I learnt that from her'.

451 Prepositions that take the dative

(1) К

К is used:

(i) To relate a part, component or supplement to the whole:

увертю́ра к «*Пи́ковой дáме*»   the overture to *Queen of Spades*

(ii) With **готóв** 'ready', **готóвиться** 'to prepare', **готóвность** 'readiness':

готóв к трудý и оборóне   ready for labour and defence

(iii) With nouns that denote emotional reaction to an event or impression:

к сожалéнию	unfortunately
к счáстью	fortunately
к моемý удивлéнию	to my surprise

(2) По

По is used:

(i) With nouns that denote means of communication:

по желе́зной доро́ге	by rail
по (а̀виа)по́чте	by (air)mail
по второ́й програ́мме	on channel two
по ра́дио, по телеви́зору/ телеви́дению	on the radio, on TV
по телефо́ну	on the telephone

(ii) In the meaning 'according to', 'by' etc.:

по приглаше́нию	by invitation
по про́сьбе	at the request of
по расписа́нию, пла́ну	according to the timetable, to plan
По мои́м часа́м (or **на** мои́х часа́х) уже́ по́лночь	By my watch it's already midnight

(iii) To denote a criterion for judgement:

Врач су́дит о здоро́вье ребёнка **по цве́ту** его́ лица́
A doctor judges the health of a child by its complexion

(iv) To denote a target, especially a moving or diffuse target (cf. **449** (1) (i)):

Откры́ли ого́нь	**по врагу́**	They opened fire on the enemy
стреля́ть	**по демонстра́нтам**	to fire on the demonstrators

Compare also **стуча́ть по столу́** 'to bang on the table' and **стуча́ть в дверь** 'to knock at the door' (see **449** (1) (i)).

(v) To define the 'frame of reference' of persons, groups, objects etc.:

инжене́р	**по профе́ссии**	engineer by profession
чемпио́н	**по бо́ксу**	boxing champion
экза́мен	**по исто́рии**	history examination

(vi) With ordinal numerals, to denote position in a scale of dimensions or priorities:

Áфрика — **вторóй по величинé** материк
Africa is the second largest continent

452 Prepositions that take the instrumental

(1) За

За links verbs of observation, supervision to their objects:

Кóшка наблюдáла	**за собáкой**	The cat was observing the dog
Он следи́л	**за развѝтием те́хники**	He was following the development of technology

(2) С

(i) The central meaning of **с** is 'with/together with/accompanied by' etc.:

мáльчик	**с ýдочкой в рукé**	a boy with a rod in his hand
человéк	**с краси́вым лицóм**	a man with a handsome face
Я согла́сен	**с вáми**	I agree with you
Он говори́т	**с акцéнтом**	He speaks with an accent
Онá слýшала	**с интерéсом**	She listened with interest
Он реши́л задáчу	**с трудóм**	He had difficulty in solving the problem

Note

(a) **Со скóростью** 'at a speed': Он éхал **со скóростью** пятьдеся́т киломéтров в час 'He was driving at a speed of fifty kilometres per hour'.

(b) **Развести́сь с** 'to divorce', **расстáться с** 'to part with', while denoting separation, retain the meaning of joint involvement.

(c) Nouns and pronouns can be linked by **с**: мы с вáми 'you and I', они́ с сестрóй 'he and his sister', отéц с мáтерью 'father and mother'. Note also хлеб с мáслом 'bread and butter'. A plural verb is used if the nouns are of equal status: Оте́ц с ма́терью **отказа́лись** помо́чь 'Father and mother refused to help'. Otherwise a singular verb is used: Мать с ребёнком **пошла́** в поликли́нику 'The mother went to the polyclinic with the child'.

(d) A nuance of purpose: обраща́ться к кому́-нибудь **с про́сьбой** 'to make a request of somebody', Премьѐр-мини́стр прие́хал в Герма́нию **с визи́том** 'The prime minister arrived in Germany on a visit'.

(e) See **94** for constructions in which 'with' is rendered by a simple instrumental (писа́ть **карандашо́м** 'to write with a pencil').

(ii) **С** is used with the names of public service vehicles when these are qualified by adjectives:

прие́хать **с ра́нним, с двухчасовы́м** по́ездом
to arrive on the early, the two o'clock train (cf. прие́хать **по́ездом** 'to arrive by train')

453 Prepositions that take the prepositional

(1) **В**

(i) **В** links verbs, adjectives, nouns denoting 'guilt', 'suspicion', 'confession', 'certainty', 'doubt', 'reproach' to their objects:

Всех шестеры́х **обвиня́ли во взры́ве комендату́ры**
All six were accused of blowing up the commandant's office

Он был аресто́ван **по подозре́нию в кра́же**
He was arrested on suspicion of theft

Он **призна́лся**	**в уби́йстве**	He confessed to the murder
Я **сомнева́юсь**	**в э́том**	I doubt that
Она́ **уве́рена**	**в себе́**	She is sure of herself
Его́ **упрека́ют**	**в ле́ни**	He is reproached with laziness

(ii) The dependent noun may also define the context of forms such as **беда́** 'trouble', **де́ло** 'matter, fact', **причи́на** 'cause' etc.:

Беда́ в том, что он её лю́бит
The trouble is that he loves her

Де́ло в том, что он ненадёжный
The fact is that he is unreliable

(2) На

The dependent noun may denote:

(i) A musical instrument:

играть **на скрипке**   to play the violin

(ii) A language:

Он говорит **на трёх**   He speaks three languages
языках

(3) О

The central meaning of **о** + prepositional is 'concerning', 'about':

думать	**о плане**	to think about the plan
закон	**о разводе**	divorce law
напоминать кому-нибудь	**о долге**	to remind someone of their duty
мысль	**о счастье**	the thought of happiness

Note
Про + accusative is a colloquial synonym of **о** 'about'.

(4) При

При can mean 'in view of', 'thanks to', 'with', 'given':

При таком таланте он станет знаменитостью
With talent like that he will become a celebrity

При её обаянии не каждая женщина помешала бы ей
блистать
With her charm not every woman would be able to prevent her
from standing out

The Conjunction

(1) Conjunctions fulfil a cohesive function in linking words and concepts to create connected speech.

(2) They fall into the following broad categories:

(i) **Co-ordinating conjunctions** link words and clauses of comparable status (bread *and* butter, young *but* experienced etc.). They subdivide into connective, adversative and disjunctive.

(ii) **Subordinating conjunctions** introduce statements that are dependent on the main clause (he said *that* he had no objection; I called the doctor, *because* I felt unwell; I want to play tennis, *if* the weather improves etc.). They subdivide into explanatory, causal, conditional, concessive, comparative and temporal conjunctions, and conjunctions of purpose and result.

Many compound conjunctions, traditionally separated by a comma, can now also be written without: ввиду́ того́ (,) что 'in view of the fact that'; до того́ (,) как 'before'; из-за того́ (,) что 'because of the fact that'; по́сле того́ (,) как 'after'; с тех пор (,) как 'since' etc. The use of a comma throws the meaning expressed by the subordinate clause into greater relief.

Co-ordinating Conjunctions

455 Connective conjunctions

(1) И 'and'

И links:

(i) Like parts of speech:

Брат **и** сестра́   Brother and sister
Она́ поёт **и** игра́ет   She sings and plays

(ii) Compatible ideas:

Свети́ло со́лнце, **и** бы́ло жа́рко
The sun was shining and it was hot

(2) И . . . и 'both . . . and'

(i) **И** . . . **и** lend greater emphasis than **и**:

Он **и** спосо́бный, **и** трудолюби́вый
He is both capable and industrious

(ii) The same meaning may be expressed:

(a) By **как** . . . **так и** (a mark of a more literary style):

Э́ти вопро́сы интересу́ют мно́гих учёных **как** в Сове́т-
ском Сою́зе, **так и** в зарубе́жных стра́нах (Vvedenskaya)
These questions interest many scholars both in the Soviet
Union and abroad

(b) With still greater emphasis, by **не то́лько** . . . **но и** (also
characteristic of a bookish style): Он говори́т **не то́лько** по-
кита́йски, **но и** по-япо́нски 'He speaks not only Chinese but also
Japanese'.

(3) Ни . . . ни 'neither . . . nor'

Он не получи́л **ни** пи́сем, **ни** газе́т
He received neither letters nor newspapers

Note

(a) The second **ни** ('nor') is preceded by a comma.

(b) **Не** is normally required only when there is a single predicate: Ни он, ни она́ **не игра́ет** (single predicate) на фле́йте 'Neither he nor she plays the flute'. Compare the absence of **не** in Она́ ни игра́ет, ни поёт 'She neither plays nor sings' and Он ни ру́сский, ни поля́к 'He is neither a Russian nor a Pole', where there are *two* predicates (**игра́ет/поёт**; **ру́сский/поля́к**). **Не** is retained, however, in constructions involving the past or future of **быть** 'to be' (or other copula): Вчера́ **не́ было**/за́втра **не бу́дет** ни хо́лодно, ни жа́рко 'Yesterday it was not/tomorrow it will neither be cold nor hot'. Note also usage with **нельзя́**: С ним **нельзя́** ни хитри́ть, ни шути́ть (Zalygin) 'With him you can neither pretend nor joke'.

(c) If there are two subjects, the predicate must be compatible with both: Ни он, ни она́ не **зна́ет** 'Neither he nor she knows' (зна́ет agrees with он and with она́), *but* Ни он, ни она́ не **зна́ли** 'Neither he nor she knew', Ни он, ни она́ не **дово́льны** 'Neither he nor she is pleased', Ни он, ни я не **говори́м** по-по́льски 'Neither he nor I speak Polish'.

456 Adversative conjunctions

(1) A 'and, but, whereas'

The conjunction **a**:

(i) links ideas which contrast without conflicting. The same parts of speech usually appear on either side of the conjunction:

Он сиди́т,	**а** я стою́	He sits and I stand
Э́то ко́шка,	**а** э́то соба́ка	That is a cat and that is a dog

(ii) introduces a positive statement via a preceding negative:

Приро́да **не** храм,	**а** мастерска́я	Nature is not a temple, but a workshop
Он **не** пи́шет,	**а** чита́ет	He is not writing but reading
Кни́га **не** бе́лая,	**а** кра́сная	The book is not white, but red

Note
The order of the clauses may be reversed:

Áстрахань, Саратов — города́ на Во́лге, **а не** на Дону́
(Vvedenskaya)
Astrakhan and Saratov are towns on the Volga and not on the
Don

(iii) introduces a supplementary statement or question:

А где други́е това́рищи?   And where are the other
                                       comrades?

Note the phrase **а вдруг?**: **А вдруг** он не во́время придёт?
'Suppose/What if he doesn't get here in time?'

(iv) introduces parenthetical statements:

Появле́ние зри́телей, **а** их бы́ло челове́к 80, сно́ва
мобилизова́ло актёров (Garin)
The appearance of the audience, and they were about 80 in
number, again stirred the actors into action

(2) Но 'but'

(i) **Но** links clauses which express incompatible ideas, e.g.

Маши́на ста́рая, **но** хоро́шая
The car is old *but* good (an arguably unexpected combination)

(ii) The conjunction is often close in meaning to **одна́ко** 'however',
несмотря́ на э́то 'despite this' (note, however, that **одна́ко** can
replace **но**, while **несмотря́ на э́то** *combines* with it, except when it
appears at the beginning of a new sentence):

Ему́ захоте́лось позвони́ть в больни́цу, **но** (= **одна́ко**/**но**
несмотря́ на э́то) он сдержа́л себя́ и позвони́л то́лько
у́тром (Panova)
He was tempted to ring the hospital **but** (= despite this)
restrained himself and didn't ring until morning

Мы овладе́ли сложне́йшими ме́тодами позна́ния, **но** ещё
пло́хо понима́ем други́х люде́й и сами́х себя́ (Kron)
We have mastered the most complex methods of cognition, **yet**
have an imperfect understanding of other people and ourselves

Note

Всё же means 'all the same', **зато** 'on the other hand':

> Дóрого, **зато** хорóшая вещь
> It's expensive, **but then** it is a quality article

(3) И, a and но

Learners sometimes experience difficulty in selecting the appropriate conjunction, especially where **a** and **но** are concerned. The following examples, each of which begins in the same way, illustrate their usage:

(i) **И** introduces additional information:

> Он молодóй **и энергúчный**
> He is young and (he is also) energetic

> Онá лю́бит кóшек **и собáк**
> She likes cats and (she also likes) dogs

(ii) **A** introduces information which contrasts with but does not conflict with the first statement:

> Он молодóй, **а онá стáрая**
> He is young, and (= whereas) she is old

> Онá лю́бит кóшек, **а он лю́бит собáк**
> She likes cats, and he likes dogs

(iii) **Но** introduces information which is in antithesis to the first statement:

> Он молодóй, **но óпытный**
> He is young, but (i.e. despite this, nevertheless) experienced

> Онá лю́бит кóшек, **но не лю́бит собáк**
> She likes cats, but she does not like dogs

Note

A and **но** sometimes appear in the same context, **но** expressing a stronger antithesis than **a**: Он хóчет, **а** я не хочý 'He wants to, and I don't'; Он хóчет, **но** я не хочý 'He wants to, but I don't'.

457 Disjunctive conjunctions

(1) Йли 'or'

Йли presents alternatives:

Это собáка **или** волк?   Is that a dog or a wolf?

Note

(a) **Йли** does not normally appear in negative contexts. Thus, 'He doesn't like football or tennis' is rendered as Он не лю́бит **ни** футбóла, **ни** тéнниса (or ни футбол, ни тéннис).

(b) 'Or' (= 'or else', 'otherwise') may be rendered as **а то/а не то/ инáче**:

На останóвках не выходи́те, **а (не) то** загуля́етесь (Panova)
Don't get out at the stops **or** you'll get lost

(2) Йли ... или (less commonly ли́бо ... ли́бо) 'either ... or'

Йли я пойду́ к нему́, **или** он придёт ко мне
Either I will go to him or he will come to me

Note

As in constructions with **ни** ... **ни** 'neither ... nor' (see **455** (3) note (c)), a compatible predicate must be found for subjects of different gender: Сéмьи, где **появи́лись** или нóвая мáма или нóвый пáпа (*Semya*) 'Families in which a new mummy or a new daddy has appeared'.

(3) Не то ... не то 'either ... or'

Не то ... **не то** may imply difficulty of identification:

До нас донёсся **не то** стон, **не то** вскрик (Trifonov)
The sound of a groan **or possibly** a scream reached our ears

(4) То ... то 'now ... now'

Он **то** краснéет, **то** бледнéет
Now he blushes, now he grows pale

(5) То ли … то ли 'maybe … maybe'

То ли … то ли implies an element of conjecture:

> И ско́лько лет ему́, сказа́ть бы́ло невозмо́жно — **то ли** под три́дцать, **то ли** за со́рок (Trifonov)
> And it was impossible to say how old he was – **maybe** getting on for thirty, **maybe** in his forties

Subordinating Conjunctions

458 Explanatory conjunctions

(1) Что 'that'

(i) **Что** is used after verbs of saying, thinking etc.:

> Он сказа́л, **что** он мне помо́жет
> He said (**that**) he would help me

Note

Что should *not* be omitted in such contexts, cf. English: 'I think (that) he's out' and Russian Я ду́маю, **что** его́ нет до́ма.

(ii) (**То**), **что** also renders the English (**preposition** +) '**-ing**':

(a) **Изве́стен** + instrumental:

> Она́ изве́стна **тем, что** переплыла́ проли́в Ла-Ма́нш
> She is famous **for having** swum the Channel

(b) **Наказа́ть за** + accusative 'to punish for':

> Ма́льчика наказа́ли **за то, что** разби́л окно́
> The boy was punished **for breaking** the window

(c) **Нача́ть с** + genitive 'to begin by':

> Она́ начала́ **с того́, что** приве́тствовала госте́й
> She began **by welcoming** the guests

(d) **Обвини́ть в** + prepositional 'to accuse of':

> Его́ обвини́ли **в том, что** он укра́л часы́
> They accused him **of stealing** the watch

(e) **Поздра́вить с** + instrumental 'to congratulate on':

Я поздра́вил его́ **с тем, что** он сдал экза́мен
I congratulated him **on passing** the examination

(f) **Привы́кнуть к** 'to get used to':

Он привы́к **к тому́, что** его́ уважа́ют
He is accustomed **to being** respected

Note

То, как; то, где; то, когда́ etc. are also possible with some verbs, e.g. **зави́сеть**: э́то зави́сит **от того́, что** он ска́жет/**где** он живёт/**как** он себя́ чу́вствует/**когда́** он ко́нчит, 'it **depends what** he says/**where** he lives/**how** he feels/**when** he finishes'.

(2) Что́бы

Что́бы + past tense is used after verbs of request, command or warning:

Скажи́ ему́, **что́бы** он не уходи́л
Tell him not to leave

Она́ предупреди́ла его́, **что́бы** он не купа́лся в о́зере
She warned him not to bathe in the lake

Она́ проси́ла, **что́бы** все вытира́ли но́ги у две́ри
She asked that everyone should wipe their feet at the door

Он приказа́л, **что́бы** нас пусти́ли во дворе́ц
He ordered that we should be admitted to the palace

See also **308** (2) note (a).

Note

Проси́ть/приказа́ть, **что́бы** are preferred in impersonal constructions. Compare use of the **infinitive** when the verbs take a direct or indirect object: Он попроси́л меня́ **откры́ть** дверь 'He asked me to open the door', Он приказа́л солда́там **стреля́ть** 'He ordered the soldiers to shoot'.

(3) Бу́дто/бу́дто бы 'as if, that', я́кобы 'allegedly, supposedly'

Бу́дто, бу́дто бы, я́кобы question the truth of a statement: Он уверя́ет, **бу́дто** сам ви́дел 'He alleges that he saw it with his own eyes'. Compare:

Арти́сты, ты́сячный раз игра́я пье́су, де́лают вид, **бу́дто** им неизве́стно — чем ко́нчится (Zalygin)
Actors performing a play for the thousandth time pretend they do not know how it will end

Он её убежда́л, **бу́дто бы** её но́вая физионо́мия лу́чше ста́рой (Zalygin)
He tried to convince her that her new face was better than her old one

Он утвержда́ет, **я́кобы** прика́з отменён
He alleges that the order has been rescinded

See **464** (2) (i) for **бу́дто** as a comparative conjunction.

459 Causal conjunctions

(1) Благодаря́ тому́ что

Благодаря́ тому́ что is associated with favourable circumstances (see **443** (1)):

Она́ сдала́ экза́мен **благодаря́ тому́ что** рабо́тала усе́рдно
She passed the examination **thanks to having** worked industriously

(2) Ввиду́ того́ что

Ввиду́ того́, что 'in view of the fact that', like **всле́дствие того́, что** 'in consequence of the fact that' and **в си́лу того́, что** 'on account of the fact that', belongs to official styles:

Ввиду́ того́, что я во вре́мя о́тпуска был бо́лен, прошу́ продли́ть мне о́тпуск
In view of the fact that I was ill while on holiday I request an extension of leave

(3) Из-за того́ что

Из-за того́ что, like **из-за** (see **443** (1)), is often associated with unfavourable circumstances:

Из-за того́ что я в ука́занный срок не верну́л книг в библиоте́ку, у меня́ бы́ли неприя́тности
I got into trouble **for not returning** the library books on time

(4) Оттого́ что

Like **от** (see **443** (3) (i)), **оттого́ что** is associated with involuntary cause:

Бы́ло нело́вко **оттого́, что** его́ заподо́зрили в жела́нии порисова́ться (Granin)
He felt awkward **at being suspected** of wishing to show off

(5) Поско́льку 'as long as'

Поско́льку ты согла́сен, я не бу́ду возража́ть
As long as you agree I won't object

(6) Потому́ что 'because'

Его́ исключи́ли из кома́нды, **потому́ что** он не прису́тст-вовал на трениро́вках
He was left out of the team because he had not attended training sessions

Note
(a) A comma separates **потому́** and **что** when the cause is emphasized, usually by the addition of бу́дто бы 'as if', ещё и 'also', мо́жет быть 'perhaps', то́лько 'only' etc. (see also **454** (2) (ii)):

ещё и потому́, что	also because
мо́жет быть потому́, что	maybe because
потому́ бу́дто бы, что	seemingly because
то́лько потому́ (or потому́ то́лько), что	only because

Его́ пригласи́ли **потому́ то́лько, что** он племя́нник режиссёра
They **only** invited him **because** he is the producer's nephew

(b) Emphasis may also be expressed by distancing **потому́** from **что**:

Потому́ бу́дто бы его́ и пригласи́ли, **что** он племя́нник режиссёра
The reason why they seem to have invited him is that he is the producer's nephew

(7)   **Так как** 'because, since'

Америка́нский учёный встре́тился с учёными университéта, **так как** круг пробле́м, над реше́нием кото́рых они́ рабо́тают, сродни́ тéмам его́ рабо́т (*Za sovetskuyu nauku*)
The American scientist met scientists in the university since the problems they are working on are akin to his own areas of interest

Note
(a)   **Потому́ что** and **так как** are virtually identical in meaning. However, clauses beginning with **потому́ что** always *follow* the main clause, while clauses in **так как** can precede or follow: Мы уста́ли, **так как** рабо́тали без переры́ва 'We were tired since we had worked without a break' or **Так как** рабо́тали без переры́ва, мы уста́ли 'Since we had worked without a break we were tired'.
(b)   **Под предло́гом что/под тем предло́гом что/под предло́гом того́ что** 'on the pretext that' denote pretended cause; **и́бо** 'for' relates mainly to high style or scientific contexts.

460   Conjunctions of purpose

Чтóбы 'in order to/in order that'
See also **309–310**.

(i)   **Чтóбы** is used:

(a)   With an **infinitive** if the subject of both clauses is the same:

Я взял ведро́, **чтóбы набра́ть** в роднике́ воды́ (Kazakov)
I took a bucket **in order to** draw some water from the spring

(b)   With the **past tense** if there is a change in subject:

Я дал ей ведро́, **чтóбы она́ могла́** набра́ть в роднике́ воды́
I gave her the bucket **so that she could** draw water from the spring

(ii) **Для того/с тем чтобы** throw the meaning of purpose into greater relief:

> Гру́зы перета́скивались в скла́ды, ... **для того́, чтобы (с тем, чтобы)** на това́ры не лил дождь (Semushkin)
> The freight was dragged over to the warehouses **so that** the merchandise should not get rained on

(iii) **Чтòбы** combines with prepositional phrases and verbs which denote purpose or desire: **добива́ться/доби́ться** + genitive 'to achieve', **забо́титься о** + prepositional 'to be concerned about', **за то** 'in favour of', **наста́ивать/настоя́ть на** + prepositional 'to insist on', **прòтив того́** 'against', **стреми́ться к** 'to strive for':

> Мы **добива́емся того́**, чтобы все голосова́ли на вы́борах
> We are trying to get everyone to vote at the election

> Я **за то (прòтив того́)**, чтобы все учи́лись ру́сскому языку́
> I am in favour of (against) everyone learning Russian

> Госуда́рство **забо́тится о том**, чтобы гра́ждане не голо-да́ли
> The state is concerned that its citizens should not go hungry

> Он **наста́ивает (на том)**, чтобы я оста́лся ночева́ть
> He insists I should stay the night

> Мы **стреми́мся к тому́**, чтобы кит был объя́влен ви́дом, находя́щимся под угро́зой исчезнове́ния
> We are striving to get the whale declared an endangered species

(iv) **Чтòбы** is normally *omitted* after verbs of motion and their equivalents if there is no change in subject: Он пришёл поговори́ть 'He came to have a chat'. However, **чтòбы** is *retained* after verbs of motion:

(a) When the action expressed by the **чтòбы** clause represents the purpose expressed by the main clause *but is not subsequent to it in time*:

> Я вы́шел из ко́мнаты, **чтòбы** доказа́ть своё безразли́чие к разгово́ру
> I left the room in order to show my indifference to the conversation

(b) When the **чтòбы** clause contains a negative subordinate infinitive:

Я вы́шел из ко́мнаты, **что́бы не разбуди́ть** ребёнка
I left the room so as not to awaken the child

(c) When the subordinate infinitive is accompanied by adverbial modifiers:

Я забра́лся на́ гору, **что́бы отту́да как сле́дует** огляде́ть окре́стность
I climbed the hill so as to survey the surrounding district properly

(v) **Вме́сто того́ что́бы** 'instead of' implies choice of a preferred alternative:

Вме́сто того́, **что́бы** отдыха́ть на пля́же, он пошёл на конце́рт
Instead of relaxing on the beach he went to a concert

Note
Что́бы does not *always* denote purpose:

Посети́тели уе́хали с тем, **что́бы** через ча́с яви́ться ещё раз
The visitors left, only **to turn up again** an hour later

461 Conjunctions of result

Так что 'so/so that'

Он провали́лся, **так что** ему́ пришло́сь пересдава́ть экза́мен
He failed, so he had to resit the examination

The conjunctions **всле́дствие чего́** 'in consequence of which' and **в результа́те чего́** 'as a result of which' are used in official registers.

462 Conditional conjunctions

(1) Е́сли 'if'

Е́сли (бы) is dealt with in **304–305**.

Note also the precautionary **на слу́чай е́сли** 'just in case':

Она́ мне дала́ свой телефо́н, **на слу́чай е́сли** придётся что́-нибудь переда́ть
She gave me her telephone number **just in case** a message needed to be passed on

See also **446** (5) (iii).

(2) Е́сли не 'unless'

Он уйдёт, **е́сли** вы **не** помеша́ете ему́
He'll go away unless you stop him

(3) При усло́вии что 'on condition that'

Она́ вы́йдет за́муж за него́ **при усло́вии, что** он уе́дет из А́нглии
She will marry him on condition that he leaves England

(4) Раз 'if, since, now that'

Раз has passed from conversational into literary style:

Раз дал сло́во, на́до его́ сдержа́ть
Now that he's given his word he should keep it

(5) Ко̀ли/ко̀ль; ко̀ль ско́ро 'if'

Ко̀ли/ко̀ль is a colloquial and obsolescent synonym of **е́сли** (**ко̀ли на то пошло́** 'for that matter/if that's the way it is') and is rarely found in written styles. **Ко̀ль ско́ро** may be used in polemic, where it raises the emotional tension:

И уж **ко̀ль ско́ро** лю́ди де́ржат живо́тных, **то** не-соверше́нство слу́жбы ветерина́рной по́мощи «бьёт» пре́жде всего́ по владе́льцам (*Semya*)
And since people keep animals, imperfections in the veterinary service hit their owners hardest

(6) Доста́точно (it is) 'sufficient/all it needs'

Доста́точно 'it is sufficient' may acquire a conditional nuance:

Доста́точно бы́ло одно́й из пуль попа́сть в ми́ну, **и** (or **как**) она́ взлете́ла бы на во́здух (Stepanov)
All it needed was for one of the bullets to hit the mine and it would have exploded

463 Concessive conjunctions

(1) Хотя́/хоть 'although'

Хотя́ (= **несмотря́ на то, что**) он тако́й молодо́й, его́ избра́ли депута́том Верхо́вного Сове́та
Although (= 'despite the fact that') he is so young he was elected a member of the Supreme Soviet

The main clause may be introduced by **а** 'but', **зато́** 'on the other hand', **но** 'but', **одна́ко** 'however':

Фёдор **хоть** и нача́льник, **но** всё-таки сосе́д (Zhukhovitsky)
Although Fedor is the boss, he is a neighbour just the same

(2) Пусть 'even if, albeit'

Пусть (**пуска́й**) is characterized by colloquial or emotive nuances:

Лю́ди всегда́ бу́дут стреми́ться к верши́нам, **пусть** да́же с ри́ском для жи́зни
People will always aim for the heights, albeit at risk to their lives

For concessive constructions with **ни** see **312**.

464 Comparative conjunctions

(1) Как 'as, like'

(i) **Как** can be used to introduce a comparison:

Верши́ны колыха́лись, **как** гре́бни волн
The summits swayed **like** the crests of waves

(ii) For additional emphasis, **так же как** or **то́чно так же как** is used:

Их на́до обуча́ть э́тому, **так же как** их у́чат чита́ть и писа́ть

They have to be taught this, **just as** they are taught to read and write

(2) Бу́дто/как бу́дто/сло́вно/то́чно 'as if'

(i) **Бу́дто** introduces statements which are seemingly at variance with reality:

Вцепи́лся глаза́ми, **бу́дто** следи́л за разду́мьями Дро́бышева (Granin)

He fastened his eyes on him as if he were following Drobyshev's meditations

See **458** (3) for **бу́дто** as an explanatory conjunction.

(ii) **Как бу́дто(бы)/сло́вно/то́чно** are used to compare similar situations:

Он перецелова́лся со все́ми, **как бу́дто** уезжа́л на не́сколько лет

He exchanged kisses with everyone, as if he were going away for several years

Усну́ла так, **как бу́дто бы** она́ что́-то соверши́ла (Zalygin)

She fell asleep as if she had accomplished something

Слу́шать его́ бы́ло тя́гостно, **то́чно** больно́го, кото́рый не жела́ет сознава́ть безнадёжность своего́ положе́ния (Granin)

It was distressing to listen to him, like listening to a sick person who is reluctant to acknowledge the hopelessness of his situation

465 Temporal conjunctions. Introductory comments

(1) Some English temporal prepositions, e.g. 'before', 'after', 'until', 'since' etc., also function as conjunctions:

Preposition	Conjunction
before dinner	**before** he arrived
after the lesson	**after** the lesson finished

Preposition	Conjunction
until Thursday	**until** we turned the corner
since May	**since** he left

(2) This does *not* apply, however, to their counterparts in Russian.

(i) The temporal prepositions are dealt with in **434** and **439**:

English	Russian
before dinner	до ýжина, **перед** ýжином
after the lesson	пòсле урóка
until Thursday	до четвергá
since May	с мáя

(ii) The equivalent conjunctions are as follows:

before	до тогó как/прéжде чем
just before	перед тем как
after	пòсле тогó как
until	(до тех пор) покá . . . не
since	с тех пор как

Note

English conjunctions such as 'when', 'if', 'until', 'as soon as' do not normally combine with the future tense, even when reference is to the future: 'when he *arrives*', 'if he *gets* here in time', 'I'll wait until you *finish/have finished*', 'I'll leave as soon as the clock *strikes* 12' etc. In Russian, however, future *meaning* is expressed by the future of the verb in such contexts: когдá он **придёт** 'when he arrives', Подождý, покá вы не **кóнчите** 'I'll wait until you finish'. (See also **264**.)

466 Temporal conjunctions which render 'before', 'after', 'by the time that', 'until', 'since'

(1) До тогó как 'before'

До тогó, **как** мы вам рассказáли о Венесуэ́ле, вы, вероя́тно, и не подозревáли, что её назвáние свя́зано с назвáнием Венéции (Vvedenskaya)
Before we told you about Venezuela you probably had no idea its name was associated with that of Venice

Note
Задо́лго до того́ как 'long before', **ещё до того́ как** 'even before'.

(2) Перед тем как 'just before'

Она́ зажгла́ све́чи **перед тем как** го́сти се́ли за стол
She lit the candles just before the guests sat down to table

Note
(a) An *infinitive* may be used in the time clause if the subject of both clauses is the same: Она́ наде́ла но́вое пла́тье **перед тем как** спусти́ться на встре́чу с гостя́ми 'She put on a new dress before going down to meet the guests'.
(b) **Перед тем как** retains the meaning of close proximity to the event which is expressed by the preposition **перед** (see **439** (1) (iii)), and can combine with adverbs and adverbial phrases which stress immediacy: **в после́дний моме́нт перед тем как** 'in the final moment before', **как раз перед тем как** 'just before', **непосре́дственно перед тем как** 'immediately before' etc.

(3) Пре́жде чем 'before'

Пре́жде чем is a synonym of **до того́ как** in strictly temporal meanings. However, *only* пре́жде чем may be used in contexts that denote:

(i) Precaution:

Ка́ждый раз пти́цы улета́ют, **пре́жде чем** я успе́ю подойти́ к ним (Aramilev)
Every time the birds fly away before I have time to approach them

(ii) Inexpediency:

Пре́жде чем осужда́ть сосе́да, на́до присмотре́ться к самому́ себе́
Before condemning one's neighbour, one should take a hard look at oneself

(iii) The dependence of the time clause on the main clause:

На́до самому́ что́-то знать, **пре́жде чем** учи́ть други́х
You must know something yourself before teaching others

(4) После того как 'after'

После того как дети легли спать, она поставила самовар
After the children had gone to bed she put on the samovar

Однажды **после того, как** отчим очень сильно его ударил,
Володя даже обратился в милицию (*Semya*)
Once after his stepfather had hit him with particular force
Volodya even went to the police

A perfective gerund may be used instead of a conjunction if the
subject of the temporal clause is the same as that of the main clause:
Сдав (= **после того как она сдала**) приёмные экзамены, она
поступила в МГУ 'Having passed the entrance examinations she
enrolled at Moscow University'.

(5) Пока

Пока means:

(i) 'By the time': **Пока** приехали пожарные, пламя удалось
потушить 'By the time the fire brigade arrived the fire had been put
out'.

(ii) 'While':

(a) When two actions or processes are running parallel:

Пока я занимаюсь, дети играют в саду
While I am studying the children play in the garden

Пока вы в пути, помещение прогреется (*Izvestiya*)
While you are on your way the building will warm up

(b) When one action or process interrupts another:

Пока мы собирались в дорогу, стало темно
While we were getting ready for the journey it grew dark

Note
Пока may be replaced by **в то время как** in these meanings. 'While'
(= 'whereas') is rendered by **в то время как/тогда как**: Он за
новый режим, **в то время как/тогда как** я решительно против it
'He is in favour of the new regime, while I am emphatically against it'.
Пока is also used in 'opportunist' contexts: Перейдём дорогу,
пока машин нет 'We'll cross the road while it's clear'.

(6) Пока́ ... не 'until'

Пока́ ... не can be used with future and past tense forms:

Я подожду́, пока́ он не **вернётся**
I shall wait until he returns

Я подожда́л, пока́ маши́на не **вы́шла** на пло́щадь
I waited until the car came out on to the square

Note

(a) The conventional negative in **пока́ ... не**.
(b) Compare Жду, **когда́** вы ко́нчите 'I am waiting for you to finish'.

(7) С тех пор как 'since'

С тех пор как он живёт в но́вом до́ме, мы ни ра́зу не встреча́лись
Since he has been living in his new house, we haven't once met

467 Other conjunctions of time

(1) Когда́ 'when, as, whenever, after'

Когда́ вы ко́нчите, бу́дем чай пить
When (after) you have finished we shall drink tea

Когда́ я возвраща́лся домо́й, я встре́тил своего́ бы́вшего учи́теля
As I was returning home I met my former teacher

(**Ка́ждый раз**), **когда́** маши́на остана́вливается, ребёнок просыпа́ется
Whenever the car stops the baby wakes up

Note

(a) For English present tense rendered by a Russian future, see **264** and **465** *Note*.
(b) A gerund may be used instead of **когда́** + finite verb if the subject of both clauses is the same: **Возвраща́ясь** домо́й, я встре́тил своего́ бы́вшего учи́теля 'While returning home I met my former teacher'.

(c) **Когда́** is also used with **ждать** and **люби́ть**: Мы жда́ли, **когда́** кто́-нибудь из девча́т поя́вится на доро́ге (Nikolaev) 'We were waiting for one of the girls to appear on the road'; — А твоя́-то, зна́чит, не о́чень лю́бит, **когда́** ты пьёшь? (Rasputin) 'So your old woman isn't very keen on you drinking?'

(d) Constructions with **слу́чай** 'case':

Иногда́ сообща́ют **о слу́чаях, когда́** води́тели наруша́ют пра́вила из-за того́, что доро́жные зна́ки пло́хо видны́ (*Nedelya*)

Sometimes there are reports of drivers committing an offence because road signs are not easily visible

(2) Как 'as, when'

(i) **Как** 'as, when' is not used independently in temporal meaning, **когда́** being preferred (see above). Alternatively, **как** may be modified to **в то вре́мя как** 'while': **В то вре́мя как** докла́дчик говори́л, я де́лал запи́ски 'While the speaker was giving his talk I made notes'. The addition of **как раз** lends a sense of immediacy: Он ре́зко оберну́лся **как раз в то вре́мя как** она́ откры́ла дверь (German) 'He turned abruptly just as she opened the door'.

(ii) **Как** is also used to denote suddenness/unexpectedness:

(a) A negative verb often appears in the main clause:

Не про́жили и двух лет, **как** получи́ли кварти́ру
They had spent less than two years there **when** they received a flat

in particular **не успе́ть** 'not to have time to, not to manage':

Не успе́л я добра́ться до две́ри, **как** свет пога́с
I hadn't managed to reach the door **when** the light went out

(b) The conjunction **едва́** 'hardly' may also appear in the main clause:

Едва́ мы добрали́сь до ле́са, как пошёл дождь
Hardly had we reached the forest **than** it began raining

(c) **Сто́ит, сто́ило** 'hardly, no sooner than' also appear:

Сто́ило ему́ сверну́ть на просёлочную доро́гу, **как** мото́р заглóх
No sooner had he turned on to a country road **than** the engine cut out

Note
Сто́ит/сто́ило combine only with *perfective* infinitives.

(3) Как вдруг 'when suddenly'

Как вдруг introduces an action which interrupts the action of the main clause:

Он застёгивал воротни́к, **как вдруг** оторвала́сь пу́говица
He was fastening his collar when suddenly a button came off

(4) Как то́лько 'as soon as'

Как то́лько он вернётся, бу́дем проверя́ть рабо́ты
As soon as he returns we shall correct the papers

Как то́лько побли́зости появля́ется враг, пингви́ны выска́кивают из воды́
As soon as an enemy appears in the vicinity the penguins jump out of the water

(5) По ме́ре того́ как 'as, in proportion as'

The conjunction **по ме́ре того́ как** '(in proportion) as' links two actions or processes advancing in parallel ('gradational' meaning):

По ме́ре того́ как поднима́лось сóлнце, день теплéл (Bunin)
As the sun rose the day was becoming warm

The Particle

(1) Particles are parts of speech which impart additional semantic nuances to other words, phrases or sentences, in most cases having no independent meanings of their own. Some, however, are poly-semantic (see **473**), precise translation often being possible only within a wider context.

(2) Particles are, in the main, a feature of colloquial Russian, where they are used to express a variety of emotions, subjective attitudes and assessments, imbuing individual speech with emotive colour and expressive spontaneity, sometimes in combination with other emotional intensifiers such as diminutives: **Ну, дава́йте, мужички́**, подни́мем за сча́стье молоды́х (Shcherbakov) 'Come on, chaps, let's raise our glasses to the happiness of the young couple'.

(3) The effect of a particle may be varied or intensified by intonation. Thus, for example, Петь **так** петь 'If we're going to sing, let's sing' can, depending on the intonational pattern with which the phrase is uttered, denote an eagerness to sing or a reluctant acceptance of the inevitable.

(4) Some particles are formally identical with conjunctions (e.g. **а**, **да**, **же**), others with adverbs (e.g. **ещё, то́лько, уже́**) or pronouns (e.g. **то**). Some are of verbal origin (e.g. **ведь, мол, пусть, хоть**).

There is considerable overlap between particles and certain inter-jections: **Ох уж** э́ти мне ро́дственники! 'Oh, these relations!', **Ну и** моро́з! 'Quite a frost!'

469 The position of the particle in the sentence

(1) Some particles always *precede* the word they qualify:

Да здра́вствует мир!	Long live peace!
Ну, пое́хали!	Right, let's go!
Пусть ска́жет	Let him tell us
Что за безобра́зие!	How disgraceful!

(2) Others always *follow* the word they qualify:

Расскажи́ **же**	Come on, tell us all about it
Помолчи́-**ка**	Do be quiet
Ты́ **ли** э́то сде́лал?	Was it you who did that?

Тепе́рь-**то** я по́нял весь у́жас своего́ положе́ния
It was now that I realized the full horror of my situation

(3) Others still may stand at the beginning or in the middle of a sent-ence (or occasionally at the end of a sentence):

Ведь он ошиба́ется *or* Он **ведь** ошиба́ется
He is wrong, you know

(4) Some, e.g. **так**, may occupy a central position between two forms:

Пить **так** пить, — ти́хо сказа́ла Га́лка (Gagarin)
'If we're drinking, let's drink', said Galka softly

470 The use of particles to impart different nuances of meaning

A phrase such as, for example, Э́то не подлежи́т сомне́нию 'That's not open to doubt', can combine with a number of different particles, each of which imparts to it a different emphasis. Thus:

(1) **Ведь** may be used to introduce a self-evident fact or to issue a gentle reminder:

Ведь э́то не подлежи́т сомне́нию
You know, that's not open to doubt

(2) **Вот** cites the statement as an example:

Вот э́то не подлежи́т сомне́нию
Now this, for instance, is beyond doubt

(3) **Да** implies that the statement can be taken for granted:

Да э́то не подлежи́т сомне́нию
Of course that is beyond doubt

(4) **Же** introduces a more categorical emphasis:

Э́то **же** не подлежи́т сомне́нию
Now that really isn't open to doubt

(5) **-то** indicates that the subject has been referred to before:

Э́то-**то** не подлежи́т сомне́нию
Now there's something that is beyond doubt

(6) **Уж** rules out any possibility of contradiction:

Уж э́то не подлежи́т сомне́нию
That is definitely not open to doubt

471 Some of the principal meanings expressed by particles

Particles are used:

(1) To **point out**:

Вот дом	Here is/There is the house
Дом **вон** там	The house is over yonder

(2) To **define or make more precise**:

Почему́ **и́менно** он протесту́ет?	Why **exactly** is he protesting?
Ро́вно в час	**Exactly** at one
Э́ти боти́нки ему́ **как раз** впо́ру	These shoes are **exactly** the right size for him

(3) To **express approximation**:

Я **почти́** гото́в	I am **almost** ready

Он **едва́ не** помеша́лся   He **almost** went out of his mind
Она́ **чуть не** умерла́ с го́ря She **very nearly** died of grief

Note
Чуть не/едва́ не combine mainly with verbs.

(4) To **restrict or exclude**:

То́лько о́н смо́жет реши́ть э́ту пробле́му
Only he will be able to solve this problem

Note
(a) **То́лько** immediately precedes the word it qualifies: Он смо́жет реши́ть **то́лько** э́ту пробле́му 'He will be able to solve only **this** problem'.
(b) It may also be used idiomatically: А он **то́лько** зна́ет, что посме́ивается 'All he can do is keep sniggering'.

472 Modal functions of particles

Particles also fulfil modal functions:

(1) **Desirability**:

Отдохну́ть **бы**!	**Oh for** a rest!
Лишь бы побо́льше вре́мени	**If only** there were more time

(2) **Command or exhortation**:

Дава́й остано́вимся!	**Let's** make a halt!

(3) **Confirmation**:

— Ты лю́бишь о́перу?	'Do you like opera?'
— **Ещё бы**!	'I'll say!'

(4) **Negation**:

Нет, он **не** чита́ет кни́гу	**No**, he is **not** reading the book
Нет **ни** мину́ты вре́мени	There's **not** a spare moment

Note
(a) The particle **не** 'not' *precedes* the word it qualifies, thus:

Не óн читáет кни́гу
He is not the one who is reading a book

Не кни́гу он читáет
It's not a book he's reading

(b) If the negated form is *not* a verb, the negative/genitive rule does *not* apply: cf. Я не ви́жу столá 'I don't see a table' and Не стóл я ви́жу 'It's not a table I see'. The negated word in such constructions (here, **стол**) bears the logical stress and is pronounced with rising intonation.

(c) 'Yes' is rendered as **нет** in a positive answer to a negative question: Вы не лю́бите кóшек? **Нет**, люблю́! 'Don't you like cats?' 'Yes, I do!'

(5) **Interrogative**:

Давнó ли он ýмер?	Is it **long** since he died?
Не óн ли опоздáл?	Wasn't it **he** who was late?
Мнóго ли там бы́ло нарóду?	Were there a **lot** of people there?
Рáзве вы не знáете?	**Surely** you know?
Неужéли он прав?	**Surely** he can't be right?

Note

(a) **Ли** follows the emphasized word, which bears the logical stress. This also applies in reported questions, where **ли** follows the 'operative' element:

Он спроси́л, **знáю ли я**	He asked if I knew
Я не пóмню, **хорóшая ли** э́то кни́га	I don't remember if that is a good book

(b) **Ли** may also express uncertainty (Не оши́бся ли он? 'Could he have made a mistake?') and may appear in rhetorical questions (Не сты́дно ли тебé? 'Aren't you ashamed of yourself?').

(c) If **ли** is omitted from a question, the word order is *not* inverted: 'Is he working?' is rendered either as Рабóтает ли он? or Он рабóтает? (no inversion, and with rising intonation on the stressed syllable).

(d) Both **рáзве** and **неужéли** 'really/surely not' imply doubt in the reliability of a statement, or a conviction that the opposite is true. **Неужéли** is much more emphatic than **рáзве**, and is commoner in spoken Russian. **Рáзве** can also denote hesitancy: **Рáзве** в кинó сходи́ть? '**I wonder if** I should go to the cinema?'

(6) **Direct speech**: the particles **де/дѐскать/мол** indicate that direct speech is being quoted:

Пётр снисходи́тельно пожа́л плеча́ми: чего́, **мол**, моро́чить го́лову (Abramov)
Peter shrugged his shoulders in a condescending way, **as if to say**, 'Pull the other one'

(7) **Probability or improbability**:

Ты, **пожа́луй**, прав	You **may well** be right
Вря́д ли он придёт	He's **hardly likely** to come
Едва́ ли мо́жно согласи́ться с ним	One can **hardly** agree with him

(8) **Comparison or similarity**: **бу́дто/как бу́дто/как бы/сло́вно** are used to compare similar events, actions etc.:

Мо́жет быть, пыль пусти́л в глаза́? — Нет, **как бу́дто** и взапра́вду уе́хал (Azhaev)
Maybe he was having us on? No, he **really does seem** to have gone

(9) **Emotional nuances**: **пря́мо, то́-то, так, уж** render emotional and expressive nuances (enthusiasm, resignation, determination, irony etc.):

Пря́мо стра́шно!	Simply terrifying!
То́-то бы́ли ра́дости!	We were **over the moon**!
Е́хать **так** е́хать!	If we're going, **let's** go!
То́же геро́й соцтруда́!	**Some** hero of socialist labour!
Вот они́, рабо́тнички!	**Some** workers!

473 The meanings of individual particles

While some particles convey one meaning only, others are poly-semantic.

(1) **А**

А is used:

(i) In prompting an answer:

Я́блоко дать, **а**? I'll give you an apple, **shall I?**

(ii) In making a request:

Помоги́ мне немно́жко, **а**? Give us a hand, **would you?**

(iii) In stating the apparently obvious:

— Что же мне тепе́рь де́лать?	Whatever should I do now?
— **А** о́чень про́сто	**Why**, it's very simple

(iv) In a conversational exchange:

— Ми́тю мо́жно?	'Can I speak to Mitya?'
— **А** он на рабо́те	**'I'm afraid** he's at work'
— **А** когда́ он бу́дет?	**'And** when will he be in?'
— **А** кто его́ спра́шивает?	**'Now**, who is this asking for him?'

(2) Бы́ло

Бы́ло is used to denote:

(i) The immediate cancellation or reversal of an action:

Пёс по́днял **бы́ло** го́лову и сно́ва опусти́л (Abramov)
The hound raised its head and lowered it again

(ii) The reversal or abandonment, often through interruption, of an action or process which has just begun:

«Ско́рая по́мощь» тро́нулась **бы́ло** вперёд, но вахтёр вдруг суетли́во замаха́л шофёру, и маши́на останови́лась (Tendryakov)
The ambulance **had begun** to move off, but the porter suddenly began waving to the driver in agitation and the vehicle stopped

(iii) The abandonment of a projected action:

Он по́днял **бы́ло** стака́н, но разду́мал
He **was about** to pick up the glass, but changed his mind

Note
(a) The verb in such constructions is almost invariably perfective. The only imperfective forms commonly found are собира́ться and хоте́ть, which are followed by a *perfective* infinitive: Он собира́лся/хоте́л **бы́ло попроси́ть** разреше́ния вы́йти, но испуга́лся 'He was **on the point** of asking permission to go out, but took fright'.

(b) **Было** also combines with perfective participles and gerunds:

У Тихоокеа́нского побере́жья вновь наблюда́ют **исчез-**
нувших бы́ло се́рых кито́в (*Selskaya zhizn*)
Grey whales, which **had been on the verge of extinction**, are
again being sighted off the Pacific coast

Останови́вшись бы́ло у перекрёстка, шофёр всё-таки
пое́хал на кра́сный свет
Having been on the point of stopping at the crossroads, the
driver jumped the lights instead

(3) Ведь

Ведь is used:

(i) To explain or justify:

Коне́чно, уме́ю стреля́ть из винто́вки, служи́л **ведь** в
а́рмии
Of course I can fire a rifle, **after all** I did do my army service

(ii) To prompt a desired answer:

Ведь ты пойдёшь в магази́н?
Now you are going to the shop, **aren't you**?

(iii) To issue a gentle reminder:

Ты **ведь** обеща́л   You did promise, **you know**

(iv) To administer a mild reproof:

Ведь я проси́ла тебя́ не   **Now** I did ask you to be quiet
шуме́ть

(4) Вот

See also **471** (1). **Вот** can be used:

(i) In combination with interrogative words:

Вот где я живу́   **That's** where I live
Вот почему́ он ушёл   **That's** why he left

(ii) For contrast:

С Ва́ней я дружу́, а **вот** с Ни́ной ника́к не ла́жу
I'm friends with Vanya, but I **just** can't get on with Nina

(iii) In warnings:

Вот всем расскажу́ об э́том
Now I'm going to tell everyone about this

(iv) In expressing feelings such as amazement, indignation etc.:

Вот дура́к!   **What** an idiot!

(5) Да

Да is used:

(i) In self-exoneration:

Да я молчу́!   **But** I am being quiet!

(ii) In consolation:

Да ты не расстра́ивайся!   **Now** don't upset yourself!

(iii) In indefinite answers:

Да я не зна́ю!   **Oh**, I don't know!

(6) Ещё

Ещё is used to express:

(i) Outrage or indignation:

Ещё учёным называ́ется!   And he calls himself a **scholar**!

(ii) Emphatic affirmation:

— Брат игра́ет в ша́хматы?   'Does your brother play chess?'
— **Ещё** как!   '**I'll say** he does!'

(iii) Emphatic denial:

— Вы го́лодны?   'Are you hungry?'
— **Ещё** чего́! Я то́лько что   '**Hungry!** I've only just had
позавтракала!   breakfast!'

(iv) A warning or threat:

Ещё уво́лят!   You'll get the sack (**if you don't
watch out**)!

(7) Же

(i) **Же** denotes categorical, insistent affirmation, often stressing the indisputability of a statement:

Ты **же** обещáл!   But you promised!

(ii) When qualifying interrogative words, **же** imparts a peremptory nuance, implying astonishment, indignation, disapproval etc.:

Кудá **же** ты идёшь?
Where do you think **you're** going?

Кто **же** так поступáет?
Now whoever behaves like **that**?

(iii) The particle can also specify precisely a place or time denoted by an adverb or adverbial phrase, e.g. здесь **же** 'at this very spot':

Приéду сегóдня **же**   I shall come **straightaway**
Там **же** живёт мой брат   **That's** where my brother lives

Тогдá **же** бы́ло произнесенó глáвное слóво совремéнной биолóгии — ген (*Russia Today*)
It was precisely at **that** point that the most important word in modern biology was uttered – gene

(iv) With demonstrative pronouns **же** conveys meanings of identity or similarity:

Мы идём по тóй **же** ýлице
We are walking down **the same** street

Он одéт в такóй **же** пиджáк
He is dressed in the **same kind of** jacket

(v) **Же** imparts an insistent or impatient nuance to imperatives:

Стой **же** спокóйно,   Now, **will** you stand still!
    наконéц!

(vi) The set phrase **нáдо же!** expresses extreme indignation:

— Э́то он так написáл?! — грóмко возмути́лась Попóва. — Нахалю́га! **Нáдо же!** ... Ну **нáдо же!** (Shukshin)
'He wrote that?!', shouted Popova indignantly. 'The impudent puppy! **What a nerve! What a confounded nerve!**'

(8) И

(i) **И** may lend emphasis to the word which *follows* it:

Я **и** стара́юсь! I **am** trying!

(ii) It can also mean 'even/also/too/as well':

Он говори́т **и** по-кита́йски He speaks Chinese **as well**

(iii) In negative statements it means 'either':

И я́ не зна́ю I don't know either

(9) -ка

(i) **-ка** may combine with the first-person perfective future of a verb to denote mild resolve:

Пойду́-**ка** домо́й **I think I might** go home

(ii) It softens the force of an imperative, expressing:

(a) Gentle exhortation:

Дай-**ка** спи́чки, Стас (Gagarin)
'**Do** give me the matches, Stas'

(b) Feelings of admiration, scorn etc.:

Смотри́-**ка**, каки́е кни́жки он чита́ет!
Just look what books he is reading!

(iii) Alternatively, it may contain a note of indignant challenge:

Посто́й-**ка** под холо́дным ду́шем!
Just you try standing under a cold shower!

(10) Ну

Ну is used:

(i) In exclamations:

Ну, уста́л! **Am I** tired!
Ну и **ну**! **Well, well!**

(ii) In emphasis:

Ну, моро́з! **Quite** a frost!

Note

Sometimes there is an element of sarcasm:

Ну, герóй!   **Some** hero!

(iii) With the perfective future to denote grudging consent:

Ну пойдём, éсли ты так хóчешь!
All right, let's go, if you are so keen!

(iv) To express impatience:

Ну, хвáтит!   That's enough of **that!**

(v) To express a peremptory imperative:

Ну, говорú!   **All right**, out with it!

(11) -то

(i) **-то** may be used to express diffidence, a reluctance to be categorical:

— Тут у вас вы́пить-**то** мóжно?
'Are you allowed to have a **drink** here?'
— Вообщé-**то** не полóжено
'**Actually** it's not normally allowed'

(ii) It is frequently used to refer to something already mentioned:

— Я вчерá и в магазúне-**то** нé был . . . (Shukshin)
'Yesterday I wasn't even **in** the shop . . .'

(iii) It may be the equivalent of English 'I mean':

— Он что, зарегистрúрован как алкогóлик? Королёв-**то**?
(Shukshin)
'Is he registered as an alcoholic? Korolev, **I mean?**'

(iv) Emphatic use is common with adverbs:

Тепéрь-то я пóнял, чтó его беспокóит
It was now that I realized what was bothering him

Сáмое стрáшное — плаву́чие мúны. **Потому́-то** кру́глые
су́тки несу́т вáхту вперёдсмотря́щие (Gagarin)
The most terrible things are mines. **That's why** the look-outs are
on 24-hour watch

(v) The particle may also be used to strengthen a negative:

Это не так-**то** про́сто   It's not so simple **at that**

(12) Уж

Уж emphasizes the main emotive content of a statement, ranging from:

(i) Confident assertion:

Уж мно́го лет в э́тих края́х нет ди́ких оле́ней (Astafev)
Now there haven't been any wild deer in these parts for many years

(ii) Resigned acceptance of the inevitable:

— Да **уж** пусть себе́   '**Oh** let them play'
игра́ют

(iii) Reassurance:

Не беспоко́йтесь, **уж** я не   Don't worry, I won't forget!
забу́ду!

(iv) Condescension:

Уж приду́мал!   That's a tall story!

(13) Хоть

Хоть can denote:

(i) A minimum requirement or expectation:
Хоть причеши́сь!   **At least** comb your hair!

(ii) An exemplary meaning:

Взять **хоть** тебя́; ты ведь ни ра́зу не пожа́ловался
Take you, **for example**; now you haven't once complained

(iii) A readiness to oblige, or to indulge a whim:

Пое́дем **хоть** за́втра!   Let's go tomorrow, **for all I
                                    care!**

(iv) Intensity or extreme manifestation (with imperatives):

Рабо́ты у него́ **хоть**   He's **up to his eyes** in work!
отбавля́й!

(14) Что

(i) In questions, **что** often emphasizes the preceding noun or pronoun:

А я́ **что**, возража́ю? — I'm not objecting, **am I**?
Ты **что**, с ума́ сошла́? — Are you mad, **or what**?

(ii) The phrase (**ну**) **что́** вы! denotes energetic denial:

Ну **что́** вы! Я вполне́ здоро́ва! — Now **come off it**! I'm perfectly fit!

474 The aggregation of particles for increased emphasis

(1) Particles may be aggregated to heighten emphasis:

(i) **А ведь/да ведь/но ведь**:

А ведь Алекса́ндр счита́лся одни́м из сильне́йших игроко́в (*Russia Today*)
And yet, you know, Aleksandr was considered to be one of the very best players

(ii) **А ещё**:

Сам не учи́лся, **а ещё** специали́стов критику́ет!
He hasn't studied himself, **yet has the nerve** to criticize the experts!

(iii) **Бы уж**:

— О го́споди, — перекрести́лась ба́ба, — молча́л **бы уж** (Belov)
'Oh, my God', the woman said, crossing herself, 'you **really ought to have** kept your mouth shut'

(iv) **Вот ещё/вот уж**:

— На́до бы его́ разыска́ть — сказа́л Пётр.
— **Вот ещё**. — нахму́рилась Ле́ля. — Бо́льше тебе́ де́лать не́чего? (Uvarova)
'I suppose we ought to go looking for him', said Peter.
'**Come off it**', said Lelya with a frown. 'Have you nothing better to do with your time?'

Вот уж не зна́ю.
I haven't the **foggiest**

(v) **Да и/да уж:**

А костёр горе́л-горе́л **да и** спали́л 1 700 гекта́ров ле́са (*Russia Today*)
And the bonfire burnt on and on and **went and** destroyed 1,700 hectares of woodland

Да уж и сама́-**то** хороша́! (Shcherbakov)
She's a fine one to talk!

(vi) **Ещё бы/ещё как:**

Ве́село на душе́! **Ещё бы:** сбыла́сь мечта́ (Sobolev)
I'm overjoyed! **You bet**, my dream has come true

Согласи́тся? **Ещё как** согласи́тся!
Will he agree? **I'll say he will!**

(vii) **Как э́то:**

Оби́дится? **Как э́то** оби́дится!
Take offence? **Not a chance!**

(viii) **Не то чтобы уж:**

А Кла́вдия была́ **не то чтобы уж** краса́вица ... (Shcherbakov)
And Claudia was **not exactly** what you might call a raving beauty ...

(ix) **Ну и; ну уж; ну уж и; ну-ка; ну что ж:**

Ну и ба́ба! — бормота́л он (Grekova)
'**What a** woman!', he murmured

Ну уж не серди́сь, я не хоте́ла тебя́ оби́деть
Come on, don't get angry, I didn't mean to offend you

Ну уж и приду́мал!
That's a tall story **if you like!**

Ну-ка, попро́буй мою́ похо́дку, — сказа́л Кондра́т (Shukshin)
'**Go on then**, do my walk', said Kondrat

Пра́вда, не стал ни поэ́том, ни певцо́м ... **Ну что ж**, не всем быть поэ́тами! (Kazakov)
It's true I became neither a poet nor a singer ... **Oh well**, not everybody can be a poet!

(x) **Так и; так уж**:

Я так и не по́нял   I **simply didn't** understand

Не бу́ду я **так уж** расхва́ливать э́ти фи́льмы (*Russia Today*)
I'm not **exactly** going to give these films rave notices

(xi) **Хоть бы/хотя́ бы/лишь бы**:

Хоть бы кто́-нибудь ми́мо прошёл ... (Gagarin)
If only someone passed this way ...

Она́ ра́да была́ бы любо́му попу́тчику, **хотя́ бы** те́хнику Мише́лю (Zalygin)
She would have been glad of any travelling companion, **even if** it was only the technician Michel

(xii) **Что же, что ж**:

Что же ты не целу́ешь меня́? — сла́бо шёпчет она́ (Kazakov)
'**Why ever** don't you kiss me?', she whispers faintly

(2) Particles may appear separately, at different points in the statement:

(i) **Ведь ... же**:

Знамени́тые спортсме́ны: боксёр Генна́дий Шатко́в, конькобе́жец Бори́с Сте́нин — кандида́ты нау́к. Но **ведь** э́то **же** едини́цы. Исключе́ние (*Russia Today*)
There are famous sportsmen who have doctorates: the boxer Gennady Shatkov, the skater Boris Stenin. **But you know**, these are isolated exceptions

(ii) **Ведь ... -то**:

Опозда́ем **ведь** на по́езд-**то**
You know, we're **going to go and** miss that train

(iii) **Ну ... же**:

Ну, ну, — серди́то доба́вил он. — **Я же** сказа́л, что иду́ (Proskurin)
'**All right**', he added angrily, 'I said I was coming, **didn't I?**'

— **Ну**, обними́тесь-**же**
– **Come on then**, give each other a hug

(iv) **Уж ... -то**:

Уйдёт. **Уж о́н-то** её зна́ет! (Koluntsev)
He'll leave. **After all**, he knows her **if anyone does**!

(3) Feelings such as indignation can generate whole strings of particles:

Ну да ведь и дура́к **же** он!
Well, really, you know, the man is a complete idiot!

(4) The phrase **куда́ там** can appear either with or without **уж**:

Про́бовали её учи́ть программи́рованию — **куда́ там**. Си́нус пу́тала с интегра́лом (Grekova)
They tried to teach her programming. **Some hope**. She confused sines with integrals

— Тепе́рь таки́х мужико́в и нет, как мой стари́к, — говори́т стару́ха.
— **Куда́ уж там**! (Rasputin)
'They don't make them like my old man any more', says the old woman.
'**No way!**'

Word Order

Introductory comments

(1) The inflected nature of Russian allows greater flexibility of word order than is possible in English, where only rigid order of words differentiates the meaning of sentences such as 'Ivan loves Masha' and 'Masha loves Ivan'.

(2) In Russian, by contrast, inflexional endings indicate the functions of words irrespective of their position in the sentence. Thus, the feminine noun accusative ending -y in **Ма́шу** identifies Masha as the object of the verb both in Ива́н лю́бит **Ма́шу** 'Ivan loves Masha' and **Ма́шу** лю́бит Ива́н 'It is Ivan who loves Masha', the difference between the two sentences being one of emphasis rather than meaning.

(3) Word order in Russian, though flexible, is by no means arbitrary, however; any disruption of the accepted or 'neutral' order throws the displaced elements into sharp relief.

(4) Questions of word order are ideally considered within the wider context of a narrative, since the order of elements in a sentence is often determined by what has gone before (see **476**) (3) (ii)).

476 'New' and 'given' information

(1) 'New' information

Each statement contains *new* information. Except in emotionally charged language, where different criteria apply (see **484**), this *new* information appears at or towards the *end* of a statement in Russian, in contrast with English, where it usually appears at or near the *beginning*. Thus, in the sentence

В Жене́ве состоя́лся   A festival took place in Geneva
фестива́ль

the festival (**фестива́ль**), as the nucleus of the new information, occupies the *final* position, while the verb **состоя́лся** 'took place' is also new but of secondary significance. **В Жене́ве** 'in Geneva', as incidental or '*given*' information (see (2)), appears in *initial* position.

Note
(a) The reverse order: **Фестива́ль состоя́лся в Жене́ве** answers the question **Где** состоя́лся фестива́ль? 'Where did the festival take place?' and can be rendered as 'The festival took place in Geneva'.
(b) In English, nouns which are the subject of *new* information are usually preceded by '*a*': 'There is **a** dog in the garden' (В саду́ есть **соба́ка**). Nouns which are the subject of *given* information are usually preceded by '*the*': '**The** dog is in the garden' (**Соба́ка** в саду́).

(2) 'Given' information

Most statements contain an item or items of '*given*' information, that is, information which is either known or presumed to be known to the reader, has been mentioned before, can be assumed from the context, or is entirely incidental to the event being described. *Given* information is never the point of the utterance. It is often circumstantial, taking the form of an adverb of time, place or manner:

Здесь удо́бно   It's comfortable **here**

5 октября́ в Жене́ве в непринуждённой обстано́вке
начали́сь перегово́ры по разоруже́нию
Disarmament talks began **in a relaxed atmosphere in Geneva
on 5 October**

(3) 'Given' and 'new' information

(i) The order 'given' information + 'new' information (with less essential preceding essential new items) is standard in a Russian sentence:

От рефóрмы цен никтó не пострадáет (*Ogonek*)
No one will suffer from the price reform

In this example, price reform (**рефóрма цен**), as a matter of common knowledge ('*given*' information), occupies initial position, while **никтó не пострадáет** 'no one will suffer' is *new* information and appears in final position.

(ii) An utterance must be considered within its overall context. Thus, in the following extracts, the *new* information at the end of each successive sentence becomes the *given* information at the start of the next:

В то врéмя я жил в мáленьком сéверном **гóроде. Гóрод** стоя́л на берегу́ **реки́. По рекé** плы́ли бéлые парохóды (Kazakov)
At that time I lived in **a** small northern **town. The town** stood on the bank of **a river.** Down **the river** sailed white steamers

На плóщади вòзле решётки стоя́т **столбы́. К столбáм** прикреплены́ желéзные **табли́чки.** Вòзле э́тих **табли́чек** останáвливаются автóбусы (Soloukhin)
On the square close to the railing stand **pillars. To these pillars** are attached iron **plaques.** Buses stop close to **these plaques**

Note
The principle that 'given' information precedes 'new' allows the differentiation of ostensibly synonymous statements such as На столé **вáза** 'There is **a vase** on the table' (answering the question **Что** на столé? 'What is on the table?') and Вáза **на столé** 'The vase is **on the table**' (answering the question **Где** вáза? 'Where is the vase?').

(iii) Sometimes the relative status of items is implied by context. Thus, in

Я включи́л рáдио и услы́шал **знакóмую баллáду. Пéла** Áлла Пугачёва
I switched on the radio and heard a **well-known ballad. It was being sung** by Alla Pugacheva

the reference in the first sentence to a well-known ballad (*new* information) determines the status of **пе́ла** 'it was being sung' as *given* information at the start of the second. **А́лла Пугачёва**, as new information, appears in *final* position, since the point of the statement is to establish, not that someone was singing a ballad (that is known from the first sentence), but *who* was singing it.

477 Relative position of subject and verb

The order of the items in an utterance containing a subject and a verb depends on which is *new* information and which is *given*.

(1) Subject + verb

In the following example the subject (**оте́ц**) represents *given* information and precedes the verb (**у́мер**), which reports *new* information:

Оте́ц у́мер   Father has died

(2) Verb + subject

The reverse order (verb + subject) is found in the following contexts; in each of them the *new* information is represented by the *noun*, which accordingly occupies *final* position:

(i) Impersonal statements, statements about the weather etc.:

Идёт дождь   It is raining
Дул све́жий ве́тер   A fresh breeze was blowing

(ii) Statements in which the verb denotes existence, non-existence, coming into existence, beginning, continuing, finishing etc.:

Наступи́ла о́сень   Autumn arrived
Идёт фильм   A film is on

Прохо́дит день, **начина́ется** друго́й — ни зву́ка (*Literaturnaya gazeta*)
One day passes, another dawns; not a sound is heard

(iii) Statements in which the verb denotes occurrence, state, process etc.:

Произошёл несча́стный слу́чай	An accident happened
Родила́сь дочь	They have had a daughter
У меня́ боли́т го́рло	I have a sore throat
Зазвони́л телефо́н	The phone began to ring

(iv) Constructions which involve the quotation of direct speech:

— Кто така́я? — **спроси́л он** вполго́лоса (Grekova)
'Who is she?', he asked *sotto voce*

Note
This also applies to statements which indicate a **source of information**: Как **сообща́ет ТАСС**... 'As **TASS reports**...'.

(v) Questions introduced by an interrogative word:

Где **живёт ва́ша дочь**?	Where does your daughter live?
Когда́ **открыва́ется магази́н**?	When does the shop open?

Note
(a) The order interrogative word + subject + predicate is compulsory with a *pronoun* subject (Почему́ **он пришёл**? 'Why has he come?'), but optional with a *noun* subject (Куда́ **лети́т самолёт**/Куда́ **самолёт** лети́т? 'Where is the aircraft flying to?').

(b) Questions which are *not* introduced by an interrogative word have the same order as a direct statement. Compare Она́ передала́ вам письмо́ '**She passed** the letter to you' and Она́ передала́ вам письмо́? '**Did she pass** the letter to you?' Alternatively, **ли** may appear as second element after the operative word (or words) in the question: Передала́ **ли** она́ вам письмо́? 'Did she pass the letter to you?' Compare **Она́** ли вам передала́ письмо́? 'Was it **she** who passed the letter to you?', **Письмо́** ли она́ вам передала́? 'Was it a **letter** she passed to you?' The order operative word + ли is also used in reported questions: Он спроси́л, **передала́** ли она́ вам письмо́ 'He asked if she had passed the letter to you'.

478 Subject, verb, object

(1) Subject + verb + object

The order subject + verb + object is encountered in the vast majority of sentences which contain these three elements:

Пётр купи́л кни́гу   Peter has bought a book

Note

(a) A *pronoun* object may precede (or follow) the verb: — **Я вас** не понима́ю, това́рищ генера́л (Grekova) 'I don't understand you, comrade general'; Он **ничего́** не ест 'He isn't eating anything'.

(b) The order *subject + object noun + verb* places unusual emphasis on the verb (or object noun): Пётр Ната́шу **уважа́ет** 'Peter **respects** Natasha' (even though he may not, for example, **like** her); Мы **дом** купи́ли 'We have bought a house'. This order is found predominantly in spoken Russian.

(c) The order *subject + verb + object* is virtually mandatory when the accusative case of subject noun and object noun is the same as the nominative, since a reversal of the order would change the meaning, cf. Кли́мат меня́ет расти́тельность 'The climate alters vegetation' and Расти́тельность меня́ет кли́мат 'Vegetation alters the climate', Мать лю́бит дочь 'The mother loves her daughter' and Дочь лю́бит мать 'The daughter loves her mother'.

(2) Object + verb + subject:

(i) The order object + verb + subject

Кни́гу купи́л Пётр

in which the subject (**Пётр**) is central to the *new* information, is rendered in English by a passive construction ('The book **was bought** by Peter') or by a construction introduced by 'It is . . .' ('**It is Peter** (and not someone else) who bought the book').

(ii) This order is also common:

(a) With an **inanimate** subject:

Меня́ разбуди́ла **гроза́**
I was awakened by a thunderstorm

А́нну Каре́нину задави́л **по́езд**
Anna Karenina was crushed by a train

(b) In sentences which contain set phrases in which the noun component is **qualified**:

Большо́е значе́ние име́ет уче́бный проце́сс
The teaching process is of great significance

Суще́ственную роль игра́л комсомо́л
A significant role was played by the Komsomol

(c) In impersonal constructions involving the third-person plural: О́вощи уже́ **выгружа́ют** 'The vegetables are already being unloaded', Вас **про́сят** к телефо́ну 'You are wanted on the phone', Её **зову́т** Ната́лья 'She is called Natalya'.

(3) Object + subject + verb

Other variants in word order depend on the relative weighting of elements in a particular context. Thus, in the example

Э́ту рабо́ту Генера́льный секрета́рь хорошо́ понима́л (*Literaturnaya gazeta*)
This was work the General Secretary understood well

the *subject* (Генера́льный секрета́рь) and *object* (э́ту рабо́ту) are *given* information, while *adverb + verb* (хорошо́ понима́л) are *new* information and appear in final position.

479 The position of the adjective

(1) The long (attributive) adjective

(i) An attributive adjective normally precedes the noun it qualifies:

И вот — оди́н из **со́лнечных ию́ньских дней** (Tokareva)
And now it was one of those sunny June days

Note
(a) See **484** (1) for stylistic variants.
(b) The attributive adjective may follow the noun in menus, stock

lists etc. (ко́фе натура́льный 'real coffee', рома́шка садо́вая 'garden camomile') and where the noun is generic (Еле́на — де́вушка у́мная 'Elena is an intelligent girl').

(c) The long adjective follows the noun when used in **predicative** meaning: Он о́чень **молодо́й** (or мо́лод) 'he is very young'.

(ii) Contrary to English practice, circumstantial information may be placed in parenthesis between the attributive adjective and the noun:

> Они́ жи́ли в большо́м, **с тремя́ этажа́ми и со мно́гими о́кнами**, особняке́
> They lived in a large detached house **with three floors and many windows**

(iii) As in English, the adjective may follow the noun, standing in apposition to it and separated from it by a comma:

> На на́рах лежа́л полушу́бок, **но́венький**, о́чень **наря́дный** (Bogomolov)
> On the bunk lay a sheepskin coat, brand-new, very smart

(2) The short adjective

A short adjective normally follows the noun, as its predicate.

Note

See **484** (1) (i) for stylistic variants and **359** (3) (ii) note (a) for the position of short-form perfective passive participles.

480 The position of the adverb

As a class which tends to convey *less essential* rather than *new* information, adverbs more often than not *precede* the verb. The adverb is usually positioned next to the verb it qualifies; in other positions it is thrown into sharp relief, since it then normally conveys new, not given, information and moves towards the end of the statement.

(1) Adverbs and adverbial phrases of time

(i) Adverbs of time usually *precede* the verb:

Он **всегда́** ошиба́ется	He always gets it wrong
Он **ещё не** просну́лся	He has not woken up yet

Вы **до́лго** жда́ли? — спроси́л Криворучко (Rybakov)
'Did you have long to wait?', asked Krivoruchko

(ii) In descriptions of incidents and events, the adverb of time is usually in initial position, followed by verb + subject, which jointly convey the *new* information:

Вдруг разда́лся вы́стрел (Rybakov)
Suddenly a shot rang out

(iii) However, adverbs and adverbial phrases that convey essential *new* information appear in *final* position: e.g. the question **Когда́** экипа́жи соверши́ли пе́рвый совме́стный полёт? '**When** did the crews make the first joint flight?' can be answered as follows:

Экипа́жи соверши́ли пе́рвый совме́стный полёт **в ию́ле 1975 го́да**
The crews carried out the first joint flight in July 1975

(2) Adverbs and adverbial phrases of place

(i) Adverbs and adverbial phrases of place also normally appear in initial position as incidental or *given* information, preceding the *new* information conveyed either by the subject alone or by the verb + subject:

В го́роде два теа́тра
There are two theatres **in the town**

Из служе́бного зда́ния вы́шел высо́кий вя́лый челове́к (Grekova)
A tall sluggish-looking man left **the service building**

(ii) However, adverbs of place that report *new* information appear in *final* position: e.g. the question **Где** располо́жена Кра́сная пло́щадь? 'Where is Red Square situated?' can be answered as follows:

Кра́сная пло́щадь располо́жена **в це́нтре Москвы́**
Red Square is situated in the centre of Moscow

(3) Adverbs and adverbial phrases of manner and degree

(i) Adverbs of manner and degree in **-o/-e** usually precede the verb or adjective:

Он **хорошо́** говори́т
He speaks well

— А вы отку́да? — **дружелю́бно** спроси́л Тёткин
(Grekova)
'And where are you from?', asked Tetkin amicably

Она́ **и́скренне** ра́да нам
She is sincerely glad to see us

Compare also adverbs of the type по-дру́жески: Он **по-дру́жески** пожа́л мне ру́ку 'He shook my hand in a friendly manner'. However, adverbs of nationality and language normally *follow* the verb: Он понима́ет **по-ру́сски** 'He understands Russian'.

(ii) A number of other adverbs of manner and degree, e.g. **во́все не** 'not at all', **едва́** 'barely', and analogous prepositional phrases also precede the verb, cf.:

Она́ **в спе́шке** забы́ла подня́ть кни́гу
In her hurry she forgot to pick up the book

481 Sentences that contain more than one adverb or adverbial phrase

The normal sequence for different types of adverb and adverbial phrase appearing within the same sentence is as follows:

1 adverbs/adverbial phrases of *time*
2 adverbs/adverbial phrases of *place*
3 other types of adverb/adverbial phrase (*manner*, *cause* etc.):

Среди́ но́чи к пере́днему кра́ю оборо́ны тайко́м под-кра́лся солда́т-разве́дчик
In the middle of the night a reconnaissance scout stealthily crept up to the front line

Ка́ждый час в на́шей стране́ от боле́зни се́рдца умира́ет 80 челове́к (*Ogonek*)
Every hour 80 people in our country die of heart disease

Неда́вно в Москве́ проводи́лся кинофестива́ль
A film festival was held recently in Moscow

В СССР бы́стро вы́росли города́ и сёла
Towns and villages sprang up quickly in the USSR

482 The position of the noun or pronoun in impersonal constructions

The accusative or dative noun or pronoun normally occupies initial position in impersonal expressions, with *new* information in final position:

Брáта лихорáдит	My brother is feverish
Дом зажглó	The house caught fire
Тáнюшке вóсемь лет	Tanyushka is eight years old
Мне хóлодно	I feel cold
Ей пришлóсь бежáть	She had to run
Нам нельзя́ бы́ло кури́ть	We were not allowed to smoke

Note

The same order applies to constructions with **нрáвиться/по-** and with **нýжен, нужнá, нýжно, нужны́**: Взрóслым понрáвился фильм 'The adults liked the film', Студéнту нужны́ дéньги 'The student needs money'. Reversal of this order throws the noun or pronoun into sharp relief: Фильм понрáвился **взрóслым**(, **но не дéтям**) 'The **adults** liked the film (, but the **children** didn't)'; Дéньги нужны́ **мне (а не ей)** 'I need the money (and she **doesn't**)'.

483 The position of particles in the sentence

For the position of particles see **469**.

484 Word order in expressive styles

A departure from neutral word order may create an expressive, emotionally charged style which is particularly characteristic of *spoken* Russian. Most parts of speech are involved:

(1) Adjectives

(i) In expressive styles short predicative adjectives may *precede* the noun, while in neutral style they *follow* the noun:

Лёгок вопро́с, **незначи́тельна** фигу́ра студе́нта (Rybakov)
The question is simple, the figure of the student insignificant (cf. neutral word order Вопро́с лёгок, фигу́ра студе́нта незначи́тельна)

(ii) This also applies to short-form participles:

Решён вопро́с о вы́ходе диспе́тчеров на пе́нсию в во́зрасте 55 лет (*Literaturnaya gazeta*)
The question of retirement for air traffic controllers at age 55 has been resolved (cf. neutral order вопро́с решён)

(iii) Conversely, attributive adjectives may *follow* the noun in expressive styles, whereas in neutral style they precede it:

Техни́ческое оснаще́ние, коне́чно, де́ло **ва́жное** (*Literaturnaya gazeta*)
Technical equipment is, of course, an important matter (cf. neutral word order ва́жное де́ло)

Compare also displacement of the adjective in:

— Да, **комфорта́бельной** э́ту маши́ну не назовёшь (Grekova)
'No, you wouldn't exactly call this vehicle comfortable'

(iv) Another expressive device is to place the verb between the attributive adjective and the noun:

Уда́чная была́ охо́та!   That **was** a successful hunt!

(2) Verb + subject

In expressive styles, *new* information may precede *given*, a reversal of neutral order:

У меня́ **голова́ боли́т**
I have a headache (cf. neutral У меня́ боли́т голова́)

Кто звони́л? **Мари́на звони́ла**
Who rang? Marina rang (cf. neutral Звони́ла Мари́на)

(3) Adverbs

(i) The order of adverbs/adverbial phrases may be reversed in expressive styles:

Хо́лодно сего́дня
It is cold today (cf. neutral Сего́дня хо́лодно)

Стально́й зуб сверка́л у него́ во рту (Rybakov)
A steel tooth glittered in his mouth (cf. neutral У него́ во рту
сверка́л стально́й зуб)

(ii) Compare also the displacement of adverbs in their function as
introductory words:

Смотре́ть э́тот фильм **стра́шно и сты́дно** (*Ekran detyam*)
It is terrible and embarrassing to see this film (cf. neutral
Стра́шно и сты́дно смотре́ть э́тот фильм)

(4) Pronouns

The pronoun may *follow* the predicate in expressive styles, often
with a concomitant change of emphasis:

— Хоро́шая пе́сня, — сказа́л Марк.
— То́лько **поёте вы́** её пло́хо, заме́тила Со́фья Алекса́н-
дровна (Rybakov)
'Nice song', said Mark.
'Except that **you** don't sing it very well', remarked Sofia Alek-
sandrovna (cf. neutral вы пло́хо её поёте)

Что сде́лал **ты́**?
What did **you** do? (cf. neutral Что ты сде́лал?)

Bibliography

Dictionaries

Russian Monolingual

Chernyshev, V. I. et al. (eds), *Словарь современного русского языка*, 17 vols, Академия наук, Moscow, 1950–65.

Evgén'eva, A. P. et al. (eds), *Словарь русского языка*, 4 vols, 2nd edn, Русский язык, Moscow, 1983.

Ozhegov, S. I., *Словарь русского языка*, 18th edn, Русский язык, Moscow, 1987.

Russian–English

Wheeler, M., *The Oxford Russian–English Dictionary*, 2nd edn, The Clarendon Press, Oxford, 1986.

Special-purpose

Alekseev, D. I., Gozman, I. G. and Sakharov, G. V., *Словарь сокращений русского языка*, Русский язык, Moscow, 1977.

Avanesov, R. I. (ed), *Орфоэпический словарь русского языка*, 3rd edn, Русский язык, Moscow, 1987.

Efremov, T. F. and Kostomarov, V. G., *Словарь грамматических трудностей русского языка*, Русский язык, Moscow, 1986.

Filin, F. P., principal editor, *Русский язык. Энциклопедия*, Советская энциклопедия, Moscow, 1979.

Treshnikov, A. F., principal editor, *Географический энциклопедический словарь*, Советская энциклопедия, Moscow, 1983.

Zaliznyak, A. A., *Грамматический словарь русского языка*, Русский язык, Moscow, 1977.

Grammars

Grammars of the Academy of Sciences of the USSR

Shvedova, N. Yu. and Lopatin, V. V., *Краткая русская грамматика*, Русский язык, Moscow, 1989.

Shvedova, N. Yu. et al. (eds), *Русская грамматика*, 2 vols, Наука, Moscow, 1982.

Vinogradov, V. V., Istrina, E. S. and Barkhudarov, S. G. (eds), *Грамматика русского языка*, 2 vols in 3 books, Академия наук, Moscow, 1960.

Others

Bivon, R., *Advanced Russian Grammar*, University of East Anglia, Norwich, 1977.

Forbes, N., *Russian Grammar*, 3rd edn, revised and enlarged by J. C. Dumbreck, The Clarendon Press, Oxford, 1980.

Miloslavsky, I. G., *Краткая практическая грамматика русского языка*, Русский язык, Moscow, 1987.

Pulkina, I. M., *A Short Russian Reference Grammar*, Progress Publishers, Moscow, 1968.

Pulkina, I. M. and Zakhava-Nekrasova, E. B., *Учебник русского языка*, Высшая школа, Moscow, 1960.

Unbegaun, B. O., *Russian Grammar*, The Clarendon Press, Oxford, 1957.

Other books on language

Akishina, A. A. and Formanovskaya, N. I., *Русский речевой этикет*, Русский язык, Moscow, 1978.

Amiantova, E. I. et al., *Сборник упражнений по лексике русского языка*, Русский язык, Moscow, 1989.

Avanesov, R. I., *Modern Russian Stress*, Pergamon, Oxford, 1964.

Barykina, A. N., Dobrovol'skaya, V. V. and Merzon, S. N., *Изучение глагольных приставок*, Русский язык, Moscow, 1979.

Bel'dyushkin, V. S. et al., *Adverbial Relations in Russian and Their English Equivalents*, Русский язык, Moscow, 1988.

Bivon, R., *Element Order* (Studies in the Modern Russian Language 7), Cambridge University Press, Cambridge, 1971.

Borras, F. M. and Christian, R. F., *Russian Syntax*, 2nd edn, The Clarendon Press, Oxford, 1979.

Bratus, B. V., *The Formation and Expressive Use of Diminutives* (Studies in the Modern Russian Language 6), Cambridge University Press, Cambridge, 1969.

Comrie, B. and Stone, G., *The Russian Language Since the Revolution*, The Clarendon Press, Oxford, 1978.

Corbett, G. G., *Predicate Agreement in Russian* (Birmingham Slavonic Monographs 7), University of Birmingham, 1979.

Davidson, R. M., *The Use of the Genitive in Negative Constructions* (Studies in the Modern Russian Language 2, in one volume with I. P. Foote, *Verbs of Motion*), Cambridge University Press, Cambridge, 1967.

Foote, I. P., *Verbs of Motion* (Studies in the Modern Russian Language 1, in one volume with R. M. Davidson, *The Use of the Genitive in Negative Constructions*), Cambridge University Press, Cambridge, 1967.

Forsyth, J., *A Grammar of Aspect. Usage and Meaning in the Russian Verb*, Cambridge University Press, Cambridge, 1970.

Forsyth, J., *A Practical Guide to Russian Stress*, Oliver and Boyd, Edinburgh and London, 1963.

Gerhart, G., *The Russian's World*, Harcourt Brace Jovanovich, New York, 1974.

Gorbachevich, K. S., *Изменение норм русского литературного языка*, Просвещение, Leningrad, 1971.

Gorbachevich, K. S., *Нормы современного русского литературного языка*, Просвещение, Moscow, 1978.

Graudina, L. K., *Вопросы нормализации русского языка*, Наука, Moscow, 1980.

Graudina, L. K., Itskovich, V. A. and Katlinskaya, L. P., *Грамматическая правильность русской речи*, Наука, Moscow, 1976.

Harrison, W., *Expression of the Passive Voice* (Studies in the Modern Russian Language 4, in one volume with J. Mullen, *Agreement of the Verb-Predicate with a Collective Subject*), Cambridge University Press, Cambridge, 1967.

Henry, P., *Manual of Russian Prose Composition*, 2nd edn, University of London Press, London, 1979.

Kaidalova, A. I. and Kalinina, I. K., *Современная русская орфография*, Высшая школа, Moscow, 1983.

Klepko, V., *A Practical Handbook on Stress in Russian*, Dover Publications, New York, 1977.

Kokhtev, N. N. and Rozental', D. E., *Популярная стилистика русского языка*, Русский язык, Moscow, 1984.

Krylova, O. and Khavronina, S., *Word Order in Russian Sentences*, Русский язык, Moscow, 1976.

Krysina, L. P., *Русский язык по данным массового обследования*, Наука, Moscow, 1974.

Miloslavsky, I. G., *Зачем нужна грамматика?*, Просвещение, Moscow, 1988.

Mullen, J., *Agreement of the Verb-Predicate with a Collective Subject* (Studies in the Modern Russian Language 5, in one volume with W. Harrison, *Expression of the Passive Voice*), Cambridge University Press, Cambridge, 1967.

Murav'eva, L. S., *Verbs of Motion in Russian*, Русский язык, Moscow, 1975.

Murphy, A. B., *Aspectival Usage in Russian*, Pergamon, Oxford, 1965.

Panov, M. V. (ed.), *Русский язык и советское общество. Социолого-лингвистическое исследование* (monograph comprising four books), Наука, Moscow, 1968.

Rassudova, O. P., *Aspectual Usage in Modern Russian*, Русский язык, Moscow, 1984.

Ridout, R. and Witting, C., *The Facts of English*, Pan Books, London, 1973.

Rozental', D. E., *А как лучше сказать?*, Просвещение, Moscow, 1979.

Rozental', D. E., *Прописная или строчная?*, Русский язык, Moscow, 1984.

Rozental', D. E., *Управление в русском языке*, Книга, Moscow, 1986.

Shapiro, A. B., *Пунктуация*, 2nd edn, Просвещение, Moscow, 1974.

Shilova, K. A. and Usmanova, E. E., *100 диалогов по телефону*, Русский язык, Moscow, 1988.

Skvortsov, L. I. (principal editor), Itskovich, V. A. and Mis'kevich, G. I., *Грамматика и норма*, Наука, Moscow, 1977.

Vasilenko, E., Egorova, A. and Lamm, E., *Russian Verb Aspects*, Русский язык, Moscow, 1988.

Vasil'eva, A. N., *Particles in Colloquial Russian*, Progress Publishers, Moscow, undated.

Vinogradov, V. V., *Русский язык*, Высшая школа, Moscow, 1972.

Vsevolodova, M. V. and Parshukova, Z. G., *Способы выражения пространственных отношений*, МГУ, Moscow, 1968.

Vvedenskaya, L. A. and Kolesnikov, N. P., *От собственных имён к нарицательным*, Просвещение, Moscow, 1981.

Wade, T., *The Gender of Soft-Sign Nouns in Russian*, Collets International, London, 1988.

Wade, T., *Prepositions in Modern Russian*, Durham Modern Language Series, 1983.

Ward, D., *Russian Pronunciation*, Oliver and Boyd, Edinburgh and London, 1958.

Ward, D., *Russian Pronunciation Illustrated*, Cambridge University Press, Cambridge, 1966.

Ward, D., *The Russian Language Today. System and Anomaly*, Hutchinson, London, 1965.

Language journals

Russian-language

Русская речь, Moscow.
Русский язык за рубежом, Moscow.

English-language

Journal of Russian Studies.

Newspapers and magazines

За советскую науку
Известия
Комсомольская правда
Литературная газета
Неделя
Огонек
Правда
Работница
Сельская жизнь
Семья
Советская Россия
Советский экран
Спутник
Экран детям
Юный натуралист

Wade, T. and White, N., *Russia Today*, 2 vols and glossary, University of Strathclyde, Glasgow, 1985 (press extracts).

Literary and other sources

By individual or joint authors

Abramov, F., *Дом*, Советский писатель, Leningrad, 1980.
Aksenov, V., *Катапульта*, Советский писатель, Moscow, 1964.
Belyakova, E., *В семье растут дети*, Русский язык, Moscow, 1983.
Bogomolov, V., *Рассказы*, Художественная литература, Moscow, 1975.
Gagarin, S., *Возвращение в Итаку*, Молодая гвардия, Moscow, 1972.
Granin, D., *Сад камней*, Современник, Moscow, 1972.
Grekova, I., *Пороги*, Советский писатель, Moscow, 1986.
Kazakov, Yu., *Selected Short Stories*, Pergamon, Oxford, 1963.
Koluntsev, F., *Ожидание*, Советский писатель, Moscow, 1969.
Kovaleva, L., *Создана семья...*, Лениздат, Leningrad, 1982.

Nikolaev, V., *Не один в пути*, Молодая гвардия, Moscow, 1974.

Orlov, V., *Серый парус карбаса*, Знание, Moscow, 1984.

Propp, V., *Русская сказка*, Издательство Ленинградского университета, Leningrad, 1984.

Rasputin, V., *Деньги для Марии*, Молодая гвардия, Moscow, 1968.

Rasputin, V., *Последний срок. Прощание с Матерой*, Советский писатель, Moscow, 1985.

Rubina, D., '*Завтра, как обычно. . .*', Юность, July 1984, 26–47.

Rybakov, A., *Дети Арбата*, Советский писатель, Moscow, 1987.

Rybakov, A., *Тяжелый песок*, Советский писатель, Moscow, 1979.

Shukshin, V., *Рассказы*, Русский язык, Moscow, 1984.

Strugatsky, A. and Strugatsky, B., *Понедельник начинается в субботу*, Юнацва, Minsk, 1986.

Tendryakov, V., *Находка*, Советская Россия, Moscow, 1966.

Tendryakov, V., *Поденка — век короткий* (and other works), Молодая гвардия, Moscow, 1969.

Tokareva, V., *Повести и рассказы*, Советский писатель, Moscow, 1987.

Trifonov, Yu., *Избранные произведения*, 2 vols, Художественная литература, Moscow, 1978.

Trifonov, Yu., *Утоление жажды*, Профиздат, Moscow, 1979.

Zalygin, S., *Южноамериканский вариант*, Московский рабочий, Moscow, 1987.

Compilations

Lebedev, V. (compiler), *Стратегия освоения*, Молодая гвардия, Moscow, 1986.

Pecheritsa, T. (compiler), *Дороги. Рассказы советских писателей*, Русский язык, Moscow, 1979 (Yu. Kazakov, Yu. Nagibin, K. Paustovky, P. Proskurin, V. Shukshin etc.).

Povolyaev, V. (compiler), *Московский рассказ*, Московский рабочий, Moscow, 1980 (Yu. Avdeenko, Yu. Kazakov, E. Khrutsky, A. Kuleshov, A. Makarov, Yu. Nagibin, V. Povolyaev, L. Sal'nikov, Yu. Trifonov, L. Uvarova, K. Vanshenkin, A. Yakhontov etc.).

Smirnov, V. (compiler), *Белый конь*, Русский язык, Moscow, 1985 (F. Abramov, V. Astaf'ev, V. Belov, V. Lebedev, E. Nosov, V. Shcherbakov, V. Shukshin, V. Sobolev, P. Vasil'ev, S. Zalygin etc.).

Zolotavkin, V. (compiler), *Проза 70-х годов*, Русский язык, Moscow, 1985 (F. Abramov, C. Aitmatov, V. Belov, D. Granin, Yu. Kazakov, Yu. Nagibin, V. Shukshin, K. Simonov, V. Soloukhin, V. Tokareva, S. Zalygin etc.).

Note
Some quotations have been taken from standard grammars of the Russian language.

Subject Index

Note: references are to *page* numbers. When English and Russian words appear together in a list, account is taken of the order of letters in both alphabets.

Word Index

The *Word Index* does not include every word that appears in the *Grammar*. It is intended to interact with the *Contents* and the *Subject Index* to facilitate access to all parts of the book. It contains all verbs with a difficult conjugation, all prepositions, conjunctions, particles, verbs and adjectives which take an oblique case, prefixes, many suffixes and other endings, and additional words and forms which illustrate significant grammatical points.

Words which appear in lists are not normally included. Thus, instead of enumerating nouns which have a locative in -ý, only the ending -ý appears in the *Word Index*, as a guide to relevant nouns. This principle is adhered to throughout the *Word Index*.

Many verb forms can be traced through their infinitives, and the forms of many nouns, pronouns, adjectives and numerals through their nominative case.

The Word Index contains references to stress patterns, except for stress in prepositions (for prepositional stress see pages 419–20).

All references are to page numbers.

a [conjunction] 407–8, 490–1, 492, 502
a [particle] 510, 515–16
-a [first name] 76
-a [f. noun] 68–71, 96
-a [f. suffix] 43
-a [gerund] 383–4, 387, 388, 391–2
-a [m. noun] 34, 68, 164, 209
-a [nouns of common gender] 37, 68
-a [place name] 78
-a [pl.-only noun] 51–2
-a [surname] 78
-á [f. adj. short form] 182
-á [m. pl. noun] 59–60, 64
-á [pl.-only noun] 51–2
-á [surname] 77
-авать 230

а вдруг 491
авеню́ 38
автобус 427
автома́т-заку́сочная 42–3
àвтомòтоклу́б [stress] 15
-аго [surname] 77
агроно́м 46
-аем [part. ending] 374
-аемый [part. ending] 361, 364–5, 376, 377, 378–9, 380
-айший 191–2
-ак [m. suffix] [stress] 63
аккомпани́ровать 101
алка́ть [stress] 235–6, 239
Алма́-Ата́ 78
а́лчный 13
-ан [part. ending] 367 [stress], 374–5